T0257204

ENGINEERING NETWORKS FOR SYNCHRONIZATION, CCS 7, AND ISDN

IEEE TELECOMMUNICATIONS HANDBOOK SERIES

The *IEEE Telecommunications Handbook Series* is designed to provide the engineer and technical practitioner with working information in the three basic fields of telecommunications: inside plant, outside plant, and administration and regulatory. This integrated series of handbooks provides practical information on the link between field experience and formal telecommunications industry standards and practices. These books are essential tools for engineers and technical practitioners who require day-to-day engineering and technical information on telecommunications systems.

If you are interested in becoming an author, contributor, or reviewer of a book in this series, or if you would like additional information about forthcoming titles, please contact:

Whitham D. Reeve
Series Editor, IEEE Telecommunications Handbook Series
Reeve Engineers
P.O. Box 190225
Anchorage, Alaska 99519-0225
(907) 243-2262
E-mail—by CompuServe: 71011.3642@compuserve.com
by Internet: w.reeve@ieee.org

Other Books in the IEEE Telecommunications Handbook Series

Boucher, *TRAFFIC SYSTEM DESIGN HANDBOOK: Timesaving Telecommuncation Traffic Tables and Programs*
1992 Softcover IEEE Order No. PP3251 ISBN 0-7803-0428-4

Carne, *TELECOMMUNICATIONS PRIMER: Signals, Building Blocks, and Networks*
Copublished with Prentice-Hall PTR
1996 Hardcover IEEE Order No. PC5670 ISBN 0-13-49026-5

Garg/Wilkes, *WIRELESS AND PERSONAL COMMUNICATIONS SYSTEMS: Fundamentals and Applications*
Copublished with Prentice-Hall PTR
1996 Hardcover IEEE Order No. PC5673 ISBN 0-13-493735-X

Nellist, *UNDERSTANDING TELECOMMUNICATIONS AND LIGHTWAVE SYSTEMS: An Entry-Level Guide, Second Edition*
1996 Softcover IEEE Order No. PP4665 ISBN 0-7803-1113-2

Reeve, *SUBSCRIBER LOOP SIGNALING AND TRANSMISSION HANDBOOK: Analog*
1992 Hardcover IEEE Order No. PC2683 ISBN 0-87942-274-2

Reeve, *SUBSCRIBER LOOP SIGNALING AND TRANSMISSION HANDBOOK: Digital*
1995 Hardcover IEEE Order No. PC3376 ISBN 0-7803-0440-3

Thomas, *CABLE TELEVISION PROOF-OF-PERFORMANCE: A Practical Guide to Cable TV Compliance Measurements Using a Spectrum Analyzer*
Copublished with Prentice-Hall PTR
1995 Hardcover IEEE Order No. PC5671 ISBN 0-13-573726-5

ENGINEERING NETWORKS FOR SYNCHRONIZATION, CCS 7, AND ISDN

Standards, Protocols, Planning, and Testing

P. K. Bhatnagar

Center for Development of Telematics
New Delhi, India

IEEE Telecommunications Handbook Series
Whitham D. Reeve, *Series Editor*

IEEE Communications Society, *Sponsor*

The Institute of Electrical and Electronics Engineers, Inc., New York

IEEE Press
445 Hoes Lane, P.O. Box 1331
Piscataway, NJ 08855-1331

Technical Reviewers

Whitham Reeve, *Reeve Engineers*
Mike Newman, *CSI Telecommunications Engineers*
Steve Cowles, *GCI Network Systems, Inc.*
Thomas Robertazzi, *SUNY/Stony Brook*
Robert McLaughlin, *Winstar Communications, Inc.*

IEEE Communications Society, *Sponsor*
COMM-S Liaison to IEEE Press, Salah Aidarous

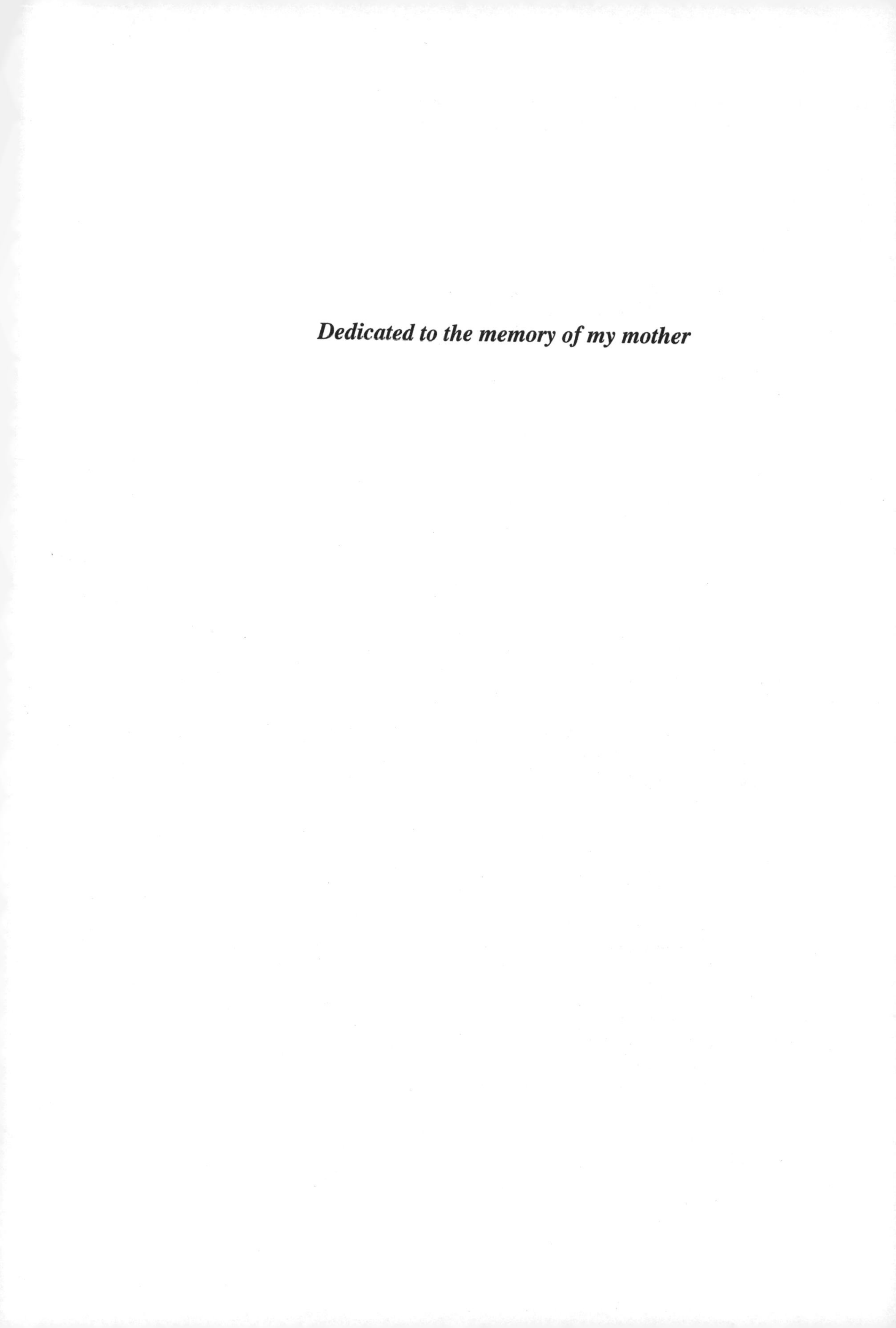

Dedicated to the memory of my mother

This book and other books may be purchased at a discount
from the publisher when ordered in bulk quantities. Contact:

IEEE Press Marketing
Attn: Special Sales
Piscataway, NJ 08855–1331
Fax: (732) 981-9334

For more information about IEEE PRESS products,
visit the IEEE Home Page: http://www.ieee.org/

10 9 8 7 6 5 4 3

ISBN 0-7803-1158-2
IEEE Order Number: PC5628

Library of Congress Cataloging-in-Publication Data

Bhatnagar, P. K. (date)
Engineering networks for synchronization, CCS 7, and ISDN: standards, protocols, planning, and testing / P. K. Bhatnagar.
p. cm.—(Telecommunications handbook series)
Includes bibliographical references and index.
ISBN 0–7803–1158–2
1. Synchronous data transmission systems. I. Title. II. Series.
TK5105.4.B49 1997
621.382′16—dc21 96–50010
CIP

Contents

Series Editor's Note

When I conceived the IEEE Press Telecommunications Handbook Series in 1990, my original focus was on telecommunications systems in North America. As a result of my own work, however, it became clear to me that I should adopt a global perspective. I had to deal with long-distance digital transmission quality problems from Alaska to just about everywhere else in the United States. In many cases, the problems are equivalent to those found internationally, and I was researching and adopting international recommendations more and more. Therefore, I was very pleased when the Series Advisory Board accepted P. K. Bhatnagar's proposal for *Engineering Networks for Synchronization, CCS 7, and ISDN.*

This volume serves to broaden the scope of the series by covering many critical engineering aspects of international telecommunications. Of particular importance in international telecommunications is the integrated services digital network (ISDN) and its impact on virtually all aspects of telecommunications systems engineering. The ISDN cannot fully function without the CCITT common channel signaling system no. 7 (CCS 7). And without digital network synchronization, neither the ISDN nor CCS 7 would be possible.

P. K. Bhatnagar's book provides a timely, practical, and unified treatment of these three subjects that will be of great interest to telecommunications engineers throughout the world. It is a welcomed and valuable addition to the IEEE Press Telecommunications Handbook Series.

Whitham D. Reeve

Foreword

The perception of the role of telecommunication networks has undergone drastic changes in recent years. Originally designed and used solely for speech communication, these networks have been increasingly deployed for carrying information in other forms: data, video, and image. The demand for new services is the inevitable outcome of changes brought about by the information age. Yet despite the fast growth of technology, the sheer size of the existing global telecommunication network dictates that the demand for new services be met by a gradual process of network evolution. Telecommunication networks must evolve in a manner that ensures backward compatability and that protects existing investments. The integrated services digital network (ISDN) is designed to meet these objectives. The policy of digitalization has been vigorously pursued by telecommunication administrations throughout the world, and with the maturation of ISDN technology, the stage is set for rapid deployment of the ISDN. This stage has been preceded by the implementation of two important infrastructural requirements, network synchronization, and the CCITT common channel signaling system no. 7 (CCS 7).

Recognizing this scenario of network evolution, P. K. Bhatnagar has chosen three important aspects of digital networks: network synchronization, CCS 7, and the ISDN. These interlinked topics are of vital interest to the industry.

Synchronization in a digital network has been compared to the role of a conductor in an orchestra. Timing is central to a digital network, and synchronization performs this function by making the nodes of the network "tick in unison." Standardization, planning, engineering, and testing of synchronization in networks based on the plesiochronous digital hierarchy (PDH) are covered in Chapters 2 and 3 of this book. The introduction of the synchronous digital hierarchy (SDH) and the consequent existence of mixed PDH-SDH networks, however, has raised new timing issues, and Chapter 15 is devoted to discussion of these aspects.

Unlike network synchronization that is implemented only in the national networks—international switching centers operate plesiochronously—CCS 7 is relevant to both national and international networks. The specification of CCS 7 protocol by the International Telegraph and Telephone Consultative Committee (CCITT), now the International Telecommunication Union-Telecommunication Standardization Sector (ITU-T), is of far-reaching significance. CCS 7 provides a common, open-ended platform for call control of new and powerful services. For instance, services in the ISDN, advanced intelligent networks, and public land mobile networks are made possible by CCS 7 call control procedures. Furthermore, CCS 7 significantly reduces call setup time and permits the establishment of a separate signaling network that can be engineered to provide highly reliable and economic operation. For these reasons, CCS 7 is fast replacing conventional channel-associated signaling systems. The focus on CCS 7 in this book is therefore well placed. In addition to an in-depth treatment of CCS 7 protocols, practical aspects such as planning, engineering, validation, and testing of CCS 7 networks have been emphasized. These issues are of day-to-day concern to the practicing engineer.

An end-to-end ISDN call involves two signaling protocols: digital subscriber signaling system 1 (DSS 1) and CCS 7. DSS 1 is employed between the ISDN user and the exchange, whereas CCS 7 is used between the exchanges involved in setting up the call. This book provides a detailed description of DSS 1 protocol and its interworking with CCS 7. Planning, testing, and services under the ISDN are also discussed. An entire chapter is devoted to packet and frame mode services in the ISDN, which will prove useful since integration of services in the ISDN cannot be complete unless packet and frame mode services are brought into its fold.

This book justifiably lays great stress on standards. Standardization has assumed an increasingly dominant role in the recent past due to globalization of economic and commercial activity, and this trend is likely to gain further momentum. Two of the three areas covered, CCS 7 and ISDN, have been the outcome of international standardization performed by the ITU. However, ITU standards are broad in scope and permit several implementation options. Regional standards have an important role to play in this context; they add details and clarifications to facilitate practical implementations. In addition to international standards, this book covers both North American and European standards. This feature should satisfy the needs of the North American and European markets.

Successful deployment of network synchronization, CCS 7, and the ISDN requires careful attention to planning, engineering, and testing issues. In my opinion, the strength of this book lies in its in-depth treatment and its focus on practical aspects. I am confident that this book will serve as a timely and valuable reference to telecommunication professionals.

P. S. Saran
Member, Telecom Commission
New Delhi, India

Preface

The evolution of telecommunication networks continues throughout the world because networks must evolve in response to demand for new features and services. The process of digitalization that began in the late 1960s is nearing completion, but this alone is not sufficient. The digital telephone network is now evolving into an integrated services digital network (ISDN). The key components of this evolution are digital network synchronization and the CCITT common channel signaling system no. 7 (CCS 7). *Engineering Networks for Synchronization, CCS 7, and ISDN* therefore focuses not only on ISDN but also on network synchronization and CCS 7 and presents a comprehensive and unified treatment of these three subjects.

Today, the telecommunication scenario is characterized by the opening up of markets and the entry of several new operators in the national networks. The resolution of interconnection and interworking issues in a multiple-operator environment requires compliance to standards. Thus, this book gives an in-depth presentation of current international and regional standards including North American and European standards. To meet the needs of network operators, planners, and practicing engineers, the planning, engineering, and testing aspects are presented with a view to bridge the gap between theory and practice. Also included is a tutorial introduction to network synchronization, CCS 7, and ISDN; thus, students of telecommunication need no specialized knowledge to follow the text. The organization and structure of the book is discussed in Chapter 1.

During the preparation of this book, several people contributed their suggestions and comments. Series editor Whitham Reeve's incisive reviews, constructive comments, and suggestions and his personal contact throughout the project were significant contributions to every stage of the work. I am thankful to the technical reviewers commissioned by the IEEE Press who reviewed the manuscript and offered many useful suggestions. I am also thankful to P. S. Saran for writing the foreword. N. K. Sinha and R. R. N. Prasad of the Indian Telecommunication Commission provided useful technical insights and advice. K. N. Gupta, currently executive director of the Centre for Development of Telematics, New Delhi, played a pioneering role in the implementation of synchronization in the Indian Telecommunication network during the 1980s, and I am thankful to him for introducing me to this subject. Savoula Amanatidis, Deborah Graffox, Lisa Dayne, and several others at the IEEE Press worked tirelessly to bring this work into shape. Special thanks also to my father, who encouraged me in this endeavor. Finally, I want to thank my wife, Manju, my daughter, Nupur, and my son, Aayush, for their understanding and support all through the long months it took to complete this book.

Although I acknowledge the support of all the people cited above, I remain responsible for the book and any residual imperfections. I welcome suggestions for improvement and for making the book more useful.

P. K. Bhatnagar
New Delhi, India

1 Introduction

Acronyms

ANSI	American National Standards Institute	MTP	Message Transfer Part
CCITT	the International Telegraph and Telephone Consultative Committee	PDH	plesiochronous digital hierarchy
CCS 7	CCITT common channel signaling system no. 7	PRS	primary reference source
DSS 1	digital subscriber signaling 1	PSTN	public switched telephone network
ETSI	European Telecommunication Standard Institute	QOS	quality of service
ISDN	Integrated services digital network	SCCP	Signaling Connection Control Part
ISUP	ISDN user part	SDH	synchronous digital hierarchy
ITU-T	International Telecommunication Union-Telecommunication Standardization Sector	SONET	synchronous optical network
		SP	signaling point
		STP	signal transfer point

The vision of uniting the world into a single cohesive unit is perhaps as old as human civilization. This dream has persisted through the centuries, despite divisions, conflicts, and wars. Modern telecommunication technology offers a step in this direction by bridging distances through reliable, efficient, and enhanced communication services anytime, anywhere. Integrated Services Digital Network (ISDN) technology is central to the modernization of telecommunication networks throughout the world. It is also one of the themes of this book.

The increasing deployment of the Integrated Services Digital Network (ISDN) in recent years is based on several sound reasons. First, the existing public switched telephone network (PSTN) is ubiquitous in which massive investments have already been made. Clearly, modernization of the telephone network must follow a course that exploits existing infrastructure. ISDN fits the bill, because it represents an evolutionary approach in which the PSTN is progressively converted to ISDN by suitable upgrades that need comparatively modest investments. Second, ISDN offers an impressive array of services involving voice, data, image, and text. It is an integrated umbrella network that embraces both circuit switched and packet switched services and provides functionality that was hitherto unavailable in existing networks, either singly or jointly. Thus, from the angle of services, ISDN permits a quantum jump. Third, ISDN is the outcome of several years of international standardization at the International Telegraph and Telephone Consultative Committee (CCITT; now ITU-T, or International Telecommunication Union-Telecommunication Standardization Sector). This has been backed by standardization at the regional level by bodies such as the American National Standards Institute (ANSI) and the European Telecommunication Standard Institute (ETSI). Thus, the ISDN offers well-standardized services. Fourth, ISDN has the potential of becoming a ubiquitous telecommunication network as the existing PSTN changes as a result of its evolution to ISDN. This alone is a major driving force in the development of new services, applications, and customer premises equipment based on the ISDN communication platform. Fifth, telecommunication networks typically incorporate more than one generation of equipment. Modernization of a large network takes several years to accomplish and is dictated by the useful life of the existing equipment and other economic factors. For example, the process of digitalization that began in the late 1960s is nearing completion now and only in the most advanced networks. Parts of the telecommunication network are still analog. Therefore, there is a need for the "new" to interwork harmoniously with the "old" and to provide backward compatibility. ISDN interworks well with the existing PSTN, packet, and other networks.

As the second half of its name suggests, ISDN requires a digital network consisting of digital switching and transport network. From this starting point, it takes three steps to accomplish an ISDN (Figure 1–1):

- Digital network synchronization
- CCITT common channel signaling system no. 7 (CCS 7)
- Implementation of ISDN functionality

The first two steps are prerequisites that should exist in the PSTN to permit its upgradation to ISDN. They are critical to the implementation of the ISDN since without synchronization, there can be no CCS 7, and without CCS 7, the ISDN is not feasible. For this reason, synchronization and CCS 7 are strongly emphasized in this book. It may be noted, however, that although synchronization and CCS 7 are essential for the ISDN, their application is by no means limited to ISDN alone. Long before the implementation of ISDN, the need for slip control was realized, and network synchronization was implemented in several countries in an essentially non-ISDN environment. Likewise, CCS 7 is a signaling system that can be applied for telephony, ISDN, and a variety of other applications.

We now turn our attention to the organization and contents of the book.

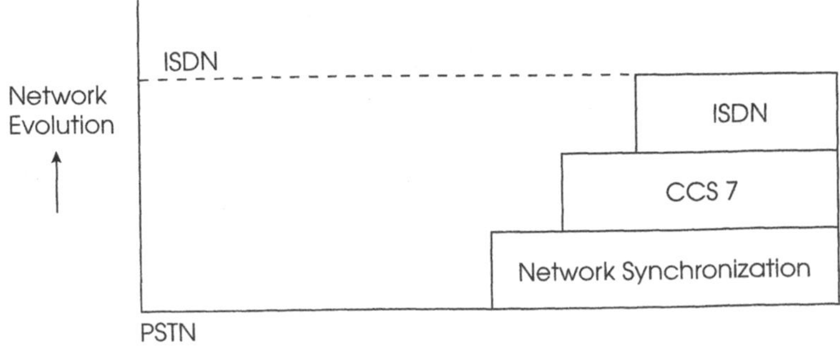

Figure 1–1 Three-step evolutionary ladder to ISDN.

Timing is a key element in the operation of modern digital networks, and synchronization is the means of providing it. Chapter 2 considers the basic concepts of network synchronization in a digital network. The mechanism of the occurrence of slips and network performance objectives for slip control are described. The parameters for clock behavior and the performance of different types of commercially available clocks are also explained. Specifications and typical configurations of reference timing sources in the context of the master-slave method of synchronization are discussed on the basis of relevant ITU-T and North American standards, and specifications of clocks to be used in the slave nodes at various hierarchical levels of the network are also presented. Jitter and wander have a major contribution in timing impairment. The jitter and wander permissible in digital networks are also discussed.

Chapter 3 is devoted to practical issues concerning network synchronization. To this end, the discussion centers on planning, testing, and monitoring synchronization networks. Planning options are considered and guidelines for implementing a reliable synchronization network are provided. The implementation of a primary reference source (PRS), transport of timing between network nodes, and intrabuilding distribution of timing are also discussed. A critical element in the success of network synchronization is the quality of the slave clocks employed. To ensure that the slave clocks behave in conformance to prescribed standards, testing and validation assume significance. Therefore, considerable attention has been devoted to the testing methodology of slave clocks under the three possible modes of operation: unstressed, stressed, and holdover. Finally, issues involved in monitoring the performance of synchronized networks are discussed.

Chapters 2 and 3 together cover network synchronization for a digital network operating on the plesiochronous digital hierarchy (PDH). Discussion of timing issues in PDH/SDH is taken up in Chapter 15.

Chapter 4 is the first in a series of chapters on the CCITT common channel signaling system no. 7 (CCS 7). Although the acronym CCS 7 has been used in this book, SS7 and #7 are also used in the literature. CCS 7 is a new and powerful signaling system that forms the basis of many telecommunication services. Chapter 4 describes the principles of CCS 7, its advantages compared with channel-associated signaling, terminology, and CCS 7 network elements such as signaling point (SP), signal transfer point (STP), and signaling links. The organization of the CCS 7 protocol structure into levels is discussed and compared with the OSI seven-layer reference model. CCS 7 is organized into four levels. The three lower levels comprise the message transfer part (MTP) of the CCS 7 protocol stack and are common to all applications. The functions of the MTP are briefly explained. The discussion about the signaling data link (level 1) is completed in this chapter. Also discussed is level 4, namely, the various user parts that sit on top of the MTP. Chapter 4 briefly covers the signaling connection control part (SCCP), which is designed to enhance the capabilities of the MTP. The concepts of connectionless and connection-oriented services are highlighted in this context. Different possibilities such as overlap and en bloc signaling and also, link-by-link and end-to-end signaling are discussed. The concepts are explained by signaling schematics corresponding to different types of calls.

Chapter 5 provides a general introduction to the ISDN, including the ISDN user-network interface reference configuration and ISDN protocol architecture. The physical layer of basic access ISDN covering the wiring, coding, framing, power feeding, and electrical characteristics at the ISDN interface is treated in depth. Layers 2 and 3 of the digital subscriber signaling 1 (DSS 1) are discussed in Chapter 8. The line transmission and coding for basic access are also explained in Chapter 5, which concludes with a brief reference to ISDN primary rate access.

Chapter 6 considers the functions of CCS 7 level 2, which is also referred to as the CCS 7 signaling link level. The formats of the three types of signal units are described. Various functions performed at this level (namely, signal unit delimitation and alignment, error detection and correction, initial alignment, error monitoring, and flow control) are explained through illustrative examples. The role of various level 2 timers and their permissible values for the ITU-T and BELLCORE specifications are also presented.

Chapter 7 deals with the signaling network functions (level 3) of CCS 7. Signaling network functions can be classified into two categories, signaling message handling and signaling network management. Both these aspects are explained with illustrative examples. Also included is a discussion on MTP restart procedure and congestion management in CCS 7 networks. The values of various level 3 timers are listed, and their roles are described.

Chapter 8 discusses two important aspects of ISDN: the services that are provided under the ISDN and the protocols required to support these services. ISDN can support a wide range of services classified under three categories: bearer services, teleservices, and supplementary services. Each category is described in detail. International and European standards on supplementary services are also listed. ISDN protocols are referred to as digital subscriber signaling 1 (DSS 1). Chapter 8 comprehensively discusses both layer 2 and layer 3 DSS 1 protocols. The format and role of various layer 3 messages have been clearly brought out by describing the DSS 1 message flow for basic call control. The requirements for the control of calls involving supplementary services are also examined. This chapter completes the description of DSS 1 protocols.

Chapter 9 provides an in-depth description of the ISDN user part (ISUP). ISUP provides call control functions for both telephony and ISDN calls. The general format of ISUP messages is followed by the ISUP signaling procedure for basic call control. Both en bloc and overlap signaling procedures are considered. The role of various ISUP messages is explained in the context of basic call control. The continuity check and supervision of speech/data circuit by the ISUP are also presented, as is the treatment of abnormal conditions such as dual seizures and the receipt of errored, unexpected, and unrecognizable messages. Various mechanisms of congestion control available in ISUP protocol are highlighted. Finally, the ISUP call setup procedure for calls that include supplementary services is considered.

Chapter 10 focuses on the planning and implementation of CCS 7 in the national network. The performance objectives for the CCS 7 network as stipulated in ITU-T recommendations are described. CCS 7 network structures are presented through the specific example of the U.S. network. Different planning options are discussed and compared. The dimensioning of signaling links is described both for en bloc and overlap signaling, and the important performance parameters that need to be monitored in a CCS 7 network are enumerated. Finally, guidelines for formulation of national CCS 7 standards are provided by highlighting some of the key areas that should be addressed as part of this activity.

Chapter 11 describes MTP and ISUP testing in CCS 7. The general requirements and functional characteristics of CCS 7 test equipment are also examined. Because CCS 7 protocol is organized in terms of levels, testing is performed for each level separately. The set of tests based on relevant ITU-T recommendations necessary for both compatibility and validation testing are described for level 2, level 3, and ISUP. On-line tests for CCS 7 are also explained.

Chapter 12 presents an overview of packet mode and frame mode bearer services in the ISDN. The call setup procedures for the minimum integration scenario (X.31, case A) and maximum integration scenario (X.31, case B) are described. Frame mode services are discussed with an emphasis on frame relaying. Protocols involved in the control (C) plane and the user (U) plane are also covered. Finally, the procedures for establishing frame mode connections in the ISDN are described on the basis of ITU-T recommendations.

Chapter 13 examines various aspects related to planning and implementation of ISDN. Included in this chapter are marketing and policy-related issues, the selection of ISDN services and applications, ISDN customer premises equipment, issues concerning the determination of ISDN tariffs, and the impact on technical plans arising from the introduction of ISDN. Also discussed is the impact of ISDN traffic on switch capacity. Various strategies for implementation of ISDN are examined. The chapter concludes with a brief introduction to quality of service (QOS) and performance requirements in the ISDN.

Chapter 14 is devoted to testing aspects in the ISDN. As for CCS 7, ISDN tests are conducted individually for each layer. Physical layer tests are described in detail. Considering the complexity and size of DSS 1 protocol, a large number of tests are prescribed for the validation of layers 2 and 3. The description of layer 2 and layer 3 tests is therefore limited to a discussion on the principles and framework of testing. The general principles of maintenance of ISDN access are also mentioned.

Chapter 15 examines timing issues arising from the introduction of the synchronous optical network (SONET)/synchronous digital hierarchy (SDH). After a brief description of the SONET and SDH frame formats, the pointer mechanism employed in SONET/SDH network elements is explained. The problem of jitter arising from pointer adjustments is discussed, particularly at the boundary of SONET/SDH with the PDH. The need for specifying a new clock for SONET/SDH is explained.

Many references listed at the end of each chapter relate to the recommendations and standards of international and regional standardization bodies. They are an authoritative source of information and need to be referred to for further study. Appendix 1 lists the addresses and other details of the various standardization bodies for procurement of these documents. Appendix 2 provides a list of ISUP messages along with their codes.

2 Digital Network Synchronization: Basic Concepts

Acronyms

ANSI	American National Standards Institute
AT&T	American Telegraph and Telephone Company
BOC	Bell operating companies
BSRF	Bell System reference frequency
CCITT	the International Telegraph and Telephone Consultative Committee
CCS 7	CCITT common channel signaling system no. 7
FISU	fill-in signal unit
FTZ	telecommunications engineering center
GPS	global positioning system
HRX	hypothetical reference connection
ISDN	integrated services digital network
LORAN-C	*lo*ng-*ra*nge *n*avigation
LSSU	link status signal unit
MRTIE	maximum relative time interval error
MSU	message signal unit
MTIE	maximum time interval error
OCXO	oven-controlled crystal oscillator
PCM	pulse code modulation
PDH	plesiochronous digital hierarchy
PLL	phase lock loop
PRS	primary reference source
SDH	synchronous digital hierarchy
SONET	synchronous optical network
SU	signal unit
TCXO	temperature-compensated crystal oscillator
TDMA	time division multiple access
TIE	time interval error
UI	unit interval
UTC	coordinated universal time

ABSTRACT

In this chapter, the basic concepts of digital network synchronization are explained. These include:

- Slip-rate objectives and synchronization methods to meet these objectives
- Description of commercially available clocks to time a digital network
- Important synchronization concepts linked to clock behavior
- Impact of jitter and wander on digital network synchronization
- Specifications and typical configurations of reference timing sources in the context of the master-slave method of synchronization

2.1 Introduction

The concept of timing is central to the operation of a digital telecommunication network. A digital network consists of digital switches interconnected by digital transmission facilities. Every switch has its own clock that determines the bit rate on the digital links emanating from it. Digital networks are based on hierarchical bit rates of 1,544 kbps and 2,048 kbps. Pulse code modulation (PCM) information is organized in frames that in turn consist of several timeslots or channels. The 8-bit timeslots repeated with a periodicity of 8 kbps form the basis for 64 kbps switched services. For a typical connection, the timeslots are switched through several offices and transported over the intervening transmission links. Frame alignment is performed by identifying the beginning of a frame in the incoming bit stream. Once alignment is achieved, other timeslots are identified and switched by virtue of their position in time with respect to the beginning of the frame. To receive and switch timeslots arriving on the incoming links correctly, the digital switches in the network must maintain the same clock rate. The goal of synchronization is to achieve a common clock rate for the digital switches. The same applies to digital cross connects.

Although digital switches and cross connects are synchronous digital equipment, a vast majority of the currently deployed transmission network is based on the plesiochronous digital hierarchy (PDH) due to the process of digitalization of the telecommunication networks. Digitalization of the transmission systems began prior to the introduction of digital switches. In accordance with the prevailing network conditions, transmission equipment such as digital multiplexers and demultiplexers were designed to accept asynchronous tributaries of varying clock rates. Synchronization of digital transmission networks was therefore not required. For synchronizing the switches, however, timing has to be transported on digital links. The timing conveyed on the links is in terms of frequency and not as date, hours, minutes, and seconds. To resolve timing issues, we need to adopt a two-pronged approach: first, to achieve synchronization of the digital switches and, second, to minimize the presence of transmission impairments such as jitter and wander that disturb timing in the bit stream.

Timing issues assume enhanced significance in an integrated services digital network (ISDN) that aims at supporting a wide range of services, both voice and nonvoice. This chapter and the next are devoted to the study of network synchronization in digital networks based on PDH. In Chapter 15, the requirements of timing and synchronization in networks based on synchronous digital hierarchy (SDH) are considered.

To ensure satisfactory provisioning of ISDN services, one requirement is to minimize the occurrence of events called slips. A *slip* involves the loss or repetition of a block of bits (frame) at the receiving end of a digital link. In the North American digital hierarchy, which is based on a first-level bit rate of 1.544 Mbps (DS-1 rate), frames consist of 193 bits: 192 data bits and 1 framing bit. In the digital hierarchy used in Europe and other parts of the world, the first-level bit rate is 2.048 Mbps. This rate uses a frame structure consisting of 256 bits per frame. Additional information on frame structure may be found in Reeve [1] and ITU-T recommendation G.704 [2]. Slips occur mainly due to differences in frequency of the clocks associated with the digital equipment at each end. Frequency inequalities between clocks lead to a buildup of phase difference that, beyond a certain value, results in a slip. Other contributors to phase variations and slips include transmission impairments such as network jitter, wander, and phase discontinuity associated with network rearrangements.

2.2 The Concept of a Slip

The concept of a slip is explained here by considering the slip events resulting from differing frequencies of network clocks.

Figure 2–1 shows a digital switch B receiving a 24-channel DS-1 bit stream from two other switches, A and C. The exchanges have local clocks with the same nominal frequency, but due to differing frequency departures from the ideal value, their actual frequencies may be different. Each digital link in the switch is terminated in a memory buffer. The PCM frames are transmitted from switch A at the bit rate determined by frequency f_a of the exchange A clock. At switch B, the clock is extracted from the incoming bit stream and the time slots are written in the memory buffer at the clock frequency f_a. The memory buffer is read, however, at the frequency f_b of the exchange B clock. Because f_a and f_b are not identical, the read and write rates differ and buffer M1 would eventually overflow or underflow, resulting in a slip. Overflow arises when writing is faster than reading ($f_a > f_b$) and a block of bits sent from switch A are lost at switch B. The underflow situation ($f_b > f_a$) has the reverse effect: a repetition of a block of bits because the same information is read twice. Similar considerations apply to the PCM frames received from exchange C, and slips occur in memory buffer M2 at a rate depending on the difference between f_b and f_c.

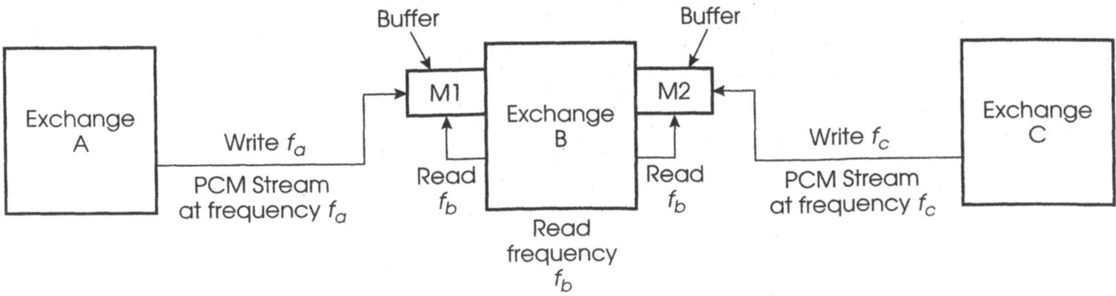

Figure 2–1 Controlled slips on memory buffers terminating PCM links.

Slips occur at the memory buffers terminating the incoming links, and they arise due to frequency inequalities of the clocks in the network. In a hypothetical situation with an absence of buffers, slips would occur in an uncontrolled manner, depending on the instantaneous value of frequency difference between the incoming bit stream and the switching office clock. With uncontrolled slips, the length of the frame is artificially shortened or lengthened. The alignment for the next frame does not appear in its expected position in time, and the frame alignment may be lost. Several frames may be lost before the frame alignment is restored. As long as the network clocks operate at different frequencies, the buffers by themselves cannot prevent slips from occurring; rather, they have the role of postponing (and to that extent, controlling) slip events by relating them to the overflow or underflow of the buffer. Slips occurring in this manner at the memory buffers are called *controlled slips*. The buffers in the switch are generally called *aligners*. The size of the aligners determines the number of bits skipped or repeated during a slip (typically one or two frames). In addition, the aligner performs the function of absorbing a certain amount of transmission impairments such as wander. It should be recognized that buffers introduce propagation delays, and the size of the buffer is based on a trade-off between delay and clock stability.

Although transmission impairments—for example, excessive errors, jitter, wander, and phase shifts due to network restoration events—may result in slips or even loss of frame alignment, the effect is limited to the link experiencing the impairment. When the frequency of a switch clock differs from those of other switches connected to it, however, frame slips are likely to occur on all the buffers terminating the incoming links. Frequency inequality has wide ramifications on network performance and is an important factor contributing to slip events. Strategies to minimize slips therefore aim at reducing frequency inequalities between the network clocks. The purpose of digital network synchronization is to perform this function by operating the network at a common clock rate.

2.3 Aligners for Terminating Digital Links

The International Telegraph and Telephone Consultative Committee (CCITT) recommendation G.810 [3] recognizes two types of aligners for terminating a digital link at the exchange. A frame aligner is designed so that the slip results in duplication or deletion of a complete PCM frame. In the other type of aligner, a slot aligner, a slip affects one or more 64 kbps timeslots.

Figure 2–2(a) shows a frame aligner designed to cause insertion or deletion of a PCM frame in the event of a slip. The aligner is a cyclic memory buffer that typically has a capacity for holding two frames. For correct reception of information, writing into the aligner is followed by reading. Initially, the read pointer is shown lagging the write pointer by one frame duration, that is, by 125 μs. When frame n has been written into the aligner and writing is to commence for the next frame, reading begins for frame n. This gap of one frame length between the read and write pointers persists as long as the write and read clocks have exactly the same rates.

When the read clock is faster, the read pointer tends to approach the write pointer. A slip occurs when the difference between them is narrowed down to one timeslot. In this condition, reading continues until the full frame has been read; then the read pointer is

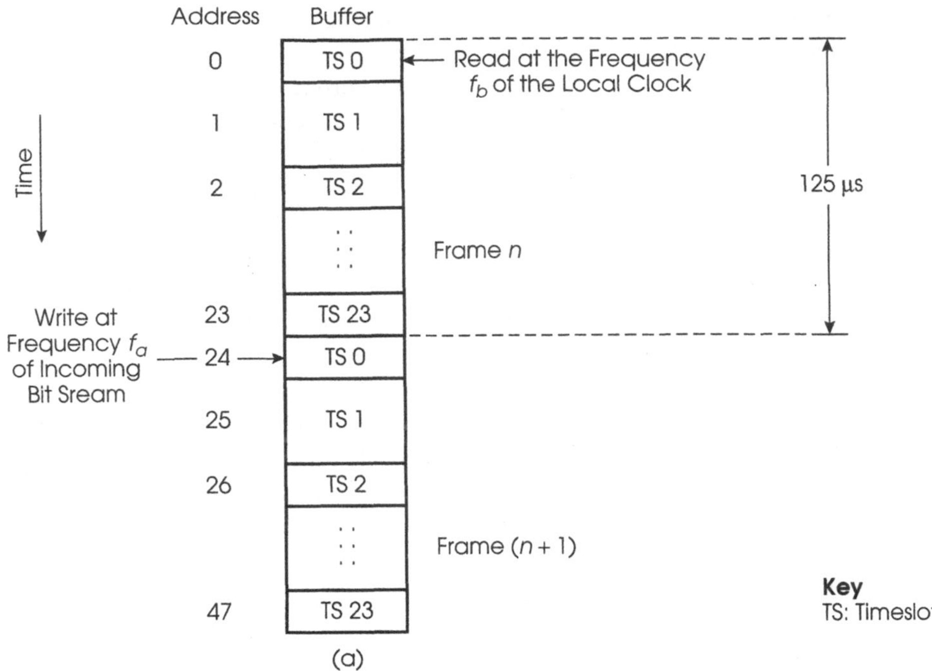

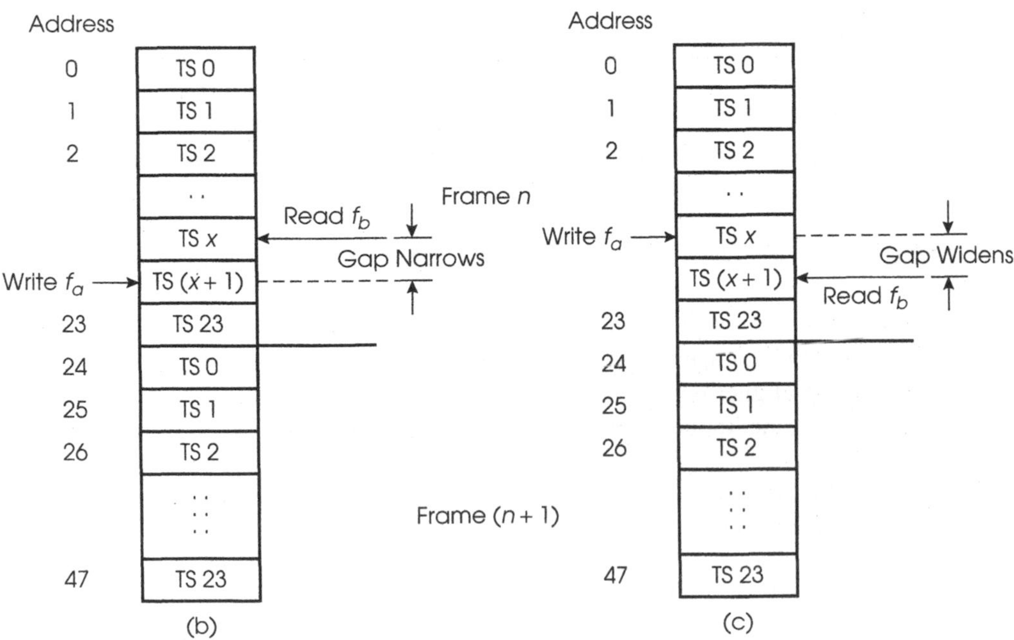

Figure 2–2 (a) Frame aligner; (b) slip-frame repeat ($f_a < f_b$); (c) slip-frame skip ($f_a > f_b$).

reset to stand on the top of the same frame. In Figure 2–2(b), reading continues up to address 23 of frame *n*, and then the read pointer is reset to address 0 of frame *n*. The same frame is therefore read twice.

When the write clock is faster, as in Figure 2–2(c), the gap between the read and write pointers widens until, due to the cyclic nature of the aligner buffer, the difference between the write and read addresses is reduced to one timeslot. In this case, the read pointer skips a frame by jumping from *n* to frame $n + 1$.

After a slip, due to modification of the read pointer, the difference of one frame length is restored between the read and write addresses. This corresponds to a phase difference of 125 μs. The next slip would follow when the frequency inequality of the two clocks causes this phase difference either to disappear or to increase to 250 μs. A slip therefore occurs when the phase of two clocks shifts by 125 μs.

2.4 Timing Impairments: Jitter and Wander

2.4.1 Jitter

Jitter is defined as short-term variations of the significant instants of a digital signal from their ideal position in time. Figure 2–3(a) shows a digital bit stream spaced uniformly in time. This represents a jitter-free signal. Figure 2–3(b) illustrates the digital bit stream impaired by the presence of jitter. The digital pulses are disturbed from their ideal positions, and the intervals between the pulses are no longer uniform. The displacement of the pulse with respect to its ideal position represents the jitter amplitude or phase variation. Jitter amplitude is specified in terms of the unit interval (UI). A UI is the interval *t* between the pulses of the jitter-free signal. The value of 1 UI for 1,544 kbps is 648 ns, and

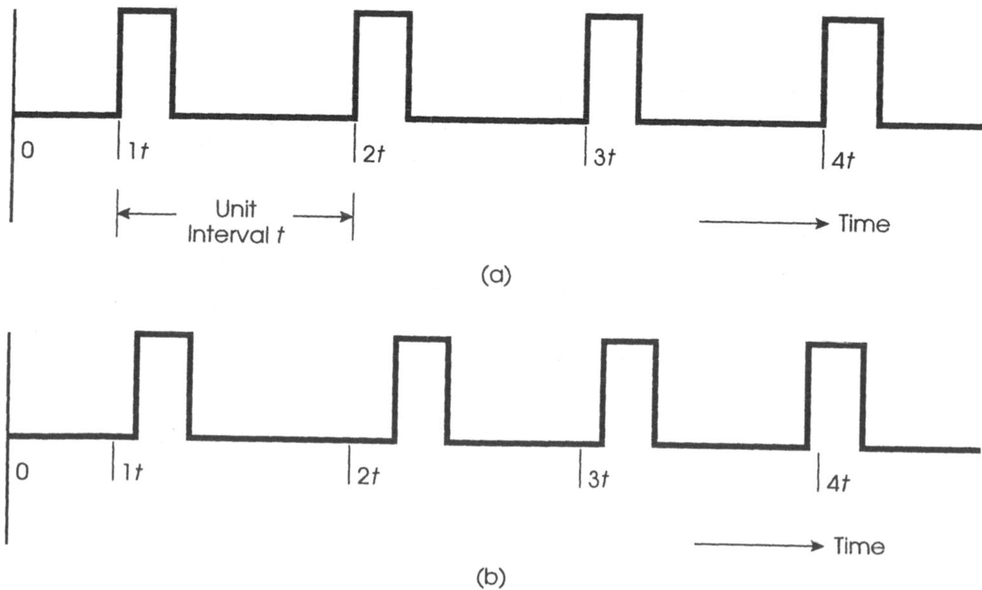

Figure 2–3 (a) Jitter-free pulses spaced uniformly in time; (b) jittered pulses.

for 2,048 kbps rates it is 488 ns. Jitter amplitude may also be specified in degrees, where 1 UI is taken as 360°. The jittered signal exhibits random variation of jitter amplitude with respect to time. These rapid phase variations have a frequency range from 10 Hz to several kHz and are referred to as short-term variations.

Several sources of jitter exist in a digital network. Regenerators and multiplexers on the transmission link are sources of jitter. The clocks that generate the digital signal themselves introduce jitter.

Regenerators are required over long transmission links. The incoming bit stream of weak and noise-laden pulses is regenerated into a new bit stream. For this purpose, timing information is extracted from the incoming pulses. The imperfections associated with the time extraction process contribute to jitter in the regenerated bit stream. Typically, a transmission link will have several regenerators along its length, and jitter will accumulate due to the cumulative effect of multiple regenerators.

Digital multiplexers and demultiplexers also introduce jitter. Digital multiplexers combine several low-rate bit streams (input tributaries) to form a single higher-rate time division multiplexed bit stream. The reverse function is performed by demultiplexers. The input bit streams to the multiplexer may have different clock rates. To generate a higher-rate bit stream, the multiplexer must equalize the bit rate of input tributaries. Justification (also called stuffing) is a commonly applied technique for equalizing bit rates of input tributaries. The term *justification* is used in printing to equalize the lengths of different lines of text with varying number of characters. To do so, additional white spaces are introduced between the words of a line of text. Similarly, to equalize the bit rates of input tributaries, additional bits are added as required. The positions of these "stuffed bits" are predetermined to ensure their removal during demultiplexing. Jitter is introduced during the justification process as well as in the waiting time for justification opportunities. Removal of stuffed bits in demultiplexers also causes jitter.

2.4.2 Wander

Wander is low-frequency jitter. In wander, the phase variations have a frequency of less than 10 Hz. Wander is generally cyclic in its incidence and is introduced largely by environmental factors, such as temperature differences over the length of a transmission link. In a synchronized network, clocks are locked to a timing reference. Because the locking mechanism is imperfect, wander is introduced.

Although complete elimination of jitter and wander in a digital network is not possible, it is necessary to control jitter and wander to minimize slip events.

The limits for jitter and wander in digital networks based on 2,048 kbps and 1,544 kbps hierarchy are specified in ITU-T recommendations G.823 [4] and G.824 [5], respectively. These are discussed in Section 2.14.

2.5 Impact of Slips

Slips may be considered as bursts of errors on the digital bit stream. The error performance objectives for the ISDN are enumerated in CCITT recommendation G.821 [6]. This recommendation, however, does not include errors resulting from slips. The controlled slip-rate objectives are specified separately in CCITT recommendation G.822 [7] (Refer to Section 2.6).

The impact of slips on CCITT common channel signaling system no. 7 (CCS 7) messages is to reduce the effective throughput of the signaling channel. CCS 7 messages are packed into data packets called signal units (SUs). The detailed format of CCS 7 messages is presented in Chapter 4. SUs are sent over a signaling link, which is a 64 kbps channel. There are three types of signal units: the message signal unit (MSU) contains signaling information, the line status signal unit (LSSU) is used for the alignment of the signaling link, and the fill-in signal unit (FISU) is sent when no signaling information is to be transmitted. In CCS 7, error correction by retransmission of the signal unit is applied only to MSUs. No error correction is applied to FISUs and LSSUs. A frame slip on a digital link that includes the signaling channel causes an error in the signal unit. If an FISU is being transmitted when the slip occurs, there is no impact on signaling. If an LSSU is involved, the link alignment procedure may be repeated. Errors in MSUs lead to retransmission with attendant reduction in the effective throughput of the signaling link.

The impact of slips varies with the type of service involved. Slips largely go unnoticed for speech, except for an occasional audible click [8]. The impact of slip is noticeable on group 3 fax transmission, wherein a slip event may mutilate four to eight scan lines [9]. Voiceband data also suffers from slips, and a single slip may cause transmission errors for up to 2 seconds. In some cases, the connection may be disconnected [10].

For the ISDN, data services are particularly sensitive to slips since, unlike the PCM encoded voice, every bit of information is significant in data transfer. Error correction is normally implemented by retransmission, and errors due to slips will increase the retransmission events, leading to a decrease in the effective data transfer throughput. When error correction measures are not implemented, slips result in a degradation of service. For services such as video telephony and videoconferencing, slips may cause a frame freeze and mutilation.

2.6 Network Performance Objectives for Slip Control

Slips cannot be entirely eliminated in a practical network. It is therefore necessary to specify the maximum permissible slip rate that would permit satisfactory provisioning of services in an ISDN.

CCITT recommendation G.822 specifies the controlled slip-rate objectives in an ISDN for an end-to-end international connection. These objectives are defined for a standard digital hypothetical reference connection (HRX) of 27,500 km length shown in Figure 2–4. The digital HRX is a model transmission connection defined in CCITT recommendation G.801 [11] for the purpose of studying and quantifying permissible limits for network performance parameters. Slips constitute one such parameter, and it is appropriate to specify the maximum permissible slip rates in relation to the HRX. The HRX has three sections: two national sections at either end and an international section interconnecting the two national networks. Measures for minimizing slip events are applied to both the international portion of the connection and the national portions, but as we shall see in Section 2.9, the methods adopted in each case differ.

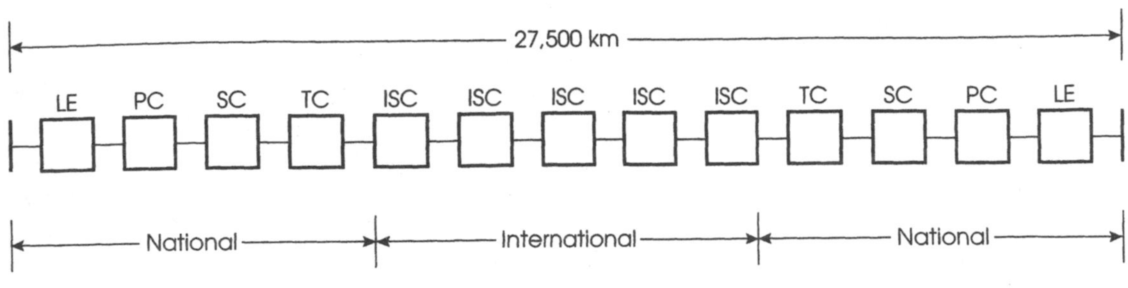

Key
LE: Local Exchange to which ISDN Subscribers are Connected
PC: Primary Center
SC: Secondary Center
TC: Tertiary Center
ISC: International Switching Center

Figure 2–4 Standard digital hypothetical reference connection.

For 64 kbps end-to-end connections, controlled slip rates are defined in three categories. Refer to Table 2–1. For most of the time (98.9%), not more than five controlled slips per day are permitted, as indicated for performance category (a). Slip rates within this threshold satisfy performance requirements for ISDN services. To account for network failures and abnormal transmission impairments, however, slip rates are allowed to exceed the above threshold for very short periods. Categories (b) and (c) specify slip rates for such abnormal situations. It is recognized that the high slip rates prescribed under categories (b) and (c) will cause a degradation of ISDN services.

In addition to prescribing the slip rate for an end-to-end international connection, a breakup of slip rates for the national and international portions of the connection is useful so that the national synchronization network may be planned and implemented to meet these objectives. CCITT recommendation G.822 specifies the allocation for the national and international portions of a connection. Furthermore, within the national network, slip allocations for the local and transit portions are suggested.

Table 2–2 indicates the prescribed allocations of controlled slip rates. The allocation for the national network is 46%. A breakup of 6% for each national transit and 40% for each local portion is given for guidance. This is understandable because the national

Table 2-1 Controlled Slip Rate Performance on a 64 kbps International Connection (CCITT G.822)

PERFORMANCE CATEGORY	MEAN SLIP RATE	PROPORTION OF TIME (TOTAL TIME ≥ 1 YEAR)
(a)	≤ 5 slips in 24 hours	> 98.9%
(b)	> 5 slips in 24 hours and ≤ 30 slips in 1 hour	< 1.0%
(c)	> 30 slips in 1 hour	< 0.1%

Table 2-2 Allocation of Controlled Slip Rates

PORTION OF HRX	ALLOWED PERCENTAGE OF PERMISSIBLE SLIP RATES
International transit	8.0%
Each national transit portion	6.0%
Each local portion	40.0%

transit portion of the network carries a high volume of traffic, and any degradation of performance will have networkwide impact. Because a large proportion of slips is permitted to occur in the local portion of the network, the quality of clocks used in the digital switching exchanges can be chosen based on their hierarchical level in the network.

By combining the objectives prescribed in Tables 2–1 and 2–2, it can be seen that for performance category (a), not more than two slips every 24 hours are permitted for the local portion of the national network. A slip budget of 6% for the national transit corresponds to a slip every 80 hours for category (a) performance. The corresponding figure for international transit works out to one slip every 60 hours.

A country's telecommunication network may be administered by several network operators or companies. These subnetworks require their own synchronization arrangement. In this situation, the permitted slip rate for the national portion of the connection is distributed between different synchronization networks by mutual agreement.

Before examining the synchronization techniques employed for minimizing slips, it is necessary to introduce some of the important parameters that characterize clock behavior and to briefly review the various types of clocks that are commercially available.

2.7 Parameters Linked to Clock Behavior

2.7.1 Frequency Accuracy and Stability

A clock is designed to operate at a certain nominal frequency. In practice, however, the clock operates at a frequency that is different from the nominal value, since in the real world, clocks are neither accurate nor stable. The measure of this difference between the nominal frequency (f_o) and the actual frequency (f_a) divided by the nominal frequency is the frequency accuracy of the clock:

$$\text{frequency accuracy} = \frac{|f_o - f_a|}{f_o}$$

A clock with the nominal frequency of 1,544 kHz operating in the frequency range of 1,544 kHz ± 0.0001 Hz has a frequency accuracy of $0.0001/(1{,}544 \times 10^3)$. This corresponds to an error of one cycle in $1{,}544 \times 10^7$ cycles. Thus, the clock will gain or lose 1 second in $1{,}544 \times 10^7$ seconds (more than 492 years).

Frequency accuracy of clocks is linked to absolute frequency. Slips depend on the relative frequency difference of the nodal clocks and not on the absolute values, however.

Consider an ideal digital network without timing impairments such as jitter and wander. If in this network all the network clocks are out by an identical margin from the nominal frequency, then there will be no slips. This situation would be identical to a network with all clocks operating precisely at their nominal frequencies. Although there are no slips in a totally synchronized network as long as frequency equality is maintained, it is not sufficient simply to maintain frequency equality. A typical connection may span several such synchronized networks. In an international call, each national part is usually independently synchronized within itself. To avoid slips on the links interconnecting the synchronized networks, it is necessary that frequency equality exists not only within each synchronized network but also between them. To fulfill this requirement, synchronized networks must provide both frequency equality and accuracy. As we shall observe in the discussion on plesiochronous operation (Section 2.9.1), the availability of at least one highly accurate and stable clock source is mandatory for each synchronized network. By using such a clock, both frequency equality and accuracy of all the network clocks can be achieved through synchronization.

Frequency stability characterizes the frequency fluctuations of a clock. It is the degree to which a clock produces the same value of frequency for a specified period of time. Figure 2–5 illustrates the concepts of frequency accuracy and stability.

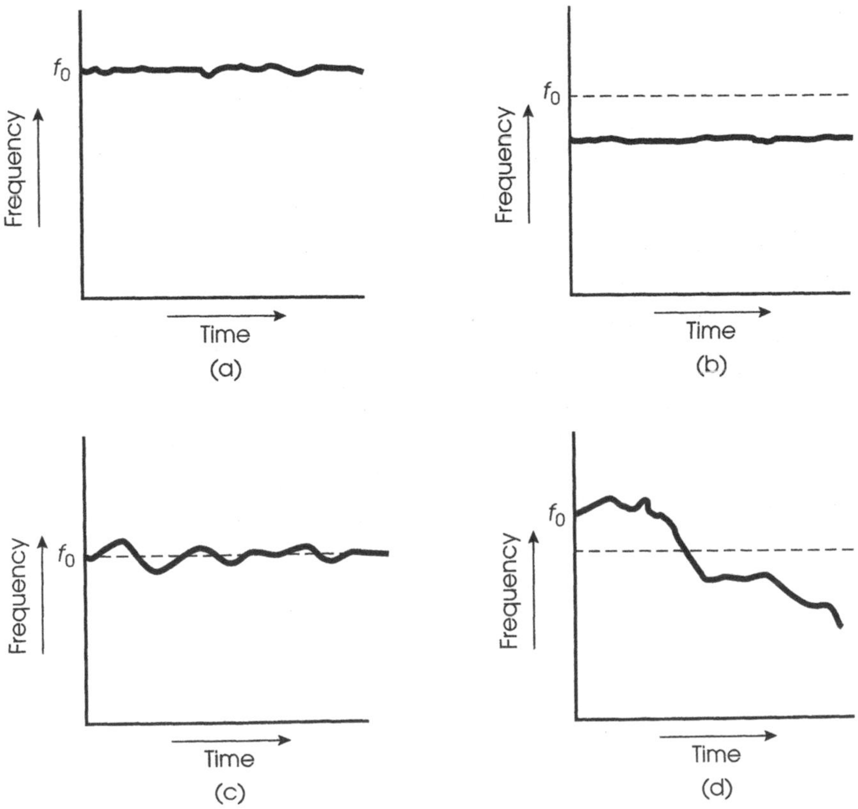

Figure 2–5 (a) Stable and accurate; (b) stable and inaccurate; (c) accurate and unstable; (d) unstable and inaccurate.

2.7.2 Time Interval Error (TIE) and Maximum Time Interval Error (MTIE)

When measuring the frequency of a clock, what is actually measured is the frequency difference with respect to another clock. For these measurements to be meaningful, the clock against which the comparison is made should have significantly higher accuracy and stability. Frequency counters usually provide the possibility to choose either their own internal oscillator or a better quality external clock for performing the comparison. Furthermore, the frequency measurements are usually comparisons of the phase relationships of clocks. Frequency can then be readily computed because there is an inverse relationship between the frequency and time period of a timing signal.

To further define clock accuracy, two parameters have been conceived: time interval error (TIE) and maximum time interval error (MTIE). TIE and MTIE specify clock inaccuracies in terms of the phase difference of the clock with respect to a reference clock. MTIE can be readily measured and can be used to determine slip intervals [12].

MTIE is defined as the maximum peak-to-peak variation in the time delay of a given timing signal with respect to an ideal timing signal within a particular period of observation. The TIE is the variation of time delay of the given timing signal with respect to an ideal timing signal at the end of the observation period.

The definitions of MTIE and TIE are illustrated in Figure 2–6(a). Recommended limits to TIE and MTIE are given in the American National Standards Institute's (ANSI) publication ANSI T.101 [12] and CCITT recommendation G.811 [13] and are discussed later in this chapter.

The concepts of TIE and MTIE may be understood by picturing two runners participating in a race. The difference in timing of the runners in completing the race is similar to the TIE, and the maximum gap between the two runners during the course of the race is similar to the MTIE. The TIE of a clock is the difference between the time taken by the clock to complete a certain number of cycles compared with the time of the same number of cycles for an ideal signal. For a stable but inaccurate clock whose frequency is greater than an ideal timing signal, the TIE at the end of the observation period S is displayed in Figure 2–6(b). The TIE for this clock increases linearly with observation period, and the MTIE and TIE are identical. Figure 2–6(c) shows the TIE versus the observation period for different cases. The long-term frequency departure is obtained by determining the MTIE and dividing it by S, where S is the duration of long-term observation period.

2.8 Atomic and Quartz Clocks

There are two categories of digital clocks: atomic clocks and quartz clocks. Three types of atomic clocks are available commercially: cesium beam clocks, rubidium clocks, and hydrogen maser clocks. Cesium beam clocks are of prime interest for telecommunication applications due to their excellent long-term frequency accuracy and stability (of the order of 1×10^{-11} or better). Cesium beam clocks are primary frequency standards. They do not require frequency calibration from any other source, and they maintain their frequency accuracy and stability throughout their operating life. The cesium beam tube is the main component of a cesium clock. The life expectancy of the tube is about 5 years. On its fail-

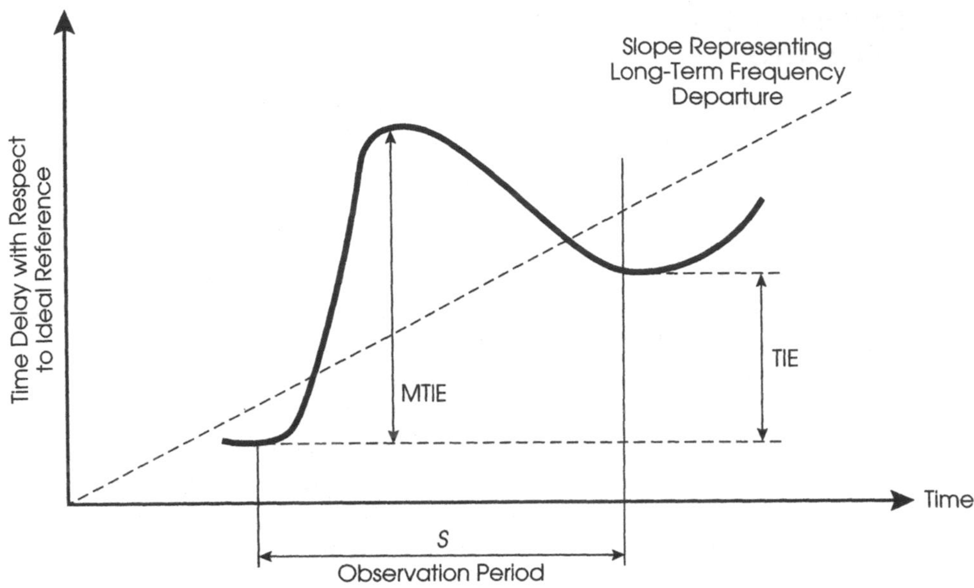

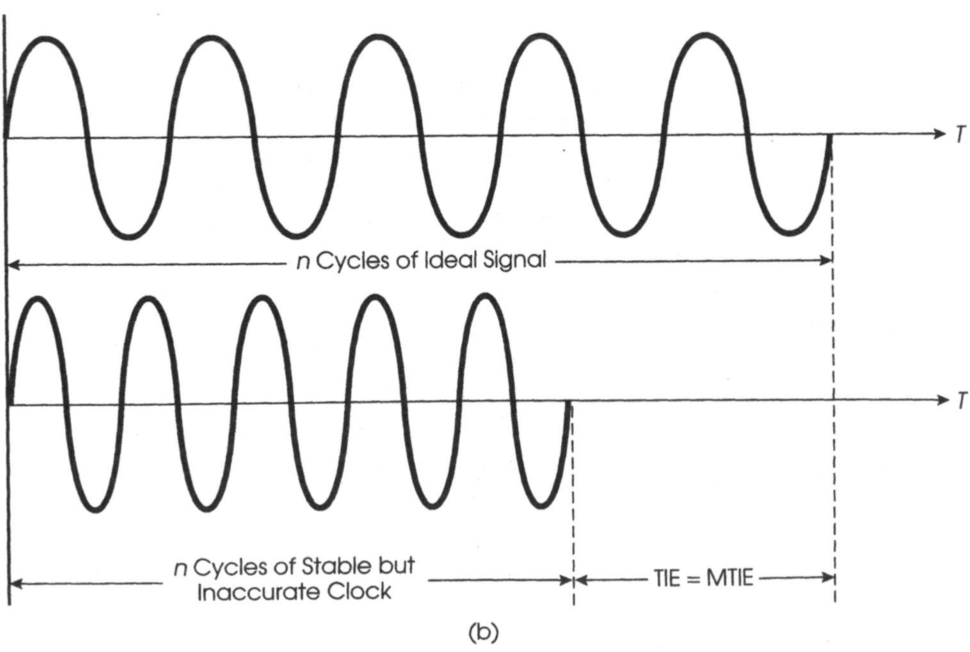

Figure 2–6 (a) Maximum time interval error and time interval error; (b) illustration of TIE; (c) example of TIE.

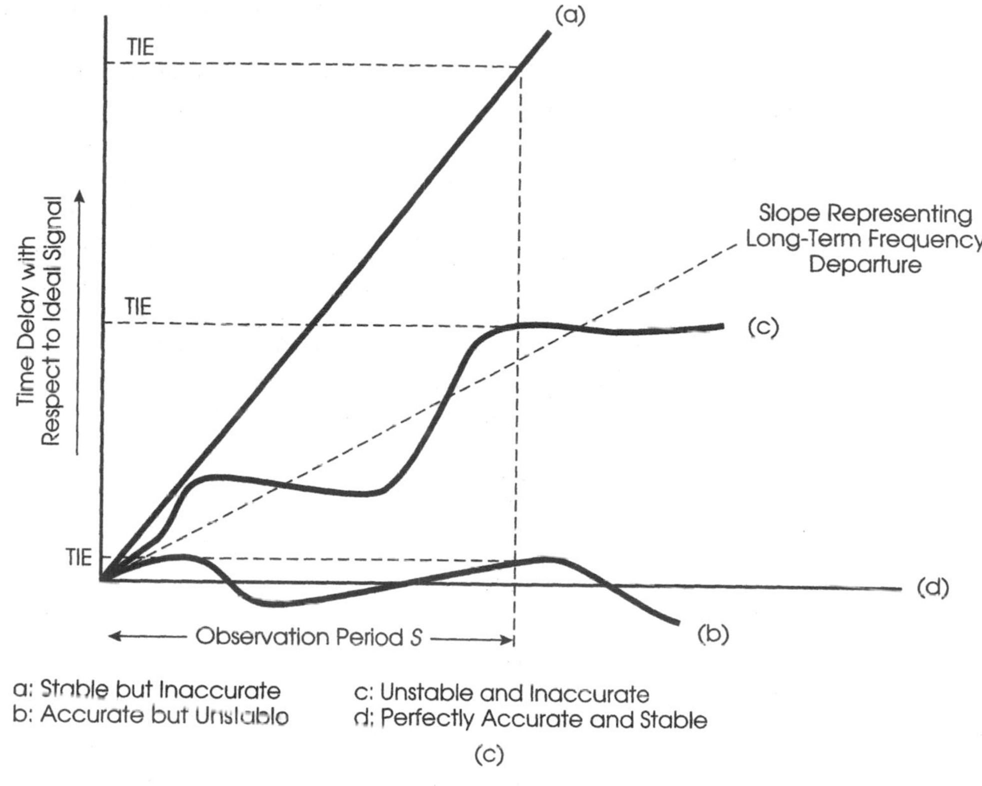

Figure 2–6 (*Continued*)

ure, the tube requires replacement. The principle of operation of a cesium beam standard is described below.

Rubidium clocks are particularly suitable for calibration and testing applications because of their excellent short-term stability and retrace capability (that is, rubidium clocks are able to reach their nominal frequency quite rapidly after a cold restart). Furthermore, they are less expensive and smaller than cesium clocks. Rubidium clocks may also be applied in the network as clocks associated with the highest hierarchy of transit switches. The long-term stability of rubidium clocks is limited to 1×10^{-11}/month, however, and this makes their use inappropriate as a primary standard for network synchronization in which better long-term stability is needed.

For the sake of completeness, mention is made of the hydrogen maser frequency standard, which is among the most expensive atomic clocks available. Despite having the best short-term and long-term frequency stability, it suffers on account of limited frequency accuracy. Therefore, the hydrogen maser is not used for network synchronization.

2.8.1 The Cesium Beam Frequency Standard

The cesium beam standard works on the principle of quantum mechanics. Atoms absorb energy during transition from a lower to higher energy level and radiate energy during a reverse transition. The radiation has very precise and constant frequency. The frequency of transition between two magnetic hyperfine levels of the fundamental state of cesium 133 amounts to 9,192,631,770 Hz. At the heart of the frequency standard is a cesium beam tube, shown in Figure 2–7(a). The output beam current is used in a feedback loop, shown in Figure 2–7(b), to provide an extremely stable and accurate primary reference frequency.

Cesium gas is heated in an oven, and a beam of cesium atoms at the desired energy level is directed by the selecting magnets into a cavity. Inside the cavity, the atoms are excited to higher energy levels by an electromagnetic field created by an injection frequency that is close to the transition frequency of the cesium atoms. The injection frequency is obtained from a combination of a precision quartz oscillator and a frequency synthesizer. When the frequency of the electromagnetic field is identical to the transition frequency of cesium atoms, a maximum number of cesium atoms undergoes the desired state transition. The atoms for which the desired transition has occurred are directed to a detector by another set of selecting magnets. The detector generates an electric current that is proportional to the number of atoms that have undergone the desired transition. The current is maximum

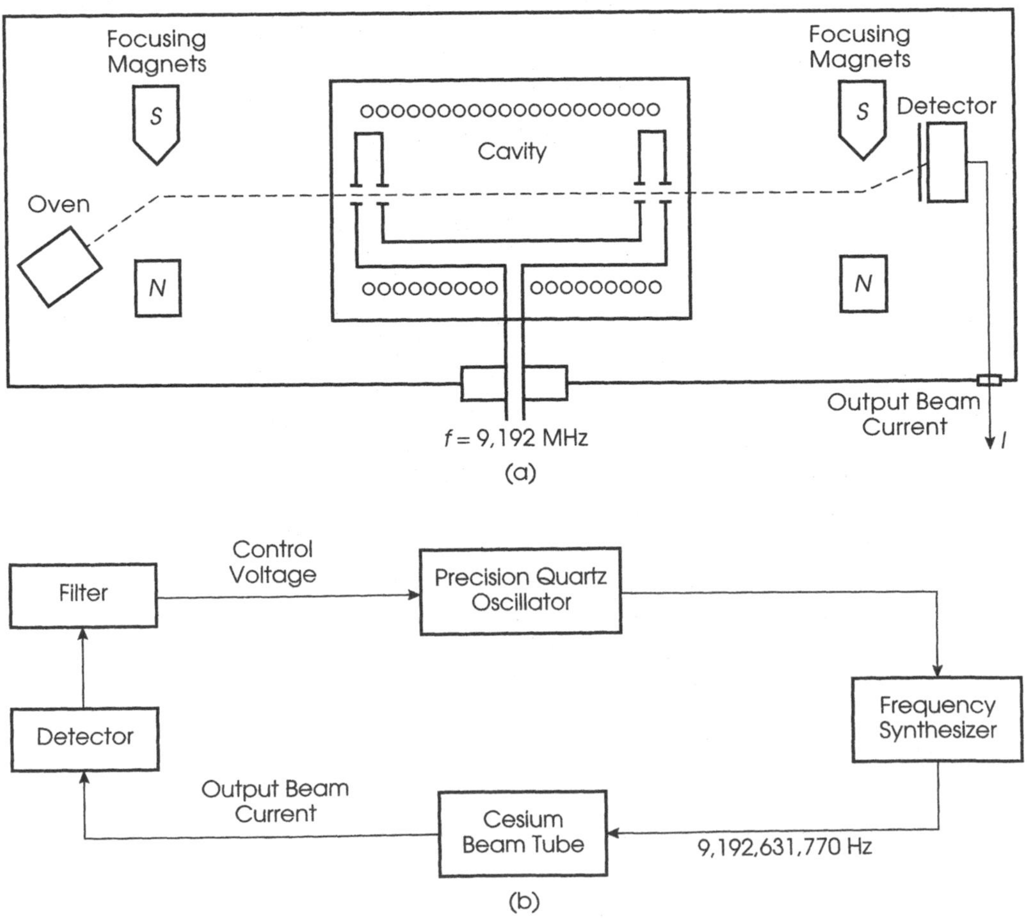

Figure 2–7 (a) A cesium beam tube; (b) cesium beam standard.

when the injection frequency is identical to the radiation frequency of cesium atoms. The detector senses the maximum beam current which is used to generate a control voltage for tuning a quartz oscillator to a highly accurate and stable frequency output of 5 MHz.

2.8.2 Quartz Clocks

A quartz clock uses a quartz crystal unit in an oscillator circuit. Quartz crystals display the piezoelectric effect. The application of pressure on quartz crystal generates charge on opposite faces of the crystal. Conversely, the application of voltage to the crystal faces causes deformation of the crystal structure. A wafer of the quartz crystal is connected to two electrodes on opposite faces and then sealed hermetically to form the crystal unit. When connected to an oscillator circuit, the crystal unit provides a reliable frequency source.

The frequency of quartz clocks vary with time due to both internal and external environmental factors. The internal factor is the aging of the quartz material. Aging is intrinsic to the quartz crystal and may arise due to changes in the quartz material, variation in the degree of contamination of the quartz wafer, redistribution of mechanical stress, or other less significant factors. Depending on the quality of the quartz material and the sophistication of the manufacturing process, quartz clocks are available in a wide range of quality. Aging rates vary from 1×10^{-4}/day to 1×10^{-11}/day. Changes in external factors such as temperature, pressure, magnetic field, and acceleration also contribute to frequency departure of quartz clocks. The frequency departure with time due to the combined effect of aging and environmental factors is called *drift*.

Among the various environmental factors, the impact of temperature variations on the frequency stability of quartz crystals is significant. The effect of temperature changes is minimized in temperature-compensated crystal oscillators (TCXOs) and oven-controlled crystal oscillators (OCXOs). In a TCXO, temperature variations are measured by a sensing device (for example, a thermistor), and a correction voltage is applied to the oscillator to compensate for the effect that temperature change has on frequency. In an OCXO, the crystal unit is enclosed in an oven that maintains the temperature within prescribed limits.

Quartz clocks are used widely in the synchronization of the digital network nodes.

2.9 Synchronization Methods

In discussing network synchronization, it is useful to identify two modes of clock operation, the plesiochronous mode and the synchronous mode. The plesiochronous mode is applied to international connections, and the synchronous mode is used for the national network.

2.9.1 Plesiochronous Mode

In this method high-quality clocks are provided in the switching offices and allowed to run independent of each other. Clocks operating autonomously in this manner are said to be free running, as no external timing control is applied on them. To meet the slip-rate objectives while operating in this mode, the clocks should have very high frequency accuracy. The following calculation will clarify this observation.

Take the example of an end-to-end HRX (shown in Figure 2–4), which has 12 links. Assuming that the total slip rate of five slips per day is uniformly distributed, five slips in 12 days will occur on each link. If the clocks at all the exchange nodes operate plesiochronously, the frequency accuracy of the clocks can be estimated as follows:

$$\text{frequency accuracy} = \frac{\text{number of slips in time } T}{\text{total number of frames in time } T}$$

$$= \frac{5 \text{ slips}}{8{,}000 \text{ (frames/sec)} \times 12 \text{ (days)} \times 24 \text{ (hours/day)} \times 60 \text{ (min/hour)} \times 60 \text{ (sec/min)}}$$

$$= 6 \times 10^{-10} \text{ per day}$$

In actual practice, the clocks used for plesiochronous operation are based on cesium beam technology. Between two cesium clocks each with an accuracy of 1×10^{-11}, a maximum frequency offset of 2×10^{-11} can occur, causing a slip in a little over 72 days, as seen from the following calculation:

$$2 \times 10^{-11} \times 8{,}000 \times 24 \times 3{,}600 = 0.0138 \text{ slip/day}$$
$$= 72.3 \text{ days/slip}$$

If cesium beam clocks are provided at all the 13 nodes of the 12-link HRX, a rate of one slip in about 6 days is expected for an end-to-end connection. This slip rate surpasses by a very large margin the prescribed objective of five slips per day. In plesiochronous working, there is no need to convey timing on the digital links. Consequently, the slips that could have occurred due to transmission link outrages, timing impairments, and other factors are not involved.

Cesium beam clocks are, however, too expensive to install and maintain in each of the numerous digital switches populating a typical national telecommunication network. The plesiochronous method is therefore not used for the national network except where there are several entities whose individual networks comprise the national network (as in the United States).

At present, plesiochronous operation is used for international links. This enables independence in planning and operation of different synchronization networks involved in an end-to-end international connection. CCITT recommendation G.810, however, does not preclude the possibility of synchronization of international links in the future.

Typically, each national network has at least one timing source based on cesium beam technology to permit plesiochronous operation on international digital links. The same timing source can also be used as a primary reference source for synchronizing the national network. The requirements of a primary reference source are examined in Section 2.10.

2.9.2 Synchronous Mode

The synchronous mode of clock working leads to network synchronization. To force the various network clocks to operate on the same frequency, each clock in the network must receive an external reference frequency.

Two techniques that have found application for synchronizing a digital network are the master-slave method and the mutual synchronization method.

Figure 2–8 illustrates the principle of the master-slave method. In the master-slave operation, as the name suggests, there is a master frequency source to which the various network clocks are locked or slaved. The master clock is the primary reference source (PRS). It delivers a frequency output called *primary reference frequency* or *timing*. In a network of practical proportions, it is not possible to supply the primary reference timing directly to each nodal clock. The primary reference timing is therefore supplied to a limited number of nodal clocks. These nodal clocks are associated with the transit exchanges at the highest level of network hierarchy and are called stratum 2 clocks. The stratum 2 clocks are locked to the primary reference timing, and they in turn supply reference timing to the stratum 3 clocks associated with exchanges at the next hierarchical level. This procedure is followed to lock all the clocks in the network.

The master-slave arrangement therefore follows the normal hierarchy of the network. The PRS clock is at the apex (stratum 1), and the slave clocks are at different levels or stratums. Timing in the network flows from top to bottom and never in the reverse direction. A higher stratum clock may feed reference timing not only to clocks at the next

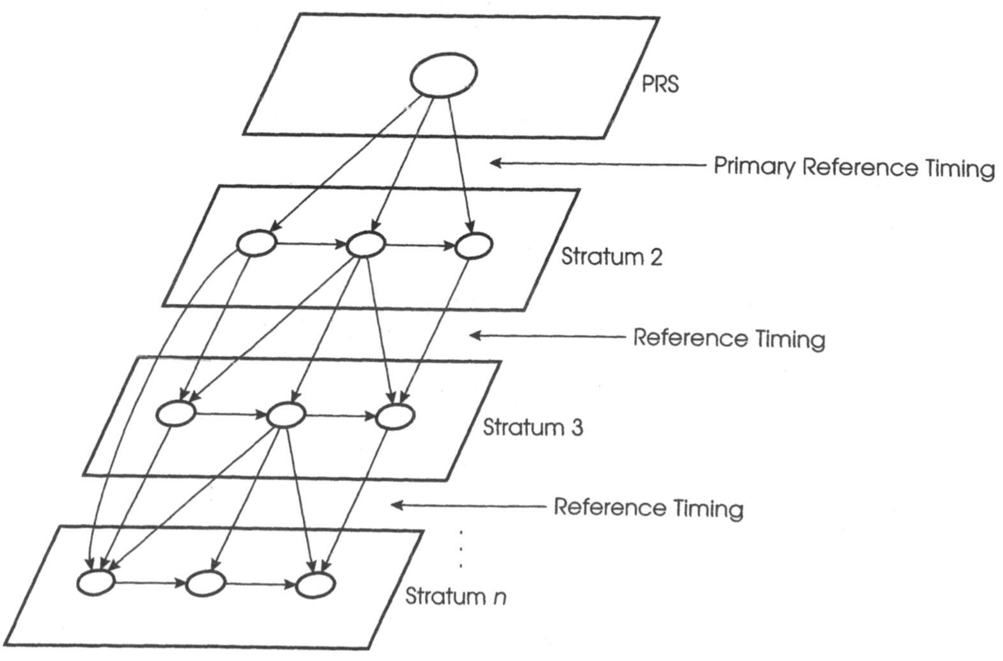

Figure 2–8 Principle of master-slave synchronization.

lower stratum but also to stratum clocks lower down in the hierarchy. For example, a stratum 2 clock may also feed stratum 4 clocks. Reference timing may also be received from a nodal clock of the same stratum. There are a few restrictions regarding the horizontal supply of reference timing. The guidelines for implementing master-slave synchronization are described in Chapter 3. For the purpose of this introductory description on the master-slave method, we have taken the PRS and stratum 1 as synonymous. A BELLCORE Technical Advisory [14] makes a distinction between the two and this is explained in the next section.

The chief merit of the master-slave method lies in its simplicity. The reference timing between network nodes is carried on existing digital links, and the traffic-carrying capacity of the links is not affected. Because there is no overhead in conveying reference timing between nodes, reliability of the synchronization network can be economically achieved by providing redundant reference timing paths to each network node.

In mutual synchronization, the various nodal clocks synchronize each other. Each network node receives the reference frequency from all other nodes and operates at a frequency that is the mean of the frequencies of all the nodes in the network. Refer to Figure 2–9. Mutual synchronization involves a mesh connection between the switching centers in the network. Such a situation does not exist in practice, particularly for the lower levels of the network hierarchy. Mutual synchronization can only apply to a small network or to a limited part of a large network. Further, although mutual synchronization achieves frequency equality, frequency accuracy cannot be ensured. It is reported that in hierarchical telecommunication networks, mutual synchronization may collapse in the event of sudden frequency changes [15]. Problems may also arise during network expansion because the addition of a new node in the network carries the risk of altering the common network frequency.

The master-slave method has found widespread application in national networks. Implementation of this technique requires two categories of equipment: a PRS, which acts as the master and which is described in the following section, and the synchronization equipment at the slave nodes, which is considered in Section 2.12.

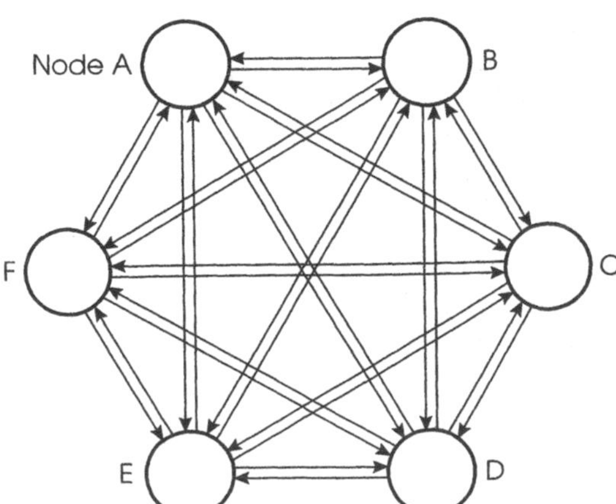

Figure 2–9 Principle of a mutually synchronized network.

2.10 Primary Reference Source (PRS)

A primary reference source (PRS) is required both for providing a frequency reference for implementing master-slave synchronization and for plesiochronous working of international links. In this section, we examine the specifications of a PRS. This is followed by a discussion on typical configurations for PRS.

2.10.1 Primary Reference Source (PRS) Specification

The PRS is an important element for synchronization because it supplies timing to the entire network. CCITT recommendation G.811 stipulates that the timing output for the PRS should be preferably at 2,048 kHz interface, although an interface at other rates—for example, 1,544 kHz, 5 MHz, or 10 MHz—may be provided by mutual agreement between network operators. ANSI T1.101 standards envisage the use of 2,048 kHz or 1,544 kHz interfaces.

The characteristics of a PRS are specified in terms of frequency accuracy, permissible phase discontinuity, and long-term phase variation at its output. The jitter value permitted at the output is not yet specified. Together, these parameters indicate the quality requirements of the primary reference timing that should be supplied by the PRS.

2.10.1.1 Frequency Accuracy

The PRS has a frequency accuracy of 1×10^{-11} or better. As discussed in Section 2.8, the only technology capable of supporting frequency accuracy of this order of magnitude is cesium beam technology. Current implementations of cesium beam clocks can even support a frequency accuracy of up to 7×10^{-12}. Although cesium beam clocks do not require frequency calibration, their accuracy is compared with the coordinated universal time (UTC). The UTC came into effect on January 1, 1972, and is the basis of time throughout the world. It provides an accuracy of about 1×10^{-13}. The UTC is implemented by using an ensemble of cesium clocks maintained under tightly controlled conditions in standardization laboratories.

ANSI T1.101 envisages two possibilities of implementing a PRS. A PRS may be implemented as a completely autonomous reference by using cesium beam clocks. Or, PRS may not be completely autonomous and may operate under the control of UTC derived frequency and time. The UTC based navigational systems such as LORAN-C (long-range navigation) or GPS (global positioning system) are used for this purpose. A description of a LORAN-C 2.048 MHz synchronization reference system is given in appendix B of ANSI T1.101. Only autonomous implementations of PRS are true stratum 1 clocks, since a stratum 1 clock is required to deliver reference timing of an accuracy of 1×10^{-11} completely autonomous of other references [14].

2.10.1.2 Phase Discontinuity (Phase Hits)

A PRS consists of a redundant configuration of cesium clocks. In the event of switching between clocks or other internal rearrangements, a phase discontinuity may arise at the output of the PRS. CCITT recommendation G.811 specifies that the phase discontinuity should be limited to one-eighth of a UI of the output signal.

2.10.1.3 Long-Term Phase Variations

The maximum permissible long-term phase variations at the output of a PRS as specified in terms of the MTIE over different observation periods are shown in Table 2–3. Figure 2–10(a) is a graph showing the MTIE versus the observation period reproduced from CCITT recommendation G.811. Figure 2–10(b) shows the wander model for a PRS.

Long-term phase variations at the output of a PRS are the combined effects of long-term frequency departure and wander of the cesium clock. The following aspects are of interest:

1. For short observation periods of less than 5 seconds (corresponding to the first row of Table 2–3), the phase variation is due to frequency departure of the cesium clock. The wander for such a short observation period is not noticeable, since the wander frequency of the clock is low. As seen from Figure 2–10(a), the frequency accuracy of the cesium clock for this observation period is specified as better than 10^{-7}.
2. For observation periods between 5 and 500 seconds (second row of Table 2–3), the frequency accuracy is specified as better than 5×10^{-9}. The phase variation due to frequency departure is $5S$ ns, where S is the observation period. The wander component is also present due to the longer observation period.
3. In the last row of Table 2–3, X represents the wander component. X has been provisionally taken as 3,000 ns (3 μs), although some administrations support a more stringent figure of 1,000 ns. The long-term frequency departure as indicated by the asymptote is 1×10^{-11}.
4. The MTIE for periods less than 0.05 second has not been defined. This corresponds to short-term phase variations or jitter that may be present in the PRS.

Table 2–3 Maximum Permissible Long-Term Phase Variation at the Output of a PRS

CCITT G.811		ANSI T1.101	
OBSERVATION PERIOD S IN SECONDS	MTIE	OBSERVATION PERIOD S IN SECONDS	MTIE
$0.05 < S \leq 5$	$100\,S$ ns	$0.05 \leq S \leq 1{,}000$	$(10 + 0.29S)$ ns
$5 < S \leq 500$	$(5S + 500)$ ns		
$S > 500$	$(0.01S + X)$ ns	$S > 1{,}000$	$(290 + 10^{-2}S)$ ns

Note: X represents the wander component. The provisional value is 3,000 ns. For values of $S < 0.05$ second, the MTIE is not specified.

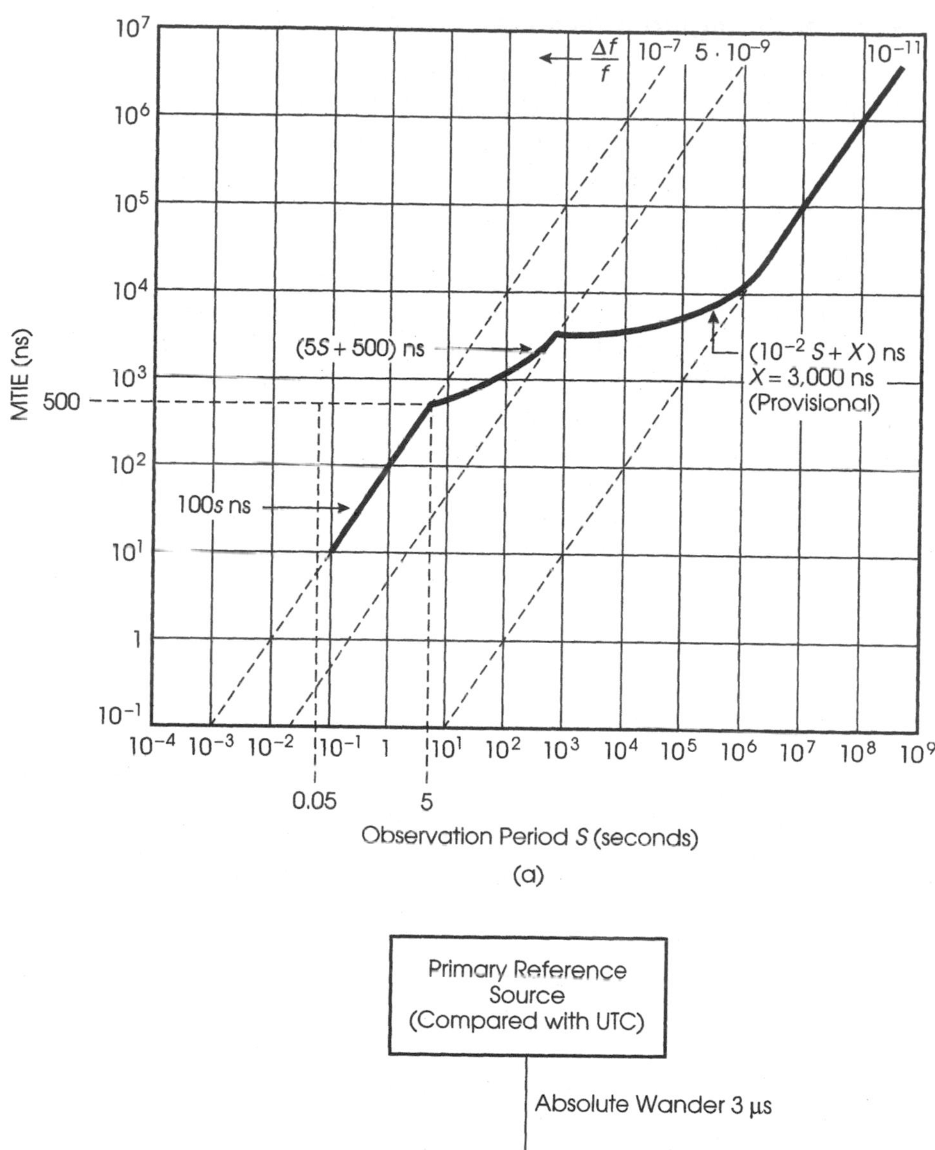

(b)

Figure 2–10 (a) Long-term phase variations versus observation time S at the output of PRS; (b) wander model for PRS (observation periods > 500 seconds).

[Part (a) reprinted from CCITT recommendation G.811 (1988). Timing requirements at the outputs of primary reference clocks suitable for plesiochronous operation of international digital links. Blue Book fasc. III. 5. Reproduced by permission.]

2.10.2 Typical Configurations for the Primary Reference Source

A typical configuration for an autonomous PRS is shown in Figure 2–11. To ensure high reliability and conformance to prescribed standards, a redundant arrangement of cesium beam oscillators is provided. Typically, three cesium beam standards, each operating at 5 MHz, are employed, although output of only one of them is used to supply the reference frequency. The triplicated arrangement ensures that a significant departure of the frequency of one of the clocks is detected by comparing it with the frequencies of the other two clocks. Each cesium oscillator monitors its own signal level and raises an alarm condition in case of failure of its output. Frequency synthesizers in each chain convert 5 MHz signals to 2,048 kHz. A comparator monitors the three frequencies to determine which two of them are close to each other. If f_1, f_2, and f_3 are the three frequencies, then $|f_1 - f_2|$, $|f_2 - f_3|$, and $|f_3 - f_1|$ are computed. Assuming that f_1 and f_2 are close to each other, one of them is switched to deliver the primary reference frequency. The switch, which is also provided in a redundant configuration, receives the alarm signals from the individual chain of cesium clocks in addition to the control signal from the comparator to select one of the outputs. The frequencies are monitored continuously by the comparator, and switching between cesium oscillators occurs based on the above criteria. To limit the

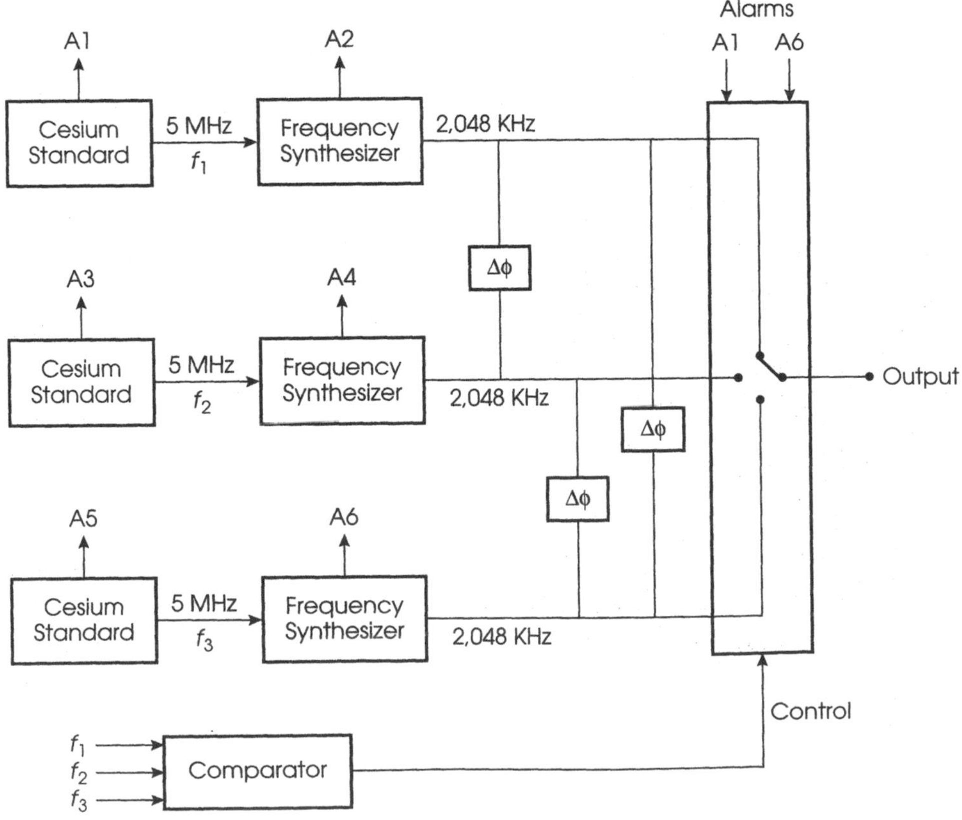

Figure 2–11 Configuration of a typical primary reference source.

phase discontinuity within one-eighth of the UI during the changeover, it is necessary to keep the phase of the three outputs close to each other. In preparation for a possible changeover, phase steppers, which keep the phase of the inactive outputs close to the one that delivers the reference frequency, may be provided.

The output of the PRS is usually a 2,048 kHz sinusoidal signal. To carry the reference frequency to time the network, a distribution arrangement is required. One possibility is to use PCM frame generators that may be timed by the primary reference signal. If the PRS is collocated with an exchange, then the exchange may perform the distribution function.

2.11 PRS Implementation in Telecommunication Networks

The original PRS for the American Telegraph and Telephone Company (AT&T) network was designed as a triplicated arrangement of cesium clocks that were located underground near the geographic center of the 48 contiguous states of the United States at Hillsboro, Missouri [16, 17]. The system delivers output frequencies, called the Bell System reference frequency (BSRF), at 20.48 MHz and 2.048 MHz. Appendix A of ANSI T1.101 describes the important parameters of the BSRF. For a long time, the BSRF was the only primary reference used in the AT&T network. Then, during the late 1980s, 14 primary reference sources were established [18]. The performance of these systems is verified using the GPS.

BELLCORE and the Bell operating companies (BOCs) are further examining various possible configurations for the PRSs. The degree of redundancy would be an important consideration and would depend on the number of offices the PRS may be required to control [14].

In Europe, the PRS in the German network is a system of cesium clocks located at the Telecommunications Engineering Center (FTZ) in Darmstadt [19]. Two primary reference clock systems, located in Paris and Lyons [20], have been established for supplying reference timing for the French telecommunication network. Geographic separation of clock systems enhances the security of reference timing by eliminating disruptions that may be caused by natural disasters or accidents. The same approach has been followed in Japan, where the PRSs are situated in Tokyo and Kyoto.

2.12 Synchronization Equipment at Slave Nodes

The synchronization equipment at the slave nodes, often called a slave or stratum clock, receives reference timing on the incoming digital links. The equipment is typically connectable to two or more links, although only one link is selected at a time. The reference timing on the link contains impairments such as jitter, wander, and errors. As long as these impairments are within permissible limits, the equipment extracts the clock, regenerates, and dejitters the reference timing. If reference timing becomes unavailable or is impaired beyond permissible limits, then a switch over to an alternative link takes place. The links carrying reference timing are selected on the basis of a predefined priority. For example, in the block schematic of the slave clock in Figure 2–12(a), where a possibility of connecting three reference timings is shown, the reference timing from port 1 normally is selected. If this reference becomes unacceptable, a switchover to the next priority timing wired to port 2 takes place. The same applies for a changeover from the priority 2 to the priority 3 reference.

At the heart of the slave clock is a phase lock loop (PLL) that phase locks a high-precision quartz oscillator to the received reference timing. In the synchronized condition, the performance of the local quartz oscillator closely matches that of the received reference clock, and the output is used to time the digital switch or nodal timing supply. A block schematic for the PLL associated with a slave clock is shown in Figure 2–12(b).

If all the reference timings to the slave node become unavailable, then the slave clock enters the holdover mode of operation. The digital memory associated with the PLL stores the control information at the instant the last reference timing was disrupted. This is used during the holdover mode to control the local quartz oscillator. After entering the holdover mode, the slave clock begins to drift slowly, depending on its performance characteristics.

From the previous discussion, three modes of operation for the slave clocks can be identified:

1. In *ideal operation,* there are no impairments on the reference timing received by the clock. This condition seldom exists in practice, but it is useful for studying clock behavior.

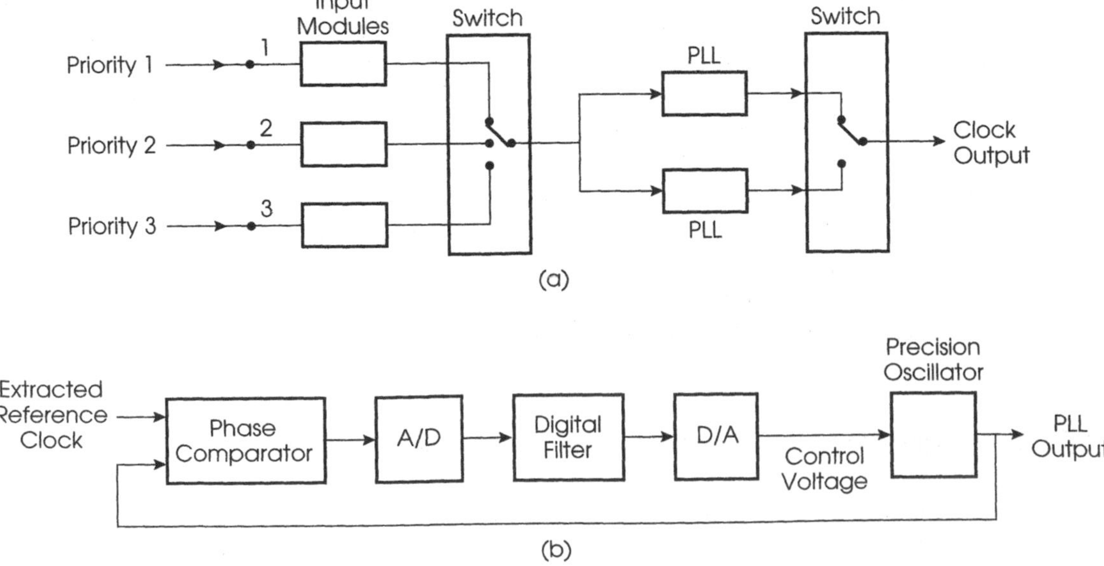

Key
PLL: Phase Lock Loop
A/D: Analog-to-Digital Converter
D/A: Digital-to-Analog Converter

Figure 2–12 (a) A typical slave clock; (b) block schematic of a PLL.

2. In *stressed operation*, the timing reference contains impairments due to jitter, protection switching, and other transmission related causes. These impairments are intrinsic to the timing distribution system. In both the ideal and stressed modes of operation, the slave clock is synchronized to the reference timing.
3. *Holdover operation* is initiated due to the unavailability of reference timing to the slave clock. The holdover operation is terminated and the synchronized operation is resumed when reference timing is restored.

2.13 Specification of Slave Clocks

CCITT recommendation G.812 [21], ANSI T1.101, and BELLCORE Technical Advisory TA-1244 [22] provide specifications for slave clocks.

2.13.1 Free-Run Accuracy, Holdover Stability, and Pull-In Range

The performance of slave clocks at various stratum levels can be specified in terms of three clock parameters: free-run accuracy, holdover stability, and the pull-in range [22].

Free-run accuracy is the frequency accuracy of a clock that has never functioned as a slave clock or has been in the holdover mode for such a long time that there is no influence of synchronized operation on its frequency accuracy.

Holdover stability is simply the amount of frequency offset that a clock has after it has lost its synchronization reference. Although such an event is rare, holdover stability is an important parameter since the slip rate depends on the holdover stability of the slave clock until reference timing is restored.

The pull-in range specifies the frequency range of the reference timing within which a slave clock can achieve and maintain synchronization. A slave clock receives timing reference from the same or a higher stratum level. In the worst case, the timing reference received by the clock may have a frequency accuracy equal to its own free-run accuracy. Therefore, to maintain synchronization, the clock should have a pull-in range equal to its own free-run accuracy. Notice that synchronization of a slave clock with a reference having frequency accuracy equal to its own does not improve the frequency accuracy of the network. Nevertheless, frequency equality between the concerned nodes is achieved, thereby minimizing slips.

2.13.2 Maximum Relative Time Interval Error (MRTIE)

Specifications of slave clocks in CCITT recommendation G.812 is based on maximum relative time interval error (MRTIE), which is similar to MTIE except that the measurement is made with respect to a real (rather than ideal) high-precision clock (for example, a cesium clock instead of UTC). The MRTIE is specified for ideal and holdover modes of operation; the specifications for the MRTIE under stressed mode are not yet finalized.

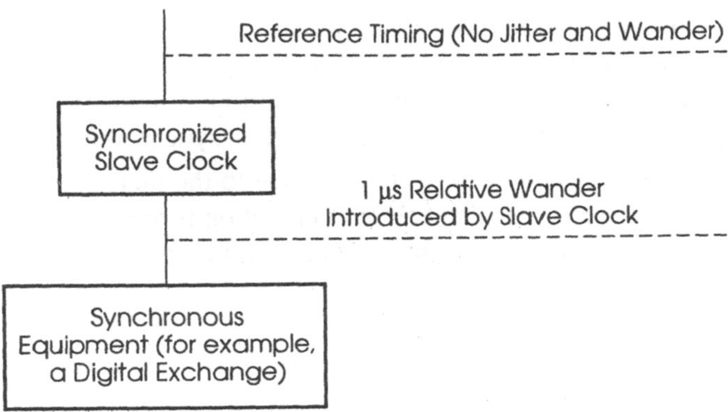

Figure 2–13 Wander model for synchronized slave clocks (observation period > 100 seconds).

In the ideal mode, the MRTIE due to wander is specified at a constant value of 1,000 nanoseconds (1 μs) for observation periods of 100 seconds and beyond. For shorter observation periods, between 0.5 and 100 seconds, MRTIE value is not yet specified.

A wander model for slave clocks in the absence of jitter and wander on the synchronizing link is shown in Figure 2–13.

In the holdover mode, the MRTIE of slave clocks depends on two factors: the initial frequency offset at the instant the clock goes into holdover mode and the holdover stability. The MRTIE for slave clocks during the holdover mode is shown in Figure 2–14. Two

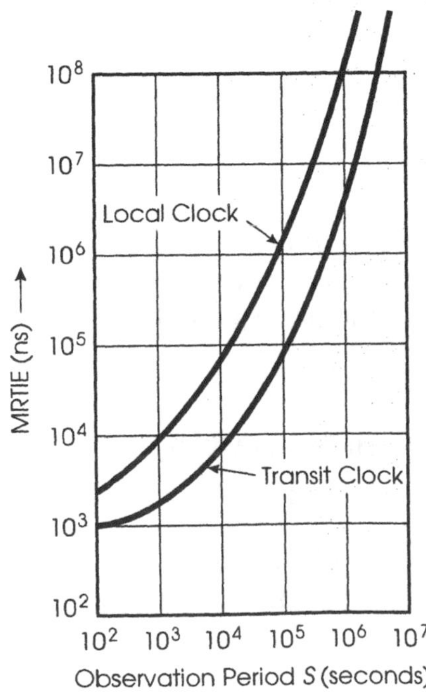

Figure 2–14 Permissible MRTIE due to wander for slave clocks in holdover mode. [Reprinted from CCITT recommendation G.812 (1988). Timing requirements at the outputs of slave clocks suitable for plesiochronous operation of international digital links. Blue Book fasc. III. 5. Reproduced by permission.]

types of clocks, local and transit, are identified in this illustration to indicate that the MRTIE depends on the application.

Table 2–4 summarizes the specifications of a PRS and transit and local slave clocks as per CCITT recommendations. Notice that in specifying clock performance in the holdover mode, CCITT recommendation G.812 [21,23] identifies no stratum levels, because the number of stratum levels depends on the specific structure of the national network.

For the North American network, different qualities of slave clocks for stratum levels 2, 3, 4, and 4E have been identified in ANSI T1.101. The specifications are summarized in Table 2–5. On the other hand, in the German network, the local exchanges use the same quality of clocks as those used for the transit exchanges. The reasons given are simplified planning and the need to reduce slip rates in lower levels of the network in view of the heavy data traffic in these levels [15]. Ultimately, the objective is to stay within the slip allocation permitted for the national part of the network and as pointed out in Section 2.6, the breakup of slip rates for the national local and national transit is only for guidance.

The additional requirements for different stratum clocks listed in Table 2–5 are based on planning and engineering considerations discussed further in Chapter 3.

In addition to the stratum clocks identified in Table 2–5, BELLCORE TA-1244 identifies a stratum 3E clock that has the capability of filtering large short-term instability in the timing reference and producing a clean timing output. This clock has better holdover performance than stratum 3 clocks and is also suitable for the synchronous optical network (SONET). A detailed discussion of stratum 3E clocks is presented in Chapter 15. The slip rate in the holdover mode for stratum 2, 3, and 3E clocks is shown in Table 2–6 [14]. It is seen that there is sufficient time available to restore references of the slave clock, as the slip rates are quite low in the holdover mode, particularly for stratum 2 and 3E clocks. Loss of timing references generates alarm conditions and with reasonable efficiency in maintenance and repair, the slip rate objectives can be readily met.

2.13.3 Phase Discontinuity

As described in Section 2.12, slave clocks typically provide redundancy in terms of the number of timing references. For applications in transit exchanges, slave clocks also provide redundant arrangement of PLLs. These features require switching between redundant elements in case of failures or during internal testing. Phase discontinuity in the output of a slave clock is likely to arise during switching from one reference timing to an-

Table 2–4 International Standards for Network Clocks

CCITT G.811, G.812			
Clock Type	Accuracy	Holdover Stability	Frequency Offset
1 (PRS)	1×10^{-11}	—	—
Transit	—	1×10^{-9} per day	5×10^{-10}
Local	—	2×10^{-8} per day	1×10^{-8}

Table 2-5 North American Standards for Network Clocks

ANSI T1.101 [12], BELLCORE TA-001244 [22], AND TA-000436 [14]					
STRATUM LEVEL	ACCURACY	HOLDOVER STABILITY	PULL-IN RANGE	MTIE DURING REARRANGEMENT (DS-1)	ADDITIONAL REQUIREMENTS
PRS	1×10^{-11}	Not applicable	Not applicable	80 ns	For PRS that is autonomous: verification to UTC. For PRS that is not completely autonomous: under control of UTC.
2 (transit)	1.6×10^{-8}	1×10^{-10} per day	1.6×10^{-8}	MTIE ≤ 1 μs Phase change slope ≤ 81 ns in any 1.326 ms	Terminate two timing references. Minor alarms: short-term loss of single reference, misframes. Major alarms: long-term loss of single reference, misframes.
3 (local)	4.6×10^{-6}	Up to 255 slips on day 1	4.6×10^{-6}	MTIE ≤ 1 μs Phase change slope ≤ 81 ns in any 1.326 ms	Terminate two timing references. Minor alarms: loss of single reference, misframes. Major alarms: loss of both timing references.
4 (channel banks, remote switch units, digital loop carrier)	32×10^{-6}	No holdover	32×10^{-6}	No requirement	Typically terminate only one timing reference.
4 E (digital PABXS)	32×10^{-6}	No holdover	32×10^{-6}	MTIE ≤ 1 μs Phase change slope ≤ 81 ns in any 1.326 ms	Terminate two timing references.

Table 2-6 Slip Rate in Holdover Mode

Stratum Level	Slips on First Day of Holdover	Slips in First Week of Holdover
2	1 or fewer	1
3E	1	13
3	17	314

other or from one PLL to another. CCITT recommendation G.812 stipulates the following requirements in this context.

(i) For a period of $2^{11} \times$ UI, phase variation should not exceed $\frac{1}{8}$ UI.

(ii) For a period exceeding (i) above, phase variation in each interval of $2^{11} \times$ UI, should not exceed $\frac{1}{8}$ UI, up to a total of 1 μs.

These specifications impose two types of requirements on the slave clocks during internal testing or rearrangements. First, to avoid sudden changes in phase, the maximum permissible rate of phase variation has been specified. Second, a ceiling on the total phase variations during such events has been imposed, which in turn limits the maximum period for which internal testing or clock rearrangements may last.

2.14 Jitter and Wander Specifications for Digital Networks

As mentioned earlier, a two-pronged approach is needed to control slips in a digital network: first, by synchronizing the network so that all the synchronous nodes operate at a common frequency, and second, by control of timing impairments such as jitter and wander. We have already discussed the first aspect. The second aspect can be addressed by specifying the maximum permissible wander for the PRS and slave clocks.

Recommendations for control of jitter and wander in digital networks based on 2,048 kbps and 1,544 kbps hierarchy are described in CCITT recommendations G.824 and G.823, respectively. These provide common standards that may be applied to various digital equipment in the network. Among other things, the standards specify the following:

- The maximum permissible jitter and wander at the output port of a digital network element.
- The amount of jitter and wander that should be tolerated at the input port of a digital network element.

To satisfy these specifications, necessary control measures are implemented at different stages: during equipment design, during planning and engineering of the network, and finally by monitoring the performance during operation.

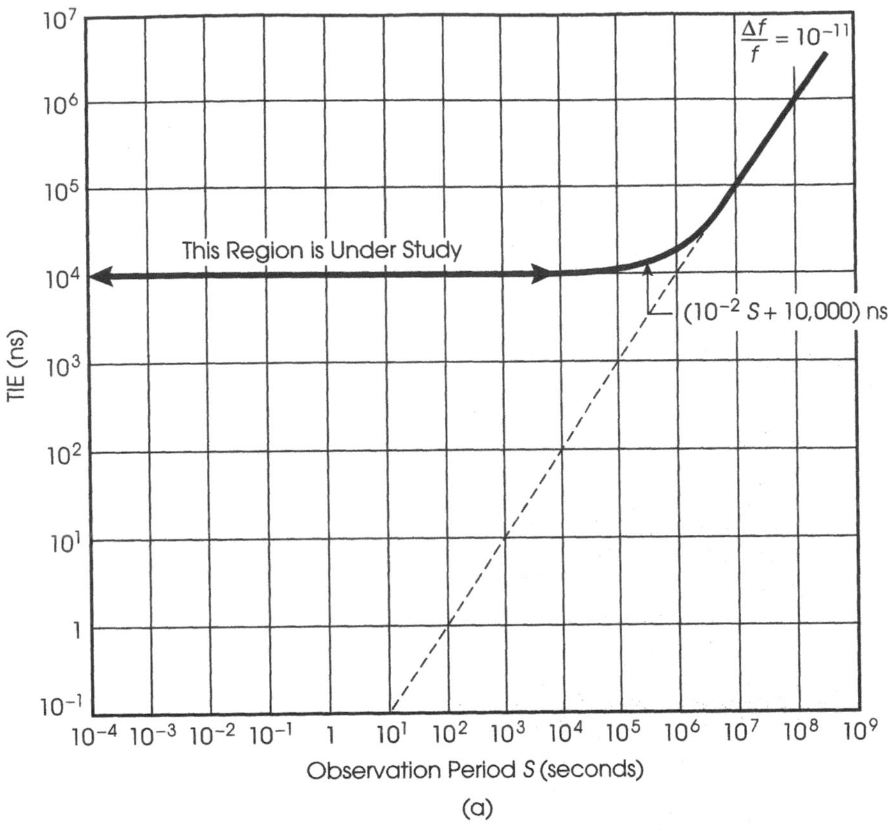

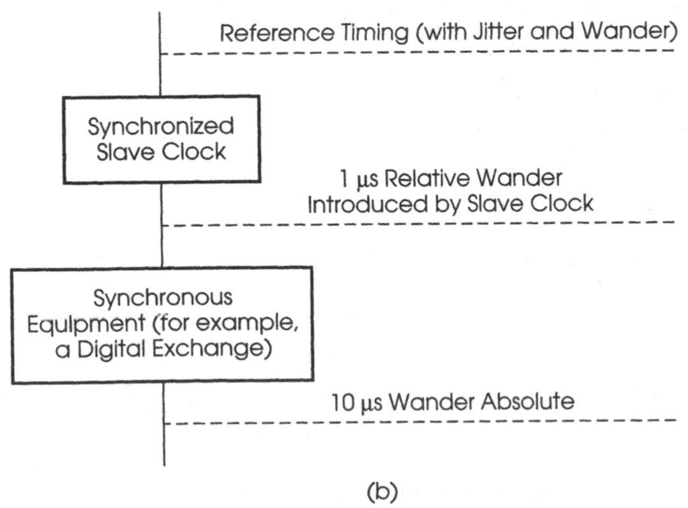

Figure 2–15 (a) MTIE versus observation period S at the output of a synchronous node when the synchronizing signal contains jitter and wander; (b) wander model for a synchronous node (observation period > 100 seconds).
[Part (a) reprinted from ITU-T recommendation G.823 (1993). The control of jitter and wander within digital networks which are based on the 2048 Kb/s hierarchy. Rev. 1. Reproduced by permission.]

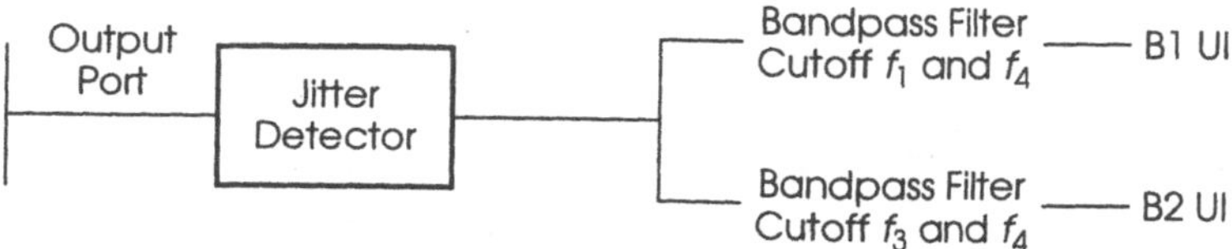

Figure 2–16 Arrangement for measuring output jitter.

2.14.1 Permissible Wander at the Output

In Section 2.12.2, the maximum permissible wander at the output of a slave clock was specified as 1 μs, assuming that the reference timing is without any impairment, that is, no jitter and wander. Recommendations G.823 and G.824 specify the maximum permissible wander at the output of a synchronous node in the presence of jitter and wander. The MTIE for an observation period of S seconds, for values of $S > 10^4$ seconds, should not exceed $(10^{-2}S + 10{,}000)$ ns. Therefore, the maximum permissible wander at the output of a synchronous node is 10 μs. The (MTIE for S less than 10^4 is not yet defined.) These specifications are shown in Figure 2–15(a). The corresponding wander model is in Figure 2–15(b).

2.14.2 Permissible Jitter at the Output

An arrangement for measuring output jitter is shown in Figure 2–16. The B1 and B2 unit intervals (UIs) of output jitter measured by this arrangement must be within the maximum permissible jitter at the output of a digital node, as specified in ITU-T recommendation G.823. These values for 2,048 kbps and 1,544 kbps rates are shown in Table 2–7.

2.14.3 Jitter and Wander Tolerance at Input Ports

The jitter and wander that should be tolerated at the input ports of digital equipment, shown in Figure 2–17, are for 2,048 kbps digital hierarchy and are based on ITU-T recommendation G.823. The mask shown in Figure 2–17 is used in testing slave clocks. This aspect is further discussed in Chapter 3.

Table 2-7 Maximum Permissible Jitter at the Output of a Digital Node

			Filter Bandwidth		
			Band-Pass Filter as in Figure 2–16		
Digital Rate	Jitter B1 UI f_1 and f_4	Limit B2 UI f_3 and f_4	f_1	f_3	f_4
2,048 kbps	1.5	0.2	20 Hz	18 kHz	100 kHz
1,544 kbps	5.0	0.1	10 Hz	8 kHz	40 kHz

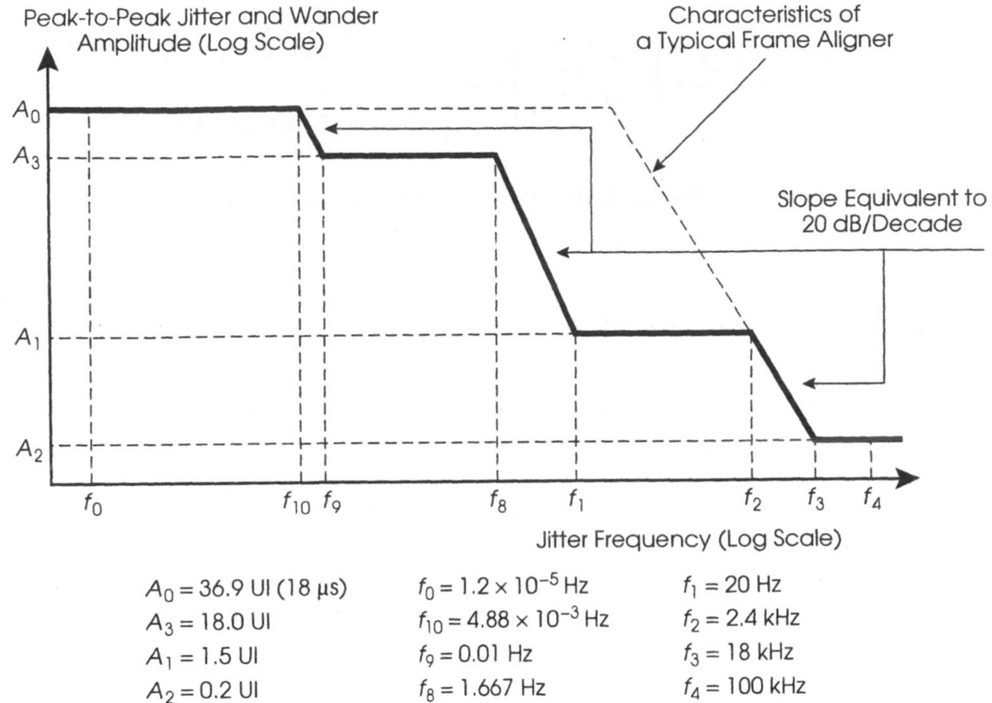

Figure 2–17 Lower limit of maximum tolerable input jitter and wander, 2,048 kbps rate.
[Reprinted from ITU-T recommendation G.823 (1993). The control of jitter and wander within digital networks which are based on the 2048 Kb/s hierarchy. Rev. 1. Reproduced by permission.]

The slave clock should be able to lock to a reference timing that contains jitter within the limits specified above. When these limits are exceeded, the reference input may be rejected.

The value A_0 represents the relative wander that may exist between an input signal to a synchronous node and the internal timing supplied by a synchronized slave clock. This is illustrated in Figure 2–18. A_0 is specified as 18 μs, and the aligner terminating the PCM link should be able to accommodate this wander. A frame aligner with a capacity to store two frames (as described in Section 2.3) can readily accommodate this wander, since after a slip event, a hysteresis of 125 μs is created between the read and write pointers. The minimum requirement is a hysteresis of 18 μs so that wander may not cause another slip immediately following a slip event.

For the terrestrial network, the path delay variations are well within the wander limit of 18 μs. In case of satellite links, variations in the position of the geostationary satellite from its ideal position causes Doppler shift, resulting in wander that may be quite large (0.5 to 2 ms). This wander is usually accommodated in the buffer stores associated with the earth station, which are much larger than the buffers in the terrestrial equipment

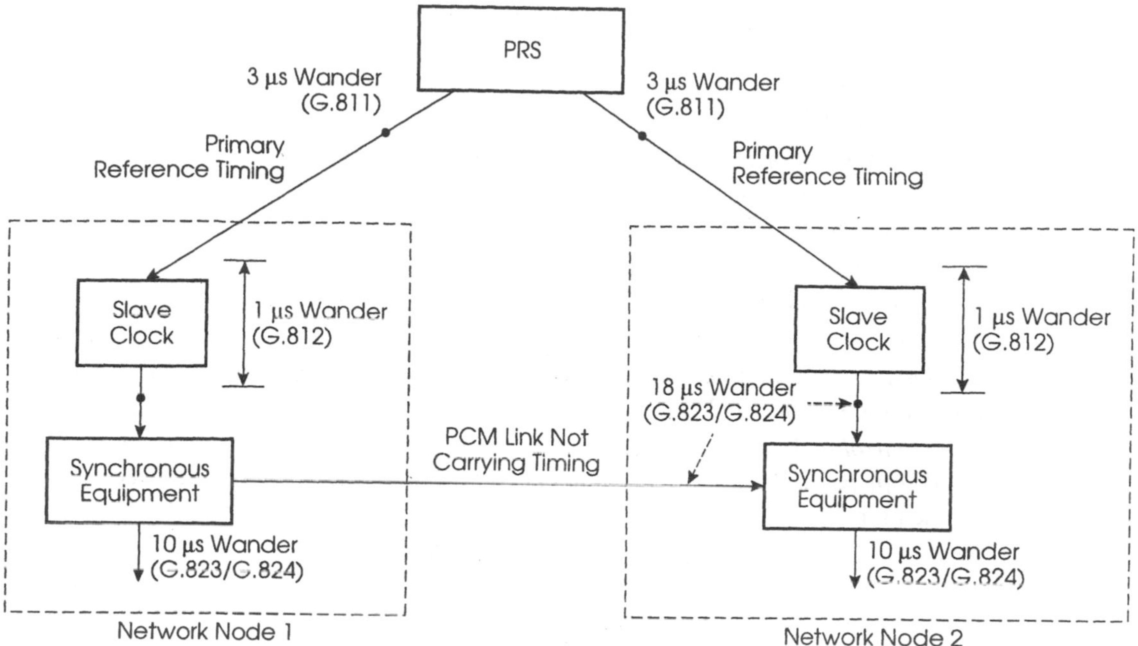

Figure 2–18 Wander model for a synchronized network.

(1,000 bits). In this case, the aligners terminating the PCM links at the exchange only need to accommodate a wander of 18 μs that may arise on the terrestrial links.

2.15 Wander Model for the Synchronized Network

The wander model for the synchronized network shown in Figure 2–18 brings together the various wander specifications discussed in this chapter.

2.16 Remarks

We have discussed the basic concepts of digital network synchronization. The specifications for the PRS and slave clocks that are required for achieving synchronization have also been described.

For international plesiochronous connections, satellite links using time division multiple access (TDMA) may be employed. Satellite links are not preferred for carrying reference timing in the national network, however. In the next chapter, we consider planning, engineering, testing, and monitoring of network synchronization.

References

[1] Reeve, W. D. *Subscriber Loop Signaling and Transmission Handbook: Digital.* IEEE Press, 1995.

[2] *General Aspects of Digital Transmission Systems: Terminal Equipments. Synchronous Frame Structure Used at Primary and Secondary Hierarchical Levels.* ITU-T recommendation G.704, rev. 1. International Telecommunication Union, 1991.

[3] *Considerations on Timing and Synchronization Issues.* CCITT Blue Book, fascicle III.5, recommendation G.810, International Telecommunication Union, 1988.

[4] *The Control of Jitter and Wander within Digital Networks Which Are Based on the 2048 kbps Hierarchy.* ITU-T recommendation G.823, rev. 1. International Telecommunication Union, 1993.

[5] *The Control of Jitter and Wander within Digital Networks Which Are Based on the 1544 kbps Hierarchy.* ITU-T recommendation G.824, rev. 1. International Telecommunication Union, 1993.

[6] *Error Performance of an International Digital Connection Forming Part of an Integrated Services Digital Network.* CCITT Blue Book, fascicle III.5, recommendation G.821. International Telecommunication Union, 1989.

[7] *Controlled Slip Rate Objectives on an International Digital Connection.* CCITT Blue Book, fascicle III.5, recommendation G.822. International Telecommunication Union, 1989.

[8] Decina, M., and U. deJulio. *International Activities on Network Synchronication for Digital Communication.* IEEE International Communications Conference, 1979.

[9] Abate, J. E., and H. Drucker. *The Effect of Slips on Facsimile Transmission.* IEEE International Conference on Communications, 1988.

[10] Drucker, H., and A. C. Morton. *The Effect of Slips on Data Modems.* IEEE International Conference on Communications, 1987.

[11] *Digital Transmission Models.* CCITT Blue Book, fascicle III.5, recommendation G.801. International Telecommunication Union, 1988.

[12] American National Standard for Telecommunications. *Synchronization Interface Standard.* ANSI T1.101-1994.

[13] *Timing Requirements at the Outputs of Primary Reference Clocks Suitable for Plesiochronous Operation of International Digital Links.* CCITT Blue Book, fascicle III.5, recommendation G.811. International Telecommunication Union, 1988.

[14] "Digital network synchronization plan." BELLCORE Technical Advisory TA-NWT-000436, issue 2, June 1993.

[15] Wolfram, E. "Digital signals with the right timing." Siemens Telecom Report 12, no. 6, 1989.

[16] Oberst, J. F. "Keeping Bell System frequencies on the beam." Bell Laboratories Record, pp. 84–89, March 1974.

[17] Abate, J. E. et al. "The switched digital network plan." Bell System Technical Journal, pp. 1297–1320, Sept. 1977.

[18] Abate, J. E. et al. "AT&T's new approach to the synchronization of telecommunication networks." IEEE Communications Magazine, pp. 35–45, April 1989.

[19] Heinz, B., and E. Steiner. "High-precision synchronisation in the ISDN." Siemens Telecom Report 11, no. 5, 1988.

[20] Charbit, R., M. Dudet, and G. Houard. "Synchronising the French digital telecommunication network." Commutation et Transmission, pp. 5–12, no. 4, 1986.

[21] *Timing Requirements at the Outputs of Slave Clocks Suitable for Plesiochronous Operation of International Digital Links.* CCITT Blue Book, fascicle III.5, recommendation G.812. International Telecommunication Union, 1988.

[22] "Clocks for the synchronized network: Common generic criteria." BELLCORE TA-NWT-001244, issue 2, Nov. 1992.

[23] *Draft Amendments to Recommendations* G.812. COM XVIII R-86-E, CCITT Study Period 1989–1992, Study Group XVIII, report R 86, p. 61, Feb. 1992.

3 Planning, Testing, and Monitoring Network Synchronization

Acronyms

ANSI	American National Standards Institute
BER	bit error rate
BITS	building-integrated timing supply
BOC	Bell operating companies
CC	composite clock
CCITT	the International Telegraph and Telephone Consultative Committee
DLC	digital loop carrier
ESF	extended superframe format
GPS	global positioning system
ITU-T	International Telecommunication Union-Telecommunication Standardization Sector
LAPD	link access procedure in D-channel
LORAN-C	long-range navigation-C
LOS	loss of signal
MTIE	maximum time interval error
MTTR	mean-time-to-repair
NMS	network management system
PDH	plesiochronous digital hierarchy
PLL	phase lock loop
PRS	primary reference source
SDH	synchronous digital hierarchy
SES	severely errored second
SF	superframe format
SONET	synchronous optical network
TIE	time interval error
TSG	timing signal generator
UTC	coordinated universal time

ABSTRACT

This chapter covers planning, testing, and monitoring of network synchronization. The topics include:

- Engineering guidelines and planning issues in digital network synchronization (discussed in the context of master-slave methodology)
- Transport of timing between network nodes
- Intrabuilding timing distribution
- Testing and validation of slave clocks
- Guidelines for monitoring the synchronization of the network

3.1 Introduction

The basic concepts, standards, and techniques in digital network synchronization were discussed in Chapter 2. In this chapter, practical issues concerning network synchronization are addressed. The principal requirement of a synchronized digital network is that it should meet the slip rate objectives. Various implementation activities—namely, planning, testing, and monitoring—are geared to meet this goal.

3.2 Network Synchronization Planning

In view of the extensive deployment of the master-slave method for synchronizing national networks, planning issues are discussed here in the context of master-slave operation. The key issues are the following:

- Primary reference source provisioning
- Timing of signal transport
- Intrabuilding timing distribution
- Avoidance of timing loops

3.2.1 Primary Reference Source (PRS) Timing

The options available to a network operator in provisioning of primary reference sources (PRSs) are as follows:

1. Obtaining the reference timing from an external agency such as an operator of international services, another operator in the national network, or a timing standards laboratory. A PRS, external to the network, may or may not contain stratum 1 clocks.
2. Owning and operating a separate PRS. Exercise of option 1 should be considered when

(a) The size of network to be synchronized is small.
(b) There are adequate guarantees on the uninterrupted availability of reference timing by the external agency.
(c) The PRS installation of the timing supplier has been inspected, and its performance in terms of frequency accuracy, phase discontinuity, and long-term phase variation has been verified.
(d) Reliable transport facilities for the reference timing are available or can be planned economically.

In addition, it is desirable that reference timing is available from two sources, at different geographic locations, so that failure of one PRS (or the associated distribution facilities) does not result in the nonavailability of a timing reference.

Although option 1 is economically attractive, due to the key significance of master timing owning and operating a separate PRS is advisable for large network operators.

For the Bell operating companies (BOCs), BELLCORE recommends that each BOC deploy its own PRSs (option 2) [1] and all large network operators in the United States have deployed their own PRSs. The benefits of option 2 are the following:

- A reduction in the number of clocks in a serial chain, thus improving the overall synchronization performance
- Ease in the administration of synchronization distribution

For additional security, it is worthwhile to provide at least two PRSs. This helps to avoid the risk of long-term disruption of reference from catastrophic events, such as a fire.

To minimize costs, a mix of options 1 and 2 can also be considered. For example, the network operator may own one PRS and make provision for obtaining standby reference timing from an external agency during contingencies.

There are two main approaches in implementing a PRS. One possibility is to implement an autonomous PRS, using cesium beam clocks that would operate independently of all other references. In this case, the PRS is also a stratum 1 clock, since it is capable of independently supplying a timing with long-term frequency accuracy of 1×10^{-11}. Alternatively, a PRS may be a nonautonomous system consisting of an internal clock that is disciplined by coordinated universal time (UTC)–derived precision radio signals such as the global positioning system (GPS) and long-range navigation (LORAN-C).

3.2.1.1 Considerations for Implementation of An Autonomous PRS

The cesium beam tube that constitutes the basic building block of a PRS has a limited operating life. A typical PRS employs three such units to form an operational system. (Refer to Figure 2–11.) When a cesium beam tube fails, the cesium standard is removed from service and sent to the manufacturer for replacement of the beam. In view of the limited number of cesium standard manufacturers worldwide, for many network operators this involves dispatching equipment overseas and a consequent increase in mean-time-to-repair (MTTR). During this period, the PRS is reduced to a duplicate arrangement of cesium standards with the accompanying inability to adopt majority logic for determining which standard should supply the primary reference timing. Therefore, networks operators may consider maintaining a spare cesium standard that could be used to restore the original configuration when the failed standard is sent for repairs. The unit sent for replacement of the tube, when received after repairs, may be kept as a spare.

The spare cesium standard should be kept as a cold (unpowered) standby and under controlled environmental conditions, similar to those prescribed for operational cesium standards. Under these conditions, the reduction in the operational life of the cesium tube is expected to be minimal. Typically, a few weeks of reduction in operational life is expected for every year of storage as cold standby. Conformance to the prescribed environmental conditions such as temperature, humidity, and vibration control is important in conserving the life of the cesium tube. In addition, the ion pump should be operated according to the prescribed procedure and schedule.

Regarding the site for the PRS, one possibility is to collocate it with a digital switch, for example, an international gateway exchange. In this case, the exchange may be used as a distributor of primary reference timing to stratum 2 clocks. Another approach is to operate the PRS from special laboratories. This option can be justified on several counts. The cesium clock and its associated equipment are radically different from digital office equipment. It therefore needs staff with skills different from the operation and maintenance staff for digital exchanges. Staff with the required expertise are more likely to be available in special laboratories. The laboratory environment, in general, can also be closely controlled and monitored. This is an important consideration because performance of cesium clocks is sensitive to factors such as temperature, humidity, altitude, magnetic field, shock, and vibrations. In some countries, underground locations are used to achieve better control on environmental conditions. When the PRS is not collocated with an exchange, PCM frame-generation equipment and digital transport facilities are required to carry the reference timing downstream to slave nodes in the network.

3.2.1.2 Considerations for Implementation of a Nonautonomous PRS

LORAN-C signal outages are low. The transmission system typically provides an availability of 99.9% that occasionally reaches 99.97% [2]. The receiver at the nonautonomous PRS may not achieve such high availability due to propagation and atmospheric conditions, however. Therefore, outages are expected in the availability of radionavigational signals, both LORAN-C and GPS. During outages, the internal clock that is disciplined by the signal must provide the accuracy of a stratum 1 clock. This requirement can be met by a clock of stratum 2 quality, since stratum 2 clocks deliver a highly accurate output during holdover. To economize on clocks, establishment of a nonautonomous PRS at a stratum 2 clock site may be considered. The existing stratum 2 clock can then be used as the internal clock of the PRS that is disciplined by LORAN-C or GPS signals.

The reliability of the PRS is a key issue. Reliability requirements for a nonautonomous PRS are specified in U.S. industry standards [3] and shown in Table 3–1.

Notice that the total system availability requirements are extremely stringent. Care also needs to be exercised in protecting the LORAN-C and GPS receiver antennas from lightning and local noise sources.

Table 3-1 Reliability Requirements for a Nonautonomous PRS

PARAMETER	DOWNTIME	AVAILABILITY
Output channel failures	0.3 minute/year	99.999943%
Total system failures	0.00001 minute/year	99.999999998%

3.2.2 Transport of Reference Timing Between Network Nodes

Currently, timing in the network is transported solely on digital transmission facilities, although analog facilities were used in earlier systems. Certain national networks employ dedicated links from PRSs to the stratum 2 clocks. For the remaining network, from stratum 2 downward, traffic-carrying links convey the timing information. To enable mutual trouble reporting, PRSs should be mesh connected.

To enhance the reliability of the synchronization network and to minimize the impact of outages or deterioration in the performance of the transmission links that carry reference timing, a slave node is generally fed by more than one reference timing. As discussed in Section 2.12, the reference timings have preassigned priorities. In the U.S. network, a synchronization node normally receives two reference timings, designated primary and secondary references. In the French network, provision has been made for up to three reference timings at the network nodes [4]. Network operators need to determine the number of reference timings to be permitted at each node. Although provisioning of a greater number of alternative timing references at the nodes enhances redundancy in timing transport, the cost of slave clocks also increases due to the increased hardware. More important, the complexity of the network increases sharply with the number of timing references. The resultant complexity increases the chances of timing loops. Timing loops must be avoided, as discussed in Section 3.2.4.

The choice of synchronization links and their ranking for assignment of priorities is an important part of the planning process. The objective is to select digital transmission links of high availability and quality.

3.2.2.1 Criteria for Selection and Prioritization

The existing digital transmission facilities interconnecting the nodes to be synchronized should be identified and listed. The transmission facilities planned to be deployed in the short and medium terms should also be noted. In addition, a list of new nodes that are planned to be included in the synchronized network is meaningful. These data are likely to enable systematic planning and to ease future modifications in the assignment of reference links and expansion of the synchronization network.

The factors to consider in choosing and ranking the synchronization links are as follows:

1. In line with the basic principle of master-slave operation, at a given node only transmission links from a clock of higher or equal stratum should be considered for the supply of reference timing.
2. Satellite links should be excluded because they are unsuitable for synchronizing the national network due to Doppler shift and the resulting excessive wander.

3. The past performance of the existing transmission links is a good guide. Parameters to consider include total outage time, jitter, wander, and bit error rate (BER). Transmission links that introduce more than 1 μs of daily wander or 2.5 μs of yearly wander should be avoided. The jitter induced on the links should be well within International Telegraph and Telephone Consultative Committee (CCITT)– specified values indicated in Chapter 2. The BER performance of the links should be examined against CCITT recommendation G.821 [5].
4. The source and routing of the links to a node should be diversified. The objective is that a fault should not simultaneously affect two reference timings. Therefore, alternative links that originate from different clocks and are routed on separate paths should be chosen. At the stratum 2 level, for example, reference timing may be made available from two PRSs over different routes. Where the provision exists for connecting up to three reference timings, the third reference may be taken from another stratum 2 clock.
5. In addition to a finite probability of failure, repeaters introduce jitter. The possibility of disruption also increases with the increase in the length of the transmission link. Therefore, the number of regenerators and the length of the transmission link should be taken into account.
6. Compared with overhead (aerial) links, buried transmission links are generally less prone to disruption events. Other things being equal, buried links usually are preferred to overhead links.
7. Transmission links with protection switching are less likely to suffer outages than those with unprotected links. Therefore, links with protection switching may be preferred. It should be recognized, however, that phase hits may occur during switching, but this problem is less severe than a total outage.
8. It is also useful to consider the characteristics of the transmission system when selecting and ranking links. Microwave systems may suffer from fading, and many T-carrier systems do not provide protection switching. Hence, optical fiber links may be preferred for timing transport.
9. When selecting the links, timing loops must be avoided.

3.2.3 Intrabuilding Timing Distribution in the U.S. Network

Several digital switches and other equipment requiring synchronization often exist in one building, particularly in large urban areas. An arrangement to supply timing within a building to synchronize a number of digital switches and other equipment has been specified in U.S. industry standards [1,2]. A single timing called building-integrated timing supply (BITS) is supplied by a nodal clock for the entire building. Only the nodal clock, generally referred to as BITS clock, receives the reference timing on digital links. All other clocks in the building are then controlled by this clock. The BITS clock is also called the timing signal generator (TSG). If all the slave clocks in the building were timed individually by external reference timing, then each slave clock would appear as a separate node in the synchronization network. With the BITS arrangement, however, the building as a whole appears as just one node in the synchronization network. The number of timing references on the synchronization map is also reduced, since timing references are only needed for the BITS clock. This arrangement, therefore, considerably simplifies the administration of the synchronization network.

Another reason for the BITS is the need to synchronize digital equipment that is not equipped to accept DS-1 signals. For example, many digital channel banks have DS-0 rate interfaces. The DS-0 rate signal represents a 64 kbps channel of the DS-1 rate bit stream. Such equipment is timed by a 64/8 kHz composite clock (CC) signal supplied by the BITS.

Figures 3–1 and 3–2 show two possible ways of distributing timing inside a building. Figure 3–1 is the recommended method of connecting the BITS [1]. Currently, the arrangement of Figure 3–2 is widely deployed but will be upgraded progressively to the scheme shown in Figure 3–1.

A slave clock may be implemented in one of the following ways:

1. Stand-alone equipment
2. Integrated (or embedded) with a digital switch or a digital loop carrier (DLC) system

Figure 3–1 represents a stand-alone implementation of the nodal clock. The TSG is synchronized by two alternative external references selected on the considerations described earlier. The TSG generates two types of timings, DS-1 timing and CC timing, which are used to synchronize all the other digital equipment in the building. This approach is recommended because it truly integrates the timing supply in the building. Depending on the site, the TSG is a stratum 2 or stratum 3 clock. The TSG must incorporate the highest quality clock within the building. For example, if one of the switches within

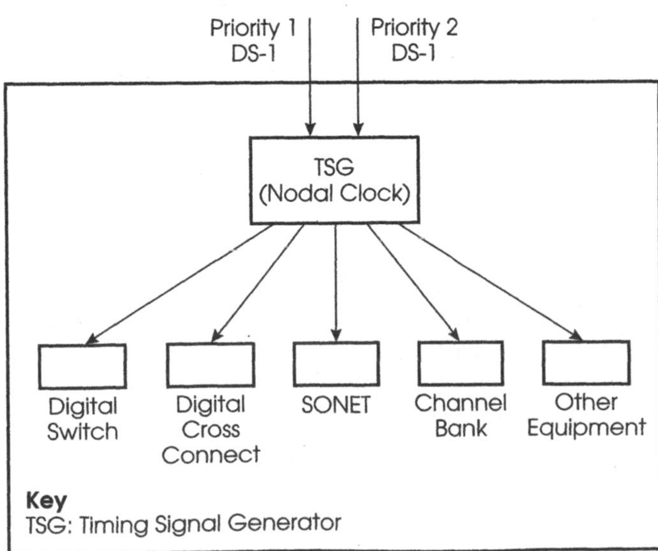

Note: Only timing signals are shown. Priority 1 and 2 DS-1 could be traffic-carrying signals connected to the TSG via bridging repeaters.

Figure 3–1 Recommended BITS implementation according to U.S. industry standards.

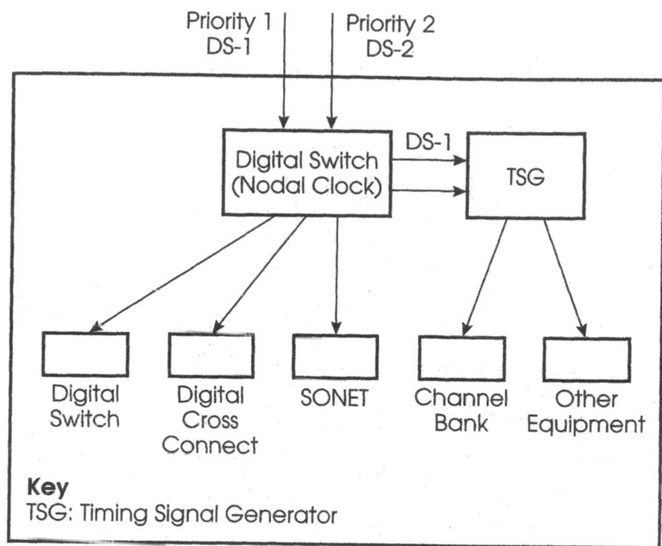

Figure 3–2 Widely used BITS implementation (not recommended): conceptual BITS.

an office has a stratum 2 clock, the TSG should have at least a stratum 2 clock. A lower stratum clock should never be used to synchronize a higher stratum clock. Stratum 4 clocks are not suitable for TSG due to their poor holdover performance. The timing sent downstream on digital links by the digital switches and cross connects will normally have the same quality as the TSG since, for the short distances involved in the distribution of timing within the building, there is very little likelihood of timing impairment or disruption. To avoid excessive propagation delays, the distribution of CC signals is limited to about 1,500 feet of 22 AWG.

In the widely used BITS implementation shown in Figure 3–2, the nodal clock is integrated in one of the digital switches in the building. The DS-1 rate signals from this switch serve to synchronize other digital switches, DLC systems, and cross connects. Traffic-carrying DS-1 rate signals are bridged to supply the TSG, which in turn generates the CC signals. This scheme is termed conceptual BITS since in reality, there are two timing sources—one supplied by a digital switch and the other by the TSG—within the building.

Network operators in the United States are progressively moving away from conceptual BITS to "true" BITS. In essence, this involves the stand-alone implementation of slave clocks in preference to their integration into a digital switch. "True" BITS is more responsive to potential changes in the network. New digital switches introduced in the network can be controlled from the existing stand-alone clock equipment in the building, and the retirement of a digital exchange or rearrangements in the building due to traffic reasons does not require that the timing paths be redesigned.

An argument in favor of embedded implementation is that network synchronization has traditionally been tied to digital switches, and switch manufacturers make provision for embedding the slave clock in the digital switch. Also, stand-alone clocks and switches are usually made by different manufacturers. When a building houses only one or two digital switches, it may be economical as well as administratively convenient to order the switch and the embedded clock from the switch manufacturer.

Failure of the stand-alone equipment that times various digital equipment in the vicinity represents a major synchronization failure. Measures to minimize failures therefore assume greater significance for stand-alone implementations. The reliability of stand-alone clock systems may be improved by a redundant architecture. The power feeding arrangement also needs to be redundant and diverse. All these measures add to the cost of implementation but are required nevertheless. The reliability objective for stand-alone clocks at stratum 2 and 3 is specified [3] in Table 3–2. The reliability requirements for stratum 4 clocks are yet to be specified in U.S. industry standards.

3.2.4 Avoidance of Timing Loops

Multiple timing references are provided to the slave clocks with the intention of improving the reliability of the synchronization network. This has a negative side effect of increasing the complexity, however, and timing loops may be formed inadvertently in certain situations, such as reconfiguration of timing references due to failures. A timing loop consists of a closed chain of clocks that are fed by a reference derived from their own output timing due to the formation of a feedback loop. The consequences are serious; the master-slave hierarchy breaks down for the concerned clocks because they are isolated from the primary reference timing. Worse still, due to undesirable feedback timing, frequency within the loop tends to become unstable.

A simple method of detecting feedback loops is described in [1] by means of an example network shown in Figure 3–3(a). The procedure arranges the nodes of the synchronization network linearly so that it becomes easy to notice the existence of timing loops, if any. The resulting representation is shown in Figure 3–3(b). The following two rules are applied to designate and arrange the nodes.

Rule 1: Stratum n clocks that receive all the reference timings from a higher stratum clock are designated as substratum $n(1)$ clocks.

As seen in Figure 3–3(a), nodes 2 and 4 at stratum 2 receive their reference timing only from stratum 1 clock. They are therefore designated as substratum 2(1). Similarly, at stratum 3, node 6 receives both its reference timings from stratum 2 clocks. Accordingly, by the application of rule 1, it gets the designation of substratum 3(1).

Rule 2: Within the same stratum, when a clock receives a timing reference from another clock, it is designated a lower substratum code than the clock supplying the reference.

Table 3-2 Reliability Objective for Stand-Alone Clocks

PARAMETER	DOWNTIME	AVAILABILITY
Output channel failures	0.3 minute/year	99.999943%
Total system failures	0.002 minute/year	99.9999996%

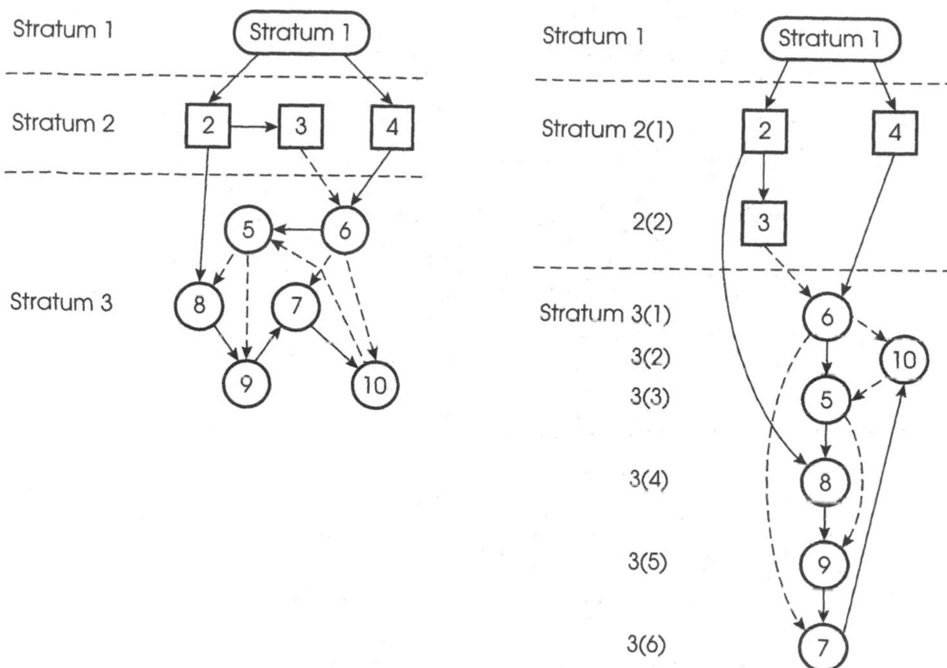

Figure 3–3 Detection of timing loops: (a) conventional layout; (b) layout with substrata. Copyright © 1993, Bellcore TA-NWT-000436. Reprinted with permission.

For example, a clock at stratum 3 receiving timing from substratum 3(1) gets a code of substratum 3(2). Likewise, a clock that receives a reference each from clocks with substratum codes 3(1) and 3(2) is assigned substratum code 3(3).

Note that the creation of substratum codes is only for the limited purpose of designation of nodes for timing loop detection; it has no relationship to the quality of the clock.

By applying the above rules, an attempt is made to arrange the nodes as shown in Figure 3–3(b). It is seen that node 6 is assigned code 3(1), since it receives both its references from a stratum 2 source. Conflicts arise in assigning substratum codes for nodes 5 and 10, however. Initially, substratum code 3(2) is assigned to node 10 based on the observation that it receives priority 2 reference from node 6. Node 5 receives its references from nodes 6 and 10 and is assigned substratum 3(3). Assignment is also made for nodes 8, 9, and 7 as shown in Figure 3–3(b). Now it is noticed that a priority 1 timing is feeding node 10. This gives rise to a conflict, since a clock with stratum code 3(6) (node 7) cannot provide reference for the clock with the previously assigned stratum code 3(2) (node 10).

An inspection of Figure 3–3(b) readily reveals timing loops in the following conditions:

1. Loop 5–8–9–7–10–5, when the priority 1 reference to node 5 fails
2. Loop 5–9–7–10–5, when priority 1 references to nodes 5 and 8 fail

The method described above can be readily applied to analyze the timing transport arrangement for the presence of timing loops in any digital network.

3.3 Testing and Validation

A critical element in the success of network synchronization is the performance of the slave clocks. Network operators should therefore establish the necessary facilities to verify and test clock performance. Two types of tests are performed on slave clocks, validation tests and installation tests. A comprehensive set of tests to evaluate performance of the equipment and to ensure that it conforms to the prescribed specifications is required for its first application in the network. These tests are called validation tests, initial service tests, or first application tests. When equipment from diverse sources are potential candidates for introduction in the network, validation testing may also be used to support technology or vendor selection. Subsequently, during installation of slave clocks at various sites, installation tests are performed to ensure the satisfactory performance of the equipment at each site.

As far as possible, the tests should attempt to test clock behavior under conditions that are expected during its actual operation in the network. The three modes of slave clock operations are the following:

1. Unstressed operation
2. Stressed operation
3. Holdover mode

Although clocks may be tested for the idealized conditions represented by the unstressed operation, of particular interest is the operation in stressed and holdover modes. In real networks, slave clocks have to function essentially under stressed conditions arising out of transmission impairments such as jitter, wander, error bursts, and phase hits due to protection switching. Since for most of its operational life the clock has to operate under stressed conditions, any testing strategy must focus on testing of the clock under these conditions.

When all input timing references are lost, the clock enters the holdover mode. In view of redundant reference timings made available to slave clocks, entry of a clock into the holdover mode rarely happens. Nevertheless, the clock's performance during these infrequent periods is critical to the minimization of slip events. The holdover performance is even more important for stratum 2 and stratum 3 clocks because they are responsible for the supply of timing to a large network downstream under stressed conditions. Thus, evaluation of clock performance during holdover is another important goal of testing.

In addition to the quality-related requirements, other functional requirements for which slave clocks need to be tested include:

- Checks on reconfiguration of the clock consequent to internal failures
- Self-diagnostic capabilities
- Generation of alarm conditions

- Acceptance of a lower-priority reference on failure of a higher-priority reference
- Entry into the holdover mode on failure of all the references
- Reversion to synchronized operation on restoration of timing references

Based on these general requirements, test setups and methodologies for slave clock testing are described below. The testing procedures are common to different stratums of slave clocks.

3.3.1 Tests on Free-Running Clocks

A test setup for measuring the time interval error (TIE) of a free-running clock is shown in Figure 3–4. The reference timing to be used for the measurement should have a very high short term stability. A cesium reference is best suited for this purpose.

The TIE meter accepts an external frequency reference at 5 MHz (or 10 MHz) from the cesium clock. As an alternative, an internal frequency reference generated by a rubidium oscillator in the TIE meter may be used. (Typically, a rubidium-based internal frequency reference is optionally available with TIE meters.) The output of the free-running clock at 1.544 Mbps (or 2.048 Mbps) primary rate is compared with the frequency reference by measuring the phase-time difference between the reference signal and the signal under test. The sampling time can be specified over a wide range, typically between 1 and 100,000 seconds. The number of samples over which the measurements are required can also be specified. For each sample time, the TIE meter computes a TIE value that may be printed or stored in a control computer. Another computed parameter is the average TIE, which is obtained by averaging the TIE for all samples. Of particular interest is the maximum time interval error (MTIE), which is the difference between two extreme readings during the observation period. Division of the MTIE by the sample time provides the frequency departure of the slave clock.

3.3.2 Tests for Synchronized Unstressed Operation

The performance of the clock under synchronized operation can be evaluated using the setup shown in Figure 3–5.

A distribution amplifier is used for the distribution of timing signal from the cesium reference. The frequency synthesizer converts the 5 MHz (or 10 MHz) reference frequency to a 1,544/2,048 kHz signal. The latter is used as external timing for the PCM

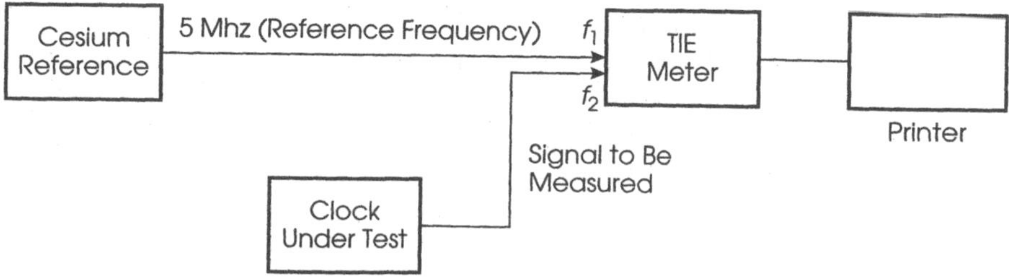

Figure 3–4 TIE measurement for free-running clock.

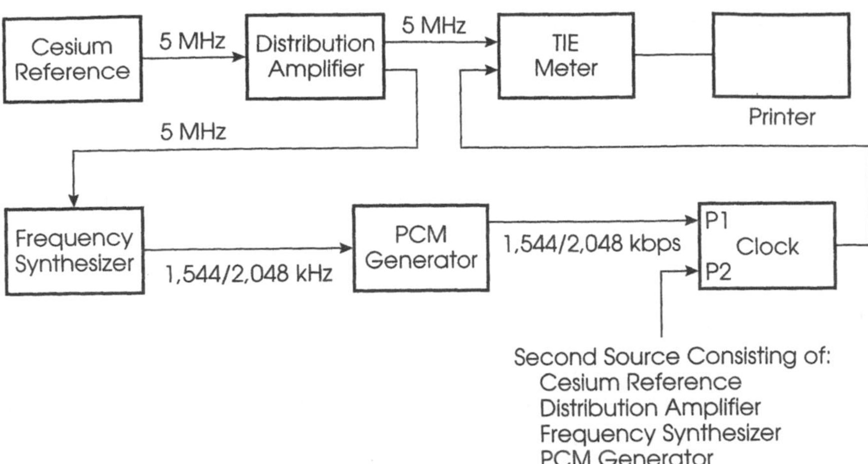

Figure 3–5 TIE measurement for a synchronized clock (unstressed operation).

generator. The PCM generator generates a primary rate PCM output at 1,544 kbps or 2,048 kbps, depending on the requirement. This is connected to the port with a preassigned priority 1 of the clock under test. A similar timing chain is created to feed the priority 2 port of the clock. If the clock is capable of accepting more than two timing references, then additional reference signals should also be connected.

After ensuring that the slave clock is locked to the reference timing on P1, TIE measurements are made. In this setup, the clock should be exactly in phase lock because no disturbances on the reference timings have been introduced. The TIE readings over a large number of sampling times should therefore be identical.

When the reference signal on port P1 is disabled, the slave clock should automatically choose the reference available on P2. The observations may be repeated with timing reference on port P2 and for any other additional input ports of the clock.

3.3.3 Tests for Synchronized Stressed Operation

The objective of stressed operation tests is to create permissible impairments on the reference timing to the slave clock. As discussed in Chapter 2, jitter is an important impairment parameter. A jitter generator is used to introduce jitter on the primary rate digital signal that is used as timing reference by the clock under test. The amplitude and frequency of jitter introduced on the reference timing is varied within the permissible limits of input jitter specified in International Telecommunication Union-Telecommunication Standardization Sector (ITU-T) recommendations G.823 and G.824 [6,7]. The permissible limits of input jitter for 2,048 kbps digital hierarchy is shown in Figure 2–17. Corresponding to the various values of input jitter, the jitter at the output of the clock is measured by a jitter receiver. These observations allow the dejitterizing capabilities of the slave clock to be evaluated in terms of its jitter transfer characteristics.

The slave clock should not reject the jittered reference timing as long as the jitter frequency and amplitude are within permissible limits. Other impairments that may be considered for stressed testing of the clock are error bursts, severely errored seconds (SESs) events, and phase hits. These impairments may be considered in combination with jitter.

The TIE measurements are made after the slave clock is synchronized to a reference timing impaired in the manner described above. Parameters such as average TIE, MTIE, and frequency departure are calculated.

To ensure that the redundant units of the slave clock are functioning normally, these observations may be repeated for all the reference input priorities and, where duplicated phase lock loops (PLLs) exist, for individual PLL chains.

3.3.4 Holdover Mode Testing

After measurements in the synchronized test mode, a loss-of-signal (LOS) condition for both reference timing sources is created to force the slave clock into the holdover mode. It is important that the holdover mode be entered from the stressed operation of the clock and not from an idealized operation; the latter does not simulate real network conditions, and the capability of the PLL to estimate the reference frequency correctly at the time of disruption cannot be properly tested.

Measurements need to be taken over several days using the TIE meter in the setup shown in Figure 3–6. From these measurements, an estimate of the various clock parameters is made.

3.3.5 Tests Prescribed for the U.S. Network

Of tests for slave clocks just described, some are appropriate for first application testing whereas others may be performed during installation. BELLCORE [1] lists the following tests and measurements:

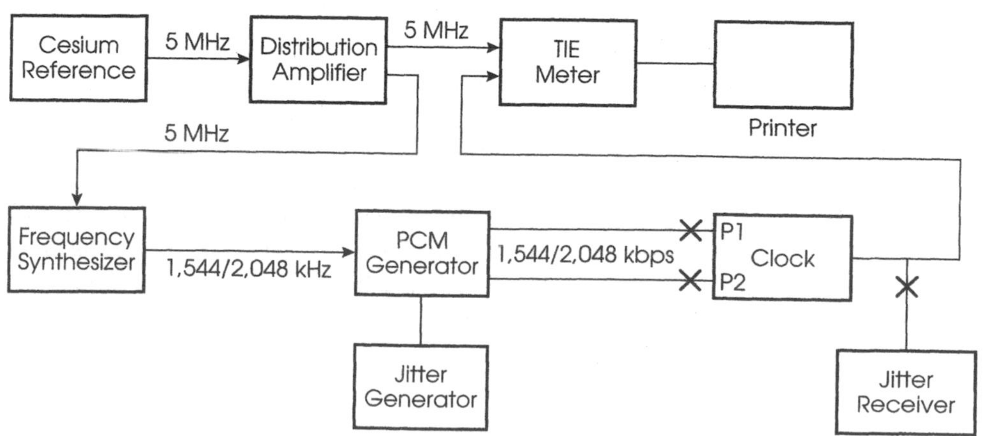

Figure 3–6 TIE measurement for a synchronized (stressed operation) clock and in holdover mode (after disabling the reference timing).

For first application:

- Free-run accuracy
- Holdover stability
- Pull-in range
- Wander and jitter generation
- Wander and jitter filtering (jitter transfer characteristics)
- Reference and hardware switching
- Alarm generation
- Correct type and number of references supported

For installation testing:

- Ability to synchronize to external reference
- Ability to switch to alternate reference when active timing fails
- Holdover performance (1 day for stratum 3, 1 week for stratum 2 and stratum 3E)
- Maintenance and operational interfaces
- One week or longer soak test

3.4 Monitoring Network Synchronization

Monitoring the synchronization network is an important operational requirement. Whereas the functioning of the slave clocks at individual sites is monitored based on the alarm conditions raised by the equipment, a "network view" of synchronized network is equally important. A first step in this direction could be to extend alarms and slip rate information from individual sites to a central facility. The number and location of such sites would depend on the size, complexity, and structure of the network. This step would provide a broad range of information to the technical staff stationed at the monitoring sites. The information may be used not only for operational purposes but also for future planning and engineering. Since telecommunication networks are monitored and managed by network management systems (NMSs), network operators should explore the possibility of integrating network synchronization monitoring within the NMS. Central offices have connections (typically, X.25 links) to network management systems, and in this case, information regarding slip rates and alarm conditions can be conveyed with other traffic statistics.

The American National Standards Institute (ANSI) [2] recommends that the following status information be available on demand at the monitoring site from stratum 2 and 3 nodes:

- Synchronization clock mode
- Synchronization reference in use
- Synchronization unit in use
- Time of most recent reference switch
- Slip rates for synchronization link

In addition, it is desirable to monitor some of the important clock parameters at the network nodes to detect and localize timing problems early. This can be achieved if the clock output is returned to a monitoring site where the frequency accuracy may be checked. For checking the frequency accuracy of stratum 2 clocks, a clock source of stratum 1 is required. From this point of view, the monitoring sites may be collocated with the PRS. This solution can be implemented in networks with multiple PRSs that are controlled by UTC timing through LORAN-C or GPS. In Section 3.2.1.2, the possibility of placing LORAN-C or GPS receivers at stratum 2 sites was mentioned. If this course is followed, monitoring sites can be chosen from among the stratum 2 locations. For networks with a limited number of PRSs, however, new monitoring sites may be needed with a stratum 1 source.

Network operators may also consider deploying additional synchronization monitoring equipment at key sites. Such equipment is offered by several clock equipment manufacturers. The equipment typically monitors a number of primary rate digital links for frequency and phase comparison with a reference clock. Potential slip situations and timing problems are analyzed, and information is conveyed to a network management system.

An issue linked with synchronization monitoring is the exchange of status information between slave clocks in the network. The existing scheme of network synchronization in which slave clocks react to timing disruptions simply by detecting the event and changing over to alternative references(s) (or entering holdover) has no mechanism for the exchange of status information between synchronization nodes. For example, a slave clock has no certain way to know whether the disruption is due to the failure of the timing transport or to a fault in the upstream clock. It also has no way to determine if and when a clock upstream enters the holdover mode.

ANSI [2] has specified that synchronization equipment accepting external timing reference should accept DS-1 rate signals with DS-1 frame format, DS-1 superframe format (SF), and DS-1 extended superframe format (ESF). Further, for the ESF, performance report messages between DS-1 terminals have been specified in BELLCORE [8]. The performance report message format is similar to the link access procedure in D-channel (LAPD) specified in ITU-T recommendation Q.921 [9] for ISDN. (LAPD is described in Chapter 8.) In addition to other status information, synchronization related status is also included in the performance report message. This arrangement will be progressively implemented by the BOCs.

3.5 Remarks

The discussion of synchronization has so far been in the context of a network based on plesiochronous digital hierarchy (PDH). Timing requirements typical to a synchronous optical network (SONET) and synchronous digital hierarchy (SDH) are considered in Chapter 15.

References

[1] "Digital Network Synchronization Plan." BELLCORE Technical Report TA-NWT-000436, issue 2, June 1993.

[2] American National Standard for Telecommunications. *Synchronization Interface Standards.* ANSI T1.101-1994.

[3] "Clocks for the Synchronized Network: Common Generic Criteria." BELLCORE Technical Reference TR-NWT-001244, issue 1, June 1993.

[4] Charbit, R., M. Dudet, and G. Howard. "Synchronising the French Digital Telecommunication Network." Commutation et Transmission, pp. 5–12, no. 4, 1986.

[5] *Error Performance of an International Digital Connection Forming Part of an Integrated Services Digital Network.* CCITT Blue Book, fascicle III.5, recommendation G.821. International Telecommunication Union, 1988.

[6] *The Control of Jitter and Wander within Digital Networks Which Are Based on the 2048 kbit/s Hierarchy.* ITU-T recommendation G.823, rev. 1, International Telecommunication Union, 1993.

[7] *The Control of Jitter and Wander within Digital Networks Which Are Based on the 1544 kbit/s Hierarchy.* ITU-T recommendation G.824, rev. 1. International Telecommunication Union, 1993.

[8] "Transport Systems Generic Requirements (TSGR): Common Requirements." BELLCORE Technical Reference, TR-NWT-000499, issue 5, Dec. 1993.

[9] *ISDN User-Network Interface—Data link layer specification.* ITU-T recommendation Q.921, rev. 1. International Telecommunication Union, 1993.

4 CCS 7: General Description

Acronyms

ACM	address complete message
ANM	answer message
ANSI	American National Standards Institute
CAS	channel-associated signaling
CCIS	common channel interoffice signaling
CCITT	The International Telegraph and Telephone Consultative Committee
CCS 7	CCITT common channel signaling system no. 7
CIC	circuit identification code
DPC	destination point code
DSS 1	digital subscriber signaling system 1
DUP	data user part
FISU	fill-in signal unit
GT	global title
HSRC	hypothetical signaling reference connection
IAM	initial address message
IN	intelligent network
ISDN	integrated services digital network
ISUP	ISDN user part
LSSU	link status signal unit
MF	multifrequency
MSU	message signal unit
MTP	message transfer part
NSDU	network service data unit
OMAP	operation and maintenance application part
OPC	origination point code
OSI	open system interconnection
PSTN	public switched telephone network
REL	release (message)
RLC	release complete (message)
SAM	subsequent address message
SANC	signaling area/network code
SCCP	signaling connection control part
SF	status field
SIF	signaling information field
SIO	service information octet
SLS	signaling link selection
SP	signaling point
SPC	stored program control
SSN	subsystem number
STP	signal transfer point
TCAP	transaction capability application part
TUP	telephone user part

ABSTRACT

The International Telegraph and Telephone Consultative Committee's (CCITT) common channel signaling system no. 7 (CCS 7) is introduced in this chapter. Included in this discussion are

- The principles, advantages, terminology, network elements, and protocol structure
- The functions of message transfer part (MTP) and various other user parts
- The characteristics of signaling data link (level 1)
- Different possibilities of signaling, such as overlap and en bloc signaling, link-by-link and end-to-end signaling
- Signaling schematics corresponding to an integrated services digital network (ISDN) call

4.1 Introduction

For almost a century since the invention of the telephone in 1876, signaling was closely linked to the circuit switched telephone network and evolved in association with developments in telephony. With the advent of stored program control (SPC) exchanges, it became possible to apply the principles of computer communications to signaling between exchanges. In 1976, the CCITT began work on a new and powerful signaling system. CCITT common channel signaling system no. 7 (CCS 7), as currently specified, is the outcome of the standardization process carried out by the CCITT during successive 4-year study periods. Although the acronym CCS 7 has been used in this book, SS 7 and #7 are also used in the literature. The first CCS 7 specifications appeared in the Yellow Book recommendations [1] in 1981. These were further refined and expanded in successive study periods, resulting in the Red Book 1985 recommendations [2], the Blue Book recommendations [3] in 1989, and the ITU-T recommendations after 1989.

Progress in international signaling (signaling between international gateway exchanges) can be divided into three stages corresponding to CCITT signaling systems no. 5, 6, and 7. CCITT signaling system no. 5, standardized in 1964, is based on the principles of channel associated signaling. The system was widely deployed. There is not a country in the world, even among the least developed, that does not use CCITT no. 5 terminal equipment in its international/intercontinental exchange [4]. In contrast to the conventional signaling techniques of CCITT no. 5, signaling system no. 6 employed common channel signaling. Many of its features influenced the development of CCS 7, including the use of a common data link to carry signaling for a large number of speech circuits, organization of signaling information in packets, detection and correction of errors, and network management. In this sense, CCITT signaling system no. 6, standardized in 1972, can be considered the predecessor to CCS 7. System no. 6 found very little application for international signaling. It was, however, designated common channel interoffice signaling (CCIS) system, adopted for the national network, and deployed quite extensively in the U.S. national network [5].

For the national network, two conventional channel-associated signaling systems have been used widely, CCITT signaling systems R1 [6] and R2 [7] (R stands for regional). The R1 signaling system is employed in the United States and Japan, whereas the R2 system is used in Europe and in most other countries. The R1 system was partially replaced by CCIS and progressively by CCS 7 in the United States and Japan. Similarly, the R2 channel associated system is being progressively superseded by the deployment of CCS 7 in other national networks.

CCS 7 has applications both for national and international signaling. The CCITT, while making recommendations for the international network, has also specified options, where appropriate, for national use. A number of such cases will be seen in the discussion on CCS 7 in Chapters 6, 7, and 9.

Unlike signaling system no. 6, which had a monolithic structure, a layered approach to protocol development is followed in CCS 7. This provides for a clear division of functions and an effective means of specifying the complex CCS 7 protocol. The layered approach did not go far enough to conform to the open system interconnection (OSI) seven-layer protocol stack [8], however. CCS 7 uses a four-layer (called levels) protocol stack instead. The reasons were that OSI protocols were concurrently under development at that time, and the initial developments in CCS 7 were focused on needs specific to telephony signaling. However, as CCS 7 evolved and matured, the modularity of structure arising from the layered concept, afforded the inclusion of several other applications. The scope of CCS 7 includes signaling in the public switched telephone network (PSTN), the ISDN, and circuit switched data services. CCS 7 is also being applied for the provision of a variety of other services, for instance, in the intelligent network, cellular mobile telephony, and network management. CCS 7 has applications both in circuit-related and non–circuit-related signaling.

A telecommunication network typically consists of different types of switching systems. Old electromechanical exchanges may coexist with modern digital switching systems. Stored program controlled (SPC) analog exchanges may also exist in the network, but electromechanical exchanges are not capable of supporting CCS 7. The SPC analog exchanges were deployed mainly in the late 1960s and early 1970s, prior to the development of CCS 7. These systems were subsequently superseded by digital switching systems. Therefore, although theoretically capable of performing CCS 7 functions, analog SPC exchanges do not usually incorporate CCS 7 capabilities. This leaves digital exchanges as a major means for deploying CCS 7.

4.2 Principles and Terminology

The principles and terminology of CCS 7 are introduced in this section through the example of the circuit switched application of CCS 7.

CCS 7 is a method of signaling that employs a single separate channel for conveying signaling information for a large number of circuit switched channels by means of labeled messages called *signal units.* From the point of view of CCS 7, a digital exchange may be considered to consist of two subsystems: one implementing functions such as call processing, maintenance, and administration, and the other implementing CCS 7 functions. Refer to Figure 4–1(a). The part of the exchange that provides CCS 7 functionality is called a *signaling point* (SP).

The common channel carrying signaling information is called a *signaling link.* Although an analog channel may also be used for this purpose, CCS 7 has been optimized

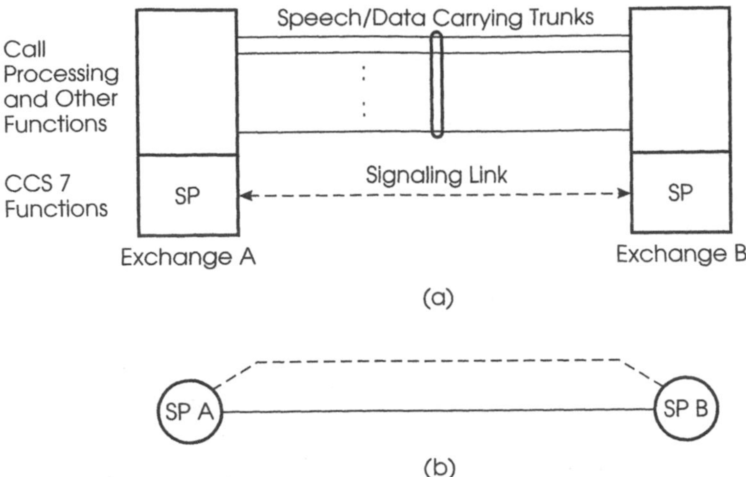

Figure 4–1 CCS 7 between two adjacent SPs: associated mode.

for operation in a digital network. Current CCS 7 implementations employ a 56 or 64 kbps timeslot of the 24-channel or 30-channel PCM frame as the signaling link. This is consistent with the progressive digitalization of the telecommunication networks and the need for faster signaling to cater to new services.

The signaling network corresponding to Figure 4–1(a) is shown in Figure 4–1(b) and consists of two signaling points, SP A and SP B, interconnected by a signaling link. This is the most elementary signaling network possible. The signal units are transported in both directions on the signaling link. In Figure 4–1, both SP A and SP B originate and terminate signal units.

CCS 7 can be used in two possible modes:

1. Associated mode
2. Quasi-associated mode

If two SPs exchange signaling messages with each other, they are said to have a signaling relation. Figure 4–1 is an example of the associated mode wherein signaling follows the same route as the circuit switched traffic.

An example of the quasi-associated mode of signaling is seen in Figure 4–2(a). The signaling for the traffic on trunks connecting exchanges A and B follows another path, namely, A–C–B. Signal transfer point C (STP C) is used for diverting signaling information from SP A to destination SP B. Notice that while SP A and SP B generate and receive messages, STP C is neither the source nor the destination for the messages. Therefore, an STP merely functions as a transit packet switcher for signaling.

An STP may be implemented in one of the following two ways:

1. As a stand-alone STP
2. As an integrated STP (SP with STP)

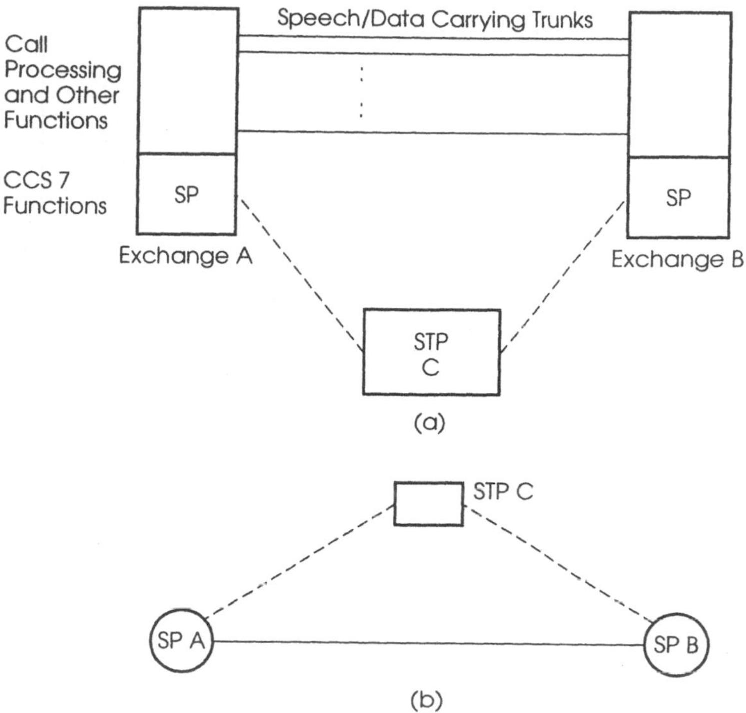

Figure 4–2 CCS 7 signaling between two adjacent SPs: quasi-associated mode.

The signaling network corresponding to Figure 4–2(a) is shown in Figure 4–2(b). The STP has no traffic carrying trunks to exchanges A and B. In such cases, the STP need not be a telephone exchange and is called a stand-alone STP.

Figure 4–3 shows an integrated SP with STP at exchange C. Exchange C functions as an SP for traffic between exchanges A and C. Signaling is carried in associated mode on signaling link 1. Similarly, signaling for traffic between exchanges B and C is carried in the associated mode on link 2. However, signaling for the trunks between exchanges A and B is carried in the quasi-associated mode on links 1 and 2. For this traffic, exchange C functions as an STP.

The mode of signaling to be used—associated, quasi associated, or a combination of the two—is determined by planning considerations specific to the requirements of individual CCS 7 networks.

Since the signaling function of the exchange is separate and distinct from the speech/data traffic in CCS 7, it is possible to visualize a telecommunication network as consisting of two separate networks, a telephone network and a signaling network as shown in Figure 4–4. Thus, the CCS 7 network has been compared to the central nervous system of a living organism [9]. Analogous to the central nervous system that controls and coordinates the living organism while remaining separate from organism's other parts, CCS 7 provides signaling for the PSTN, the ISDN, or any other network falling within its field of application.

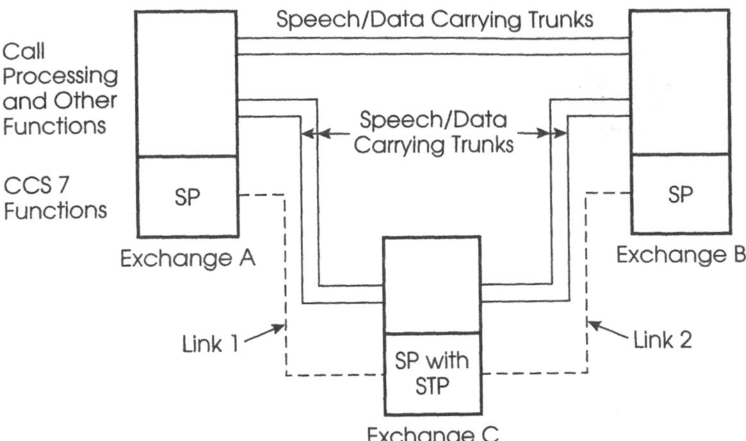

Figure 4–3 CCS 7 Signaling between SPs: associated mode and quasi-associated mode using integrated STP.

Just as every exchange in the telephone network has a unique numbering code, a unique "point code" is assigned to each SP/STP to identify them in the signaling network. Thus, each node in the CCS 7 network can be addressed by its point code.

Based on the amount of signaling information to be transported between two SPs, more than one signaling link may be required in parallel. Even when only one signaling link is sufficient to carry the signaling traffic, a second link is required to avoid disruption of signaling during failures. The links should follow diverse routes between SPs to ensure that the physical damage on one route will not affect the signaling traffic. A number of signaling links that directly interconnect two SPs form a *link set.* Refer to Figure 4–5.

A predetermined path that a message takes between an origination SP and a destination SP through a succession of SPs/STPs and the interconnecting signaling links constitutes a *signaling route* for that signaling relation. There may be several signaling routes

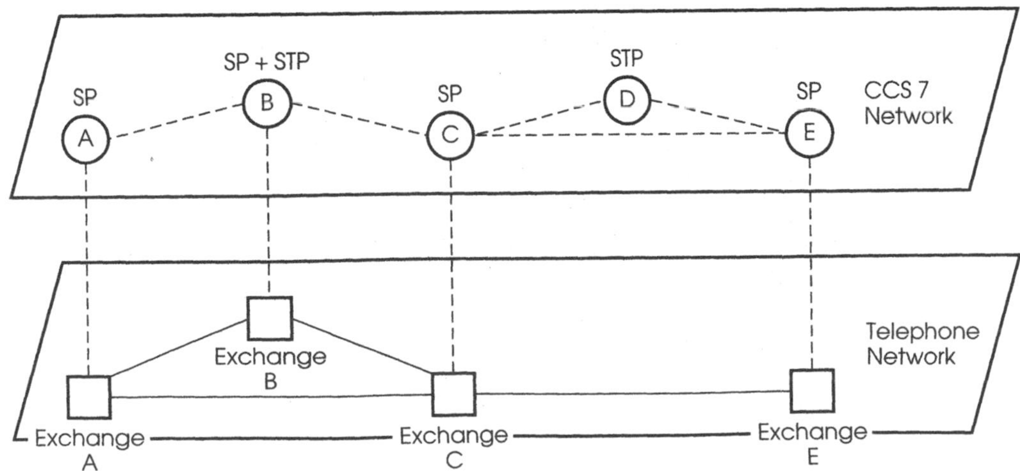

Figure 4–4 Separate signaling and telephone networks.

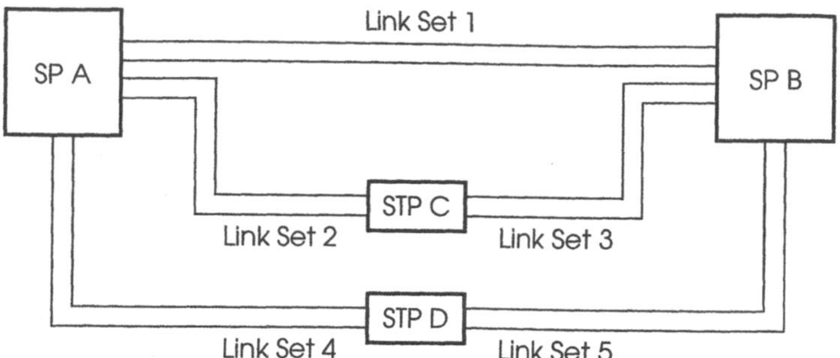

Figure 4–5 Illustration of signaling link set, route, and route set.

that a message can take between the origination and destination SP. These signaling routes are collectively termed the *signaling route set* for that signaling relation.

For the signaling relation between SP A and SP B, the routes are

Route 1: A–B and includes link set 1

Route 2: A–C–B and includes link sets 2 and 3

Route 3: A–D–B and includes link sets 4 and 5

These three routes constitute a route set for the signaling relation SP A–SP B in Figure 4–5.

4.3 Pros and Cons: CCS 7 versus Channel-Associated Signaling (CAS)

In channel-associated signaling (CAS), a dedicated signaling link is required for each speech channel. Interexchange signaling consists of both line signals and register signals. Line signals indicate the basic state of a trunk, such as a seizure. Register signals typically consist of the address information (digits of the called party and calling number identification) that is stored in registers and passed from one exchange to the other. The dedicated link, provided for each speech channel, is used to convey the line signals. When a 24-channel or 30-channel PCM system interconnects two exchanges, the dedicated signaling channels for each speech channel are multiplexed and carried in one signaling channel for the 30-channel E1 signal and in 24-channel DS-1 signal by robbed bit.

An example of CAS between two exchanges connected by 2,048 kbps, 30-channel PCM links is shown in Figure 4–6. Timeslot 16 is used to convey line signals (such as seizure and clear forward) for the traffic in the remaining channels 1 to 15 and 17 to 31. (Timeslot 0 is used for frame alignment.) The register signals (called party address information) are carried in individual speech channels, using, for example, multifrequency (MF) senders and receivers. After the connection is established, the MF sender and receiver can be released and used for another call setup. Therefore, MF senders and receivers are provided in a common pool and dimensioned based on the volume of traffic. In Figure 4–6, three channels are used for line signaling (timeslot 16 in each 2,048 kbps PCM) for a total of 90 speech/data channels.

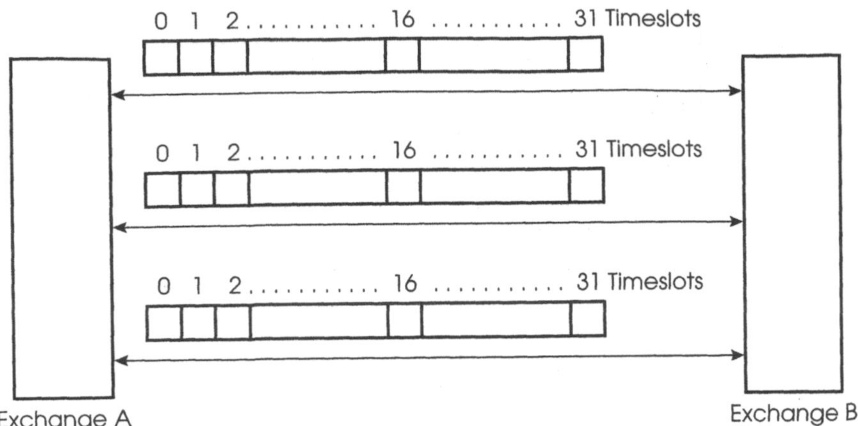

Figure 4–6 Example of channel-associated signaling.

On the other hand, if CCS 7 is used between exchanges A and B, then only one timeslot is required for signaling since one signaling channel is able to cater to a large number of speech/data channels. Refer to Figure 4–7. It is not necessary to use timeslot 16; any timeslot *x*, in any one of the three 2,048 kbps PCM links, may be chosen. To provide greater reliability, however, two channels will be employed in practice.

For higher volumes of traffic, CCS 7 is economical in the use of PCM channels. The above example pertains to CCS 7 in the associated mode. The savings in 64 kbps channels is even more pronounced when the quasi-associated mode is used. The additional channels made available may be used to carry circuit switched traffic.

Channel-associated signaling is intrinsically slow, resulting in longer call setup times. Because of the high speed of signaling (at 64 kbps), CCS 7 provides an efficient signaling system with much shorter call setup time.

Channel-associated signaling has several built-in rigidities. For example, register signals can be transferred only at the time of call setup. Since the speech path is also used for signaling, there is no possibility of signaling during the "talking phase" of the call.

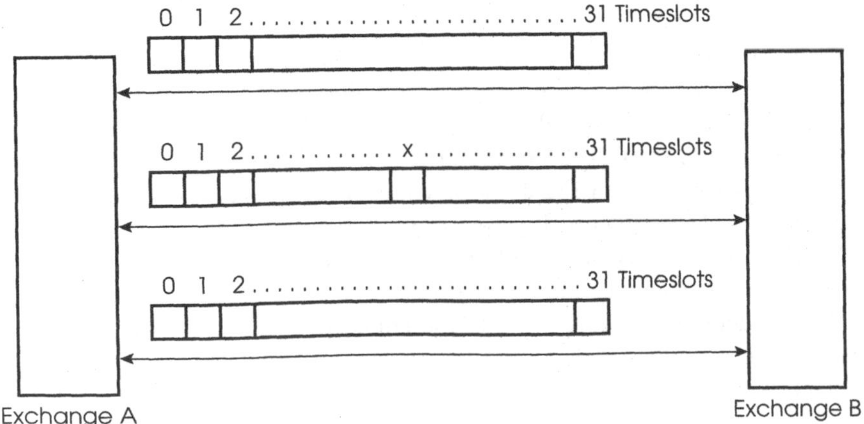

Figure 4–7 Example of CCS 7.

A significant advantage of CCS 7 is in the range of services that the system can support. Because CCS 7 supports signal units of variable lengths, and because messages up to 279 octets (an octet consists of 8 bits of information) are supported, much more signaling information can be exchanged than is possible with CAS. Furthermore, in contrast to the rather limited set of signals that can be supported with CAS, many message types can be specified. The structured nature of CCS 7 protocol enhances modularity and provides a flexible method for future enhancements, thus allowing the relatively easy introduction of new and advanced services.

Despite the advantages described above, a large-scale flash-cut transition from CAS to CCS 7 may be neither advisable nor practical. Rather, a phased approach over a relatively long time, say 5 to 10 years, may be more appropriate. A large network usually contains a mix of switching systems. The cost of upgrading or replacing switches that do not possess CCS 7 functionality should be examined in the context of the type and extent of new services planned for the network. Since switching systems with and without CCS 7 capabilities may coexist in the network, many of the advantages of CCS 7 may not be realized on a large scale. The CCS 7 exchanges in the network necessarily require interworking with the non–CCS 7 exchanges, and cost savings in terms of signaling equipment may not be significant, at least in the early stages of introduction of CCS 7. In addition, a host of other issues need consideration in the implementation of CCS 7 in the network; these aspects are detailed in Chapter 10.

In CAS, the speech path and signaling path for any given call are the same. A failure in the path will usually result in call setup failure, whereas successful call setup implies that the speech path is good and that conversation can proceed. In CCS 7, however, due to separation of speech and signaling paths, the actual establishment of the speech path cannot be readily confirmed. Therefore, a continuity test has been specifically designed in CCS 7 to address this problem. However, the continuity test introduces considerable delay in call setup, and, in a large trunk group, it will significantly add to the call holding time. To alleviate this problem, CCS 7 provides various continuity test options, such as test on all calls, even-numbered calls only, odd-numbered calls only, test on every Nth call (where N=1 to 15), or no test whatsoever. Continuity test parameters are established during circuit provisioning and apply on a trunk group basis.

4.4 Organization of Signaling Information

Signaling information exchanged between SPs is organized into packets of data called *signal units.* The signal units are of three types; fill-in signal units (FISUs), link status signal units (LSSUs), and message signal units (MSUs). CCS 7 protocol requires constant bidirectional flow of information on the signaling link at a standard bit rate (for example, 64 kbps). During periods when no useful signaling information is to be exchanged by the SPs, FISUs are sent, which is better than keeping the link idle because the presence of FISUs helps to monitor the link for errors continuously. LSSUs are used to exchange information about the status of the signaling link interconnecting two adjacent SPs. LSSUs are exchanged, for example, when a link is to be brought into service. MSUs, the third type of signal unit, are used to exchange signaling information between SPs pertaining to a call. The expressions message signal unit (MSU) and signaling message are used synonymously in the literature.

Table 4–1 Summary Table

SIGNAL UNIT	LENGTH	INCLUDES
FISU	6 octets	FISU fields
LSSU	7 or 8 octets	FISU fields + SF
MSU	Up to 279 octets	FISU fields + SIO + SIF

Signal units are composed of a number of fields, each with a specific name and purpose. All FISUs are identical in length (six octets). The fields of the FISU are repeated in the LSSU; in addition, a status field (SF) that conveys the status of the link is added. The SF is either one or two octets long; thus, LSSUs may be seven or eight octets long. The MSU contains two more fields in addition to the fields of the FISU: the service information octet (SIO) and the signaling information field (SIF). The length of MSUs may vary widely due to the SIF, whose size may vary from 2 to 272 octets, depending on the signaling information to be conveyed. See Table 4–1.

Signal unit formats and the role of various component fields, along with the description of CCS 7 protocols, are discussed in Chapters 6, 7, and 9. Refer to Figure 6–1 for the basic format of signal units.

4.5 Layered Approach in CCS 7

The structuring of CCS 7 protocols into layers was influenced by the open system interconnection (OSI) reference model specified in CCITT recommendation X.200 for the exchange of information between users in a communication system. The OSI model partitions the protocol into seven functional blocks called layers, numbered from 1 to 7, as shown in Figure 4–8. The lowest layer is called the physical layer. It includes, as the name suggests, the mechanical and electrical characteristics of the system. It also defines the format followed in the transmission of information bits. Each layer adds some specific functionality to the system and uses the functions and capabilities provided by the lower layers

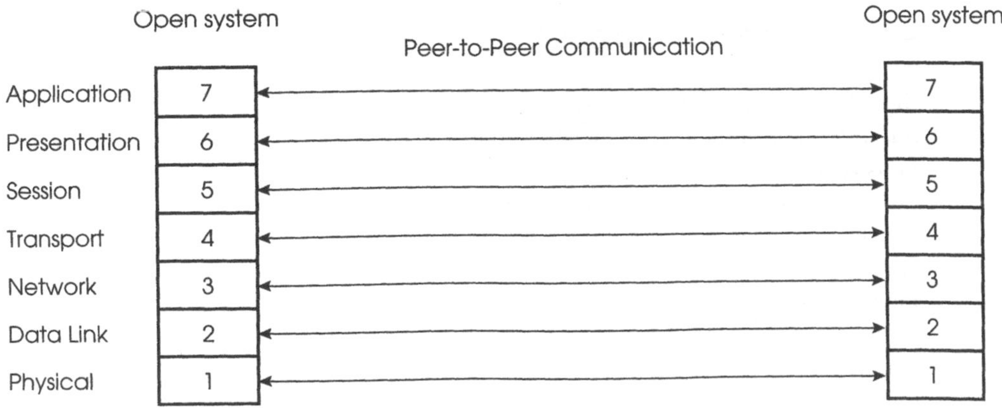

Figure 4–8 OSI seven-layer reference model.

in the discharge of its functions. Furthermore, within the system, layers communicate only with neighboring layers. For example, layer 3 communicates with layers 2 and 4 only.

CCS 7 protocol is partitioned into four levels (the term *level* is used to differentiate it from the OSI layers):

Level 1: physical
Level 2: data link
Level 3: network
Level 4: user part(s)

Levels 1 to 3 together transfer signaling messages between network nodes reliably and accurately. They also provide the functions necessary for the management of the network. Levels 1 to 3 are therefore collectively called the message transfer part (MTP) of CCS 7 protocol. These levels focus on the transport of the messages as opposed to the end purpose or application.

The application of signaling to meet specific goals is the function of level 4. Many functional blocks in level 4 representing specific applications use the common message transport facilities offered by the MTP. Since these functional blocks are users of the MTP, they are referred to as user parts. Several user parts may exist simultaneously at level 4. Examples of user parts are the telephone user part (TUP) for signaling in telephony, the ISDN user part (ISUP), and the transaction capability application part (TCAP). The ISUP covers both telephony and the ISDN.

The signaling connection control part (SCCP) is also a user of the MTP. SCCP can be viewed as an enhancement over the MTP transfer capabilities. It was developed subsequently to the MTP, and together with the MTP it provides the capabilities corresponding to layers 1 to 3 of the OSI model. SCCP, in turn, has other users at level 4 itself, an example is the TCAP. Notice that the ISUP can be a user of SCCP in addition to being a user of the MTP. The CCS 7 protocol stack is shown in Figure 4–9.

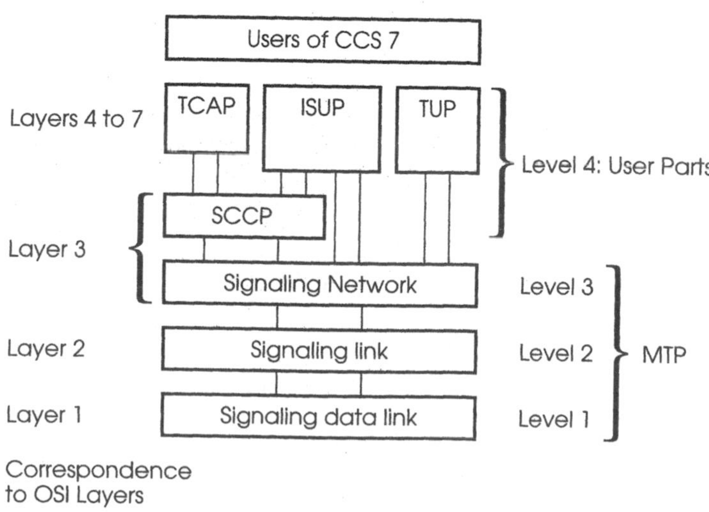

Figure 4–9 CCS 7 protocol stack.

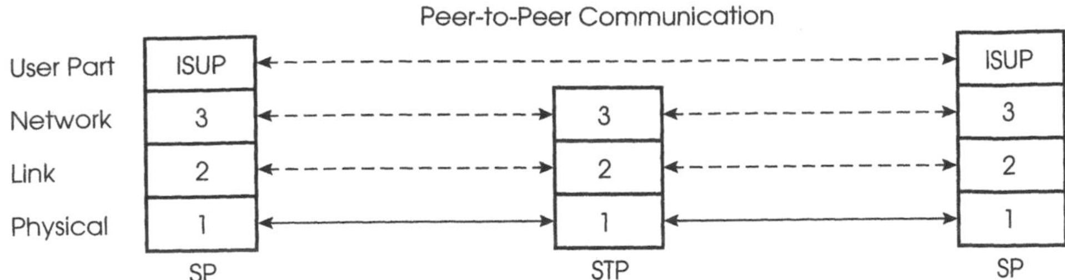

Figure 4–10 CCS 7 in an ISDN.

The CCS 7 protocol stack is implemented at each SP in the CCS 7 network. User parts are provided based on the services to be supported. For example, the CCS 7 network in the ISDN uses the ISUP at the SPs. Refer to Figure 4–10. At an STP, only the MTP is present; the user parts are not installed. Ultimately, all communication between SPs takes place at the physical level. Functionally, however, the various levels of CCS 7 at an SP can be considered to communicate with the corresponding levels of another SP. This is peer-to-peer communication (peer: one of equal standing with another), shown by dotted lines in Figure 4–10.

Table 4–2 lists the CCITT/ITU-T recommendations concerning various functional blocks of CCS 7. Also given are corresponding requirements in the United States as specified by the American National Standards Institute (ANSI) and BELLCORE.

Table 4–2 Standards on CCS 7

CCS 7 FUNCTIONS	CCITT/ITU-T RECOMMENDATIONS	ANSI STANDARDS	BELLCORE STANDARDS
MTP	Q.701 [10] to Q.704 [13]	ANSI T1.111-1992 [39] and ANSI T1.111a-1994 [40]	TR-NWT-00246 [46]
TUP	Q.721 [14] to Q.725 [18]	—	
ISUP	Q.761 [19] to Q.764 [22], Q.767 [23]	ANSI T1.113-1992 [41] and T1.113a-1993 [42]	
DUP	Q.741 [24]	—	
SCCP	Q.711 [25] to Q.716 [28], Q.716 [29]	ANSI T1.112-1992 [43]	
TCAP	Q.771 [30] to Q.775 [34]	ANSI T1.114-1992 [44]	
OMAP	Q.750 [35], Q.752 [36] to Q.754 [38]	ANSI T1.116-1990 [45]	

Section 4.6 introduces the MTP, and Section 4.7 briefly discusses the ISUP and SCCP. Other user parts listed in Table 4–2—namely, the TUP, the data user part (DUP), the TCAP, and the operation and maintenance application part (OMAP)—are not used for ISDN call control and are therefore outside the scope of this book.

4.6 The Message Transfer Part (MTP)

The MTP is made up of three lower layers, 1, 2, and 3. The MTP is basic to CCS 7 protocol and is a mandatory requirement for every implementation, irrespective of the field of application.

4.6.1 Signaling Data Link (Level 1)

The flow of signaling information takes place through the physical transmission link interconnecting the SPs. A signaling data link consists of two transmission paths operating together in opposite directions at the same data rate and utilized solely and exclusively for conveying signaling information between two SPs.

The signaling data link usually consists of digital transmission channels. Although rarely used in the current scenario of digitalization of telecommunication networks, an analog link with modems, operating at lower bit rates (as low as 2.4 kbps for telephony application), is also specified in CCITT recommendations. For the U.S. network, analog signaling data links are not specified [46].

CCS 7 can operate both on terrestrial and satellite links. Satellite links should be avoided as far as possible, however, due to the large delays inherent in their use.

For a digital signaling data link, the CCITT recommended bit rate is 64 kbps. For the U.S. network, the standard bit rate is 56 kbps, but 64 kbps may be used when links with this bit rate are available [46].

The 64 kbps digital transmission channel may be derived from a 1,544 kbps, 2,048 kbps, or 8,448 kbps digital multiplex system, as per functional characteristics specified in CCITT recommendations G.703 [47] and G.704 [48]. For example, timeslot 16 may be used in the 30-channel 2,048 kbps PCM system. The timeslot carrying the CCS 7 signaling information is semipermanently connected to the common channel signaling equipment at the two end SPs. Alternatively, suitable interface equipment to perform this function may be employed. Refer to Figure 4–11.

The availability and error rates permissible over a digital signaling data link are identical to the usual requirements applicable to digital circuits described in CCITT recommendations G.821 [49] and ANSI T1.510 [50]. There are no special requirements for CCS 7.

4.6.2 Signaling Link Functions (Level 2)

A brief overview of level 2 functions is presented here; they are considered in greater detail in Chapter 6. The signaling data link, which consists of physical facilities, is prone to transmission errors. But accurate transport of signaling information is an essential requirement in CCS 7. Level 2 provides the necessary error detection and correction

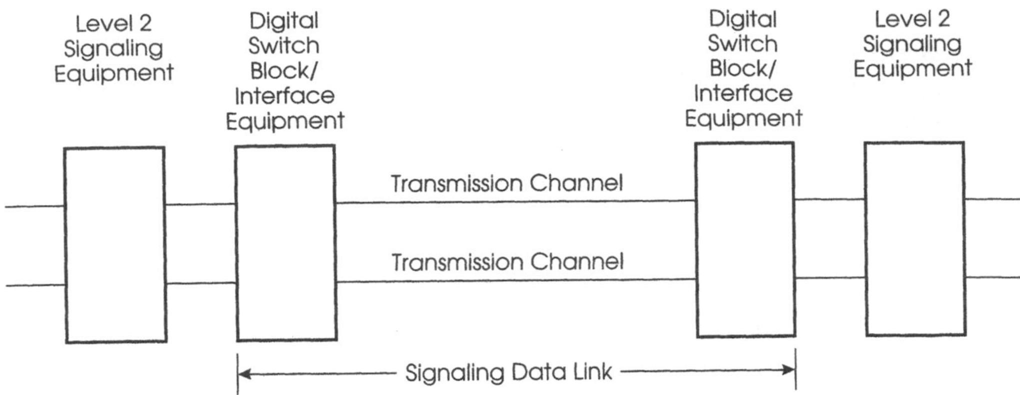

Figure 4–11 Functional configuration of signaling data link.

mechanisms so that the signaling messages are conveyed from one SP to another without loss, repetition, missequence, or errors. A signaling data link so enhanced (in its capabilities by level 2 functions) is called a signaling link. A signaling link may therefore be visualized as an ideal bidirectional transport channel between two adjacent SPs.

Since the signal units contain a variable number of octets, demarcation of one signal unit from another is done by a flag of one octet. The flag has a distinctive pattern, and a mechanism is provided so that the flag pattern is not imitated by the remaining data in a signal unit.

Level 2 also provides for error monitoring so that a signaling link with excessive errors may be removed from service. By exchanging LSSUs, level 2 performs such functions as indicating the onset and abatement of congestion and "proving a link" that is, validating a link for its ability to carry signaling traffic before bringing it into service.

To perform these functions, FISUs and LSSUs are exchanged between adjacent SPs. FISUs and LSSUs are not involved at levels 3 and 4. Refer to Figure 4–12.

4.6.3 Signaling Network Functions (Level 3)

The signaling network functions relate to the entire CCS 7 network. An important function of level 3 is to deliver messages generated by a user part at an SP to the corresponding user part in the destination SP. The message may be transported through one or more intermediate STPs. In Figure 4–13(a), MSUs generated by the ISUP of SP A are de-

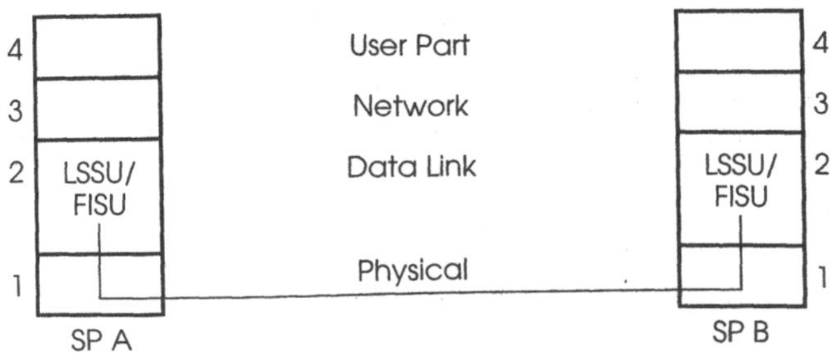

Figure 4–12 Signal units exchanged between level 2 of adjacent SPs.

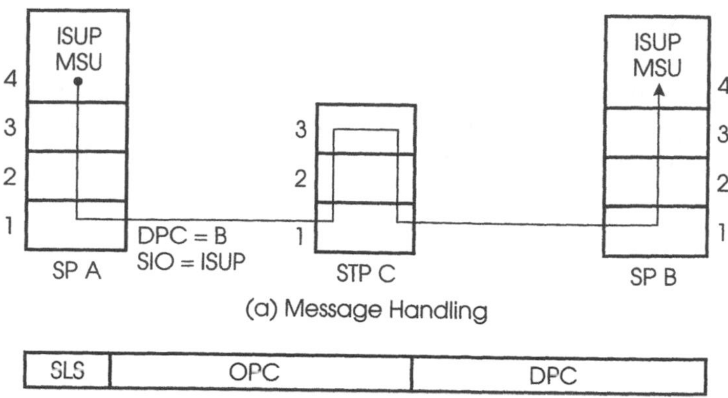

Key
SLS: Signaling Link Selection
OPC: Origination Point Code
DPC: Destination Point Code

(b) Routing Label

Figure 4–13 Transport of level 4 messages: (a) Message Handling; (b) Routing Label.

livered to the ISUP of SP B via an STP C. This function is called *message handling*. The level 3 functions at SP A, STP C, and SP B work in cooperation to perform the message transfer. The MSU contains a routing label that specifies the point codes of the origination and destination SPs (origination point code, OPC, and the destination point code, DPC) besides a signaling link selection (SLS) field. Refer to Figure 4–13(b).

The routing toward the destination SP is decided by examining the DPC in the routing label and determining the signaling link that the message should use toward the destination SP. Typically, more than one signaling link toward a destination exists, and signaling messages are distributed on the links as evenly as possible to avoid congestion due to uneven load. Load balancing is performed by using the SLS field.

When there is no direct route to the destination SP, the originating SP first routes the message to an STP. The STP examines the DPC and then routes the message toward the destination. Once the message reaches the destination SP, it needs to know the user part to which the message is to be delivered. A field in the MSU (service indicator) is analyzed to determine the user part. The service indicator has 4 bits; therefore, an MTP can address only up to 16 user parts.

Apart from the message handling function, level 3 also performs signaling network management. It consists of signaling link management, traffic management, and route management. The objective of these management functions is to ensure a high degree of reliability and availability of the signaling network. For network management functions, messages are exchanged between level 3 of the SPs/STPs. For example, in the case of a link failure, level 3 of the SP detecting the failure needs to inform the adjacent SP of the failure so that the two SPs can divert messages carried by the failed link to an alternative available link. Therefore, in addition to the exchange of MSUs by the users of MTP, MSUs are also exchanged between level 3 of the SPs/STPs. The various level 3 MSUs are described in Chapter 7.

4.7 User Parts

The users of the MTP are the telephone user part (TUP), the ISDN user part (ISUP), the data user part (DUP), and the signaling connection control part (SCCP). The ISUP provides the functionality of both the TUP and the DUP. In addition, it supports ISDN services. Apart from being the user of the MTP, the ISUP may be optionally the user of the SCCP, if certain innovative features, such as signaling unrelated to a circuit switched connection, are required. Apart from the MTP, which has been discussed already, only the ISUP and the SCCP are relevant for ISDN applications. These are discussed in the following sections.

4.7.1 ISDN User Part (ISUP)

In this section, a few examples of the application of the ISUP are presented; Chapter 9 is devoted to a detailed study of the ISUP.

The ISDN user part supports both basic bearer services and supplementary services for voice and nonvoice application in an ISDN. In addition, circuit switched telephone service and data services are also supported.

The first specification of ISUP was published in the CCITT Red Book recommendations in 1985. These were revised and expanded in the Blue Book in 1989 and subsequent ITU-T recommendations in 1993. The ISUP is described in recommendations Q.761 to Q.764. In addition, the Q.73x series of recommendations deal with ISDN supplementary services and the ISUP protocol to support these services. The ISUP for the international network is specified in Q.767.

The MSUs that originate and terminate in the ISUP are referred to as ISUP messages. Figure 4–14 shows an ISDN call setup using ISUP messages between an originating and a terminating exchange through a transit exchange.

In the ISDN, signaling between the ISDN user and the exchange follows digital subscriber signaling system 1 (DSS 1) protocol specified in ITU-T recommendations Q.921 [51] and Q.931 [52]. This is called user-to-network or access signaling. The corresponding standards for North America are specified in ANSI T1.602 [53] and ANSI T1.605 [54]. DSS 1 protocol is organized on the principles of the OSI reference model. It uses a common D-channel for signaling associated with two B-channels (for basic rate access ISDN) or 30 B-channels (for primary rate access ISDN). The D-channel has a bit rate of 16 kbps for the basic access and 64 kbps for primary access. In view of difference in requirements of subscriber access signaling from the interexchange signaling, the DSS 1 and CCS 7 signaling systems are different and distinct. In Figure 4–14, setup, call proceeding, alerting, connect, and disconnect are DSS 1 messages. The initial address message (IAM) and address complete message (ACM) are ISUP messages of CCS 7. Notice that release (REL) and release complete (RLC) messages exist in both DSS 1 and CCS 7. Although they have identical nomenclature, the formats of these messages in the two protocols are different and distinct.

Two signaling possibilities exist for the ISUP, *en bloc* operation and *overlap* operation. Figure 4–14 shows en bloc operation. The calling user supplies the digits corre-

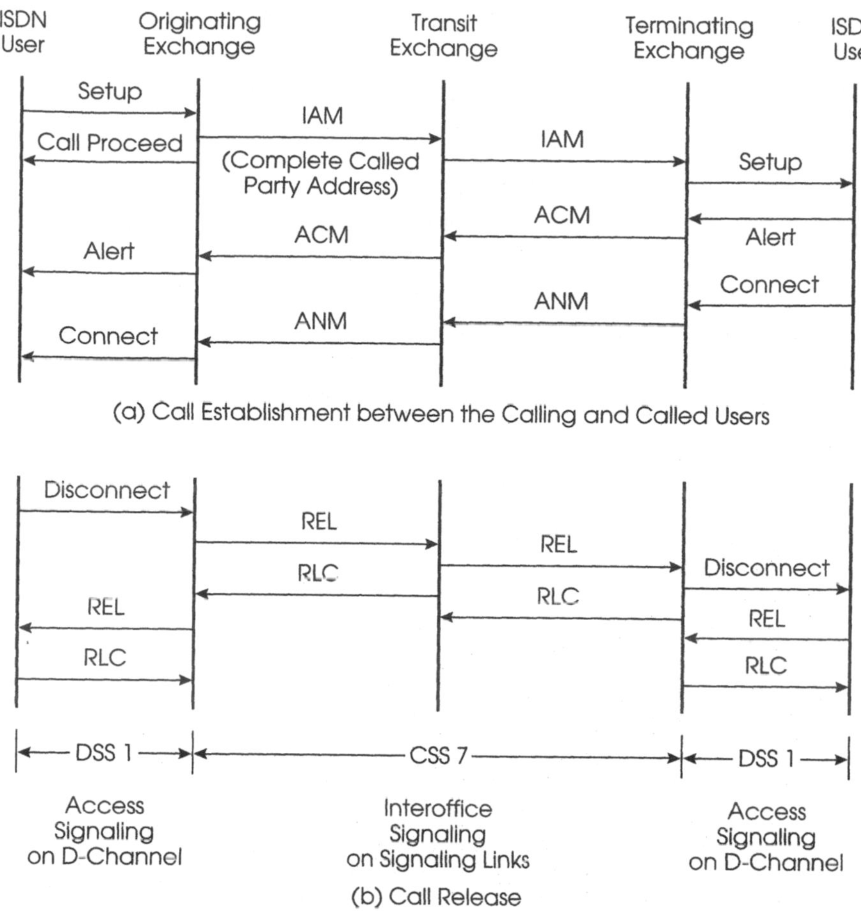

Figure 4–14 ISUP messages for a successful ISDN call (en bloc operation).

sponding to the address of the called user and these digits are carried to the originating exchange in the setup message. In en bloc operation, the originating exchange commences signaling only after receiving all the digits for the called user. Upon receipt of the setup message, the ISUP in the originating exchange generates an IAM. The IAM which contains the address of the called user, is sent on a signaling link by the MTP. Selection of a suitable interexchange circuit takes place between the originating exchange and the transit exchange to set up a circuit switched connection between the two exchanges. The ISUP in the transit exchange generates another IAM that is routed on a signaling link by the MTP to the ISUP in the terminating exchange. A circuit switched connection is established between the transit and the terminating exchanges. Furthermore, on receipt of the IAM message, the terminating exchange sends a setup message (access signaling) to the called user and receives an alerting signal from the user. The ISUP in the terminating exchange now sends the ACM to the originating exchange via the transit exchange. Upon receipt of the ACM, the originating exchange sends an alerting message to the calling user. The calling user hears the ring back tone. When the called user answers the call, the connect message is received at the terminating (destination) exchange. The ISUP in the destination exchange generates an answer message (ANM) that is sent to the originating exchange, which in turn sends a connect message to the calling user. A switched connection between the calling and called users is established, and the call enters the "talking phase" (cut-through).

In the ISDN, the call can be released by either user. Assuming that a release is initiated by the calling user, a disconnect message goes to the originating exchange, which in turn sends a release (REL) ISUP message to the transit exchange. The transit exchange sends a release message to the terminating exchange and a release complete (RLC) message to the originating exchange. The terminating exchange sends a disconnect message to the called user and an RLC ISUP message to the transit exchange.

An alternative to en bloc operation is the overlap operation where, unlike en bloc operation, the called user address is sent in parts. Each exchange sends an IAM after it has received enough digits to route the call to the next exchange. Additional digits are sent in one or more subsequent address messages (SAMs). The terminating exchange, however, sends the ACM only after receiving all the digits.

The distinction between en bloc and overlap operations lies only in the call setup. Call setup for overlap operation is shown in Figure 4–15. Which alternative to use is based on planning considerations described in Chapter 10.

The above example illustrates the use of a few ISUP messages. Many more exist for dealing with different call scenarios, including unsuccessful calls and calls with different ISDN supplementary services. In the example, the originating, transit, and terminating ex-

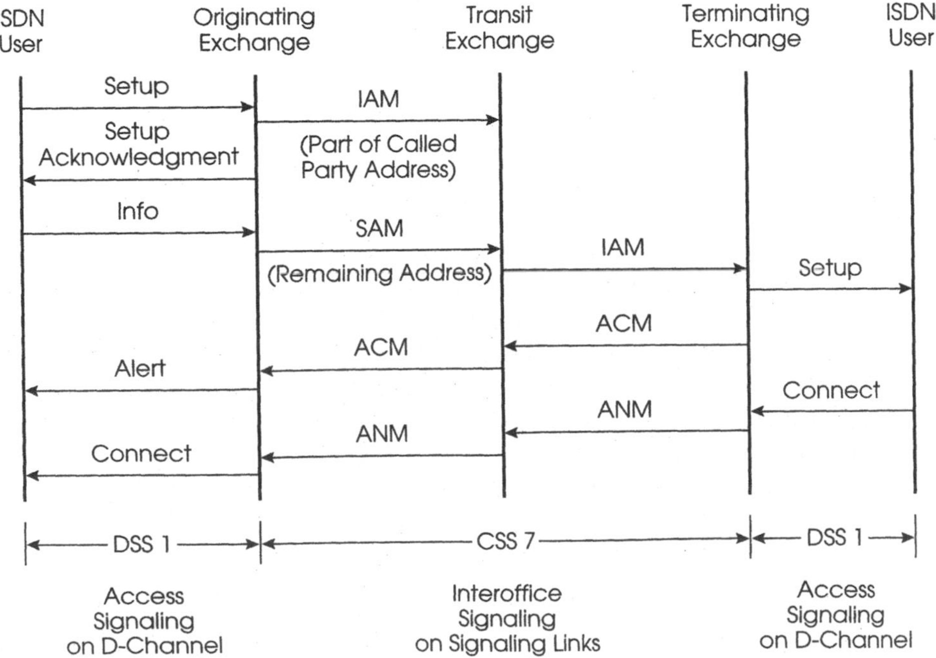

Figure 4–15 ISUP messages for ISDN call setup (overlap operation).

changes implement SP functions; that is, all the four levels of the CCS 7 protocol are implemented. The signaling is performed link by link for the circuit switched connection between the exchanges in question.

In addition to the link-by-link signaling, the ISUP procedures also include the possibility of end-to-end signaling, in which case the signaling relation exists only between the end exchanges. The transit exchanges function as STPs. End-to-end signaling may or may not be related to a circuit switched connection. Accordingly, end-to-end signaling may be provided in the ISUP in two ways: by using the existing transport capability of the MTP, in which case the end-to-end signaling is related to a circuit switched connection, or by using enhanced transport capabilities provided by the SCCP. End-to-end signaling supported by the SCCP need not be related to a circuit switched connection.

Figure 4–16 illustrates end-to-end signaling using MTP functionality only. The method is known as the pass-along method. Notice that the circuit identification code (CIC) in the ISUP messages contains the identity of the physical trunk on which the circuit switched connection is established.

Signaling without being related to a circuit switched connection is implemented using SCCP functions. This makes implementation of certain additional services—for example, signaling between end exchanges prior to call setup or after call disconnection—possible. Services such as intelligent network (IN) services and mobile telephony require the SCCP. The next section contains a brief overview of SCCP functions.

4.7.2 Signaling Connection Control Part (SCCP)

The SCCP is an enhancement of transport oriented MTP functions. It brings the capabilities of CCS 7 protocol at par with layers 1 to 3 of the OSI model. Applications that require enhanced transport capabilities are users of the SCCP.

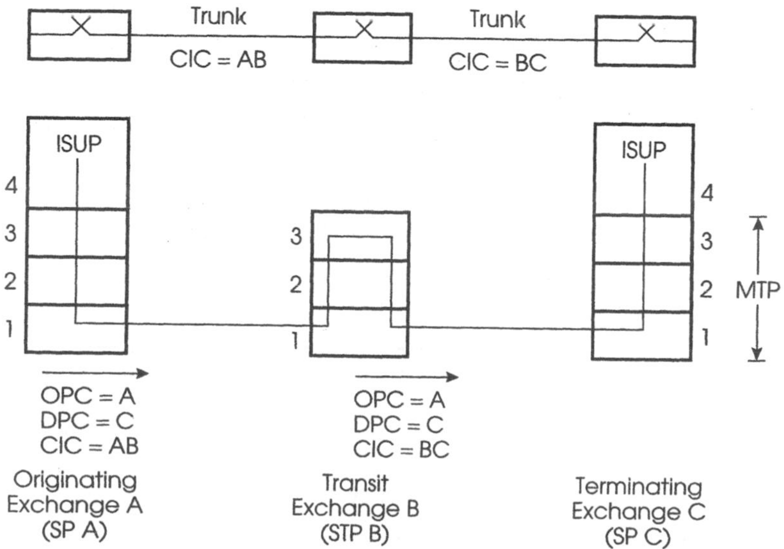

Figure 4–16 End-to-end signaling using MTP (pass-along method).

Two key enhancements are provided by the SCCP, the extended addressing capability and the provision of both connectionless and connection-oriented services.

4.7.2.1 Enhanced Addressing Capability

The number of users of the MTP is limited to 16, due to the 4-bit service indicator used for addressing. The SCCP provides addressing for up to 255 users by employing subsystem numbers (SSNs). Refer to Figure 4–17. The SSNs provide a distribution mechanism that enables the SCCP to deliver a message to the desired application. In this way, the use of SSNs is local to the SP.

At the CCS 7 network level, an enhancement of the addressing facility is provided by global title (GT) translation. The SCCP gives its users the option to supply a GT. The GT is an address that uniquely identifies an application (a user of the SCCP) residing in a CCS 7 node. The GT is translated into a DPC and SSN either at the originating SP itself or at any other node that maintains the translation table. The DPC enables the MTP to reach the desired node. The SCCP in the destination node then analyzes the SSN to reach the desired application. The SCCP-based routing using GT is illustrated in Figure 4–18, in which GT translation is done at STP B.

4.7.2.2 Connectionless and Connection-Oriented Services

In contrast to the MTP, which provides only a connectionless class of service, the SCCP caters to both connectionless and connection-oriented services. The MTP maintains a connectionless flow of messages, since it simply transports messages received from level 4 and does not recognize the messages as pertaining to a specific transaction (for example, a call). Messages are sent singly and independently of one another. Therefore, all messages are unconnected or unrelated to each other as far as the MTP is concerned. It is another matter that the messages for a specific transaction are delivered in sequence because the same SLS value is assigned to them, but this does not alter the basic nature of connectionless service provided by the MTP to its users. (During the early stage of definition of the CCS 7 protocol, the circuit switched connection was the primary application and the connectionless service provided by MTP was adequate.)

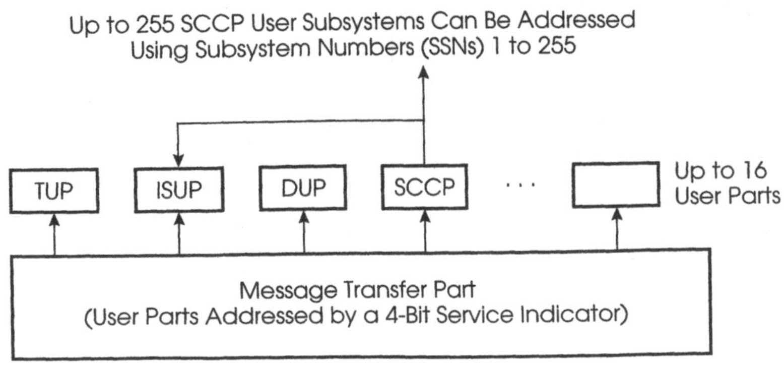

Figure 4–17 Addressing by subsystem numbers.

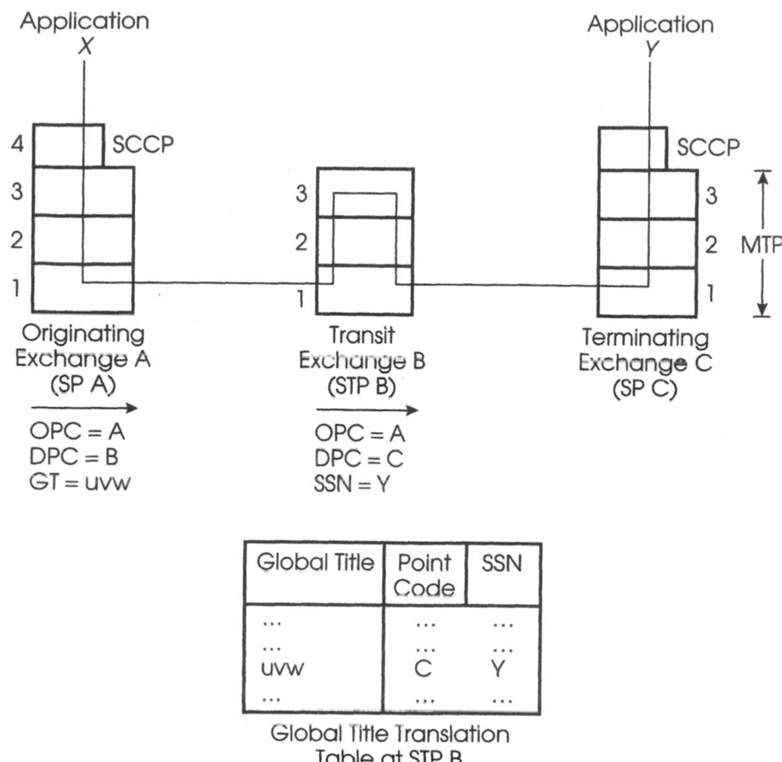

Figure 4–18 Addressing by global title translation.

The SCCP provides the following services:

Class 0: basic conncctionless service
Class 1: sequenced connectionless service
Class 2: basic connection-oriented service
Class 3: flow control connection-oriented service

In basic connectionless service, a block of information from the SCCP user in the originating SP is transported to the SCCP user in the destination SP. The maximum size of this block (called the network service data unit, NSDU), is up to 255 octets when addressing is not by global title. The information block is not broken into segments while being transported. The service is a pure connectionless service, and sequencing of messages is not ensured.

The class 1 sequenced connectionless service is the equivalent of the MTP connectionless service. Although the service is connectionless, sequencing of messages is performed.

In the class 2 basic connection-oriented service, a bidirectional transfer of NSDUs between the SCCP user in the node of origin and the SCCP user in the destination node is performed by a signaling connection. Since a number of such signaling connections may be multiplexed on the same signaling relation, it is necessary to assign a pair of reference numbers, called local reference numbers, for a signaling connection. To ensure message sequencing, messages with the same local reference numbers are assigned the same SLS.

The class 3 connection-oriented service provides more features than class 2 service, such as flow control (for congestion management) and detection when message missequence occurs.

4.8 CCS 7 Numbering and Network Structure

The network structure and numbering aspects of CCS 7 are described in the CCITT/ITU-T recommendations listed in Table 4–3. For the sake of completeness, the table also lists the relevant international recommendations on CCS 7 testing and the complimentary U.S. industry standards.

4.8.1 CCS 7 Numbering

The worldwide CCS 7 network consists of the international CCS 7 network and various national CCS 7 networks. This division permits independent management of the national and international networks; thus, independent numbering schemes are essential.

The numbering scheme listing the point codes for the international network is specified in ITU-T recommendation Q.708 [56]. The number of bits to be used in the point

Table 4-3 CCS 7 Standards on Network Structure, Numbering, and Testing

CCS 7: Other Aspects	CCITT Recommendations	ANSI/BELLCORE
Signaling network structure	Q.705 [55]	BELLCORE TA-NWT-00246 [46]
International SP codes	Q.708 [56]	—
Hypothetical signaling reference connection	Q.709 [57]	
SS7 test specification (general)	Q.780 [58]	
MTP level 2 test specification	Q.781 [59]	ANSI T1.234-1993 [66]
MTP level 3 test specification	Q.782 [60]	
TUP test specification	Q.783 [61]	—
ISUP test specification	Q.784 [62]	ANSI T1.236-1993 [67]
ISUP supplementary service test specification	Q.785 [63]	
SCCP test specification	Q.786 [64]	ANSI T1.235-1993 [68]
TCAP test specification	Q.787 [65]	—

code is 14. (The standard routing label for international CCS 7 network has 32 bits; 14 bits each for the OPC and DPC and 4 bits for the SLS.) The point code is structured into three subfields (refer to Figure 4–19):

- Zone identification, a 3-bit field, that permits partitioning the international network into eight zones. Zones 2 through 7 have been specified, and zones 0 and 1 are currently spare. Figure 4–20 shows a map identifying the zones.
- Area/network identification, an 8-bit field, provides a maximum of 256 geographical areas within each zone. A country is assigned one or more of these geographical areas.
- Signaling point identification consisting of 3 bits makes a provision for up to eight international signaling points within each area.

For a country that has more than eight international SPs, additional area/network identification codes are allotted. For example, for the United States signaling area/network code (SANC) values 3-020 through 3-059 are allotted. Here "3" represents the zone number and the next three digits are the decimal values for the 8-bit area/network identification.

The numbering of SPs in the national network is determined by the appropriate national agency. A 14-bit point code may also be used for numbering of SPs in the national network. This is not mandatory; a 24-bit code is used in the U.S. network. These issues are discussed as part of planning considerations in Chapter 10.

4.8.2 CCS 7 Performance Objectives

The performance objectives for CCS 7 need to be closely aligned to the services carried by the network. Two major objectives are as follows:

1. High availability of the CCS 7 network. An availability figure of 99.9998% for any particular signaling route set is specified. This corresponds to a maximum permissible downtime of 10 minutes in a year.
2. The maximum permissible signaling delay. To specify this parameter, a hypothetical signaling reference connection (HSRC) is used as a model. The HSRC consists of two end SPs and a succession of STPs, with or without SCCP functions, interconnected by signaling data links. The HSRC has an international section and two national sections (one at either end). The values of maximum

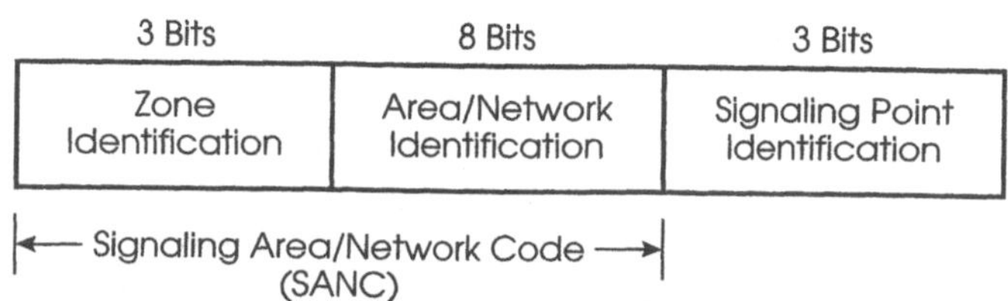

Figure 4–19 Format for international signaling point code.

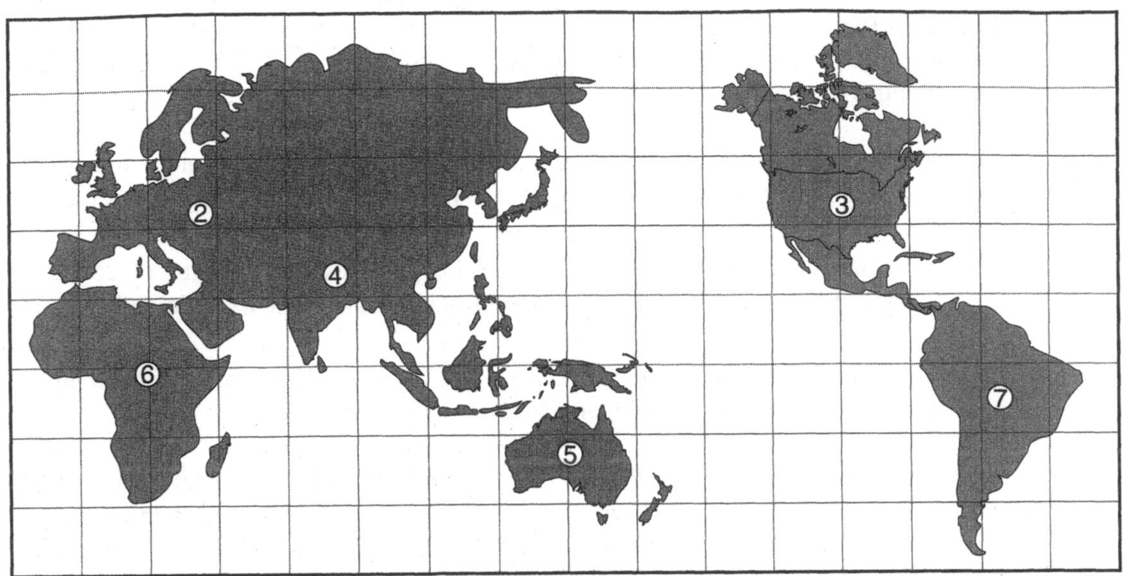

Figure 4–20 International CCS 7 numbering zones.

signaling delays for the international component and the national components for the HSRC are stated in CCITT recommendation Q.709 [57] and are discussed in Chapter 10.

Besides addressing other technoeconomic issues, the network structure for CCS 7 has to be planned and engineered to meet performance objectives. The performance, network, and other matters allied to planning and engineering are covered in Chapter 10.

4.9 Remarks

CCS 7 is an important infrastructure that serves as a platform for various services in the network. As discussed, different user parts cater to different services, and the MTP and SCCP provide the transfer protocols of CCS 7. Since this book focuses on ISDN services, only those protocols that are relevant to the ISDN were introduced in this chapter. Detailed descriptions of CCS 7 protocol follow in Chapters 6 and 7. ISUP is discussed in Chapter 9. Planning and testing are crucial to the success of CCS 7. These are considered in Chapters 10 and 11.

References

[1] *Specifications of Signaling System No. 7.* CCITT Yellow Book, vol. VI, fascicle VI.6, recommendations Q.701–Q.741. International Telecommunication Union, 1981.

[2] *Specifications of Signaling System No. 7.* CCITT Red Book, vol. VI, fascicle VI.6, recommendations Q.701–Q.714. International Telecommunication Union, 1985.

[3] *Specifications of Signaling System No. 7.* CCITT Blue Book, fascicle VI.7, recommendations Q.701–Q.716; fascicle VI.8, recommendations Q.721–Q.766; and fascicle VI.9, recommendations Q.771–Q.795 (three volumes). International Telecommunication Union, 1989.

[4] Chapius, R. J., and A. E. Joel Jr. *Electronic Computers and Telephone Switching.* North Holland Publishing Company, 1990.

[5] "Common channel interoffice signaling." Bell System Technical Journal (special issue), Feb. 1978.

[6] *Specifications of Signaling System R1.* CCITT Blue Book, vol. VI, fascicle VI.4, recommendations Q.310–Q.331, International Telecommunication Union, 1989.

[7] *Specifications of Signaling System R2.* CCITT Blue Book, vol. VI, fascicle VI.4, recommendations Q.400–Q.490. International Telecommunication Union, 1989.

[8] *Data Communications Network—Open System Interconnection (OSI). Model and Notation, Service Definition.* CCITT Blue Book, fascicle VIII.4, recommendations X.200–X.219. International Telecommunication Union, 1989.

[9] Roehr, W. C., Jr. "Inside SS7 no. 7: A detailed look at ISDN's signaling system plan." Data Communication, pp. 120–128, Oct. 85.

[10] *Specifications of Signaling System No. 7: Functional Description of the Message Transfer Part of Signaling System No. 7.* ITU-T recommendation Q.701, rev. 1. International Telecommunication Union, 1993.

[11] *Specifications of Signaling System No. 7: Signaling Data Link.* CCITT Blue Book, fascicle VI.7, recommendation Q.702. International Telecommunication Union, 1988.

[12] *Specifications of Signaling System No. 7: Signaling Link.* ITU-T recommendation Q.703, rev. 1. International Telecommunication Union, 1993.

[13] *Specifications of Signaling System No. 7: Signaling Network Functions and Messages.* ITU-T recommendation Q.704, rev. 1. International Telecommunication Union, 1993.

[14] *Specifications of Signaling System No. 7: Telephone User Part. Functional Description of the Signaling System No. 7 Telephone User Part (TUP).* CCITT Blue Book, fascicle VI.8, recommendation Q.721. International Telecommunication Union, 1988.

[15] *Specifications of Signaling System No. 7: Telephone User Part. General Function of Telephone Messages and Signals.* CCITT Blue Book, fascicle VI.8, recommendation Q.722. International Telecommunication Union, 1988.

[16] *Specifications of Signaling System No. 7: Telephone User Part. Formats and Codes.* ITU-T recommendation Q.723, rev. 1. International Telecommunication Union, 1993.

[17] *Specifications of Signaling System No. 7: Telephone User Part. Signaling Procedures.* ITU-T recommendation Q.724, rev. 1. International Telecommunication Union, 1993.

[18] *Specifications of Signaling System No. 7: Telephone User Part. Signaling Performance in the Telephone Application.* ITU-T recommendation Q.725, rev. 1. International Telecommunication Union, 1993.

[19] *Specifications of Signaling System No. 7: ISDN User Part. Functional Description of the ISDN User Part of Signaling System No. 7.* ITU-T recommendation Q.761, rev. 1. International Telecommunication Union, 1993.

[20] *Specifications of Signaling System No. 7: ISDN User Part. General Function of Messages and Signals.* ITU-T recommendation Q.762, rev. 1. International Telecommunication Union, 1993.

[21] *Specifications of Signaling System No. 7: ISDN User Part. Formats and Codes.* ITU-T recommendation Q.763, rev. 1. International Telecommunication Union, 1993.

[22] *Specifications of Signaling System No. 7: ISDN User Part. Signaling Procedures.* ITU-T recommendation Q.764, rev. 1. International Telecommunication Union, 1993.

[23] *Specifications of Signaling System No. 7: ISDN User Part. Application of ISDN User Part of CCITT Signaling System No. 7 for International ISDN Interconnections.* ITU-T recommendation Q.767. International Telecommunication Union, 1991.

[24] *Specifications of Signaling System No. 7: Data User Part.* CCITT Blue Book, fascicle VI.8, recommendation Q.741. International Telecommunication Union, 1988.

[25] *Specifications of Signaling System No. 7: Signaling Connection Control Part. Functional Description of the Signaling Connection Control Part.* ITU-T recommendation Q.711, rev. 1. International Telecommunication Union, 1993.

[26] *Specifications of Signaling System No. 7: Signaling Connection Control Part. Definition and Function of SCCP Messages.* ITU-T recommendation Q.712, rev. 1. International Telecommunication Union, 1993.

[27] *Specifications of Signaling System No. 7: Signaling Connection Control Part. SCCP Formats and Codes.* ITU-T recommendation Q.713, rev. 1. International Telecommunication Union, 1993.

[28] *Specifications of Signaling System No. 7: Signaling Connection Control Part Procedures.* ITU-T recommendation Q.714, rev. 1. International Telecommunication Union, 1993.

[29] *Specifications of Signaling System No. 7: Signaling Connection Control Part (SCCP) Performances.* ITU-T recommendation Q.716, rev. 1. International Telecommunication Union, 1993.

[30] *Specifications of Signaling System No. 7: Transaction Capabilities Application Part. Functional Description of Transaction Capabilities.* ITU-T recommendation Q.771, rev. 1. International Telecommunication Union, 1993.

[31] *Specifications of Signaling System No. 7: Transaction Capabilities Application Part. Transaction Capabilities Information Element Definitions.* ITU-T recommendation Q.772, rev. 1. International Telecommunication Union, 1993.

[32] *Specifications of Signaling System No. 7: Transaction Capabilities Application Part. Transaction Capabilities Formats and Encoding.* ITU-T recommendation Q.773, rev. 1. International Telecommunication Union, 1993.

[33] *Specifications of Signaling System No. 7: Transaction Capabilities Application*

Part. Transaction Capabilities Procedures. ITU-T recommendation Q.774, rev. 1. International Telecommunication Union, 1993.

[34] *Specifications of Signaling System No. 7: Transaction Capabilities Application Part. Guidelines for Using Transaction Capabilities.* ITU-T recommendation Q.775, rev. 1. International Telecommunication Union, 1993.

[35] *Specifications of Signaling System No. 7: Signaling System No. 7 Management. Operations, Maintenance, and Administration Part of Signaling System No. 7—Management Overview.* ITU-T recommendation Q.750, rev. 1. International Telecommunication Union, 1993.

[36] *Specifications of Signaling System No. 7: Signaling System No. 7 Monitoring and Management.* ITU-T recommendation Q.752, rev. 1. International Telecommunication Union, 1993.

[37] *Specifications of Signaling System No. 7: Operations, Maintenance, and Administration Part of Signaling System No. 7.* ITU-T recommendation Q.753, rev. 1. International Telecommunication Union, 1993.

[38] *Specifications of Signaling System No. 7: Operations, Maintenance, and Administration Part of Signaling System No. 7. Management Application Service Elements Definition.* ITU-T recommendation Q.754, rev. 1. International Telecommunication Union, 1993.

[39] American National Standard for Telecommunications. *Signaling System Number 7 (SS7)—Functional Description of the Signaling System Message Transfer Part (MTP).* ANSI T1.111-1992.

[40] American National Standard for Telecommunications. *Signaling System Number 7 (SS7)—Message Transfer Part (MTP). Numbering of Signaling Point Codes.* ANSI T1.111a-1994 (supplement to ANSI T1.111-1992).

[41] American National Standard for Telecommunications. *Signaling System Number 7 (SS7)—Integrated Services Digital Network (ISDN) User Part.* ANSI T1.113-1992.

[42] American National Standard for Telecommunications. *Signaling System Number 7 (SS7)—Integrated Services Digital Network (ISDN) User Part (N × DS0 Multi-Rate Connection).* ANSI T1.113a-1993 (supplement to ANSI T1.113-1992).

[43] American National Standard for Telecommunications. *Signaling System Number 7 (SS7)—Signaling Connection Control Part (SCCP).* ANSI T1.112-1992.

[44] American National Standard for Telecommunications. *Signaling System Number 7 (SS7)—Transaction Capability Application Part (TCAP).* ANSI T1.114-1992.

[45] American National Standard for Telecommunications. *Signaling System Number 7 (SS7)—Operations, Maintenance and Administration Part (OMAP).* ANSI T1.116-1990.

[46] "Specifications of signaling system number 7." BELLCORE Technical Reference TR-NWT-00246, issue 2, June 1991; rev. 1, Dec. 1991; rev. 2, Dec. 1992; rev. 3, Dec. 1993.

[47] *General Aspects of Digital Transmission Systems; Terminal Equipments—Physical Characteristics of Hierarchical Digital Interfaces.* ITU-T recommendation G.703, rev. 1. International Telecommunication Union, 1991.

[48] *General Aspects of Digital Transmission Systems; Terminal Equipments—Synchronous Frame Structures Used at Primary and Secondary Hierarchical Levels.* ITU-T recommendation G.704, rev. 1. International Telecommunication Union, 1991.

[49] *Error Performance of an International Digital Connection Forming Part of an Integrated Services Digital Network.* CCITT Blue Book, vol. III, fascicle III.5, recommendation G.821. International Telecommunication Union, 1989.

[50] American National Standard for Telecommunications. *Network Performance Parameters for Dedicated Digital Services—Specifications.* ANSI T1.510-1994.

[51] *Digital Subscriber Signaling System No. 1: ISDN User-Network Interface—Data Link Layer Specification.* ITU-T recommendation Q.921, rev. 1. International Telecommunication Union, 1993.

[52] *Digital Subscriber Signaling System No. 1: ISDN User-Network Interface Layer 3 Specification for Basic Call Control.* ITU-T recommendation Q.931, rev. 1. International Telecommunication Union, 1993.

[53] American National Standard for Telecommunications. *Integrated Services Digital Network (ISDN)—Data-Link Layer. Signaling Specification for Application at User-Network Interface.* ANSI T1.602-1989.

[54] American National Standard for Telecommunications. *Integrated Services Digital Network (ISDN)—Layer 3. Signaling Specification for Circuit-Switched Bearer Service for Digital Subscriber Signaling System Number 1 (DSS1).* ANSI T1.605-1990.

[55] *Specifications of Signaling System No. 7: Message Transfer Part. Signaling Network Structure.* ITU-T recommendation Q.705, rev. 1. International Telecommunication Union, 1993.

[56] *Specifications of Signaling System No. 7: Message Transfer Part. Numbering of International Signaling Point Codes.* ITU-T recommendation Q.708, rev. 1. International Telecommunication Union, 1993.

[57] *Specifications of Signaling System No. 7: Message Transfer Part. Hypothetical Signaling Reference Connection.* ITU-T recommendation Q.709, rev. 1. International Telecommunication Union, 1993.

[58] *Specifications of Signaling System No. 7: Signaling System No. 7 Test Specification—General Description.* ITU-T recommendation Q.780, rev. 1. International Telecommunication Union, 1993.

[59] *Specifications of Signaling System No. 7: Message Transfer Part Level 2 Test Specification.* ITU-T recommendation Q.781, rev. 1. International Telecommunication Union, 1993.

[60] *Specifications of Signaling System No. 7: Message Transfer Part Level 3 Test Specification.* ITU-T recommendation Q.782, rev. 1. International Telecommunication Union, 1993.

[61] *Specifications of Signaling System No. 7: TUP Test Specification.* CCITT Blue Book, fascicle VI.9, recommendation Q.783. International Telecommunication Union, 1988.

[62] *Specifications of Signaling System No. 7: ISUP Basic Call Test Specification.* ITU-T recommendation Q.784, rev. 1. International Telecommunication Union, 1993.

[63] *Specifications of Signaling System No. 7: ISUP Protocol Test Specification for Supplementary Services.* ITU-T recommendation Q.785. International Telecommunication Union, 1991.

[64] *Specifications of Signaling System No. 7: Signaling Connection Control—Part Test Specifications.* ITU-T recommendation Q.786. International Telecommunication Union, 1993.

[65] *Specifications of Signaling System No. 7: Transaction Capabilities Part. Test Specification.* ITU-T recommendation Q.787. International Telecommunication Union, 1993.

[66] American National Standard for Telecommunications. *Signaling System Number 7 (SS7)—MTP Levels 2 and 3 Compatibility Testing.* ANSI T1.234-1993.

[67] American National Standard for Telecommunications. *Signaling System Number 7 (SS7)—MTP ISDN User Part Compatibility Testing.* ANSI T1.236-1993.

[68] American National Standard for Telecommunications. *Signaling System Number 7 (SS7)—SCCP Class 0 Compatibility Testing.* ANSI T1.235-1993.

5 Introduction to ISDN

Acronyms

AMI	alternate mark inversion
ANSI	American National Standards Institute
BER	Bit error ratio
CCITT	the International Telegraph and Telephone Consultative Committee
CCS 7	CCITT common channel signaling system no. 7
CRC	Cyclic redundancy check
DSL	digital subscriber loop
DSS 1	digital subscriber signaling system 1
EC	echo canceller
ETSI	European Telecommunication Standards Institute
ISDN	integrated services digital network
ISUP	ISDN user part
ISW	inverted synchronized word
ITU-T	International Telecommunication Union-Telecommunication Standardization Sector
LAPD	link access procedure on D-channel
LT	line termination
NPCU	normal power consumption unit
NT	network termination
OSI	open system interconnection
PABX	private automatic branch exchange
PCM	pulse code modulation
PCU	power consumption unit
PSTN	public switched telephone network
RPCU	restricted power consumption unit
SDL	system description language
SW	synchronization word
TA	terminal adapter
TCM	time compression multiplex
TEI	terminal endpoint identifier
TE1	terminal equipment type 1 (ISDN terminals)
TE2	terminal equipment type 2 (non-ISDN terminals)
2B1Q	2-binary, 1-quaternary

ABSTRACT

This chapter begins with a general introduction to the integrated digital services network (ISDN). The discussion includes:

- ISDN user-network interface reference configuration
- Protocol architecture in the ISDN
- Physical layer for the basic access ISDN, covering the wiring, coding, framing, power feeding, and electrical characteristics at the ISDN interface
- The transmission code 2B1Q (2-binary, 1-quarternary) used on the digital subscriber loop and a brief description of the primary access ISDN

5.1 Introduction

ISDN stands for integrated services digital network. This identifies the two key elements of the ISDN:

1. The integration of services
2. Provisioning of these services in a digital network

The goal of the ISDN is to provide a variety of services—speech, text, data, image, video, and their appropriate combinations—through a single unified and standardized access at the customer's premises. The means of accomplishing this goal is the digital network.

The earliest and the most widespread service is plain telephony offered through the public switched telephone network (PSTN); for text communication, a separate telex network was deployed. In the pre-ISDN scenario, new services were offered, primarily by means of dedicated networks. Even when implemented through the PSTN, each service required a separate access at the customer premises. It is clear that such an approach could not be sustained indefinitely; the complexity and costs mounted with the increase in the number of services due to multiplicity of dedicated networks, customer interfaces, and terminals.

The technical possibility of integrating various services in a common network arose from the digitalization of the existing telephone network. It needs to be emphasized that the ISDN was not the cause, but rather the consequence, of digitalization. The replacement of analog switching and transmission systems by digital systems took place as part of the digitalization process. In the ISDN, the subscriber loop was also digitalized, thereby providing an end-to-end digital connectivity. Thus, the ISDN may be viewed as the final step in the process of digitalization of telephone networks. CCITT common channel signaling system no. 7 (CCS 7), which provides major enhancements in the signaling capability of the exchanges, was already under development when the idea of the ISDN took root in the late 1970s and early 1980s. The potential of CCS 7 to fulfill the requirements for the ISDN was amply demonstrated when, by exploiting the modular nature of CCS 7 protocol, the ISDN user part (ISUP) was developed. Furthermore, the additional processing requirements for supporting the ISDN in digital exchanges could be adequately fulfilled by the availability of more powerful processors and the development of modular architecture for digital exchanges. Modular architecture permitted an increase in the call processing capability of the exchanges in economic steps. All these trends were discernible in the late 1970s, and it was in this context that the International Telegraph and Telephone Consultative Committee (CCITT; now the International Telecommunication Union-Telecommunication Standardization Sector, or ITU-T) took up the process of defining and standardizing the ISDN during its 1980–84 study period. The first standards on the ISDN were the Red Book recommendations [1]. Subsequently, during its two consecutive 4-year study periods, CCITT came up with an extensive body of recommendations, covering various aspects of the ISDN and its interworking with other networks. Concurrently, regional standards were framed by other standardization bodies, for example, the European Telecommunication Standards Institute (ETSI), American National Standards Institute (ANSI), and BELLCORE.

The ISDN has evolved from the telephony network, and this helps protect the enormous investments already made in the PSTN throughout the world. Thus, telecommunication administrations and network operators have the possibility of upgrading their PSTN progressively to the ISDN at a pace dictated by their specific needs. Because a 64 kbps channel represents the basic building block for both the switching and transmission systems in the PSTN, the ISDN provides services based on the 64 kbps bit rate and its multiples. The digitalization of the local loop is also performed on existing pair of copper lines. This is essential because investments made in local line plants the world over are very substantial. Broadly, the additional elements required in an ISDN over the existing digital telecommunication network may be summed up as follows:

1. Digitalization of the local loop by providing appropriate terminations at either end capable of transferring digital signals. The termination at the ISDN user end is called the network termination (NT), and that at the other is called the line termination (LT). The NT represents an interface between the user and the network, since it is connected to the digital subscriber loop (DSL) on the network side and the ISDN equipment on the user side. In addition, the transmission of digital signals on the local loop is performed using a specified transmission code.
2. ISDN terminals capable of operating at bit rates of 64 kbps and its multiples and a standardized arrangement for their connection to the NT in the customer's premises by internal wiring.
3. Deployment of the digital subscriber signaling system 1 (DSS 1). DSS 1 protocol is implemented in ISDN terminals and the local exchanges. DSS 1 is not required in the transit exchanges.
4. Provision of additional call processing and other software in the local exchanges to support ISDN calls.
5. Provision of the ISDN user part (ISUP) in the CCS 7 protocol implementation in all the digital exchanges, both local and transit, that route ISDN calls.

These additional elements are shown in Figure 5–1.

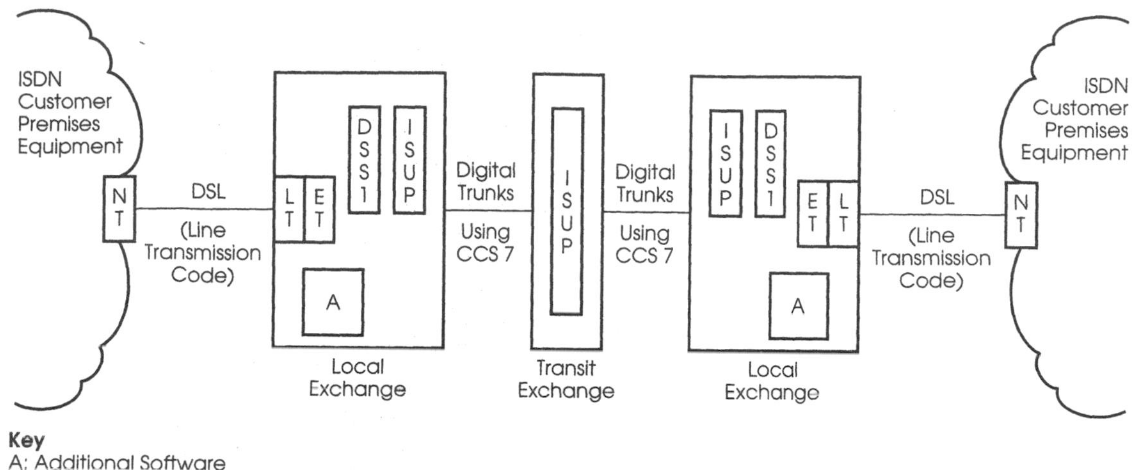

Figure 5–1 Additional elements in an ISDN.

There are two types of ISDN, basic rate and primary rate. Basic rate ISDN is supported on the two-wire line between the customer and the exchange. It provides a bit rate of 144 kbps, which is organized into three channels:

- Two information channels, called B-channels, each at 64 kbps. These channels can be used for two independent and, possibly, simultaneous calls.
- A signaling channel, called the D-channel, at 16 kbps. This channel carries the signaling according to DSS 1 protocol for the calls established through the B-channels.

Primary rate ISDN is supported on a 2,048 kbps or 1,544 kbps PCM between the customer and the exchange. It consists of 30 B-channels for the 2,048 kbps rate or 23 B-channels for the 1,544 kbps bit rate. The D-channel in both the cases carries the signaling at 64 kbps.

Apart from the 64 kbps circuit switched connections, the ISDN also supports multirate calls, that is, calls with bit rates that are multiples of 64 kbps. Examples of these are 2×64 kbps, 384 kbps, 1,536 kbps, and 1,920 kbps. For basic rate ISDN, only 2×64 kbps calls can be supported. With primary rate ISDN, other multirate calls are also possible.

5.2 Customer Premises in the ISDN

The customer premises configuration is defined in ITU-T recommendations (I-series). The term *user* is employed to denote the ISDN subscriber (or customer), and the customer premises configuration is called the *user-network* interface. A reference configuration, shown in Figure 5–2, is defined for the user network interface. The reference configuration is characterized by reference points R, S, T, and U. The overall functionality of the user-network interface may be divided into functional blocks, and the reference points

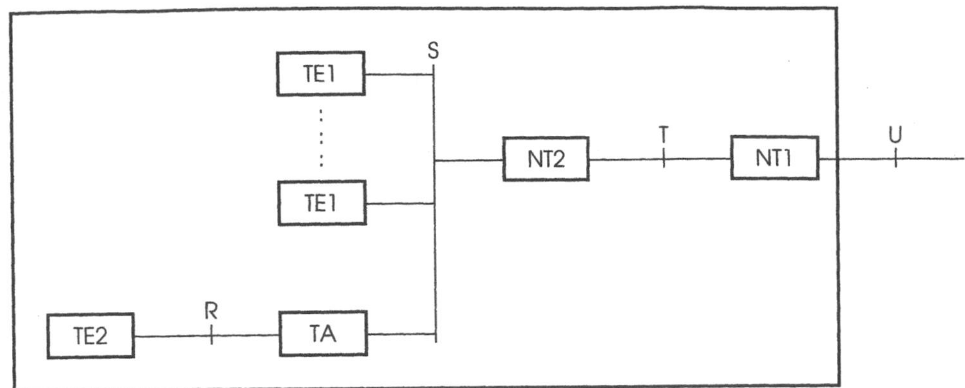

Key
TE1: ISDN Terminals
TE2: Non-ISDN Terminals
TA: Terminal Adapter
NT2: Network Termination 2
NT1: Network Termination 1
R, S, T, U: Reference Points

Figure 5–2 ISDN user-network interface reference configuration.

may be viewed as interfaces to these blocks. The functional blocks provide a basis for the realization of customer premises equipment. Individual pieces of equipment may be designed to coincide with the functional blocks or their appropriate combinations. The ISDN terminals are connected to reference point S. They are referred to as terminal equipment 1 (TE1). Reference point R has been defined to permit the use of existing non-ISDN terminals by the ISDN user. All non-ISDN terminals, designated terminal equipment 2 (TE2) in the figure, are connected at reference point R. An appropriate terminal adapter (TA) is provided between reference points R and S for connection of these terminals to the ISDN. This is a useful feature, since ISDN users would normally require interconnection capabilities to other networks using the existing non-ISDN terminals. For example, to interconnect the existing group 3 facsimile terminal, the ISDN subscriber uses an analog-to-S (A/S) TA. For access to an X.25 packet switched network, an X.25-to-S (X.25/S) TA is employed. In summary, this arrangement permits two categories of terminals in the ISDN customer premises: ISDN terminals (TE1) directly connectable to the S-interface and non-ISDN terminals (TE2) that are connected at the R-interface and require appropriate terminal adapters.

The two network terminations in the user-network interface are NT1 and NT2. NT1 terminates the digital subscriber line. The other side of NT1 represents reference point T. NT2 provides an interface between reference points S and T and is typically implemented as an ISDN private automatic branch exchange (PABX).

As noted earlier, physical pieces of equipment may not correspond, one to one, to the functional blocks of the reference configuration. More than one block may be implemented as a single piece of equipment. In implementations where NT2 is missing, the S and T reference points coincide, and there is only the S reference point. Since only NT1 is present in such situations, it is designated simply as NT. Also, TAs are missing when non-

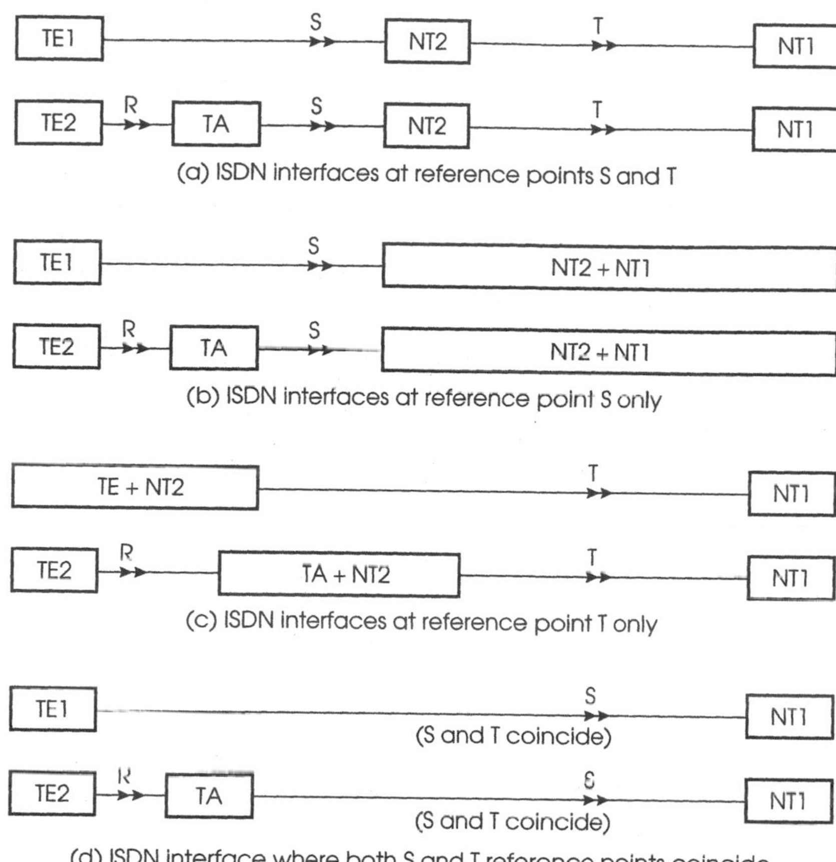

Figure 5–3 Examples of reference configuration.
[Reprinted from ITU-T recommendation I.411 (1993). ISDN user-network interfaces—Reference configurations. Rev. 1. Reproduced by permission.]

ISDN equipment is not present in the customer premises. These possibilities are summarized in ITU-T recommendation I.411 [2] and are shown in Figure 5–3.

5.3 Protocol Architecture in the ISDN

There are two protocols in the ISDN: protocol for the transfer of user information in the B-channels and protocol for the transfer of signaling information in the D-channel. These protocols are structured in terms of the layering concept of the open system interconnection (OSI) reference model. The physical layer (layer 1) is common to both protocols and corresponds to the specifications laid down in ITU-T recommendation I.430 [3] for basic access and recommendation I.431 [4] for the primary access ISDN. The protocol architecture is shown in Figure 5–4.

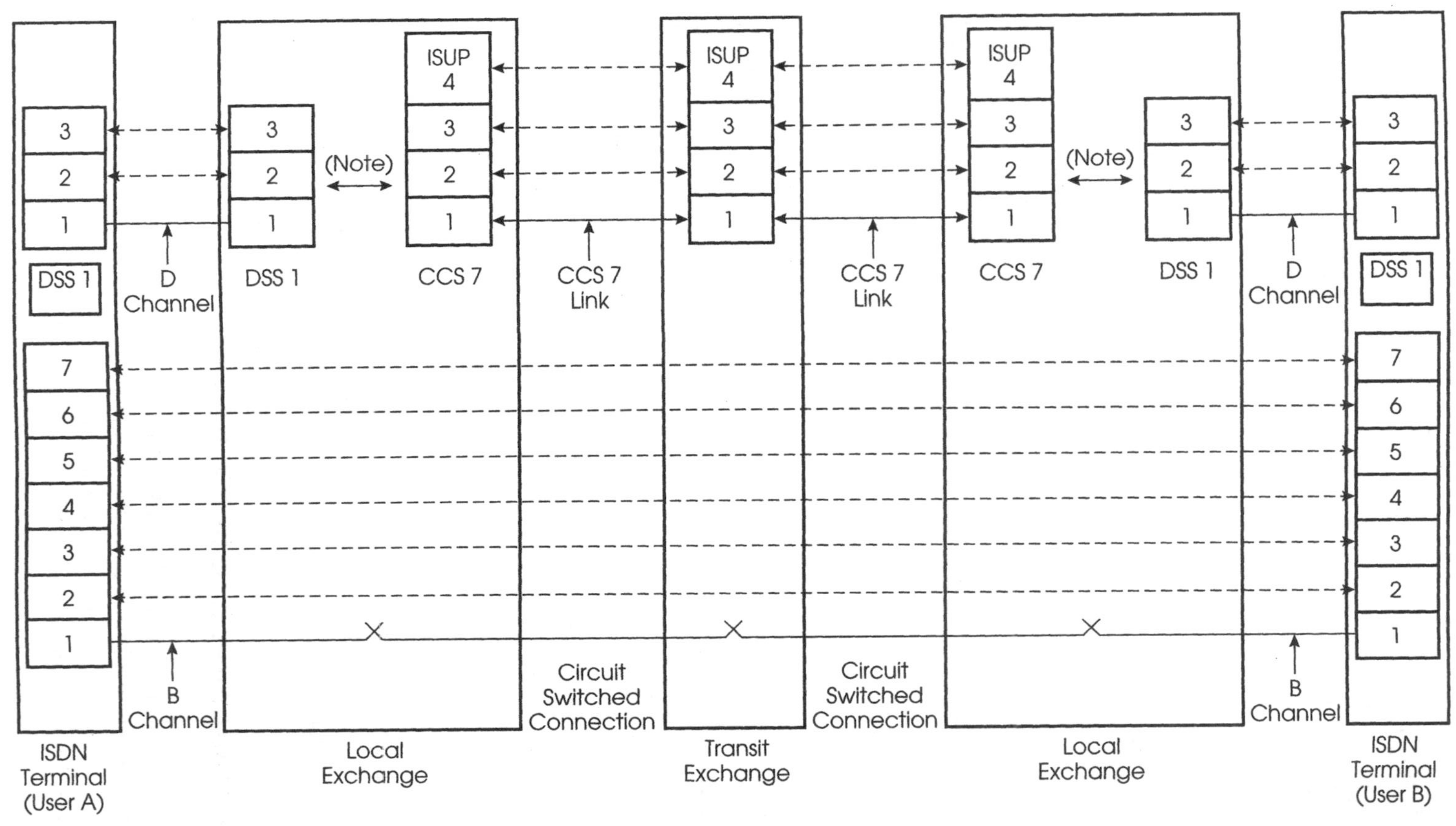

Note: Interworking between DSS 1 and CCS 7-ISUP protocols.

Figure 5–4 Protocol architecture in an ISDN.

For the transport of circuit switched user information, the ISDN merely provides the physical layer functions. Layers 2 to 7 are implemented only in the ISDN terminals, and the network is completely transparent to these functions. In this discussion, layers 2 to 7 for B-channel protocols are not considered. These layers are implemented in the ISDN terminals based on the nature of the service offered to the customer.

Layers 2 and 3 of the DSS 1 (which operates between the ISDN user and the local ISDN exchange) are implemented in both the terminals and the local exchange. The signaling link used for this purpose is the D-channel. Signaling in the D-channel is an example of common channel signaling, since the D-channel is a separate channel used for signaling corresponding to the calls established through the B-channels. However, the DSS 1 is different from CCS 7 protocol because of the differences in the functional requirements of the two systems. A call between two ISDN customers switched through more than one ISDN digital exchange requires both DSS 1 and CCS 7 protocols. DSS 1 protocol is required at either end between the local ISDN exchange and the ISDN terminals, whereas CCS 7 is needed between the ISDN exchanges. Since both signaling systems are required for the control of an ISDN call, protocol conversion must take place at the local exchanges. The interworking between DSS 1 and CCS 7 is specified in ITU-T recommendation Q.699 [5].

5.4 Physical Layer in Basic Access

The physical layer defines the means of transmission of information on the B-channels and signaling on the D-channel. It includes the wiring arrangements and power feeding for the user network interface elements, data transport between the NT and the TEs, procedure for activation and deactivation of terminals, synchronization, electrical interfaces, and mechanical interfaces. It also includes the line transmission coding on the digital subscriber loop.

5.4.1 Wiring Arrangement

The wiring in the ISDN user premises consists of a passive bus that runs from the NT to all the TEs in the premises. Refer to Figure 5–5(a). The bus must have a minimum of four wires: a pair each for transfer of information from NT to TEs and vice versa. Twisted unshielded cooper wire is used for this purpose. In addition, a third pair may be provided as an option to power the TEs from the NT. To connect the NT and TE on the bus, an eight-pin plug and jack arrangement, standardized according to ISO 8877 [6], is used; see Figure 5–5(b). The TEs have a connecting cord that is terminated on a plug. The length of the connecting cord should not be more than 10 meters. A similar arrangement exists for connecting the NT; in this case, however, the length of the connecting cord must not exceed 3 meters. The sockets that take the plug are provided either directly on the passive bus or through a short stub connection, not exceeding 1 meter in length. The sockets are positioned along the length of the bus cable depending on the intended location of the TEs and the NT in the user premises. The connection of the cord to the NT or the TE may be either by permanent hard wiring or through a plug and jack arrangement.

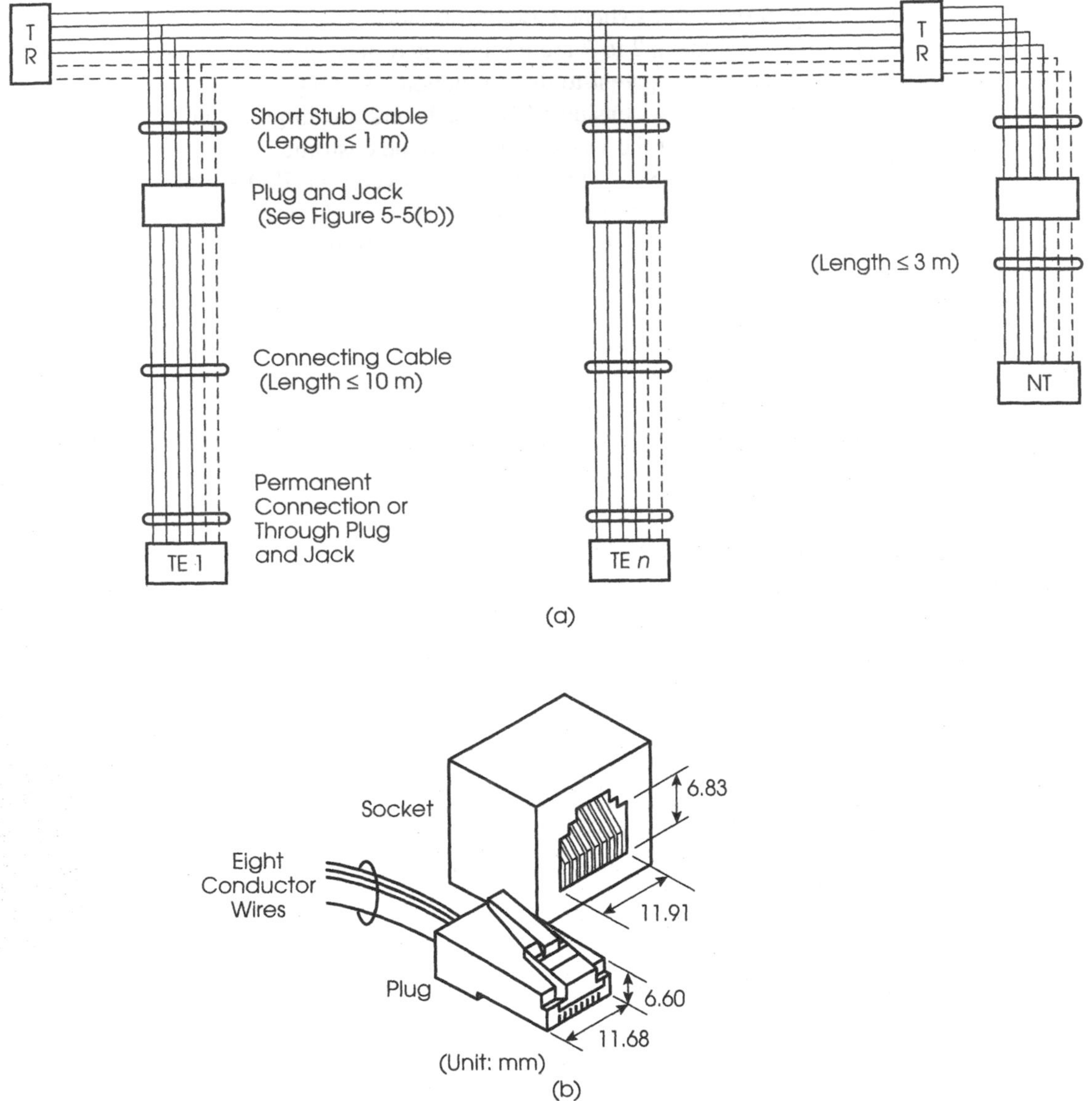

Figure 5–5 Reference configuration for wiring: (a) wiring arrangement; (b) plug and socket.

Two types of wiring arrangements are identified in ITU-T recommendation I.430:

1. Point to point
2. Point to multipoint

The point-to-point arrangement has one transmitter and one receiver. Refer to Figure 5–6, where a single TE is connected to the NT. Due to the bidirectional nature of in-

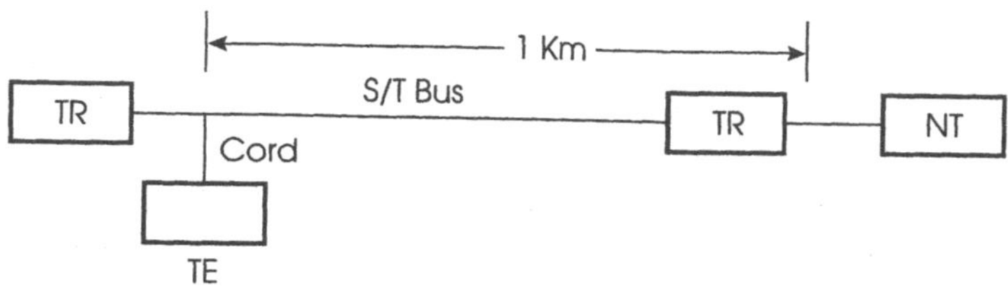

Figure 5–6 Point-to-point configuration.

formation flow, the TE or the NT acts as a transmitter or receiver, depending on the direction of information transfer. The TE can be placed up to a distance of 1 kilometer from the NT. With this arrangement, attenuation should not exceed 6 dB, and the round trip delay should be in the range of 10 to 42 μs.

The point-to-multipoint arrangement involves a single transmitter connected to several receivers or several transmitters connected to a single receiver. This is the case with the S-interface when several TEs are involved in bidirectional information exchange with the NT. Figure 5–2 shows that the S-interface has the capability of point-to-multipoint operation. On the other hand, the T-interface only supports a point-to-point configuration.

The point-to-multipoint arrangement is used when several TEs exist in the ISDN customer premises. Two alternatives are available for arranging the TEs:

1. Short passive bus
2. Extended passive bus

The short passive bus configuration can support a maximum of eight TEs. The configuration permits placement of TEs at random points throughout the length of the bus. Refer to Figure 5–7. Due to this flexibility of arrangement, the short passive bus is widely used in customer premises. However, since the terminals are at different distances from the NT, the signal pulses sent out by the TEs are received at the NT at different times. Hence, the bus length is limited by the maximum round trip delay for which the NT is designed. The maximum round trip delay corresponds to the farthest terminal from the NT and is specified at 14 μs. The minimum round trip delay is specified at 10 μs and corresponds to a TE placed along with the NT. Based on these figures, the maximum distance of a TE from the NT is of the order of 100 to 200 meters: 100 meters when a low impedance cable with characteristics impedance of 75 Ω is used, and 200 meters for a high im-

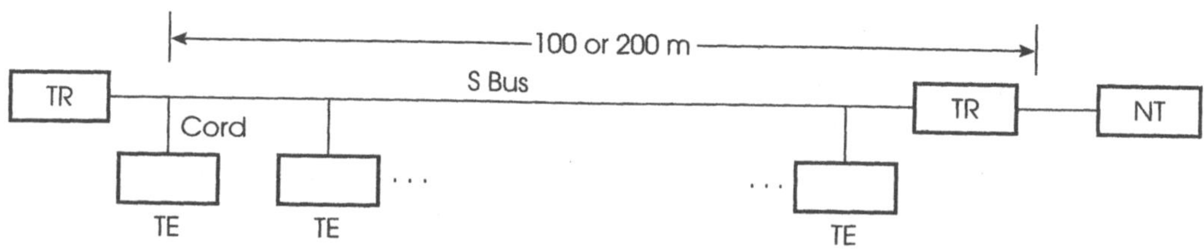

Figure 5–7 Short passive bus: point-to-point configuration.

pedance cable of 150 Ω characteristic impedance. The NT is usually placed at one end of the bus; for this situation, the length of the short passive bus is 100 to 200 meters.

The extended passive bus wiring configuration is shown in Figure 5–8. This arrangement is useful when the distance of the terminals from the NT is expected to be large. The TEs are clustered toward the far end of the bus; thus, the difference in the round trip delays for the different TEs is restricted to a small value of 2 μs. The extended passive bus supports a length of 100 meters to 1 kilometer. Up to four TEs can be supported, and the maximum spacing between them should range from 25 to 50 meters.

The application of the point-to-point and point-to-multipoint configurations in structured cabling system at the customer's premises has been described in Reeve [7].

5.4.2 Power Feeding

The power available from the exchange on the digital subscriber loop at the NT1 is insufficient to meet the power requirements of ISDN terminals connected on the S-interface. To reduce power consumption, the TE is deactivated when no call is in progress. In the deactivated state, the TE goes into a low power consumption mode. Whenever required, the functions of the TE are restored by following an activation procedure. (Activation and deactivation procedures are described in Section 5.4.3.5.) Yet despite this power saving measure, ISDN terminals typically require far more power than that available from the exchange. Therefore, power is provided locally from the mains supply at the customer premises. Batteries, as a backup to the mains power, may be provided as an option. The local power supply can be functionally considered as part of the NT. NT also receives power from the network, that is, from the local exchange. Since the NT has both these power sources, one of the important methods for powering the terminals is to feed power across the interface from the NT.

5.4.2.1 Powering of Terminals Across the Interface

From the point of view of power feeding, there are two possible conditions:

1. Normal power condition
2. Restricted power condition

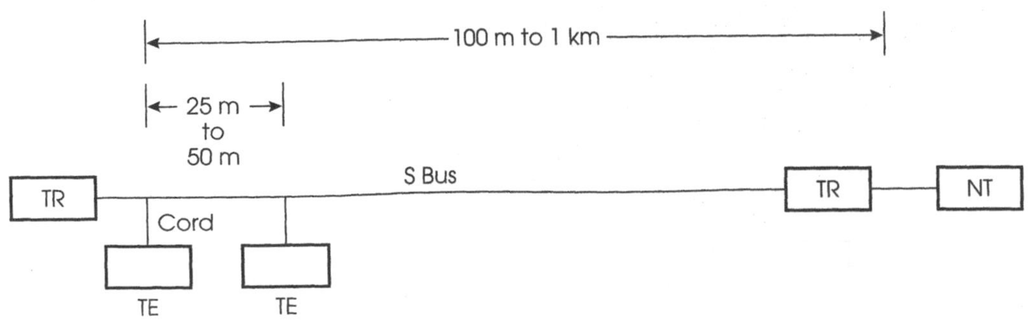

Figure 5–8 Extended passive bus: point-to-point configuration.

The normal power condition applies when the locally supplied power (for example, mains supply) is available. When locally supplied power is not available, the only power source is the network power, which corresponds to the restricted power condition. During restricted power condition, only one terminal, specifically designated for this purpose, is kept operational. This terminal provides at least the basic telephony functions.

The power feeding arrangement to TEs is shown in Figure 5–9. The NT can supply power to the TEs in two ways:

1. By the use of additional pair of wire (shown as dotted lines in Figure 5–5(a))
2. By phantom power feeding on the same four wires used for information transfer between the NT and the TEs (power source 1 supplies the power in this case)

For supply of power by an additional pair of wires, power source 2 shown in Figure 5–9 is used. Power sink 2 represents the power consumed at the TEs. Pins 7 and 8 in the eight-pin plug and jack arrangement are used in this case. See also Table 5–1, which shows the assignment of pins for the eight-pin plug and jack.

The phantom power feeding technique permits the use of the same four wires that are involved in information transfer between the NT and TEs. The pair of wires on pins 3

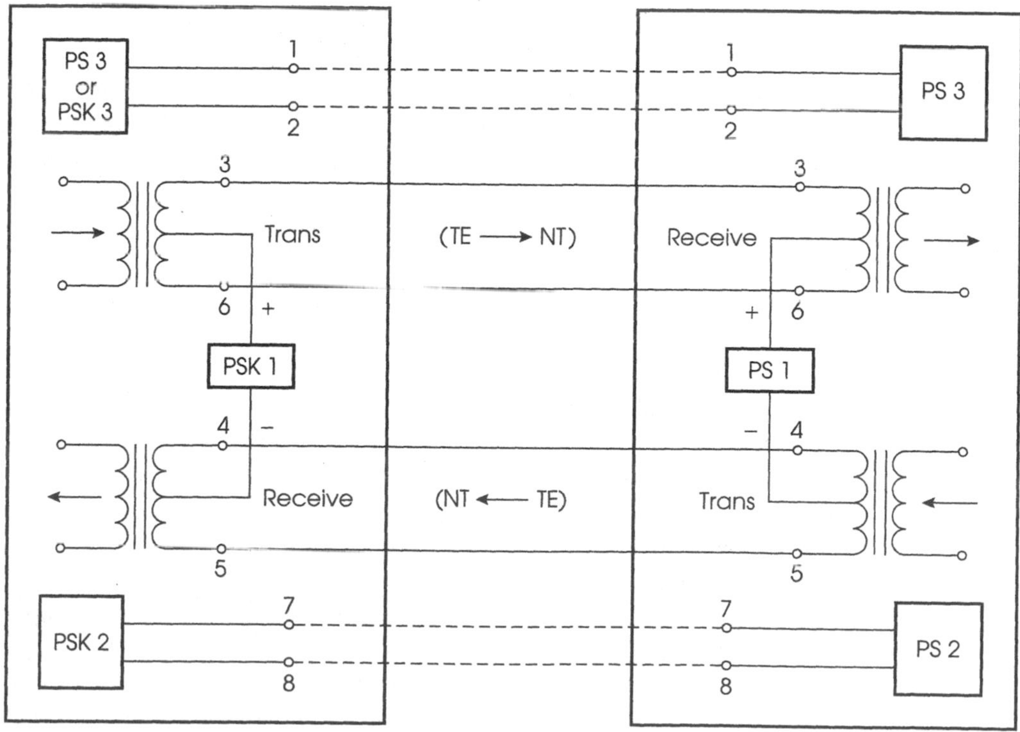

Key
PS: Power Source
PSK: Power Sink; Represents the Power Consumed by the TEs

Figure 5–9 Power feeding arrangement.

Table 5-1 Assignment of Pins for the Eight-Pin Plug and Jack

Pin No.	Function: TE	Function: NT	Polarity
1	Power source 3	Power sink 3	+
2	Power source 3	Power sink 3	−
3	Transmit	Receive	+
4	Receive	Transmit	+
5	Receive	Transmit	−
6	Transmit	Receive	−
7	Power sink 2	Power source 2	−
8	Power sink 2	Power source 2	+

through 6 (of the plug and jack) is for transmission of digital information from the TE to the NT, whereas the wire pair on pins 4 and 5 is for information transfer from the NT to the TE. The polarity shown for these pins in Table 5–1—namely, positive for pin 3 and negative for pin 6—indicates the polarity of the framing pulse in the frames from the NT to the TE. Likewise, the polarity on pins 4 and 5 refer to the polarity of framing pulses in the frames from the NT to the TE. As noted earlier, these four wires also provide for power transfer from the NT to the TEs, that is, from power source 1 to power sink 1.

The polarity of power transfer shown in Table 5–1 for power source 1 refers to normal power conditions. When the local power supply is disrupted, the NT indicates the onset of "restricted power condition" to the TEs by a reversal of polarity. On sensing this polarity reversal, the terminal designated for restricted power operation continues to function, while the others are shut down.

The main characteristics of power source 1 are as follows:

- Power source 1 may supply power for normal or restricted power condition or for both.
- The location of power source 1 can be inside the NT or external to it. In either case, from a functional viewpoint it is considered to be a part of the NT. This is necessary because it is the responsibility of the NT to detect the absence of the local power supply and to indicate the onset of restricted power condition to the TEs.
- For normal condition, power source 1 must supply at least 10 watts of power to the TEs. The maximum power that a TE is permitted to consume when drawing power from power source 1 is 1 W. In ITU-T recommendation I.430, the power consumption by the TEs is indicated in terms of power consumption units (PCUs). For normal condition, PCUs are called normal power consumption units (NPCUs). One NPCU is equal to 100 mW. Thus, the maximum power that a TE is permitted to consume under normal conditions is 10 NPCUs. This power consumption is applicable for a TE in the activated state. For a deactivated TE, the normal power consumption is limited to 1 NPCU (100 mW).
- Under normal power conditions, the nominal voltage to be supplied by power source 1 is 40 V at the output of the NT. The permitted tolerances are 5% and

–15%. The maximum voltage permitted at the interface of a TE is 40V +5% (42V), and the minimum voltage is 40V –40% (24 V).

- Under restricted power conditions, at least 420 mW of power must be supplied at the output of the NT. Taking 20 mW as the power loss on the S-interface, 400 mW are available for the TEs. For restricted power conditions, a restricted power consumption unit (RPSU) is defined in ITU-T recommendation I.430. One RPSU is equal to 95 mW. Out of the 400 mW available for the TEs, up to 380 mW (4 RPSUs) may be consumed by a designated terminal to provide at least the basic telephony service, and 20 mW may be consumed by the other TEs to perform certain minimum functions, such as maintaining their identity (terminal identity is indicated by a terminal endpoint identifier (TEI), described in Chapter 8), and for the detection of line conditions. The nominal voltage at the inputs of the TEs in this case is 40 V with a tolerance of 5% (42 V) to –20% (32 V). The power consumption of 380 mW by the designated TE in the restricted power condition arises only during the activated state of the TE. If the designated TE is in a deactivated state, the permissible power consumption is limited to 25 mW. Figure 5–10 provides a summary of power consumed using power source 1.

Power source 2 must supply at least 8 W (80 NPSUs) of power under normal power condition. Under restricted power condition, it should supply a minimum power of about 2 W (21 RPSUs). The nominal voltage at the output of NT must be 40 V with a tolerance range of 5% to 20%. The same figures apply for the voltage at the input of the TEs.

A terminal that is powered across the interface, using either of the two power sources PS1 or PS2, should have an arrangement to detect the presence or absence of this power.

In addition to the two methods of power feeding described above, there is also a possibility of one TE (using power source 3 shown in Figure 5–9) supplying power to another TE. Power sink 3 resides in the TE that is receiving power. The pair of wires required for this purpose are connected at pins 1 and 2.

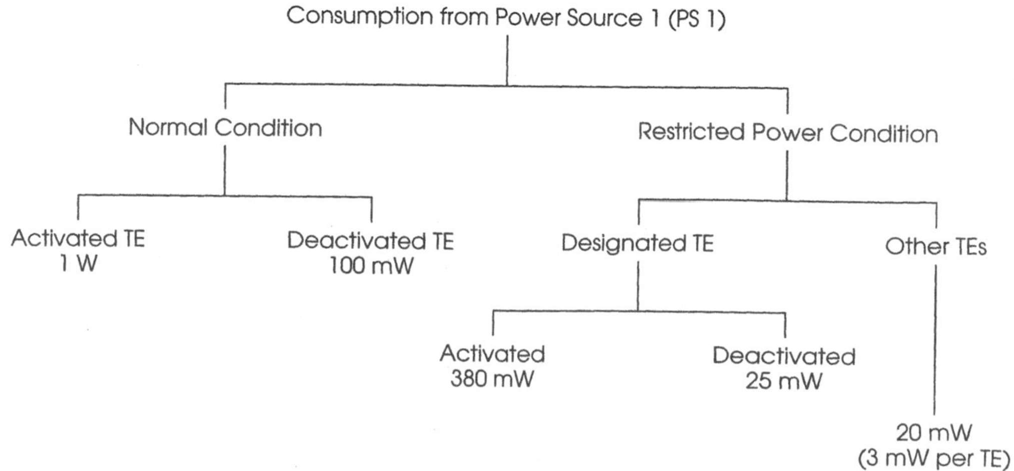

Figure 5–10 Power consumption from PS 1.

5.4.2.2 TEs Powered Locally

For TEs powered locally, the terminals are powered individually by the local supply. Although the locally powered TEs should always have an arrangement to detect failure of the local power, they may or may not have an arrangement to detect the presence of PS1 or PS2. When the local power fails, the TEs (which can detect the presence of PS1) may receive up to 3 mW of power to enable them to maintain their TEI assignment. For TEs not possessing this capability, no power is delivered by PS1, even in the case of failure of the local power.

It is not necessary that the same method of powering is used for all terminals connected to a basic access. Some TEs may be powered locally, and others may be supplied power across the interface by PS1 or PS2. Again, there may be locally powered TEs that are able to detect PS1 or PS2 and also TEs that are locally powered but without the capability of detecting PS1 or PS2. TEs may also be fed power on a separate wire pair from another TE using PS3.

With such diverse possibilities, administrations must decide on the methods of power feeding to be adopted. The European standards envisage the requirement of power feeding across the interface as well as local powering of terminals. Furthermore, locally powered terminals must have the capability to detect the presence or absence of PS1 or PS2 [8]. TEs such as IBM PCs with add-on cards and audiographic terminals that require considerable power for their normal operation are typically powered locally because large amounts of power cannot be fed across the interface. On the other hand, it may be possible to feed the normal power requirements of ISDN terminals such as ISDN telephones by PS1 or PS2.

5.4.3 Data Transport between NT and TEs

To understand data exchange between the NT and the TEs, it is necessary to consider the following two aspects:

1. *Coding,* that is, the way in which binary data is represented as electrical signals on the bus
2. *Framing,* which specifies the way binary information is organized and grouped into frames.

5.4.3.1 Coding

The code chosen for the S-interface is a modification of alternate mark inversion (AMI) code. The code is designed such that the electrical pulses representing the logical 1's and 0's do not result in a DC offset voltage that might interfere with the detection of signals at the receiver. The four wires of the passive bus, on which the exchange of information takes place, have a finite inductance and capacitance. The bus can therefore be visualized as a low-pass filter. A high pulse would result in charging and a low pulse in discharging of the bus. Thus, there is a need to balance the high and low pulses so that storage of energy on the bus and creation of a DC offset is avoided.

A three-level code is chosen in which a logical 1 is the absence of signal, whereas logical 0's are transmitted as alternating high and low pulses; an example is shown in Fig-

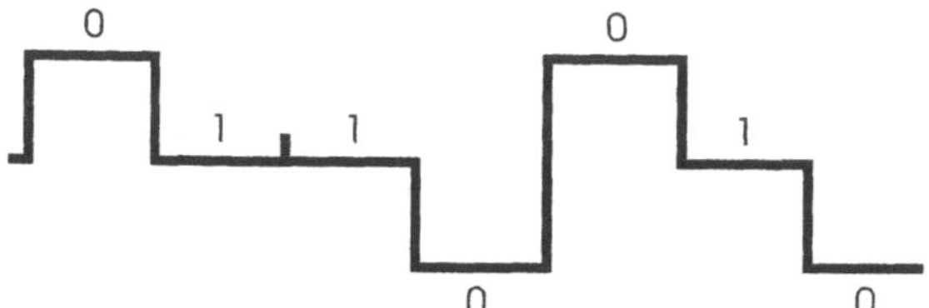

Figure 5–11 Code for binary information 0110010.

ure 5–11. It may be noticed that to ensure DC balance, the number of logical 0's must be even. This requirement is satisfied during framing, as discussed in the next section.

In the point-to-multipoint configuration, where several TEs may attempt to simultaneously transmit on the bus, it is necessary to examine the resultant signal on the bus and its interpretation by the NT. For simultaneous transmission by two TEs, A and B, the various possibilities are shown in Table 5–2.

Except for the last two rows, which correspond to simultaneous transmission of binary zeros with opposite polarity, the resultant binary value is equivalent to an "AND" operation. During framing, the condition corresponding to last two rows is avoided.

5.4.3.2 Framing

The data exchanged between the NT and the TEs is organized into groups of bits called frames. Apart from the usable bit rate of 144 kbps for basic access ISDN, additional information is to be exchanged between the NT and the TEs to perform certain management functions. Two such functions, maintaining an even number of binary 0's for DC balance and avoiding simultaneous transmission of 0's of the same polarity by the terminals, have already been mentioned. To take all these requirements into account, the bit rate on the S-interface is kept at 192 kbps. A frame is composed of 48 bits, which is transmitted in 250 microseconds. Thus, 4,000 frames are transmitted in 1 second in either direction. The frame structure for the two directions is shown in Figure 5–12. Notice that there are a few differences in the frames transmitted in the two directions, namely, NT to TE and TE to NT. The common aspects are considered first.

A fundamental requirement of framing is to delineate one frame from the other. This is achieved by creating a code violation at the beginning of each frame. A code vio-

Table 5–2 Resultant Signal for Simultaneous Transmission by Two Terminals

TERMINAL A	TERMINAL B	RESULTANT SIGNAL
1 (no signal)	1 (no signal)	1 (no signal)
0 (H or L)	1 (no signal)	0 (H or L)
1 (no signal)	0 (H or L)	0 (H or L)
0 (H)	0 (H)	0 (H)
0 (L)	0 (L)	0 (L)
0 (H)	0 (L)	1 (no signal)
0 (L)	0 (H)	1 (no signal)

Note: H = high pulse, L = low pulse.

lation means that the rule of alternate high and low pulses for coding logical 0 is not followed. A framing bit F of logical 0 with a code violation indicates the beginning of a new frame. Thus, if the last logical 0 in the previous frame is a high pulse, bit F will also be a high pulse. If the previous logical 0 is a low pulse, bit F will be a low pulse. In Figure 5–12, the F bit is taken as a high pulse. To avoid the DC imbalance caused by the F bit, a balancing bit L with a reverse polarity immediately follows the F bit.

The usable information in the frame structure consists of the following:

- B1 octet (one B-channel)
- D bit (D-channel)
- B2 octet (other B-channel)
- D bit
- B1 octet
- D bit
- B2 octet
- D bit

Thus, 16 bits of a B1-channel are carried per frame. With the transmission of 4,000 frames/second, a 64 kbps B1-channel bit rate is obtained. The same applies for the B2-channel. For the D-channel, 4 bits are transmitted in each frame, providing a 16 kbps bit rate.

To ensure that a transmission error (which may also result in a code violation) is not confused as the beginning of a frame, a second code violation is introduced at the first logical 0 found in the B1-channel or the D-channel. If, however, the B1 octet and the D-channel happen to carry all 1's, then the second code violation is provided by the F_A bit (called the auxiliary framing bit). F_A appears at the fourteenth bit position for frames in either direction. Therefore, the beginning of a frame is known for certain latest by the fourteenth bit position.

The remarks made so far are common to the frame structures in either direction. The differences are now discussed.

In the NT to TE direction, a balancing bit is sent as the last bit of the frame. This is the balancing bit over bits 3 to 47 of the frame. In the TE to NT direction, however, balancing is done after each B-channel octet and each D-channel bit. There are five other bits in the frame format in the NT to TE direction: bits N, A, M, E, and S. Bit N, which immediately follows the F_A bit, is set to the value of F_A. Bit A is used for activation, M for multiframing (Section 5.4.3.3), and E bit for resolving D-channel access (discussed in the next section). The use of bit S is not yet specified by the ITU.

The TEs determine the beginning of each frame received from the NT by detecting the line code violations that are deliberately built into the frames, as explained above. Frame alignment is assumed to occur when three consecutive pairs of line code violations are detected and the two violations in each pair are not spaced by more than 14 bits. A TE assumes that it has lost frame alignment when 500 μs (corresponding to the time period of two frames) have elapsed without detecting valid pairs of code violations.

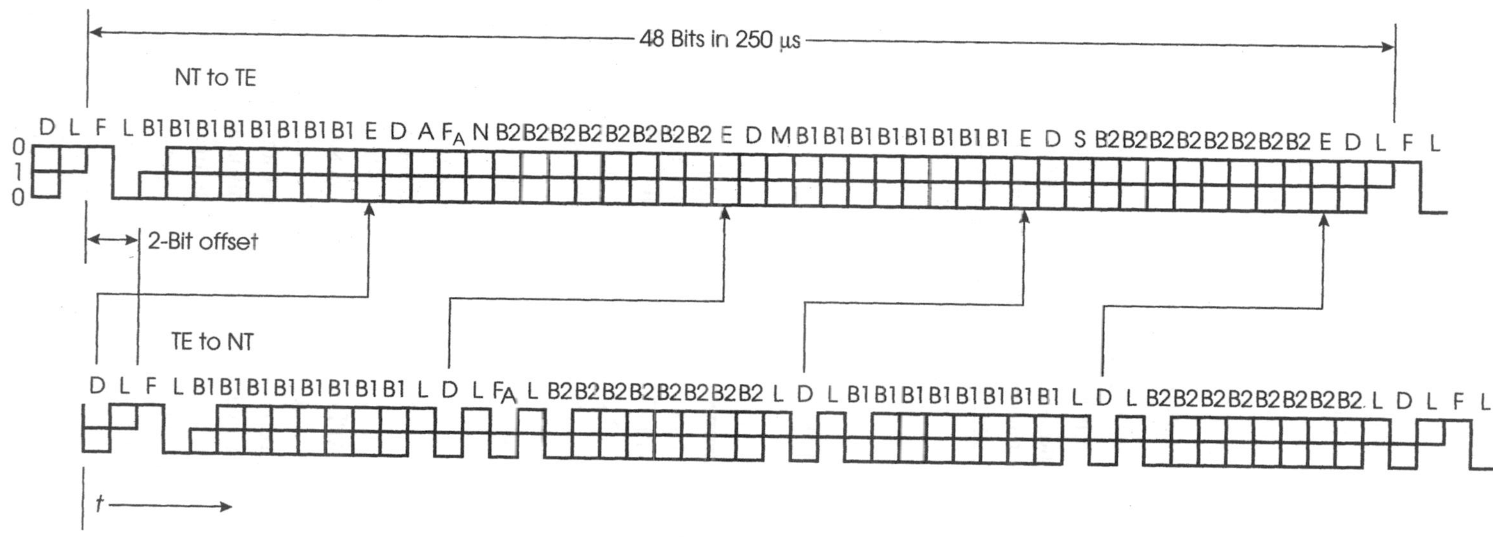

Figure 5–12 Frame structure.
[Reprinted from ITU-T recommendation I.430 (1993). Basic user-network interface layer 1 specification. Rev. 1. Reproduced by permission.]

5.4.3.3 Multiframing: M Bit

As an option, the frames may be organized into multiframes. A multiframe consists of 20 frames. To identify a multiframe, the M bit of every twentieth frame in the NT to TE direction is set to 1; in all other frames, it is kept 0. The purpose of multiframing is to obtain some additional bits for exchange of information between the TEs and the NT for maintenance and other purposes. In the TE to NT direction, these additional bits are obtained by robbing a bit in the F_A position in every fifth frame. In all other frames, F_A is kept at logical 0.

5.4.3.4 Resolving D-Channel Access: E Bit

In the NT to TE direction, a D-channel echo bit, designated the E bit, is sent. This bit is used to resolve the contention for access of the D-channel by the terminals. More than one terminal may like to send signaling (and other information corresponding to the slow bit rate services) on the D-channel at the same time. This results in a contention for access of the D-channel that needs to be resolved so that only one terminal at a time transmits on the D-channel. The problem of contention does not exist for the B-channels, since one terminal has access to one B-channel (B1 bits) and the other has access to the other (B2 bits). B1 and B2 are separated in time. Furthermore, a terminal begins transmission on the B-channel only after gaining access to the D-channel.

A terminal that is in an active state and has not yet gained access to the D-channel sends no signals (this is equivalent to a sequence of logical 1's) on the D-channel. On receiving the D bit, the NT simply loops it back in the E-bit position on the frame sent toward the TE. This is shown by arrows in Figure 5–12. At the same time, the terminal continuously monitors the D echo channel (E bit). It counts the number of consecutive 1's received in the E bit. As long as the TE receives 1 on the E bit, it knows that there is no other terminal sending a 0 in the D-channel. The value of the number of 1's counted by the terminal is designated as C. C is reset to zero whenever a 0 is received in the E bit and is incremented by one whenever a 1 is received. When the value of C reaches 11, the count is no longer incremented and C stays at this value even as more 1's are received on the D echo channel.

When a certain value of C is reached—that is, when the terminal has received a certain number of consecutive E bits as 1—it concludes that the D-channel is free. The terminal can now begin transmission by sending the sequence 01111110 as part of the link access procedure on D-channel (LAPD) under layer 2. This sequence represents the flag of the layer 2 frames. (The frame format for layer 2 frames is described in Chapter 8.)

A situation may arise where two terminals begin transmission in the D-channel at exactly the same time. Therefore, while transmitting information on the D-channel, the TE continues to monitor the echo channel and compares the value with the last transmitted bit in the D-channel. If the transmitted bit is the same as the received echo, the TE continues to transmit. If the two are different, the TE stops transmission in the D-channel (that is, it sends a sequence of logical 1's) and begins monitoring the D-channel.

Since the D-channel may carry signaling information as well as other information—for example, data for slow rate services—it is necessary to assign priority to a TE that wants to send signaling information. Accordingly, the following two priority classes have been defined:

1. Priority class 1 is assigned to TEs wanting to send signaling information on the D-channel.
2. Priority class 2 is assigned to TEs that need to send other information.

Within each class there is a further classification, a normal level and a lower level. After a TE has successfully completed transmission of frames in the D-channel, it is put at a lower level within the same priority class so that other TEs in the same class get a fair chance to access the D-channel. The priorities are implemented using the value of the counter C, described above. Table 5–3 shows the value of counter C for each priority and level.

5.4.3.5 Activation and Deactivation of Terminals and the NT

To save power when not in use, the terminals may be deactivated by the network. Activation may be initiated by the terminal itself (prior to making a call) or by the network (for an incoming call). Activation restores the full functionality of the TE so that it is ready to handle an originating or an incoming call. Similarly, the NT may also be activated or deactivated.

Activation (or deactivation) of the TE is meaningful only for terminals connected to the interface. Therefore, it is necessary to specify the criteria by which a TE can determine whether it is connected or disconnected. When a TE is powered across the interface, the detection of power source 1 (PS1) or power source 2 (PS2) by the TE indicates that it is connected to the interface. For a TE that is not powered across the interface, the connection or disconnection status may be determined on the basis of one of the following criteria:

- Detection of power source 1 or 2
- Presence of the local power supply

The connection status is sent by the TE to the management entity by the primitive MPH-INFORMATION INDICATION (connected). The disconnection status is conveyed by the primitive MPH-INFORMATION INDICATION (disconnected).

The activation request is conveyed to the physical layer by layer 2 by a primitive PH-ACTIVATE REQUEST (PH-AR). Layer 1 then follows an activation procedure and, after successful activation, informs layer 2 by another primitive PH-ACTIVATE INDICATION (PH-AI).

As part of the activation procedure, the following information signals are exchanged between a TE and the NT:

Table 5–3 Values of C

Priority Class 1		Priority Class 2	
Normal Level	Lower Level	Normal Level	Lower Level
8	9	10	11

INFO 0: no signal (used in both directions, NT to TE and TE to NT)

INFO 1: a continuous signal with the following sequence: a positive 0, a negative 0, and six 1's (used in the TE to NT direction)

INFO 2: frame with all bits of B, D, and D echo channels set to 0. Bit A is set to 0. N and L bits are set according to the normal coding rules (used in the NT to TE direction).

INFO 3: synchronized frames with operational data on the B and D channels (used in the TE to NT direction)

INFO 4: frames with operational data on B, D, and D echo channels. Bit A is set to 1.

These information signals are used to accomplish the activation and deactivation of both the NT and the TE. In all, eight states, F1 through F8, are specified for the TEs, whereas four states, G1 through G4, are defined for the NT.

5.4.3.5.1 Activation and Deactivation of the TEs

A simplified system description language (SDL) representation of the activation and deactivation of a TE is shown in Figure 5–13. The sequences followed for the activation are described next.

A TE with the disconnected status transmits INFO 0 (that is, no signal) to the NT. This is called the *inactive state* of the TE (designated F1 state).

On detection of the presence of PS1 or PS2, the TE goes into state F2. In this state, the TE may or may not be receiving signals from the NT and has not determined the nature of the received signals, if any. Therefore, F2 is called the *sensing state.* During the F2 state, the TE continues to send INFO 0 (no signals) on the interface. The TE has a connected status and this fact is conveyed to the management entity by sending a primitive MPH-II (connected). The TE now goes into state F3, namely, the deactivated state. Refer to Figure 5–13(a) and 5–13(b).

The process of activation commences when layer 1 in the TE receives an activation request (by a primitive PH-AR from layer 2). It initiates a timer T3 and starts sending INFO 1 to the NT. At this stage the TE is awaiting response from NT and is said to be in state F4 (awaiting signal). See Figure 5–13(c).

On the first receipt of a signal from the NT, the TE discontinues sending INFO 1 (it does not send any signal, which is the same as sending INFO 0) and examines whether INFO 2 or INFO 4 has been received. The TE is in state F5 (identifying input). See Figure 5–13(d).

If the TE identifies that INFO 2 has been received from the NT, it sends INFO 3 and goes into state F6. This is called the synchronized state. Frame alignment has been achieved at this stage, since the TE is able to identify INFO 2, which has the normal frame structure. The TE sends INFO 3 (synchronized frames with operational data on B and D channels). See Figure 5–13(e).

The TE now awaits normal frames (INFO 4) from the NT. On receipt of INFO 4, the activation is complete. A primitive PH-AI indicating that the terminal has been activated is sent to layer 2. Likewise, a primitive MPH-AI is sent to the management entity. This activated state of the TE is called the F7 state. See Figure 5–13(f).

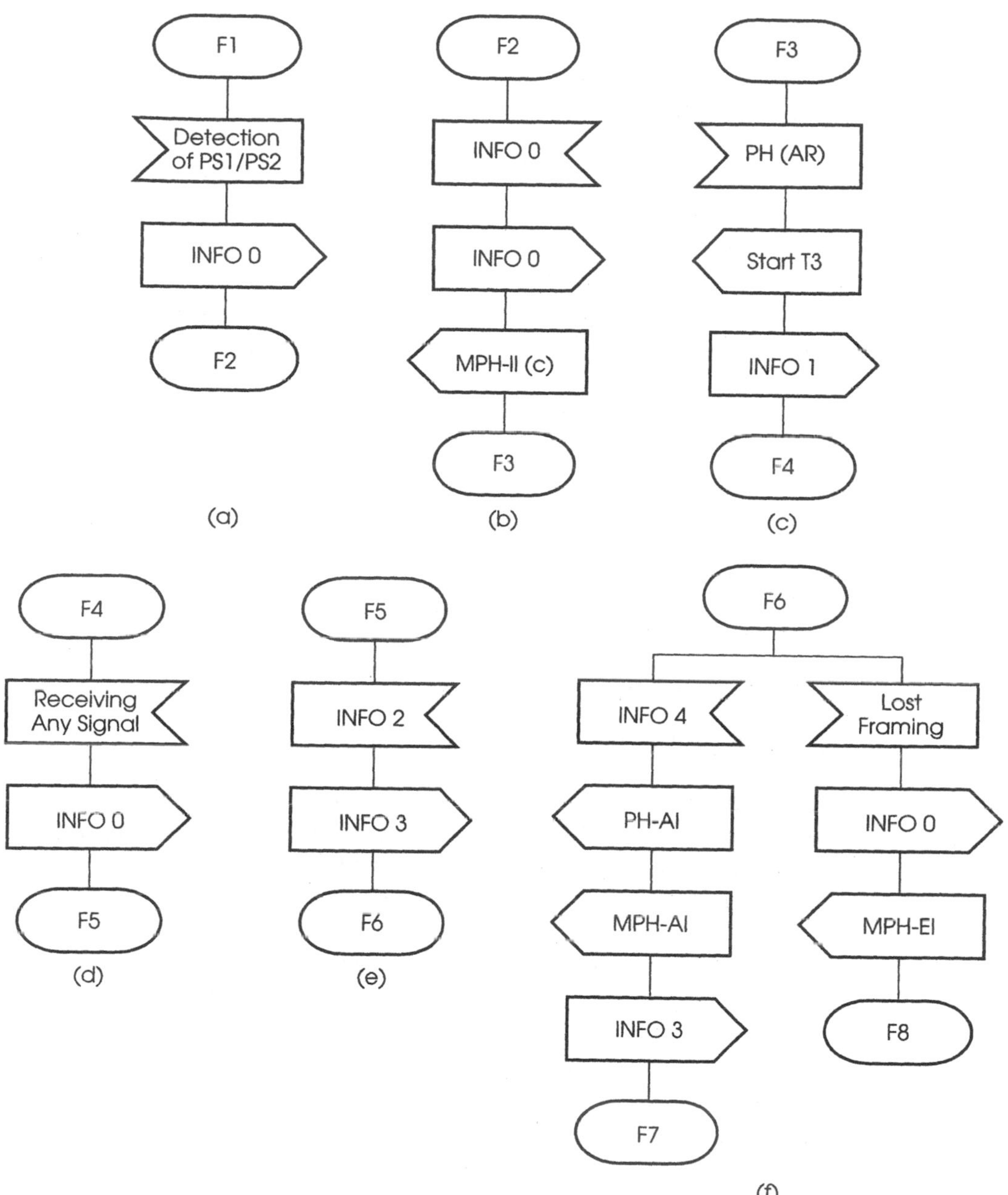

Figure 5–13 A simplified SDL representation of the activation/deactivation procedure for terminals.

If framing is lost, the terminal stops sending signals, informs the management entity, and goes into the F8 state (lost framing). See Figure 5–13(f).

To perform the activation of the terminal in a reasonable time, the maximum permissible time for different steps in the process are prescribed [3]. Two examples are cited here. On receipt of a signal from NT, a TE in the F4 state must discontinue sending INFO

1 within 5 ms. Furthermore, a TE should reach the synchronized state within 100 ms of the receipt of INFO 2.

Figure 5–13 is a simplified SDL for the activation process. The following additional points, not shown in this figure, may therefore be noted:

- Disappearance of power source 1 or 2, from any states F2 to F8, results in return to the F1 (inactive) state.
- Expiry of timer 3 while the terminal is in states F4, F5 or F6 results in a return to the deactivated state (F3).
- Loss-of-frame alignment may also occur when the TE is in the synchronized state (F6). In this case also, the TE goes to state F8 (lost framing).

5.4.3.5.2 Activation and Deactivation of NTs

Four states, designated G1 to G4, are defined for the NT:

1. The G1 state is the deactivated state of the NT when it is not transmitting any signal (that is, it is sending and receiving INFO 0).
2. In the G2 state, the NT is awaiting activation. It sends INFO 2 and waits for the reception of INFO 3.
3. The G3 state is the active state of the NT. The NT sends INFO 4 and receives INFO 3 from the TE.
4. The G4 state is the state where the NT wishes to deactivate.

The NT may be activated from the network side (for example, when an incoming call is received) or by one of the ISDN terminals when a call origination is required. Figure 5–14 shows the activation of the NT from the network side.

For an NT in the G1 state, the request to begin activation is received by layer 1 in the primitive PH-AR. (The NT may also begin activation when it receives INFO 1 from one of the TEs.) The NT sends INFO 2 and starts timer 1. This takes the NT to the G2

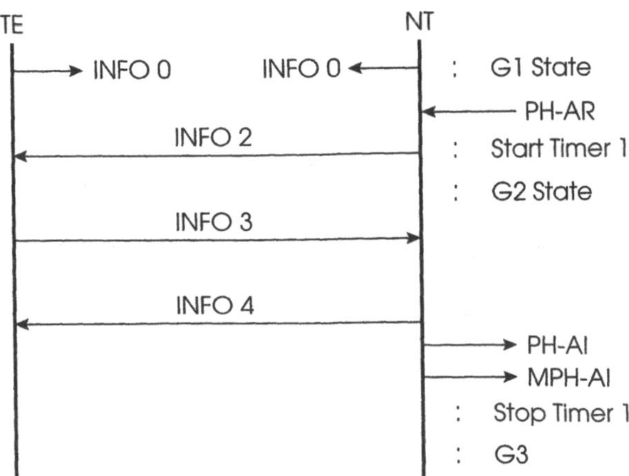

Figure 5–14 Activation of the NT.

(awaiting activation) state. On receiving INFO 2, the TE responds by INFO 3, as already shown in Figure 5–13(e).

When the NT receives INFO 3, while in G2 state, it responds with INFO 4. After the exchange of these frames, NT sends primitives PH-AI and MPH-AI to layer 2 and to the management entity, respectively. Timer 1 is stopped, and NT reaches the active G3 state.

If timer 1, started at the beginning of state G2, expires (due to, for example, nonreceipt of INFO 3 from the TE), then the NT stops sending any signals (sends INFO 0), and the G4 state is reached.

5.4.4 Timing Aspects

The TEs are timed by the frames received from the NT. TEs extract timing from the received frames and send out frames toward the NT based on this timing. However, the output of the TE contains jitter due to two factors. First, jitter is introduced during timing extraction by the TE, and second, the TE itself adds jitter to the output pulse stream. ITU-T recommendation I.430 specifies the maximum jitter permissible, as follows:

- Timing extraction jitter should be within –7% to +7% of the bit period.
- The total phase deviation between the output and input pulses (this also includes the timing extraction jitter) of a TE should be within –7% to +15% of the bit period.

The above specifications apply to TEs employed for both point-to-point and point-to-multipoint configurations.

The NT is timed by the network. It locks to the timing available on the PCM highway, in the case of primary access, and to the bit stream available on the digital subscriber loop, for basic access. This timing in turn is used by the TEs on the S-interface. The peak-to-peak jitter specified at the output of the NT is 5% of the bit period.

5.4.5 Electrical Characteristics

The terminating resistance (TR) at either end of the passive bus should be 100 Ω with a tolerance of ±5%. The two terminating resistances in parallel give an effective resistance of 50 Ω. The pulse characteristics of the signals has been specified for impedance loads of 50 Ω and 400 Ω [3]. The former corresponds to a point-to-point configuration with the assumption that there is no line impedance; the latter relates to a point-to-multipoint configuration with eight TEs transmitting logical 0's simultaneously.

The nominal amplitude of the pulses corresponding to the individual bits of the 48-bit frame is specified as 750 mV, zero to peak. These pulses may either be positive or negative.

At the nominal bit rate of 192 kbps, the 48-bit frame is transmitted in 250 μs. Thus, the pulse width is about 5.21 μs. The bit-rate tolerance is specified as ±100 ppm. Therefore, the pulse width may vary slightly from the nominal value of 5.21 μs. The pulse mask shown in Figure 5–15, for a load impedance of 50 Ω, is based on a pulse width of 5.21 μs. The dotted line indicates the nominal pulse shape. The outer envelope indicates the maxi-

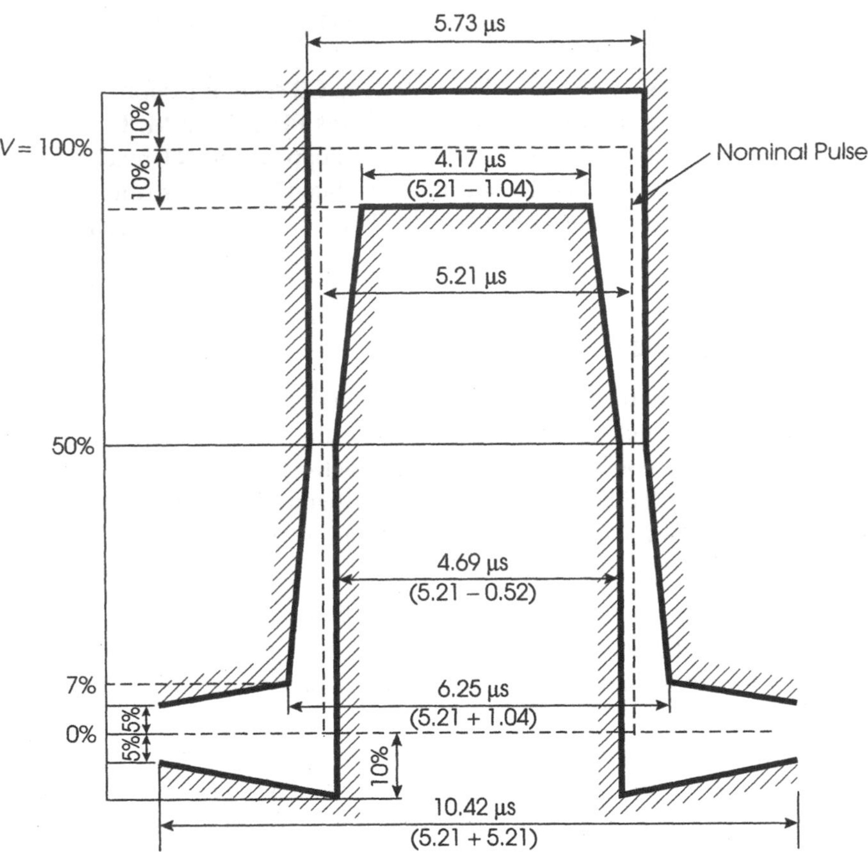

Note: For clarity of presentation, the above values are based on a pulse width of 5.21 μs.

Figure 5–15 Pulse mask for a load impedance of 50 Ω. [Reprinted from ITU-T recommendation I.430 (1993). Basic user-network interface layer 1 specification. Rev. 1. Reproduced by permission.]

mum permissible pulse width and amplitude. The inner envelope corresponds to the minimum permissible values of pulse width and amplitude. The pulse should lie between the mask, except for an overshoot at the leading edge of the pulse. The overshoot has been quantified as follows:

1. The overshoot should not exceed 5% of the pulse amplitude that the signal will attain at the midpoint of the pulse. The midpoint of the pulse corresponds to the peak amplitude.
2. Within a duration of less than 0.25 μs, half the amplitude of the overshoot must be reached.

Figure 5–16 shows the pulse mask for a load of 400 Ω.

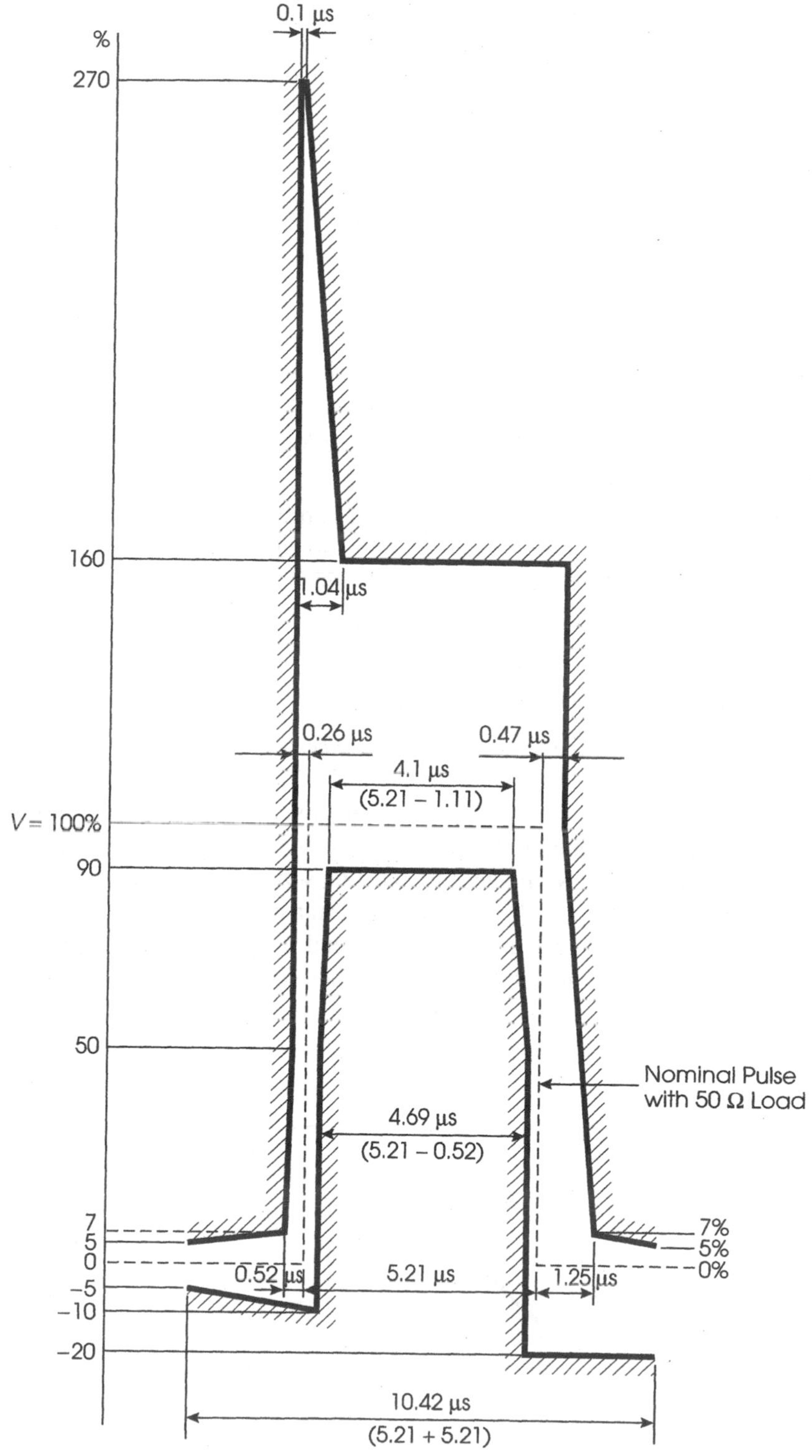

Figure 5–16 Pulse mask for a load impedance of 400 Ω.
[Reprinted from ITU-T recommendation I.430 (1993). Basic user-network interface layer 1 specification. Rev. 1. Reproduced by permission.]

Since the NT and TEs act as receivers and transmitters, depending on the direction of information exchange, both the output and input impedances for the NT and the TE should be specified. The values are as follows:

1. Output impedance when the NT is transmitting and input impedance when the NT is receiving should not exceed the template shown in Figure 5–17. The following conditions apply:
   - The NT is transmitting pulses other than those corresponding to the logical 0's.
   - The rms value of the applied voltage is 100 mV.
   - The frequency range is 2 kHz to 1 MHz.

   When the NT is transmitting logical 0's, the output impedance of the NT should be ≥ 20 Ω.
2. Output impedance when the TE is transmitting and input impedance when the TE is receiving should conform to the impedance template shown in Figure 5–18. All other conditions and values are identical to those stated above for the NT.

5.4.6 Line Transmission and Coding for Basic Access

The bit rate to be supported on the line between the exchange and the ISDN customer premises is 160 kbps in both directions. This includes 144 kbps for the 2B+D channels and 16 kbps to support additional functions, such as framing, timing, operation, and maintenance. In keeping with the basic philosophy of designing the ISDN as an evolution over the existing PSTN, this bit rate must be supported on the two-wire metallic pair employed in the PSTN. To allow bidirectional transmission, the line termination at the ISDN exchange end and the NT at the customer end function as both transmitters and receivers (transceivers). The digital subscriber loop therefore consists of two transceivers connected by a pair of wires.

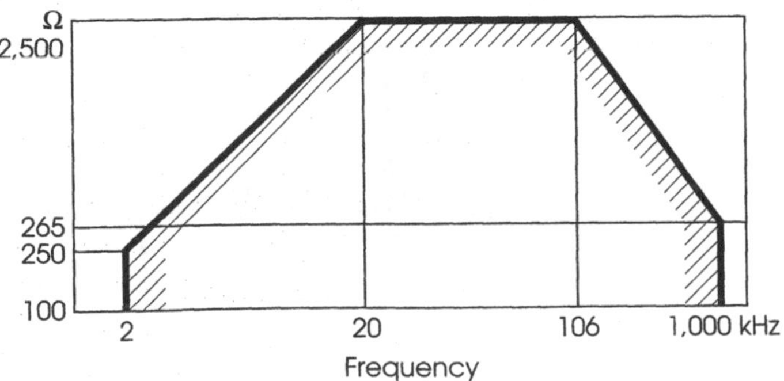

Figure 5–17 NT impedance template.
[Reprinted from ITU-T recommendation I.430 (1993). Basic user-network interface layer 1 specification. Rev. 1. Reproduced by permission.]

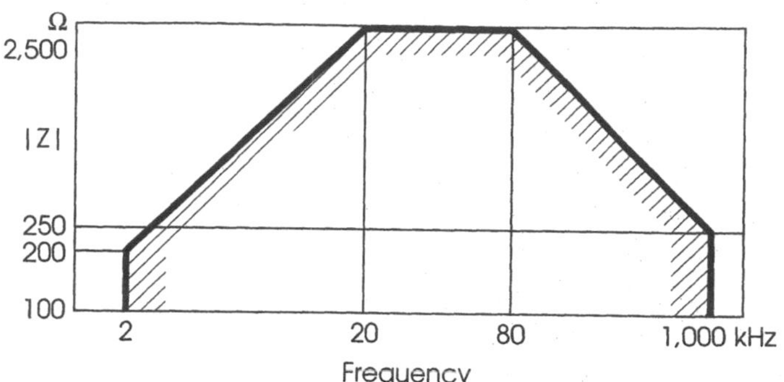

Figure 5–18 TE impedance template.
[Reprinted from ITU-T recommendation I.430 (1993). Basic user-network interface layer 1 specification. Rev. 1. Reproduced by permission.

Regarding the method of transmission, two techniques have been employed, time compression multiplex (TCM) and echo canceller (EC) with hybrid. Early implementations of the ISDN were based on the TCM method. Time compression, taken in the literal sense, is not feasible since, clearly, time cannot be compressed. In the context of this method, however, it means a reduction in transmission time in each direction to less than half, by more than doubling the transmission rate. Accordingly, transmission takes place alternately in either direction, in quick bursts, at slightly more than 320 kbps. Therefore, although transmission occurs in one direction at a time, bidirectional information transfer at 160 kbps is achieved. The bursts are sent at more than double the bidirectional bit rate to allow for a small time gap between opposite directions of transmission. This minimizes the possibility of collision (or overlap). Due to quick data bursts to and fro, the method is also referred to as the Ping-Pong method.

The principal disadvantage of the TCM technique lies in the requirement of higher transmission bandwidth in either direction. This limits the range of transmission.

In current ISDN implementations, the TCM method has been superseded by the EC method, which permits full duplex transmission. Since transceivers in the NT and the LT are both transmitting and receiving at the same time, the echo of the transmitted signal will interfere with the signal received from the distant end. Echo signals may arise at the hybrid (near end echo), at specific points on the line (at bridged taps and where change of wire gauge occurs), and at the hybrid at the distant end (far-end echo). Thus, the received signal is the cumulation of the signal transmitted from the distant end and the echo signal. Echo cancellers are provided at both the ends to cancel the echo signals. The echo canceller simulates the expected echo signal, and this is subtracted from the received signal. The simulated echo signal corresponds to only the near-end echo. (The far-end echo is not as pronounced, and it is not possible to simulate echo signals arising at random points on the line. For this reason, it is desirable to avoid bridged taps and other causes of transmission discontinuity on the line.) If the signal sequences transmitted in either direction are identical, the echo canceller may mistakenly assume that the signal received from the distant end is the echo of the transmitted signal. To prevent this, the signals are scrambled before transmission.

Table 5-4 Quaternary Symbols

FIRST BIT	SECOND BIT	QUATS (Q)
1	0	+3
1	1	+1
0	1	−1
0	0	−3

Several alternative line codes can be employed with the echo-cancellation technique. The 2B1Q (2-binary, 1-quaternary) line code, a four-level code, has been standardized by BELLCORE [9] for use by BOCs in the United States. The following description is based on this standardization.

Successive pairs of scrambled bits of the binary data stream on the line are grouped together and coded into quarternary symbols, called quats. The first bit of the pair represents the sign, and the second bit represents the magnitude. Refer to Table 5–4.

The bit stream emanating from the S/T interface on the DSL is first scrambled, coded into quats as shown in Table 5–4, and transmitted on the line. At the LT, descrambling is performed and the quats are converted into the bit pattern. The same is true for transmission in the reverse direction. As seen from Table 5–5, 18 bits are coded into nine quats. Therefore, the baud rate with this coding is only 80 bauds.

The mask for the electrical signals on the line is shown in Figure 5–19. The voltage levels at points A to H completely define the pulse mask. These values, for the normalized pulse (relative to peak) and for the four quat symbols, are given in the accompanying table. The columns for quat symbols +3, +1, −1, and −3 are obtained by multiplying the normalized pulse voltage levels by 2.5, 5/6, −5/6, and −2.5. The pulse mask in the figure is drawn for the normalized pulse.

The pulses transmitted on the DSL should be received by the receiver at the other end with a Bit Error Ratio (BER) of less than 1E10-7.

Table 5-5 2B1Q Encoding of 2B + D Bit Fields

	B1-CHANNEL		
b11 b12 q1	b13 b14 q2	b15 b16 q3	b17 b18 q4
	B2-CHANNEL		
b21 b22 q5	b23 b24 q6	b25 b26 q7	b27 b28 q8
	D-CHANNEL		
	d1 d2 q9		

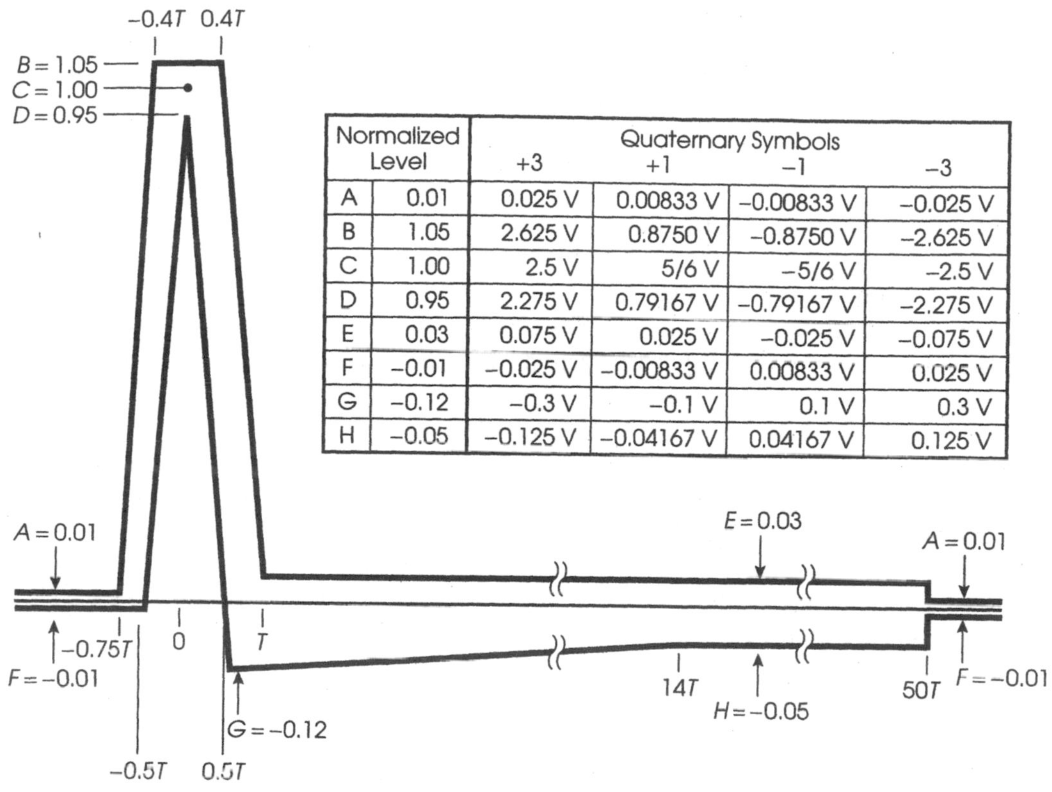

Normalized Level		Quaternary Symbols +3	+1	−1	−3
A	0.01	0.025 V	0.00833 V	−0.00833 V	−0.025 V
B	1.05	2.625 V	0.8750 V	−0.8750 V	−2.625 V
C	1.00	2.5 V	5/6 V	−5/6 V	−2.5 V
D	0.95	2.275 V	0.79167 V	−0.79167 V	−2.275 V
E	0.03	0.075 V	0.025 V	−0.025 V	−0.075 V
F	−0.01	−0.025 V	−0.00833 V	0.00833 V	0.025 V
G	−0.12	−0.3 V	−0.1 V	0.1 V	0.3 V
H	−0.05	−0.125 V	−0.04167 V	0.04167 V	0.125 V

Figure 5–19 Normalized pulse from the NT or LT transmitter. [Copyright © 1991, BELLCORE TR-NWT-000 393. Reprinted with permission.]

5.4.7 Frames and Multiframes on the Digital Subscriber Loop (DSL)

The bit rate of 160 kbps on the DSL is composed of the following:

- 128 kbps for the two B-channels
- 16 kbps of D-channel
- 4 kbps of M-channel bits for maintenance purposes
- 12 kbps of synchronization word (SW)

The bit stream of 160 kbps is organized into frames. BELLCORE [9] has standardized a frame of 120 quat positions, as shown in Figure 5–20. At the 160 kbps rate, the frame duration is 1.5 ms (160,000/240 seconds).

The first nine quat symbols—namely, +3 +3 −3 −3 −3 +3 −3 +3 +3—correspond to the SW. This sequence indicates the beginning of a frame. Next are quats corresponding to the 2B+D bits repeated 12 times in succession. A total of 108 quats (12 × 9 quats of

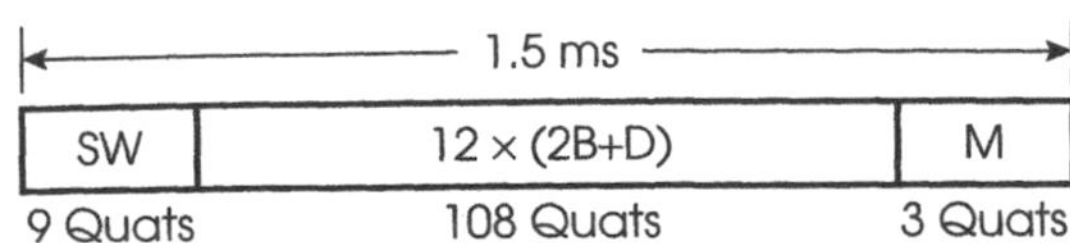

Figure 5–20 Frame configuration at the U reference.

Table 5–4) are required. The frame also contains three quats corresponding to 6 M-channel bits.

To provide for additional functions, a multiframe configuration is used by building a superframe composed of eight frames (duration 12 ms). Superframe synchronization is carried out by an inverted synchronization word (ISW) with the following sequence:

$$-3\ -3\ +3\ +3\ +3\ -3\ +3\ -3\ -3$$

To identify a superframe, the first frame, and every ninth frame thereafter, begins with the ISW instead of an SW.

With 6 bits (M1 to M6) of M-channel in each basic frame, 48 bits of M-channel are available for a superframe. These bits are used for various purposes in the NT to LT and LT to NT directions. For example:

- One of the M bits, designated "act," is used in the start-up procedure of the NT and the LT.
- There are 12 bits for the cyclic redundancy check (CRC).
- Another bit, called the far-end block error (febe), is used to communicate failure of the CRC check.
- A pair of bits ps1 and ps2 by which the NT communicates the status of the power supply at the NT end are used in the NT to TE direction. (Status includes both mains and secondary supplies normal, failure or unavailability of one of the two supplies, and failure or imminent failure of both the supplies.)
- The ntm bit is used by the NT to indicate to the exchange that it is under testing by the customer.
- The S/T-interface activity indicator (sai) is another M bit sent by the NT to the LT. It is used to communicate that there is activity (that is, that INFO 1 or INFO 3 has been received by the NT) at the S/T-interface. It is set to 1 in case of activity.

5.4.8 Start-Up Procedure

Once put into service, the DSL operates continuously. During normal operation, the NT is synchronized to the LT. The timing supplied by the LT is the same as the exchange timing. The system operates in the master-slave mode, with the LT functioning as the master and NT as the slave. Therefore, the signals sent out by the NT toward the LT are synchronized to the signals received by it from the LT. When the NT temporarily loses synchronization, it sends out signals based on the time supplied by a local oscillator. This oscillator should have the accuracy of a stratum 4 clock. (Stratum clocks are described in Chapter 2.)

The goal of the start-up procedure is to establish a synchronized operation with a view to establish bidirectional communication on the line. The start-up procedure is used when the system is brought into service for the first time or when normal operation is to be restored after service disruption.

Start-up may be initiated by either the NT or the LT and involves an exchange of signals between the two.

Figure 5–21(a) illustrates the start-up procedure for the DSL in combination with the activation of the TE and the NT on the S/T-interface. The process is initiated by a call origination at the deactivated TE. A call origination request causes an activation request primitive (PH-AR) from layer 2 to layer 1. The TE sends an INFO 1 signal to the NT. In this example, the NT is in the reset state and initiates the start-up procedure.

The NT initiates the procedure, at time T0, by sending a tone signal designated TN (tone from the NT) on the line. The TN consists of an alternate pattern of four +3 quats followed by four −3 quats. The length of this pattern is equal to six frame lengths (720 quats). The tone is sent up to time instant T1. The duration of the tone is 9 ms, which is the time for transmission of six frame lengths.

This procedure may be followed by an optional signal called SN1. SN1 has the structure of a basic frame. Since there are no operational data on the 2B+D and M-channels from the S/T interface, the NT generates a bit pattern of all 1's for these channels. This is coded into quats and sent after scrambling on the line. The NT now ceases to transmit (time instant T2).

During the period T0 to T2, the NT transmits and the LT only receives; it does not send any signal toward the NT. (An exception is when the LT has also initiated the start-up procedure independently and simultaneously.) The LT starts transmission (at T3) after detecting stoppage of transmission by NT. It successively sends signals designated SL1 (duration T3 to T4), SL2 (duration T4 to T6), and SL3 (duration T7 onwards), as shown in Figure 5–21(a). Transmission of SL1 is optional. The pattern of pulses in SL1 is identical to SN1. SL2 has the basic frame structure, with bits of the 2B+D channel set to 0 by the LT. While receiving SL2, the NT sends SN2 signals (T5 to T6). SN2 signals are identical to the basic frame, with all bits corresponding to 2B+D channels set to 1. This is followed by transmission of SN3 signals (T6 onwards).

The full operational capability of NT is established at time T6, whereas the LT becomes fully operational by time T7. After NT becomes fully operational, it sends INFO 2 to the TE on the S/T-interface and SN3 signals over the line to the LT, with the maintenance bit sai set to 1. Subsequently, when INFO 3 is received by the NT from the TE, it sends SN3 toward the LT, with the maintenance bit act set to 1. The activation is completed when the SL3 signal with act bit equal to 1 is received by the NT and the latter sends INFO 4 to the TE.

Both SN3 and SL3 are signals with operational information on 2B+D channels. This means that the NT and the LT are no longer generating the bit pattern for these channels but are simply passing on the data received by them. For example, the NT passes the user data received on the S/T-interface on the line. Transparent passage of information by the NT and the LT continues as long as the DSL is in service. Moreover, unlike other signals used in the start-up process, SN3 and SL3 signals also include ISW. Therefore, the multiframing capability of the NT and the LT is also established. SN3 and SL3 signals continue on the line indefinitely until deactivation is performed on network request. Figure 5–21(b) shows the deactivation of S/T interface on the request of the network.

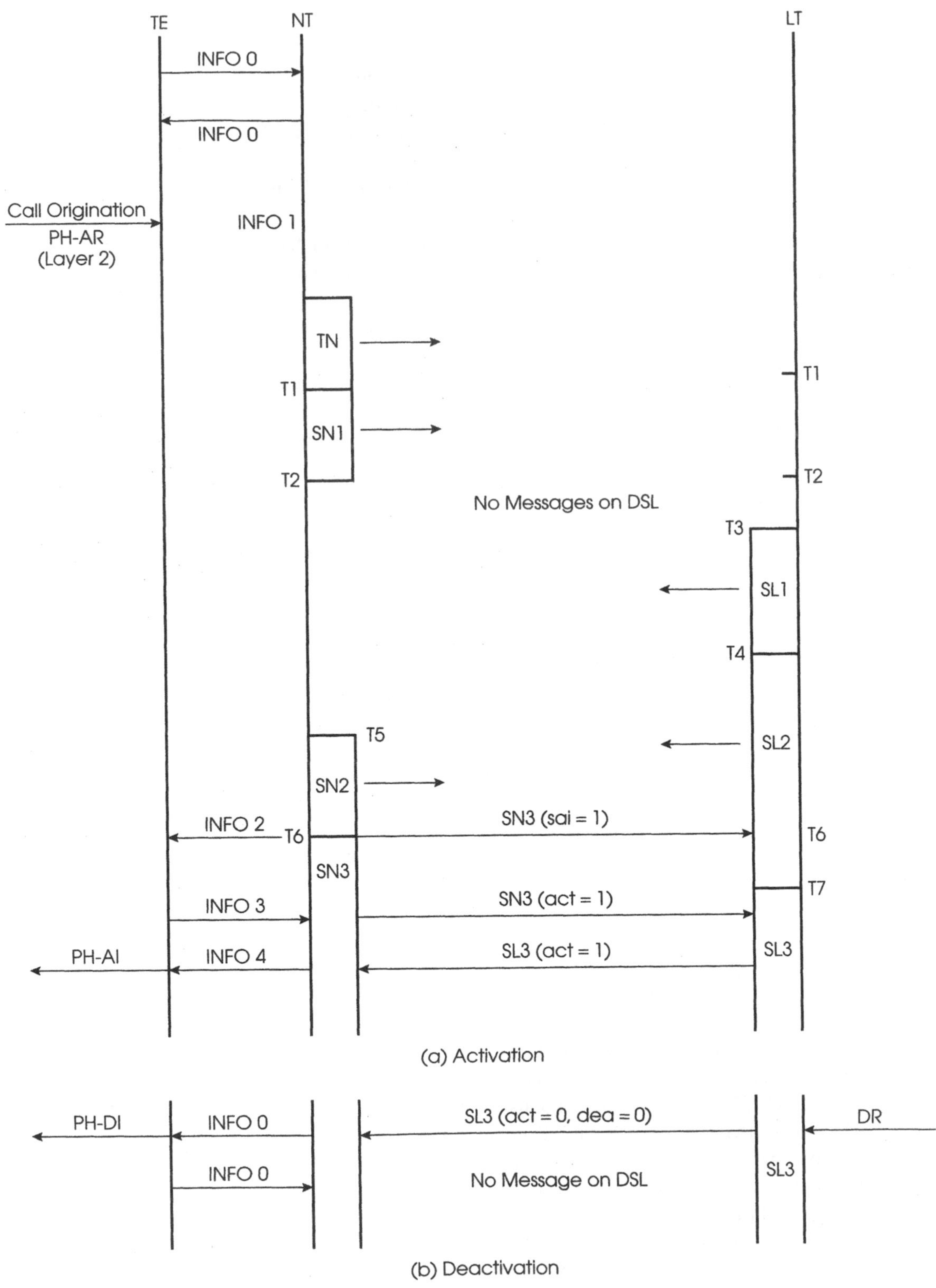

Note: dea is called the turn-off bit. LT sets it to binary zero to inform NT that it is turning-off.

Figure 5–21 Start-up procedure and activation/deactivation of the S/T-interface.

5.5 Primary Rate ISDN

As noted earlier, primary rate ISDN is based on 1,544 kbps or 2,048 kbps bit rates, which are identical to the 24-channel and 30-channel PCM systems, respectively. The main characteristics of the physical layer in this case may be summarized as follows:

- ISDN primary rate access is based on a point-to-point configuration. Thus, multiple terminals cannot be connected. Typically, an ISDN PABX is provided at the primary rate ISDN's customer premises to which the terminals are connected.
- Due to the point-to-point configuration, the problem of access contention does not exist.
- Power feeding is local. Therefore, there is no requirement to supply power to the interface.
- In addition to the 64 kbps B-channels, H0- (at 384 kbps) and H1-channels are also supported. The H1-channel may be either at 1,536 kbps (H11-channel) or at 1,920 kbps (H12-channel).
- The interface is always in the active state.

References

[1] *Integrated Services Digital Network.* Red Book, vol. III, fascicle III.5, I-series recommendations of the CCITT. International Telecommunication Union, 1985.

[2] *ISDN User-Network Interfaces—Reference Configurations.* ITU-T recommendation I.411. International Telecommunication Union, 1993.

[3] *ISDN User-Network Interface—Basic User-Network Interface. Layer 1 Specification.* ITU-T recommendation I.430. International Telecommunication Union, 1993.

[4] *ISDN User-Network Interface—Primary User-Network Interface. Layer 1 Specification.* ITU-T recommendation I.431. International Telecommunication Union, 1993.

[5] *Interworking between the Digital Subscriber System Layer 3 Protocol and the Signalling System No. 7 ISDN User Part.* CCITT Blue Book, fascicle VI.6, recommendation Q.699. International Telecommunication Union, 1988.

[6] Information Technology—Telecommunication and Information Exchange between Systems—Interface connector and contact assignment for ISDN—Basic Access Interface located at reference point S and T. ISO/IEC 8877: 1992.

[7] Reeve, W. D. *Subscriber Loop Signaling and Transmission Handbook: Digital.* IEEE Press, 1995.

[8] *ISDN Basic User Network Interface Layer 1 Specification and Test Principles.* European Telecommunication Standard ETS 300 011:1992.

[9] "Generic requirements for ISDN basic access digital subscriber lines." BELLCORE Technical Reference TR-NWT-000393, issue 2, Jan. 1991.

6 Functions of the CCS 7 Signaling Link Level

Acronyms

ACM	address complete message	RTB	retransmission buffer
AERM	alignment error rate monitor	SF	status field
BIB	backward indicator bit	SIB	status indication busy
BSN	backward sequence number	SIE	status indication emergency alignment
CCS 7	CCITT common channel signaling system no. 7	SIF	signaling information field
CK	check field	SIN	status indication normal alignment
CRC	cyclic redundancy check	SIO	service information octet; also, status indication out of alignment
FIB	forward indicator bit	SIOS	status indication out of service
FISU	fill-in signal unit	SIPO	status indication processor outage
FSN	forward sequence number	SP	signaling point
IAM	initial address message	SU	signal unit
LI	length indicator	SUERM	signal unit error rate monitor
LSSU	link status signal unit		
MSU	message signal unit		
PCR	preventive cyclic retransmission		
REL	release (message)		

ABSTRACT

This chapter is concerned with the functions of the signaling link level including:

- The formats of the three types of signal units
- The various functions performed at this level, including signal unit delimitation and alignment, error detection and correction, initial alignment, error monitoring, and flow control
- The purpose of the various level 2 timers and their permissible value ranges

6.1 Introduction

The signaling data link carries signaling information for a large number of speech/data channels. This information must be conveyed with a high degree of reliability and accuracy. One important goal of the CCITT common channel signaling system no. 7 (CCS 7) signaling link level is to ensure accurate transport of signaling information in the CCS 7 network. To meet this objective, error detection and correction functions are provided. Although signaling information is conveyed on a physical (error-prone) link, the functions performed at the signaling link level have the effect of providing an ideal, error free transport mechanism for signaling information to level 3 of the CCS 7 protocol stack.

Furthermore, for the signaling information to be meaningful, it must be organized. In CCS 7, signaling information is organized in packets, called signal units (SUs). An SU represents the basic building block of signaling information. SUs are of variable length, which imposes the requirement of marking or flagging the beginning and end of each SU in the data stream. Level 2 performs this function of signal unit delimitation.

The signaling link level performs preliminary checks on the data received at either end of the link to verify that the data conforms to the format of signal units. This initial acceptance procedure is termed *signal unit alignment.* Successful signal unit alignment indicates that the SUs transmitted on the link have not been corrupted in a manner that prevents the receiving signaling point (SP) from recognizing them as valid signal units. However, errors may exist that escape detection during the initial acceptance procedure. Error detection checks are therefore conducted on each signal unit separately.

Error detection and correction functions represent an overhead on the signaling network resources. Error correction is implemented by retransmission of the signal units received in error. Excessive errors (with the consequent need for retransmission) reduce the effective throughput of the signaling link. The link is therefore continuously monitored to ensure that the error rate is within permissible limits. When the error rate becomes excessive, the link is removed from service. Similarly, procedures exist for bringing links into service. The initial alignment procedures are designed to perform these functions.

Error rate monitoring is performed not only during the operation of the link but also by performing the initial alignment procedure when the link is brought into service. To facilitate a description of the error monitoring performed on the link, two functional entities are identified in ITU-T recommendation Q.703 [1]: the alignment error rate monitor (AERM) for monitoring errors during link alignment and the signal unit error rate monitor (SUERM) for monitoring during the in-service operation of the link. The detection of congestion is also performed at the signaling link level.

The functions performed at level 2 are as follows:

- Signal unit delimitation
- Signal unit alignment
- Error detection
- Error correction
- Initial alignment
- Signaling link error monitoring
- Flow control

The functions to be performed at level 2 (and also at other levels) are implemented at the signaling points constituting the CCS 7 network. Although the physical realization of level 2 functions may differ from system to system, a generic name, *signaling link terminal,* is used for an entity within a signaling point that performs the various level 2 functions. A

CCS 7 network typically has a number of links connecting a signaling point to other signaling points. The signaling link terminal realizes the level 2 functions for one signaling link.

In the succeeding sections, the various signaling link functions are described.

6.2 Signal Unit Formats

A signal unit forms the basic building block of signaling information. There are three types of SUs: the fill-in signal unit (FISU), the link status signal unit (LSSU), and the message signal unit (MSU).

In view of the high availability requirement of the CCS 7 network, the signaling links are monitored at all times. Even when no signaling information need be conveyed on the link, FISUs are sent on the link so that faulty links may be quickly identified and taken out of service. FISUs are generated and received only between level 2 of the adjacent signal points; higher levels are not involved.

The LSSU, as the name suggests, is used to convey the status information between adjacent signaling points. LSSUs are involved during first-time initialization and during recovery of the link after a failure. Like FISUs, LSSUs are also exchanged between the level 2 functions of adjacent SPs.

MSUs convey the signaling information between the user parts (level 4) of the adjacent signaling points. The initial address message (IAM), address complete message (ACM), and the release message (REL) are examples of MSUs exchanged between user parts. In addition, information between signaling points at level 3 for the management of the signaling network is carried in MSUs. Signal unit formats are shown in Figure 6–1.

Notice that the signal units are composed of fields. Since FISUs and LSSUs implement level 2 functions, the description and purpose of the various fields comprising these two types of signal units are presented in this chapter. MSUs are also created at level 2, but some fields are relevant to the functions of level 3 and level 4. These are considered in Chapters 7 and 8.

FISUs are composed of seven fields that are common to LSSUs and MSUs as well:

- Flag, for signal unit delimitation
- Check field (CK), for error detection
- Forward sequence number (FSN)
- Forward indicator bit (FIB)
- Backward sequence number (BSN)
- Backward indicator bit (BIB)
- Length indicator (LI)

The FSN, FIB, BSN, and BIB together provide a mechanism for implementing the error correction function. The LI field indicates the number of octets between the LI and CK fields. The LI field identifies the type of signal unit as follows:

- LI = 0 for fill-in signal units (because there are no octets between the LI and CK fields except for two spare bits)

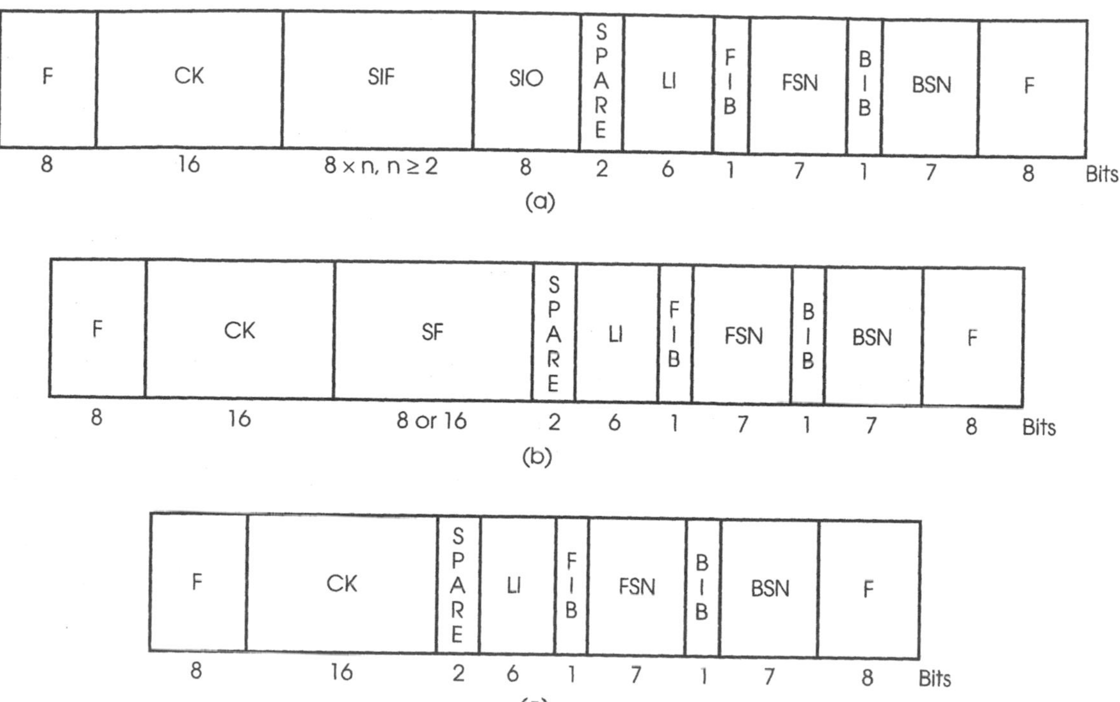

Figure 6–1 Signal unit formats: (a) message signal unit (MSU), LI > 2; (b) link status signal unit (LSSU), LI = 1 or 2; (c) fill-in signal unit (FISU), LI = 0.

- LI = 1 or 2 for LSSUs
- LI > 2 for MSUs (the value of LI is set to 63 when the signaling information field has more than 62 octets)

In addition to the common fields, the LSSU contains an additional field called the status field (SF) whose function is to indicate the link status. The MSU, on the other hand, contains two additional fields, the signaling information field (SIF) and the service information octet (SIO).

6.3 Signal Unit Delimitation

A unique 8-bit flag indicates the beginning of a signal unit. Signal units follow one after the other on the signaling link. Therefore, the beginning of a signal unit also indicates the end of the preceding signal unit. In rare cases, however, (for example, in congestion conditions), more than one flag may exist between two signal units.

A bit pattern of 01111110 is used for the flag. To ensure that a bit pattern imitating the flag does not occur inside a signal unit, the transmitting SP inserts a zero after five consecutive 1's in the signal unit bit pattern. This is done without examining the value of the

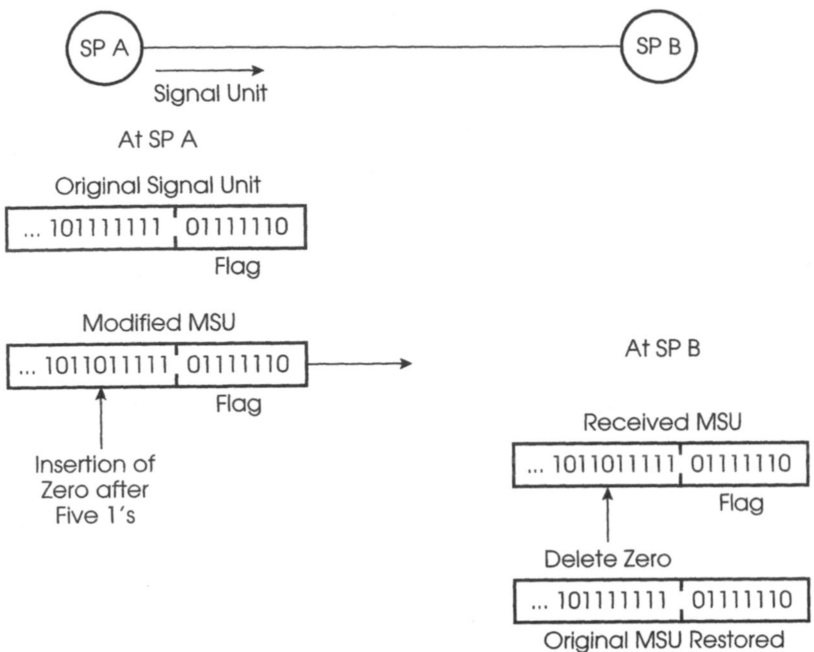

Figure 6–2 Prevention of flag imitation.

next bit in the signal unit. Thus, even if the actual data includes five 1's followed by a zero, a zero is still inserted. This procedure simplifies the process of bit insertion. After zero bit insertions, the flag is prefixed and the signal unit is transmitted. At the receiving SP, the flag is detected and removed. The signal unit is then searched for the existence of a sequence of five consecutive 1's, and whenever such a sequence is found, the following zero (that was inserted at the transmitting SP) is removed. The original contents of the signal unit are thus restored. Figure 6–2 illustrates the zero insertion and deletion procedure.

6.4 Signal Unit Alignment

Preliminary checks are made to identify signal units in the data stream received on the link. Seven or more consecutive 1's are detected as an error condition. Checks are also made on the length of the signal unit. The length of a signal unit should be in multiples of 8 bits; the minimum and maximum permissible length is 6 octets and 279 octets, respectively. If any of these checks fail, the data is discarded until a pattern corresponding to a flag is received.

6.5 Error Detection

After a signal unit is identified based on the procedure described above, error detection is performed by the use of the standard CCITT 16-bit cyclic redundancy check (CRC) on each signal unit. The check bits are generated by the transmitting SP on the bits constituting all other fields of the signal unit except the flag. The check bits are then appended as a two-octet check (bit) field (CK) at the end of the signal unit, and the signal unit is transmitted over the link. At the receiving SP, the check bits are independently calculated in an identical manner, and the result is compared with the CK in the signal unit. A mismatch is interpreted as an error in the received signal unit, and the error correction procedure (described in the next section) is applied.

6.6 Error Correction

Two methods of error correction are available, the basic method and the preventive cyclic retransmission (PCR) method. In both methods, error correction is implemented by retransmission of signal units. While in the basic method, retransmission occurs only when the transmitting SP is informed by the receiving SP about the signal units that are received in error; in the PCR method, retransmission takes place for the signal units whose correct reception is not yet confirmed by the receiving SP, provided that no new MSUs or LSSUs are required to be sent.

In both methods, the SP, while transmitting an MSU on the link, also stores it in a retransmission buffer (RTB) in preparation for a possible subsequent retransmission. Detailed discussion on the methods is presented in Sections 6.6.1 and 6.6.2. In Section 6.6.3, the criteria for selecting the error correction method is discussed.

6.6.1 Basic Method

Each SU is assigned a sequence number by the originating SP. The sequence number is contained in the forward sequence number (FSN) field. The FSN is incremented linearly as MSUs are transmitted. The FSN therefore uniquely identifies an MSU. FISUs or LSSUs are sent with an FSN value of the last MSU sent. In view of the 7-bit capacity of the field, the FSN has a range of 0 to 127. When an FSN value of 127 is reached, it is set to 0 for the next MSU sent. The numbering scheme dictates that no more than 127 MSUs be stored for retransmission in the RTB. The numbering of signal units is performed independently at the two SPs interconnecting the link. Refer to Figure 6–3 for an illustrative example.

The error correction procedure operates independently in the two directions. At the receiving end, both the correct and errored receptions of signal units are acknowledged. A

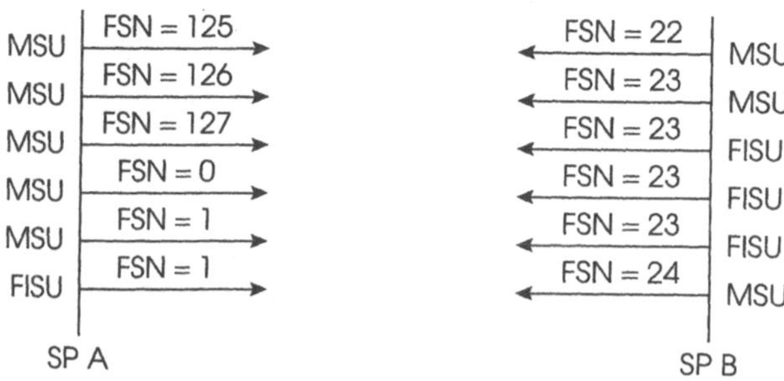

Figure 6–3 Assignment of forward sequence number in signal units.

positive acknowledgment is sent for an error-free case, whereas a negative acknowledgment indicates an error condition. To minimize retransmission events, only MSUs are retransmitted. The errored reception of FISUs and LSSUs is noted for the purpose of error rate monitoring of the link.

Acknowledgment information is integrated within the signal units transmitted by an SP. FSN, BSN, FIB, and BIB are the fields used for this purpose. Although the bit rate on the signaling link is the same in either direction (for example, 64 kbps), the number of signal units transmitted on the link by the two SPs during a time interval may not be identical due to the varying lengths of signal units. Consequently, a number of signal units may be received by an SP before a signal unit containing an acknowledgment is sent.

6.6.1.1 Positive Acknowledgment

After a received signal unit has passed the error detection check based on the CRC polynomial, the length indicator field is examined to determine the type of signal unit. For a received MSU, if the FSN is one more than the FSN of the last accepted signal unit and the received FIB is equal to the last sent BIB, then the MSU is considered to be received in correct sequence and free of errors. In this case, level 2 accepts the MSU and delivers it to level 3 of the MTP. A positive acknowledgment is sent to the other SP in the next signal unit transmitted. In this signal unit, the FSN of the last correctly received MSU is sent back as the BSN. The FIB and the BIB are left unchanged. Initially, when the link is aligned, the FIB and BIB each equal one. Therefore, as long as the MSUs are received correctly in either direction, FIB and BIB each equal one.

Positive acknowledgment is detected by examining the FIB in the received message. If the value of the FIB is the same as that sent by the SP in the previous signal unit, a positive acknowledgment is detected. The positive acknowledgment of an MSU also indicates the acceptance of all previously unacknowledged MSUs.

Figure 6–4 illustrates the error free condition. When an MSU is sent by SP A on the signaling link, the contents are saved in an RTB. In the example, two MSUs with FSN values of 125 and 126 are saved in the RTB. A positive acknowledgment is to be returned to SP A by SP B. The MSU indicating positive acknowledgment has BSN equal to 126. When a signal unit with a BSN value of 126 is received by SP A, the MSUs with FSN values of 125 and 126 are deleted from the retransmission buffer. Subsequent signal units are sent by SP B with the same BSN until a new acknowledgment is required to be sent.

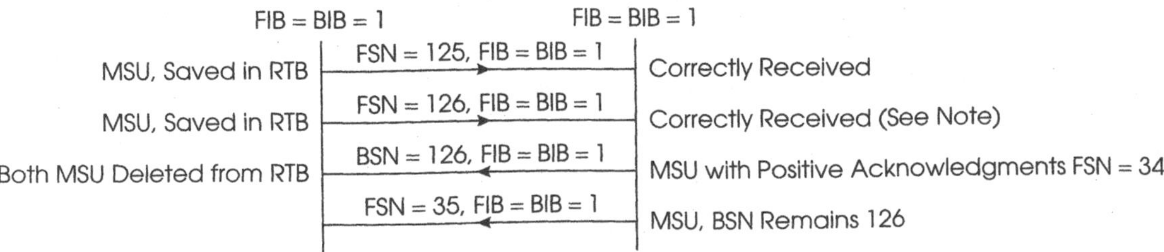

Note: FSN is one more than the last correctly received FSN, and the received FIB is equal to the last sent BIB (both are 1).

Figure 6–4 Error-free case, positive acknowledgments.

6.6.1.2 Negative Acknowledgment

If an MSU with an error is received at an SP, the message is discarded and not delivered to level 3 of the MTP. The SP then sends a negative acknowledgment in the next signal unit. In this signal unit, the FSN of the errored message is not transferred as the BSN; instead, the BSN field continues to retain the FSN of the last correctly received MSU. In addition, the BIB is inverted. An example of the retransmission mechanism is shown in Figure 6–5.

A negative acknowledgment is detected when the received BIB is not in the same state as the previously sent FIB. The BSN value indicates the point up to which messages have been correctly received by the distant SP. Accordingly, all messages with an FSN value greater than the received BSN are sent, one by one, by fetching them from the retransmission buffer. Furthermore, the FIB value is inverted in all messages beginning from the first retransmitted message. Until all the messages in the retransmission buffer are retransmitted, no fresh MSUs are sent.

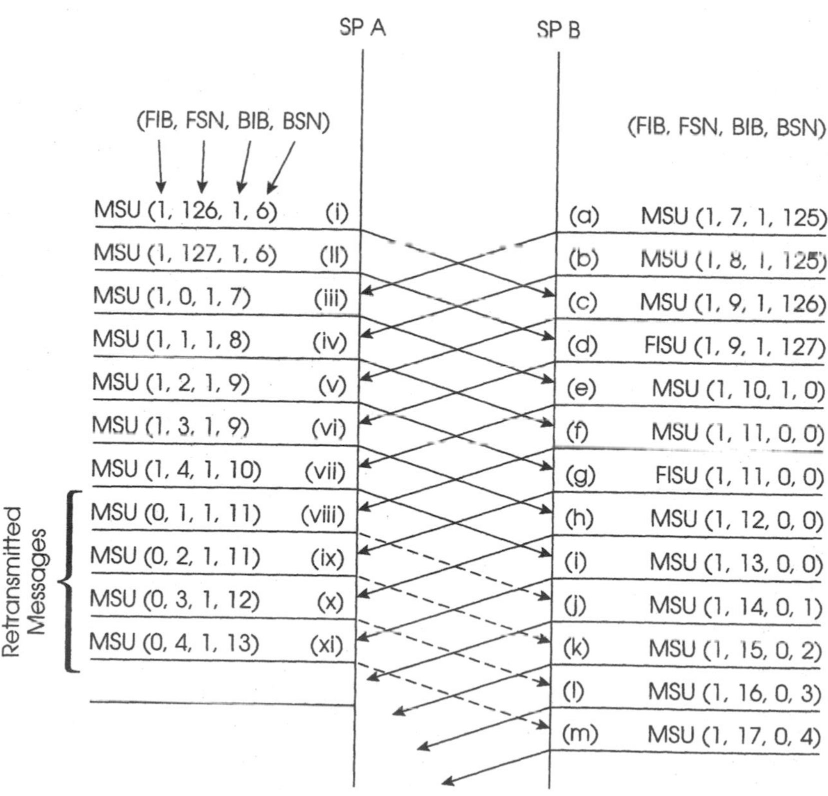

Notes: 1. MSU (iv) sent by SP A is received in error at SP B.
2. Negative acknowledgment sent by SP B in MSU (f). (BIB is inverted and BSN contains the last correctly sent FSN.)
3. SP A detects negative acknowledgment upon the receipt of message (f) and resends all MSUs after the last positive acknowledgment.

Figure 6–5 Retransmission in basic error correction method.

An "excessive delay of acknowledgment" timer T7 is used when an unreasonably long period has elapsed after the transmission of a message unit and no acknowledgment, either positive or negative, has been received from the remote terminal. On expiration of timer T7, it is concluded that a link failure has occurred, and an indication to this effect is given to level 3.

6.6.2 Preventive Cyclic Retransmission (PCR) Method

In the preventive cyclic retransmission method, there are no negative acknowledgments. Whenever no new signal units are to be sent, the SP cyclically transmits the MSUs available in the retransmission buffer. When new signal units are to be transmitted, they take priority over the retransmission of MSUs. If already in progress, retransmission is interrupted to allow for the transmission of new signal units. During periods when neither new signal units are available for transmission or cyclic retransmission is required, fill-in signal units are transmitted on the signaling link.

The signal units for which positive acknowledgment has been received are deleted from the retransmission buffer. Because transmission of new MSUs takes priority over retransmission, in the event of high signaling load on the link, the rate of cyclic retransmission may be reduced. The retransmission buffer has the limited capacity to store up to 127 messages, and the effectiveness of error correction may suffer. To remedy such situations, a forced retransmission procedure is prescribed wherein transmission of new MSUs is suspended temporarily and all unacknowledged MSUs in the retransmission buffer are transmitted one by one.

To permit forced retransmission, a count is kept for the number of MSUs available for retransmission (N1) and the corresponding number of octets in these MSUs (N2). Thresholds are set for these parameters, and whenever one of them is reached, the forced retransmission of MSUs that have not been retransmitted even once is commenced until all such MSUs are retransmitted. The forced retransmission continues cyclically until both parameters are within the threshold values. Subsequently, the normal preventive cyclic retransmission procedure is resumed.

The threshold values for N1 and N2 can usually be set by man-machine command. These need to be set with care. When the threshold values are set too high, the effectiveness of error correction may be reduced since forced retransmission may occur too infrequently. On the other hand, low thresholds may lead to frequent entry and exit from the forced retransmission procedure.

The maximum possible value for which N1 can be set is 127, because no more than 127 MSUs can be available for retransmission due to the limits of 0 to 127 for forward sequence numbers. In the absence of errors, the maximum value for N2 is calculated as follows: If TL is the time interval between the transmission of a message by an SP and the receipt of positive acknowledgment from the distant end and Teb is the emission time for one octet of SU, then

$$N2 = \frac{TL}{Teb} + 1$$

For a 64 kbps signal link, Teb = $\frac{1}{8{,}000}$ second. TL includes a two-way propagation delay on the link and the processing time at the distant SP.

Link failure is indicated to level 3 if an MSU remains unacknowledged by the remote end for an unusually long period. As previously noted, timer T7 is used for this purpose.

6.6.3 Criteria for Selection: Basic versus Preventive Cyclic Retransmission (PCR)

In a signaling network, both the basic and PCR methods may coexist. However, the same method should be used by the adjacent SPs for a signaling link. The criteria for choosing the method is the propagation delay expected on the signaling link. The basic method is applied where the one-way propagation delay is less than 15 ms. The PCR method is suitable for signaling links where the one-way propagation delay is equal to or greater than 15 ms. Where the signaling link is provided by means of satellite links, only the PCR method is used. If, in a link set, one or more signaling links are provided by satellite while the other links are provided by terrestrial transmission, then it is recommended that all the links in such a link set use the PCR method of error correction even though the terrestrial signaling links may have a propagation delay of less than 15 ms [1,2]. This guideline minimizes the possibility of different methods of error correction being applied at the two ends of the same link.

6.7 Initial Alignment Procedure

The initial alignment procedure is applied both for first-time initialization of the link to bring it into service and to recover from a failure. Initial alignment is performed independently for each link; during the alignment of one link, other links are not involved. Initial alignment is requested by level 3 by sending a "start" indication to layer 2. Level 3 has the status of the various links connected to the SP. It requests emergency initial alignment if there are no other in-service links between the two SPs. Normal initial alignment is requested when at least one in-service link already exists between the SPs.

As part of the procedure, LSSUs are exchanged between the two signaling link terminals. To ensure that the link is of good quality, it is monitored for errors at either end by sending LSSUs for a specified period. This procedure is referred to as *proving* the link. A shorter proving period is used for emergency alignment. The status field (SF) of an LSSU includes the information shown in Figure 6–6.

Spare	Status Indication
5 bits	C B A

Note: The status field shown above consists of one octet. The three least-significant bits are coded as follows:

C	B	A	Status Indication
0	0	0	O: Out of Alignment
0	0	1	N: Normal Alignment
0	1	0	E: Emergency Alignment
0	1	1	OS: Out of Service
1	0	0	PO: Processor Outage
1	0	1	B: Busy

Figure 6–6 Status field format.

A number of stages or states are involved in the execution of the initial alignment procedure. Figure 6–7 shows the state transition diagram.

As long as the signaling link terminal is powered off, there is no activity on the link. With power on, the terminal sends a status indication out of service (SIOS) in the LSSUs by coding the status field with OS. Each LSSU with SIOS has the following contents: FSN = BSN = 127, and FIB = BIB = 1. These are continuously sent on the link until a "start" is given by level 3 to commence link alignment. Upon receipt of the start indication, the signaling terminal sends status indication out of alignment (SIO) continuously. Simultaneously, timer T2 is started. If the initial alignment procedure has also been started at the distant SP, the terminal should receive signal units from the distant end. An LSSU with SIO, status indication normal alignment (SIN), or status indication emergency alignment (SIE) is expected. If, in the meantime, a "stop" indication is received from level 3, the procedure is suspended (idle state). If none of the above happens, the process of sending an SIO is terminated by time out of T2, thereby suspending the procedure.

If the distant terminal is also attempting the initial alignment of the link, the near terminal receives an SIO, SIN, or SIE. SIN is received when level 3 of the distant SP perceives that the normal initial alignment is to be performed. SIE indicates a request for emergency alignment. Before making a decision, the signaling terminal consults the information available from the local level 3. If an emergency situation is indicated, then irrespective of the SIN or SIE received from the distant SP, emergency proving is used. Similarly, if an SIE is received from the distant end, then emergency proving is adopted even when the local level 3 indicates a normal situation.

Thus, normal proving is to be performed only when a normal situation is indicated at both ends of the link. The "aligned" state is indicated when the near signaling terminal is transmitting an SIN or SIE and either SIN, SIE, or SIOS has not yet been received from the distant terminal. (SIOS indicates that the distant SP has aborted the initial alignment process.) Timer T3 is used for the forced exit from this state.

Once SIN or SIE status indications are received from the distant SP, proving of the link commences. During normal proving, an SIN is sent by both ends. During emergency proving, two cases may arise:

- When both terminals perceive emergency condition, both terminals send SIE.
- When one terminal perceives a normal condition and the other an emergency condition, the terminal perceiving the normal condition sends an SIN and the other sends an SIE.

The nominal values of proving periods are specified in ITU-T recommendation Q.703 as follows:

Normal proving: period $P_n = 2^{16}$ octet transmission time
Emergency proving: period $P_e = 2^{12}$ octet transmission time

The normal proving period specified for North America is shorter: 2^{12} octet transmission time [2]. Timer T4 is used for the proving period. Expiration of timer T4 in-

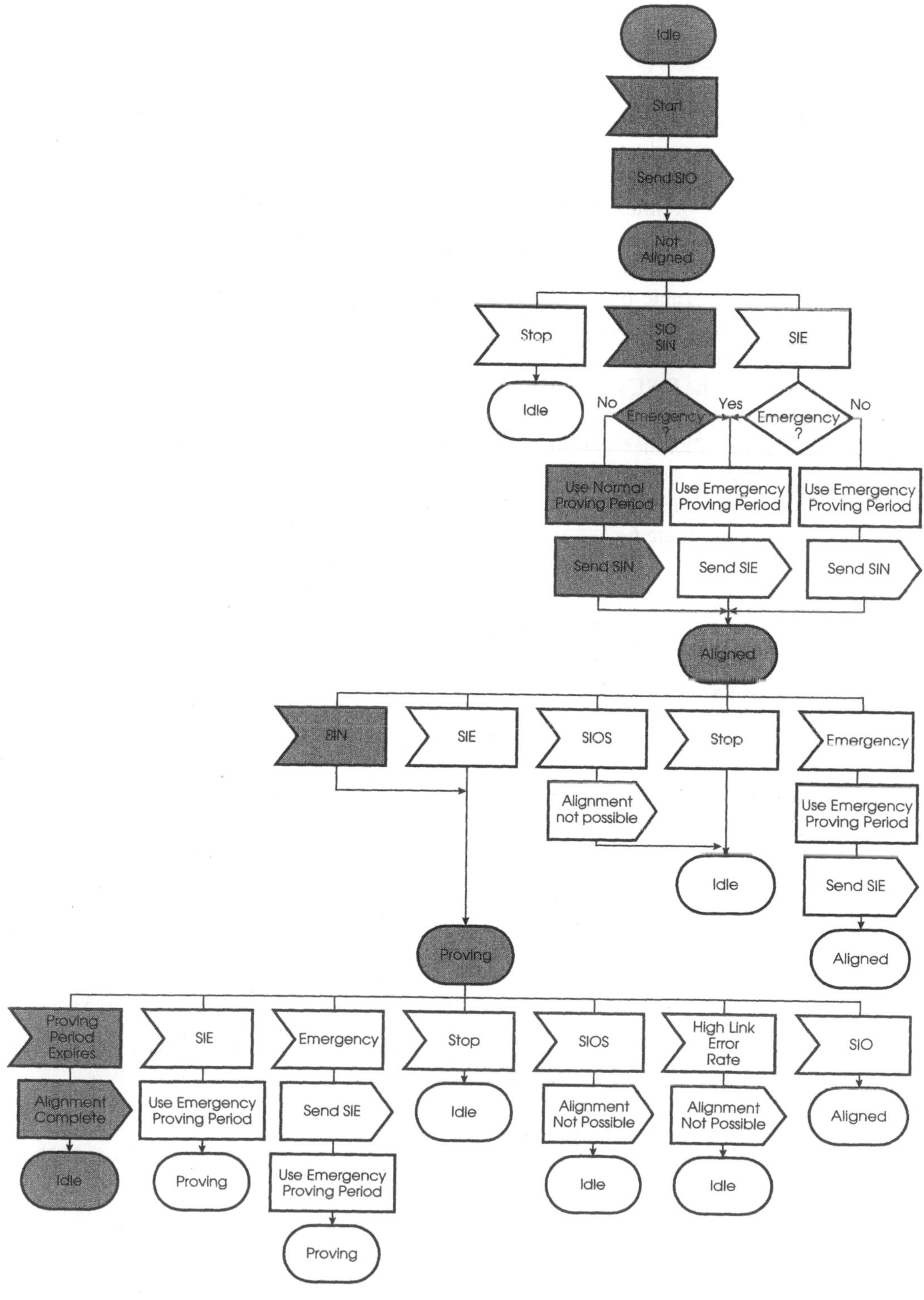

Figure 6–7 Outline of initial alignment procedure.

dicates successful proving unless the proving period has been previously aborted up to four times.

After successful proving, the signaling terminal enters the "aligned ready" state provided that it does not detect any local processor outage. Processor outage is described in the next section. The aligned ready state begins with the terminal sending the FISUs on the link. Simultaneously, timer T1 is started. Until proving is completed at the remote terminal, the FISUs are not received from the remote terminal. Up to five provings are permitted. The value of timer T1 should be chosen to permit time for these provings (normal proving period) at the remote terminal. Therefore, $T1 = 5 \times P_n$ + safety margin. For example, if the proving period timer T4 is set to the ITU-T–prescribed nominal value of 8.2 seconds (refer to Table 6–1), then five normal provings will take no more than 42 seconds. In this case, after including a safety margin (say, 3 seconds), timer T1 may be set at a value of 45 seconds. (As seen in Table 6–1, the value range of T1 is 40 to 50 seconds.) Upon receiving the FISUs or MSUs from the remote terminal, timer T1 is stopped and the terminal enters the "in-service" state. The terminal now sends the FISUs or MSUs as required. If timer T1 times out, then the terminal goes into the "idle" state, and SIOS are sent on the link.

Figure 6–8 illustrates the initial alignment procedure corresponding to the path with shaded boxes in Figure 6–7.

Table 6–1 Level 2 Timer Values

TIMER	ITU-T	BELLCORE
T1: timer "aligned ready"	40 to 50 seconds	13 to 30 seconds; nominal value 13 seconds
T2: timer "not aligned"	5 to 50 seconds T2 low[a]: 5 to 50 seconds T2 high[a]: 70 to 150 seconds	5 to 14 seconds; Nominal value 11.5 seconds or 16 to 30 seconds; nominal value 23 seconds
T3: timer "aligned"	1 to 1.5 seconds	5 to 14 seconds; nominal value 11.5 seconds
T4: proving period timer	Normal proving: 7.5 to 9.5 seconds; nominal value 8.2 seconds Emergency proving: 400 to 600 ms; nominal value 500 ms	At 56 kbits/second Normal proving: nominal value 2.3 seconds; range ± 10% Emergency proving: 0.6 seconds; nominal value ± 10%
T5: timer "sending SIB"	80 to 120 ms	80 to 120 ms
T6: timer "remote congestion"	3 to 6 seconds	3 to 6 seconds for 56 or 64 kbps
T7: timer "excessive delay of acknowledgment"	0.5 to 2 seconds (for PCR method: 0.8 to 2 seconds)	0.5 to 2 seconds for 56 or 64 kbps

[a]When automatic allocation method is used at MTP level 3 (refer to Chapter 7).

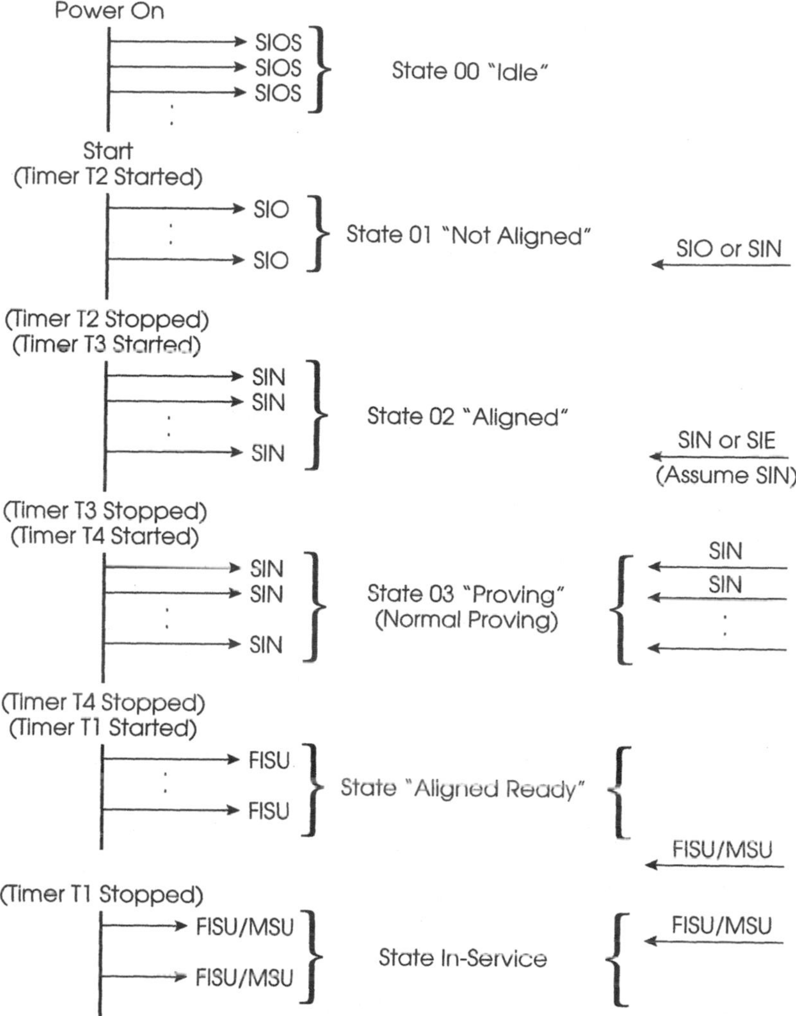

Figure 6–8 Initial alignment procedure (ideal case) corresponding to the shaded boxes of Figure 6–7.

6.8 Processor Outage

The processor outage condition relates to a situation where the signaling link cannot be used due to failure conditions at level 3 and above. Signaling messages can no longer be transferred from level 2 to higher levels. The processor outage condition may not affect all the links at an SP. Upon recognizing a local processor outage, level 2 sends the information to the remote signaling link terminal by means of an LSSU with the status field coded for "status indication processor outage" (SIPO). It also discards any messages re-

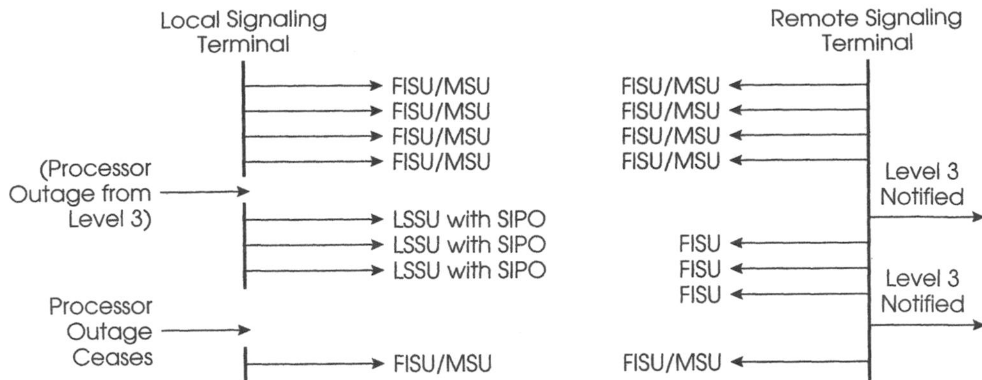

Figure 6–9 Processor outage.

ceived from the distant terminal. Upon receiving SIPO status, the distant terminal notifies its own MTP level 3 and commences to send FISU messages. Figure 6–9 illustrates the above description. During processor outage, local or remote, timers T5, T6, and T7 are stopped.

6.9 Error Rate Monitoring

Error rate monitoring of the signaling link is performed both during the in-service operation of the link and during proving of the link. The signal unit error rate monitor (SUERM) performs in-service monitoring, while the alignment error rate monitor (AERM) is employed for error monitoring during proving.

6.9.1 Signal Unit Error Rate Monitor (SUERM)

The SUERM is a linear counter that operates on the leaky bucket principle. The counter is initially set to zero. The counter is incremented for each signal unit received in error. It is decremented by one after reception of a block of D signal units, unless the counter is already zero. When a threshold value of *T* is reached for the SUERM, level 2 reports the condition to level 3, which removes the link from service.

For a 64 kbps signaling link, the values of *D* and *T* are 256 and 64, respectively. Figure 6–10 shows the operation of the SUERM for a 64 kbps link.

Monitoring of the link for errors permits the removal of the link from service in case of excessive errors. Furthermore, if preliminary checks as described in Section 6.4 fail, then the SUERM enters the "octet counting mode." The octet counting mode continues until the next error-free signal unit is received or until the link goes out of service. For every block of *N* octets counted during the octet counting mode, the SUERM is incremented by one. The octet counting mode performs two functions. First, it allows for discarding of data when signal units cannot be identified from the received data. Second, it

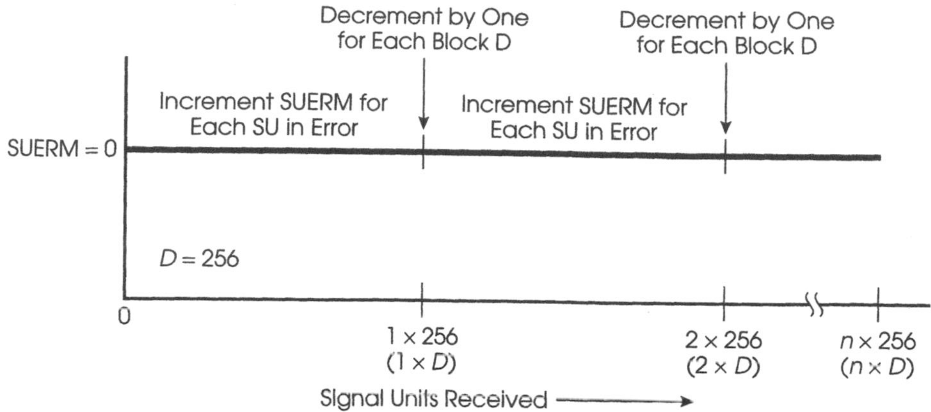

Figure 6–10 Signal unit error rate monitor.

contributes to the incrementing of the SUERM. Thus, if the octet counting mode continues for a significant period, then the link is taken out of service. For example, if the octet counting mode is entered when the SUERM is zero, the link will be removed from service after the receipt of $N \times 64$ octets that fail the preliminary tests. The values of *T, D,* and *N* are given in Table 6–2.

6.9.2 Alignment Error Rate Monitor (AERM)

The AERM is a linear counter employed to monitor errors during the normal and emergency proving of the link. It is initialized to zero upon entry to the proving state of the initial alignment procedure. The counter is incremented for every LSSU received in error. If the octet counting mode is entered during the proving period, then the counter is incremented for every block of *N* octets counted. If the counter reaches a threshold value Ti, then the proving period is aborted. Different threshold values, Tin and Tie, are used for normal and emergency proving, respectively. If the proving is aborted *M* times, then the terminal enters the idle state and the link is taken out of service.

The values of different parameters associated with AERM for the ITU-T recommendations and the BELLCORE standards are shown in Table 6–3.

Table 6–2 SUERM Parameters

	ITU-T Recommendation [1]		BELLCORE [2]
	64 kbps	Lower Bit Rates,	Both 56 kbps and 64 kbps
T	64 SUs	32 SUs	64 SUs
D	256	256	256
N	16	16	16

Table 6-3 AERM Parameters

PARAMETER	VALUE
Tin	4
Tie	1
M	5
N	16

6.10 Flow Control

The flow control procedure is used for overload control at level 2. An example of overload is the reception of too many MSUs by a signaling terminal from the distant signaling terminal. Level 2 may not be able to process them fast enough for transfer to level 3, which causes congestion to develop. The mechanism for detecting the onset of congestion (and its abatement) is implementation dependent. It should be implemented such that the unstable operation by way of frequent onset and abatement of congestion is avoided.

When the signaling terminal perceives a congestion condition, it sends an LSSU with status indication busy (SIB) on the link to the remote transmitting end. It also suspends acknowledgment of message units. The LSSU SIB is sent at a periodicity determined by timer "remote busy" T5 (80 to 120 ms).

To prevent the indication of a link failure to level 3 that would result from the expiration of excessive acknowledgment delay timer T7, timer T7 is reset every time an SIB signal is received at the remote end. Further, when the first SIB signal is received at the transmitting remote end, it starts a longer supervision timer T6. Refer to Figure 6–11. T6 is called "timer remote congestion" (duration 3 to 6 seconds), and expiration of this timer results in link failure indication to level 3.

When the signaling terminal perceives the abatement of the congestion condition, it discontinues the periodic transmission of the SIB signal and commences normal operation by acknowledging the MSUs received from the remote end. When messages with acknowledgment are received at the remote end, it stops timer T6, and normal operation at both ends ensues.

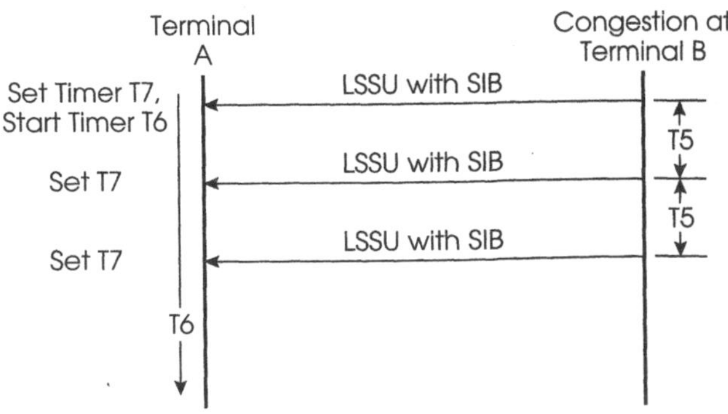

Figure 6–11 Flow control: congestion at terminal B.

6.11 Remarks

Out of seven level 2 timers, T1 to T4 are employed during the initial alignment procedure. T5 and T6 relate to control flow function, and T7 is involved in the error correction function for both the basic and PCR methods. Timer values have been listed in Table 6–1.

REFERENCES

[1] *Specifications of Signaling System No. 7: Signaling Link.* ITU-T recommendation Q.703, rev. 1. International Telecommunication Union, 1993.

[2] "Specifications of signalling system number 7." BELLCORE Technical Report TR-NWT-000242, vol. 1, issue 2, chap. T1.1113, June 1991; rev. 1, Dec. 1991; rev. 2, Dec. 1992; rev. 3, Dec. 1993.

7 Signaling Network Functions in CCS 7

Acronyms

CBA	changeback acknowledgment
CBD	changeback declaration
CCS 7	CCITT common channel signaling system no. 7
CIC	circuit identification code
COA	changeover acknowledgment
COO	changeover order
DPC	destination point code
ECA	emergency changeover acknowledgment
ECO	emergency changeover order
FSN	forward sequence number
ISDN	integrated services digital network
ISUP	ISDN user part
ITU-T	International Telecommunication Union-Telecommunication Standardization Sector
LFU	link forced uninhibited (signal)
LIA	link inhibit acknowledgment (signal)
LIN	link inhibit (signal)
LLT	link local inhibit test (signal)
LRT	link remote inhibit test (signal)
LUA	link uninhibit acknowledgment (signal)
LUN	link uninhibit (signal)
MIM	managment inhibit message
MSU	message signal unit
MTP	message transfer part
OPC	origination point code
PCM	pulse code modulation
RCT	route-set-congestion-test (message)
RST	route set test (message)
SCCP	signaling connection control part
SDLC	signaling data link connection
SI	service indicator
SIF	signaling information field
SIO	service information octet
SLC	signaling link code
SLS	signaling link selection
SP	signaling point
STP	signal transfer point
TFA	transfer allowed (message)
TFC	transfer controlled (message)
TFP	transfer prohibited (message)
TFR	transfer restricted (message)
TRA	traffic restart allowed (message)
TUP	telephone user part
UPU	user part unavailable

ABSTRACT

This chapter deals with the signaling network functionality (level 3) of CCITT common channel signaling system no. 7 (CCS 7), including:

- Signaling message handling and network management aspects
- The message transfer part (MTP) restart procedure specified by the International Telecommunication Union-Telecommunication Standardization Sector (ITU-T)
- International standards and the North American standards concerning signaling network functions
- ITU-T recommended level 3 timer values and the role of various timers in supervising level 3 functions.

7.1 Introduction

Signaling network (level 3) functions are implemented at each signaling point (SP) to permit transfer of signaling messages and to manage the CCS 7 network. In contrast to the signaling link (level 2) functions that are performed individually and separately for each signaling link, level 3 functions relate to overall network aspects.

More specifically, signaling network functions can be classified into two categories:

1. Signaling message handling
2. Signaling network management

Signaling message handling functions ensure that the messages originating at a user part of an SP are transferred to the corresponding user part in the destination SP. The transfer may take place through a number of intermediate signal transfer points (STPs). Similarly, messages generated by level 3 of the originating SP terminate in level 3 of the destination SP. These messages are used for performing the functions of level 3.

Both level 3 and level 4 messages are basically message signal units (MSUs). The messages are distinguished from one another by the value of the service information octet (SIO) in the MSU, as described in Section 7.2.1.

To accomplish message transfer, each node in the signaling network must be uniquely identified by a point code. The point codes of the two endpoints of the message transfer are contained in a routing label provided in the MSU. Therefore, at any node of the CCS 7 network, it is possible to ascertain the origination and destination of the message by examining the routing label. Signaling message handling functions make extensive use of the routing label for the transfer of messages in the network. The routing label format is described in Section 7.2.2.

The signaling network management functions aim at ensuring a minimum disruption to CCS 7 traffic in the event of failures. Since failure of a signaling connection has an impact on a large number of speech or data channels, the availability requirements are very stringent for the CCS 7 network. Therefore, when planning and engineering the CCS 7 network, adequate redundancy must be provided in the provisioning of signaling links.

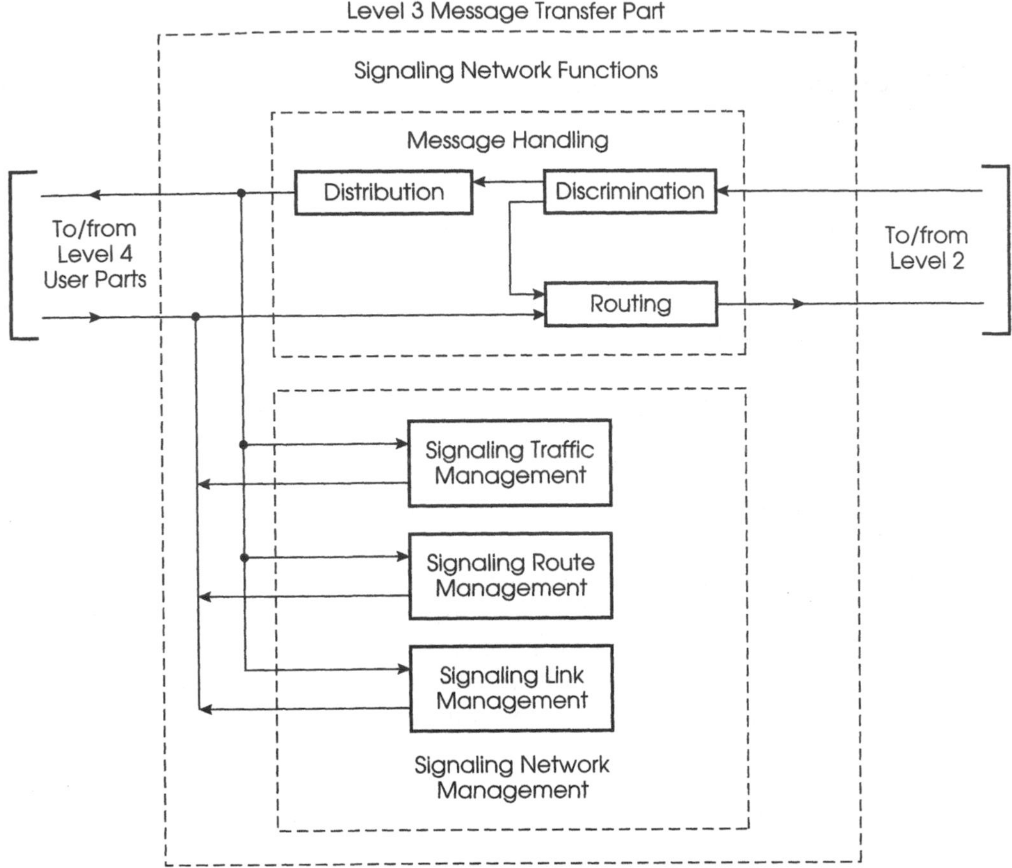

Figure 7–1 Main functional blocks.

Signaling network management functions are directed toward managing the network redundancies to achieve the high-availability requirement. For example, the management functions provide for network reconfiguration in response to failures and for traffic control in the event of congestion.

The major functional blocks constituting the level 3 message transfer part (MTP) are shown in Figure 7–1. Before discussing the functions performed by level 3 MTP, it is useful to describe the various fields that are involved in implementing these functions.

7.2 Level 3 Message Format

The structure of level 3 messages is shown in Figure 7–2(a). For the sake of comparison, the message formats of other user parts are also shown; refer to Figures 7–2(b) through 7–2(d). Although all other fields are identical, the format of the signaling information field (SIF) and the label contained therein depends on the user part involved. There are four types of labels: types A, B, C, and D. Type A is used for level 3 MTP. Types B, C, and D correspond to the telephone user part (TUP), the integrated services digital network

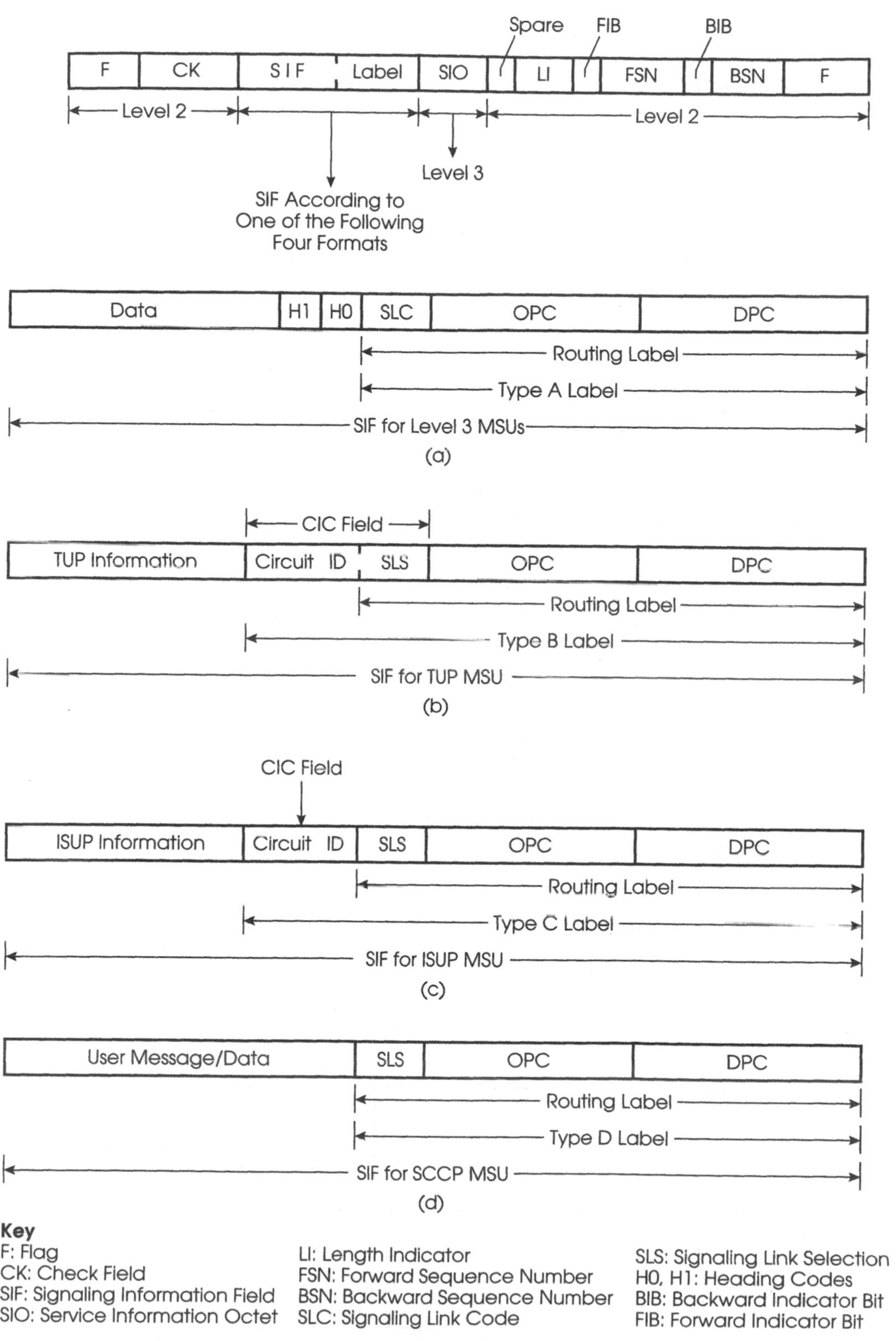

Figure 7–2 Message signal unit formats: (a) SIF for level 3 MSUs; (b) SIF for TUP MSU; (c) SIF for ISUP MSU; (d) SIF for SCCP MSU.

(ISDN) user part (ISUP), and signaling connection control part (SCCP) messages, respectively.

Notice that for level 3 MSUs, the routing label and the label are the same. In the case of signaling for circuit switched applications such as telephony (TUP) and ISDN (ISUP), the label includes the circuit identification code (CIC). The CIC contains the identity of the physical circuit that carries the call for which the signaling information is meant. The signaling link selection (SLS) field is used for load sharing between signaling links. For TUP messages, the SLS is part of the CIC field, whereas for ISUP messages, the SLS and the CIC are separate fields. Instead of an SLS, level 3 MSUs have the signaling link code (SLC) field. The SLC identifies the signaling link connecting the origination and destination SPs for the message. If the message is not related to any particular signaling link, the code 0000 is used. The lengths of the fields are not shown in Figure 7–2; they will be indicated during detailed discussions of the functions performed by the various fields.

There are a number of level 3 MSUs; a total of 27 messages are defined in ITU-T recommendation Q.704 [1]. These messages are classified into nine groups depending on the nature of functions for which the messages are employed. A 4-bit heading code H0 identifies the message group. Heading code H1, also 4 bits long, is used for identifying a message within the group. Together, H0 and H1 fields identify the level 3 message. The SIF of a level 3 message may also include a data field of variable length ($8 \times n$ bits, where n is the number of octets). For certain level 3 messages, the data field may be missing, whereas for others, the data field provides any additional information that needs to be conveyed as part of the message. The format of different level 3 messages is describe later in this chapter.

The following fields are used in the implementation of level 3 functions:

- The service information octet (SIO)
- The routing label

7.2.1 Service Information Octet (SIO)

The format of the SIO is shown in Figure 7–3. The SIO consists of two blocks, a service indicator (SI) and a subservice field. SI and subservice field codes as defined in ITU-T recommendation Q.704 [1] are shown in Tables 7–1 and 7–2, respectively.

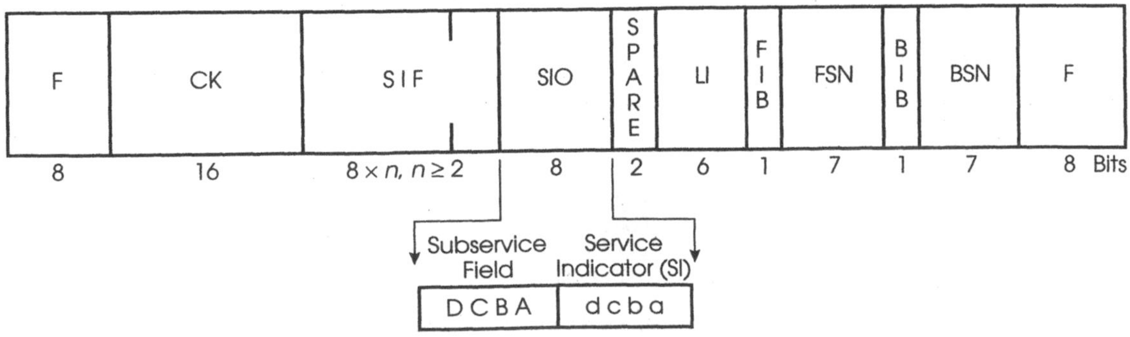

Figure 7–3 Service information octet (SIO).

Table 7-1 Service Indicator (SI) Codes

Code D C B A	Meaning	
0 0 0 0	Signaling network management	Level 3 message
0 0 0 1	Signaling network testing and maintenance	
0 0 1 0	Spare	
0 0 1 1	SCCP	
0 1 0 0	Telephone user part (TUP)	Level 4 message
0 1 0 1	ISDN user part (ISUP)	
0 1 1 0	Data user part (call and circuit related)	
0 1 1 1	Data user part (facility registration and cancellation)	
1 0 0 0	Reserved for MTP testing user part	
1 0 0 1 to 1 1 1 1	Spare	

The SIO is used for distribution of MSUs to level 3 or to the concerned user part, depending on the value of the SI code. For example, a message originating in the ISUP has an SI code 0101 inserted at the originating SP. Level 3 of the destination SP examines the SI code and determines that the MSU has been generated by the ISUP of the originating SP. The message is therefore distributed to the ISUP at level 4. Similarly, if the MSU received at an SP contains an SI code 0000, level 3 determines that the MSU is meant for signaling network management at level 3.

The 4 bits of the SI provide 16 possible codes. As seen from Table 7–2, ITU-T recommendations leave eight spare codes. These may be appropriately used in the national networks. In the United States network, three of these spare codes—namely 0001, 1101, and 1110—are used. Code 0001 is specified for "signaling network testing and maintenance specific message," and 1101 and 1110 are reserved for individual network use [2].

The signaling messages for a call may involve a number of signaling networks. For instance, signaling for an international call involves the international CCS 7 network and the national CCS 7 networks of the calling and called sides. These networks are structurally independent of one another. Refer to Figure 7–4.

The 4-bit subservice field enables distinction between the national CCS 7 network and the international CCS 7 network. The network indicator bits C and D are used for this purpose. Bits A and B that are spare may be used for assigning up to four priority levels

Table 7-2 Subservice Field Codes

Bits D	C	B A	Meaning
0	0	Spare	International network
0	1	Spare	Spare for international use
1	0	Spare	National network
1	1	Spare	Reserved for national use

Note: Bits D and C constitute the network indicator code.

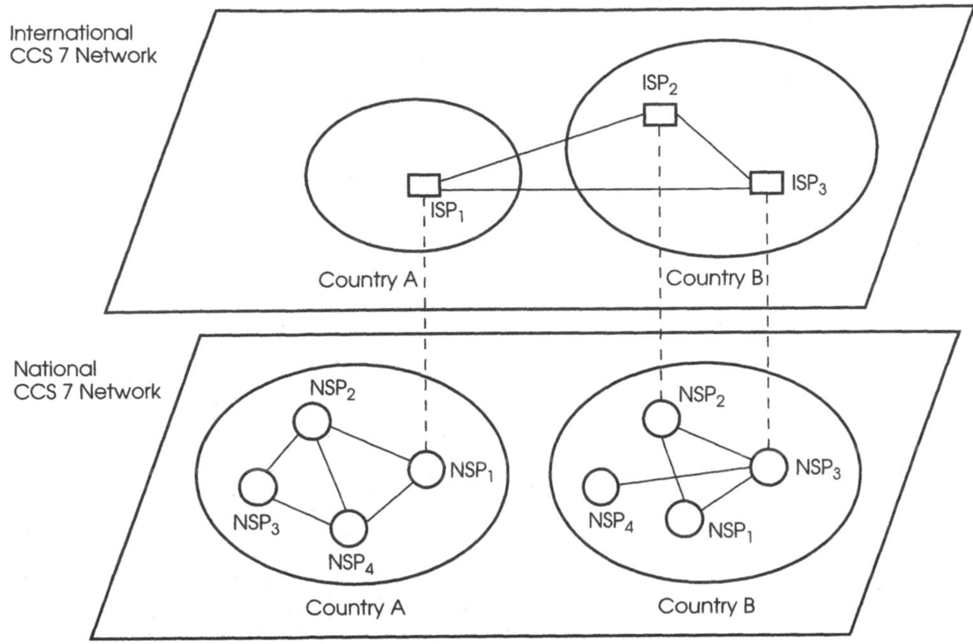

Key
ISP: International Signaling Point
NSP: National Signaling Point

Figure 7–4 Structurally independent international and national CCS 7 networks.

for MSUs in the national network. (Priority levels for MSUs are listed in Table 7–4, Section 7.6.11.)

The network indicator code 11, reserved for national use, may be used to define a second national CCS 7 network. This is relevant, for instance, when two different versions of CCS 7, such as CCITT Red Book and Blue Book versions, are implemented in the national network. With this arrangement, the protocol interworking aspects need to be considered only at the interface signaling points.

7.2.2 The Routing Label

The standard routing label, as specified for the international network in ITU-T recommendation Q.704, has a length of 32 bits divided into three fields:

1. Destination point code (DPC)
2. Origination point code (OPC)
3. Signaling link selection (SLS)

As mentioned in Section 7.2, the last field is called the signaling link code (SLC) for MTP management messages.

Figure 7–5 Standard routing label.

Figure 7–6 Routing label for the U.S. network.

The DPC identifies the SP where the message is to be delivered, whereas the OPC indicates the originating SP for the message. The function of the SLS is for load sharing between the signaling links, as discussed in Section 7.3.3. The standard routing label is shown in Figure 7–5.

Since the OPC and DPC fields are 14 bits long, a maximum of 16,344 SPs can exist in the international CCS 7 network. The standard routing label format may also be adopted for the national network when the ultimate number of SPs is unlikely to go beyond this value. In larger national networks, a modified label structure should be used. In the U.S. network for which the routing label is specified in the American National Standards Institute (ANSI) standards [3], the DPC and OPC are 24 bits long and the SLS consists of 5 bits. Refer to Figure 7–6.

7.3 Signaling Message Handling

The signaling message handling functions have three components:

1. Message discrimination function
2. Message distribution function
3. Message routing function

7.3.1 Message Discrimination and Message Distribution Functions

For a message received by an SP, the discrimination function compares the DPC in the routing label with the point code of the SP. If the two match, the discrimination function concludes that the message is meant for this SP. The next step is to determine the user part to which the message has to be supplied. This is accomplished by the distribution function. The distribution function examines the 4-bit service indicator (SI) in the service information octet (SIO) of the received MSU. The SI points to the user part for which the MSU is intended. The MSU is then delivered to the desired user part. Figure 7–7 illustrates the message discrimination and distribution functions.

If the distribution function determines that the user part identified in the SI does not exist in the SP and the received MSU cannot be delivered to the user part, a user part un-

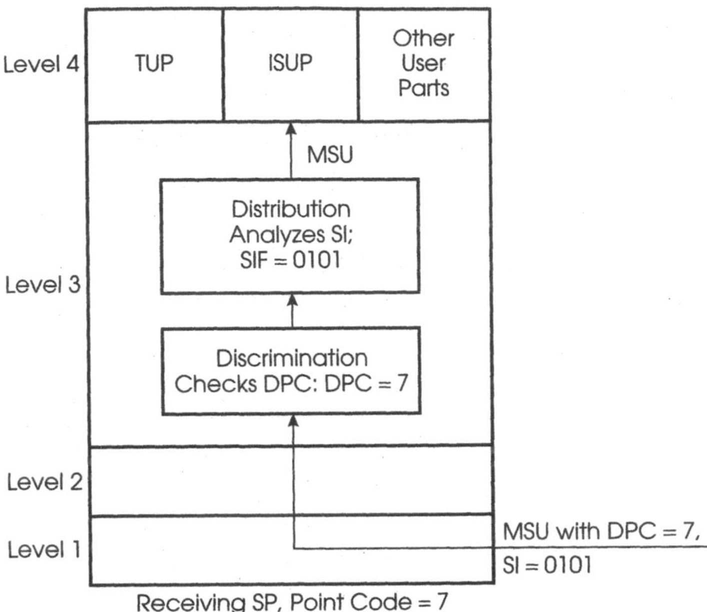

Figure 7–7 Message discrimination and distribution.

available (UPU) message is sent to the originating SP. The format of the UPU message is shown in Figure 7–8. The 4-bit field, marked ZYXW in the figure, provides the identity of the user part not found at the destination SP. For example, if SP A sends an ISUP message to SP B and if the ISUP does not exist at SP B, then level 3 of SP B returns a UPU message with the ZYXW bits coded as 0101. This indicates to SP A that ISUP is not available at SP B. The 4-bit field, marked DCBA in Figure 7–8, indicates the reasons for unavailability of the user part. On receiving a UPU message, the concerned user part in the originating SP should reduce its traffic appropriately.

If the DPC contained in a received message is different from the point code of the SP, the discrimination function knows that the message is not meant for this SP and a signal transfer function is to be performed, provided that the STP functionality is available in the SP. In this case, the message is confined to level 3, and further processing of the message is performed by the routing function.

When signaling network management functions are to be performed, messages are not delivered to a user part. Thus, an MSU with a service indicator code of 0000 (first row of Table 7–1) is processed at level 3 and does not require distribution to any of the level 4 user parts.

7.3.2 Message Routing Function

The message routing function in an SP is concerned with outgoing signaling messages. When a message is to be sent by a user part, the message routing function in level 3 determines the signaling link on which the message is to be sent. While doing so, the rout-

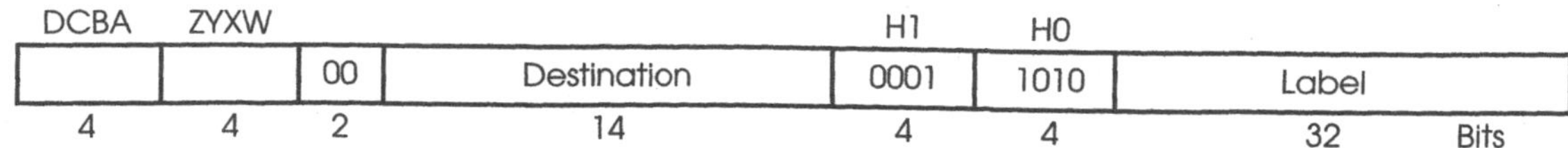

Notes:

1. Bits ZYXW are coded as follows:

   Bit Z Y X W

   0 0 1 1 SCCP
   0 1 0 0 TUP
   0 1 0 1 ISUP
   0 1 1 0 DUP
   1 0 0 0 MTP Testing User Part

   (All other combinations are spare.)

2. Bits DCBA are coded as follows:

   Bit D C B A

   0 0 0 0 Unknown
   0 0 0 1 Unequipped Remote User
   0 0 1 0 Inaccessible Remote User

   (All other combinations are spare.)

3. The destination refers to the SP that generates the UPU message.

Figure 7–8 Format of the UPU message.

ing function also ensures the balancing of the load between links if several links are available toward the destination SP.

Each node in the CCS 7 network maintains a routing table. The table is examined in combination with the DPC in the message to determine the outgoing signaling link sets available to route the message. The outgoing signaling link is then decided using the SLS field to ensure the balancing of the load.

While for most messages it is sufficient to examine the DPC to determine the route, additional information may be needed for certain messages. For example, at an international gateway exchange, two sets of point codes are to be handled, one for the national network and one for the international network. In this case, the network indicator field is examined to determine the relevant point code numbering scheme. In addition, special routing rules may be applied for certain level 3 network management messages. For example, a signaling link test message has to be routed only on the signaling link under test.

Figure 7–9 illustrates the routing function where SP A (point code 5) routes a message originating in its ISUP to SP B (point code 12). Figure 7–10 shows the routing function for an STP. The message received from SP B is first checked by the discrimination function and then routed based on the DPC.

7.3.3 Load Sharing

The purpose of load sharing is to balance the signaling traffic among available links to achieve a near uniform level 2 processing load for the signaling terminals associated with the links. This is necessary because unbalanced loading may cause congestion on some of the links.

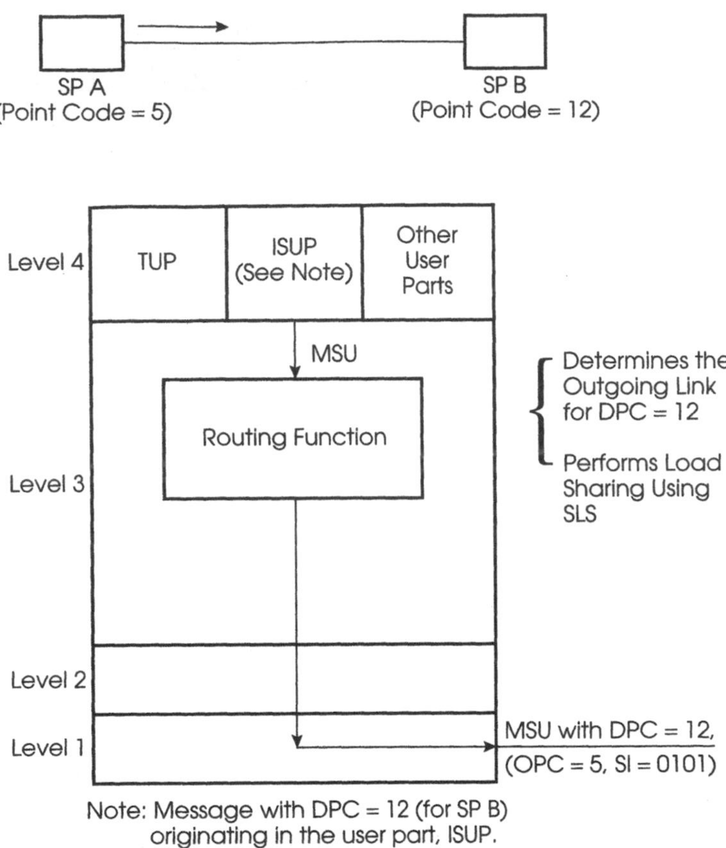

Figure 7–9 Routing function at SP A.

In its simplest form, load sharing may be performed for links within a single link set. The 4-bit SLS field permits load sharing between a maximum of 16 links of a link set, as shown in Figure 7–11. For example, a message originating at SP A may be assigned an SLS value 0000 and sent on link 1. The next message may be assigned an SLS code 0001 and sent on link 2 toward the destination. In this manner, SLS values may be assigned and messages distributed over the links in a link set.

Another more complex case is of load sharing between links not belonging to the same link set. This corresponds to a situation where more than one link set exists toward the destination SP. One or more signaling link sets operating on the basis of load sharing constitute a combined link set. In Figure 7–12, an example of a combined link set for the signaling relationship between SP A and SP D is shown. A message originating in SP A for destination SP D can be routed via a link in link set 1 or link set 2. Similarly, a choice exists between link set 3 or link set 4 at STP B. The routes are A–B–D, A–C–D, and A–B–C–D. The least significant bit in the SLS is used to select one of the two link sets at SP A. This gives a possibility of using the remaining 3 bits for sharing load for up to eight

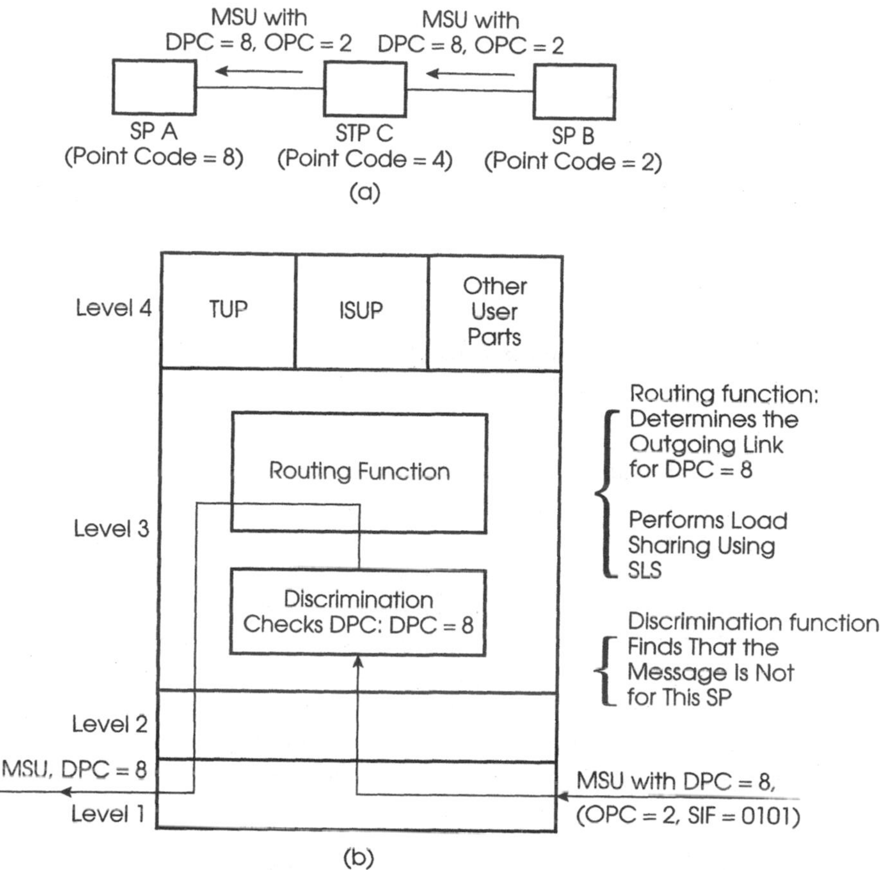

Figure 7–10 Routing function at STP C.

links in each link set. At STP B, another bit is used for selection between link sets 3 or 4, leaving a possibility of selection of one out of four links in each of these link sets.

While implementing load sharing based on the above principles, care should be taken to ensure that all messages for a given user transaction in one direction take the same route. This is necessary to avoid missequencing of the messages, since messages taking different routes may suffer different delays. In the example of Figure 7–12, if a

SLS = 0000 (Link 1)
SLS = 0001 (Link 2)
SLS = 0010 (Link 3)
⋮
SLS = 1111 (Link 16)
SP A SP B

Figure 7–11 Load sharing between 16 links in one link set for messages from SP A to destination SP B; associated mode of signaling.

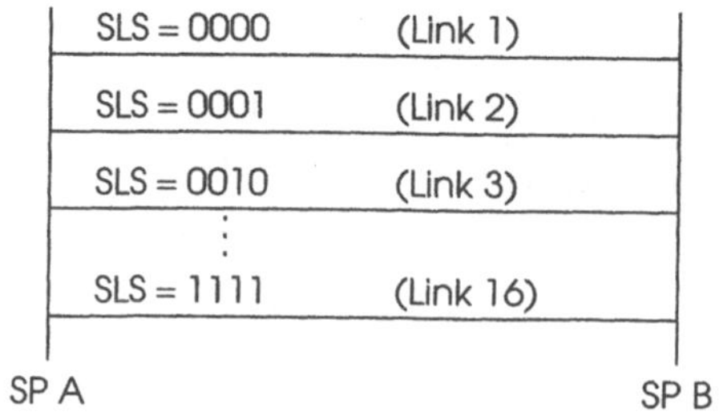

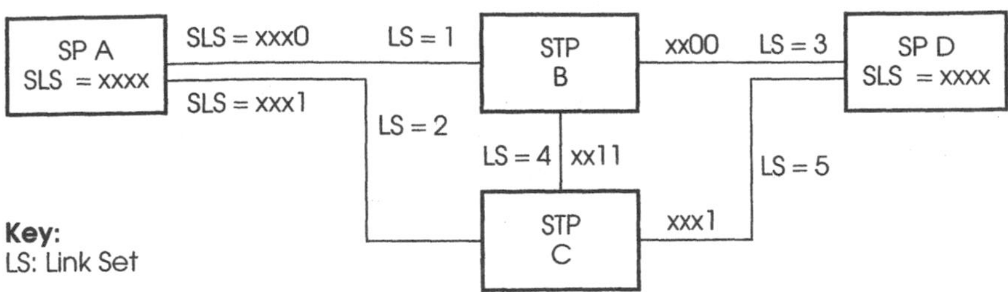

Figure 7–12 Load sharing in a combined link set.

telephone call is made from exchange A to exchange D, all forward messages from SP A to SP D for the call should take the same route, say route A–B–D. This is done by using the same SLS code for these messages. All the backward messages for this call may, however, follow a different route, such as D–C–A.

The SLS load-sharing method does not provide for the even sharing of the load in all cases. The load distribution is not exactly equal in a link set where the number of links is not a power of 2, that is, 1, 2, 4, 8. For example, if the number of links in a link set is seven, the 16 possible SLS values may be distributed as follows: three SLS codes each for two links and two SLS codes each for the remaining five links. In this case, equal load distribution results for five links, while the other two links (with three SLS codes) carry higher traffic.

7.3.3.1 Load Sharing in the U.S. Network

The basic structure of the U.S. national CCS 7 network is shown in Figure 7–13. An SP is connected to a pair of STPs by a pair of link sets, one link set to each STP. The links are called A-links. The two STPs in the pair are interconnected by signaling links called C-links. The STP pair is called a mated STP pair. One mated STP pair is connected to an-

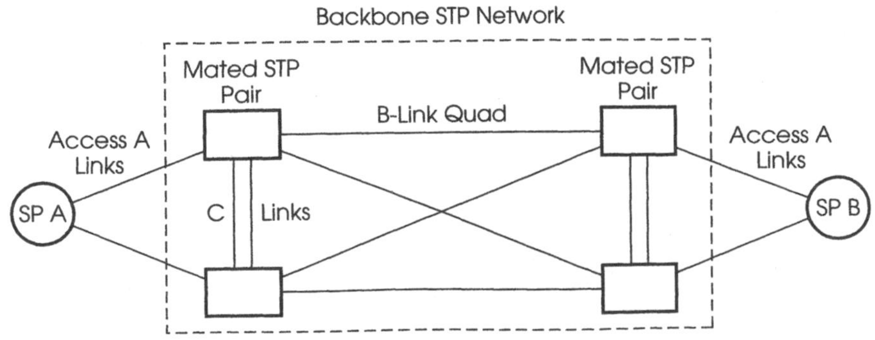

Figure 7–13 Structure of the CCS 7 network with single hierarchy of STPs.

other STP pair by a signaling link quad structure, called B-links. A number of STP pairs so interconnected form the "backbone" STP network. Note that the designation of links (namely, A, B, and C) is only for the purpose of readily identifying their position in the CCS 7 network structure; they do not possess any other distinguishing characteristics.

The network of Figure 7–13 is an example of a single-level STP hierarchy. Depending on factors such as the volume of traffic and the capacity of an individual STP, signaling networks with two levels of STP hierarchy may also be implemented [4].

The load sharing in the U.S. network is performed on the basis of the 5-bit SLS field. For load sharing in a combined link set, the link set is chosen on the basis of the least significant bit of SLS. When this bit is 0, the message is routed on link set 1. For the next message, this bit is 1 and the message is sent over link set 2. Prior to sending the message on the chosen link set, the least significant bit is rotated, (that is, it is moved to the leftmost position), and all other bits are shifted right by one bit position. Refer to Figure 7–14(a). The bit rotation permits link set selection at the next node based on the least significant bit. Link set selection proceeds independently at each node while following a uniform procedure of selection based on the least significant bit position. An example of end-to-end routing is given in Figure 7–14(b).

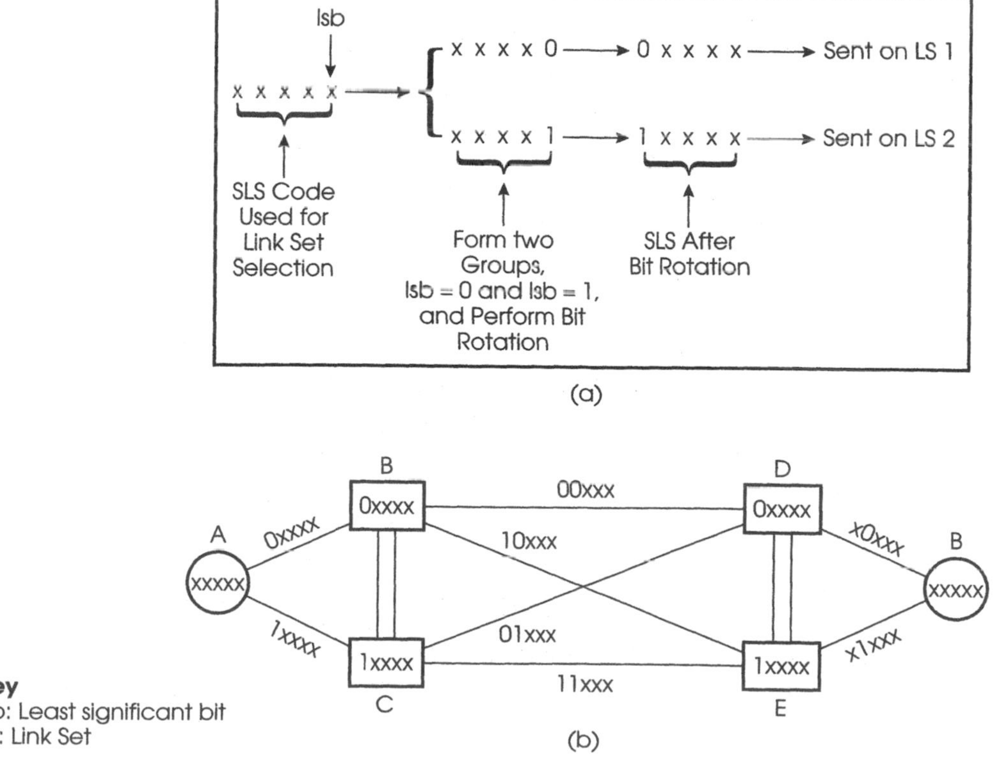

Figure 7–14 Example of end-to-end routing: (a) load sharing at an SP; (b) example of end-to-end routing.

7.4 Signaling Network Management

Signaling network management primarily provides two functions: reconfiguration in the event of failures and traffic management during congestion. Failures may occur in any of the elements constituting the CCS 7 network: the signaling links, the SPs, and the STPs. Signaling routes consist of these network elements, and failures may render some of the routes unavailable for signaling. In the event of failures, signaling traffic is diverted to alternative links and routes. For congestion in parts of the signaling network, the traffic has to be reduced until congestion abates. Based on these considerations, signaling network management consists of three broad functions:

1. Signaling link management
2. Signaling traffic management
3. Signaling route management

7.5 Signaling Link Management

The signaling link management functions in an SP are designed to control the links connected to the SP and to maintain a certain minimum capability of carrying signaling traffic, both under normal operation and in the event of failures.

The following procedures are performed:

- Link activation
- Link restoration
- Link deactivation
- Link set activation

A signaling link may be either "available" or "unavailable" for carrying signaling traffic. A number of conditions may render a signaling link unavailable. One condition, obviously, is the failure of the link. The link is recognized by level 3 as failed when a failure condition is conveyed by level 2.

Another unavailable condition may be the "inactive" status of the link. Initially, at the time of installation, all the links in a link set are out of operation and are considered "inactive." The links are activated one by one by performing the level 2 initial alignment procedure described in Chapter 6. After the successful completion of alignment at both ends, the link has the status "active" and is ready to be brought into service by level 3. This process of making a signaling link ready to carry signaling traffic is called *link activation.* In a link set, a certain number of links must be "active" to carry the anticipated signaling traffic. As a result of failures, however, the number of active links may fall below the minimum required threshold. New links are brought into service, and link activation is required in this situation. Link activation may also be initiated in response to increased signaling traffic so that additional links may be brought into service.

7.5.1 Signaling Data Link and Signaling Terminal Allocation

Each signaling link in operation consists of a signaling data link with a signaling terminal at either end. Prior to the initiation of link activation, it is necessary to allocate a signaling data link and signaling terminals. A signaling data link is essentially a timeslot of a pulse code modulation (PCM) system used for conveying signaling information. When not associated with a signaling terminal, this timeslot may be used for carrying circuit switched speech or data traffic. To make the timeslot available for signaling in such cases, the associated circuits are blocked at both ends. The signaling terminals at an SP may be a pooled resource, and any signaling terminal from the common pool may be assigned to a signaling data link to constitute a signaling link.

Depending on the degree of automation in performing these procedures, three alternatives are specified:

1. Basic signaling link management
2. Automatic allocation of signaling terminals only
3. Automatic allocation of both signaling data link and signaling terminals

In basic signaling link management, signaling data links and signaling terminals are manually allocated to constitute a signaling link. The basic method represents a minimum capability that should be available for the international signaling network.

In automatic allocation of signaling terminals only, an idle signaling terminal is chosen, if available. An idle terminal is one that is not connected to a signaling data link. If an idle terminal is not available, then a terminal associated with a signaling link for which the initial alignment procedure could not be completed successfully may be chosen. The signaling terminals chosen automatically at either end are then assigned to a manually selected signaling data link.

For automatic allocation of both signaling terminal and signaling data link, the procedure followed for allocation of signaling terminal is the same as described above.

Regarding the automatic allocation of signaling data link, the same signaling data link has to be assigned at either end. (In fact, this requirement has to be met regardless of the method chosen.) Therefore, the SP that makes the selection of signaling data link first, conveys the identity of the data link to the other SP by sending a signaling data link connection (SDLC) order message. The format of this message is shown in Figure 7–15.

Referring to Figure 7–16, assume that SP A is the first to select a signaling data link. It then sends the circuit identification code (CIC) of the data link in a 12-bit field as part of the SDLC order message to SP B on one of the active links connecting the SPs.

Spare	Signaling Data Link Identity	Heading Code H1	Heading Code H0	Label		
0000	xx. x	0001	1000	SLC	OPC	DPC
4	12	4	4	4	14	14 Bits

Figure 7–15 Signaling data link connection (SDLC) order message.

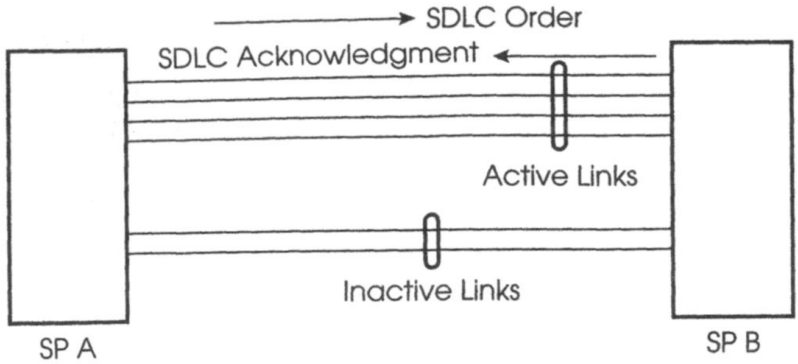

Figure 7–16 Automatic allocation of the signaling data link.

The link used to send the SDLC order message is determined by the SLS in the routing label. On receipt of the message, SP B sends a signaling–data link–connection acknowledgment message. The format of this message is shown in Figure 7–17. The H1 field in the acknowledgment message indicates one of the following three possibilities:

Bits D C B A

0 0 1 0	connection-successful signal
0 0 1 1	connection-not-successful signal
0 1 0 0	connection-not-possible signal

A connection-successful signal corresponds to a positive acknowledgment. It is sent after the receiving end has successfully assigned a signaling terminal. Both ends can now attempt activation of the signaling link as described in the next section. A connection-not-successful signal indicates a request for the selection of an alternative link. Accordingly, the sending end generates a new signaling–data link–connection order specifying an alternative data link. The chosen alternative data link is the one with the highest priority among the inactive links. If the receiving SP is not able to assign a signaling terminal, a negative acknowledgment is sent in the form of a connection-not-possible signal.

Timing supervision is provided by timer T7. If an acknowledgment is not received for a signaling–data link–connection order within time T7, the order is repeated. The value of T7 is specified in the range of 1 to 2 seconds.

If both ends send the signaling–data link–connection order at the same time, possibly for different signaling data links, the choice made by the higher-order point code pre-

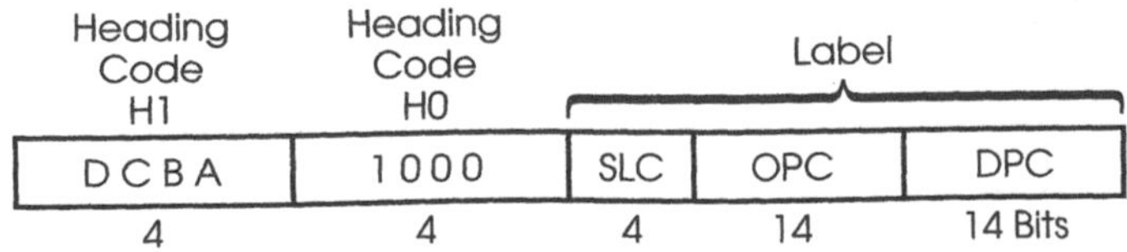

Figure 7–17 Signaling–data link–connection (SDLC) acknowledgment message.

vails. Thus, the signaling point with the higher-order point code will not send an acknowledgment message while awaiting acknowledgment for its own signaling–data link–connection order.

7.5.2 Signaling Link Activation

The signaling link activation procedure is shown in Figure 7–18. An inactive link reaches an active status when the initial alignment procedure has been successfully completed at level 2. In case the initial alignment procedure fails, it is repeated after a time delay T17. The delay is introduced to avoid oscillation of initial alignment failure and link restart. The value of timer T17 should be between 800 and 1,500 ms. After the successful completion of the level 2 initial alignment procedure at both ends, the link reaches an active status. Before making the link available for signaling traffic, however, a signaling link test is performed on the link as specified in CCITT recommendation Q.707 [5]. (The test is also performed during link restoration.) The link carries signaling traffic only after successful completion of the link test. The actual link test is described in Chapter 11.

7.5.3 Signaling Link Restoration

Signaling link restoration refers to the procedure to be followed to bring a previously failed link back into service. Before attempting restoration, the traffic of the failed link is diverted to other active links according to the changeover procedure described in Section 7.6.1. (The changeover procedure is part of signaling traffic management function.) An attempt to restore the link is then made by performing the link activation procedure described above. Successful alignment is followed by the signaling link test. Upon

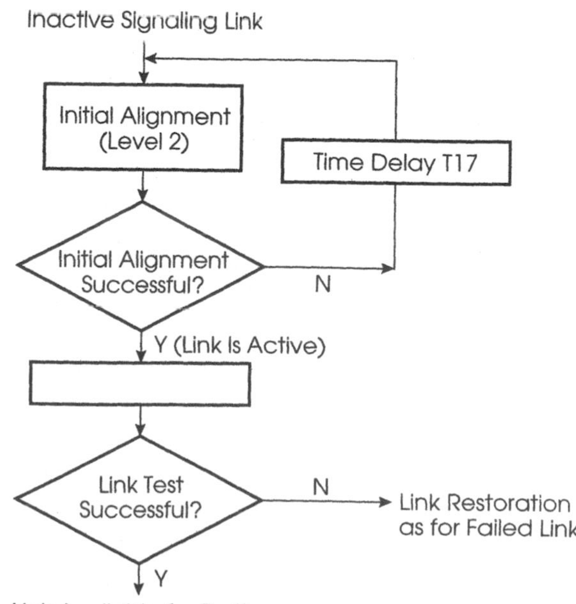

Figure 7–18 Signaling link activation.

satisfactory completion of the signaling link activation procedure, the link is restored. The link may carry signaling traffic after the changeback procedure (Section 7.6.2).

If the link activation is not successful, further action depends on the method followed for link management. For basic signaling link management, the signaling data link or signaling terminal is replaced manually.

For the signaling link management procedure corresponding to automatic allocation of signaling terminals only, a new signaling terminal is assigned automatically, and the restoration of the link is reattempted using the same signaling data link. If the restoration attempt is not successful, it is reasonable to assume that the signaling data link is faulty. Therefore, another available signaling data link in the link set is manually assigned to the signaling terminal and another link activation is attempted.

For the procedure corresponding to automatic allocation of both signaling data link and signaling terminal, failure of the initial alignment or link test is followed by the automatic allocation of a new signaling data link or signaling terminal.

7.5.4 Signaling Link Deactivation

A link can be deactivated provided that it is not carrying any signaling traffic. Therefore, before deactivation, signaling traffic from the link to be deactivated is diverted to other links by a changeover procedure conducted at either end of the link. The need for link deactivation may arise when the number of active links in a link set exceeds a maximum threshold. In such a case, the link with the minimum priority may be deactivated; thus, the timeslot associated with the signaling data link is made available for carrying circuit switched traffic. The signaling terminal associated with the deactivated link is then assigned to a common pool of free signaling terminals.

In basic link management, link deactivation is manually initiated, whereas in automatic link management, deactivation is initiated automatically.

7.5.5 Signaling Link Set Activation

The signaling link set activation procedure is performed when all the links in a link set require activation, as would be the case when none of the links in the link set is active. This situation arises when a link set is to be brought into service for the first time or when a link set is to be restarted after failure of all the links. Processor restart in an SP would also require activation of the connected link sets.

Depending on the urgency to reestablish signaling on the link set, two alternatives are available:

1. Link set normal activation
2. Link set emergency restart

In link set normal activation, normal proving takes place. In link set emergency restart, emergency proving of the links is performed at level 2 to shorten the activation time. In both cases, signal link activation is attempted simultaneously on as many links in the link set as possible. Signaling traffic may commence as soon as the first link is successfully activated.

7.6 Signaling Traffic and Signaling Route Management

When a signaling link becomes unavailable (for example, due to failure), it is necessary to divert the signaling traffic carried by the unavailable link to other available links. Similarly, when a signaling route to a destination becomes unavailable, the traffic needs to be diverted to other signaling routes to the destination. The redistribution of traffic is also required on restoration of a signaling link or signaling route. In the event of congestion at an SP, the traffic to that SP should be reduced until the congestion conditions abate. Traffic diversion is also involved in the failure of an SP and its subsequent restoration. An important objective of traffic management is that signaling messages should not be lost and their sequence be correctly maintained during traffic redistribution.

The following procedures are available for signaling traffic management:

- Changeover (Section 7.6.1)
- Changeback (Section 7.6.2)
- Forced rerouting (Section 7.6.4)
- Controlled rerouting (Section 7.6.7)
- Management inhibiting (Section 7.6.9)
- MTP restart (Section 7.6.10)
- Signaling traffic flow control (Section 7.6.11)

Signaling route management is concerned with the availability of signaling routes between signaling points. The procedures used for this purpose are

- Transfer prohibited (Section 7.6.3)
- Transfer restricted (Section 7.6.5)
- Transfer allowed (Section 7.6.6)
- Signaling route set test (Section 7.6.8)
- Signaling route set congestion and transfer controlled (Section 7.6.12)

7.6.1 Changeover

The changeover procedure is used to divert signaling traffic from a link that has become unavailable to other alternative available links, without loss, duplication, or missequencing of messages. The links to which the traffic of the unavailable link is diverted may be carrying their own traffic. The existing signaling traffic on these links should not be disturbed as a result of the changeover.

The procedure consists of the following steps:

1. On determining that an existing in-service link can no longer be used, an SP stops the transmission and reception of MSUs on the link.
2. The SP next checks for the availability of an alternative active link or links. Here, three cases may arise as follows (cases 1 and 2 correspond to the changeover to links within the same link set):

Case 1: When an active and unblocked link, not carrying traffic, is available in the same link set, the changeover procedure is initiated on this link. This case corresponds to Figure 7–19(a).

Case 2: When one or more links already carrying traffic are available within the same link set, one or more alternative links may be selected for attempted changeover of traffic. This case is shown in Figure 7–19(b). When the traffic to be diverted is low, only one of the alternative available links may be used. When only one link is used, the link with the highest priority is selected.

Case 3: When no alternative links in the link set (to which the unavailable link belongs) are available, an alternative route to the concerned remote signaling point is selected. An example is shown in Figure 7–19(c).

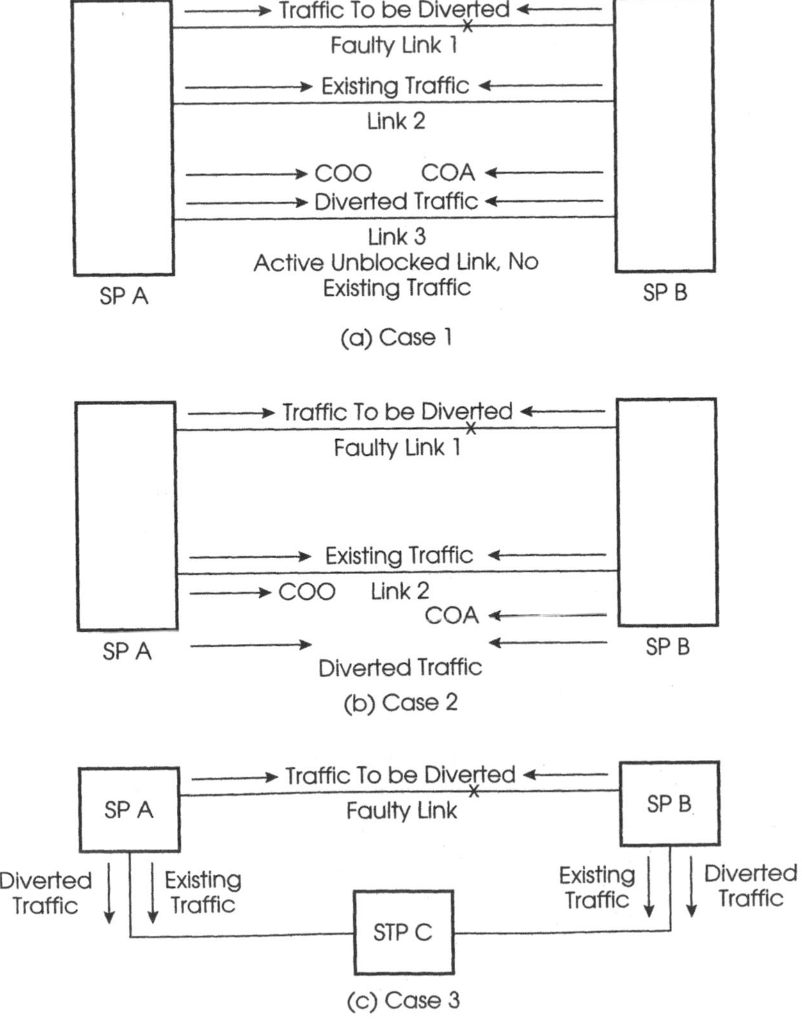

Figure 7–19 Examples of changeover.

3. The SP initiating changeover sends a changeover order (COO) message to the remote SP on an alternative link as determined in step 2. The remote SP responds by a changeover acknowledgment (COA). Both the COO and COA are sent without priority along with existing signaling traffic. The SP sending the COO expects to receive the COA from the remote SP within time T2. The value for timer T2 (waiting for changeover acknowledgment) has been specified as 700 to 2,000 ms. When the signaling route is known to contain satellite sections, the minimum limit is 1,400 ms.

The formats for the COO and COA are identical except for different values of the H1 field (see Figure 7–20). In addition to the DPC and OPC, the label contains the identity of the link that has become unavailable in the SLC field.

4. Changeover without losing, duplicating, or missequencing the messages is the objective of buffer updating. In the changeover order, the SP sends a 7-bit forward sequence number (FSN) of the last correctly received message on the deactivated link. The SP also receives similar information from the remote SP in the changeover acknowledgment message. With the identity of the last correctly received message, the level 2 retransmission buffer of the unavailable link is updated at both ends.
5. The messages already stored in retransmission and the transmission buffers are now sent on the alternative links. The diverted traffic has no priority over the traffic that may already exist on the alternative links.

If timer T2 expires and no COA message is received from the other SP, then the new traffic is nevertheless started on the alternative links. The retrieval function (steps 4 and 5 above) is not performed, however; thus, in this case, a few messages may be lost. An identical procedure is followed if a COO or a COA is received with an unreasonable value of FSN. Another abnormal condition may be the receipt of a COA message by an SP that has not sent a COO message previously. In this case, the COA message is ignored.

After an SP recognizes the need for a changeover, the diversion of signaling traffic should be performed as speedily as possible. Therefore, as part of MTP performance parameters ITU-T recommendation Q.706 [6] prescribes the maximum permissible time limit

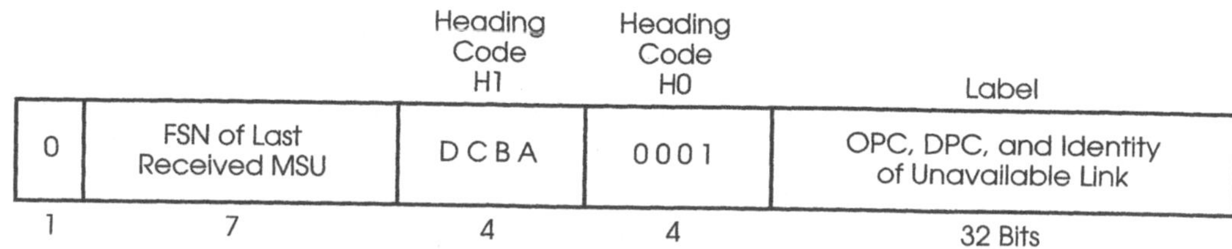

Figure 7–20 Format of changeover order (COO) and changeover acknowledgment (COA) messages.

for sending a COO message after the link has become unavailable. This time should not exceed 500 ms. Similarly, the permissible time limit within which the COA message must be sent by an SP after the receipt of a COO message (answer time to COO) is specified at 300 ms. These values also hold good for an emergency changeover, described in the next section.

7.6.1.1 Emergency Changeover

If the signaling link becomes unavailable through failure of the associated signaling terminal, it may not be possible to obtain the FSN of the last correctly received message from level 2. In this eventuality, the SP, while initiating changeover, sends an emergency changeover order instead of the normal changeover order described in the previous section. The remote SP responds by sending back an emergency changeover acknowledgment. The format for the emergency changeover message is shown in Figure 7–21.

Figure 7–22 shows an example in which SP A initiates emergency changeover. As indicated in the figure, the following steps are performed:

1. Level 3 at SP A finds that it is not possible to obtain the last accepted FSN from level 2 corresponding to signaling link 1.
2. Since a problem exists with level 2 corresponding to link 1, further MSUs generated by the ISDN user part (ISUP) for this link are stored in a level 3 buffer instead of being sent to level 2 for transmission.
3. Based on considerations discussed in the previous section (cases 1, 2, and 3), an alternative link is determined for diversion of traffic. Assuming that link 2 is to be used for changeover, an emergency changeover order (ECO) is sent on this link to remote SP B.
4. On receipt of an emergency changeover acknowledgment (ECA) from remote SP B, SP A starts transmission of MSUs beginning with the MSUs stored in the buffer.

If however, SP B initiates (normal) changeover, then SP A receives the changeover order and attempts to update the level 2 retransmission buffer using the FSN received in the changeover message. Irrespective of the success of buffer updating, an emergency changeover acknowledgment is sent by SP A to the remote SP. Upon receipt of the emergency changeover acknowledgment, the signaling traffic is diverted to the alternative

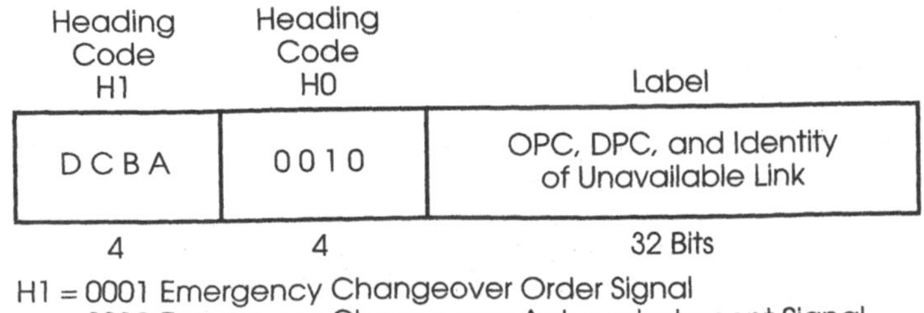

Figure 7–21 Format of emergency changeover messages.

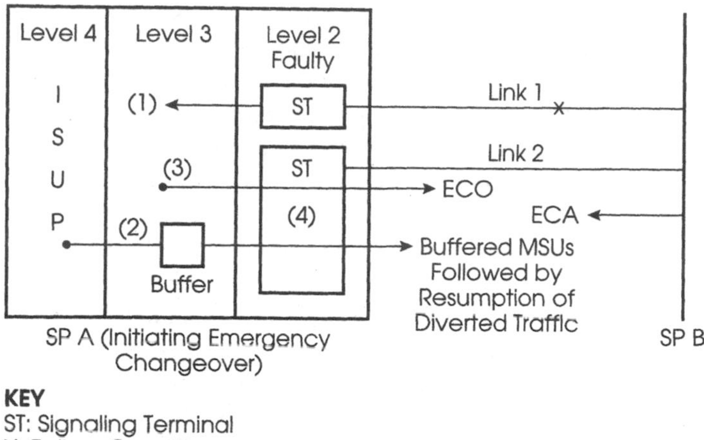

Figure 7–22 Example of emergency changeover.

links. However, messages stored in the transmission and retransmission buffers of the unavailable link are not transmitted.

Thus, temporary disruption of signaling traffic of the failed link is expected to occur during emergency changeover. Another point of difference from the normal changeover procedure is that the link from which traffic has been diverted is taken out of service by sending "out of service" LSSUs (SIOS) on the link.

7.6.1.2 Time-Controlled Changeover

Time-controlled changeover is employed when it is not possible or desirable to exchange COO and COA messages between the signaling points. An example is the changeover for a link that has been inhibited. (Link inhibition is described in Section 7.6.9.) Traffic of the inhibited link should be diverted to alternative links without causing the inhibited link to fail. Since a changeover order would cause the link to fail, exchange of COO and COA messages should be avoided.

The signaling point deciding on the changeover diverts the signaling traffic of the inhibited link to alternative links after a delay of time T1. The T1 timer (the timer to avoid missequencing on changeover) has a range of 500 to 1200 ms. When satellite links are used, the range specified is 800 to 1200 ms.

7.6.2 Changeback

The changeback procedure reverses the function of changeover by restoring the traffic carried by the link prior to changeover. This is needed when an unavailable link from which the traffic had been diverted by the changeover procedure becomes available. The alternative links continue to carry their own signaling traffic.

The first step in the changeback procedure is to determine which alternative links are carrying the diverted traffic as a consequence of changeover. The procedure described below applies to diversion of traffic from one alternative link to a new available link.

The concerned traffic on the alternative link is stopped, and all new messages corresponding to this traffic are stored temporarily in a changeback buffer. A changeback declaration (CBD) message is then sent on the alternative link. This message indicates to the remote SP that no further messages corresponding to the traffic being diverted will be received on the alternative link. The remote SP sends a changeback acknowledgment (CBA). Upon receipt of this message, the SP restarts the traffic on the new available link.

If a changeback acknowledgment is not received in response to a changeback declaration within a period T4, then the CBD is repeated. On the second attempt, a new timer T5 is started. Even if no CBA is received before the expiration of time T5, the traffic is restarted on the link made available. However, a maintenance function is informed about the lack of receipt of changeback acknowledgment. The value range of both timers T4 and T5 is identical at 500 to 1200 ms. (For satellite links, the lowest value is 800 ms.) In a particular implementation, the values of T4 and T5, although lying in the permissible range, may be different.

Figure 7–23 shows the format of the changeback message. Notice the presence of an 8-bit changeback code field. This field is useful when an SP initiates changeback on several alternative links at the same time. After stopping the concerned traffic on each alternative link, a changeback declaration is sent on each alternative link with a different value of changeback code. Any new messages to be transmitted to the remote SP for the concerned traffic may be stored in changeback buffers. The remote SP returns a changeback acknowledgment with the same changeback code as in the changeback message being acknowledged. This enables the SP to determine the alternative link whose signaling traffic is to be sent on the newly available link. The messages stored in the changeback buffer are sent on the new link followed by the restored signaling traffic. An example of the changeback procedure is shown in Figure 7–24.

There is also a special case of changeback, where one of the SPs has undergone MTP restart (discussed in Section 7.6.10) and then a changeback is initiated due to links made available towards the restarted SP. To minimize the possibility of missequencing, the SP adjacent to the restarted SP waits for a timer T3 before resuming traffic on the newly available links. The value range of timer T3 is the same as that of T4 and T5 timers.

7.6.3 Transfer Prohibited

The transfer prohibited message is sent by an STP to adjacent SPs when a particular destination becomes inaccessible to the STP. Consider Figure 7–25. Assume that the link BC is unavailable. If link BD also becomes unavailable, then signaling point D is no

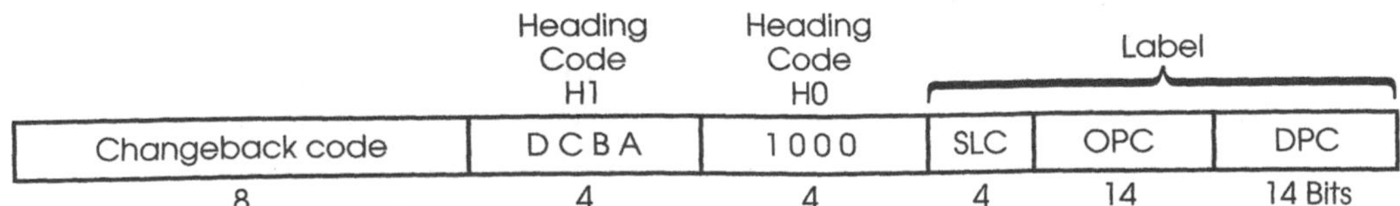

Figure 7–23 Changeback message.

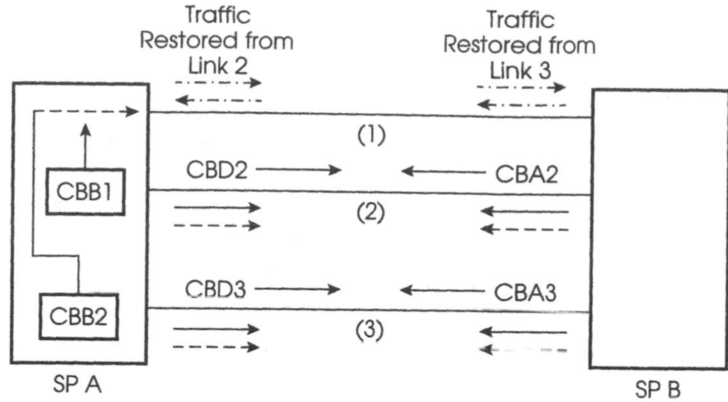

Notes:

Link 1: Newly activated link.

Links 2, 3: Alternative links ——→ traffic for changeback.
- - - -→ own traffic of the links.
-·-·-·→ restored traffic

CBD2 is changeback declaration with changeback code = *x* (for example).
CBA2 is changeback acknowledgment with changeback code = *x*.

CBD3 is changeback declaration with changeback code = *y* (for example).
CBA3 is changeback acknowledgment with changeback code = *y*.

CBB1 and CBB2 are changeback buffers for link 1 and link 2 respectively.

Time supervision: Timers T4 and T5.

Figure 7–24 Changeback from more than one alternative link (changeback buffers shown for SP A only).

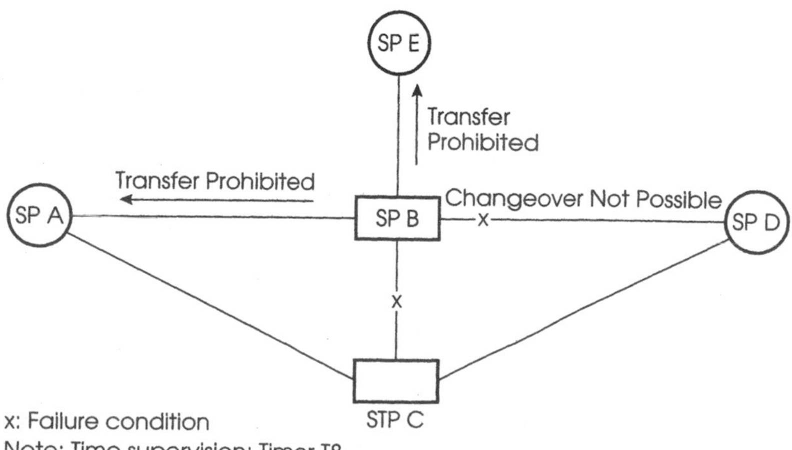

Figure 7–25 Example of the use of transfer prohibited message and forced rerouting.

longer accessible from STP B. Because no alternative links are available between B and D, changeover is not possible. The messages for the unavailable link BD, stored in the retransmission buffer at STP B, are discarded. The fact that messages to destination D can no longer be transferred by STP B is conveyed to the adjacent SPs A and E so that they do not send messages destined for SP B. This is done by transfer prohibited messages to SP A and SP E. Transfer prohibited messages are always sent to adjacent SPs.

The transmission of a transfer prohibited message may take place by the broadcast method or the response method. With the broadcast message, the STP sends transfer prohibited messages to all adjacent SPs when it recognizes that a destination is inaccessible. With the response method, the STP sends transfer prohibited messages only to the SPs that have sent messages to it meant for the inaccessible destination.

Timer T8 (the transfer prohibited inhibition timer) is started both for the broadcast method and the response method. It has a range of 800 to 1,200 ms. A transfer prohibited message is sent only if timer T8 is not running, since the running of timer T8 indicates that the sending of a transfer prohibited message is already in progress. Hence, timer T8 avoids repetition of transfer prohibited messages. The format of the transfer prohibited message is shown in Figure 7–26.

7.6.4 Response to Transfer Prohibited: Forced Rerouting

The SP receiving the transfer prohibited message performs forced rerouting. Forced rerouting is part of the traffic management function. Referring to the example of Figure 7–25, SP A, upon receipt of the transfer prohibited message, stops the traffic pertaining to the route A–B–D and stores such messages in the forced rerouting buffer. It then determines an alternative route—for example, route A–C–D—via STP C. The traffic to destination D is then restored over the new route, starting with the messages stored in the forced rerouting buffer.

7.6.5 Transfer Restricted

The transfer restricted procedure is prescribed as a national option; it is not implemented in the international CCS 7 network. In this procedure, as opposed to the total prohibition of messages to a destination in the transfer prohibited procedure, an STP notifies adjacent SPs, by means of transfer restricted messages, that they should no longer send their messages to the restricted destination if possible. This procedure may be used, for instance, when congestion exists on a link set between the STP and the destination SP.

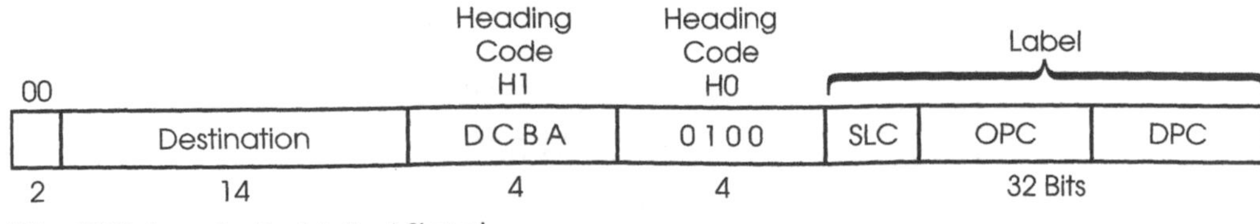

Figure 7–26 Transfer prohibited message.

Transfer restriction in such situations helps avoid further overloading of the congested part of the network.

The format of the transfer restricted message is the same as for transfer prohibited message. The heading codes H0 and H1 are 0100 and 0011, respectively. The transfer restricted procedure is prescribed for the U.S. network [2].

7.6.6 Transfer Allowed

When a previously inaccessible SP becomes accessible to an STP, an indication is given to other adjacent SPs by means of transfer allowed messages. In Figure 7–27, if a previously unavailable link BD is restored, then SP D becomes accessible from STP B. To enable SPs A and E to route their messages to destination D via STP B, STP B sends transfer allowed messages to SPs A and E. Since STP C still is inaccessible from STP B, transfer allowed message cannot be sent to STP C. The format of the transfer allowed message is shown in Figure 7–28.

7.6.7 Response to Transfer Allowed: Controlled Rerouting

Upon receiving a transfer allowed message from an adjacent STP, an SP initiates controlled rerouting. The transmission of messages toward the destination on the alternative route is stopped. In the example of Figure 7–27, at SP A, traffic toward SP D carried along route A–C–D is stopped and further traffic for SP D is stored in a controlled rerouting buffer. Simultaneously, timer T6 is started. Upon expiration of timer T6, the traffic toward destination D is started on the normal route A–B–D, beginning with the messages stored in the controlled rerouting buffer. The delay introduced by timer T6 reduces the possibility of out-of-sequence reception of messages at the destination SP D. The value of the timer is between 500 and 1200 ms. For satellite links, the lower limit of the range is raised to 800 ms. Table 7–3 shows the before and after routing from SP A and SP E to SP D.

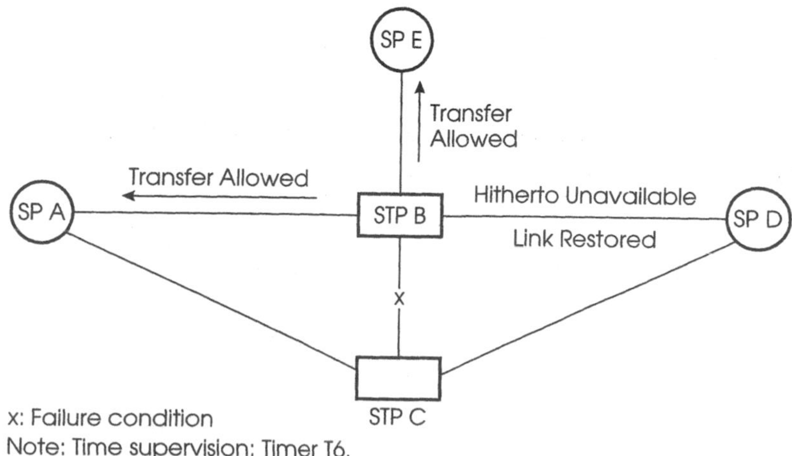

Figure 7–27 Example of the use of the transfer allowed message and controlled rerouting.

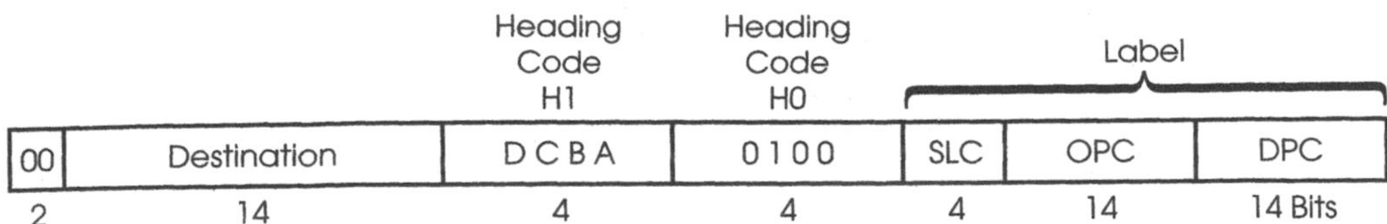

Figure 7–28 Transfer allowed message.

7.6.8 Signaling Route Set Test

A signaling route set test is a signaling route management function employed when an SP receives a transfer prohibited or transfer restricted message for a particular destination from an adjacent STP. The purpose of this test is to find out when the transfer prohibited or restricted condition ceases to exist so that traffic to the destination may be routed through the STP. A signaling route set message whose format is shown in Figure 7–29 is sent from the SP to the STP that had previously sent the transfer prohibited or transfer restricted message.

The destination field contains the point code of the destination SP for which a transfer prohibited or transfer restricted message had been received and toward which the availability of a signaling route through the STP is being tested.

Figure 7–30 shows an example of a route set test procedure. The signaling routes between SP A and SP D are A–C–D and A–B–D. Assuming that the link set between STP C and SP D becomes inaccessible or restricted, STP C sends a transfer prohibited (TFP) or transfer restricted (TFR) message to SP A. SP A now sends signaling route set test (RST) messages to STP C at intervals of T10 until a transfer allowed message is received from STP C. Timer T10 is called "waiting to repeat signaling route set test message" and has a value in the range of 30 to 60 seconds. When the transfer prohibited or restricted condition ceases to exist, a transfer allowed (TFA) message is sent by STP C to SP A, and SP A thereafter commences signaling traffic to destination SP D on the route A–C–D.

7.6.9 Management Inhibiting

A link that experiences either too many changeovers or changebacks in a short period or a significant error rate may require maintenance and testing. For this purpose, the link is inhibited, that is, it can no longer carry signaling traffic generated by the user parts.

Table 7–3 Routing Table for Destination D Before and After Controlled Rerouting Corresponding to Figure 7–27

	At SP A		At SP E	
Link	Before	After	Before	After
Normal	—	A–B–D	—	E–B–D
Alternative	A–C–D	A–C–D	—	—

		Heading Code H1	Heading Code H0	Label		
00	Destination	D C B A	0 1 0 1	SLC	OPC	DPC
2	14	4	4	4	14	14 Bits

H1 = 0001 for Signaling Route Set Test Message for Prohibited Destination
= 0010 for Signaling Route Set Test Message for Restricted Destination

Figure 7–29 Signaling route set test message.

However, the link carries test and maintenance messages and its status remains unchanged for level 2. Inhibiting is a signaling traffic management function and may be requested by either end of the link.

Inhibition of a signaling link takes place only if inhibition does not result in SP destinations becoming inaccessible. A link remains inhibited until it is uninhibited by a management action or by a routing function when the latter finds that a destination has become inaccessible and there are inhibited links in the link set to that destination. By uninhibiting in such situations, isolation of a destination from the signaling network is avoided. Uninhibiting is requested by the SP that originally requested inhibition. Forced uninhibiting can be requested by either SP.

The management inhibit message (MIM) contains only three fields: the label and the two heading codes H0 and H1. The SLC in the label field indicates the signaling link to be inhibited or uninhibited. A total of eight management inhibit messages, corresponding to different H1 codes, are specified. Refer to Figure 7–31.

An example of the inhibiting and uninhibiting procedures is shown in Figure 7–32. A possible scenario is presented, illustrating the use of link inhibit (LIN), link inhibit acknowledgment (LIA), link local inhibit test (LLT), link remote inhibit test (LRT), link uninhibit (LUN), and link uninhibit acknowledgment (LUA) signals. Other scenarios are also possible. Timers T22 and T23 are used to implement an inhibit test procedure. The basic purpose of this procedure is to ensure that the same inhibition status exists on both ends of the link. LLT messages are sent with a periodicity of T22 by the SP that initiated inhibition. LRT messages are sent with a periodicity of T23 by the SP that accepted link inhibition. The values of these timers have been provisionally set in the range of 3 to 6 minutes. However, when the status of link is not the same at either end (for example, if an

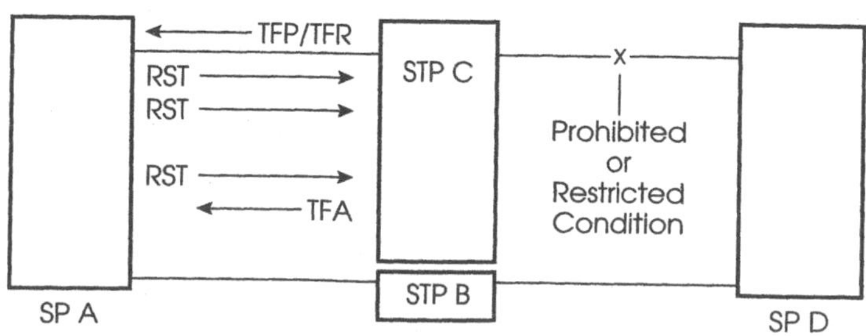

Figure 7–30 Example of signaling route set test procedure.

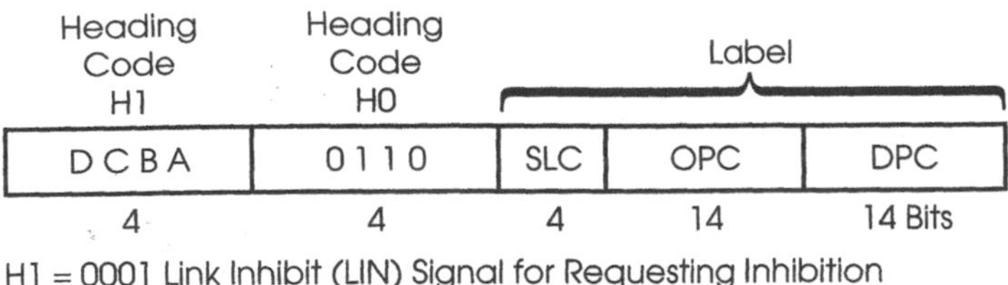

H1 = 0001 Link Inhibit (LIN) Signal for Requesting Inhibition of a Link
= 0010 Link Uninhibit (LUN) Signal for Requesting Uninhibition of a Previously Inhibited Link
= 0011 Link Inhibited Acknowledgment (LIA) Signal for Providing Acknowledgment to a LIN Request
= 0100 Link Uninhibited Acknowledgment (LUA) Signal for Acknowledgment of LUN Request
= 0101 Link Inhibit Denied (LID) Signal for Denying or Rejecting LIN Request
= 0110 Link Forced Uninhibited (LFU) Signal
= 0111 Link Local Inhibit Test (LLT) Signal
= 1000 Link Remote Inhibit Test (LRT) Signal

Figure 7–31 Format of management inhibit messages.

LLT message is received at an SP and it finds that the link is not remotely inhibited), then the SP sends a link forced uninhibit (LFU) message and the inhibited status is also canceled at the other end. Similar action is taken when an SP receives an LRT message and the link in question is not locally inhibited.

For an LIN request, if the other end does not send an LIA within the expiration period of timer T14, then the LIN request is sent again. A maximum of two attempts are permitted for attempting link inhibition. The value of timer T14 is 2 to 3 seconds. Similarly, timers T12 and T13 are provided for uninhibit and forced uninhibit acknowledgments, respectively. The permissible value range for both these timers is 800 to 1,500 ms.

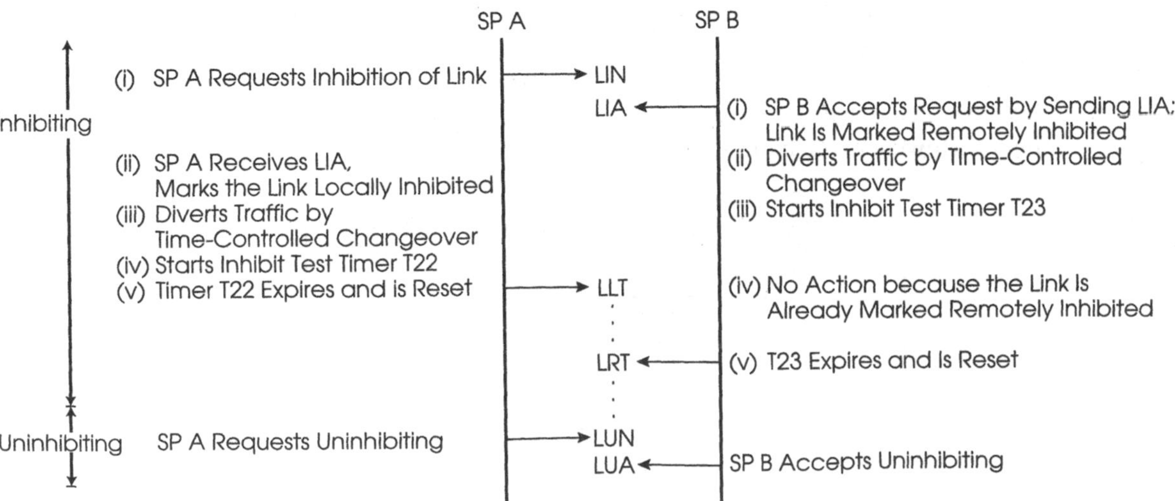

Figure 7–32 Example of management inhibiting and uninhibiting.

7.6.10 Message Transfer Part (MTP) Restart

An SP or an STP is completely isolated from the network when signaling links to adjacent nodes become unavailable. An SP may also be completely isolated from the network by maintenance action while attempting restoration of a partially isolated SP, especially when less severe actions at restoration are unsuccessful. MTP restart attempts to bring the hitherto isolated SP or STP into the network by restoring signaling traffic to adjacent nodes. The procedure was designated SP restart in the CCITT Blue Book recommendations [7]. Due to problems in implementation, however, a revised procedure was subsequently specified in the Q.704 ITU-T recommendation of 1993 [1]. This section is based on the revised procedure.

During the period that an SP remains isolated from the network, the status of the signaling network might undergo changes. For instance, transfer prohibited or restricted conditions may arise for certain destinations. Since the SP is isolated, it has no means of receiving transfer prohibited or transfer restricted messages and updating its routing data. Thus, when the MTP restarts at an SP, it becomes necessary that routing tables are updated according to the existing status of the signaling network. The exchange of network status information is therefore central to the MTP restart procedure. It is also important that the procedure be completed expeditiously; this minimizes the probability of occurrence of network status changes during the implementation of the restart procedure. For time supervision during the MTP restart, timers T18 and T20 are used.

To provide network status, the adjacent nodes of the network send two types of messages to the SP under MTP restart. Adjoining STPs send transfer prohibited (TFP) or transfer restricted (TFR) messages, if certain destinations are inaccessible or restricted from the concerned STP. (Transfer restricted procedure is a national option. Refer to Section 7.6.5.) The other message sent is the traffic restart allowed (TRA) message. A TRA message is sent after the adjacent node has sent all the TFP and TFR messages. For an adjacent accessible node that has no signal transfer function, only a TRA message is sent to the restarting node. No TRA message is received from an adjacent node found to be inaccessible during the MTP restart procedure. The format of the TRA message is shown in Figure 7–33.

Referring to Figure 7–34, assume that the routing tables at C prior to isolation of STP C were as follows:

For destination A: normal: C–A; alternative: C–E–A

For destination B: normal: C–B; alternative: C–E–B

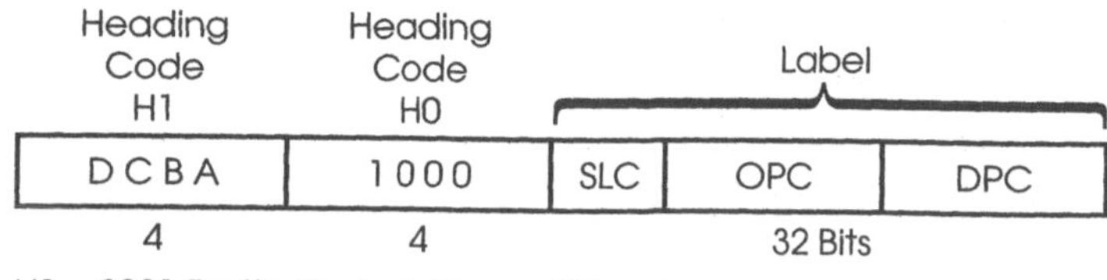

Figure 7–33 Format of traffic restart allowed message.

For destination D: normal: C–D; alternative: C–E–D

For destination E: normal: C–E; alternative: C–D–E

For destination F: normal: C–F; alternative: C–D–F

For destination G: normal: C–D–G; alternative: C–F–G

For destination H: normal: C–F–H; alternative: C–D–H

Assume that while STP C is isolated, link sets at G–D and H–F become unavailable and that link set BC has also failed. During the isolation, transfer prohibited messages for destination G would be sent by STP D for all accessible adjacent nodes, namely, STP E, STP F, and SP H. Similar action would be taken by STP F for destination H. Due to isolation of STP C from the network, TFP messages would not be sent to it, and although the routing tables at all the concerned nodes would be updated, routing tables at STP C would remain unchanged.

The MTP restart begins when the first link to an adjoining node becomes serviceable at level 2. At this moment, timers T18 and T20 are started. The MTP restart procedure for an STP has two phases. The first phase is completed upon the expiration or stopping of timer T18; the second phase ends upon the expiration or stopping of overall supervision timer T20. For MTP restart of an SP (that is, where no transfer function is involved), timer T18 is not used. In this case, only the first phase of the procedure is relevant, and the entire time corresponding to the T20 timer is available for the first phase.

To begin with, it is preferable to activate one link in each link set using the level 2 emergency alignment procedure. This would permit the accessibility of adjacent nodes as early as possible, and the network status information will be made available from these nodes to enable updating of the routing table at the restarting SP. For the example of Figure 7–34, a link in each of the link sets C–A, C–D, C–E, and C–F are activated first. (Since the link set CB is assumed to be faulty, links in that link set remain unavailable.) As soon as a link in link set CD becomes available, the TFP message for destination G is sent by STP D to the restarting STP C. This is followed by a TRA message by STP D to STP C. Similarly, STP F sends a TFP message for destination H to STP C, followed by a TRA message. STP E has no TFP or TFR message to send; it sends a TRA message to STP C. SP A and SP B have no transfer function; they send a TRA message to STP C. Notice that since link set BC is in a failed condition, the TRA message from SP B to STP C is routed via STP E.

As a consequence of the reception of a TFP message from STP D, the normal route

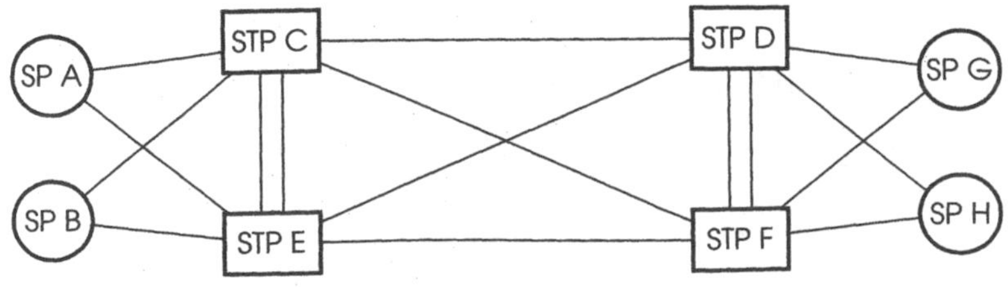

Figure 7–34 Example network for MTP restart; restarting node is STP C.

C–D–G for destination G is removed from the routing table in the restarting node C. The routing table is also modified for destination H. These actions are supervised by timer T18. Timer T18 usually is stopped when TRA messages have been received from all adjacent nodes. A decision to stop timer T18 may also be made, however, when a sufficient number of links have been activated to carry the signaling traffic and enough TRAs have been received to provide a high level of confidence in the updated routing tables. The criteria for determining these aspects are network and implementation dependent.

In the second phase of the procedure, which is applicable only if the restarting node has a signal transfer function, transfer prohibited and transfer restricted messages are sent by the restarting STP to all the adjacent nodes in the broadcast mode. The objective is to inform the adjacent nodes about limitations in transferring messages by the restarting STP arising out of network status. For Figure 7–34, since link set CB is unavailable, restarting STP C sends transfer prohibited messages for destination B to the adjacent nodes A, D, E, and F. When all the TFP and TFR messages have been sent, timer T20 is stopped and the second phase of the MTP restart procedure is completed. The value of timer T20 should be from 59 to 61 seconds.

After timer T20 is stopped or expires, the restarting SP sends traffic restart allowed messages to all adjacent nodes. Internal to the SP, the restarting MTP informs its user parts of the accessibility or otherwise of each SP. In addition, timer T19 is started whenever a TRA message is sent to an adjacent SP. This completes the MTP restart procedure.

Timer T19 is a supervision timer used to prevent possible Ping-Pong of the TFP, TFR, and TRA messages. It has a value range of 67 to 69 seconds. If any TRA message is received from an adjacent SP while timer T19 is running, then the TRA message is discarded and no further action is necessary. However, if a TRA message is received when no associated timer T19 is running, then the SP sends the necessary TFP and TFR messages followed by a TRA message to the concerned adjacent SP.

7.6.10.1 Actions at a Node Adjacent to the Restarting Node

Referring to Figure 7–34, wherein STP C is under MTP restart, an adjacent node such as STP D assumes that STP C is restarting by one of two possible ways:

1. When the first link in a direct link set (for example, the first link in link set CD) is brought into service at level 2. In this case, timer T21 is started. STP D sends any TFP and TFR messages and then finally sends a TRA message to the restarting node. When the TRA message is received from the restarting STP C, timer T21 is stopped. The value range for timer T21 is 63 to 65 seconds.

   Similar actions take place at the various nodes adjacent to the restarting node. For an adjacent node that has user parts, such as SPA, an MTP-RESUME primitive is sent to the various local users after the stoppage or expiration of the timer T21, indicating that users can now send messages to the restarting node (and to other nodes that may have become accessible as a result of the accessibility of the restarting node).
2. When another route to C becomes available (for example, route D–E–C). In this

case, any TFP and TFR messages are sent to the restarting node via the route made available. The MTP-RESUME primitive is sent to all local users, indicating the possibility of resuming user signaling to the restarting node. An adjacent node with transfer capability also sends the necessary TFP and TFR messages and finally a TRA message on the available route to the restarting node.

7.6.11 Signaling Traffic Flow Control

There may be occasions when a network experiences congestion. Mechanisms to deal with congestion are described in the following sections.

7.6.11.1 Signaling Link Congestion

As discussed in Chapter 6, when the level 2 transmission and retransmission buffers are occupied beyond an implementation-specified threshold, level 2 advises level 3 about the onset of link congestion. Conversely, when the buffer occupancy falls below a specified threshold, a congestion abatement condition is indicated for the link. To avoid excessive oscillation between the congestion onset and congestion abatement conditions, the congestion abatement threshold is set at a lower occupancy than the congestion onset threshold.

For the international CCS 7 network, a signaling link is either congested or not congested. Because there is no mechanism to characterize the degree of congestion of a signaling link, there is only one congestion onset and one congestion abatement threshold.

For national CCS 7 networks, an option exists to define up to four congestion states (an uncongested state and three congestion states representing different degrees of signaling link congestion). Depending on whether the MSUs are assigned congestion priority, the following two alternatives exist:

1. National signaling network using multiple congestion states with congestion priority
2. National signaling network using multiple congestion states without congestion priority

Insofar as the congestion aspects are concerned, national CCS 7 networks may be implemented either on the same basis as the international network or according to one of these two national options mentioned.

7.6.11.1.1 National Signaling Network Using Multiple Congestion States with Congestion Priority

Multiple congestion states with congestion priority has been chosen for the U.S. network [2,3]. In this option, up to four congestion thresholds, numbered from 0 to 3, can be defined. The value 0 corresponds to an uncongested condition whereas values 1 through 3 indicate an escalating scale of link congestion. Congestion abatement thresholds (each with lower occupancy value than the corresponding onset threshold) are also defined. Figure 7–35 illustrates two examples of how congestion thresholds are used.

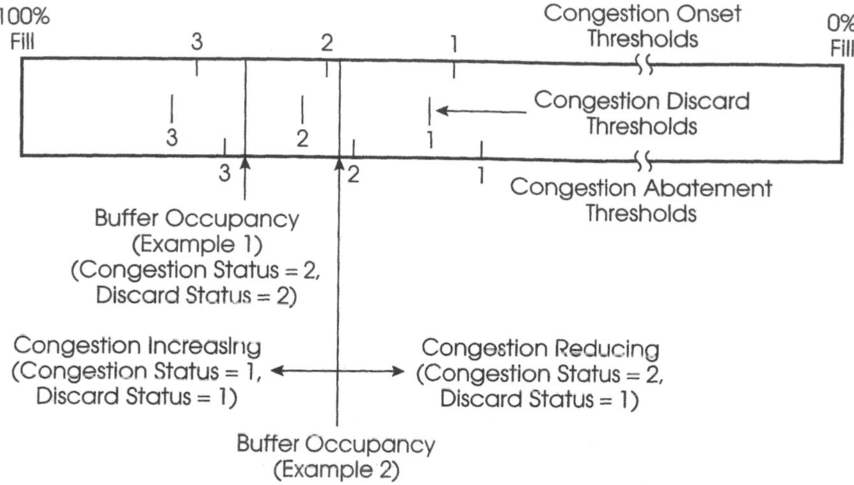

Figure 7–35 Congestion thresholds for the national CCS 7 network.

Link congestion conditions are controlled by discarding some of the MSUs being received at level 3 so that they are not passed on to level 2 for transmission on the signaling link. The selective discarding of MSUs is based on the relative importance of the MSUs. The MSU is assigned one of the four congestion priorities by the user part generating the MSU at level 4. The priority is set in bits A and B of the subservice field of the MSU, as shown in Table 7–4. See also Figure 7–3 and Table 7–2.

In addition to the congestion onset and abatement thresholds, discard thresholds are defined for each congestion level. The discard threshold is set for a higher value of buffer occupancy than the corresponding congestion onset threshold.

With the buffer occupancy as shown in example 1 of Figure 7–35, the link is at congestion status 2 since the occupancy exceeds the second congestion onset threshold. The occupancy is also greater than congestion discard threshold 2, so the link has a congestion discard status of 2.

The decision whether to discard the message or to allow it to be transmitted on the congested link is made by comparing the congestion priority with the congestion status of the link and, if necessary, with the discard status of the link. This is shown in Figure 7–36.

Table 7–4 Congestion Priorities

Bits		
A	B	Meaning
0	0	Congestion priority 0: MSU discarded for congestion levels 1 to 3
0	1	Congestion priority 1: MSU discarded for congestion levels 2 and 3
1	0	Congestion priority 2: MSU discarded for congestion level 3
1	1	Congestion priority 3: MSU not discarded

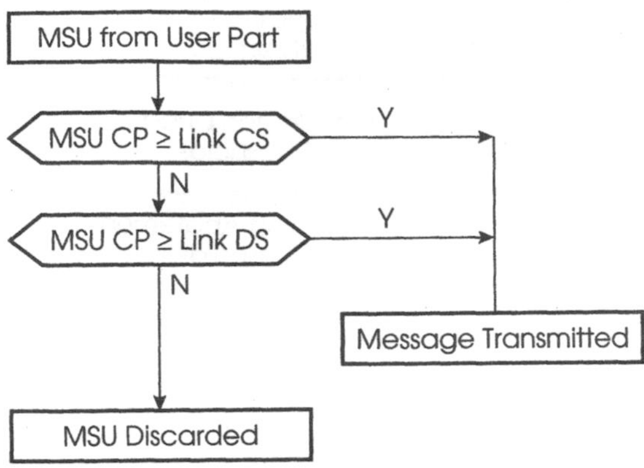

Key
CP: Congestion Priority of the MSU
CS: Congestion Status of the Link
DS: Discard Status of the Link

Figure 7–36 Handling messages at level 3 under signaling link congestion.

The link congestion status for buffer occupancy lying between the congestion onset threshold and the corresponding congestion abatement status depends on whether the link occupancy is increasing or decreasing. Example 2 in Figure 7–35 represents this situation.

Contrary to the national option described above, MSUs are not discarded by the MTP for the international network; they are assigned congestion priorities and discarded if necessary by the generating user part.

7.6.11.1.2 National Signaling Network Using Multiple Congestion States without Congestion Priority

Another national option is a signaling network that has multiple signaling link congestion states but without congestion priority. It is an alternative to the national option using multiple signaling link congestion states with congestion priority discussed above. This option is not used in the U.S. network [2,3]. In this case, the criteria for assigning different congestion states to the signaling links is different. Instead of defining a pair of congestion onset and congestion abatement thresholds for each congestion state, only one pair of congestion onset and congestion abatement thresholds is defined. During congestion, different congestion states are determined on the basis of how long the congestion conditions last. An example of signaling link congestion status based on this principle is shown in Figure 7–37. The congestion status of the signaling link is shown by the nodes, and transition from one congestion state to another is shown by directed edges (a),(b), . . . , (e). The conditions for transition are explained below.

1. As soon as the buffer occupancy exceeds the congestion onset threshold, that is, $L > L_o$, the signaling link goes directly to the highest congestion state 3 (edge a). As long as L is greater than L_o, the link stays at congestion state 3.
2. While in congestion state 3, if the buffer occupancy becomes less than the congestion abatement value—that is, $L < L_a$—then the time for which this condition prevails is measured. For a time T_y, if L remains less than L_a, then the link

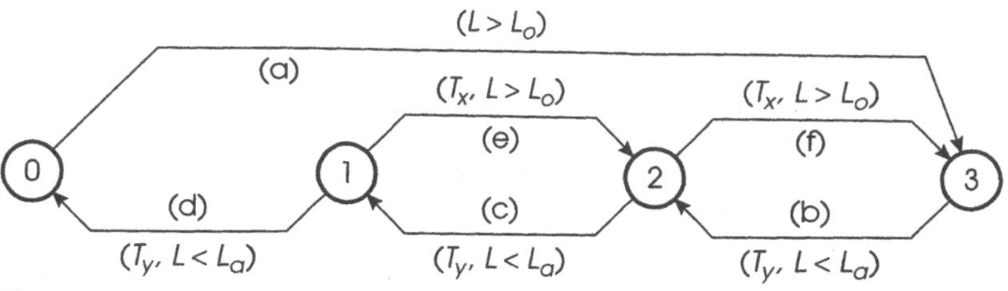

Key
L: Buffer Occupancy
L_o: Congestion Onset Threshold
L_a: Congestion Abatement Threshold
T_x: Time Interval for Incrementing Congestion Status
T_y: Time Interval for Decrementing Congestion Status

Figure 7–37 Signaling link congestion status using multiple signaling link congestion without congestion priority.

is assigned a congestion status 2 (edge b). The same criteria applies for transition from state 2 to 1 (edge c) and from state 1 to 0 (edge d).

3. While the link is in congestion state 1, if the buffer occupancy remains higher than the congestion onset threshold for a period T_x, then the link is assigned congestion status 2 (edge e). A similar argument applies for transition from state 2 to state 3 (edge f).

L_o, L_a, T_x, and T_y are implementation-dependent parameters.

7.6.12 Signaling Route Set Congestion

At an originating SP, a congestion status is associated with each signaling route set. In the international network, if a link in the signaling route toward a given destination becomes congested, then the signaling route toward the destination is also considered to be congested. When the multiple congestion levels option is used, the congestion status of the route is the same as the congestion status of the link with the highest congestion level.

The congestion status of a signaling route set can be updated by two procedures:

1. Transfer controlled procedure
2. Signaling route set congestion test procedure

The first procedure is applicable for international networks. It can also be used for national networks that do not use multiple levels of congestion. Both procedures are required for national networks that implement multiple congestion levels.

The transfer controlled procedure uses the transfer controlled (TFC) message whose format is shown in Figure 7–38.

The use of the TFC message in an international network is illustrated in Figure 7–39. Upon detecting congestion, STP B informs SP A by a TFC message containing the point code of SP C as the destination. Upon receipt of the TFC message, SP A takes actions to decrease the transmission of messages to SP C via STP B. As long as the congestion lasts,

		Heading Code H1	Heading Code H0	Label		
00	Destination	D C B A	0 0 1 1	SLC	OPC	DPC
2	14	4	4	4	14	14 Bits

Notes:
1. SLC in the routing label is set to 0.
2. H1 = 0010.
3. The two most significant bits are spare in the international network. For national networks with multiple congestion priority, however, these may be used to provide congestion status of the destination.

Figure 7–38 Format of transfer controlled (TFC) message.

STP B sends a TFC message to SP A after every eight messages. For the national option with multiple congestion levels, the TFC message sent by STP B also indicates the level of congestion. In addition to the reduction of traffic to SP C, SP A also periodically sends a route-set-congestion test (RCT) message to the destination SP (in this case, SP C). By this message, SP A requests an update of the latest congestion status. The format of the RCT message is shown in Figure 7–40.

Timer T16 is started at SP A after sending the RCT message. The value of the timer is 1.4 to 2 seconds. SP A expects a TFC message providing the current congestion status in response to the RCT message. If a TFC message is received before timer T16 expires, then the congestion status for the route set toward destination SP C is updated with the value provided in the TFC message. If timer T16 expires without receiving a TFC message, then SP A lowers the congestion level by one. The periodicity of sending RCT messages is determined by timer T15, whose value is specified from 2 to 3 seconds.

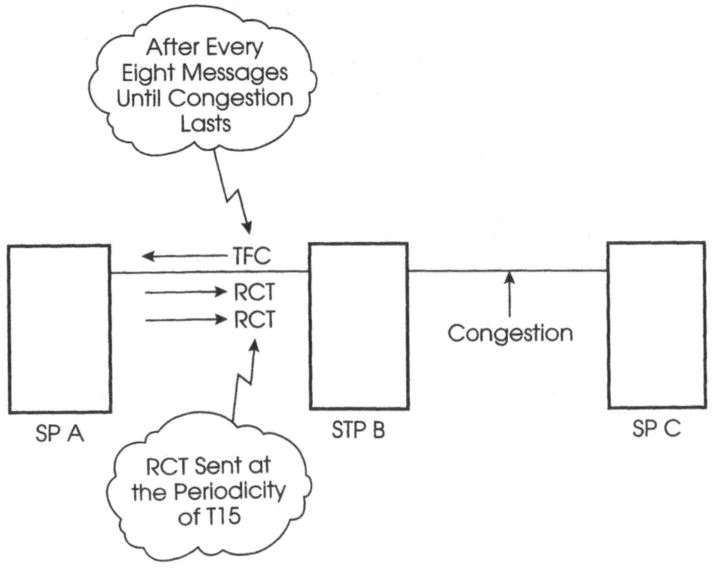

Figure 7–39 Example of the use of TFC and RCT messages.

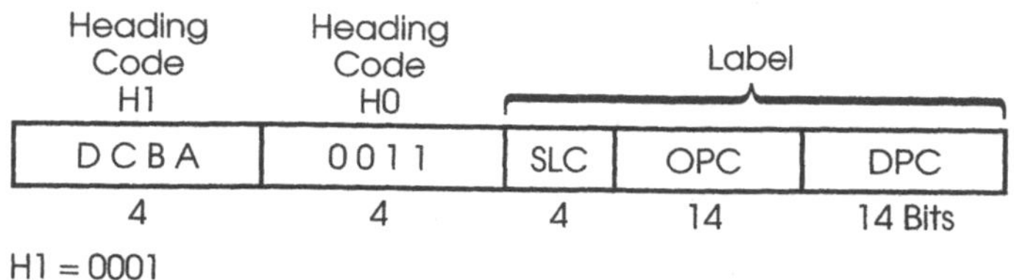

Figure 7–40 RCT message format.

7.7 Summary of Level 3 Timers

The various level 3 timers described in this chapter are listed in Table 7–5. The values in parentheses are applicable where routes with long propagation delays are used. The timer values are per ITU-T recommendation Q.704. For the U.S. network, timers T1 to T17 are identical in their use and value ranges. Timers T22 and T23, however, are designated T20

Table 7-5 ITU-T Recommended Level 3 Timer Values

USE	RANGE
T1 To avoid missequencing on changeover	500 (800) to 1,200 ms
T2 Waiting for changeover acknowledgment	700 (1,400) to 2,000 ms
T3 Time-controlled diversion delay to avoid missequencing on changeback	500 (800) to 1,200 ms
T4 Waiting for changeback acknowledgment (first attempt)	500 (800) to 1,200 ms
T5 Waiting for changeback acknowledgment (second attempt)	500 (800) to 1,200 ms
T6 Delay to avoid message missequence on controlled rerouting	500 (800) to 1,200 ms
T7 Waiting for signaling data link connection acknowledgment	1 to 2 seconds
T8 Transfer prohibited inhibition	800 to 1,200 ms
T9 Not used	
T10 Waiting to repeat signaling route set test message	30 to 60 seconds
T11 Transfer restricted timer	30 to 90 seconds
T12 Waiting for uninhibit acknowledgment	800 to 1,500 ms
T13 Waiting for force uninhibit	800 to 1,500 ms
T14 Waiting for inhibition acknowledgment	2 to 3 seconds
T15 Waiting to start signaling route set congestion test	2 to 3 seconds
T16 Waiting for route set congestion status update	1.4 to 2 seconds
T17 Delay to avoid oscillation of initial alignment failure and link restart	800 to 1,500 ms
T18 Within an SP with MTP restart for supervision of links and link set activation and routing data updating	Implementation and network dependent
T19 Supervision timer during MTP restart to avoid ping pong between TFA, TFR, and TRA messages	67 to 69 seconds
T20 Overall MTP restart timer at the SP whose MTP is restarting	59 to 61 seconds
T21 Overall MTP restart timer at an SP adjacent to the restarting SP	63 to 65 seconds
T22 Local inhibit test timer	3 to 6 minutes (provisional)
T23 Remote inhibit test timer	3 to 6 minutes
T24 Stabilization timer after removal of local processor outage	500 ms (provisional)

and T21, respectively, and the value range of each of these timers is 90 to 120 seconds. There are also other differences, especially with respect to timers related to the MTP restart procedure. Timers applicable to the U.S. network are listed in a BELLCORE standard [2].

REFERENCES

[1] *Specifications of Signaling System No. 7: Signaling Network Functions and Messages.* ITU-T recommendation Q.704, rev. 1. International Telecommunication Union, 1993.

[2] "Signaling network functions and messages." BELLCORE Technical Reference TR-NWT-000246, vol. 1, issue 2, chap. T1.111.4, June 1991.

[3] American National Standard for Telecommunications. *Signaling System Number 7 (SS7)—Functional Description of the Signaling System Message Transfer Part (MTP).* ANSI T1.111-1992.

[4] "Signaling network structure." BELLCORE Technical Reference TR-NWT-000246, vol. 1, issue 2, chap. T1.111.5, June 1991.

[5] *Testing and Maintenance.* CCITT Blue Book, vol. VI, fascicle VI.7, recommendation Q.707. International Telecommunication Union, 1989.

[6] *Specifications of Signaling System No. 7: Message Transfer Part. Signaling Performance.* ITU-T recommendation Q.706, rev. 1. International Telecommunication Union, 1993.

[7] *Signaling Network Functions and Messages.* CCITT Blue Book, fascicle VI.7, recommendation Q.704. International Telecommunication Union, 1989.

8 ISDN: Services and Protocols

Acronyms

ABRM	asynchronous balanced response mode
AOC	advice of charge
ARM	asynchronous request mode
ASP	assignment source point
CCBS	call completion to busy subscriber
CD	call deflection
CFB	call forwarding busy
CFNR	call forwarding no reply
CFU	call forwarding unconditional
CH	call hold
CLIP	calling line identification presentation
CLIR	calling line identification restriction
COLP	connected line identification presentation
COLR	connected line identification restriction
CONF	conference calling
CRED	credit card calling
CT	call transfer
CUG	closed user group
CW	call waiting
DID	direct dialing in, or direct inward dialing
DISC	disconnect frame
DLCI	data link connection identifier
DM	disconnect mode frame
DSS 1	digital subscriber signaling system 1
EA	extension of address
FCS	frame check sequence
FRMR	frame reject frame
HDLC	high-level data link control
ISDN	integrated services digital network
ISPABX	ISDN public automatic branch exchange
ISUP	ISDN user part
ITU-T	International Telecommunication Union-Telecommunication Standardization Sector
LAPB	link access protocol balanced
LAPD	link access procedure on D-channel
LH	line hunting
MCID	malicious call identification
MLPP	multilevel precedence and preemption service
MSN	multiple subscriber number
NRM	normal request mode
OCB	outgoing call barring
OSI	open system interconnection
PSTN	public switched telephone network
RDTD	restricted differential time delay
REL	release
REJ	reject
REL COMP	release completed
RNR	receive not ready
RR	receive ready
SABME	set asynchronous balanced mode extended
SAP	service access point
SAPI	service access point identifier
TASI	time-assigned speech interpolation
TEI	terminal endpoint identifier
TS	timeslot
UA	unnumbered acknowledgment frame
UI	unnumbered information frame
UUI	user-to-user information
UUS	user-to-user signaling

ABSTRACT

Continuing beyond the introduction to the integrated services digital network (ISDN) presented in Chapter 5, this chapter discusses two important aspects of ISDN: the services provided under the ISDN and the protocols required to support these services. More specifically, the following aspects are covered:

- Basic services in the ISDN; bearer and teleservices
- ISDN supplementary services
- Standards on ISDN services
- Link access procedure for the D-channel: layer 2 in DSS 1
- Layer 3 protocol in digital subscriber signaling system 1 (DSS 1)

8.1 Introduction

Services under the ISDN are many and varied. A clear view of ISDN services is essential both for terminal equipment manufacturers and network operators. Therefore, ISDN services should be described under a formal framework, step-by-step. The International Telecommunication Union-Telecommunication Standardization Sector (ITU-T) has addressed this issue by defining a framework for service description in recommendation I.130 [1]. Using this framework, the services are described in three main stages or steps. Sections 8.2 to 8.6 are devoted to the study of ISDN services. Taken together, these services represent a set of capabilities available in the ISDN. Using the services as building blocks, a large number of ISDN applications can be implemented based on the specific needs and requirements of the customers. ISDN applications are covered in Chapter 13, as part of the discussion on planning aspects of the ISDN.

The physical layer (layer 1) was considered in Chapter 5. The remaining two layers of the digital subscriber signaling system 1 (DSS 1) are discussed in this chapter. ITU-T recommendations Q.920 [2] and Q.921 [3] specify the layer 2 functions of DSS 1, and the layer 3 functions of DSS 1 are specified in recommendations Q.930 [4], Q.931 [5], and Q.932 [6]. Layer 2 and layer 3 functions are described in Sections 8.7 and 8.8, respectively.

This chapter considers only the circuit switched services and corresponding protocols. Packet mode services and protocols needed to support them are the subject of Chapter 12.

8.2 ISDN Services

ISDN services are described in three stages. Stage 1 involves description of the service from the user's point of view; implementation aspects are not covered. In this description, each service is defined in terms of a set of "attributes." An attribute represents a specific characteristic of a service. Thus, by using a number of attributes, all the characteristics of a service can be described. Some of the attributes may be common to several services, others may be specific to a service. For example, the information transfer rate is an attribute common to all circuit switched services. However, the value of this attribute—

namely, the bit rate that a service supports—may vary from service to service. A general discussion on the use of attributes for description of services is presented in ITU-T recommendation I.140 [7].

Stage 2 covers the functionality required from the network and, to some extent, from the terminal equipment for implementation of the service. Stage 3 involves the detailed specification of protocol and formats required for such implementation. Since ISDN service implementation requires two protocols, CCS 7 and DSS 1, a stage 3 description is provided separately for each protocol.

Services in the ISDN may be classified into two categories:

1. Basic services
2. Supplementary services

Basic services are further classified into bearer services and teleservices. Services are provided to the end users not only through the functions contained in the customer premises equipment but also by the functional capability of the network interconnecting the users through a switched connection. It is therefore important to characterize the requirements to be met by the network for the provision of these services. Bearer services are meaningful in this context because they define the transmission capacity and functions required from the network. The functionality provided by the user terminals is not included in bearer services; they merely provide the capability and means to transfer the information between the ISDN user-network interfaces. On the other hand, teleservices provide service capability right up to the point of use, namely, the user. As a consequence, they also include the terminal equipment functions. Telephony, facsimile, telex, teletex are examples of teleservices. It is important to note that a teleservice requires the use of an appropriate bearer service, since it is the latter that provides the underlying network support.

True to their name, supplementary services supplement or augment a basic service by providing additional features and capabilities. Supplementary services are not standalone; they are always offered in association with a basic service. Several supplementary services may be associated with a basic service, depending on the needs of the user.

Figure 8–1 shows the access points where ISDN services may be offered to the customer. Bearer services are offered at reference points S/T, whereas teleservices are provided to the user of the ISDN terminal equipment. Since supplementary services exist only in association with the bearer or teleservices, they are offered at the access point of the concerned basic service.

8.3 ISDN Bearer Services

Bearer services have been described in ITU-T recommendation I.210 [8] in terms of 13 different attributes, classified under the following three categories:

1. Information transfer attributes
2. Access attributes
3. General attributes

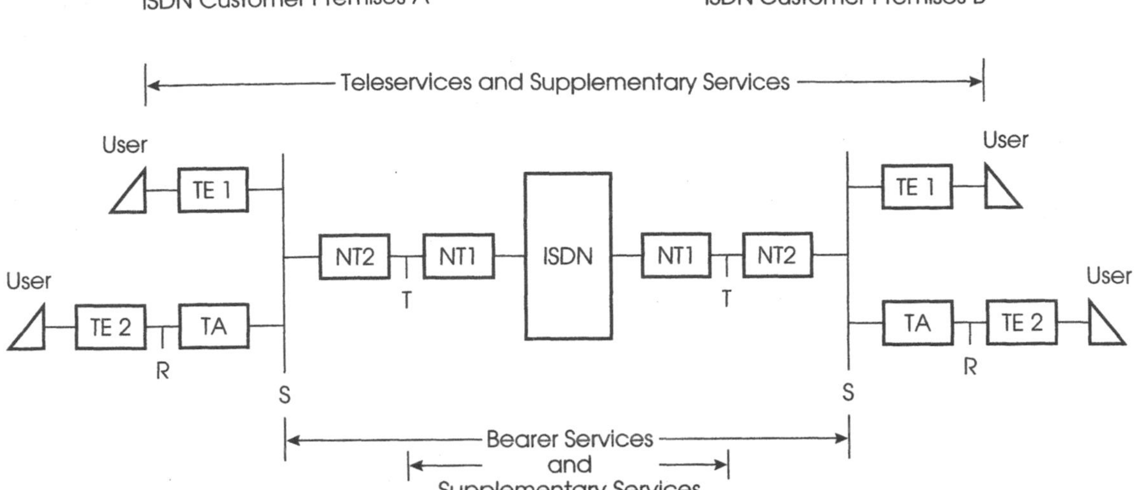

Figure 8–1 Customer access to ISDN services.

8.3.1 Information Transfer Attributes

Information transfer attributes specify the capability of the ISDN network for transferring information between the ISDN user network interfaces at the access points S/T. Table 8–1 lists various information transfer attributes and their possible values. Out of seven attributes listed in this category, the first four (information transfer mode, information transfer rate, information transfer capability, and structure) are called dominant attributes. The remaining three are referred to as secondary attributes.

The dominant attributes are used to categorize different bearer services. In Section 8.3.3, 10 categories of ISDN services are identified. Since the ISDN is capable of transferring information both in the circuit switched and packet switched modes, the bearer service may be either a circuit switched service or a packet switched service. For circuit switched bearer services, further classification results from several possible bit rates of information transfer, for example, 64 kbps, 2 × 64 kbps, and other multiples of thc 64 kbps rate. For the packet switched connection, the information transfer rate is specified in terms of throughput.

Several capabilities of information transfer are available in ISDN bearer services, including speech, and audio information at three different bandwidths, video, and unrestricted digital information. For 7 kHz audio, the encoding is per ITU-T recommendation G.722 [9]. For unrestricted digital information transfer, the ISDN should ensure unaltered transfer of bit sequence at the specified bit rate between the access points. For speech and audio information, unrestricted digital information transfer is not mandatory but can be used.

The structure attribute refers to the capability of the ISDN to deliver information at the destination access point in the same structure in which it was presented at the origination access point. One example of a structure in circuit switched information transfer is 8 kHz integrity, which involves transfer of 8,000 samples every second. Information is

Table 8-1 Bearer Service Attributes and Their Values

ATTRIBUTES	POSSIBLE VALUE OF ATTRIBUTES	
A. Information transfer attributes		
1. Information transfer mode	Circuit	Packet
2. Information transfer rate	Bit rate 64, 2 × 64, 384, 1,920; other multiples of 64 kbps	Throughput
3. Information transfer capability	Unrestricted digital, speech, 3.1 kHz audio, 7 kHz audio, 15 kHz audio, video, others for further study	
4. Structure	8 kHz integrity, service data unit integrity, RDTD	
5. Establishment of communication	Demand, reserved, permanent	
6. Symmetry	Unidirectional, bidirectional symmetric bidirectional asymmetric	
7. Communication configuration	Point-to-point, multipoint, broadcast	

Notes:

1. 7 kHz audio has been renamed "unrestricted digital information with tones and announcements." Also refer to Figure 8–22(c).

2. RDTD stands for restricted differential time delay. (Refer to Section 8.3.3.5.)

demarcated in 125 μs time intervals, and all bits submitted within this interval at one user network interface are transferred to another user-network interface in a single 125 μs interval. For the packet switched connection, the structure may be in the form of service data unit integrity.

The secondary attributes are establishment of communication, symmetry, and communication configuration.

Possible options in the establishment of communication attribute are on-demand communication, reserved communication, and permanent communication. On-demand communication signifies the establishment of the connection (and its subsequent release) as soon as possible following a request. Reserved communication is established for a predetermined duration. The connection establishment and disconnection times are indicated while making the request. This option is particularly suited for videoconferencing subscribers because the time for the videoconference is generally fixed in advance. For permanent communication, although the time for establishment of connection is specified, the duration of the connection is not mentioned.

The communication is termed *bidirectional symmetric* when the transfer of information through the ISDN takes place at a bit rate that is identical in both directions. When the bit rates in the two directions differ, the communication is *bidirectional asymmetric.* Furthermore, for certain applications, the transfer of information in only one specified direction may be required. For example, in monitoring and surveillance, unidirectional bearer capability is usually sufficient.

Point-to-point communication takes place in a normal circuit or packet switched connection between two S/T reference points. A multipoint communication configuration arises for three-party calling and conference calls. Broadcast communication is essentially unidirectional information transfer from one S/T reference point to several other S/T reference points simultaneously.

8.3.2 Access Attributes and General Attributes

Access attributes describe the means of accessing network functions or facilities as seen at the access points, namely, S or T reference points. Two attributes fall under this category:

1. Access channel and rate
2. Access protocols

Refer to Table 8–2 for access attributes and their possible values. For signaling, the access channel is the D-channel with bit rates of 16 kbps for basic rate access and 64 kbps for primary rate access. For user information, the access channel may be a B-channel or one of the alternatives shown in the table. It is important to specify the protocols employed at the access reference points. Table 8–2 lists the relevant ITU-T recommendations regarding access protocols for both signaling and user information.

From the point of view of protocol layers, the bearer services include the three lower layers for DSS 1 protocol as specified in ITU-T recommendations I.430 [10] and I.431 [11] for the physical layer, Q.920 [2] and Q.921 [3] for layer 2, and Q.930 [4] and Q.931 [5] for layer 3. The signaling information is carried in the D-channel. As seen from Table 8–2, included in the signaling access protocols are several other ITU-T recommendations, for example, X.25 [12], X.30 [13], X.31 [14], V.110 [15], and V.120 [16]. Rec-

Table 8–2 Access Attributes and Their Possible Values

1. Access channel and rate D(16), D(64), B, H0, H11, H12
2.1 Signaling access protocol layer 1 ITU-T rec. I.430/I.431, X.30, X.31, V.110, V.120
2.2 Signaling access protocol layer 2 ITU-T rec. Q.920, Q.921, X.31, X.25
2.3 Signaling access protocol layer 3 ITU-T rec. Q.930, Q.931, X.30, X.31, X.25, V.110
2.4 Information access protocol layer 1 ITU-T rec. I.430, I.431, I.460, X.30, X.31, V.110, V.120, G.711, G.722
2.5 Information access protocol layer 2 HDLC LAPB, ITU-T rec. Q.920, Q.921, X.25, X.31
2.6 Information access protocol layer 3 ITU-T rec. T.70-3, X.25, X.31

ommendations X.30, V.110, and V.120 are concerned with the use of different types of non-ISDN data terminal equipment in the ISDN through the use of terminal adaptors. Recommendation X.31 specifies the protocol for the support of packet mode services in the ISDN.

The general attribute category lists the supplementary services that can be provided in association with the bearer service, the quality of service requirements, interworking capabilities, and other operational and commercial requirements linked to the bearer service. The access attributes and general attributes are collectively called qualifying attributes.

8.3.3 Bearer Service Categories

ITU-T recommendation I.230 [17] identifies the various bearer service categories based on the different combinations of the dominant attribute values. The individual bearer service within the category is identified by the secondary attributes, whereas the qualifying attributes further specify a bearer service. In this chapter, only the circuit switched bearer services are considered. Packet mode bearer services will be discussed in Chapter 12. A total of ten circuit switched bearer service categories have been identified in ITU-T recommendation I.231 [18]. The first eight bearer services were defined in the Blue Book; the last two were added in subsequent recommendations.

The circuit mode bearer services so far identified by the ITU-T are listed below and further explained in the following paragraphs. The use of "8 kHz" in the name of bearer service categories refers to the sampling rate of 8,000 per second and should not be confused to mean analog bandwidths.

- 64 kbps unrestricted, 8 kHz structured bearer service category
- 64 kbps, 8 kHz structured bearer service category usable for speech information transfer
- 64 kbps unrestricted, 8 kHz structured bearer service category usable for 3.1 kHz audio information transfer
- Alternate speech/64 kbps unrestricted, 8 kHz structured bearer service category
- 2 × 64 kbps unrestricted, 8 kHz structured bearer service category
- 384 kbps unrestricted, 8 kHz structured bearer service category
- 1,536 kbps unrestricted, 8 kHz structured bearer service category
- 1,920 kbps unrestricted, 8 kHz structured bearer service category
- Circuit mode 64 kbps 8 kHz structured multiuse bearer service category
- Multirate unrestricted 8 kHz structured bearer service category

The bearer service categories enumerated above have bit rates of 64 kbps or its multiples. Thus, bearer services permit the setting up of both 64 kbps and multirate connections. The use of PCM timeslots for transporting different types of multirate calls for a 2,048 kbps digital path is summarized below. Timeslots 0 and 16 are not used. Therefore, timeslots 15 and 17 are considered consecutive time slots, and 30 timeslots are available for carrying bearer information.

- For 2 × 64 kbps: a pair of consecutive timeslots (TS) are used for each call, for example, timeslots 1 and 2 for call 1, TS 2, and TS 3 for the next call, and so on. A total of 15 2 × 64 kbps calls can be carried in the 30 timeslots available in a 2,048 kbps digital path.
- For 384 kbps: six consecutive timeslots are used for each call. A total of five 384 kbps calls can be carried.
- For 1,536 kbps: 24 consecutive timeslots are used, for example, TS 1 to TS 15 and TS 17 to TS 25. Thus, only one 1,536 kbps call can be carried. Timeslots 26 to 31 can be used, if necessary, to carry up to six 64 kbps or three 2 × 64 kbps calls.
- For 1,920 kbps: 30 consecutive timeslots, 1 to 15 and 17 to 31.

8.3.3.1 64 kbps Unrestricted, 8 kHz Structured Bearer Service Category

The 64 kbps unrestricted, 8 kHz structured bearer service is recommended as "essential" for the international network [18]. The values of the dominant attributes are evident from the service designation. The secondary attribute values are as follows:

Establishment of communication: demand, reserved or permanent

Symmetry: bidirectional symmetric or unidirectional

Communication configuration: point-to-point or multipoint

This bearer service category may be offered with different combinations of secondary attribute values, as shown in the tree structure of Figure 8–2. Out of the 12 combinations, two combinations, demand–bidirectional point-to-point and permanent–bidirectional point-to-point are mandatory [18]; the remaining are optional.

The unrestricted attribute associated with this service ensures that bit integrity will be preserved during information transfer. Therefore, the service can support a wide range of applications, including speech, 3.1 kHz audio, and transparent access to X.25 packet switch network.

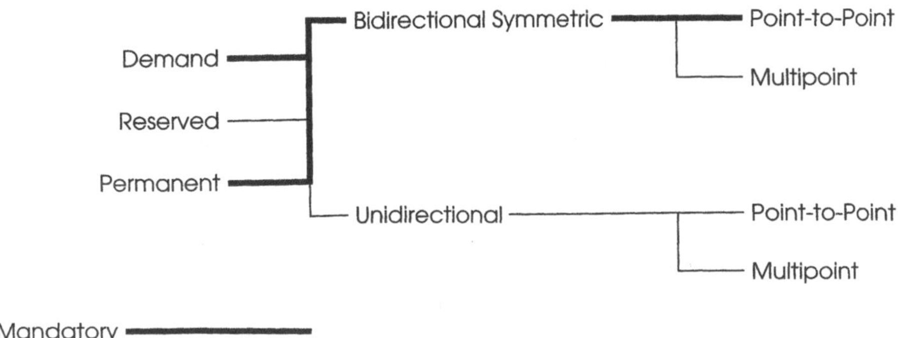

Figure 8–2 Combination of secondary attributes.

8.3.3.2 64 kbps, 8 kHz Structured Bearer Service Category Usable for Speech Information Transfer

The 64 kbps, 8 kHz structured bearer service category usable for speech information transfer, recommended as "essential" for the international network [18], is used to support speech application. Speech is encoded according to A-law or μ-law as stated in ITU-T recommendation G.711 [19]. The 64 kbps encoding of speech, sent out on the B-channel, may take a path through the network that includes both digital and analog transmission. The network may also provide for echo cancellation, analog-to-digital conversion, and low bit rate voice encoding. Unlike unrestricted digital transfer, bit integrity is not assured by the network.

The combinations of secondary attributes shown in Figure 8–2 also apply for this service. The mandatory combinations are the same as for 64 kHz unrestricted digital service.

8.3.3.3 Circuit Mode 64 kbps, 8 kHz Structured Bearer Service Category Usable for 3.1 kHz Audio Information Transfer

The circuit mode 64 kbps, 8 kHz structured service usable for 3.1 kHz audio information transfer is similar to the speech bearer service. It is intended for data transmission via modems and for facsimile group 1, 2, and 3 applications. Unlike speech, however, there is no echo cancellation, no low bit rate encoding, and no use of time-assigned speech interpolation (TASI) during transport through the network. The network may include both digital and analog transmission. In this case also, bit integrity is not assured.

The combinations of secondary attributes and those marked essential are identical to the bearer services described above.

8.3.3.4 Alternate Speech/64 kbps Unrestricted, 8 kHz Structured Bearer Service Category

The capability of alternate speech and 64 kbps unrestricted digital transfer within the same call is provided by alternate speech/64 kbps unrestricted, 8 kHz structured bearer service. At the time of call setup, when service request is made, the user also specifies the initial mode, speech or data. Subsequently, during the call, requests for change of mode can be made as required. When the change of mode from speech to 64 kbps unrestricted is requested, the network disables speech processing devices (for example, echo cancellers) from the transmission path. These devices are reinserted when speech mode is required.

The calls may be made using a single terminal with composite functions for handling both speech and data. Another alternative is to use two separate terminals, one for speech and the other for data. However, the use of separate terminals is not convenient, because the change of mode entails call transfer between terminals.

This service is not intended for unidirectional communication. Hence, out of the combination of secondary attributes listed in Figure 8–2, only six combinations are applicable. The service is not recommended as "essential" for international connections.

When offered in the national ISDNs, the essential combinations are identical to those specified for the bearer service described above.

8.3.3.5 2 × 64 kbps Unrestricted, 8 kHz Structured Bearer Service Category

The 2 × 64 kbps unrestricted, 8 kHz structured bearer service provides the unrestricted transfer of user information on the two 64 kbps B-channels. The 8 kHz integrity, along with the restricted differential time delay (RDTD) feature, is provided. Hence, the timeslots sent to the network from the transmitting S/T-interface should be delivered to the receiving S/T-interface with a differential time delay of less than 50 ms.

8.3.3.6 Other Multirate Bearer Services

The bit rates supported are 384 kbps, 1,536 kbps, and 1,920 kbps. The bit rates cannot vary call by call. Thus, a user subscribing to 384 kbps service is provided a 384 kbps bandwidth for every call. Unrestricted transfer of information is permitted under these services. The 384 kbps bearer service finds application in videoconferencing. Higher bit rates afforded by 1,536 kbps and 1,920 kbps bearer services can be employed for high-speed data transfer, facsimile, and video applications.

8.3.3.7 64 kbps, 8 kHz Structured Multiuse Bearer Service Category

The 64 kbps, 8 kHz structured multiuse bearer service is useful for transfer of information between multiuse terminals. Examples of multiuse terminals include 7 kHz telephones and combined group 3 and group 4 fax machines. The service provides a 64 kbps unrestricted bearer for calls between two multiuse terminals. Calls between a multiuse terminal and an ISDN speech or a 3.1 kHz audio terminal are also supported. For calls between a multiuse terminal and an ISDN speech terminal, 64 kbps bearer usable for speech is provided. On the other hand, calls between a multiuse terminal and an ISDN 3.1 kHz audio terminal make use of 64 kbps bearer usable for audio information. Calls between a multiuse terminal and the PSTN are also supported. In this case, the network supports either speech or 3.1 kHz audio, depending on the request. As noted earlier, the network provides speech processing functions, such as echo cancellers, for supporting speech.

8.3.3.8 Multirate Unrestricted 8 kHz Structured Bearer Service Category

The multirate unrestricted 8 kHz structured bearer service permits the user to request a specific bit rate from the ISDN on a call-to-call basis. It supports the establishment and release of circuit switched connections providing unrestricted information transfer in integer multiples of 64 kbps, up to the maximum rate of the interface (128, 192, ... , 1,920 kbps). The originating user of the service indicates the required information transfer rate and the called party number. The network establishes the connection supporting the requested bit rate. The bit rate remains constant throughout the duration of the call.

8.4 ISDN Teleservices

Teleservices are characterized by the presence of higher-layer end-to-end protocols. A detailed description of these protocols for the various teleservices is outside the scope of this book, but necessary references are included followed by a brief description.

The teleservices identified in the relevant ITU-T recommendations are as follows:

- Telephony (recommendation I.241.1) [20]
- Teletex (recommendation I.241.2) [21]
- Telefax group 4 (recommendation I.241.3) [22]
- Mixed mode (recommendation I.241.4) [23]
- Videotex (recommendation I.241.5) [24]
- Telex (recommendation I.241.6) [25]
- Telephony 7 kHz (recommendation I.241.7) [26]

The telephony teleservice in the ISDN is akin to conventional telephony. It provides subscribers with a two-way speech connection at an audio bandwidth of 3.1 kHz. The relevant encoding law—A-law or μ-law—is applied. Digital signal processing such as the use of echo cancellation may also be employed by the network.

The teletex teleservice is used to transfer documents coded according to a standardized character set specified in ITU-T recommendation T.61 [27]. A teletex call involves preparing the document in the local mode using a teletex terminal, storing it in a memory associated with the terminal, and then transporting the information through the ISDN to the called teletex terminal where it is stored in the memory associated with the called terminal. Thus, the call involves an automatic memory-to-memory transfer of documents. The smallest unit of the teletex information is one page, and a document may consist of several pages.

The teletex call may be established either as a circuit switched connection over a B-channel or as a packet switched connection using a B- or D-channel. Signaling access protocols are the three layers of DSS 1 protocols. Information access layer 1 protocols are either I.430 or I.431, depending on whether the teletex call is associated with the basic rate or primary rate ISDN access. Layer 2 and 3 information access protocols for the circuit switched teletex connection are according to ITU-T recommendation X.75 [28] and ISO 8208 [29], respectively. The corresponding protocols for packet switched connections are X.25 LAPB and X.25 (packet layer protocol). In addition, higher-layer protocols specified in the T-series ITU-T recommendations are implemented in the teletex equipment at the two ends of the connections. These protocols are T.70 [30], T.62 [31], T.61, and T.60 [32] for layers 4 to 7, respectively.

The telefax group 4 teleservice provides ISDN users with end-to-end facsimile communication using standardized coding and communication protocols. Unlike teletex, which is limited to textual information that has to be keyed in before transmission, telefax provides the flexibility and convenience of sending existing printed text, line drawings, pictures, graphs, or virtually anything that can be put on paper. Information access protocols are the same as for teletex. Layer 4 to 7 protocols are T.70 for layer 4, T.62 for layer 5, T.400 [33] for layer 6, and T.503 [34], T.521 [35], and T.563 [36] for layer 7.

With both teletex and telefax group 4 circuit switched connections, the following eight supplementary services described in Section 8.5 may be provided:

1. Closed user group
2. Multiple subscriber number
3. User-to-user signaling
4. Calling line identification presentation
5. Calling line identification restriction
6. Connected line identification presentation
7. Connected line identification restriction
8. Direct dialing in (called direct inward dialing, DID, in the United States)

For packet switched connections of these two teleservices, the supplementary services that may be supported are not yet identified.

The mixed mode teleservice permits a mix of both teletex coded and telefax coded information. The higher layer protocols correspond to the following ITU-T recommendations:

- Layer 4: recommendations X.224 [37] and X.214 [38]
- Layer 5: recommendations X.225 [39] and X.215 [40]
- Layer 6: recommendations T.61, X.226 [41], and X.216 [42]
- Layer 7: recommendations T.501 [43], T.522 [44], and T.561 [45]

The videotex teleservice is similar to the existing videotex service. Text, still pictures, graphics, and audio information can be retrieved from a database by the ISDN user of this service.

ITU-T recommendations on telex teleservice are not yet mature, and there is little motivation for further work since the service is unlikely to find widespread application in the ISDN.

The 7 kHz telephony teleservice enables the user to receive high-quality speech and sound in the frequency range of 50 Hz to 7,000 Hz. A 7 kHz telephone is required for this purpose. By the use of a fallback arrangement, it is possible for the 7 kHz terminal to communicate with a user with a 3.1 kHz conventional telephone.

8.5 ISDN Supplementary Services

ISDN supplementary services can be classified under the following categories:

- Number identification supplementary services
- Call offering supplementary services
- Call completion supplementary services
- Multiparty supplementary services
- Community of interest supplementary services

- Charging supplementary services
- Additional information transfer

Throughout this discussion, the "served user" is one to whom a particular ISDN supplementary service is provided.

8.5.1 Number Identification Supplementary Services

Grouped under the number identification supplementary services category are calling line identification presentation (CLIP), calling line identification restriction (CLIR), connected line identification presentation (COLP), connected line identification restriction (COLR), direct dialing in (DID), multiple subscriber number (MSN), malicious call identification (MCID), and subaddressing supplementary services.

8.5.1.1 Calling Line Identification Presentation (CLIP)

CLIP provides the ISDN number of the calling party to the called party during the ringing phase (call setup) of the call. The number supplied may also include the subaddress. The ISDN terminal at the called subscriber displays the calling party number supplied by the network. Prior information of the calling subscriber number enables the called party to decide whether or not to answer the call. This service may be offered as a subscription or as a standard feature by the network provider. All incoming calls to subscribers with CLIP service are displayed with the exception of the following two cases:

1. When the calling party subscribes to the CLIR supplementary service (CLIR forbids the display of the calling number)
2. When the ISDN is unable to obtain the calling party number. This may happen when the call spans more than one network. For example, part of the call may be routed through a public switched telephone network (PSTN), and the latter may not be able to supply the calling line identity to the ISDN to which the called party is connected. In these cases, the called party is informed by the network about the unavailability of the calling party number.

In the United States, this type of service is currently available to non-ISDN customers and is known as caller ID and calling number delivery.

There may be occasions when a non-ISDN network delivers the calling party number to the destination ISDN (that is, the ISDN to which the called subscriber is connected) but without an indication of whether or not the presentation of the calling party number is permitted. In such cases, the decision to provide CLIP can be taken independently by the destination ISDN [46].

8.5.1.2 Calling Line Identification Restriction (CLIR)

The CLIR supplementary service is offered to the calling party and prevents the presentation of the calling ISDN number and the subaddress (if any) to the called party. As a consequence, this service prevents the use of the CLIP supplementary service by the called party. The service may be offered as a subscription or as a generally available service. For obvious reasons, however, it is not meaningful to offer CLIP and CLIR on a general basis in the same network. It should also be possible to override the operation of CLIR for calls to a category of subscribers. For example, it is not desirable to withhold calling ISDN number for calls made to police, fire, and other emergency services. The CLIR service may be made available on a permanent basis—that is, for all calls from the calling party—or may be provided on a call-by-call basis on specific request of the calling user. Whenever a call originating in an ISDN is routed through or destined to a non-ISDN network, the CLIR indication may not be carried to the destination network. In such cases, if the calling party number is available to the destination network, then the destination network is authorized to decide about presenting or restricting the calling party address [47]. Many state public service commissions in the United States require that CLIR be provided at no charge to customers requesting it. In these states, unrestricted transmission of the calling number has been viewed as an invasion of privacy.

8.5.1.3 Connected Line Identification Presentation (COLP)

The COLP supplementary service is offered to the calling party. When the call is answered, the ISDN number to which the call has been switched is conveyed to the calling party. The terminal of the calling party displays the connected number (not to be confused by the display of digits sent out during call origination, which is a feature of the terminal). The COLP confirms to the calling party that it is connected to the intended called party. The connected number may be provided entirely by the network, entirely by the terminal of the connected called party, or partially by the network and the rest by the terminal of the connected party. A useful enhancement to this service could be the display of the connected number before the called party answers. This feature is under study in the ITU-T.

8.5.1.4 Connected Line Identification Restriction (COLR)

The COLR supplementary service is offered to the called subscriber. This service prevents the operation of the COLP service. When subscriber A with COLP service subscription is connected to subscriber B with COLR service subscription, calling subscriber A is prevented from receiving the ISDN number of subscriber B. This service may be provided either on a permanent or temporary basis. Permanent basis means that once the service is subscribed, it is available for all calls. When provided on a temporary basis, the subscriber indicates a preference (whether COLR should apply or not) for each incoming call separately.

8.5.1.5 Direct Inward Dialing Service

The direct inward dialing service allows an incoming call to be directly routed to an ISDN number connected to an ISDN public automatic branch exchange (ISPABX) without the intervention of the ISPABX operator. This supplementary service is akin to the DID facility available in the PSTN.

8.5.1.6 Multiple Subscriber Number (MSN) Supplementary Service

The multiple subscriber number (MSN) supplementary service allows the assignment of unique directory numbers to the various terminals connected at the S-interface. Incoming calls at the ISDN basic access can therefore be terminated on the desired terminal based on the directory number. As a consequence, several directory numbers are required at a single ISDN basic access. Each administration has to decide the maximum number of directory numbers to be permitted on one basic access.

8.5.1.7 Malicious Call Identification (MCID) Supplementary Services

The malicious call identification supplementary service (MCID) is offered to the called subscriber. On the request of the called party, it permits, on a per call basis, recording of the calling party's directory number in the destination exchange. The information recorded in the destination exchange for the call should consist of the following:

- Called party number
- Calling party number
- Date and time of the call

As an option, the calling party subaddress may also be recorded if it is provided by the originating ISDN access.

For a call originating from an exchange that is not capable of sending the calling line identity to the next exchange in the connection, the calling party number is not available at the destination exchange. In this case, the destination exchange only knows the incoming circuit on which the call has been received. To identify the calling number in this situation, it is useful to hold the connection so that the call may be physically traced. As a national option, the ability to hold the connection exists in association with the MCID.

8.5.1.8 Subaddressing Supplementary Services

The subaddressing supplementary service extends the addressing capability of an ISDN access. The additional digits comprising the subaddress may be used to identify different terminals within an ISDN installation. In contrast to the multiple subscriber number (MSN) and direct dialing in (DID supplementary services), subaddressing does not form part of the ISDN numbering plan. Thus, subaddressing digits are transported transparently by the network and have only significance at the two endpoints of the connection, namely, the calling and the called ISDN users.

8.5.2 Call Offering Supplementary Services

The call offering supplementary services are call transfer (CT), call forwarding busy (CFB), call forwarding no reply (CFNR), call forwarding unconditional (CFU), call deflection (CD), and line hunting (LH).

8.5.2.1 Call Transfer (CT)

Call transfer supplementary service allows an ISDN subscriber (served* user A) to transfer an existing call to a third party. For the existing call, the served user may be either a calling or a called party. There are three possible variations of call transfer:

1. Normal call transfer
2. Single-step call transfer
3. Explicit call transfer

The normal call transfer can be described in the following steps:

1. Served user A has an already-existing connection to another user B. User A makes a request to the network to transfer the call to user C.
2. The network puts the existing call on hold. (Call hold is described in Section 8.5.3.2.) The connection between users A and B remains intact.
3. User A dials the number of user C.
4. The network informs users B and C about the call transfer. Furthermore, it provides users B and C with each other's address. This, however, depends on the supplementary services available to users B and C. For example, if user B has the CLIR supplementary service, his address cannot be provided to user C. (Step 4 is optional.)
5. When the call between users A and C is established, user A requests the network to complete the call transfer.
6. The network disconnects the connection between users A and B and establishes a connection between users B and C, thus completing the call transfer.

If the call between users A and C is not established (user C may be busy or the call attempt may be unsuccessful), user A still has the possibility of communicating with user B on the original connection. As an alternative, call transfer to a user other than user C can also be attempted. This also holds when the network is unable to establish a connection between users B and C.

In the normal call transfer procedure, the original connection can be retrieved in cases of failure to transfer the call. In the single-step call transfer procedure, the served user simply provides the address of user C to the network. The network disconnects the connection between users A and B and proceeds to establish connection between users B and C. There is no possibility of retrieval of the original connection should the call transfer fail.

In the explicit call transfer procedure, served user A puts the existing connection on hold and establishes a connection with third party C. The served user then explicitly requests the network to perform call transfer. In this case, the network has no knowledge of the intention of the served user to transfer the call to the third party C until the explicit call

---

*Served user is the ISDN subscriber to whom the supplementary service is being provided.

request is made. This is not so in normal call transfer, since the network knows that the new connection is to be established between users B and C (step 3 above) as soon as it receives the digits dialed for connection between users A and C.

The three scenarios of call transfer described above require varying degrees of involvement (and, as a consequence, control) of the served user in affecting call transfer. The explicit call transfer provides maximum control; with the single-step procedure, the control is minimal.

8.5.2.2 Call Forwarding Services

Forwarding of calls to a specified number can be provided using these services. Three options exist in this regard:

1. Call forwarding unconditional (CFU)
2. Call forwarding no reply (CFNR)
3. Call forwarding busy (CFB)

These options are offered as separate supplementary services. An ISDN user may subscribe to one or more of these services. In view of the similarities in the procedures for subscription, activation, and operation of these services, it is sufficient to describe only one of them in detail. The CFU supplementary service is described in this section.

When an ISDN user subscribes to the CFU service, all incoming calls are diverted to a prespecified alternative number. The call diversion takes place unconditionally, irrespective of the state of the called user's access (for example, busy or idle). Since the subaddress digits only have an end-to-end significance, these digits are transported transparently by the network.

The user subscribing to this service—namely, the served user—is also referred to as the forwarding user or called user. The alternative number to which the call is forwarded is called the forwarded to user. The call forwarding supplementary service may be subscribed to separately with each basic service available to the served user, or, in the alternative, the service may be subscribed to collectively for all the available basic services. For example, one user who has telephony and facsimile services may like call forwarding to be applied only to telephone calls. On the other hand, another subscriber may like all telephone calls made to the subscriber's office after office hours forwarded to the subscriber's home telephone and all facsimile group 4 calls forwarded to another number.

The served user activates the CFU service by sending the forwarded to number and the basic service to which the CFU activation applies to the network.

The network provides an appropriate response to the activation request. The response varies, depending on the options subscribed by the served user. Examples of options are:

- Notifying the served user whenever a call has been forwarded
- Notifying the calling party if the call has been forwarded
- Notifying the served user if the CFU is currently active or inactive

Within the ISDN, multiple call forwardings are permitted: A calls B, B forwards the call to C, C forwards to D, and so on. Forwarding is permissible only when the concerned users have subscribed to CFU as well as the basic service to which CFU is associated. The number of forwardings are limited to between three and five for each call. The user at the final destination of the call receives an indication that the incoming call is a forwarded call. Additional information, such as the number originally called and the last number that forwarded the call, may also be indicated.

With call forwarding busy (CFB), call forwarding takes place only when the served user is busy, whereas call forwarding no reply (CFNR) results in call forwarding when the served user does not answer within a specified time.

8.5.2.3 Call Deflection (CD)

The call deflection service is distinguished from other call forwarding services by its real time nature. The service is invoked by the served user on the arrival of an incoming call. Instead of answering an incoming call, the served user deflects it to a third party (the deflected to number). The operation of the service is based on the options supplied by the served user while subscribing for the service:

- The served user indicates whether the served user's number is permitted to be presented to the deflected to number.
- The served user also indicates whether the calling user should receive notification that the call has been deflected to another number. If the served user prefers that a notification be sent to the calling user, then it may be with or without the deflected to number. This should also be indicated at the time of service subscription.

On receiving an incoming call and deciding that the call should be deflected, the served user requests the network and supplies the deflected to number. The request for deflection and supply of the number to the network may be performed manually or automatically by a terminal preprogrammed to do so. If the served user ISDN access has the commonly used point-to-multipoint configuration, then the network may receive conflicting responses from different terminals. One terminal may immediately request call deflection; another terminal may connect to the call or put the call in alerting state. In this case, the call deflection request will be ignored by the network.

The actions performed by the network also depend on when the call deflection request is made. When the network receives a call deflection request before alerting, the call to the served user is cleared. If the request is received after alerting, the network has the alternative possibility of retaining the call to the served user until alerting commences at the deflected number. As for other call forwarding services, multiple-call deflection requests are permissible subject, of course, to the subscription of the service by other users involved in multiple-call deflection.

The user who finally receives the deflected call is always informed by the network that the call has been deflected. Furthermore, as an option, the user may also receive the originally called number, the last deflected number, and the causes of the original and last deflections.

8.5.2.4 Line Hunting (LH)

The line hunting supplementary service permits incoming calls to be offered in a distributed manner to a group of ISDN interfaces. The group of ISDN interfaces is called the line hunting group. The distribution of calls may be made sequentially, or a uniform distribution of calls to each member of the line hunt group may be attempted. An ISDN interface may have several ISDN directory numbers associated with it, based on the MSN supplementary service. At present, the line hunting group is not composed of these ISDN directory numbers. Thus, incoming calls are distributed only on the basis of ISDN interfaces, with each interface having a single ISDN number. The call waiting supplementary service should not be provided to a line in the hunt group, since this service interferes with the sequential or uniform distribution of calls to the hunt group. Call waiting is discussed in Section 8.5.3.1.

8.5.3 Call Completion Supplementary Services

Four supplementary services are offered under this category:

1. Call waiting (CW)
2. Call hold (CH)
3. Completion of calls to busy subscribers (CCBS)
4. Terminal portability

8.5.3.1 Call Waiting (CW)

When an ISDN user is engaged on an existing call and no free B-channel is available on the ISDN interface, the call waiting service allows the user to be informed of the arrival of an incoming call. The user may then decide to accept, ignore, or reject the incoming call. The service may be offered with several possible variations:

- The service may be provided as a subscription or to all users without a subscription.
- The notification of call waiting to the served user may be provided by means of out-of-band indication or by in-band signals (for example, call waiting tones).
- The calling user may be notified that the call is waiting at the destination, or the caller may simply receive a ringback without any knowledge that the call is waiting.
- Since several ISDN numbers may exist for an ISDN interface (for example, through the MSN supplementary service), the call waiting service may be offered to each number individually, to a subset of ISDN numbers, or to all numbers at the ISDN interface.

Two timers, T1 and T2, are used in the operation of call waiting service. When the network offers the call under the call waiting service, the terminal of the served user should respond within time T1. Timer T1 has a value of a few seconds. On receipt of this response, the network informs the user who originated the waiting call that the destination has been offered the call. As an option, information that the call is under waiting may also be presented. The served user now has three options, as mentioned earlier:

1. Accept the waiting call
2. Ignore the waiting call
3. Reject the waiting call

To accept the waiting call, the served user may terminate the existing call, thus making the B-channel available. Another possibility is to use call hold supplementary service (refer to Section 8.5.3.2) to make a B-channel available. The served user can then answer the waiting call. The network expects the served user to answer the waiting call before the expiry of timer T2. The value of this timer is between 0.5 and 2 minutes.

To ignore the waiting call, the served user may continue with the existing call, leading to the expiry of timer T2. The network thereupon takes the following steps:

1. Informs the served user that the call is no longer waiting
2. Informs the calling party that the call cannot be connected
3. Releases the call

The served user can reject the call by informing the network before the expiry of timer T2. In this case, actions similar to "ignoring of waiting call" are performed by the network.

8.5.3.2 Call Hold (HOLD)

The call hold supplementary service enables a user to interrupt communications on an existing call temporarily and to reestablish communication later on, if necessary. When the call hold service is invoked, the B-channel associated with the call is made free. As an option, when the call hold is in operation, a B-channel may be kept reserved to allow the user to make an outgoing call or to accept an incoming call (as in call waiting). The existing call can be retrieved subsequently by the served user, if desired. Reservation of more than one B-channel is not permissible.

The call hold service can be invoked by either party to a call, the calling user or the called user, provided that the call hold service is available to them both. Similarly, either party can clear the call while the call is in the held state.

The calling user can invoke the service any time after the call has been answered but before the call is terminated. As an option, the call hold may be invoked by the calling user when the call is being alerted at the called user interface or when all the information necessary for completion of the call has been supplied by the calling user.

The called user can invoke the service any time after the call is answered and before call clearing commences. The call hold service may be provided on subscription or may be made generally available.

8.5.3.3 Completion of Calls to Busy Subscribers (CCBS)

Although identified as one of the supplementary services for the ISDN, the completion of calls to busy subscribers service, to be provided to the calling user, is yet to be defined by the ITU. On finding the called number busy the calling user will have the possibility of activating this service and requesting the network to establish the connection when the called user becomes free.

8.5.3.4 Terminal Portability

The terminal portability supplementary service, as the name indicates, permits the user to move the ISDN terminal from one socket to another within the same basic access during the active phase of the call. When the terminal is unplugged from the original socket, the call is temporarily suspended; it is resumed when the terminal is replugged into another socket. The B-channel assigned to the call is not assigned to any other call during this procedure. The service also allows the user to replace the ISDN terminal by another compatible terminal during the active phase of a call. The service can be provided to both the calling and the called users.

8.5.4 Multiparty Supplementary Services

Multiparty supplementary services permit communication between more than two users. Two services have been identified in this category, conference calling (CONF) and three-party supplementary services.

8.5.4.1 Conference Calling (CONF)

The objective of the CONF service is to allow several users to communicate with each other simultaneously in a conference-like fashion. For the sake of orderly communication and for utilizing the various features provided by the service, one of the users is designated the conference controller. The served user is usually the conference controller. Other users are called conferees. The features provided by this service include adding new users, dropping existing users from the conference, temporarily isolating one or more existing users from the conference, and splitting the conference into two groups of users. Since multiple calls are involved, it is necessary for these calls and the conference as a whole to be identified by call reference numbers. The conference controller provides the call reference numbers, termed as *call ID,* to the network.

To invoke the service, the served user supplies a call reference number to the network, that the served user has assigned to the conference call to be established. This number is called the root call ID. The conference controller then supplies the directory numbers of the other conferees to be included in the conference.

The various conferees may be distributed over different exchanges in the network. The network checks whether the requested conference call can be setup. This check includes the following:

- A bearer capability compatibility check; that is, whether all the conferees in the conference can be provided with the bearer capability required for the call. For example, for audioconferencing, circuit mode 64 kbps, 8 kHz structured bearer service usable for speech is required by each conferee.
- A supplementary service compatibility check
- A check on the state of each connection
- A check to determine if the conference resources required from the network can be allotted

The conference resource required is typically a "bridge" in one of the exchanges. Circuit switched connections are established from each conferee to the bridge, which acts as a point of interconnection. The bridge will usually be in the exchange to which the conference controller is connected, but it can also be located in any other suitable exchange.

After performing the checks listed above, the network connects the requested conferees in a conference. The conference controller may request adding new conferees or dropping existing conferees. The conferees can disconnect themselves from the conference or, if needed, put themselves on hold.

A provision also exists for the conference controller to request disconnection from the conference. In this case, the other conferees can continue to communicate and disconnect themselves as required.

8.5.4.2 Three-Party Supplementary Service

The three-party service involves the served user and two other users. A three-way communication is established, and each user can communicate with the other two.

Served user A invokes this service only after establishing connections to users B and C. The call to one user (for example, user B) should be in the active state, and the other call should be in the held state. After the service is provided, all three users are in an active three-way communication. The served user can perform the following controlling functions:

- Disconnect a user from the three-way communication (results in an active call between the served user and the other user)
- Disconnect both the users
- Communicate with any one user in privacy by keeping the other user on hold

8.5.5 Community of Interest Supplementary Services

The community of interest supplementary services are aimed at a group of users who share special communication needs. Five supplementary services have been specified to meet these requirements: the closed user group (CUG), the private numbering plan, multilevel precedence and preemption service (MLPP), priority service, and outgoing call barring.

8.5.5.1 Closed User Group (CUG)

A closed user group consists of a group of users who have a restricted access arrangement. There can be several closed user groups in a network, and a user can be a member of one or more CUGs. The main categories of access restrictions that may apply to a member are the following:

1. Calls permitted within the CUG only
2. Calls within the CUG and incoming calls only from users outside the CUG
3. Calls within the CUG and outgoing calls to users outside the CUG
4. Calls within the CUG with both incoming and outgoing calls to users outside the CUG

The first category is the most restrictive, whereas there are no access restrictions in the last category. Within the first category, further access restrictions may be imposed, namely, barring incoming calls or barring outgoing calls. Several scenarios of access restrictions can be built by combining different restriction possibilities.

When a user is a member of more than one CUG, one CUG is registered with the network as the preferential CUG. Thus, when the user dials without identifying the CUG, the network takes the preferential CUG as the default while routing the calls.

8.5.5.2 Private Numbering Plan (PNP)

The private numbering plan supplementary service has not yet been defined by the ITU.

8.5.5.3 Multilevel Precedence and Preemption Service (MLPP)

The multilevel precedence and preemption service allows several levels of call priority and provides special arrangements for handling of these calls. The priority of calls are assigned with the following precedence levels:

- Precedence level 0
- Precedence level 1
- Precedence level 2
- Precedence level 3
- Precedence level 4 (routine; lowest)

A subscriber to the MLPP service may be assigned one of the precedence levels. While making a call, the subscriber assigns a precedence level to the call. This level should be lower than or equal to the precedence level assigned to the subscriber at the time of service subscription. If the call is to be completed in the normal course, then there is no impact of the MLPP service. However, when the call cannot be completed in the normal course, the MLPP service provides for special handling of the call.

A call may not be completed because of the unavailability of either the network resources (for example, no free circuits) or due to the lack of access resources (for example, no free B-channel). As part of special handling of the call, it may be necessary to free network resources engaged on a call with lower precedence. For this purpose, preemption of calls with a lower level of precedence may be attempted. A preemption notice is sent to both the parties involved in the call.

If the called party is busy on an existing call with a lower level of precedence, then this call would have to be preempted to complete the higher precedence call. However, this is not done unless the called party agrees to the preemption by acknowledging a preemption notification sent by the network.

An important aspect of the MLPP service is its restricted scope of application. The MLPP service applies only to users who have subscribed to the service. Thus, calls made by or to non-MLPP users cannot be preempted.

8.5.5.4 Priority Service

The priority service accords preferential treatment to calls originating from certain subscribers or destined to a specific group of numbers. The group of subscribers provided with the priority service on originated calls are called A priority subscribers. The group of numbers to which calls are given priority treatment are called B priority subscribers. B priority numbers can include destinations such as fire, medical emergency services, and police. The priority treatment of calls concerns preferential path selection for the calls by the network. For example, for a priority call experiencing trunk blocking, the exchange may attempt repeated call rerouting.

Two categories of priority A subscribers are envisaged: Category I subscribers have all their outgoing calls treated as priority calls, and category II subscribers indicate priority status on a call-to-call basis by using a special service code during call setup.

8.5.5.5 Outgoing Call Barring

Restrictions to making outgoing calls can be provided to subscribers of this service in two ways:

1. General outgoing call barring, where outgoing access is barred except for a few emergency numbers
2. Special outgoing call barring, wherein outgoing access may be restricted in a specific predefined manner, such as barring outgoing access to national or international calls

This service may be provided separately for each basic service. For example, a subscriber may subscribe to this service for telephony calls, but not for group 4 facsimile calls. To invoke the call barring service, the subscriber is assigned a code. When the subscriber subscribes to outgoing call barring in association with more than one basic service, separate codes are assigned corresponding to each basic service.

8.5.6 Charging Supplementary Services

8.5.6.1 Credit Card Calling (CRED)

The credit card calling service is yet to be defined in the ITU-T.

8.5.6.2 Advice of Charge (AOC)

The advice of charge service is usually offered to the calling user, except when reverse charging is applicable. The user is informed of the usage-based charges levied on the call. Depending on when the charging information is made available to the user, the service has the following three variations:

1. AOC at call setup
2. AOC during the call
3. AOC at the end of the call

AOC at call setup provides the user with advance information regarding the charging rate for the call being setup. AOC is supplied during call setup or at the time of connection at the latest. If a charging rate change occurs during the call, the new rate is supplied to the user as soon as it becomes applicable.

AOC during the call involves the supply of charge information while the call is in its active phase. The information supplied may take several forms, such as to supply cumulative call charges with continuous updating or to supply an incremental increase in charges as the call progresses in time. Charge information may be supplied as an actual charge amount or as the number of charge units. Other charge-related information such as the duration of the call, the type of charging (normal, credit card, or reverse), and the charging rate may also be included.

In AOC at the end of the call, the charging information supplied is similar to AOC during the call except that the charges relate to the entire call.

8.5.6.3 Reverse Charging

Calls are usually charged to the user who makes the call, but the reverse charging service allows for a flexible arrangement of charging so that calls need not always be charged to the calling user. The service can be provided with the following options:

1. Entire call charges are levied on the called user. The reverse charging request can be made either by the calling user at the call setup or by the called user any time during the call.
2. Call charges are shared between the calling and the called user. Request for reverse charging can be made either by the calling user or the called user during the active phase of the call. Charges before the request is made are levied on the calling user, and those after the request are levied on the called user.
3. Reverse charging is performed by the network unconditionally, that is, the

called user is charged for the entire call without any explicit request for reverse charging from either of the users.

8.5.7 Additional Information Transfer

At present, only the user-to-user signaling service is defined under the additional information transfer category.

8.5.7.1 User-to-User Signaling

The user-to-user signaling (UUS) supplementary service allows the exchange of a limited amount of user-generated information between the calling and the called ISDN users over the D-channel. For example, in association with a speech call, short textual messages can also be exchanged by means of this service. The information, called user-to-user information (UUI), is passed transparently through the network; it has significance only at the two endpoints. UUS service is currently available only in association with circuit switched calls.

Depending on the stage of the call when UUI exchange is performed, three types of UUS services can be conceived:

Service 1: user information can be transferred during the setup and clearing phases of the call along with the call control messages.

Service 2: user information can be transferred only during the setup phase of the call, but the information is sent in messages that are separate from the call control messages.

Service 3: user information can be transferred by means of separate messages at any time during the active phase of the call; for example, information may be exchanged during conversation in a speech call.

Services 1 and 2 are activated by the calling user during call setup. Service 3 is requested by the called user during the active phase of the call.

Since the information transfer takes place on the D-channel, it is necessary to limit the length of information exchange. Message length is limited to 128 octets. Thus the users subscribing to the UUS supplementary service have the facility to send short messages of up to 128 octets in addition to speech communication. An attractive application of this service arises when the called user is unavailable. In this case, the calling user can send short messages, and the ISDN telephone of the called user stores the messages. The messages can be displayed to the called user subsequently.

8.6 International and European Standards on Supplementary Services

Tables 8–3 and 8–4 list the international and European standards on the description of supplementary services. The standards appearing in these tables are listed from [46] through [179].

Table 8–3 International Standards on Supplementary Services

SERVICE	STAGE 1	STAGE 2	STAGE 3 USING CCS 7	STAGE 3 USING DSS1
Number identification supplementary services:				
DID	I.251.1	Q.81 § 1	Q.731 § 1	Q.951 § 1
MSN	I.252.2	Q.81 § 2	—	Q.951 § 2
CLIP	I.251.3	Q.81 § 3	Q.731 § 3	Q.951 § 3
CLIR	I.251.4	Q.81 § 3	Q.731 § 4	Q.951 § 4
COLP	I.251.5	Q.81 § 5	Q.731 § 5	Q.951 § 5
COLR	I.251.6	Q.81 § 5	Q.731 § 6	Q.951 § 6
MCID	I.251.7			
Subaddressing	I.251.8	Q.81 § 8	Q.731 § 8	Q.951 § 8
Call offering supplementary services:				
CT	I.252.1			
CFB	I.252.2	Q.82 § 2	Q.732 § 2	
CFNR	I.252.3	Q.82 § 2	Q.732 § 3	
CFU	I.252.4	Q.82 § 2	Q.732 § 4	
CD	I.252.5	Q.82 § 3	Q.732 § 5	Q.952 § 2-5
LH	I.253.6	Q.82 § 4		
Call completion supplementary services:				
CW	I.253.1	Q.83 § 1	Q.733 § 1	Q.953 § 1
Call hold	I.253.2	Q.83 § 2	Q.733 § 2	Q.953 § 2
CCBS	I.253.3	Q.83 § 3	Q.733 § 4	
Terminal portability				
Multiparty supplementary services:				
CONF	I.254.1	Q.84 § 1	Q.734 § 1	Q.954 § 1
Three-party	I.254.2	Q.84 § 2	Q.734 § 2	Q.954 § 2
Community of interest supplementary services:				
CUG	I.255.1	Q.85 § 1	Q.735 § 1	Q.955 § 1
PNP	I.255.2			
MLPP	I.255.3	Q.85 § 3	Q.735 § 3	Q.955 § 3
Priority service	I.255.4			
Outgoing call barring	I.255.5			
Charging supplementary services:				
CRED	I.256.1	Q.86 § 1		
AOC	I.256.2	Q.86 § 2		
Reverse charging	I.256.3	Q.86 § 3		
Additional information transfer supplementary services:				
UUS	I.257.1	Q.87 § 1	Q.737 § 1	Q.957 § 1

Table 8-4 European Standards on Supplementary Services

Service	Stage 1	Stage 2	Stage 3 Using CCS 7	Stage 3 Using DSS1
Number identification supplementary services:				
DID	ETS 300 062:1991	ETS 300 063:1991		ETS 300 064:1991
MSN	ETS 300 050:1991	ETS 300 051:1991		ETS 300 052:1991
CLIP	ETS 300 089:1992	ETS 300 091:1992		ETS 300 092:1992 and Amendment 1 (1993)
CLIR	ETS 300 090:1992	ETS 300 091:1992		ETS 300 093:1992
COLP	ETS 300 094:1992	ETS 300 096:1992		ETS 300 097:1992
COLR	ETS 300 095:1992	ETS 300 096:1992		ETS 300 098:1992
MCID	ETS 300 128:1992	ETS 300 129:1992		ETS 300 130:1992
Subaddressing	ETS 300 059:1991	ETS 300 060:1991		ETS 300 061:1991
Call offering supplementary services:				
CT				
CFB	prETS 300 199:1992	prETS 300 203:1992		
CFNR	prETS 300 201:1992	prETS 300 205:1992		
CFU	prETS 300 200:1992	prETS 300 204:1992		
CD	prETS 300 202:1992	prETS 300 206:1992		
LH				
Call completion supplementary services:				
CW	ETS 300 056:1991	ETS 300 057:1992		ETS 300 058:1991
Call hold				
CCBS				
Terminal portability	ETS 300 053:1991	ETS 300 054:1991		ETS 300 055:1991
Multiparty supplementary services:				
CONF	ETS 300 183:1992	ETS 300 184:1993		ETS 300 185:1993
Three-party	ETS 300 186:1993	ETS 300 187:1993		ETS 300 188:1993
Community of interest supplementary services:				
CUG	ETS 300 136:1992	ETS 300 137:1991		ETS 300 138:1992
PNP				
MLPP				
Priority service				
Outgoing call barring				
Charging supplementary services:				
CRED				
AOC (at call setup)	ETS 300 178:1992	ETS 300 181:1993		ETS 300 182:1993
AOC (during call)	ETS 300 179:1992	ETS 300 181:1993		ETS 300 182:1993
AOC (end of call)	ETS 300 180:1992	ETS 300 181:1993		ETS 300 182:1993
Reverse charging				
Additional information transfer supplementary services:				
UUS	prETS 300 284:1993	prETS 300 285:1993		prETS 300 286:1993

8.7 Mutual Interaction between Supplementary Services

A typical ISDN user may subscribe to several supplementary services in association with the same basic service. It is therefore necessary to consider the impact of supplementary services on each other. The impact of each service on all others is included in stage 1 descriptions of the services. In this section, a few examples are presented as illustrations.

One obvious case arises from the diverging customer needs that the CLIP and CLIR services are intended to satisfy. Calling line identity cannot be presented if the calling user has the calling line identity restriction service.

Another example of interaction between CLIR and call transfer was mentioned in step 4 of section 8.5.2.1.

A user who has invoked the three-party supplementary service cannot invoke explicit call transfer to transfer either of the two calls. To transfer such calls, the user will have to first cancel the three-party service.

The CUG supplementary service has areas of interaction with many other supplementary services. As discussed in Section 8.5.5.1, this service involves various types of access restrictions that limit the operation of the various call diversion services when CUG users are involved. Access restrictions imposed by CUG also apply to conference calls.

When outgoing call barring (OCB) along with one or more call diversion services is active, incoming calls requiring diversion have to be treated on the basis of the outgoing restriction imposed by the OCB service.

8.8 Link Access Procedure in D-Channel (LAPD)

Layer 2 of ISDN is called the link access procedure on D-channel (LAPD). The physical link (layer 1) for both basic and primary rate ISDN was described in Chapter 5. Recall that in the open system interconnection (OSI) reference model, each layer establishes communication with a corresponding layer in an adjacent entity (peer-to peer communication) by making use of the functions provided by the lower layers. Likewise, the link layer makes use of the physical link to perform its functions.

In addition to the LAPD protocol, the D-channel can also support link access protocol balanced (LAPB), which is layer 2 protocol for X.25 public switched packet data networks. Both LAPB and LAPD are based on high-level data link control (HDLC) protocol. In contrast to LAPB, where a single data link connection is to be established, several logical data link connections on the D-channel may be required in the case of LAPD. This is a special requirement in ISDN and is taken care of by the addressing mechanism to be discussed shortly.

Data link specifications are contained in two ITU-T recommendations, Q.920 and Q.921. Recommendation Q.920 deals with the general aspects of the data link. The detailed procedures are covered in recommendation Q.921.

The principal purpose of the D-channel is to carry signaling information for the control of calls established in the B-channels. To transfer signaling information between layer 3 entities residing in the terminal equipment and the ISDN exchange, layer 2 is requested to perform certain functions by layer 3. In other words, layer 2 provides a service to layer 3 for the exchange of signaling information. The delivery of service by layer 2 to layer 3 is by means of primitives and is said to take place at a hypothetical service access point (SAP).

The SAP is the point where layer 3 accesses (that is, receives) a service provided by layer 2. Refer to Figure 8–3. The SAP shown in this figure corresponds to the signaling information exchanged between layer 3 entities at an ISDN terminal and the serving exchange.

The D-channel may also be used for slow rate packet data and other services. Therefore, in addition to exchange of signaling information, the layer 3 entities at the two ends may also need to communicate to provide these services. In this situation, layer 3 may request layer 2 to provide more than one service and several SAPs may exist, one SAP for every service provided by layer 2. Since there is a single data link between the exchange and the ISDN access, it is necessary that the frames (information exchanged by layer 3 entities is structured into frames) identify the service access point, to which they are related. Each SAP is therefore assigned a unique number called a service access point identifier (SAPI). Refer to Figure 8–4.

The design of the LAPD must also consider the fact that several terminals may be connected at the S/T-interface of an ISDN access. To identify the terminal for which the frames are meant, each terminal in an ISDN access is assigned a number called the terminal endpoint identifier (TEI).

SAPI and TEI taken together are called the data link connection identifier (DLCI). They provide a mechanism of using the single D-channel to establish independent information exchanges between several terminals at an ISDN access and the exchange, with one or more SAPs for each terminal. This capability is illustrated in Figure 8–5, where several logical data link connections are shown to be multiplexed on a single data link. In the figure, terminal A and the ISDN exchange have two SAPs, one for packet data and the other for signaling information. Terminal B has a single SAP. The SAPI for signaling information has a value 0, whereas the SAPI for packet data is 16. The TEI value is common to all SAPIs within a terminal, thus, each terminal has a single TEI value. In the example of Figure 8–5, terminals A and B have TEI values of 88 and 8, respectively. For a broadcast link, however, the ISDN exchange uses a common TEI value (127) for all terminals because all the terminals have to be addressed at the same time.

Because the LAPD is based on the HDLC protocol, it is useful to examine the operational modes available in HDLC. The terminals interconnecting an HDLC data link may function as a primary-secondary pair or as a pair with both terminals incorporating com-

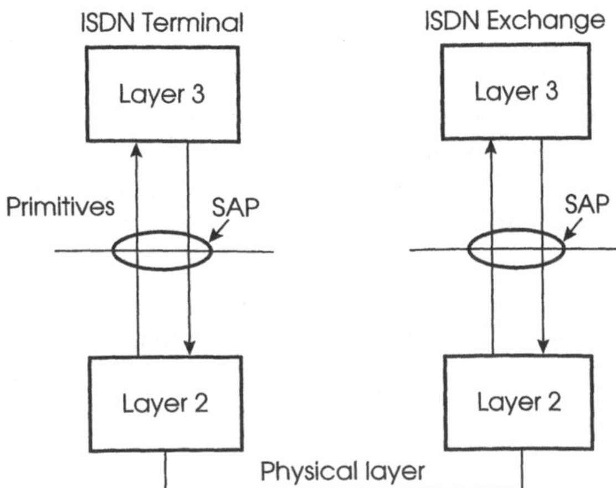

Figure 8–3 Concept of service access point (SAPI).

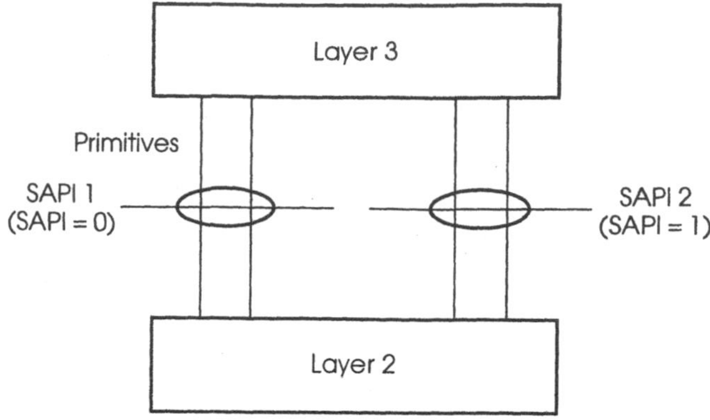

Figure 8–4 Example of more than one service access point.

bined primary and secondary functions. A primary terminal is like the master; it assumes full responsibility of error control and flow control on the link.

Three modes of operation are defined in HDLC:

1. Normal response mode (NRM): the secondary terminal can initiate data transfer only on the explicit permission of the primary terminal.
2. Asynchronous response mode (ARM): a secondary terminal is permitted to initiate transmission without an explicit permission from the primary.

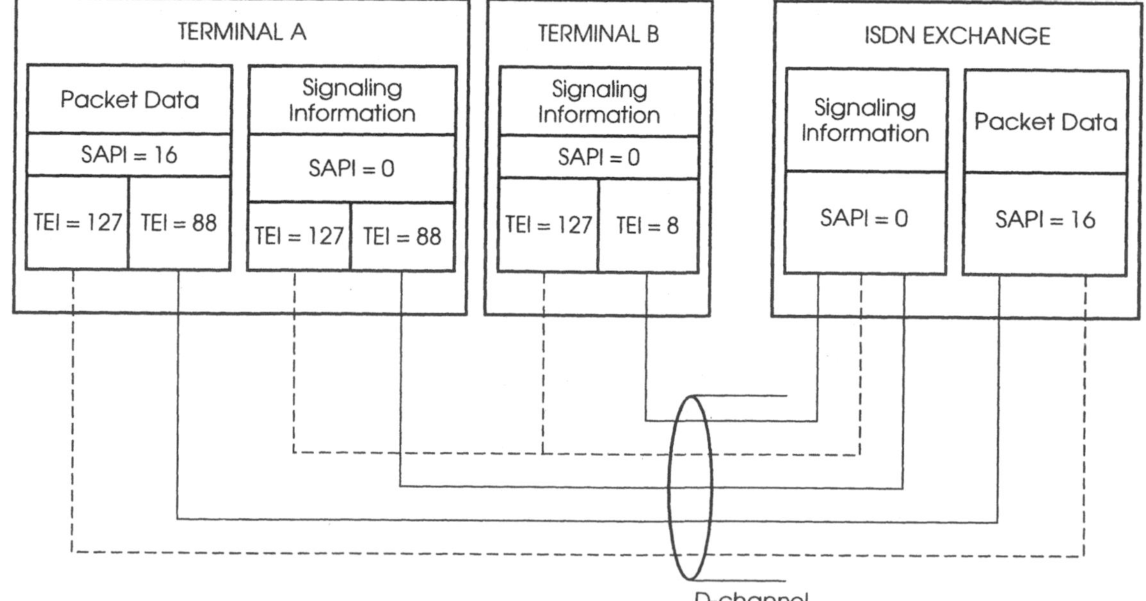

Figure 8–5 Multiplexing several logical data link connections.

3. Asynchronous balanced response mode (ABRM): both ends have combined primary and secondary terminals. Thus, both ends have equal and identical responsibility for error and flow control on the link. Either side may send commands and responses without any explicit authorization from the other end.

In LAPD (as well as in LAPB), the ABRM mode of operation is adopted. Two versions of this mode are possible: normal, using modulo 8 operation, and extended, which employs modulo 128 operation. In LAPB, either of the two modes can be used. Modulo 8 means that the frames are assigned numbers successively from 0 to 7. In modulo 128, the frames have numbers from 0 to 127. In LAPD, only modulo 128 operation is prescribed.

8.8.1 Services Provided by Layer 2

As noted earlier, layer 2 provides services to layer 3. It also provides certain administrative services and services to the layer 2 management entity, as shown in the tree structure of Figure 8–6. To provide these services, layer 2 establishes a data link connection with the peer layer 2 entity. When the service is no longer required, the data link connection is released.

The information flowing on the D-channel is structured into frames. Frame formats are discussed in the next section.

It is seen from Figure 8–6 that layer 2 provides unacknowledged information transfer service to both layer 3 and the management entity. In unacknowledged information transfer, layer 2 at the sending end does not receive any acknowledgment from the peer layer 2. This, however, does not preclude the possibility of an acknowledgment from

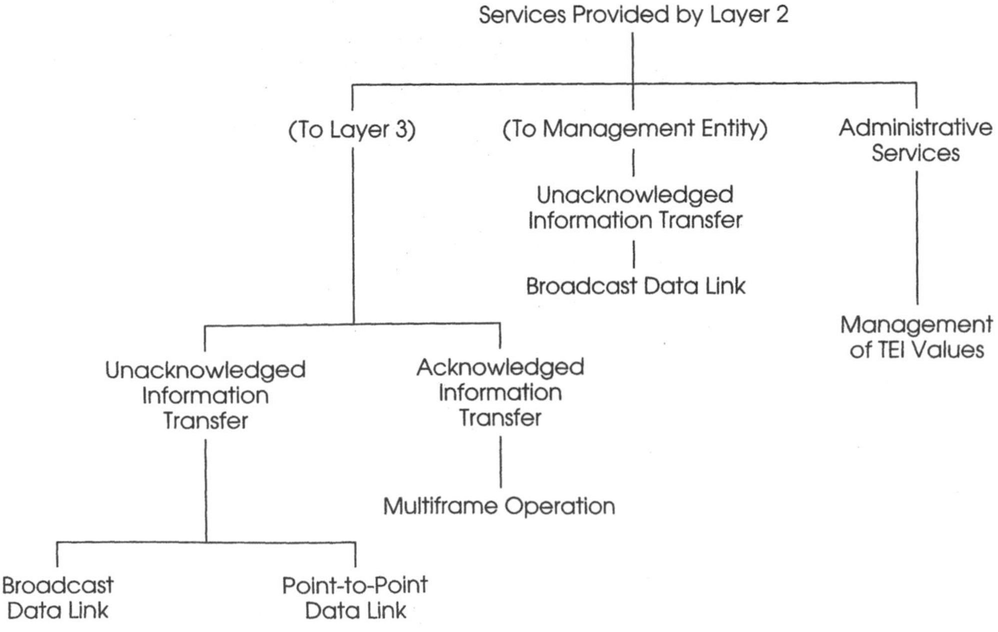

Figure 8–6 Services provided by layer 2.

higher layers. For unacknowledged information transfer to layer 3, the data link connection may be either point-to-point or broadcast. However, unacknowledged information transfer to management entity is by means of broadcast data link connection only.

Acknowledged information transfer service is provided only to layer 3, not to the management entity. Important characteristics of acknowledged information transfer are as follows:

- The integrity of data transfer is ensured.
- Frames are numbered, and their proper sequence is checked by layer 2 at the receiving end.
- Flow control and error correction are available.
- The service involves bidirectional flow of multiple frames between the peer layer 2 entities. The data link is therefore said to be under multiple frame operation.

The administrative service provided by layer 2 mainly relates to the management of TEI values for the terminal. This includes assignment and removal of TEI values. The assigned values are also checked. The procedure for TEI management is discussed in Section 8.8.4.

The provision of these services by layer 2 requires not only the exchange of frames on the data link between the two layer 2 entities, but also the exchange of primitives between layers 2 and 3 and between layer 2 and the management entity. As already mentioned, the exchange of primitives between layers 2 and 3 are considered to occur at the service access point.

The details of the different fields in the frame and their role in performing various layer 2 functions are discussed in Sections 8.8.2 and 8.8.3.

8.8.2 Frame Format

The 16 kbps bit stream in the D-channel is organized into frames. A frame, the basic unit of information, is composed of several fields. The structure of LAPD frames is shown in Figure 8–7.

The frames are formed by layer 2 at the sending end. This delimitation function involves the insertion of single octet flags at the beginning and end of the frame. The address field (two octets) provides the identity of the logical data link to which the frame relates. The control field consists of one or two octets. There are several types of frames, and this field identifies the type of frame. Moreover, the control field also carries the sequence number of the frames when necessary. Frames with sequence numbers have a control field of two octets; a single octet control field suffices for frames without sequence numbers. The frame check sequence (FCS) field consists of two octets. This field is used for error correction.

Notice that in the two formats shown, the only difference lies in the presence or absence of the information field. The information field mainly consists of layer 3 information. Typically, frames without the information field (format A) are used when layer 2 has to send frames to peer layer 2 and no layer 3 information is to be carried. The length of frames without the information field is fixed: five octets between flags for frames without sequence numbers and six octets for those with sequence numbers. When present, the information field has a variable length, the permissible length is up to 260 octets.

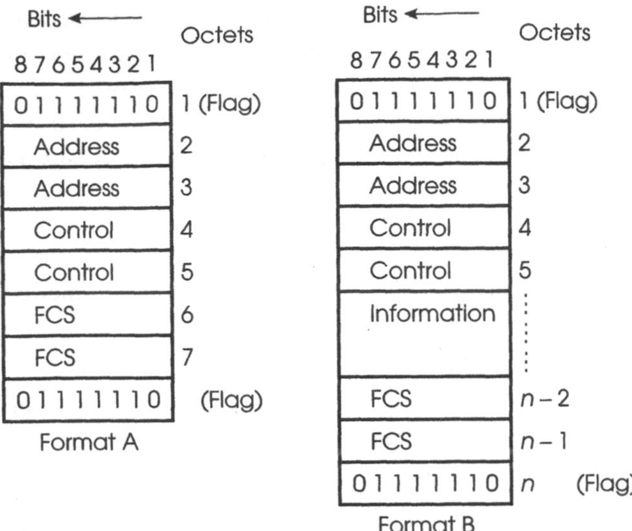

Figure 8–7 LAPD frame formats.

8.8.3 Functions Performed by Layer 2

Broadly, the functions performed by layer 2 are the following:

- Structuring the 16 kbps D-channel bit stream into frames
- Error detection and correction
- Addressing to allow several data link connections on a channel
- Sequencing to ensure that the transmitted frames are received in the correct order at the receiving end
- Flow control to regulate the flow of frames to avoid congestion

8.8.3.1 Delimitation Function: Opening and Closing Flags

Flags are used to indicate the beginning and end of a frame. The beginning of a frame is identified by a sequence of 8 bits, namely, 01111110. In addition to the opening flag, an identical closing flag is used to indicate the end of the frame. The transceivers in the terminals and the exchange are designed to accept more than one consecutive flag, although in certain applications, the closing flag can be used to indicate the beginning of the next frame.

To ensure that the contents of the frame do not contain the same bit sequence as the flag, a zero insertion and deletion procedure is performed. The procedure is similar to the one described in Section 6.3 for CCS 7 signal units. An extra 0 is inserted by the sending side after a contiguous sequence of five 1 bits. The first task of the receiving side is to identify the flags and discard them. Then, the removal of any 0's inserted by the transmitter is performed on the remaining data.

8.8.3.2 Error Detection

The last two octets before the closing flag are called the *frame check sequence* (FCS) octets. Error detection is performed by means of a cyclic redundancy check polynomial, which computes and appends the frame check sequence octets before the frame is transmitted. On the receiving side, the FCS octets are computed independently by employing the same cyclic check redundancy polynomial on the received data. A match between this computed value and the FCS octets received in the frame signals a correctly received frame. A mismatch indicates an error condition.

In addition to the above procedure, the receiving side also makes certain broad checks to ensure that the received frame conforms to the prescribed frame format. A frame is considered as invalid—that is, received in error—in each of the following situations:

- Not properly bounded by the flags
- Frames whose length is not an integer number of octets
- Frames without a sequence number of fewer than five octets
- Frames with a sequence number of fewer than six octets
- Frames with a single octet address field
- In the address field, frames containing a SAPI that is not supported by the receiver

If the frame is valid, the receiver proceeds to process the received frame; otherwise, the frame is discarded.

8.8.3.3 Address Field: Multiplexing Logical Data Links

The role of a SAPI and a TEI in multiplexing logical data links has already been explained. The address field consists of two octets and identifies the device and the service (signaling or packet data) to which the frame relates. It therefore includes both the SAPI and TEI. Figure 8–8 shows the address field format.

The 6-bit SAPI field permits the definition of up to 64 service access points. In ITU-T recommendation Q.921, only a few SAPI values have been assigned so far, as seen in Table 8–5.

The 7-bit TEI field provides for 127 TEI values. The TEI uniquely identifies the terminal on the passive S bus. Normally, two terminals cannot have the same TEI (except for the broadcast mode). In certain situations, however, a terminal may have more than one

8	7	6	5	4	3	2	1	Octet
SAPI						C/R	EA 0	2
TEI							EA 1	3

Key
EA: Address Field Extension Bit
C/R: Command/Response Bit
SAPI: Service Access Point Identifier
TEI: Terminal Endpoint Identifier

Figure 8–8 Address field format. [Reprinted from ITU-T recommendation Q.921 (1993) ISDN user-network interface—Data link layer specifications. Rev. 1. Reprinted by permission.]

Table 8-5 Assignment of SAPI Values

SAPI VALUE	RELATED ENTITY
0	Call control procedure (signaling information)
1–15	Packet mode communication using Q.931 call control
16	X.25 packet mode communication
17–31	Reserved for future standardization
63	Layer 2 management procedures
All others	Not available for recommendation Q.921 procedures

TEI value, for example, a terminal providing two separate but identical applications, say packet mode communication using Q.931 call control procedures. In this case, the same SAPI value (SAPI = 1) has to be assigned for both applications since the two applications are identical. In order to identify different logical data links for the two applications, it is necessary to assign two TIE values to the terminal.

The assignment of TEI values to a terminal can be performed by both automatic and nonautomatic means. Automatic allocation is carried out by the network, whereas nonautomatic assignment is performed by the user. The TEI values used are as follows:

0–63 for nonautomatic assignment

64–126 for automatic assignment

127 for the broadcast mode

The assignment procedure is described in Section 8.8.4.1.

The first bit in each octet of the address field is the extension of address (EA) bit. EA = 0 indicates the first octet of the address field. The EA is set to 1 in the second octet.

Depending on the application, frames may represent commands sent from one side to the other to perform specific tasks. The other side may send back responses to the received commands. Commands and responses can flow in either direction, user to network and network to user. The command/response (C/R) bit indicates whether the frame corresponds to a command or a response. Table 8–6 shows the values for C/R bit in the two directions:

8.8.3.4 The Control Field: Frame Types, Sequencing, Error Correction, and Flow Control

The control field identifies the type of the frame:

1. Information (I) frames are used to transfer information between layer 3 entities, as noted earlier.

Table 8-6 Values for C/R Bits

DIRECTION	COMMAND	RESPONSE
Network to user	1	0
User to network	0	1

2. Supervisory (S) frames play a role in error correction and flow control.
3. Unnumbered (U) frames provide additional control functions.

Control field formats corresponding to these frame types are shown in Figure 8–9.

All frames contain a poll/final (P/F) bit. In a command frame, the P/F bit is called the *P bit.* The P bit is set to 1 if the data link entity is soliciting a response from the peer data link entity. In the response frame, the P/F bit is called the F bit. An F bit set to 1 indicates that the response frame is being transmitted in answer to the command frame soliciting a response.

8.8.3.4.1 Information Frames

Information frames are assigned consecutive sequence numbers, *N(S),* as they are sent out by the transmitter. The values of *N(S)* assigned to information frames in the two directions are independent of each other. The sequence number of the next expected I-frame from the other side is provided in the *N(R)* field. *N(R)* also serves as an acknowledgment to the receiving side that frames sent out by it earlier with *N(S)* from 0 to *N(R)* – 1 have been correctly received. This mechanism of acknowledging more than one frame at a time provides the capability of sending different number of frames in the two directions. Thus, depending on the application, the two sides send information frames as required

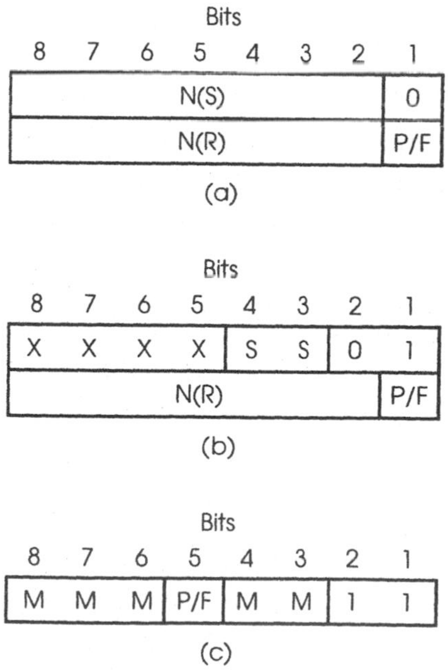

Bits

8	7	6	5	4	3	2	1
N(S)							0
N(R)							P/F

(a)

Bits

8	7	6	5	4	3	2	1
X	X	X	X	S	S	0	1
N(R)							P/F

(b)

Bits

8	7	6	5	4	3	2	1
M	M	M	P/F	M	M	1	1

(c)

Key
N(S): Transmitter Send Sequence Number
N(R): Transmitter Receive Sequence Number
S: Supervisory Function Bit
M: Modifier Function Bit
P/F: Poll Bit (P) When the Frame is Issued as a Command; Final Bit (F) When the Frame is a Response Frame
X: Reserved, Set to 0

Figure 8–9 Control field formats: (a) information frames, I format; (b) supervisory frames, S format; (c) unnumbered frames, U format.

and need not send an acknowledgment each time a frame is correctly received from the other end. *N(S)* and *N(R)* cycle in the range of 0 to 127 (modulo 128, extended mode of operation). Theoretically, up to 127 frames can remain unacknowledged before an acknowledgment is sent. However, the maximum number (k) of I-frames that may remain unacknowledged has been specified at the following values:

- For basic access signaling information, $k = 1$.
- For basic access packet information, $k = 3$.
- For both primary access signaling and packet information, $k = 7$.

Information frames are always used as command frames.

As will be seen in the discussion on establishment of a logical data link, when the link is first setup, the I-frames are transmitted beginning with $N(S) = 0$, $N(R) = 0$. To manage the values of *N(S)* and *N(R)* at the two ends, local variables *V(R)*, *V(S)*, and *V(A)* are used at either end. *V(S)* is used to set the *N(S)* value in the next I-frame to be transmitted. *V(R)* indicates the *N(S)* value expected in the I-frame to be received next from the distant end. The third variable, *V(A)*, is used to indicate the *N(R)* value of the transmitted frame whose acknowledgment is expected next.

In summary, I-frames are numbered and, in an error-free situation, must be received in correct sequence. Their error-free reception must be acknowledged. Acknowledgments may be sent either along with an I-frame or by a supervisory frame. I-frames are used as commands for transferring information between peer layer 3 entities.

8.8.3.4.2 Supervisory Frames

Supervisory frames do not contain the *N(S)* field. Refer to Figure 8–9(b). The *N(R)* field conveys acknowledgment for correctly received frames. Bits 3 and 4 of the first octet of the *S* format control field are used to distinguish between the three types of supervisory frames that are defined for LAPD. These are

1. Receive ready (RR) supervisory frame
2. Receive Not Ready (RNR) supervisory frame
3. Reject (REJ) Supervisory frame

(HDLC also includes a fourth type, selective reject, to request retransmission of only a single I-frame.)

The RR supervisory frame, as its name suggests, is sent by a data link entity to indicate that it is ready to receive frames from the other side. The *N(R)* value in the frame signals acknowledgment of frames received with sequence numbers up to $N(R) - 1$. In addition, the RR frame serves to cancel the effect of any RNR frame sent earlier. The RR command frame with the P bit set to 1 is used to solicit information from the peer data link entity about its status.

The RNR supervisory frame has functions that are reverse of those of an RR frame. It is used by the data link layer entity to indicate a busy condition. The *N(R)* field in the frame has the usual function of acknowledgment. An RNR command with the P bit set to 1 is also used to find the status of the peer data link entity.

The REJ supervisory frame is used to request retransmission of I-frames starting with the frame numbered *N(R)*. The REJ frame may also be used in canceling the busy condition indicated by an RNR frame sent earlier. Moreover, like the RNR command, an REJ command may be used to obtain the status of a peer data link entity.

Each type of S-frame described above may be used as a command or response frame. An example of error correction by retransmission involving an exchange of I- and S-frames between layer 2 entities is presented in Figure 8–10.

In addition to acknowledgments, supervisory frames provide the capability of flow control and error correction by retransmission. To reduce the flow of received frames when the data link entity perceives congestion, it can request its peer data link entity to temporarily suspend transmission of frames by sending an RNR frame.

8.8.3.4.3 Unnumbered Frames

The control field for unnumbered frames is shown in Figure 8–9(c). Different combinations of M bits are used to define seven different types of U-frames, which are listed below. They do not contain any sequence number and are used to provide additional data link control functions. Some U-frames are used as commands and others as responses, as indicated in parentheses.

- Set asynchronous balanced mode extended (SABME) frame (command)
- Disconnect (DISC) frame (command)
- Disconnect mode (DM) frame (response)
- Unnumbered acknowledgment (UA) frame (response)
- Frame reject (FRMR) frame (response)
- Unnumbered information (UI) frame (command)

UI are frames that are used in the TEI management procedure described in the next section. An example of the use of other frames appears in Section 8.8.5.

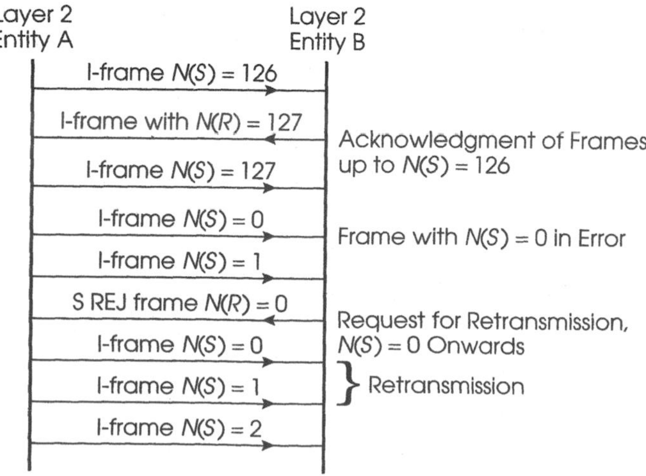

Figure 8–10 Error correction by retransmission.

8.8.4 Terminal Endpoint Identifier (TEI) Management

The following procedures are used for TEI management:

1. The TEI assignment procedure is used for assignment of TEI values to terminals that are connected for the first time or that have been reconnected after being moved.
2. The TEI check procedure is used periodically by the network to ensure that the TEI values have been assigned correctly; for example, this procedure checks that two terminals in an ISDN basic access have not been assigned the same value.
3. The TEI removal procedure is used by the network to deallocate a TEI value previously assigned to a terminal.
4. The TEI identity verify procedure is employed by the user to verify the identity of the terminals connected to the S/T-interface.

Unnumbered information (UI) frames are exchanged between the network and the user for the management of TEI values. The information field in the UI-frame has the format as shown in Figure 8–11. The first octet is the management entity identifier. At present, recommendation Q.921 specifies only TEI management procedures. In the future, other management procedures may be added, and this is the rationale for providing a management entity identifier. The value of the management entity identifier for the TEI management procedure is coded as 0000 1111. The reference number occupies the second and third octets. The function of the reference number is discussed in the next section. The fourth octet refers to message type. In all, there are seven types of messages involved in the implementation of the TEI management procedures. The codes for these message types are listed in Table 8–7. The use of the message type, reference number, and action indicator, which appear in Figure 8–11 and Table 8–7, is explained with reference to the TEI assignment procedure in the next section.

8.8.4.1 *TEI Assignment Procedure*

The requirements for the assignment of the TEI are as follows:

- An ISDN terminal may be assigned a TEI value either by the user (nonautomatic assignment) or by the network (automatic assignment).

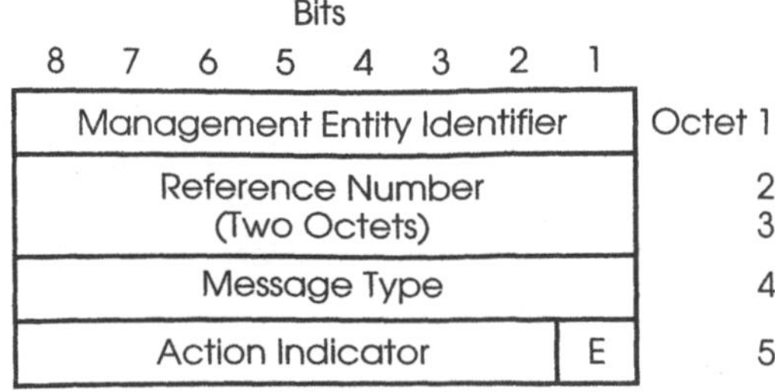

Figure 8–11 Messages used for TEI management (information field of UI-frames).

Table 8–7 Codes for Messages Concerning TEI Management Procedures

Reprinted from ITU-T recommendation Q.921 (1993) ISDN user-network layer 2 specifications—Data link layer specifications. Rev. 1. Reproduced by permission.

Message Name	Management Entity Identifier	Reference Number Ri	Message Type	Action Indicator Ai
Identity request (user to network)	0000 1111	0-65535	0000 0001	Ai = 127; any TEI value acceptable
Identity assigned (network to user)	0000 1111	0-65535	0000 0010	Ai = 64–126; assigned TEI value
Identity denied (network to user)	0000 1111	0-65535	0000 0011	Ai = 64–126; denied TEI value Ai = 127; no TEI value available
Identity check request (network to user)	0000 1111	Not used (coded 0)	0000 0100	Ai = 127; check all TEI values Ai = 0–126; TEI value to be checked
Identity check response (user to network)	0000 1111	0-65535	0000 0101	Ai = 0–126; TEI value in use
Identity remove (network to user)	0000 1111	Not used (coded 0)	0000 0110	Ai = 127; request for removal of all TEI values Ai = 0–126; TEI value to be removed
Identity verify (user to network)	0000 1111	Not used (coded 0)	0000 0111	Ai = 126; TEI value to be checked

- The possibility of moving a terminal from one socket to another socket in the same basic access or to a socket in another basic access of the same or a different local exchange must be supported.
- There should be no need to preregister or provide prior information to the network before connecting a new ISDN terminal.
- It may be necessary to assign more than one TEI to an ISDN terminal that supports more than one service with the same SAPI value.
- Different terminals in the same access should not be assigned the same TEI.

On the user side, the management entity has the record of the TEI values. On the network side, a record of the TEI values is also maintained by the management entity in the ISDN exchange. This entity is aptly called the assignment source point (ASP).

Automatic assignment of TEI consists of the following steps. This procedure is illustrated in Figure 8–12.

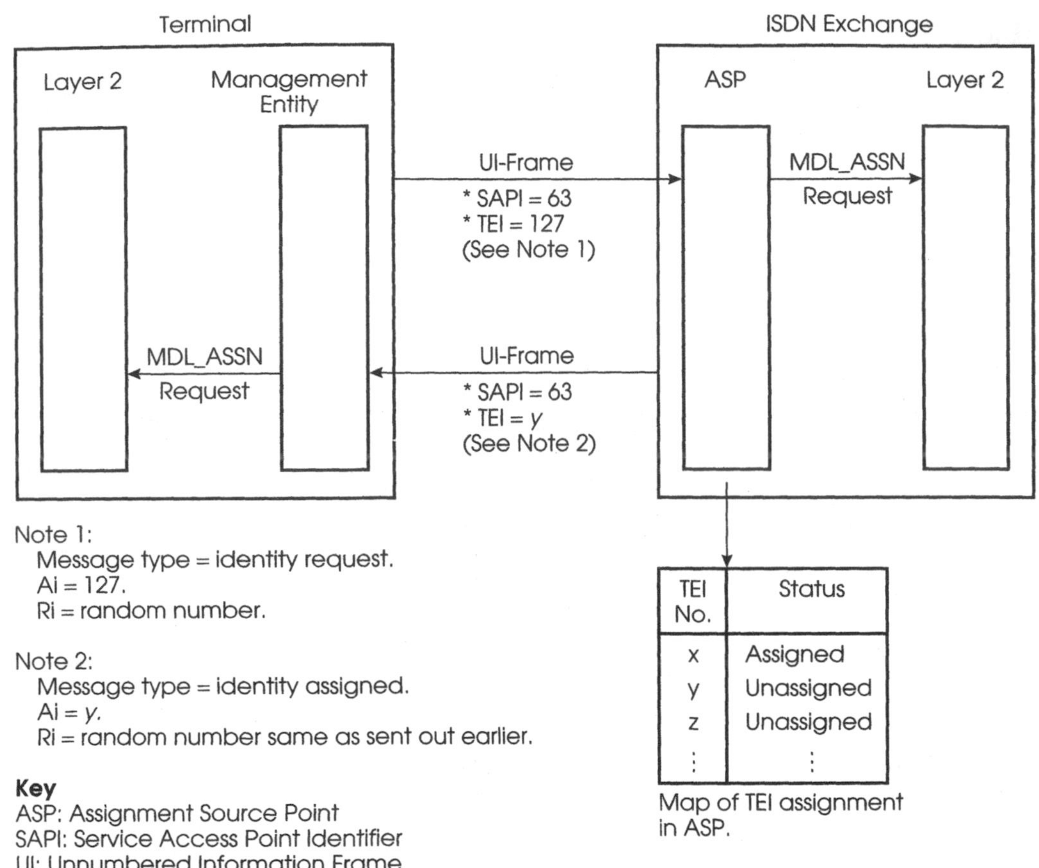

Figure 8–12 TEI automatic assignment procedure (successful assignment).

1. The management entity at the user side initiates a request for TEI assignment by generating an unnumbered information (UI) frame, complete with the flag, FCS, and other layer 2 fields. The SAPI is set at 63 (refer to Table 8–5). The TEI for the broadcast mode, 127, is used. The frame also includes the following (also refer to the first row of Table 8–7):
   (a) The message type, of one octet, which indicates the nature of the request. In this case, the message type is "identity request" (that is, the management entity is requesting assignment of an identity code, namely, the TEI). The code used is 00000001.
   (b) The reference number, Ri, of two octets, to differentiate between different terminals that may simultaneously request TEI assignment. The reference number is generated by the management entity using a random-number generator. Two octets of Ri accommodate a random number in the range of 0 to 65,535. The possibility of generating identical random numbers for two simultaneous TEI assignment requests is extremely remote.

(c) The action indicator, Ai, set to 127. It indicates that any TEI value in the permissible range (64 to 126, for automatic assignment) may be allotted.

Timer T202 is also started at the user end.

2. Upon receiving the UI-frame, the ASP refers to the map of TEI assignments available with it. An unused TEI is selected and conveyed to layer 2 by means of a primitive MDL-ASSIGN REQUEST.
3. The ASP generates a UI-frame with the message type "identity assigned" if a TEI value has been assigned. The Ai contains the value of the TEI selected for assignment. The UI-frame is transmitted to the user end.
4. On receipt of the UI-frame, the management entity at the user side checks the Ri to ensure that the primitive received indeed corresponds to the TEI assignment request sent earlier. If the Ri value matches, then timer T202 is stopped.
5. The assigned TEI is conveyed by the management entity to layer 2 of the terminal using the MDL-ASSIGN REQUEST primitive.

   If the ASP is unable to assign a TEI—for example, due to nonavailability of an unused TEI value—then the UI-frame sent to the user side contains the message type "identity denied." The Ai field in this case contains 127, which corresponds to the broadcast mode. Thus, no TEI assignment is made.
6. The management entity also checks for anomalies such as the assignment of a TEI value by the network that already exists as per the record available with the management entity. In such a case, the management entity may initiate a TEI identity verify or TEI removal procedure.

The six steps described above complete the automatic TEI assignment procedure. If no response is received from the network before expiry of timer T202, or if a UI-frame with an identity denied message is received, a fresh request for TEI assignment using a new Ri value is made. Timer T202 has a value of 2 seconds. Repeat requests can be made up to N202 times, where N202 is a system parameter. The default value for N202 is 3.

For nonautomatic assignment of TEI, the management entity on the user side assigns the terminal identity in the range 0 to 63 and informs layer 2 using the primitive MDL-ASSIGN REQUEST.

8.8.4.2 TEI Check Procedure

An ISDN terminal may be removed from the S/T-interface or moved to another basic access. It is therefore necessary for the ASP to suitably update the TEI map so that it reflects the current situation.

When the status of all the TEI assignments at an ISDN interface are required by the network, a UI-frame with the message type "identity check request" is sent by the network to the user. The Ai value is set at 127. On the other hand, if the network desires to make a check on a particular TEI, then this TEI value is set in Ai. Also refer to Table 8–7.

In Figure 8–13, the network sends Ai = 127 to ascertain the TEI values of all the terminals. The SAPI is set at 63 and the TEI at 127. All three terminals connected at the

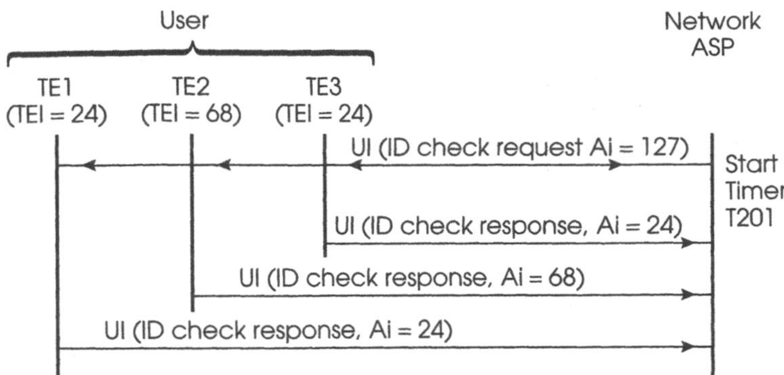

Figure 8–13 Example of the TEI check procedure.

interface respond with UI-frames with the message type "identity check response." The TEI value is set in the Ai field. Different random reference numbers—say, Ri1, Ri2, and Ri3—are sent by terminals TE1, TE2, and TE3, respectively.

The network finds that two TEI values are equal to 24. That they relate to different terminals is readily known due to different Ri values. Thus, besides permitting the network to determine the current TEI assignments, the check procedure also provides the capability of detecting assignment of the same TEI value to more than one terminal.

Timer T201 is used for time supervision. It is started at the network side when the UI-frame with an identity check request is sent and stopped when a UI-frame with an identity check response is received.

When the check procedure is used to ascertain whether a particular TEI is currently assigned at the ISDN access and if no UI-frame (with identity check response) is received before the expiry of timer T201, the procedure repeats once more after resetting timer T201. If following this second attempt no response is received from the terminal side, then the ASP concludes that the TEI value being checked is not assigned to any terminal and is available for reassignment to a terminal.

As a result of the TEI check procedure, the map of TEI assignment maintained by the ASP is updated.

8.8.4.3 TEI Removal Procedure

The TEI removal procedure may be initiated at either end, the user side or the network side. When the procedure is initiated at the network side, a UI-frame with the message type "identity remove" is sent to the user side. Refer to row 6 of Table 8–7. The TEI value to be removed is set in the Ai field of the frame. When all the TEI values at an S/T-interface are to be removed, the Ai field is coded as 127. The information that a TEI removal request has been made by the ASP is conveyed to the layer 2 entity on the network side using an MDL_REMOVE request primitive. The identity remove message is sent twice in succession to avoid the risk of message loss.

When the TEI removal procedure is initiated at the user side, the management entity informs the layer 2 at the user side by using the MDL_REMOVE request primitive. The TEI value to be removed is contained in the Ai field of this primitive.

8.8.4.4 TEI Identity Verify Procedure

The implementation of the TEI identity verify procedure is optional for both the network and the user side. As seen in Section 8.8.4.2, the TEI check procedure is normally initiated by the network. However, in certain situations, the user side may also verify the identity of a terminal connected at the S/T-interface. The TEI identity verify procedure enables the user to make such a request.

The user side sends a UI-frame with the message type "identity verify request." The other fields are set according to row 7 of Table 8–7. Upon receiving the message, the network side begins the TEI check procedure described earlier. The TEI identity verified procedure is supervised at the user side by timer T202.

8.8.5 Multiple Frame Operation Procedure

Multiple frame operation consists of three phases:

1. Establishing a data link connection
2. The bidirectional transfer of multiple frames between data link entities
3. Disconnection of the data link

8.8.5.1 Establishing a Data Link Connection

To provide bidirectional flow of layer 2 frames between the terminal and the network, it is essential that a data link be established between the two endpoints. Unnumbered frames listed in Section 8.8.3.4.3 are used for this purpose.

A request for establishing a data link originates at layer 3, either in the terminal or the network. Layer 3 makes this request by using a primitive called DL_ESTABLISH request. The end that initiates the procedure sends an SABME frame command. The P bit in the command is set to 1. Simultaneously, timer T200 is started.

If upon examination of the SAPI and TEI in the SABME command the other end finds that the data link can be set up, it responds by an unnumbered acknowledgment (UA) frame. The F-bit in the UA-frame is set to the same binary value as the P bit in the SAMBE command. Layer 2 also reports to layer 3 by the DL_ESTABLISH indication primitive that a data link is being established.

On receipt of the UA response frame, timer T200 is stopped. The control variables *V(S), V(R),* and *V(A)* are set to 0. These control variables are used in association with the send sequence number *N(S)* and the receive sequence number *N(R)* during multiple-frame transfer on the data link. Layer 2 informs layer 3 that its request for establishing a data link connection has been executed. This is done by sending the DL_ESTABLISH CONFIRM primitive.

An example of the data link establishment procedure is shown in Figure 8–14, in which the terminal is assumed to initiate the procedure.

The data link is now ready for multiple-frame operation involving information and supervisory frames with proper sequence numbers. Recommendation Q.931 stipulates that timer T203 may be started as an option. Timer T203 is for supervising the start of

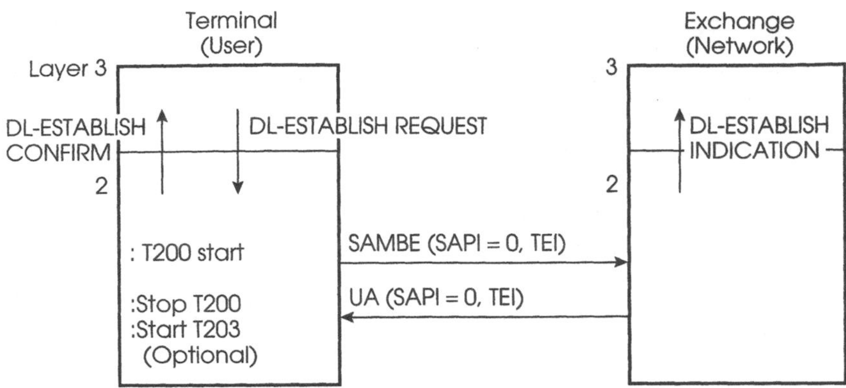

Figure 8–14 Data link establishment procedure.

multiframe operation after the link is set up. It represents the maximum time allowed without frames being exchanged. The default value for T203 is 10 seconds.

If the side receiving the SABME command determines (after examining the TEI and SAPI) that it is not in a position to set up the data link, it sends a disconnect mode (DM) response frame with the F bit equal to the P bit of the received SABME command. On receiving the DM frame, layer 2 informs layer 3 that the data link has not been established. A primitive DL-RELEASE-INDICATION is used for this purpose.

If timer T200 expires without either UA or DM response from the other side, the SABME command may be retransmitted up to N200 (default value 3) times. Each time the SABME command is sent, timer T200 is reset. If no response is received after N200 retransmissions, then layer 3 is informed accordingly by DL-RELEASE-INDICATION primitive. In addition, an error indication is sent to the management entity by MDL-ERROR-INDICATION primitive.

8.8.5.2 Multiple Frame Transfer between Data Link Entities

A request is made by layer 3 to layer 2 for transmission of information to the peer layer 3 entity. The information is contained in the primitive DL-DATA-REQUEST. The data link entity generates an I-frame and packs the information received from layer 3 into the information field of the frame. The *N(S)* and *N(R)* values are set equal to two control variables, *V(S)* and *V(R),* respectively. An I-frame is transmitted, and, simultaneously, timer T200 is started. In addition, the value of *V(S)* is incremented in preparation for the transmission of the next frame.

Upon receipt of a valid I-frame, the layer 2 entity sends the contents of the information field to layer 3 by means of the primitive DL-DATA-INDICATION. On receiving an I-frame, the data link entity may respond with one of the following frames:

- Receive ready (RR) frames indicate that it is ready to receive further frames. It also contains the acknowledgment of the received frame and may be used to find out about the status (for example, busy status) of the other side.

- If the data link entity determines a busy condition, it should request the other end not to send any frames for the time being. This may be done by sending receive not ready (RNR) frame.

If the data entity wishes to send information to the other side, I-frames are sent.

An example of multiframe operation is provided in Figure 8–15. A brief explanation follows.

(1) and (2): The establishment of a data link is completed. The control variables at either end are initialized to 0.

(3): The transmission of multiple frames begins with the sending of an I-frame by end A.

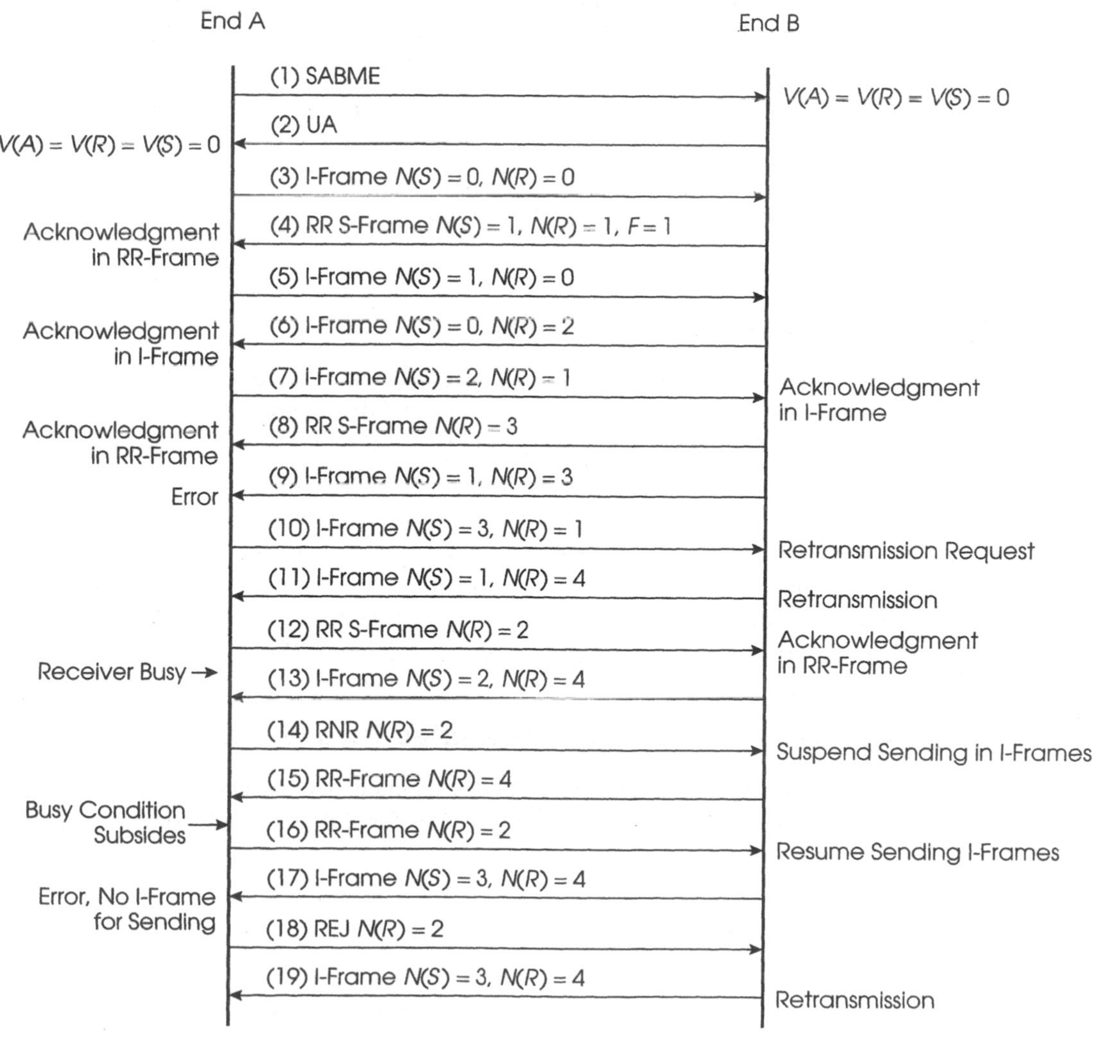

Figure 8–15 Example of a multiframe operation.

(4): End B receives the frame correctly. End B sends an RR-frame indicating that it is ready to receive further frames. The F bit is set at 1 in the RR-frame. Correct reception of the received I-frame is also acknowledged.

(5), (6), and (7): The exchange of I-frames takes place.

(8): An RR-frame is sent by end A.

(9): An I-frame sent by end B is received in error at end A.

(10): End A in the next I-frame also indicates the reception of an errored I-frame by means of the value set in *N(R)*.

(11): The I-frame sent earlier is repeated by end B.

(12): The RR-frame sent by end A includes acknowledgment of the correct reception of the I-frame.

(13): An I-frame is sent by end B.

(14): The level 2 entity at end A perceives a busy condition. Accordingly it sends a receive not ready (RNR) frame. End B suspends the sending of I-frames.

(15): An RR-frame is sent by end B.

(16): The busy condition abates at end A. An RR-frame is sent by end A.

(17): An I-frame is sent by end B.

(18): The I-frame is received in error at end A. However, it has no I-frame to send. Therefore, to request retransmission, end A sends an REJ frame.

(19): On reception of the REJ frame, end B retransmits the I-frame.

8.8.5.3 Disconnection of Data Link

To terminate the multiframe operation, layer 3 makes a request to layer 2 by the DL_RELEASE request primitive. Layer 2 then sends a DISC frame on the data link to the other end with the P bit set to 1. Timer T200 starts. Refer to Figure 8–16. Layer 2 at the other end responds with a UA-frame with the F bit set to the same value as the P bit in the received DISC frame. Layer 2 also sends the DL_RELEASE indication primitive to its layer 3. Upon receipt of the UA message, layer 2 at the end that initiated the disconnection confirms the termination of multiframe operation to layer 3 by the DL_RELEASE confirm primitive. Timer T200 is stopped. If timer T200 expires before receiving the UA message, then the procedure is repeated after resetting timer T200.

8.8.6 Summary of Layer 2 Timers and Associated Parameters

Table 8–8 lists layer 2 timers and other associated parameters as standardized in ITU [3]. Table 8–9 provides the corresponding values for Bell operating companies [180].

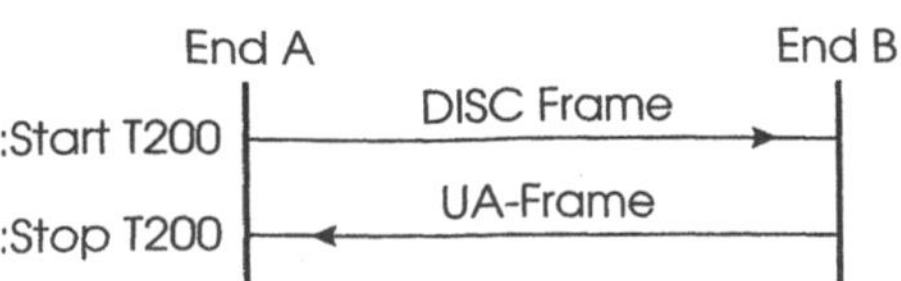

Figure 8–16 Termination of the multiframe operation.

Table 8-8 ITU-T Recommended Values for Layer 2 Timers and Parameters

TIMER/PARAMETER	APPLICATION	VALUE
T200	Point-to-point LAPD at 16 kbps and 64 kbps	1 second
T201	TEI assignment procedure at ASP	1 second
T202	TEI assignment procedure, user side	2 seconds
T203	Point-to-point LAPD at 16 and 64 kbps	10 seconds
N200	Point-to-point LAPD at 16 and 64 kbps	3
N201	Point-to-point LAPD at 16 and 64 kbps	260
N202	TEI assignment procedure, user side	3

Table 8-9 BELLCORE Recommended Values for Layer 2 Timers and Parameters

	VALUE	
TIMER/PARAMETER	RANGE	DEFAULT SETTING
T200	1 to 20 seconds in steps of 0.5 s	1 second
T201	0.5 to 5 seconds in steps of 0.1 s	1 second
T202	0.5 to 10 seconds in steps of 0.1 s	2 seconds
T203	10 to 300 seconds in steps of 10 s	10 seconds
N200	1 to 10 in steps of 1	3
N201	—	260
N202	—	3

8.9 Layer 3 Protocol in Digital Subscriber Signaling System 1 (DSS 1)

Layer 3 protocol specifies the various functions required for establishing, maintaining, and releasing circuit switched, packet switched, and user-to-user signaling connections. The protocol applies equally to both basic and primary access connections. For establishing a call in the B-channel, layer 3 selects and assigns one of the B-channels available at the user-network interface. It also requests the network to provide the necessary bearer capability required to support the service request. Layer 3 functions also permit the implementation of various supplementary services. Since a variety of ISDN equipment may be present at each ISDN access, layer 3 also checks for compatibility. Furthermore, the use of a separate D-channel allows transfer of information, irrespective of the state of the call.

A sequence of layer 3 messages are exchanged between the user and the network for call control at both the calling and called ends. The messages are carried in the information field of the frames created at layer 2 and make use of the data link connection established on the D-channel.

The ITU-T recommendations covering layer 3 procedures are summarized in Table 8–10.

Table 8–10 International Standards on ISDN User Network Interface Layer 3

RECOMMENDATION	TOPIC
Q.930	Describes the general aspects of layer 3 protocols and functions
Q.931	Procedures for circuit switched, packet switched, and user-to-user signaling connections for both basic rate and primary ISDN interfaces
Q.932	Protocols for supplementary services
Q.933	Procedures for frame mode bearer capabilities
Q.939	Coding of compatibility information elements to various bearer and teleservices

Layer 3 protocols for circuit switched connections are discussed in the following sections. Protocols for the support of supplementary services are also covered. Procedures for packet switched connections and frame mode bearer capabilities are considered in Chapter 12.

8.9.1 Format of Layer 3 Messages

The layer 3 message format is shown in Figure 8–17. Each message consists of two parts, a common header part that is mandatory for every message and a number of information elements. Information elements consist of one or more octets of information, coded in a prescribed manner. The amount of information carried by a layer 3 message varies widely with the type of message. Thus, the number and type of information elements vary from message to message. Furthermore, for a given message, some of the information elements may be mandatory, whereas the others may be optional. If a layer 3 message information exceeds 260 octets, which is the maximum permissible size for the I-field in LAPD, it becomes necessary to segment the message before sending it on the data link. The segments are then reassembled by layer 3 at the receiving end.

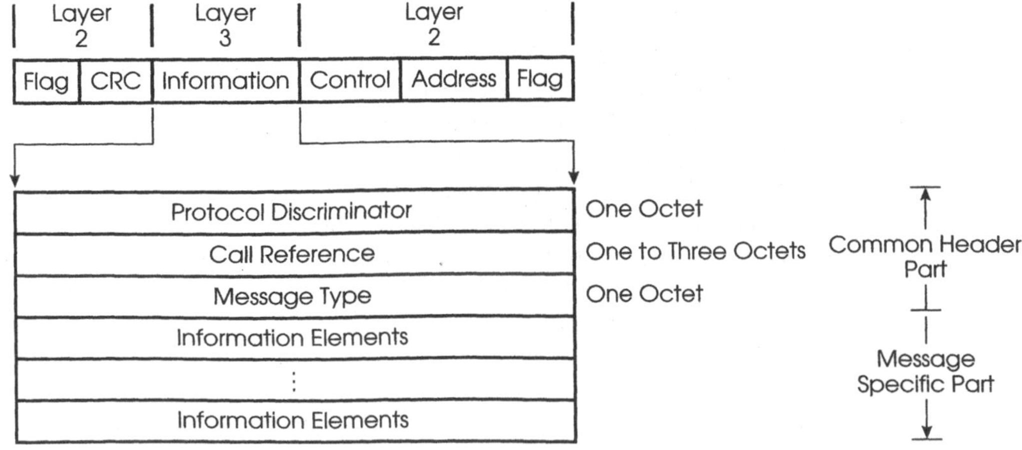

Figure 8–17 Layer 3 message format.

Table 8–11 Protocol Discriminator Coding

8765 4321	Meaning
0000 0000 to 0000 0111	Used to define protocols concerning user-to-user signaling
0000 1000	Q.931 call control messages
0001 0000 to 0011 1111	[a]
0100 0000 to 0100 1111	Reserved for national use
0101 0000 to 1111 1111	[a]

[a] Reserved for other network layer or layer 3 protocols, including X.25.

The header consists of the following:

- Protocol discriminator
- Call reference value
- Message type

8.9.1.1 Protocol Discriminator

The protocol discriminator octet is used to distinguish a Q.931 call control message from messages of other protocols. Table 8–11 shows the coding scheme for protocol discriminator octet. For recommendation Q.931, the protocol discriminator is coded 0000 1000.

When user-to-user supplementary service is to be supported through a signaling connection, it is necessary to specify the protocol in which the user-to-user information is carried. Codes 0000 0000 to 0000 0111 are provided for this purpose.

8.9.1.2 Call Reference

Layer 3 messages are sent on a data link for control of different calls. To identify messages corresponding to a particular call, a call reference is assigned at the beginning of the call and exists until the call is terminated or suspended.* The call reference is always assigned at the originating ISDN interface. Once a call is terminated (or suspended), the call reference number used for the call can be assigned to a subsequent call.

The call reference information element format is shown in Figure 8–18. It essentially consists of two parts, a call reference value and a flag. The call reference value is typically one octet long for basic access, whereas for primary access, a two-octet reference value is usually used.

The flag permits the use of the same reference number for two calls originating in opposite directions on the layer 2 logical link. The side that allocates the call reference

*A call is normally suspended to implement the Terminal Portability Supplementary Service (See Section 8.5.3.4.)

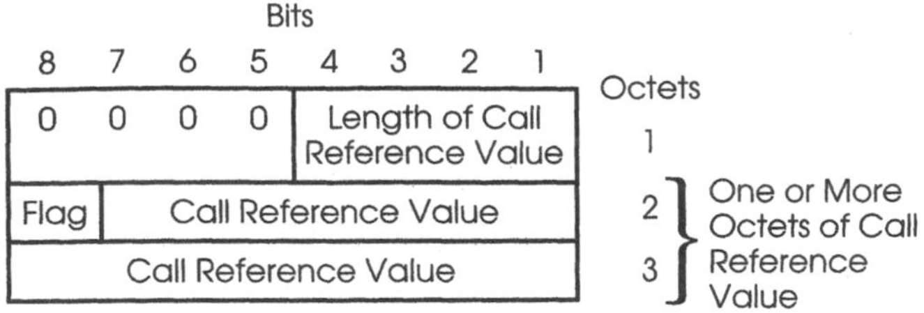

Figure 8–18 Call reference information element.

sets the flag to 0; the other side sets the flag to 1. Thus, if the two sides allocate the same call reference for different calls on the same logical data link connection, then the calls are distinguishable by the value of the flag.

8.9.1.3 Message Type

The message type information element identifies the message. It consists of a single octet in which the message type is coded using the seven least significant bits. Bit 8 is reserved for future use.

The following example illustrates the use of messages in the control of a successful basic circuit switched call connection between two ISDN users. Refer to Figure 8–19.

EXAMPLE 8-1

When the calling terminal originates a call, a SETUP message is sent from the terminal to the originating ISDN exchange. Two possibilities exist with regard to the contents of the setup message:

1. The entire information necessary for establishing the call may be sent to the network in one step in the setup message. This is called en bloc sending of information. Refer to Figure 8–19(a).
2. The information may be sent in more than one installment. This is called the overlap sending of information. Refer to Figure 8–19(b). The setup message should contain enough information to permit the originating exchange to begin processing of the call through the network. The originating exchange acknowledges this by sending a SETUP ACK message to the calling terminal. The calling terminal then sends the remaining information through one or more information (INFO) messages. When all the information is received, the originating exchange sends a CALL PROC message to the calling terminal.

In either case, the originating ISDN exchange checks whether the information received in the SETUP message is complete. If so, it initiates further processing of the call and the call proceeds in the network, possibly via several transit exchanges, to the terminating ISDN exchange. Simultaneously, the originating exchange informs the calling terminal that complete information has been received and that the call is proceeding through the network. This is done by sending a CALL PROC message to the calling terminal. The call proceeding message also informs the calling terminal of the B-channel it should use for the call.

On receiving the call, the terminating ISDN exchange also generates a setup message and sends it to the called ISDN access. A compatibility check is made to ascertain whether a free terminal of the appropriate type is available. If the compatibility check is successful, the terminal identified as the called terminal for the call sends an alerting (ALERT) message to the terminating ISDN exchange. When the call is answered, the called terminal sends a connect (CONN) message to the terminating ISDN exchange. The information is sent through the network to the originating exchange, which in turn generates a connect message for the calling terminal. The latter now sends a CONN ACK message to the originating ISDN exchange. The information is transferred through the network to the terminating exchange. The terminating exchange then sends the connect acknowledge message to the called terminal. The connection on the B-channel is now established.

In the ISDN, either side can initiate the release of the connection. In Figure 8–19, the called side is shown to initiate release. A disconnect (DISC) message is sent to the terminating exchange. The information is conveyed through the network to the originating exchange, which sends a DISC message to the calling terminal. As shown in the figure, the release of connection is completed by means of the release (REL) and release completed (REL COMP) messages.

Example 8–1 is based on a successful call. Additional messages are required for various other cases that may arise in the call control procedure of a circuit switched call. Additional messages are also required for control of packet mode connection and user-to-user signaling. A list of messages for basic call control specified in ITU-T recommendation Q.931 is shown in Table 8–12. The table also contains a brief description of each message, the direction of transmission (user to network, network to user, or both directions), its significance (local, access, dual, or global), and its applicability to the type of connection (circuit mode, packet mode, or user signaling connection).

A message has local significance when it has relevance only in the originating or terminating ISDN access. One example is the CALL PROC message. When sent by the originating ISDN exchange, it informs the calling terminal that the call is being processed through the network and that all the information required for the call has been received. The calling terminal therefore need not send any more information. The relevance or significance of the message in this case is limited to the originating ISDN access.

A message has access significance when it has relevance at both the originating and terminating ISDN access. Such messages need to be transported transparently by the network from one ISDN access to another, but no processing is performed on the contents of the message. NOTIFY message is one such example; it has significance at both the ISDN accesses, since it may contain information regarding call suspension that needs to be passed on from one access to the other.

A message with dual significance is relevant in either originating or terminating access and also in the network.

Messages of global significance have relevance everywhere, in the originating and terminating access and also in the network. Examples include ALERT, SETUP, and DISC messages.

The classification of messages according to their significance, as shown in Table 8–12, is useful in the study of interworking between DSS 1 protocol and CCS 7 with the ISDN user part (ISUP). This aspect is specified in ITU-T Recommendation Q.699 [181].

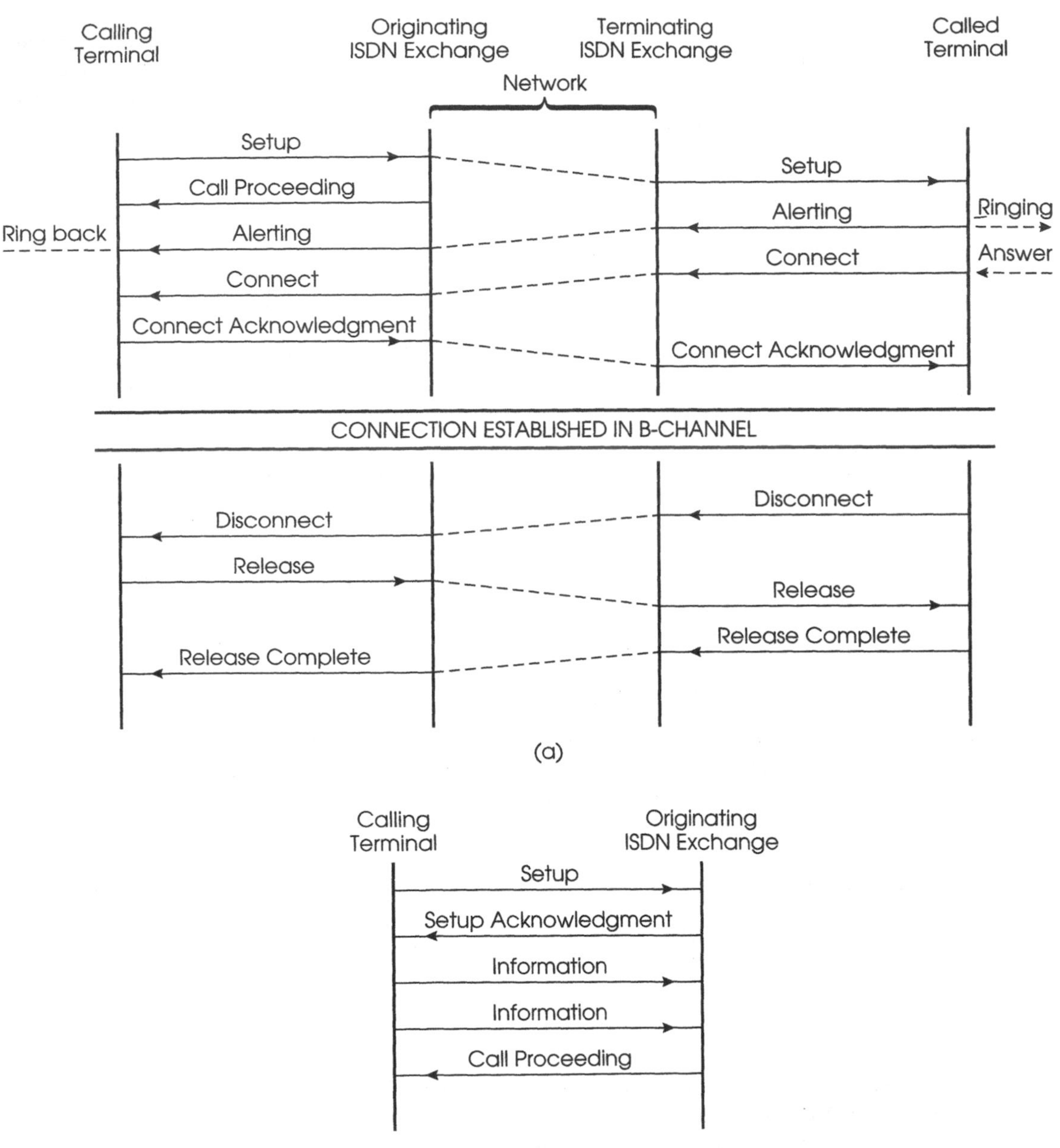

Figure 8–19 DSS 1 message flow for a successful circuit switched call: (a) en bloc mode of sending information; (b) overlap sending.

Table 8-12 Layer 3 Messages

Coding Type	Message Name	Purpose	Significance	Direction	Connection (Circuit/ Packet/ User signal)
76 54321					
00 00000	Escape to nationally specified message types				
00.....	*Call establishment messages:*				
00001	ALERTing	Alerting of called user initiated	Global	Both	All
00010	CALL PROCeeding	Call establishment initiated	Local	Both	All
00111	CONNect	Acceptance of the call by called user	Global	Both	All
01111	CONNect ACKnowledge	Indicates establishment of connection	Local	Both	All
00011	PROGress	Indicates status of call progress	Global	Both	Circuit
00101	SETUP	To initiate call establishment	Global	Both	All
01101	SETUP ACKnowledge	Call establishment initiated, but more information may be required	Local	Both	Circuit/ user signal
Call information phase messages:					
01 00110	RESume	Request to resume a suspended call	Local	u→n	Circuit
01 01110	RESume ACKnowledge	Indicates completion of call resumption	Local	n→u	Circuit
01 00010	RESume REJect	Indicates failure to resume a suspended call	Local	n→u	Circuit
01 00101	SUSPend	Request to suspend a call	Local	u→n	Circuit
01 01101	SUSPend ACKnowledge	Completion of call suspend	Local	n→u	Circuit
01 00001	SUSpend REJect	Indicates failure to suspend a call	Local	n→u	Circuit
01 00000	USER INFOrmation	Information transfer for user-to-user signaling	Access	Both	User signal
Call clearing messages:					
10 00101	DISConnect	*u* → *n*: request to clear end-to-end connection *n* → *u*: end-to-end connection cleared	Global	Both	Circuit/ packet
01101	RELease	Indicates release of channel and call reference	Local	Both	All
11010	RELease COMPlete	Channel and call reference released; channel available for reuse	Local	Both	All
00110	RESTart	To bring the indicated channels to idle condition	Local	Both	Circuit/ user signal
01110	RESTart ACKnowledge	Indicates that the request in RESTart message has been completed	Local	Both	Circuit/ user signal

(continued)

Table 8-12 Layer 3 Messages (*Continued*)

Coding Type	Message Name	Purpose	Significance	Direction	Connection (Circuit/ Packet/ User signal)
Miscellaneous messages:					
11 00000	SEGment	Partitioning of long messages	Local	Both	All
11 11001	CONgestion CONtrol	To indicate initiation or termination of flow control on the transmission of USER INFO message	Local	Both	User signal
11 11011	INFOrmation	To provide additional call-related information	Local	Both	Circuit/ User signal
11 01110	NOTIFY	Provide information regarding a call	Access	Both	Circuit
11 11101	STATUS	Response to a STATUS ENQ message	Local	Both	All
11 10101	STATUS ENQuiry	To solicit a status information from peer layer 3	Local	Both	All

Note: $u \rightarrow n$: user to network
$n \rightarrow u$: network to user

8.9.2 Message Specific Part: Information Elements

As seen from Figure 8–17, in addition to the header, each message contains one or more information elements. Information elements may consist of a single octet or a variable number of octets. Again, two types of formats are specified for the single-octet information elements. The various permissible formats are shown in Figure 8–20.

8.9.3 Basic Call Control Procedure

The basic circuit switched call procedure was briefly described earlier in this chapter. A detailed description of the procedure is now presented. The call procedure may be studied for the following three cases:

1. Call establishment at the originating ISDN interface (outgoing call)
2. Call establishment at the destination ISDN interface (incoming call)
3. Call clearing

8.9.3.1 Call Establishment at the Originating ISDN Interface

A call is initiated by the calling user by sending a SETUP message to the network. The contents of SETUP message for circuit switched connections are shown in Figure 8–21. Notice that out of the large number of information elements that can exist in the message specific part, only the presence of the bearer capability information element is mandatory. The

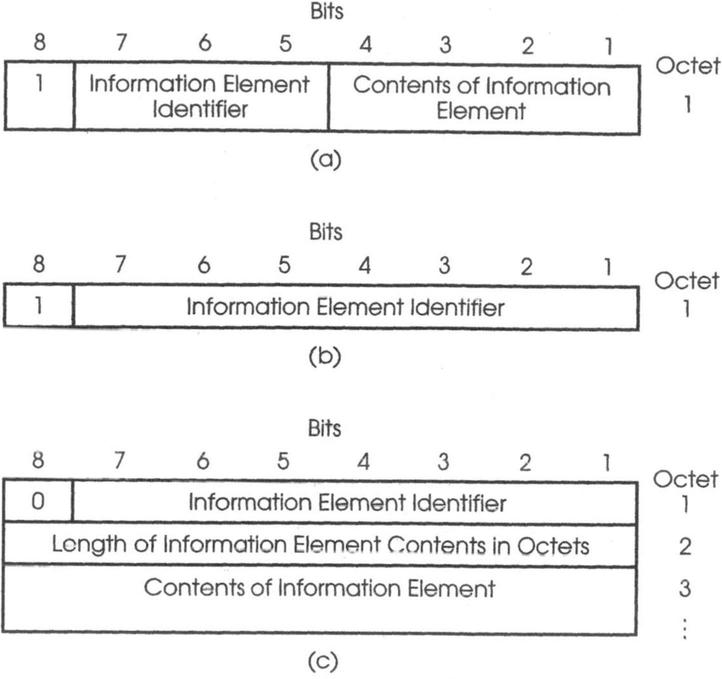

Figure 8–20 Information element formats: (a) single octet (type 1); (b) single octet (type 2); (c) variable length.
[Reprinted from ITU-T recommendation Q.931 (1993) ISDN user-network layer 3 specification for basic call control. Rev. 1. Reproduced by permission.]

rest are optional, and their presence in the message depends on requirements of information during a particular call. Thus, the length of the message varies widely case by case.

The SETUP message in the user-to-network direction must specify the bearer capabilities required from the network for the call request. No default bearer capability can be used by the network in the absence of the bearer capability information element.

Readers may recall the discussion on bearer services and the associated attributes in Section 8.2. The bearer capability information element contains the bearer attribute requirements for the call. An example of this element is shown in Figure 8–22.

The calling user may also be provided with the possibility of specifying more than one bearer capability option for a call. For example, the calling user may like to indicate the bearer capability of unrestricted digital as the first priority and restricted digital as the next option if the network is unable to meet the first priority option. In this case, there will be two bearer capability information elements in the SETUP message, one each for the two bearer capability options. To provide these options, the network implements the bearer change procedure. The use of this procedure is optional. The repeat indicator, a single-octet information element, is typically used in the bearer service change procedure. In general, the repeat indicator is included in a layer 3 message when the same information element appears more than once in the message. The function of the repeat indicator information element is to provide a prioritized list for selecting one of the options.

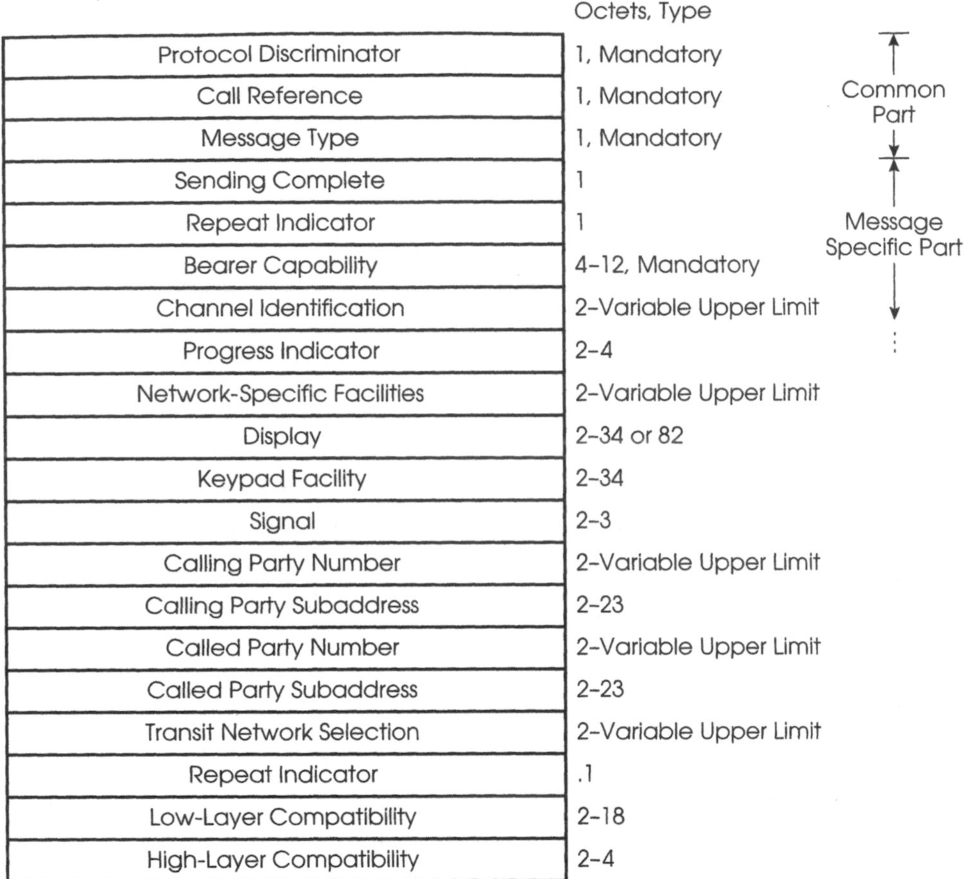

Figure 8–21 SETUP message for a circuit switched connection.

Figure 8–23 illustrates the case when the bearer change procedure is not available. An availability of bearer service change is shown in Figure 8–24.

If the user monitors the B-channels associated with the D-channel, the SETUP message is sent only if an associated B-channel is free. If the user does not monitor the B-channels, it sends a SETUP message anyway. Before the call is established, the calling user and network need to decide about the B-channel to be used for the call. The channel identification information element is used for B-channel selection and is shown in Figure 8–25.

For an originating call, the user informs the network of one of the following alternatives by the channel identification information element:

1. The channel on which the call should be connected is indicated and the network should only use the indicated channel.
2. The preferred channel is indicated. However, any other channel that may be selected by the network is also acceptable.
3. No preferred channel is indicated and the network may select any channel.

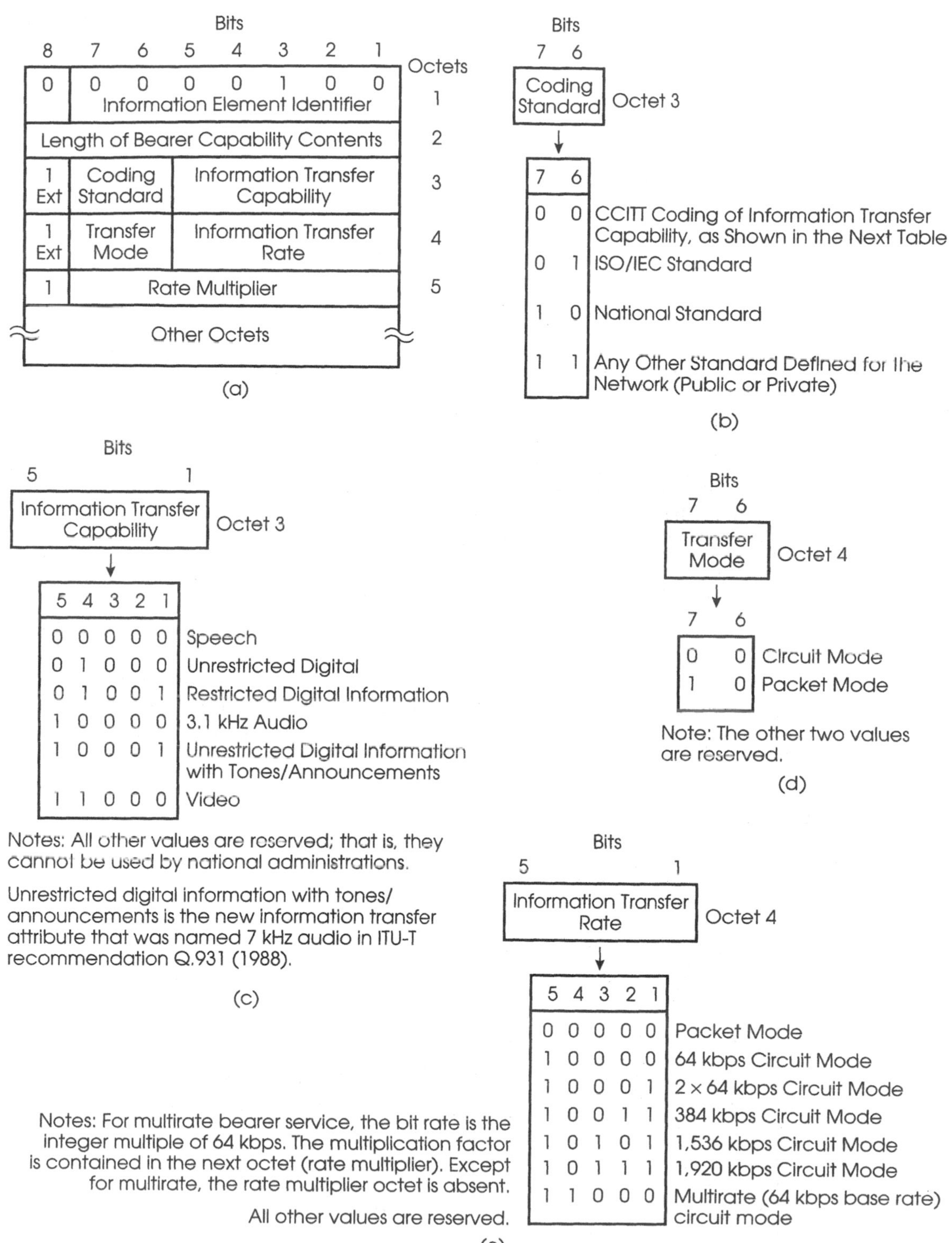

Figure 8–22 An example of bearer capability information element: (a) format; (b) coding standard field; (c) information transfer capability field; (d) transfer mode field; (e) information transfer rate field.

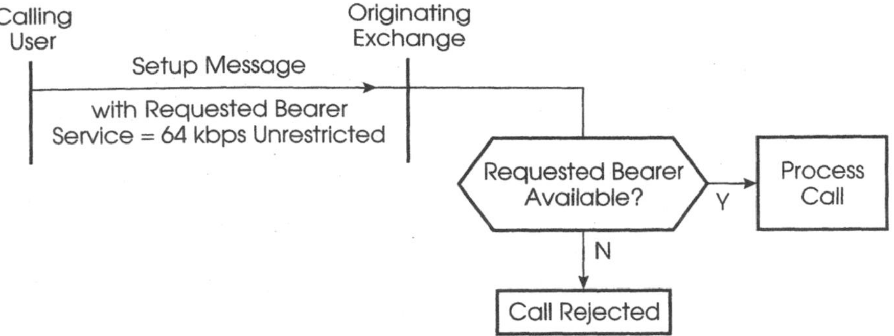

Figure 8–23 Bearer change procedure not available.

The last option is taken by the network if the channel identification information element is missing in the SETUP message. It is important to note that the B-channel selection is limited to the channels associated with the same D-channel. Recommendation Q.931 stipulates that for a basic access point-to-multipoint ISDN user, the terminals should not indicate any preferred channel for circuit switched basic call control unless one of the B-channels is already being used by the terminal. When the information channel required is the D-channel (for packet data, for example), an indication is given to the network (by setting bit 3 of octet 3 to 1).

The network indicates the selected channel to the user by means of the channel identification information element in the first message returned by the network after the reception of the SETUP message. This could be the CALL PROC message (for enbloc

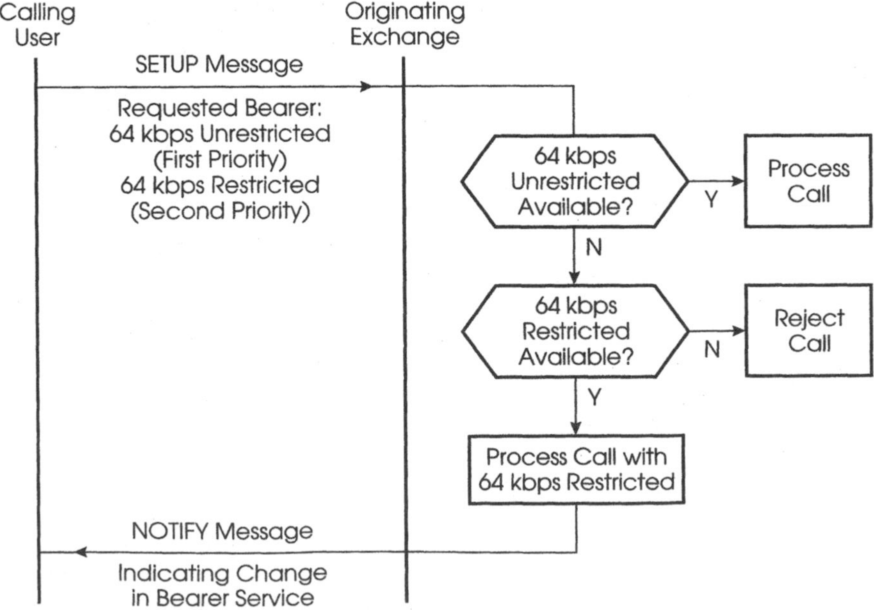

Figure 8–24 Bearer change procedure available.

Bits 8	7	6	5	4	3	2	1	Octets
0	0 Information Element Identifier	0	1	1	0	0	0	1
Length of Channel Identification Contents								2
1 Ext	Interface Identifier Present	Interface Type	0 Spare	Preferred/ Exclusive	D-Channel Indicator	Information on Channel Selection		3

Coding for Octet 3:

Bit 7: Interface Identifier Present

0: The S/T-Interface Is the One that Includes the D-Channel Carrying This Information Element; thus, the Interface Has Been Identified Implicitly.

1: The Interface Is Explicitly Specified in Octets After Octet 3 (Not Shown in This Figure)

Bit 6: Type of Interface: 0 (Basic), 1 (Primary)

Bit 5: Spare

Bit 4: Preferred/Exclusive

0: Indicated Channel Is Preferred

1: The Indicated Channel Only Should be Used.

Bit 3: D-Channel Indicator

0: The Channel Identified Is Not a D-Channel

1: The Channel Identified Is a D-Channel

Bits 2 1: Information Channel Selection

0 0 No B Channel Is Indicated

0 1 B1 Channel

1 0 B2 Channel

1 1 Any Channel

Figure 8–25 Channel identification information element.

sending) or SETUP ACK message (for overlap message). The format of these messages is shown in Figures 8–26 and 8–27.

If the B-channel cannot be assigned to the user, then a REL COMP message is sent to the calling user. Refer to Figure 8–28. The release complete message contains a cause information element. The contents of this information element (called cause value), details the reason (or cause) for sending the message. A cause value (= 34) indicates that no channel could be assigned by the network for the call.

Reverting to the contents of the SETUP message, for en bloc sending, complete information necessary for processing the call is expected by the network. To convey the called party number and subaddress, two possibilities exist:

1. The information may be carried in the called party number and called party subaddress information elements of the SETUP message. The format of these two information elements is shown in Figures 8–29 and 8–30. The type of number field in Figure 8–29 may indicate an international number, a national number, a subscriber number, a network specific number (call to an operator)

Field	Octets, Type
Protocol Discriminator	1, Mandatory
Call Reference	2-Upper Limit Variable, Mandatory
Message Type	1, Mandatory
Bearer Capability	4-12
Channel Identification	2-Upper Limit Variable
Progress Indicator	2-4
Display	2-34 or 82
High-Layer Compatibility	2-5

Figure 8–26 CALL PROC message.

Field	Octets, Type
Protocol Discriminator	1, Mandatory
Call Reference	2-Upper Limit Variable, Mandatory
Message Type	1, Mandatory
Channel Identification	2-Upper Limit Variable
Progress Indicator	2-4
Display	2-34 or 82
Signal	2-3

Figure 8–27 SETUP ACK message.

Field	Octets, Type
Protocol Discriminator	1, Mandatory
Call Reference	2-Upper Limit Variable, Mandatory
Message Type	1, Mandatory
Cause	2-32 (See Note)
Display	2-34 or 82
Signal	

Note: Cause value is mandatory in the first call clearing message.

Figure 8–28 REL COMP message.

Bits

8	7	6	5	4	3	2	1	Octets
	Called Party Number							
0	1	1	1	0	0	0	0	1
	Information Element Identifier							
Length of Called Party No. Information								2
1 Ext	Type of Number			Numbering Plan Identification				3
0 Spare	Digits (IA5 Characters Set) (See note)							4 ⋮

Note: The number of digits appear in multiple octet 4's in the same order in which they would be entered; that is, the number digit which would be entered first is located in the first octet 4.

Figure 8–29 Called party number information element. [Reprinted from ITU-T recommendation Q.931 (1993) ISDN user-network layer 3 specification for basic call control. Rev. 1. Reproduced by permission.]

or an abbreviated number. The numbering plan identification field may indicate the ISDN plan (E.164), the data numbering plan (X.121) or the telex numbering plan (F.69).

2. The information may be carried in the keypad facility information element using the IA5 character set. Refer to Figure 8–31. The maximum length of this information element is 34 octets.

Although either possibility may be used, it is mandatory that the network at least recognize the information supplied through the first option.

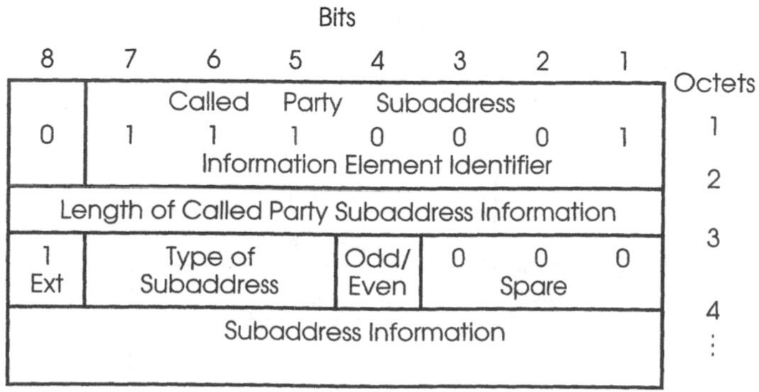

Figure 8–30 Called party subaddress information element. [Reprinted from ITU-T recommendation Q.931 (1993) ISDN user-network layer 3 specification for basic call control. Rev. 1. Reproduced by permission.]

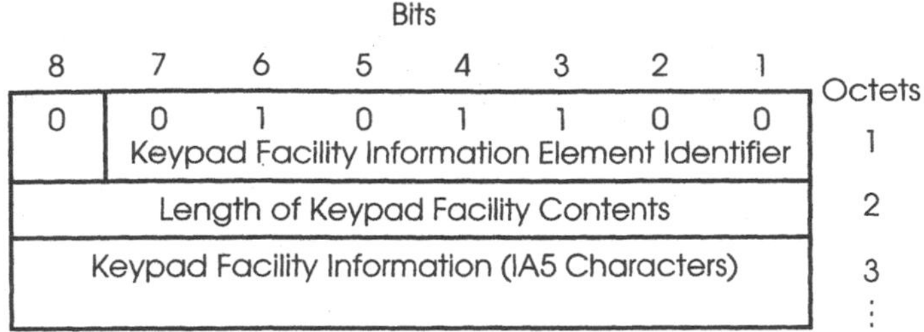

Figure 8–31 Keypad facility information element.
[Reprinted from ITU-T recommendation Q.931 (1993) ISDN user-network layer 3 specification for basic call control. Rev. 1. Reproduced by permission.]

Two possible methods exist to indicate to the originating exchange that all the information about the called party number has been delivered:

1. By the use of a separate sending complete information element in the setup message
2. By including a "#" character in the called party number information element itself

The originating exchange must implement at least one of these possibilities.

For overlap sending, the SETUP message may contain either no information or only partial information regarding the called party number. Upon receipt of the SETUP message, the network sends the SETUP ACK message and starts timer T302. Figure 8–32 shows the use of timers during call setup in the overlap method.

If no information about the called party number is received in the SETUP message, then the network may send a tone to the user using the signal information element in the SETUP ACK message. The function of the signal information element is to provide information for the tones that may be provided to the user. The signal information element has

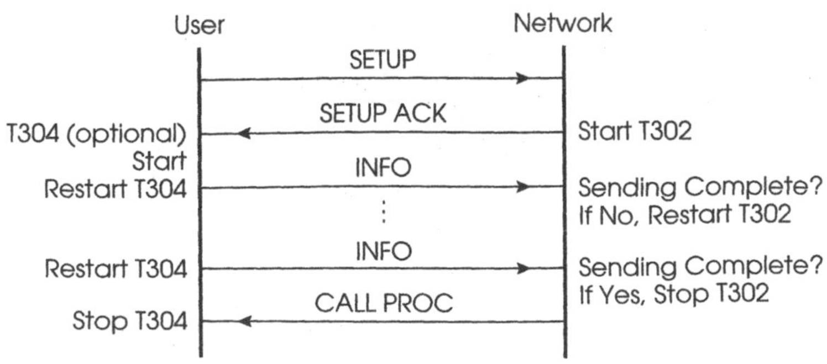

Figure 8–32 Use of timers during call setup in overlap signaling.

an octet named signal value that indicates the type of tone to be fed to the user. For example, an all-zero signal value code indicates to the user terminal that dialtone should be fed. Other combinations represent different tone conditions such as ring back tone, congestion tone, answer tone, busy tone, and call waiting tone.

For the sake of symmetry, the user may also start timer T304 upon receipt of the SETUP ACK message. Timer T304 is optional. Every time the INFO message is sent, timer T304 is restarted. One or more INFO messages may be sent by the user. As with the case of the setup message in en bloc sending, the called party number may be supplied in the INFO message either by using the called party number information element or by keypad sending. Upon receipt of each INFO message, the network checks for the receipt of complete information. If complete information has not been received, timer T302 is restarted. The format of the INFO message is shown in Figure 8–33.

In the final INFO message sent by the user, a sending complete information element (refer to Figure 8–33) is included in the INFO message to indicate that all the information necessary for processing the call has been sent. Timer T302 is stopped when the INFO message indicates that all information has been sent. A CALL PROC message is now sent to the user. Upon receipt of this message, the user stops timer T304.

8.9.3.2 Call Establishment at the Destination ISDN Access

1. When the ISDN call arrives at the destination ISDN exchange, it selects an idle B-channel to the called user interface.
2. A SETUP message is generated by the exchange and sent to the called user on a layer 2 data link connection. Two cases may arise:
   - If multiple terminals exist at the called user interface, then the SETUP message is included in an unnumbered information (UI) frame and sent in broadcast mode (TEI – 127).
   - For a single terminal configuration at the called user interface, a point-to-point data link is established for sending the message.

Field	Octets, Type
Protocol Discriminator	1, Mandatory
Call Reference	2-Upper Limit Variable, Mandatory
Message Type	1, Mandatory
Sending Complete	4-12
Display	2-Upper Limit Variable
Keypad Facility	2-34
Signal	2-3
Called Party Number	2-5

Figure 8–33 INFO message.

3. Compatibility check is applied to both multiple terminal and single terminal configurations. The check is performed at the called user interface on the following two aspects:
   - Checking the address supplied in the SETUP message (step 3 a)
   - Checking that the called user interface is able to support the services offered by the network as indicated in the SETUP message (step 3 b)

   (a) The called party number in the SETUP message is checked with the number assigned to the called user. If the subaddressing information element is included in the message, then it is also matched with the subaddresses existing at the called interface. If the check is successful, then step 3b is performed. If the check fails, then the call is ignored.

   (b) Upon receiving the SETUP message, each terminal at a multiterminal user interface, checks to determine if it can communicate with the calling terminal. For this purpose, the following information elements of the SETUP are examined:
   - Bearer capability
   - High-layer compatibility
   - Low-layer compatibility

   The bearer capability and the low-layer compatibility information elements relate to the bearer service requirements for the call, for example, the information transfer rate and information transfer capability (speech, video). Each terminal checks whether it can support these requirements. The high-layer compatibility element indicates the teleservice requirements, for example, speech, facsimile group 4, and teletex. Thus, if facsimile group 4 service is indicated in the SETUP message, then a telephone meant for speech service concludes that it is not compatible and ignores the SETUP message. On the other hand, a group 4 facsimile terminal would determine that it is compatible and would therefore respond. If several terminals at the called user interface are compatible, then the one that responds first is used for the call.
4. If no terminal at the called user interface is able to establish compatibility, then for multi-terminal configuration, either the call is ignored or a REL COMP message with cause value 88 (incompatible destination) is returned. For a single-terminal configuration, the latter course of action is followed.
5. A compatible terminal to be used for the call may be either a non-automatic answering terminal (for example, a simple ISDN telephone) or an automatic answering terminal (for example, a group 4 facsimile terminal). A nonautomatic answering terminal may respond with a CALL PROC message. This message is optional and may be sent to achieve symmetry with the message exchange at the calling interface. When a CALL PROC message is received at the destination ISDN exchange, this information is conveyed through the network to the originating ISDN exchange. In turn, the latter sends a CALL PROC message to the calling user. Following the CALL PROC message, an ALERT message is sent by the called terminal, indicating that the called user is being alerted for responding to the call. This information is also communicated to the originating exchange, which sends an ALERT message to the calling user. An automatic

answering terminal may also respond with a CALL PROC message. This message is optional. No alerting is required in this case, since the terminal answers automatically.

6. When the called user answers either by automatic or nonautomatic means, a CONN message is sent to the network. A CONN message is also sent to the calling user by the originating ISDN exchange. Upon receipt of CONN ACK to these CONN messages, the call is established.

   The three messages, CALL PROC, ALERT, and CONN, involved in the call establishment procedure described above have identical information elements:

   - Protocol discriminator (mandatory, one octet)
   - Call reference (mandatory, two or more octets)
   - Message type (mandatory, one octet)
   - Channel identification (optional, two octets or more)
   - Display (optional, two to 34 or 82 octets)

The CONNECT ACK message is also composed of the same information elements, except for the channel identification information element, which is missing in this case.

8.9.3.3 Call Clearing

An ISDN call can be cleared at any time by either the calling or the called user. For this purpose, a DISC message is sent by the user wishing to clear the call. The format of the DISC message is shown in Figure 8–34.

When the user sends the DISC message, it starts timer T305 and disconnects the B-channel used by the call. However, the B-channel is not available to any other call at this stage. The value of timer T305 is 30 seconds. Refer to Figure 8–35.

When the network (either the originating or terminating exchange) receives the DISC message, it initiates necessary action to release the circuit switched connection between the originating and the terminating exchanges involved in the call. The network also disconnects the B-channel used for the call and sends a REL message to the user. Furthermore, the network starts timer T308. The value of timer T308 is 4 seconds.

Field	Octets, Type
Protocol Discriminator	1, Mandatory
Call Reference	2-(No Upper Limit Variable Specified), Mandatory
Message Type	1, Mandatory
Cause	4-32
Progress Indicator	2-4
Display	2-34 or 82
Signal	2-3

Figure 8–34 DISCONNECT message.

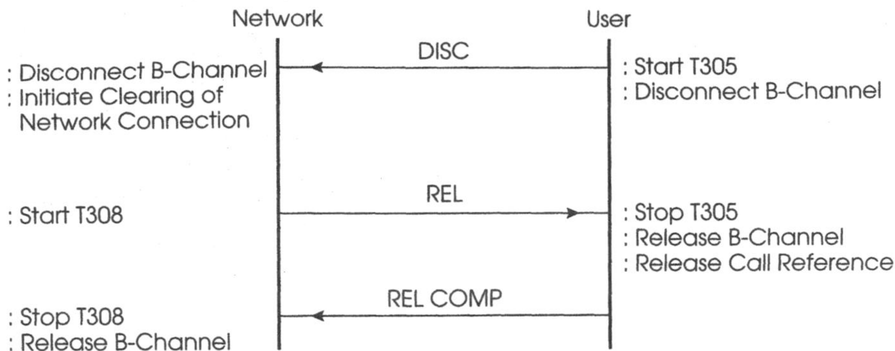

Figure 8–35 Example of call clearing.

Upon receiving the REL message, the user stops timer T305 and releases the B-channel. The B-channel can now be used for another call to the ISDN interface. The user also releases the call reference value and sends a REL COMP message to the network.

When received by the network, the REL COMP message results in the release of the B-channel; a new call can be offered on this channel to the user. The network stops timer T308 and releases the call reference value associated with the call.

The REL and REL COMP messages have identical information elements, as follows:

- Protocol discriminator (mandatory)
- Call reference (mandatory)
- Message type (mandatory)
- Cause
- Display

What happens if timer T305 or T308 associated with the call release procedure described above expires? Figure 8–36(a) illustrates a case where no response to DISC message is received from the network. Timer T305 therefore expires at the user side. Timer T305 is not restarted; instead, timer T308 is now started at the user end, and simultaneously, the user sends a REL message to the network. The REL message contains the same cause number as originally sent in the DISC message. If the network responds to the REL message, then normal call clearing takes place. If timer T308 expires a second time and no response is received from the network, then the user places the B-channel under maintenance and the call reference is released. Figure 8–36(b) shows the consequences of expiry of timer T308 at the network side.

8.9.4 Control of ISDN Supplementary Services

The call control procedure discussed so far relates to a basic ISDN call. The signaling requirements for number identification supplementary services such as CLIP and CLIR can be met by the same messages, information elements, and signaling procedures

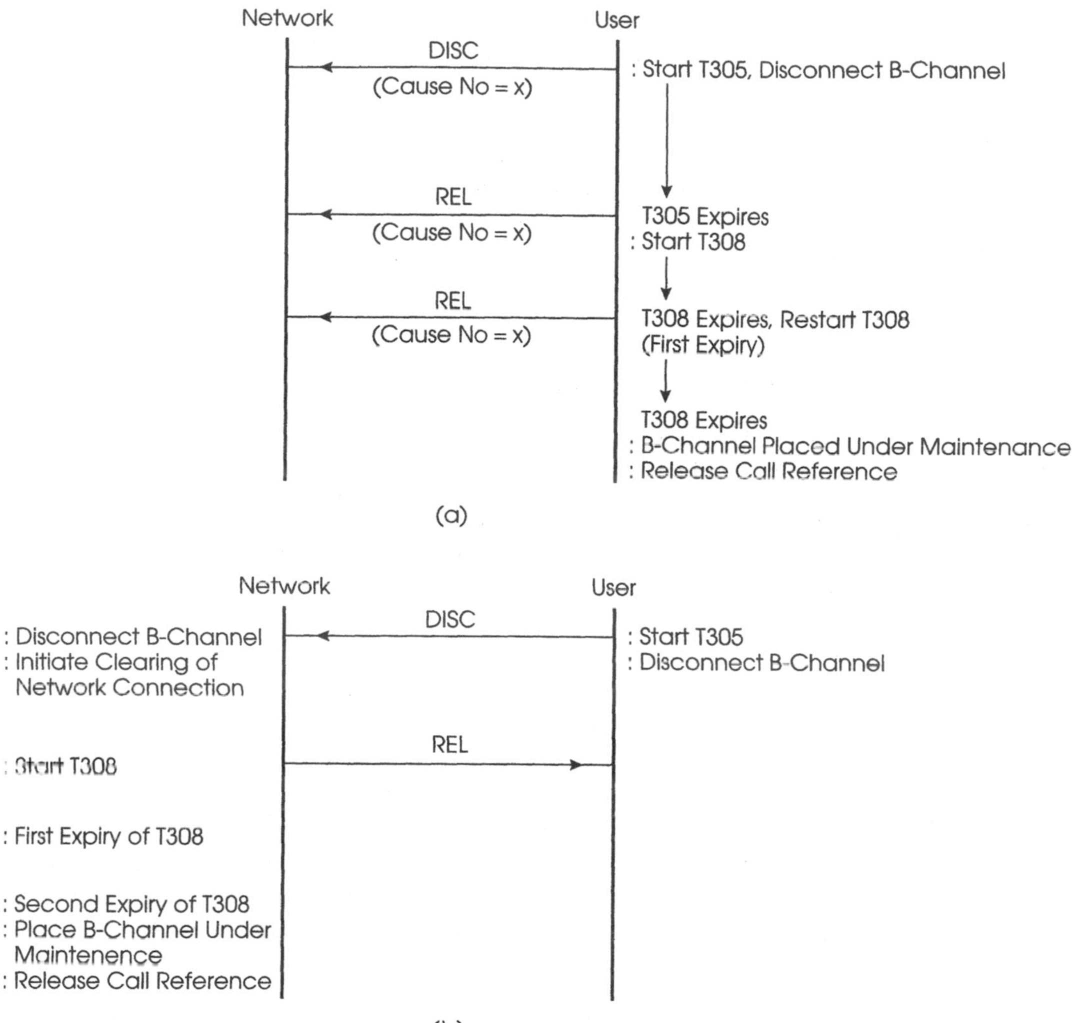

Figure 8–36 Expiry of timers during call clearing: (a) Timer Expiry at the user side; (b) Timer Expiry at the network side.

that are used for the control of basic calls. For other supplementary services, however, additional protocols are required along with the basic call control procedure. Three protocols are available for this purpose:

1. Keypad protocol
2. Feature key management protocol
3. Functional protocol

The first two are called stimulus mode protocols since they are based on the caller sending information (stimuli) appropriate to the supplementary service directly to the network. The information, which is composed of characters (numbers, symbols, alphabets), is simply passed on by the terminal to the network; no intelligent processing by the terminal is involved.

When keypad protocol is employed, the keypad facility information element in the SETUP and INFO messages is used to convey the caller generated information to the network. (Refer to Figure 8–31 for the format of keypad facility information element.) Similarly, the network communicates with the user by means of display information element.

Feature key management protocol requires two additional elements:

1. Feature activation
2. Feature indication

These two information elements are not needed for basic call control. For supplementary services using feature key management protocol, however, the feature activation information element is included in the SETUP and INFO messages for conveying information in the user to network direction; the feature indication information element is included in the opposite direction. Discussion on feature keypad management protocol is not pursued any further in this book. Readers may refer to ITU-T recommendation Q.932 for details.

Since additional information for the supplementary service is merely passed on to the network by the terminals in the stimulus mode, the introduction of new services does not require new terminals or an upgrade of the existing ones. Upgrades are, however, required in the ISDN exchanges when new services are implemented.

In functional protocol, the terminal functionality is used to generate coded information for transfer to the network. Unlike the stimulus method, the terminal is aware of the supplementary service being provided and participates in the processing required for this purpose. Because the communication between the called user and the ISDN exchange is no longer direct, the intelligent processing performed by the terminal can provide a friendly interface to the user. At the same time, a standardized communication procedure between the terminal and the exchange for each supplementary service is required. To implement this standardized procedure for supplementary service control, eight additional messages have been defined: FACILITY, HOLD, HOLD ACKNOWLEDGE, HOLD REJECT, REGISTER, RETRIEVE, RETRIEVE ACKNOWLEDGE, and RETRIEVE REJECT. The role of some of these messages is seen in the next section.

ITU-T recommendations foresee that one or more of the supplementary service control protocols may exist in a network. Functional protocol is generally used except when the support of stimulus mode is specifically subscribed by the user.

The use of control procedures is illustrated by the example of the call hold supplementary service in the following section.

8.9.4.1 Control Procedure for the Call Hold Supplementary Service

Call hold supplementary service was described in Section 8.5.3.2. Signaling for this service is discussed in this section using functional protocol as well as keypad protocol.

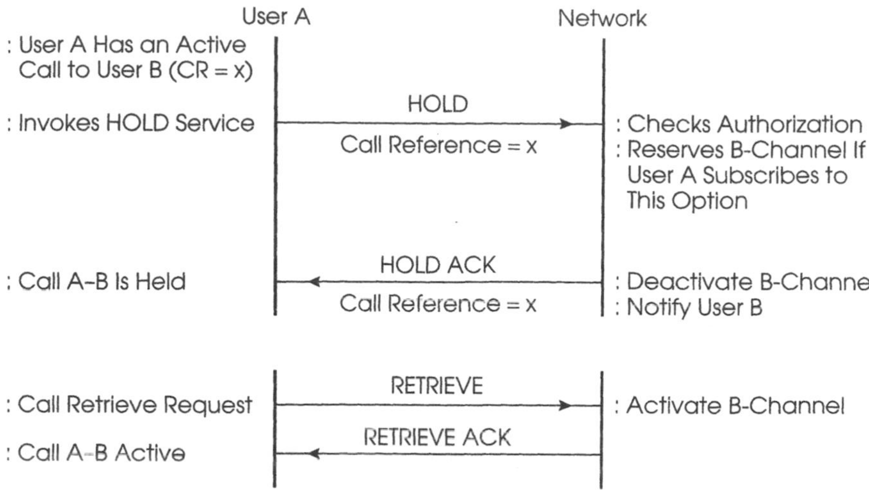

Figure 8–37 Signaling for call hold supplementary service using functional protocol.

8.9.4.1.1 Using Functional Protocol

An example of the use of functional protocol is shown in Figure 8–37. It is assumed that user A has an existing active call to user B. User A initiates the call hold service, and a HOLD message is sent by the user to the network. The HOLD message has four information elements: the usual three mandatory information elements followed by an optional display information element. The call reference in the HOLD message is the same as for the existing call that is to be placed on hold.

The network checks whether user A is a subscriber of the call hold service. It also reserves a B-channel if user A subscribes to the reservation option. The network thereafter acknowledges the hold request by means of a HOLD ACK message. This message has a format identical to the HOLD message.

The network deactivates the B-channel being used for the existing call. The call is put under hold. The network also notifies user B.

If the network cannot accept the HOLD request for certain reasons (for example, user A may not be a valid subscriber of the service), then a HOLD REJ message is returned and the existing call remains active. In addition to the mandatory information elements, the HOLD REJ message has two optional information elements, cause and display. The reason for rejecting the service request is provided in the cause information element.

When user A wishes to retrieve call A–B, user A sends a RETRIEVE message to the network. The network responds by a RETRIEVE ACK message and activates the B-channel connection.

8.9.4.1.2 Using Keypad Protocol

The information carried by the keypad information element is interpreted by the network to ascertain the supplementary service requested by the user. The keypad codes used for indicating the various services are network dependent. The exchange of DSS 1 messages in this case is shown in Figure 8–38.

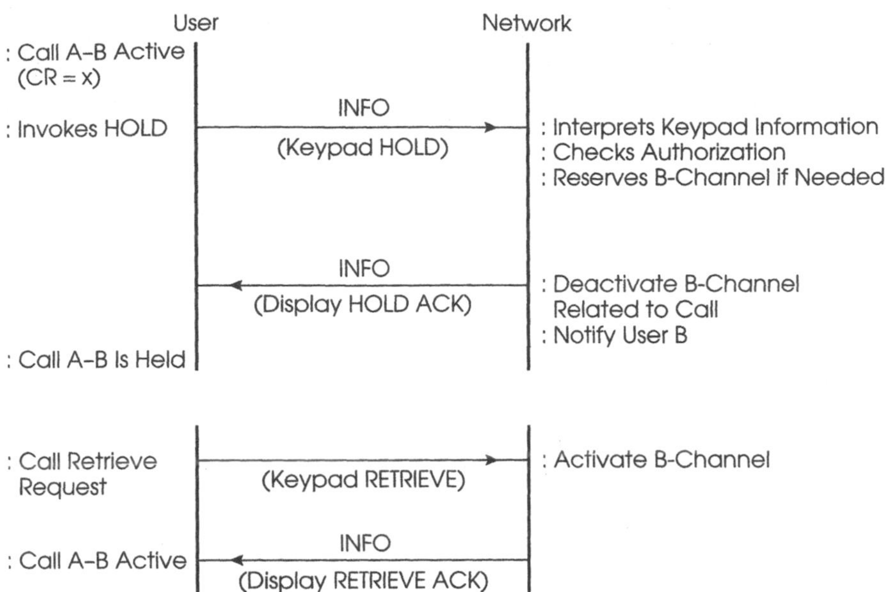

Figure 8–38 Signaling for call hold supplementary service using keypad protocol.

8.10 Remarks

The description of the ISDN services presented in this chapter amply demonstrates the variety and flexibility of features available in the ISDN. Reliable voice communication and the transmission of data, image, and video are requirements common to all sectors of economic activity. Thus, the ISDN has the potential of widespread application. To realize this potential, ISDN services must focus on the specific needs and requirements of the end user. This issue is part of the ISDN planning aspects and is addressed in Chapter 13.

The discussion of layers 2 and 3 of the DSS 1 completes the description of ISDN protocols. The scope of DSS 1 protocols is limited to the ISDN user network interface and the ISDN exchanges to which the ISDN interfaces are connected. However, an ISDN call typically spans several exchanges. Much like the runners in a relay race, layer 3 DSS 1 information must be handed over to the CCS 7 ISUP messages at the origination and destination exchanges. In the next chapter, the basic call control and ISUP procedures for supplementary services are discussed.

References

[1] *General Modeling Methods. Method of the Characterization of Telecommunication Services Supported by an ISDN and Network Capabilities of an ISDN.* CCITT Blue Book, fascicle III.7, recommendation I.130. International Telecommunication Union, 1988.

[2] *Digital Subscriber Signaling System No. 1: ISDN User-Network Interface. Data Link Layer—General Aspects.* ITU-T recommendation Q.920, rev. 1. International Telecommunication Union, 1993.

[3] *ISDN User-Network Interface—Data Link Layer Specification.* ITU-T recommendation Q.921, rev. 1. International Telecommunication Union, 1993.

[4] *ISDN User-Network Interface Layer 3—General aspects.* ITU-T recommendation Q.930, rev. 1. International Telecommunication Union, 1993.

[5] *ISDN User-Network Interface Layer 3 Specifications for Basic Call Control.* ITU-T recommendation Q.931, rev. 1. International Telecommunication Union, 1993.

[6] *Generic Procedures for the Control of ISDN Supplementary Services.* ITU-T recommendation Q.932, rev. 1. International Telecommunication Union, 1993.

[7] *Attributes Technique for the Characterization of Telecommunication Services Supported by an ISDN and Network Capabilities of an ISDN.* ITU-T recommendation I.140, rev. 1. International Telecommunication Union, 1993.

[8] *Principles of Telecommunication Services Supported by an ISDN and the Means to Describe Them.* ITU-T recommendation I.210, rev. 1. International Telecommunication Union, 1993.

[9] *7 kHz Audio-Coding within 64 kbit/s.* CCITT Blue Book, fascicle III.4, recommendation G.722. International Telecommunication Union, 1989 (copies of the digital test sequences described in Appendix II of rec. G.722 are also available on three floppy disks). Also: *Testing Signal-to-Total Distortion Ratio for 7 kHz Audio-Codecs at 64 kbit/s Connected Back-to-Back.* ITU-T recommendation G.722A. International Telecommunication Union, 1993.

[10] *Basic User-Network Interface—Layer 1 Specification.* ITU-T recommendation I.430, rev. 1. International Telecommunication Union, 1993.

[11] *Primary Rate User-Network Interface—Layer 1 Specification.* ITU-T recommendation I.431, rev. 1. International Telecommunication Union, 1993.

[12] *Interface between Data Terminal Equipment (DTE) and Data Circuit Terminating Equipment (DCE) for Terminals Operating in the Packet Mode and Connected to Public Data Networks by Dedicated Circuits.* ITU-T recommendation X.25. International Telecommunication Union, 1993.

[13] *Support of X.21, X.21 bis, and X.20 bis based data terminal equipment (DTEs) by an integrated services digital network (ISDN).* ITU-T recommendation X.30, rev. 1. International Telecommunication Union, 1993.

[14] *Support of Packet Mode Terminal Equipment by an ISDN.* ITU-T recommendation X.31, rev. 1. International Telecommunication Union, 1993.

[15] *Support of Data Terminal Equipment with V-Series Type Interfaces by an Integrated Services Digital Network.* ITU-T recommendation V.110, rev. 1. International Telecommunication Union, 1992.

[16] *Support by an ISDN of Data Terminal Equipment with V-Series Type Interfaces with Provision for Statistical Multiplexing.* ITU-T recommendation V.120, rev. 1. International Telecommunication Union, 1992.

[17] *Definition of Bearer Service Categories.* CCITT Blue Book, fascicle III.7, recommendation I.230. International Telecommunication Union, 1988.

[18] *Circuit-Mode Bearer Service Categories.* CCITT Blue Book, fascicle III.7, recommendation I.231. International Telecommunication Union, 1988.

[19] *Pulse Code Modulation (PCM) of Voice Frequencies.* CCITT Blue Book, fascicle III.4, recommendation G.711. International Telecommunication Union, 1988.

[20] *Teleservices Supported by an ISDN: Telephony.* CCITT Blue Book, fascicle III.7, recommendation I.241.1. International Telecommunication Union, 1988.

[21] *Teleservices Supported by an ISDN: Teletex.* CCITT Blue Book, fascicle III.7, recommendation I.241.2. International Telecommunication Union, 1988.

[22] *Teleservices Supported by an ISDN: Telefax.* CCITT Blue Book, fascicle III.7, recommendation I.241.3. International Telecommunication Union, 1988.

[23] *Teleservices Supported by an ISDN: Mixed Mode.* CCITT Blue Book, fascicle III.7, recommendation I.241.4. International Telecommunication Union, 1988.

[24] *Teleservices Supported by an ISDN: Videotex.* CCITT Blue Book, fascicle III.7, recommendation I.241.5. International Telecommunication Union, 1988.

[25] *Teleservices supported by an ISDN: Telex.* CCITT Blue Book, fascicle III.7, recommendation I.241.6. International Telecommunication Union, 1988.

[26] *Teleservices Supported by an ISDN: Telephony 7 kHz.* ITU-T recommendation I.241.7. International Telecommunication Union, 1993.

[27] *Character Repertoire and Coded Character Sets for the International Teletex Service.* ITU-T recommendation T.61, rev. 1. International Telecommunication Union, 1993.

[28] *Packet-Switched Signaling System between Public Networks Providing Data Transmission Services.* ITU-T recommendation X.75, rev. 1. International Telecommunication Union, 1993.

[29] *Information Technology—Data Communications. X.25 Packet Layer Protocol for Data Terminal Equipment.* ISO 8208/ IEC, 2nd ed., 1990.

[30] *Network-Independent Basic Transport Service for the Telematic Services.* ITU-T recommendation T.70, rev. 1. International Telecommunication Union, 1993.

[31] *Control Procedures for Teletex and G4 Facsimile Services.* ITU-T recommendation T.62, rev. 1. International Telecommunication Union, 1993.

[32] *Terminal Equipment for Use in the Teletex Service.* ITU-T recommendation T.60, rev. 1. International Telecommunication Union, 1993.

[33] *Introduction to Document Architecture, Transfer, and Manipulation.* CCITT Blue Book, fascicle VII.6, recommendation T.400. International Telecommunication Union, 1988.

[34] *A document Application Profile for the Interchange of Group 4 Facsimile Documents.* ITU-T recommendation T.503, rev. 1. International Telecommunication Union, 1991.

[35] *Communication Application Profile BT0 for Document Bulk Transfer Based on the Session Service.* ITU-T recommendation T.521, rev. 1. International Telecommunication Union, 1992.

[36] *Terminal Characteristics for Group 4 Facsimile Apparatus.* ITU-T recommendation T.563, rev. 2, International Telecommunication Union, 1993.

[37] *Protocol for Providing the OSI Connection-Mode Transport Service.* ITU-T recommendation X.224, rev. 1. International Telecommunication Union, 1993.

[38] *Information Technology—Open Systems Interconnection: Transport Service Definition.* ITU-T recommendation X.214, rev. 1. International Telecommunication Union, 1993.

[39] *Session Protocol Specification for Open Systems Interconnection for CCITT Applications.* CCITT Blue Book, fascicle VIII.5, recommendation X.225. International Telecommunication Union, 1988.

[40] *Session Service Definition for Open Systems Interconnection for CCITT Applications.* CCITT Blue Book, fascicle VIII.4, recommendation X.215. International Telecommunication Union, 1988.

[41] *Presentation Protocol Specification for Open Systems Interconnection for CCITT Applications.* CCITT Blue Book, fascicle VIII.5, recommendation X.226. International Telecommunication Union, 1988.

[42] *Presentation Service Definition for Open System Interconnection for CCITT Applications.* CCITT fascicle V.III.4, Blue Book, recommendation X.216. International Telecommunication Union, 1988.

[43] *Document Application Profile MM for the Interchange of Formatted Mixed Mode Document.* ITU-T recommendation T.501, rev. 1. International Telecommunication Union, 1993.

[44] *Communication Application Profile BT1 for Document Bulk Transfer.* ITU-T recommendation T.522, rev. 1. International Telecommunication Union, 1992.

[45] *Terminal Characteristics for Mixed Mode of Operation MM.* CCITT Blue Book, fascicle VII.7, recommendation T.561. International Telecommunication Union, 1988.

[46] *Calling Line Identification Presentation.* ITU-T recommendation I.251.3, rev. 1. International Telecommunication Union, 1992.

[47] *Calling Line Identification Restriction.* ITU-T recommendation I.251.4, rev. 1. International Telecommunication Union, 1992.

[48] *Direct-Dialing-In.* ITU-T recommendation I.251.1, rev. 1. International Telecommunication Union, 1992.

[49] *Multiple Subscriber Number.* ITU-T recommendation I.251.2, rev. 1. International Telecommunication Union, 1992.

[50] *Connected Line Identification Presentation.* CCITT Blue Book, fascicle III.7, recommendation I.251.5. International Telecommunication Union, 1988.

[51] *Connected Line Identification Restriction.* CCITT Blue Book, fascicle III.7, recommendation I.251.6. International Telecommunication Union, 1988.

[52] *Malicious Call Identification.* ITU-T recommendation I.251.7, rev. 1. International Telecommunication Union, 1992.

[53] *Sub-Addressing Supplementary Service.* ITU-T recommendation I.251.8, rev. 1. International Telecommunication Union, 1992.

[54] *Call Transfer.* CCITT Blue Book, fascicle III.7, recommendation I.252.1. International Telecommunication Union, 1988.

[55] *Call Forwarding Busy.* ITU-T recommendation I.252.2, rev. 1. International Telecommunication Union, 1992.

[56] *Call Forwarding No Reply.* ITU-T recommendation I.252.3, rev. 1. International Telecommunication Union, 1992.

[57] *Call Forwarding Unconditional.* ITU-T recommendation I.252.4, rev. 1. International Telecommunication Union, 1992.

[58] *Call Deflection.* ITU-T recommendation I.252.5, rev. 1. International Telecommunication Union, 1992.

[59] *Line Hunting (LH).* CCITT Blue Book, fascicle III.7, recommendation I.252.6. International Telecommunication Union, 1988.

[60] *Call Waiting (CW) Supplementary Service.* ITU-T recommendation I.253.1. International Telecommunication Union, 1990.

[61] *Call Hold (CH).* ITU-T recommendation I.253.2, rev. 1. International Telecommunication Union, 1992.

[62] *Completion of Call to Busy Subscribers.* CCITT Blue Book, fascicle III.7, recommendation I.253.3. International Telecommunication Union, 1988.

[63] *Conference Calling (CONF).* CCITT Blue Book, fascicle III.7, recommendation I.254.1. International Telecommunication Union, 1988.

[64] *Three-Party Supplementary Service.* ITU-T recommendation I.254.2, rev. 1. International Telecommunication Union, 1992.

[65] *Closed User Group.* ITU-T recommendation I.255.1, rev. 1. International Telecommunication Union, 1992.

[66] *Private Numbering Plan (PNP).* CCITT Blue Book, fascicle III.7, recommendation I.255.2. International Telecommunication Union, 1988.

[67] *Multi-Level Precedence and Preemption Service (MLPP).* ITU-T recommendation I.255.3. International Telecommunication Union, 1990.

[68] *Priority Service.* ITU-T recommendation I.255.4. International Telecommunication Union, 1990.

[69] *Outgoing Call Barring.* ITU-T recommendation I.255.5. International Telecommunication Union, 1992.

[70] *Credit Card Calling (CRED).* CCITT Blue Book, fascicle III.7, recommendation I.256.1 International Telecommunication Union, 1988.

[71] *Advice of Charge (AOC).* CCITT Blue Book, fascicle III.7, recommendation I.256.2. Geneva, 1988. Also: *Advice of Charge: Charging Information at Call Set-Up Time.* ITU-T recommendation I.256.2a, International Telecommunication Union, 1993. *Advice of Charge: Charging Information During the Call.* ITU-T recommendation I.256.2b. International Telecommunication Union, 1993. *Advice of Charge: Charging Information at the End of the Call.* ITU-T recommendation I.256.2c. International Telecommunication Union, 1993.

[72] *Reverse Charging.* ITU-T recommendation I.256.3, rev. 1. International Telecommunication Union, 1992.

[73] *User-to-User Signaling.* ITU-T recommendation I.257.1, rev. 1. International Telecommunication Union, 1992.

[74] Direct Dialing-in. CCITT Blue Book, fascicle VI.1, recommendation Q.81 § 1. International Telecommunication Union, 1988.

[75] *Multiple Subscriber Number.* ITU-T recommendation Q.81 § 2. International Telecommunication Union, 1992.

[76] *Calling Line Identification, Presentation (CLIP) and Calling Line Identification Restriction (CLIR).* ITU-T recommendation Q.81. § 3, rev. 1. International Telecommunication Union, 1991.

[77] *Connected Line Identification, Presentation, and Restriction (COLP) and (COLR).* ITU-T recommendation Q.81 § 5, rev. 1. International Telecommunication Union, 1991.

[78] *Sub-Addressing (SUB).* ITU-T recommendation Q.81 § 8, rev. 1. International Telecommunication Union, 1992 (published with Q.81 § 2).

[79] *Call Forwarding.* ITU-T recommendation Q.82 § 2, rev. 1. International Telecommunication Union, 1993.

[80] *Call Deflection.* ITU-T recommendation Q.82 § 3. International Telecommunication Union, 1993.

[81] *Line Hunting.* CCITT Blue Book, fascicle VI.1, recommendation Q.82 § 4. International Telecommunication Union, 1988.

[82] *Call Waiting (CW).* ITU-T recommendation Q.83 § 1, rev. 1. International Telecommunication Union, 1991.

[83] *Call Hold.* ITU-T recommendation Q.83 § 2, rev. 1. International Telecommunication Union, 1992.

[84] *Completion of Call to Busy Subscriber.* CCITT Blue Book, fascicle VI.1, recommendation Q.83 § 3. International Telecommunication Union, 1988.

[85] *Terminal Portability.* ITU-T recommendation Q.83 § 4. International Telecommunication Union, 1991 (published with Q.83 § 1).

[86] *Conference Calling (CONF).* ITU-T recommendation Q.84 § 1. International Telecommunication Union, 1993.

[87] *Three-Party Service.* ITU-T recommendation Q.84 § 2. International Telecommunication Union, 1992.

[88] *Closed User Group.* ITU-T recommendation Q.85. § 1, rev. 1. International Telecommunication Union, 1992 (published with Q.85 § 3).

[89] *Multi-Level Precedence and Preemption (MLPP).* ITU-T recommendation Q.85. § 3. International Telecommunication Union, 1992 (published with Q.85 § 1).

[90] *Credit Card Call.* CCITT Blue Book, fascicle VI.1, recommendation Q.86 § 1. International Telecommunication Union, 1988.

[91] *Advice of Charge (AOC).* CCITT Blue Book, fascicle VI.1, recommendation Q.86 § 2. International Telecommunication Union, 1988.

[92] *Reverse Charging (REV).* ITU-T recommendation Q.85 § 3. International Telecommunication Union, 1993.

[93] *User-to-User Signaling (UUS).* ITU-T recommendation Q.87 § 1, rev. 1. International Telecommunication Union, 1993.

[94] *Direct Dialing-In.* ITU-T recommendation Q.731. § 1. International Telecommunication Union, 1992.

[95] *Calling Line Identification Presentation (CLIP).* ITU-T recommendation Q.731 § 3. International Telecommunication Union, 1993.

[96] *Calling Line Identification Restriction (CLIR).* ITU-T recommendation Q.731 § 4. International Telecommunication Union, 1993.

[97] *Connected Line Identification Presentation.* ITU-T recommendation Q.731 § 5. International Telecommunication Union, 1993.

[98] *Connected Line Identification Restriction.* ITU-T recommendation Q.731 § 6. International Telecommunication Union, 1993.

[99] *Sub-Addressing (SUB).* ITU-T recommendation Q.731 § 8. International Telecommunication Union, 1992 (published with Q.731 § 1).

[100] *Call Forwarding Busy.* ITU-T recommendation Q.732 § 2. International Telecommunication Union, 1993.

[101] *Call Forwarding No Answer.* ITU-T recommendation Q.732 § 3. International Telecommunication Union, 1993.

[102] *Call Forwarding Unconditional.* ITU-T recommendation Q.732 § 4. International Telecommunication Union, 1993.

[103] *Call Deflection.* ITU-T recommendation Q.732 § 5. International Telecommunication Union, 1993.

[104] *Call Waiting (CW).* ITU-T recommendation Q.733 § 1. International Telecommunication Union, 1992.

[105] *Call Hold.* ITU-T recommendation Q.733 § 2. International Telecommunication Union, 1993.

[106] *Terminal Portability.* ITU-T recommendation Q.733 § 3. International Telecommunication Union, 1993.

[107] *Conference Calling (CONF).* ITU-T recommendation Q.734 § 1. International Telecommunication Union, 1993.

[108] *Three-Party Service.* ITU-T recommendation Q.734 § 2. International Telecommunication Union, 1993.

[109] *Closed User Group.* ITU-T recommendation Q.735 § 1, rev. 1. International Telecommunication Union, 1992.

[110] *Multi-Level Precedence and Preemption (MLPP).* ITU-T recommendation Q.735 § 3. International Telecommunication Union, 1993.

[111] *User-to-User Signaling (UUS).* ITU-T recommendation Q.737 § 1. International Telecommunication Union, 1993.

[112] *Direct Dialing-In.* ITU-T recommendation Q.951 § 1. International Telecommunication Union, 1992.

[113] *Multiple Subscriber Number.* ITU-T recommendation Q.951 § 2. International Telecommunication Union, 1992.

[114] *Calling Line Identification Presentation (CLIP).* ITU-T recommendation Q.951 § 3. International Telecommunication Union, 1993.

[115] *Calling Line Identification Restriction (CLIR).* ITU-T recommendation Q.951 § 4. International Telecommunication Union, 1993.

[116] *Connected Line Identification Presentation.* ITU-T recommendation Q.951 § 5. International Telecommunication Union, 1993.

[117] *Connected Line Identification Restriction.* ITU-T recommendation Q.951 § 6. International Telecommunication Union, 1993.

[118] *Sub-Addressing (SUB).* ITU-T recommendation Q.951 § 8. International Telecommunication Union, 1992.

[119] *Call Deflection.* ITU-T recommendation Q.952 § 2–5. International Telecommunication Union, 1993.

[120] *Call Waiting (CW).* ITU-T recommendation Q.953 § 1. International Telecommunication Union, 1992.

[121] *Call Hold.* ITU-T recommendation Q.753 § 2. International Telecommunication Union, 1993.

[122] *Conference Calling (CONF).* ITU-T recommendation Q.954 § 1. International Telecommunication Union, 1993.

[123] *Three-Party Service.* ITU-T recommendation Q.954 § 2. International Telecommunication Union, 1993.

[124] *Closed User Group.* ITU-T recommendation Q.955 § 1. International Telecommunication Union, 1992.

[125] *Multi-Level Precedence and Preemption (MLPP).* ITU-T recommendation Q.755 § 3. International Telecommunication Union, 1993.

[126] *User-to-User Signaling (UUS).* ITU-T recommendation Q.957 § 1. International Telecommunication Union, 1993.

[127] *ISDN; Direct Dialing In (DDI) Supplementary Service. Service Description.* ETSI, European Telecommunication Standard ETS 300 062:1991.

[128] *ISDN; Multiple Subscriber Number (MSN) Supplementary Service. Service Description.* ETSI, European Telecommunication Standard ETS 300 050:1991.

[129] *ISDN; Calling Line Identification Presentation (CLIP) Supplementary Service. Service Description.* ETSI, European Telecommunication Standard ETS 300 089:1992.

[130] *ISDN; Calling Line Identification Restriction (CLIR) Supplementary Service. Service Description.* ETSI, European Telecommunication Standard ETS 300 090:1992.

[131] *ISDN; Connected Line Identification Presentation (COLP) Supplementary Service. Service Description.* ETSI, European Telecommunication Standard ETS 300 094:1992.

[132] *ISDN; Connected Line Identification Restriction (CLIR) Supplementary Service. Service Description.* ETSI, European Telecommunication Standard ETS 300 095:1992.

[133] *ISDN; Malicious Call Identification (MCID) Supplementary Service. Service Description.* ETSI, European Telecommunication Standard ETS 300 128:1992.

[134] *ISDN; Subaddressing (SUB) Supplementary Service. Service Description.* ETSI, European Telecommunication Standard ETS 300 059:1991.

[135] *ISDN; Call Forwarding Busy (CFB) Supplementary Service. Service Description.* ETSI, Proposed European Telecommunication Standard prETS 300 199:1992.

[136] *ISDN; Call Forwarding No Reply (CFNR) Supplementary Service. Service Description.* ETSI, Proposed European Telecommunication Standard prETS 300 201:1992.

[137] *ISDN; Call Unconditional (CFU) Supplementary Service. Service Description.* ETSI, Proposed European Telecommunication Standard prETS 300 201:1992.

[138] *ISDN; Call Deflection (CD) Supplementary Service. Service Description.* ETSI, Proposed European Telecommunication Standard prETS 300 202:1992.

[139] *ISDN; Call Waiting (CW) Supplementary Service. Service Description.* ETSI, European Telecommunication Standard ETS 300 56:1991.

[140] *ISDN; Terminal Portability (TP) Supplementary Service. Service Description.* ETSI, European Telecommunication Standard ETS 300 53:1991.

[141] *ISDN; Conference Call Add-On (CONF) Supplementary Service. Service Description.* ETSI, European Telecommunication Standard ETS 300 183:1992.

[142] *ISDN; Three Party (3PTY) Supplementary Service. Service Description.* ETSI, European Telecommunication Standard ETS 300 186:1993.

[143] *ISDN; Closed User Group (CUG) Supplementary Service. Service Description.* ETSI, European Telecommunication Standard ETS 300 136:1992.

[144] *ISDN; Advice of Charge: Charging Information at Call Setup (AOC-S) Supplementary Service. Service Description.* ETSI, European Telecommunication Standard ETS 300 178:1992.

[145] *ISDN; Advice of Charge: Charging Information During the Call (AOC-D) Supplementary Service. Service Description.* ETSI, European Telecommunication Standard ETS 300 179:1992.

[146] *ISDN; Advice of Charge; Charging Information at the End of the Call (AOC-E) Supplementary Service. Service Description.* ETSI, European Telecommunication Standard ETS 300 180:1992.

[147] *ISDN; User-to-User Signaling (UUS) Supplementary Service. Service Description.* ETSI, European Telecommunication Standard ETS 300 284:1993.

[148] *ISDN: Direct Dialing In (DDI) Supplementary Service. Functional Capabilities and Information Flows.* ETSI, European Telecommunication Standard ETS 300 063:1991.

[149] *ISDN; Multiple Subscriber Number (MSN) Supplementary Service. Functional Capabilities and Information Flows.* ETSI, European Telecommunication Standard ETS 300 051:1991.

[150] *ISDN; Calling Line Identification, Presentation and Restriction (CLIP and CLIR) Supplementary Service. Functional Capabilities and Information Flows.* ETSI, European Telecommunication Standard ETS 300 091:1992.

[151] *ISDN; Connected Line Identification Presentation and Restriction (COLP and COLR) Supplementary Service. Functional Capabilities and Information Flows.* ETSI, European Telecommunication Standard ETS 300 096:1992.

[152] *ISDN; Malicious Call Identification (MCID) Supplementary Service. Functional Capabilities and Information Flows.* ETSI, European Telecommunication Standard ETS 300 129:1992.

[153] *ISDN; Subaddressing (SUB) Supplementary Service. Functional Capabilities and Information Flows.* ETSI, European Telecommunication Standard ETS 300 060:1991.

[154] *ISDN; Call Forwarding Busy (CFB) Supplementary Service. Functional Capabilities and Information Flows.* ETSI, Proposed European Telecommunication Standard prETS 300 203:1992.

[155] *ISDN; Call Forwarding No Reply (CFNR) Supplementary Service. Functional Capabilities and Information Flows.* ETSI, Proposed European Telecommunication Standard prETS 300 205:1992.

[156] *ISDN; Call Forwarding Unconditional (CFU) Supplementary Service. Functional Capabilities and Information Flows.* ETSI, Proposed European Telecommunication Standard prETS 300 204:1992.

[157] *ISDN; Call Deflection (CD) Supplementary Service. Functional Capabilities and Information Flows.* ETSI, Proposed European Telecommunication Standard prETS 300 206:1992.

[158] *ISDN; Call Waiting (CW) Supplementary Service. Functional Capabilities and Information Flows.* ETSI, European Telecommunication Standard ETS 300 57:1992.

[159] *ISDN; Terminal Portability (TP) Supplementary Service. Functional Capabilities and Information Flows.* ETSI, European Telecommunication Standard ETS 300 54:1991.

[160] *ISDN; Conference Call Add-on (CONF) Supplementary Service. Functional Capabilities and Information Flows. Service Description.* ETSI, European Telecommunication Standard ETS 300 184:1993.

[161] *ISDN; Three Party (3PTY) Supplementary Service. Functional Capabilities and Information Flows.* ETSI, European Telecommunication Standard ETS 300 187:1993.

[162] *ISDN; Closed User Group (CUG) Supplementary Service. Functional Capabilities and Information Flows.* ETSI, European Telecommunication Standard ETS 300 137:1991.

[163] *ISDN; Advice of Charge (AOC) Supplementary Service. Functional Capabilities and Information Flows.* ETSI, European Telecommunication Standard ETS 300 181:1992.

[164] *ISDN; User-to-User Signaling (UUS) Supplementary Service. Functional Capabilities and Information Flows.* ETSI, European Standard Telecommunication Standard ETS 300 285:1993.

[165] *ISDN; Direct Dialing In (DDI) Supplementary Service. Digital Subscriber Signaling One (DSS 1) Protocol.* ETSI, European Telecommunication Standard ETS 300 064:1991.

[166] *ISDN; Multiple Subscriber Number (MSN) Supplementary Service. Digital Subscriber Signaling One (DSS 1) Protocol.* ETSI, European Telecommunication Standard ETS 300 052:1991.

[167] *ISDN; Calling Line Identification, Presentation (CLIP) Supplementary Service. Digital Subscriber Signaling One (DSS 1) Protocol.* ETSI, European Telecommunication Standard ETS 300 092:1992; amendment 1, 1993.

[168] *ISDN; Calling Line Identification, Restriction (CLIR) Supplementary Service. Digi-*

tal Subscriber Signaling One (DSS 1) Protocol. ETSI, European Telecommunication Standard ETS 300 093:1992.

[169] *ISDN; Connected Line Identification Presentation (COLP) Supplementary Service. Digital Subscriber Signaling One (DSS 1) Protocol.* ETSI, European Telecommunication Standard ETS 300 097:1992.

[170] *ISDN; Connected Line Identification Restriction (COLR) Supplementary Service. Digital Subscriber Signaling One (DSS 1) Protocol.* ETSI, European Telecommunication Standard ETS 300 098:1992.

[171] *ISDN; Malicious Call Identification (MCID) Supplementary Service. Digital Subscriber Signaling One (DSS 1) Protocol.* ETSI, European Telecommunication Standard ETS 300 130:1992.

[172] *ISDN; Subaddressing (SUB) Supplementary Service. Digital Subscriber Signaling One (DSS 1) Protocol.* ETSI, European Telecommunication Standard ETS 300 061:1991.

[173] *ISDN; Call Waiting (CW) Supplementary Service. Digital Subscriber Signaling One (DSS 1) Protocol.* ETSI, European Telecommunication Standard ETS 300 58:1992.

[174] *ISDN: Terminal Portability (TP) Supplementary Service. Digital Subscriber Signaling One (DSS 1) Protocol.* ETSI, European Telecommunication Standard ETS 300 55:1991.

[175] *ISDN; Conference Call Add-On (CONF) Supplementary Service. Digital Subscriber Signaling One (DSS 1) Protocol. Service Description.* ETSI, European Telecommunication Standard ETS 300 185:1993.

[176] *ISDN; Three Party (3PTY) Supplementary Service. Digital Subscriber Signaling One (DSS 1) Protocol.* ETSI, European Telecommunication Standard ETS 300 188:1993.

[177] *ISDN; Closed User Group (CUG) Supplementary Service. Digital Subscriber Signaling One (DSS 1) Protocol.* ETSI, European Telecommunication Standard ETS 300 138:1992.

[178] *ISDN; Advice of Charge (AOC) Supplementary Service. Functional Capabilities and Information Flows. Digital Subscriber Signaling One (DSS 1) Protocol.* ETSI, European Telecommunication Standard ETS 300 182:1993.

[179] *ISDN; User-to-User Signaling (UUS) Supplementary Service. Digital Subscriber Signaling One (DSS 1) Protocol.* ETSI, European Telecommunication Standard ETS 300 286:1993.

[180] "Network interface description for national ISDN-1 customer access." BELLCORE Technical Reference TR-NWT-000776, issue 2, Feb. 1993.

[181] *Interworking between the Digital Subscriber Signaling System Layer 3 Protocol and the Signaling System No. 7 ISDN User Part.* CCITT Blue Book, fascicle VI.6, recommendation Q.699. International Telecommunication Union, 1988.

9 CCS 7 ISDN User Part

Acronyms

ACC	automatic congestion control
ACM	address complete message
ANM	answer message
BLA	blocking acknowledgment (message)
BLO	blocking (message)
BOCs	Bell operating companies
CALL PROC	call proceed (message)
CC	continuity check
CCR	continuity check request (message)
CCS 7	CCITT common channel signaling system no. 7
CGB	circuit group blocking (message)
CGBA	circuit group blocking acknowledgment (message)
CGU	circuit group unblocking (message)
CGUA	circuit group unblocking acknowledgment (message)
CIC	circuit identification code
CLIP	calling line identification presentation
CLIR	calling line identification restriction
CON	connect, a message used in ISUP protocol
CONN	connect, a message used in DSS 1 protocol
CONN ACK	connect acknowledge (message), a message used in DSS 1 protocol
COT	continuity (message)
CPG	call progress (message)
CQM	circuit group query message
CQR	circuit group query response (message)
DISC	disconnect, a message in DSS 1 protocol
DSS 1	digital subscriber signaling system 1
IAM	initial address message
IDR	identification request (message)
IRS	identification response (message)
ISDN	integrated services digital network
ISUP	ISDN user part
ITU-T	International Telecommunication Union-Telecommunication Standardization Sector
MCID	malicious call identification
MTP	message transfer part
REL	release (message)
RLC	release complete (message)
RSC	reset circuit (message)
SAM	subsequent address message
SCCP	signaling connection control part
SIF	signaling information field
SP	signaling point
TMR	transmission medium requirement parameter
UBA	unblocking acknowledgment (message)
UBL	unblocking (message)
UCIC	unequipped circuit identification (message)
UPA	user part available (message)
UPT	user part test (message)
UPU	user part unavailable (message)

ABSTRACT

The integrated services digital network (ISDN) user part (ISUP) was briefly described in Chapter 4. A detailed description follows in this chapter. The aspects covered here include:

- General format of ISUP messages.
- ISUP signaling procedures for basic call control for en bloc and overlap signaling along with the structure and role of various ISUP messages in the implementation of these procedures.
- Continuity check for circuit switched speech/data circuits.
- Supervision of speech/data circuits by the ISUP, namely, circuit group query, blocking, unblocking, and resetting circuits and circuit groups.
- Treatment of abnormal conditions, such as dual seizures and the receipt of errored, unexpected, or unrecognizable messages, message parameters, or parameter values.
- Congestion control.
- ISUP signaling procedures associated with supplementary services.

9.1 Introduction

The ISDN user part (ISUP) finds application in both international and national networks for signaling of circuit switched connections. Contrary to the impression created by its name, the ISDN user part is not limited only to connections in the ISDN. The circuit switched connections may relate to an ISDN, analog network, or a mixed analog and digital network. As explained in Chapter 4, ISUP uses the services offered by the message transfer part (MTP). In some cases, the services of the signaling connection control part (SCCP) may also be used.

9.2 ISUP Message Format

It may be recalled from Figure 7–2 that the signaling information field (SIF) for an ISUP message consists of a routing label type C and the ISUP information.

The general format of an ISUP message is shown in Figure 9–1. The message has the following components:

- Label type C, consisting of a routing label and a circuit identification code (CIC).
- A message type code to identify the ISUP message.
- A mandatory fixed part, consisting of those fixed-length parameters that must always be present in a particular type of message. The sequence of occurrence and the length of these parameters is predefined for each message type. Therefore, there is no need to include the name of the message and its length.

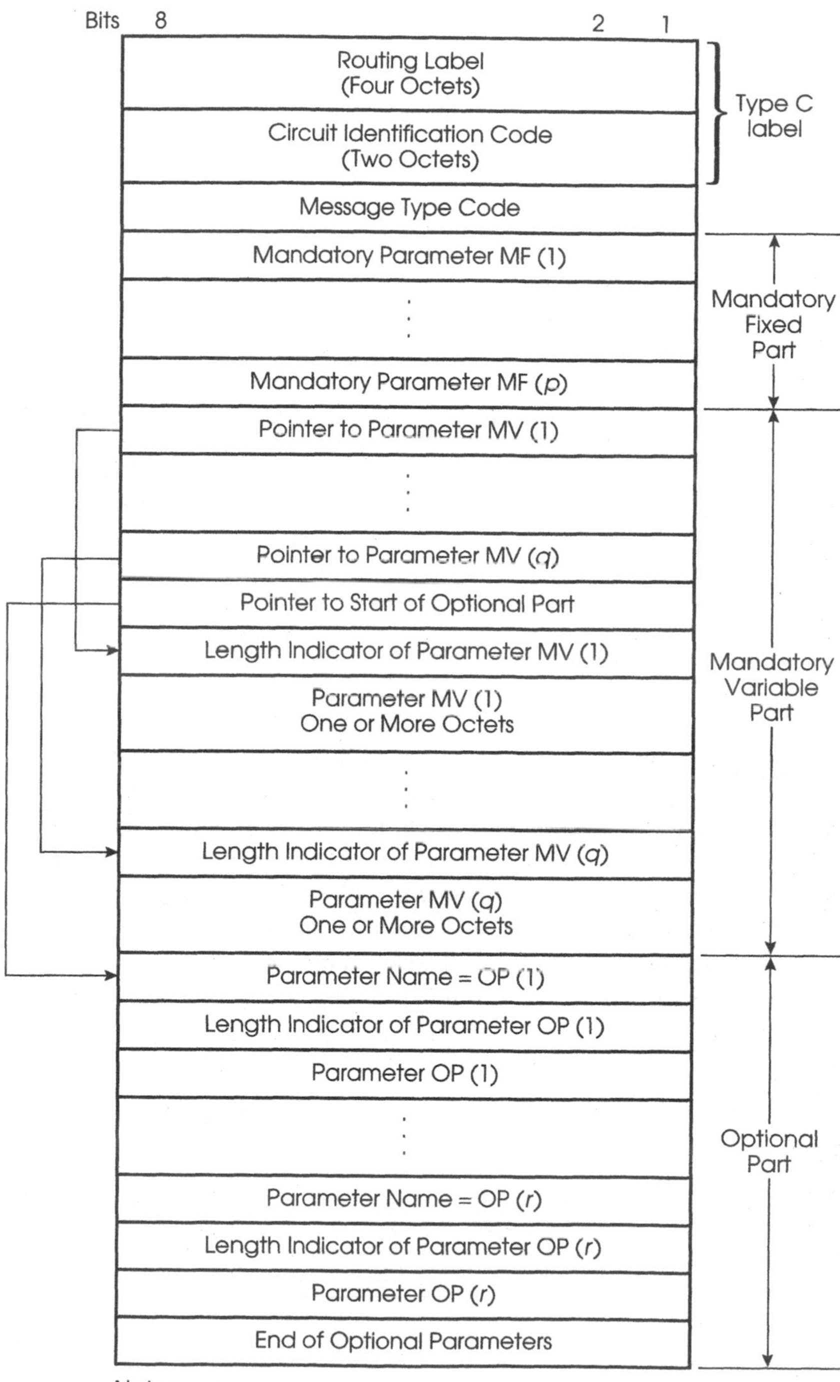

Notes:
1. MF(1) to MF(*p*) are mandatory fixed parameters.
2. MV(1) to MV(*q*) are mandatory variable parameters.
3. OP(1) to OP(*r*) are optional parameters.

Figure 9–1 General format of ISUP messages.

- A mandatory variable part, consisting of parameters of variable lengths whose presence in the message is mandatory. Due to the variable lengths, a pointer indicating the beginning of the parameter and a length indicator is included for each mandatory variable parameter in the message. There is no need to indicate the names of the parameters, since the parameters to be included and their sequence are predefined for each message type.
- Optional parameters that may be either fixed or variable in length may or may not occur in a particular type of message. The sequence in which the optional parameters occur in a message is not fixed. Therefore, for each optional parameter present in a message, the parameter name is included. Normally, the same optional parameter does not appear more than once in a message.

The CIC identifies the circuit to which the signaling message refers. The format of the circuit identification field is shown in Figure 9–2(a).

EXAMPLE 9-1

For identification of timeslot 12 in a 30-channel PCM system numbered 20, the contents of the circuit identification field are shown in Figure 9–2(b). The five least-significant bits are used to identify a timeslot in the range of 0 to 31. The remaining 12 bits indicate the number of the PCM system. The spare bits are coded with zeros.

For multirate connections, the CIC indicated in the message is the lowest-numbered CIC of the multiple 64 kbps circuits used. It was indicated in Chapter 8 that contiguous timeslots are assigned for a multirate connection. For example, in a 2,048 kbps digital path, a 384 kbps connection may use timeslots 1 to 6. In this case, the CIC in the message is coded for timeslot 1. Other timeslots in the connection need not be explicitly indicated in the message because they are known to be contiguous.

The message type code field identifies an ISUP message. A total of 45 ISUP messages are specified in International Telecommunication Union-Telecommunication Standardization Sector (ITU-T) recommendations Q.762 [1] and Q.763 [2]. A list of these messages and their codes is given in Appendix 2.

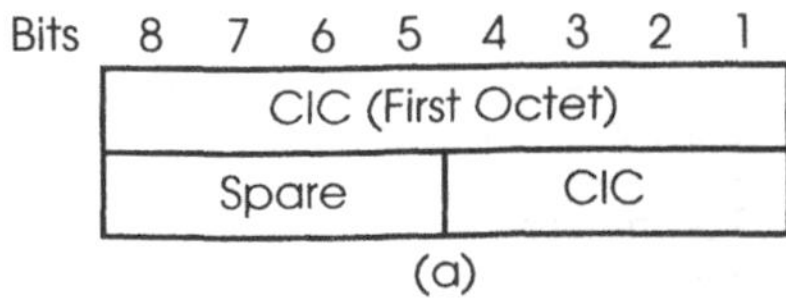

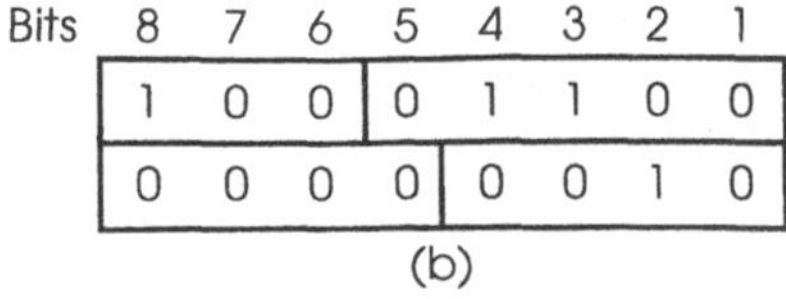

Figure 9–2 (a) Circuit identification code field format; (b) example of a circuit identification field.

9.3 ISUP Signaling Procedures for Basic Call Control

The ISUP signaling procedure for basic call control—that is, for calls that do not include any supplementary services—is described in this section. Both en bloc and overlap methods of signaling are considered. In en bloc operation, the originating exchange commences signaling only after receiving all the digits for the called subscriber. In overlap operation, on the other hand, the exchange commences signaling as soon as it has received sufficient digits to route the call to the next exchange. The ISUP signaling procedures for basic call control are specified in ITU-T recommendation Q.764 [3].

9.3.1 Basic Call Control for En Bloc Signaling

Before pursuing this section, readers should refer to Section 4.7, which presents an introductory discussion of ISDN call control using ISUP messages. Attention may be paid in particular to Figures 4–14 and 4–15, which depict calls corresponding to en bloc and overlap operation, respectively. The exchanges involved in the connection are two local exchanges that originate and terminate the call and one or more transit exchanges.

9.3.1.1 Connection Setup

All the information necessary for establishing the call is sent by the calling party to the originating exchange in the SETUP message of digital subscriber signaling system 1 (DSS 1) protocol. The originating exchange examines the SETUP message to determine whether the information received is complete in all respects. The SETUP message always contains a bearer capability information element (refer to Figure 8–21). Among other things, the bearer capability information element indicates to the originating exchange the details of the type of connection required for the call. Recall that the information transfer capability, information transfer rate, and rate multiplier fields in the bearer capability information element (Figure 8–22) indicate the type of connection needed for the call. For example, the call may be of one of the following types:

- Speech
- 64 kbps unrestricted
- 64 kbps unrestricted preferred
- Multirate unrestricted connection types at 2 × 64 kbps, 384 kbps, 1,536 kbps, or 1,920 kbps

This information, along with the called party number, is used in the originating exchange to decide the next exchange to which the call should be routed and in the selection of a free and suitable circuit to that exchange.

Some of the information contained in the SETUP message is also of relevance to the next exchange for the purpose of call control. This information is therefore transferred or mapped to the initial address message (IAM) of the ISUP and sent to the next exchange.

The IAM is usually the longest ISUP message. The mandatory fixed and variable parameters of the IAM are shown in Figure 9–3. In addition, there can be up to 29 optional parameters. Many of these parameters are useful for carrying signaling information for the support of supplementary service and are not relevant for basic call control.

The *nature of the connection indicator* parameter is set by the originating exchange to indicate the following three aspects of the connection (refer to Table 9–1):

1. Need for continuity check
2. Echo cancellation
3. Use of satellite circuits

As noted in Section 4.3, a continuity check may be required in CCITT common channel signaling system no. 7 (CCS 7) since, due to the separation of speech and signaling, the actual establishment of speech connection can not be readily verified. This may not be necessary in all cases, however. A continuity check is not needed where the transmission system interconnecting the exchanges has a means of indicating failure conditions to the exchange. When failure conditions on the transmission links cannot be communicated, a continuity check is useful. Two examples of where a continuity check will be needed are transmission links with TDMA satellite systems and digital access cross-connect systems. As noted in Chapter 4, in high traffic exchanges, a continuity check adds considerably to the connection setup time. In such situations, a continuity check may be performed less often (for example, on every alternate call) and not on a per call basis. The procedure for performing a continuity check is described in Section 9–4.

If the originating exchange determines that echo control is required for the call, it enables the outgoing half echo control device and sets bit E to 1 (Table 9–1).

If a satellite circuit is selected by the originating exchange during call setup, then

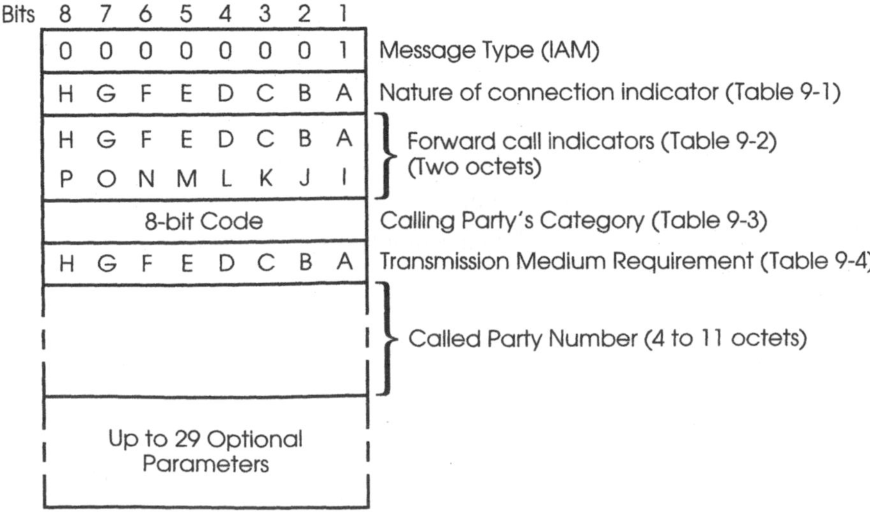

Figure 9–3 Initial address message (IAM).

Table 9–1 Nature of Connection Indicator Parameter

Bits		
Bits B	A	Satellite indicator
0	0	No satellite circuit in the connection
0	1	One satellite circuit in the connection
1	0	Two satellite circuits in the connection
1	1	Spare
Bits D	C	Continuity check indicator
0	0	No continuity check required
0	1	Continuity check required on this circuit
1	0	Continuity check performed on a previous circuit
1	1	Spare
Bits E		
0		Outgoing half echo control device not included
1		Outgoing half echo control device included
Bits F–H		Spare

the satellite indicator bits are set to indicate *one* satellite circuit in the connection. When a terrestrial link is chosen, the satellite indicator is set to *no* satellite circuit in the connection.

The signaling capabilities required from the network are included in the *forward call indicator* parameter. The originating exchange sets appropriate values based on the type of service requested in the SETUP message. For example, for 64 kbps unrestricted data transfer, bits H and G will be set for ISUP required all the way. (Refer to Table 9–2.) Other network signaling capabilities included are ISUP preferred and ISUP not required. In the latter case, any other signaling system (for example, R2 MFC) may be used for the connection. (R2 MFC is an analog multifrequency tone signaling method.) The type of CCS 7 signaling—namely, end-to-end or link-by-link—is also indicated in the forward call indicator parameter. The forward call indicator also informs the next exchange in the connection about the nature of the calling party: ISDN access or non-ISDN.

The coding of the *calling party's category* parameter is shown in Table 9–3. For calls dialed by an operator, the provision to indicate the language spoken by the operator exists. This feature is useful for international ISDN calls.

The transmission requirements for the call are indicated by the *transmission medium requirement* parameter shown in Table 9–4.

The called party number is included in the *called party number* parameter. This parameter has a variable length of 4 to 11 octets. A pair of digits is packed in one octet. If the called party address has an odd number of digits, a filler code containing 0000 is inserted immediately following the last digit. The nature of the address (for example, national or international number) and the numbering plan followed for the called party number (for example, the ISDN numbering plan according to ITU-T recommendation E.164) are also included in the called party address parameter. Figure 9–3 shows an example of a called party number. At this stage, the connection is completed only in the backward direction, that is, between the originating exchange and the calling party access.

After sending the initial address message, the originating exchange starts timer T7 (awaiting address complete timer, with a value range of 20 to 30 seconds). If the address complete message is not received before the expiry of timer T7, the connection is released

Table 9-2 Forward Call Indicator Parameter

Bits			Description
Bit	A		National/international call indicators
	0		Call to be treated as a national call
	1		Call to be treated as an international call
Bits	C	B	End-to-end method indicator
	0	0	No end-to-end connection available (only link-by-link method)
	0	1	Pass-along method available
	1	0	SCCP method available
	1	1	Pass-along and SCCP methods available
Bit	D		Interworking indicator
	0		No interworking encountered (CCS 7 all the way)
	1		Interworking encountered
Bit	F		ISDN user part indicator
	0		ISUP not used all the way
	1		ISUP used all the way
Bits	H	G	ISUP preference indicator
	0	0	ISUP preferred all the way
	0	1	ISUP not required all the way
	1	0	ISUP required all the way
	1	1	Spare
Bit	I		ISDN access indicator
	0		Originating access non-ISDN
	1		Originating access ISDN
Bits	K	J	SCCP method indicator
	0	0	No indication
	0	1	Connectionless method available
	1	0	Connection-oriented method available
	1	1	Connectionless and connection-oriented methods available
Bit	L		Spare
Bits	P–M:		Reserved for national use

and an indication is returned to the calling party using DSS 1 protocol. The connection in the backward direction is also released.

When the information required to be sent to the next exchange is more than 272 octets long, the initial address message is segmented by the originating exchange. In this case, a second segment that contains the remaining part of the message is sent immediately following the first segment. One optional parameter in the IAM is the *optional forward call indicators* parameter; a bit in this parameter is set to indicate to the next exchange that the IAM is in two segments.

Out of the 29 optional parameters that can exist in the IAM a few parameters are discussed here by way of illustration. An optional parameter, the *calling party number* parameter, may be used by the originating exchange to convey the calling party's address. The calling party's address may be sent without a request or on the basis of a specific request from the destination exchange.

The optional *user service information* parameter has the same format as the bearer capability information element of the SETUP message of DSS 1 protocol. (Refer to Chapter 8 for the format of the SETUP message.) Thus, the bearer capability information can be mapped directly onto this parameter. Likewise, the *user teleservice information*

Table 9-3 Calling Party's Category Parameter

CODE	MEANING
00000000	Calling party's category unknown
00000001 to 00000101	Operator, French, English, German, Russian, and Spanish languages in ascending order of binary values
00000110 to 00000100	Available to administrations for selection of a particular language by mutual agreement
00001001	Reserved
00001010	Ordinary calling subscriber
00001011	Calling subscriber with priority
00001100	Voiceband data call
00001101	Test call
00001110	Spare
00001111	Pay phone
00010000 to 11011111	Reserved for national use
11111111	Spare

Note: In national calls, the code 00001001 may be used to indicate that the called party is a national operator.

Table 9-4 Transmission Medium Requirement Parameter

CODE	MEANING
00000000	Speech
00000001	Spare
00000010	64 kbps restricted
00000011	3.1 kHz audio
00000100	Reserved for alternate speech/64 kbps unrestricted, beginning with speech
00000101	Reserved for alternate 64 kbps unrestricted/speech, beginning with 64 kbps unrestricted
00000110	Reserved for 64 kbps preferred
00000111	Reserved for 2 × 64 kbps unrestricted
00001000	Reserved for 384 kbps unrestricted
00001001	Reserved for 1,536 kbps unrestricted
00001010	Reserved for 1,920 kbps unrestricted
00001011 to 11111111	Spare

parameter is another optional parameter which is identical in format to the high-layer compatibility information element of DSS 1.

For call setup propagation delay, a *propagation delay counter* parameter can be used in the IAM. A record of propagation delay experienced in the connection is useful in deciding the need for echo control. The propagation delay counter consists of one octet in which the propagation delay, in milliseconds, is stored in the binary form. In the IAM sent by the originating exchange, the counter is usually set to zero. In each succeeding exchange thereafter, the propagation delay counter is updated. This obviously requires that the exchanges maintain information on propagation delay for each circuit.

When the IAM sent by the originating exchange is received in a transit exchange, a free and suitable circuit to the next exchange is selected based on the called party address and the connection type specified in the transmission medium requirement parameter.

In certain cases, the transit exchange may alter the signaling information received from the preceding exchange while formulating the IAM for the next exchange. For example, the nature of connection indicator may be altered to reflect the characteristics of the outgoing circuit selected. The satellite indicator (bits A and B) in this parameter is incremented from its earlier value (that is, the value received from the previous exchange) if the outgoing circuit selected is a satellite circuit.

The transmission path is cut through in both directions at a transit exchange as soon as it sends the IAM to the next exchange. However, where request for a continuity check has been received in the IAM, the connection of transmission paths occurs only after the completion of continuity check. Timer T8 is associated with the continuity check procedure. It is started on receipt of continuity check request and stopped upon successful completion of the check. The continuity check procedure is explained in Section 9.4.

When the transit exchange receives an IAM with the indication that the message is segmented, it starts timer T34 and awaits the second segment of IAM. Although the message segments are sent sequentially by the originating exchange, in rare cases, such as due to signaling network rearrangements, the second segment may be delayed or even lost. Timer T34 is useful in such situations. This timer is stopped when the second segment is also received; the call then proceeds in a normal manner. The second segment is discarded if it is received after the expiry of T34. Thereafter, the call proceeds in the normal manner, using only the contents of the first segment of the IAM. Timer T34 lies between 2 and 4 seconds.

When the IAM reaches the destination exchange, the called party number is examined to determine if the connection is allowed. When the connection is allowed, the terminating exchange communicates with the called party's access by sending a SETUP message. A call proceed (CALL PROC) message from the called party may be received in response. (As explained in Chapter 8, the use of a CALL PROC message by the destination access is optional.)

Irrespective of the receipt of CALL PROC message, an address complete message (ACM) is sent by the destination exchange as a backward signaling message. The format of the ACM is shown in Figure 9–4.

Two cases may arise at the destination exchange:

1. *Case 1:* The terminating exchange decides on its own (without receiving any indication to this effect from the called party access) that the complete address of the called party has been received.

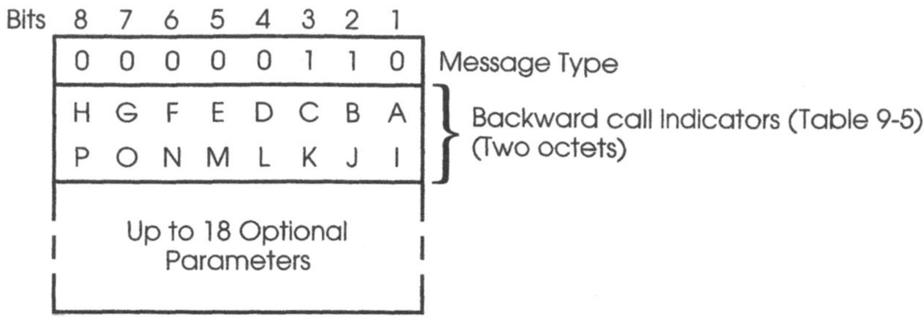

Figure 9–4 Address complete message (ACM).

2. *Case 2:* The terminating exchange determines that the called party's complete address has been received only on receipt of an indication to this effect from the called party's access.

In the first case, the ACM is sent as soon as it is determined that the complete address of the called party has been received at the destination exchange, even though no indication has been received from the called party's ISDN access so far. Because the status of the called party access is unknown at this moment and the called party is an ISDN subscriber, the backward call indicator parameter in the ACM is set as follows (refer to Table 9–5):

Called party status indicator: no indication (bits C and D are set to 0)
ISDN access indicator: ISDN (bit M is set to 1)

The ISDN terminal at the destination access may be either the nonautomatic answering type or it may possess automatic answering capabilities. When the terminal at the called party ISDN access is a nonautomatic answering terminal, the destination user is alerted and this fact is conveyed to the terminating exchange by the DSS 1 ALERT message. Thereafter, the terminating exchange (which has already sent the ACM) sends a CALL PROGRESS (CPG) message in the backward direction toward the originating exchange. Figure 9–5 shows the interworking between the DSS 1 and ISUP CCS 7 messages at the terminating exchange for this situation.

For better understanding of the CCS 7–DSS 1 interworking, the terminating exchange may be considered to perform the following three functions:

1. Incoming CCS 7 ISUP functions by which the terminating exchange sends and receives ISUP messages from the preceding exchange in the connection
2. Call control functions, such as determining the status of the called party and switching the connection
3. Outgoing DSS 1 functions by which the terminating exchange communicates with the called party access

The signals shown in lowercase letters—for example, setup indication and setup confirm—are internal to the exchange software. ISUP and DSS 1 messages are shown in uppercase letters.

Table 9-5 Backward Call Indicator Parameter

Bits B	A	Charge indicator
0	0	No indication
0	1	No charge
1	0	Charge
1	1	Spare
Bits D	C	Called party's status indicator
0	0	No indication
0	1	Subscriber free
1	0	Connect when free
1	1	Spare
Bits F	E	Called party's category indicator
0	0	No indication
0	1	Ordinary subscriber
1	0	Pay phone
1	1	Spare
Bits H	G	End-to-end method indicator
0	0	No end-to-end method available (only link by link method)
0	1	Pass-along method available
1	0	SCCP method available
1	1	Pass-along and SCCP methods available
Bit I		Interworking indicator
0		No interworking encountered
1		Interworking encountered
Bit J		End-to-end information indicator
0		No end-to-end information available
1		End-to-end information available
Bit K		ISUP indicator
0		ISUP not used all the way
1		ISUP used all the way
Bit L		Holding indicator
0		Holding not requested
1		Holding requested
Bit M		ISDN access indicator
0		Terminating access non-ISDN
1		Terminating access ISDN
Bit N		Echo control device indicator
0		Incoming half echo control device not included
1		Incoming half echo control device included
Bits P	O	SCCP method indicator
0	0	No indication
0	1	Connectionless method available
1	0	Connection-oriented method available
1	1	Connectionless and connection-oriented methods available

The format of the CPG message is shown in Figure 9–6. The CPG is always sent in the backward direction. It contains two mandatory parameters, the message type and the event information parameter. Besides these mandatory parameters, up to 18 optional parameters may be present. The purpose of CPG is to convey the occurrence of an event during call setup to the originating exchange. In turn, the latter informs the calling party of the event. In this case, the event to be conveyed is about alerting of the called party. Thus,

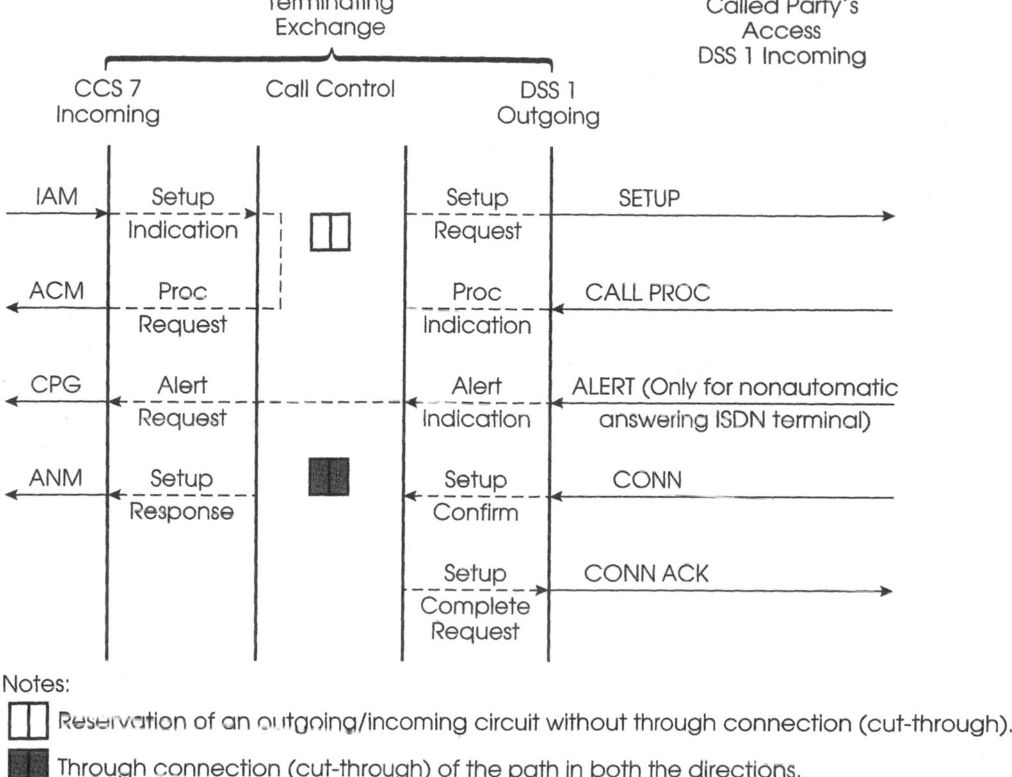

Figure 9–5 Interworking between the CCS 7 ISUP and the DSS 1 at the terminating exchange: Case 1.

as seen from Table 9–6, bits A to G of the event information parameter should be set to 0000001. Since an indication of the occurrence of an event is to be supplied to the calling party, there is no presentation restriction, and bit H is set to 0.

When the terminal at the called party ISDN access is an automatic answering terminal, the ALERT message is not received; consequently, there is no need to send the CPG message.

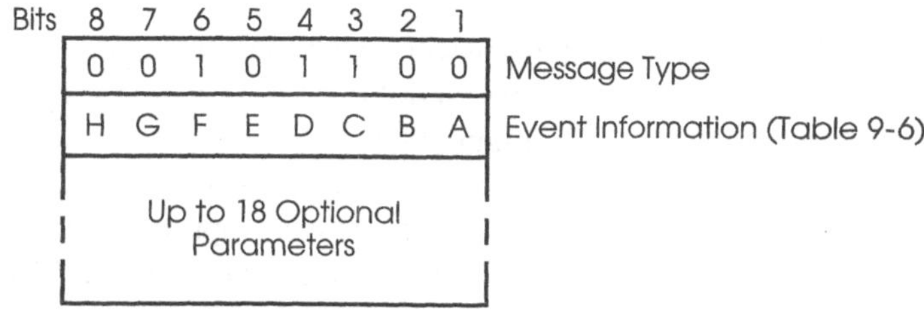

Figure 9–6 Call progress (CPG) message.

Table 9–6 Format of Event Information Parameter

Bits G F E D C B A	Event indicator
0 0 0 0 0 0 0	Spare
0 0 0 0 0 0 1	Alerting
0 0 0 0 0 1 0	Progress
0 0 0 0 0 1 1	In-band information or an appropriate pattern is now available
0 0 0 0 1 0 0	Call forwarded on busy
0 0 0 0 1 0 1	Call forwarded on no reply
0 0 0 0 1 1 0	Call forwarded unconditional
0 0 0 0 1 1 1 to 1 1 1 1 1 1 1	Spare
Bit H	**Event presentation restricted indicator**
0	No indication
1	Presentation restricted

For both automatic and nonautomatic answering terminals, a CONN message is sent to the terminating exchange from the destination access when the call is answered. The terminating exchange on reception of this message performs the following actions:

- Cuts through the path in both directions: toward the called party access and the preceding exchange
- Sends an answer message (ANM) as a backward signal

The format and functions of the ANM are discussed later in this chapter.

The actions performed by the terminating exchange in the second case depend on the type of ISDN terminal at the destination access. For a nonautomatic answering ISDN terminal, the ALERT message is sent to the terminating exchange, and only then is the ACM sent in the backward direction toward the preceding exchange.

Since the status of the called party access is known from the ALERT message and the called party is an ISDN subscriber, the backward call indicator parameter in the ACM is set as follows (refer to Table 9–5):

Called party's status indicator: subscriber free (bits C and D are set to 1 and 0, respectively)

ISDN access indicator: ISDN (bit M set to 1)

When the called subscriber answers, a CONN message is received at the terminating exchange from the called access, and the ANM is sent in the backward direction. The flow of messages is as shown in Figure 9–7.

The ANM has only one mandatory parameter, the message type, but up to 20 optional parameters can be included. When several optional parameters are present, the length of the ANM may exceed 272 octets; in this case, the ANM message is segmented. One of the optional parameters is the backward call indicators parameter (Table 9–5). Thus, information about the connection, such as whether ISUP has been used all the way

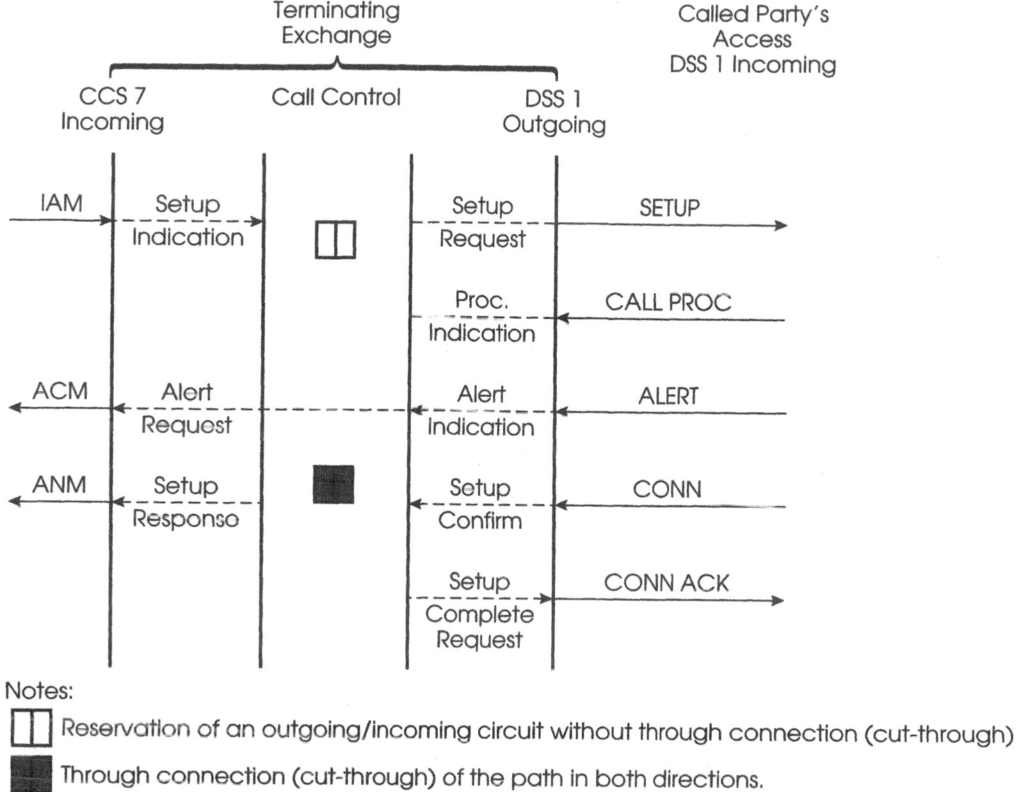

Figure 9–7 Interworking between the CCS 7 ISUP and the DSS 1 at the terminating exchange—non-automatic answering ISDN terminal: Case 2.

and the use of an echo control device, can be sent back to the originating exchange. Another optional parameter is the *optional backward indicators* parameter, which includes a segmentation indicator to inform whether the ANM message is segmented.

For an automatic answering ISDN terminal, no ALERT message is sent by the ISDN access, but only a CONN message when the call is answered. In this case, the terminating exchange sends a single ISUP message called the connect (CON) message. This backward message indicates to the preceding exchanges that the called party address is complete and that the call has been answered. Thus, the functions of the ACM and ANM are combined in the CON message. The message flow for this case is shown in Figure 9–8.

The CON message has two mandatory parameters, message type and backward call indicators parameters. In addition, up to 19 optional parameters may be specified, many of which are useful in supporting supplementary services.

When an ACM is received at an intermediate exchange it simply passes the ACM, without change, to the preceding exchange. At the same time, timer T9 (awaiting answer timer) is started. Timer T9 is stopped when an ANM is received. The value of this timer should be kept between 2 to 4 minutes, as recommended in ITU-T recommendation Q.118 [4]. If timer T9 expires, then the connection is released.

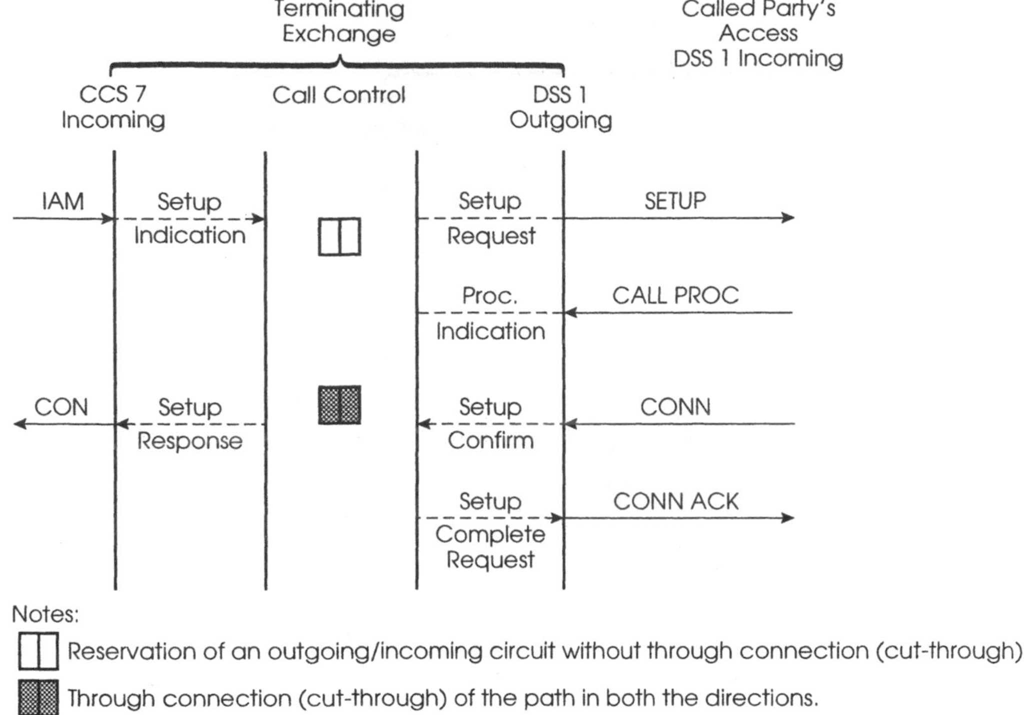

Figure 9–8 Interworking between the CCS 7 ISUP and the DSS 1 at the terminating exchange—Automatic answering ISDN terminal: Case 2.

When the CON message is received at an intermediate exchange, it is sent unchanged to the preceding exchange. When the ACM is received at the originating exchange, the following actions are taken:

- Timer T7, which was started on sending the IAM, is stopped.
- An awaiting answer timer T9 is started.
- The called party's status indicator is examined.

Based on the examination of called party's status indicator (bits D and C of backward call indicator parameter, refer to Table 9–5), two cases corresponding to case 1 and case 2 described earlier may arise:

1. The called party's status indicator in the ACM contains *no indication.* The originating exchange therefore waits for further ISUP messages. Subsequently, ISUP messages corresponding to one of the following alternatives may be received at the origination exchange:
   - If the called terminal is a nonautomatic answering ISDN terminal, a CPG message is received. In this case, the originating exchange sends an ALERT DSS 1 message to the calling party's ISDN access. Next, the origination ex-

change receives an ANM indicating that the connection has been completed. The originating exchange then performs the following functions:
  - The transmission path is cut through in the forward direction.
  - Timer T9 is stopped.
  - If charging is controlled by the originating exchange, then charging of the call is commenced.
  - A CONN DSS 1 message is sent to the calling party.
- If the called terminal is an automatic answering terminal, no CPG is received by the originating exchange; only an ANM is received when the called party answers. Actions identical to those described above, (namely, through connection of the transmission path, stopping timer T9, commencement of charging if necessary, and sending a connect (CONN) message to the calling party) are performed.

2. The called party's status indicator in the ACM contains a *subscriber free* indication. Therefore, an ALERT message is sent to the calling party. In addition, timer T7 is stopped and timer T9 is started. The ACM is followed by ANM, and actions identical to those described for the first case are performed.

If an ISUP message CON is received in place of an ACM and an ANM (this happens when the called ISDN terminal has the automatic answering feature), then timer T7 is stopped. Timer T9 is not involved in this case. Other actions (namely, through connection of the transmission path in the forward direction, commencement of charging, if necessary, and informing the calling party by a CONN DSS 1 message) are also performed.

9.3.1.2 Connection Release

Release of an ISDN connection may be initiated by either side, the calling party or the called party, and the procedure to be followed in the two cases is identical. In the following description, release by the called party is assumed.

The called side sends a disconnect (DISC) DSS 1 message to the terminating exchange. The terminating exchange releases the switched transmission path in both the directions. It also sends a release (REL) ISUP message to the preceding exchange. At the same time, timers T1 and T5 are started at the terminating exchange. Upon receipt of an REL message, the release of the switched path is initiated at an intermediate exchange, timers T1 and T5 are started, and the REL message is sent to the preceding exchange in the connection. Also upon completion of the release of the switched path, a release complete (RLC) message is sent back to the preceding exchange in the connection. When the REL message reaches the originating exchange, the transmission path is released in both directions and a DISC DSS 1 message is sent to the calling party access.

Upon receipt of the RLC message, timers T1 and T5 are stopped at the concerned exchange. Figure 9–9 shows the exchange of messages for normal call release initiated by the called party.

Figure 9–10 shows the format of the REL message. The REL message consists of two mandatory parameters, the message type and the cause indicators. In addition, up to 12 optional parameters are specified. The coding of the cause indicators parameter is

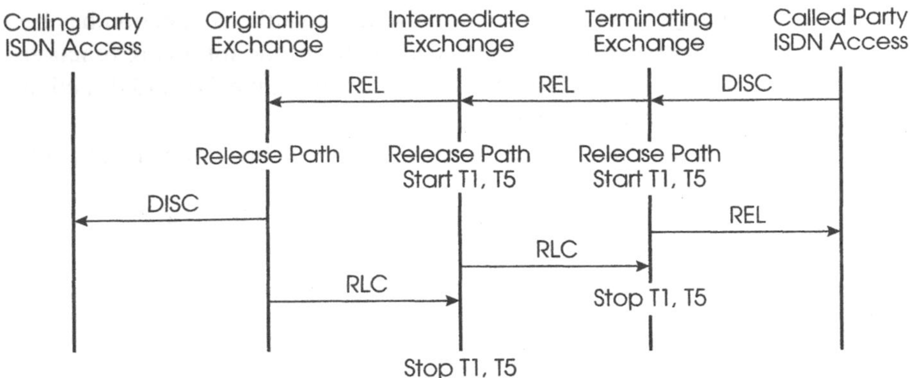

Figure 9–9 Normal call release initiated by the called party.

shown in Table 9–7, which reveals that the cause indicators parameter specifies not only a particular condition or cause but also the location to which this condition relates. It may also contain a variable-length field for including associated diagnostic information, if any. For this reason, the cause indicators parameter is of variable length: two octets and above. The purpose of cause indicators in a release message is to indicate the reasons for release of the call. The cause indicators parameter is an optional parameter in several ISUP messages.

The cause value is a 7-bit field in the cause indicators parameter. Thus, up to 127 cause values can be specified in the range of 1 to 127. A few examples of cause values are as follows:

- Unallocated (unassigned number): the called party number is in a valid format but is currently unassigned: Cause value = 1.
- Misdialed trunk prefix: Cause value = 5.
- Normal call clearing: Cause value = 16.
- Invalid number format (address incomplete): Cause value = 28.
- Facility reject: the supplementary service requested by the user cannot be provided by the network. Cause value = 29.

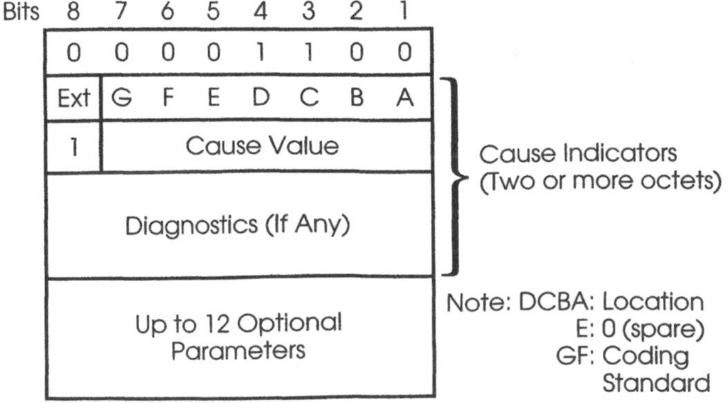

Figure 9–10 Release (REL) message.

Table 9-7 Coding of the Cause Indicators Parameter

Bits	Meaning
Ext bit	
0	Octet continues through the next octet
1	Last octet
Bits 7 6	Coding standard
0 0	ITU standardized coding (for cause values)
0 1	Reserved for other international standards
1 0	National standards
1 1	Standard specific to identified location[a]
Bit 5	Spare (set to 0)
Bits 4 3 2 1	Location
0 0 0 0	User
0 0 0 1	Private network serving the local user
0 0 1 0	Public network serving the local user
0 0 1 1	Transit network
0 1 0 0	Public network serving the remote user
0 1 0 1	Private network serving the remote user
0 1 1 1	International network
1 0 1 0	Network beyond interworking point[b]

[a]Other standards to be used only when the desired cause (or condition) is not available in the list of cause values standardized by the ITU.

[b]All other values are reserved.

- Switching equipment congestion: Cause value = 42.
- Bearer capability not authorized: Cause value = 57.
- Identified channel does not exist: Cause value = 82.
- Mandatory information element is missing in a message: Cause value = 96.

The cause indicators parameter is used both for CCS 7 ISUP messages and the DSS 1. Complete specifications are found in ITU-T recommendation Q.850 [5].

As noted above, for normal call release initiated by either the calling or the called party, the REL message contains a cause value of 16.

The release complete (RLC) message can have only up to three parameters: message type, cause indicators, and end of optional parameters. Only the message type parameter is mandatory.

When an RLC message is not received at an exchange before the expiry of timer T1, the REL message is retransmitted and timer T1 is started again. The value of T1 ranges from 15 to 60 seconds. Thus, REL is sent repeatedly at the periodicity of timer T1 in the expectation of receiving an RLC message. If timer T5 (range of 5 to 15 minutes) also expires and the RLC message is not received, then the following actions are taken by the exchange:

- It sends a reset circuit (RSC) message and starts timer T17. (RSC is a single-octet message consisting of only message type parameter.)
- It removes the circuit from service.
- It alerts maintenance personnel.
- It stops timer T1.

Figure 9–11 shows the role of various timers when an RLC message is not received at an intermediate exchange in response to an REL message sent to the originating exchange. In this example, the originating exchange on receipt of a reset message should send an RLC message, and if the circuit is already not in idle state, then the circuit should be made idle. Upon receipt of an RLC message, timer T17 is stopped. Other possibilities also exist, such as where the originating exchange is not able to bring the circuit in idle condition and therefore RLC cannot be sent to the intermediate exchange.

9.3.2 Basic Call Control for Overlap Signaling

In view of the similarities in call control procedures, only the points of difference from en bloc signaling are described in this section.

As soon as sufficient information is available to route the call, the IAM is sent by the originating exchange. The IAM in overlap signaling has essentially the same information as the IAM in en bloc signaling except that all the digits of the called party are not included. Therefore, the remaining digits are carried in one or more subsequent address messages (SAMs). The format of the SAM is shown in Figure 9–12.

Cut-through of the transmission path in the backward direction takes place immediately following the sending of IAM, as is the case with en bloc signaling.

Upon receipt of the IAM, the intermediate exchanges attempt to perform call routing by selecting a free and suitable circuit to the next exchange. If however, the informa-

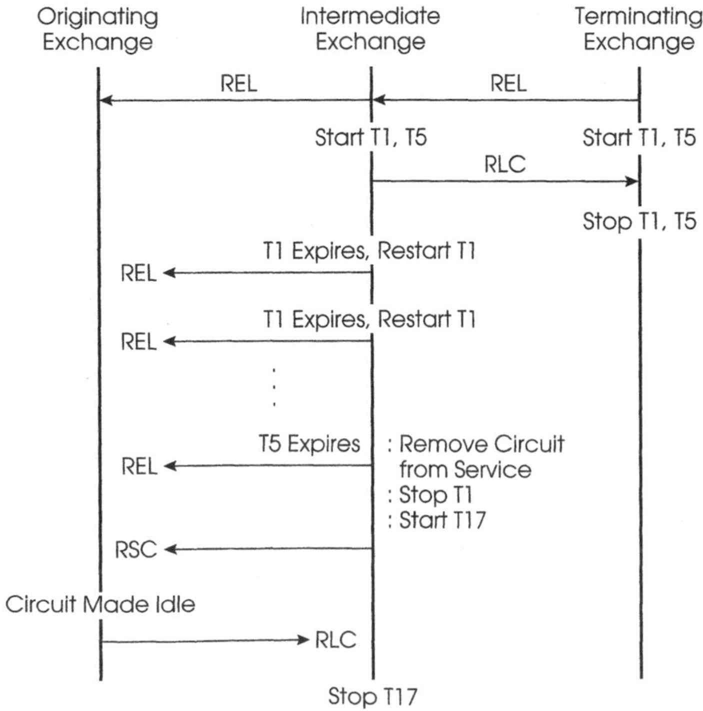

Figure 9–11 Call release when the RLC message is not received in response to the REL message.

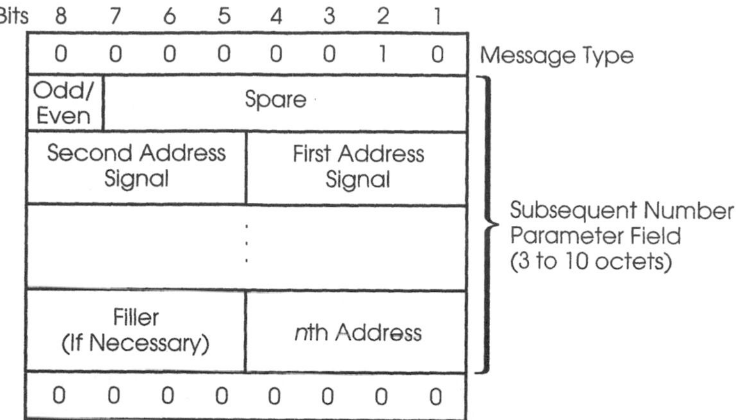

Figure 9–12 Subsequent address message (SAM).

tion in the IAM is not sufficient to perform this function, then the intermediate exchange waits for the receipt of one or more SAMs until the number of digits of the called party is sufficient to route the call. While sending the IAM to the next exchange, the intermediate exchange includes all the digits received thus far in the SAMs. The transmission path is through-connected in both directions after sending of the IAM. The continuity check is performed the same way as with en bloc signaling.

If the calling party number is not received in the IAM and the destination exchange requires this information, it can send a backward message called an "information request" message. Simultaneously, timer T33 is started. This message is relayed by the intervening transit exchanges to the originating exchange. The originating exchange then sends an "information" message, containing the calling party's number, in the forward direction to the next exchange. The message is repeated by the intermediate exchanges to the destination exchange. If an information message is not received at the destination exchange before the expiry of timer T33, then the connection is released. Timer T33 has a range of 12 to 15 seconds. The use of information request and information messages is limited to national ISDN calls.

The formats of the information request and information messages are shown in Figures 9–13 and 9–14, respectively. Besides seven optional parameters, the information request message has a mandatory information request indicators parameter. The coding for

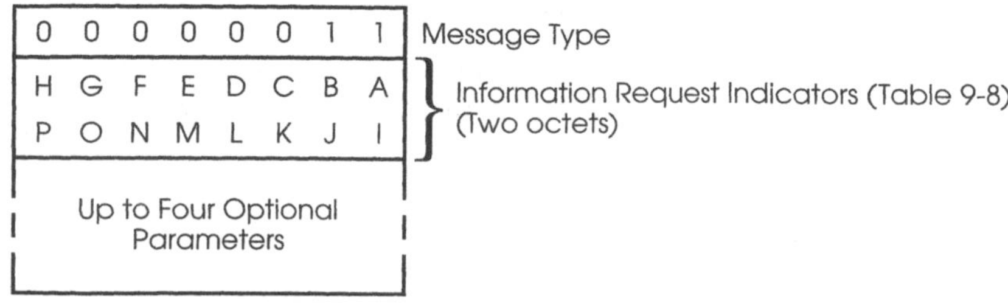

Figure 9–13 Information request message.

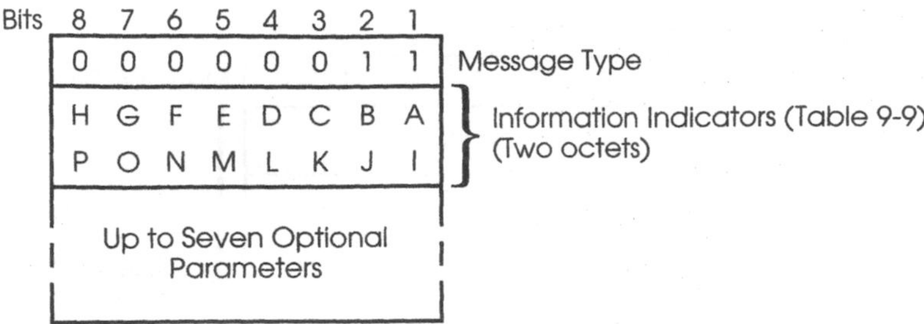

Figure 9–14 Information message.

this parameter is given in Table 9–8. The mandatory parameter for information message is information indicators parameter whose coding is shown in Table 9–9. These messages are also used in en bloc signaling. They are useful in implementing supplementary services, such as malicious call identification.

9.4 Continuity Check (CC)

A request for a continuity check (CC) may be made by an exchange to the next exchange in the connection. As mentioned earlier, this request is contained in the IAM. Simultaneously, the requesting exchange connects a transceiver to the go and return paths of the outgoing circuit. Upon receiving the request, the next exchange connects a check loop to the go and return paths of the incoming circuit. A tone is sent on the go path and received on the return path. The check tone frequency should be 2000 ± 20 Hz. A continuity check is successful when the tone is properly received. This information is sent to the next exchange in a continuity (COT) message, whose format is shown in Figure 9–15.

An example of a successful continuity check is shown in Figure 9–16. The originating exchange makes a continuity check request to an intermediate exchange (bits D and C in the continuity check indicator of the IAM are set to 0 and 1, respectively. Refer to Table 9–1). The check tone is sent, and timer T24 is started to supervise the process. The value of timer T24 should be less than 2 seconds.

Table 9–8 Coding of the Information Request Indicators Parameter

Bit A	Calling party address request indicator
Bit B	Holding indicator
Bit C	Spare
Bit D	Calling party's category request indicator
Bit E	Charge information request indicator
Bits G and F	Spare
Bit H	Malicious call identification request indicator
Bits L–I	Spare
Bits P–M	Reserved

Note: For each indicator bit, a 1 represents a request for information and a 0 signifies the absence of a request.

Table 9–9 Coding of the Information Indicators Parameter

Bits B A	Calling party address response indicator
0 0	Calling party address not included
0 1	Calling party address not available
1 0	Spare
1 1	Calling party address included
Bit C	Hold provided indicator
0	Hold not provided
1	Hold provided
Bits E and D	Spare
Bit F	Calling party's category response indicator
0	Calling party's category not included
1	Calling party's category included
Bit G	Charge information response indicator
0	Charge information not included
1	Charge information included
Bit H	Solicited information indicator
0	Solicited
1	Unsolicited
Bits L–I	Spare
Bits P–M	Reserved

Upon the receipt of the IAM containing the continuity check request, the intermediate exchange connects a loop and starts timer T8, which has a permissible range of 10 to 15 seconds. The intermediate exchange also informs the terminating exchange that a continuity check is being performed on the previous section of the connection. This is done by appropriately coding the continuity check indicator in the IAM (bits D and C are set to 1 and 0, respectively, as seen from Table 9–1). Timer T8 is also started at the terminating exchange upon receipt of the IAM.

Upon the proper receipt of the check tone, the originating exchange concludes that the continuity check is successful. Timer T24 is stopped, and the transceiver is removed. The originating exchange conveys the successful completion of the CC to the intermediate exchange using the COT message. Upon receipt of the COT message, the intermediate exchange removes the check loop and stops timer T8. It relays this message to the terminating exchange so that the terminating exchange also knows of the successful completion of the continuity check on the previous section of the connection. The terminating exchange thereafter stops timer T8.

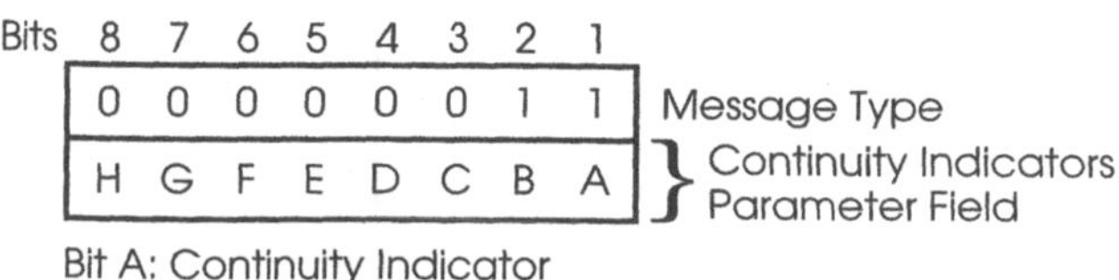

Figure 9–15 Continuity (COT) message format.

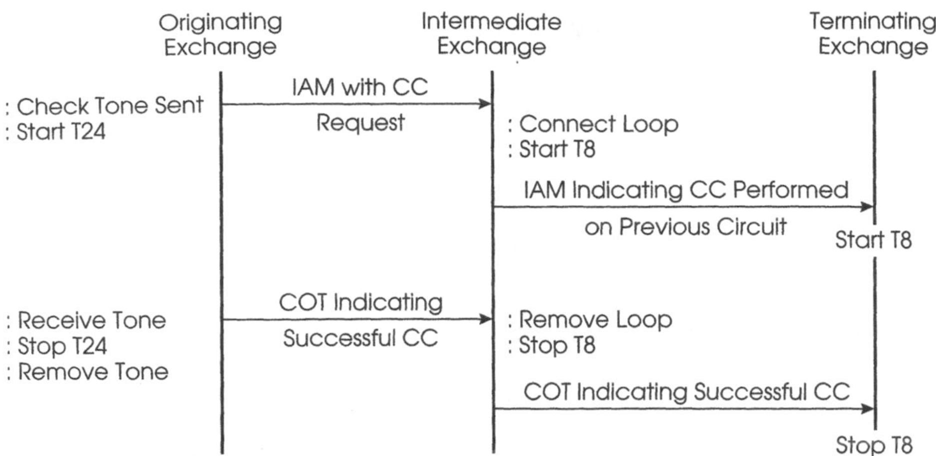

Figure 9–16 Successful continuity check (CC): CC request in an IAM.

Figure 9–17 shows an example of continuity check failure involving two exchanges; an originating exchange and a terminating exchange. The continuity check is considered failed when the transceiver determines an improper receipt of the check tone or when the tone is not received before the expiry of timer T24. In this situation, the originating exchange informs the terminating exchange regarding failure of continuity check in the COT message. Upon the failure of the CC on one circuit, a repeat attempt is permitted on another circuit. Therefore, upon receiving a CC failure, the terminating exchange starts timer T27 to await a request for a repeat continuity check from the originating exchange. The value of T27 is 4 minutes. If the repeat request is not received (as in Figure 9–17), timer T27 expires and the terminating exchange clears the connection.

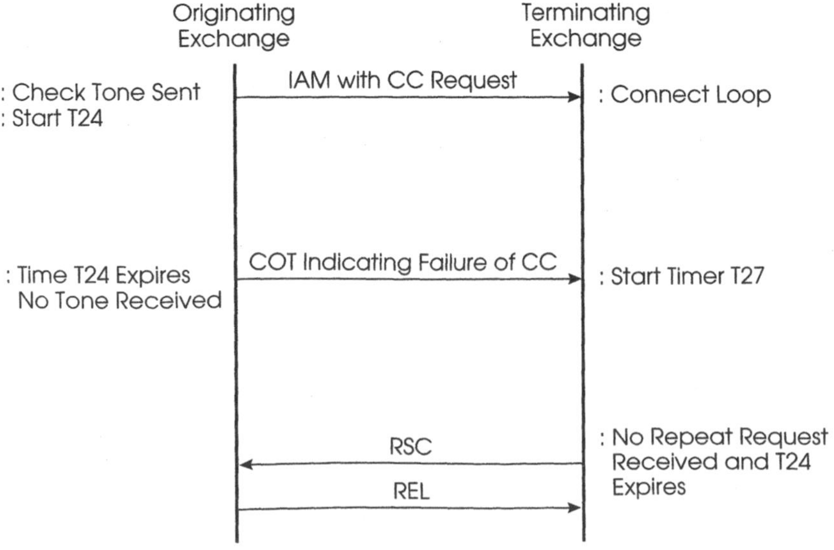

Figure 9–17 Example of continuity check (CC) failure: CC request in an IAM.

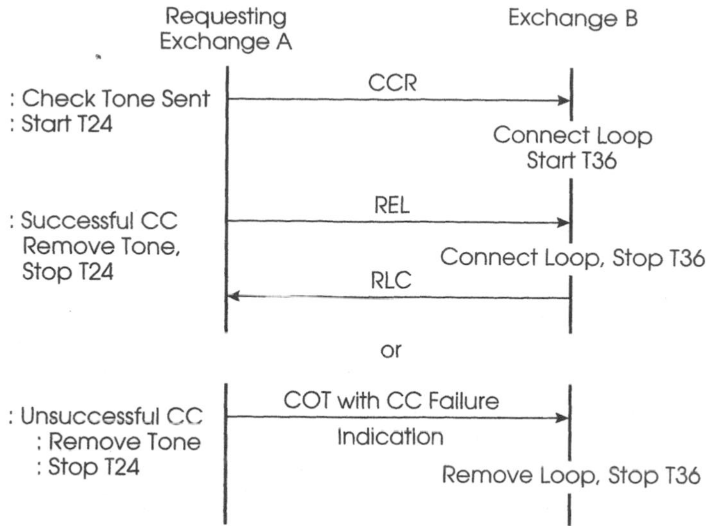

Figure 9–18 An example of continuity check using CCR message.

Another failure condition arises when timer T8 expires before a COT message is received at the intermediate or terminating exchange. In this case, the connection is cleared.

The procedure described above involves a continuity check, section by section, during normal call setup. It may also be necessary to perform a CC on a circuit as a routine or an on-demand test. A continuity check request (CCR) message is used for this purpose. A CCR message has just one parameter, the message type (coded 00010001), to identify the message. The CC in this case is based on a test call involving the circuit being checked. An example of continuity check using CCR message is shown in Figure 9–18. Timer T36 has a range of 10 to 15 seconds.

9.5 Supervision of Speech/Data Circuits by ISUP

A number of ISUP messages are used in the supervision of speech/data circuits served by CCS 7. They provide the facility to audit, block, unblock, and reset circuits, either individually or in a group. These actions allow recovery from abnormal conditions and permit testing of circuits.

9.5.1 Circuit Group Query

To audit—that is, to find the state of circuits—an exchange can make a query to another exchange using the circuit group query procedure. Two messages are employed: the sending exchange transmits a circuit group query message (CQM) and the receiving exchange responds with a circuit group query response message (CQR).

The format of a circuit group query message is shown in Figure 9–19. The message contains a range and status parameter. This parameter is also used in several other ISUP messages where it has both the range and status subfields, hence its name. For the CQM,

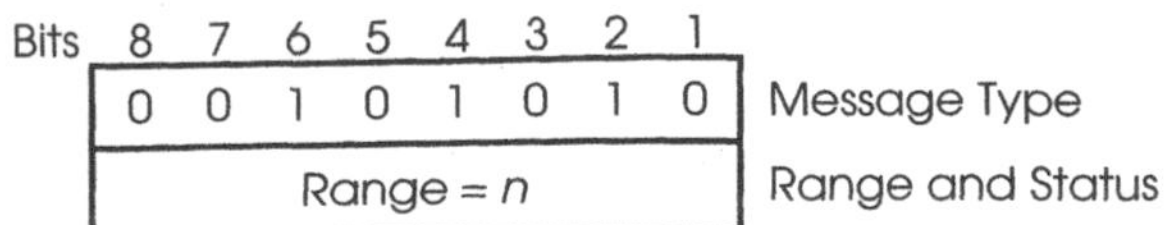

Figure 9–19 Circuit group query message (CQM).

however, the status subfield is not relevant and is therefore missing. For the CQM, the valid range value (n) should be from 0 to 31. The value of n is kept one less than the number of circuits to be queried ($n = 0$ indicates that the query is for a single circuit and $n = 31$ signifies that the states of 32 circuits are required). The sending exchange indicates the identity of the first circuit in the group in the CIC (refer to Table 9–1). Timer T28 is started when the message is sent. The value of timer T28 is 10 seconds. If timer T28 expires before the receipt of the CQR message, then the maintenance system is informed by the sending exchange.

The format of the CQR is given in Figure 9–20. One octet each is used to furnish the state of a circuit. Thus, if the state of six consecutive circuits is to be furnished beginning from circuit number p (= 10), then the range octet has the value $n = 5$, to indicate circuits 0 through 5. The states of these circuits will be furnished in six octets of the circuit state indicator parameter field. The circuit number p is indicated in the CIC field of the ISUP message.

As seen from Table 9–10, a circuit may be under different states. When a circuit is blocked, it cannot be used for setting up connections, except for those relating to test calls. A circuit may be blocked in three different ways: by the exchange to which it belongs (local blocking), by another exchange (remote blocking), or both locally and remotely. Remote blocking is performed by means of circuit blocking messages, described later in this chapter. Finally, the circuit may be in an active state wherein it can be used for normal traffic. These four states (the active state and the three blocked states) are represented by a pair of bits AB in the circuit state indicator.

Blocking of circuits may arise in the following two situations:

1. Maintenance blocking
2. Hardware blocking

A circuit can be maintenance blocked even when it is in use on an existing connection, namely, incoming busy or outgoing busy. After the connection is released (in the normal course), however, it is no longer available for call processing.

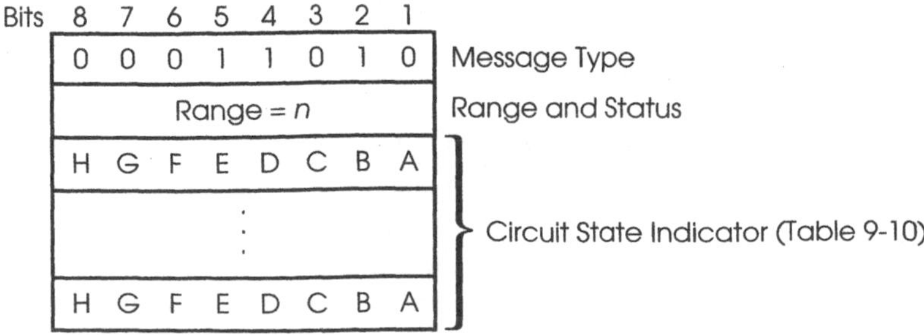

Figure 9–20 Circuit group query response (CQR) message.

Table 9–10 Coding of the Circuit State Indicator Parameter

Case (a): For bits D C = 0 0		
Bits B	A	Maintenance blocking state
0	0	Transient
0	1	Spare
1	0	Spare
1	1	Unequipped
Case (b): For bits D C not equal to 0 0		
Bits B	A	Maintenance blocking state
0	0	No blocking (active)
0	1	Locally blocked
1	0	Remotely blocked
1	1	Locally and remotely blocked
Bits D	C	Call processing state
0	1	Circuit incoming busy
1	0	Circuit outgoing busy
1	1	Idle
Bits F	E	Hardware blocking state (see note)
0	0	No blocking (active)
0	1	Locally blocked
1	0	Remotely blocked
1	1	Locally and remotely blocked
Bits H	G	Spare

Note: If bits FE are not coded 00, bits DC must be coded 11.

When a circuit is hardware blocked, the existing connection, if any, involving the circuit is released. Therefore, hardware blocking cannot coexist with the circuit being incoming or outgoing busy (refer to the note to Table 9–10).

A representation of the various states described above are covered by case (b) of Table 9–10. Case (a) indicates the state of a circuit when it is unequipped or in a transient state. Transient states may arise either during call processing (for example, awaiting receipt of backward signal, after the IAM has been sent) or during maintenance (awaiting acknowledgment for blocking or unblocking a message sent earlier to a remote exchange).

9.5.2 Blocking and Unblocking of Circuits or Circuit Groups

The messages used for blocking and unblocking of circuits are

- Blocking
- Blocking acknowledgment
- Unblocking
- Unblocking acknowledgment

These messages consist of a single-octet message type parameter.

9.5.2.1 Blocking of Circuits

Figure 9–21 illustrates the blocking procedure. Requesting exchange A sends a blocking (BLO) message to exchange B for the circuit indicated in the CIC field of the message. Receiving exchange B processes this message, and after marking the circuit "remotely blocked," it returns a blocking acknowledgment (BLA) message to exchange A, which marks the circuit "locally blocked." At the requesting exchange, timers T12 and T13 are used for time supervision.

Figure 9–22 illustrates the situations where blocking is attempted during call setup for the same circuit that is being used for that call setup. Two cases may arise:

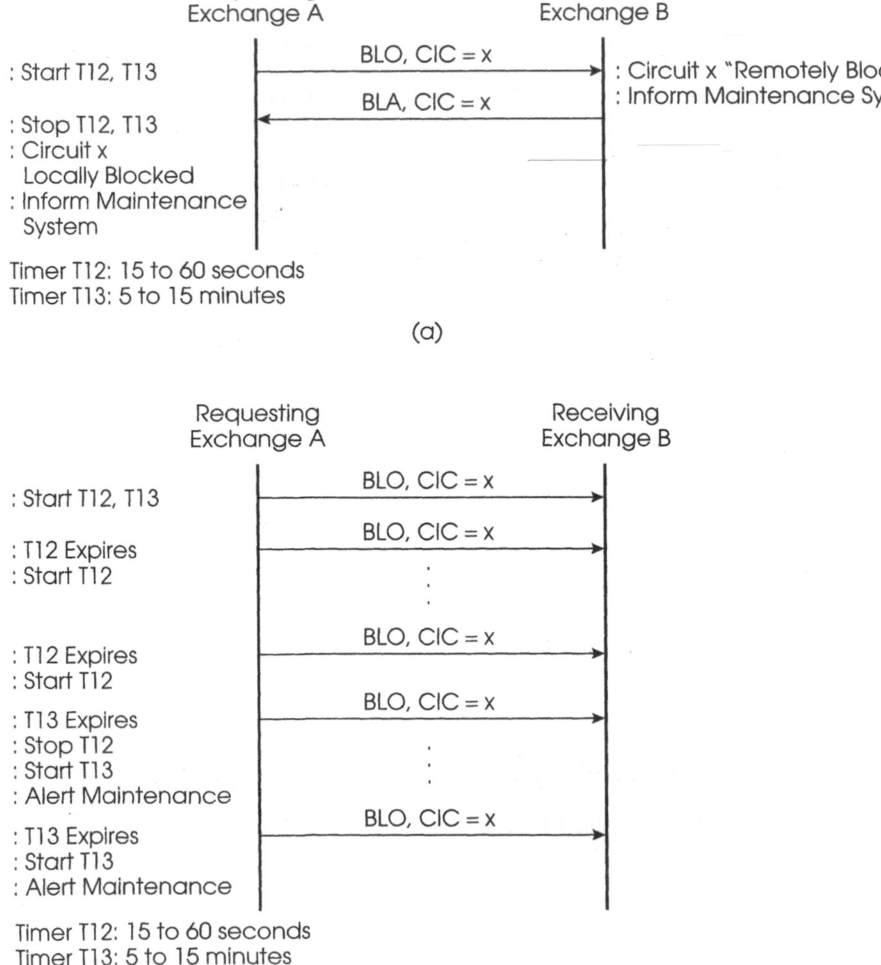

Figure 9–21 (a) Successful blocking of a circuit in first attempt; (b) unsuccessful blocking: maintenance intervention.

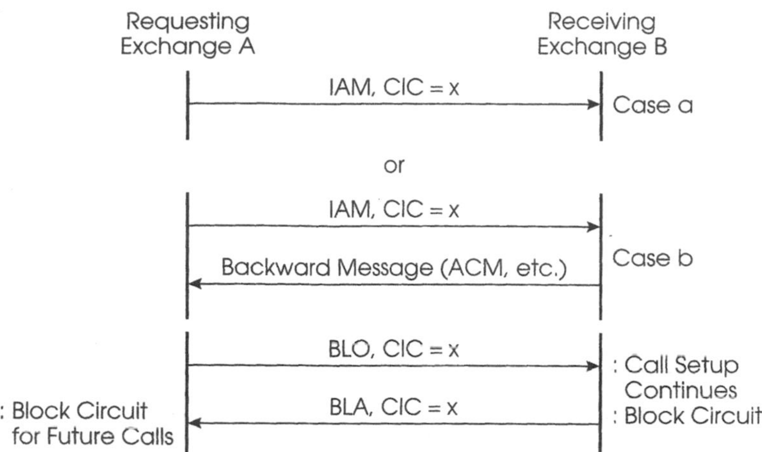

Figure 9–22 Blocking of a circuit being used in call setup.

- Case a: Blocking message received after IAM has been previously received for the same circuit.
- Case b: Blocking message received after IAM has been sent for the circuit and at least one backward message has been received.

Treatment of these cases is identical, as can be seen from Figure 9–22.

Figure 9–23 shows a situation where an exchange has sent a blocking message. Instead of receiving a blocking acknowledgment, however, an IAM with the same circuit is received. If the IAM refers to the normal call, then it is discarded and the blocking message is repeated. For test calls, if possible, the call should be put through. If this is not possible, then the IAM should be discarded and the blocking message repeated.

9.5.2.2 Unblocking of Circuits

A simple example of unblocking circuits is shown in Figure 9–24. The unblocking procedure is similar to that of blocking and uses unblocking (UBL) and unblocking acknowledgment (UBA) messages. Timers T14 and T15 are used. These timers are identical

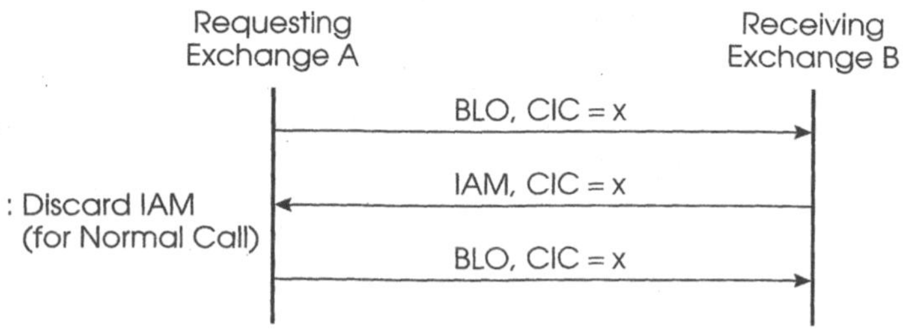

Figure 9–23 IAM in response to blocking (BLO) message.

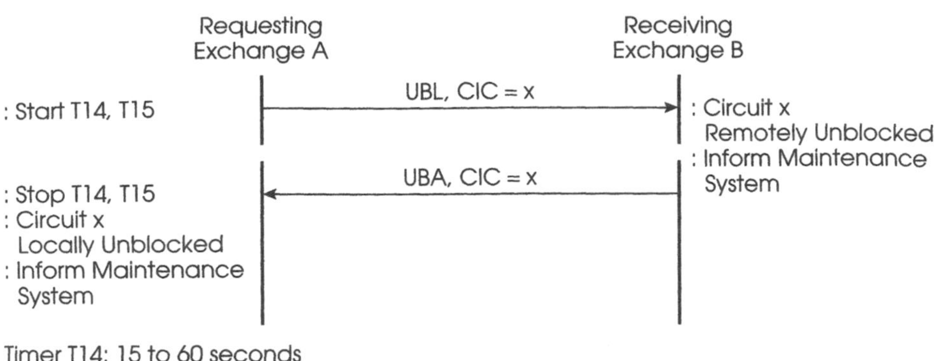

Figure 9–24 Successful unblocking of a circuit in the first attempt.

in value range and similar in functions to timers T12 and T13, respectively. (See the previous section).

9.5.3 Blocking and Unblocking of Circuit Groups

Four ISUP messages are employed in blocking and unblocking of circuit groups:

1. Circuit group blocking (CGB) message
2. Circuit group blocking acknowledgment (CGBA) message
3. Circuit group unblocking (CGU) message
4. Circuit group unblocking acknowledgment (CGUA) message

All the messages have an identical format, as shown in Figure 9–25.

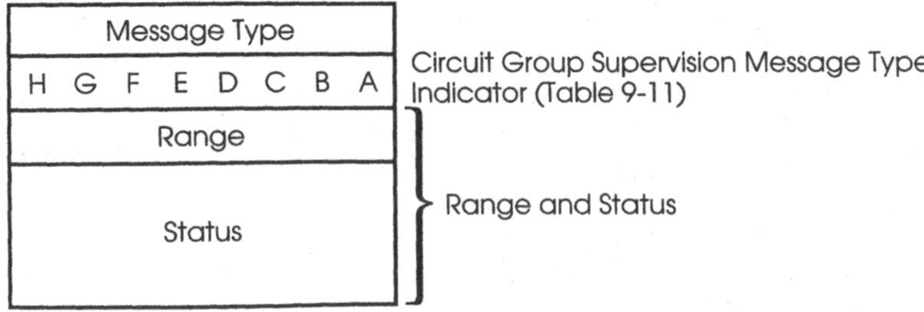

Note: Codes for different messages types are as follows:

Message	Code
CGB	00011000
CGBA	00011010
CGU	00011001
CGUA	00011011

Figure 9–25 Circuit group blocking and unblocking messages.

Coding for the range subfield has already been described in connection with the circuit group query message. In the status field, corresponding to each circuit between 1 and 32, a status bit denotes two conditions: 0 for no indication and 1 for blocking. If p is the circuit identity as provided in the CIC and n is the value in the range subfield, then bits p to $p + n - 1$ are the status bits of relevance in the message. Provision of status bits corresponding to individual circuits allows flexibility in specifying the circuits in the group. For example, for circuit group blocking, status bits corresponding to only those circuits that need to be blocked are set to 1; other bits are kept at 0. The setting of the type indicator bits (see Table 9–11) enables hardware or maintenance blocking, as required.

Figure 9–26 shows maintenance-oriented blocking for specified circuits in a group of circuits. Comparison with Figure 9–21(a) shows that the procedure is similar to blocking of individual circuits.

If the CGBA message is not received from the receiving exchange, then the CGB message is repeated at the periodicity of T18. If timer T19 also expires, then maintenance personnel are alerted and retransmission of CGB continues at a periodicity of T19 until maintenance intervention takes place. Thus, the procedure in this case also is similar to the corresponding procedure for blocking of individual circuits depicted in Figure 9–21(b).

Maintenance-oriented unblocking of circuit groups follows a procedure similar to unblocking of individual circuits. A group of circuits in a maintenance-oriented blocking state can be unblocked only by a maintenance-oriented CGU message, not by a hardware-oriented CGU. Similarly, hardware-oriented blocking requires unblocking by a hardware-oriented CGU, that is, a CGU with indicator bits B and A set at 0 and 1, respectively. Timers T20 (15 to 60 seconds) and T21 (5 to 15 minutes) are used for unblocking of circuit groups.

9.5.4 Reset of Circuits and Circuit Groups

The purpose of reset messages is to bring circuits or group of circuits into the idle state. This may be necessary in several situations. An example of the use of the reset circuit (RSC) message was presented in Figure 9–11 wherein, while attempting connection release, timer T5 expires and no RLC message is received in response to an REL message sent earlier.

Digital exchanges typically maintain a map in software indicating the state of various circuits associated with the exchange. This map must conform to the physical state of the circuits. For example, a circuit that is in use in an outgoing call setup must have the state "outgoing busy" in the memory map. If, due to memory mutilation, the circuit is indicated "idle," then there is a possibility of selection of a busy circuit for a subsequent

Table 9–11 Coding of the Circuit Group Supervision Message Type Indicator

Bits B	A	Type indicator
0	0	Maintenance oriented
0	1	Hardware failure oriented
1	0	Reserved for national use
1	1	Spare
Bits C to H		Spare

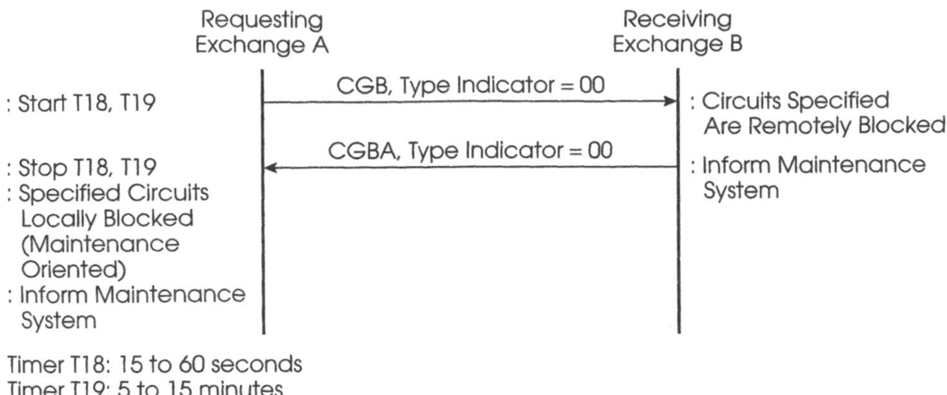

Figure 9–26 Successful blocking of a circuit in the first attempt.

call. In this case, the circuit should be reset to idle by a reset message. When several circuits are involved, a group reset message is needed. The format of a circuit group reset message is identical to the CQM format shown in Figure 9–19.

9.6 Treatment of Abnormal Conditions

9.6.1 Dual Seizures

Since the circuits served by CCS 7 are capable of both way working, a method of circuit selection that would minimize the possibility of dual seizure is necessary. Dual seizure arises when two adjacent exchanges in a connection attempt to seize the same circuit almost simultaneously. This is commonly called *glave.*

Two alternative methods have been specified in ITU-T recommendation Q.764. For the BELL operating companies (BOCs) in the U.S. network, BELLCORE recommends method 1 [6]. Other telephone companies may use method 2. The actual method used is by agreement between telephone company administrations.

In method 1, an opposite order of circuit selection is used at the two exchanges connected by a both-way circuit group. Opposite selection of circuits is performed as follows. The exchange with the higher point code (as explained in Chapter 4, each node in the CCS 7 network is assigned a point code that uniquely identifies a node within the network) selects an available circuit in the decreasing order of CIC numbers, whereas the other exchange selects circuits in increasing order of CIC values. Alternatively, the exchange with the higher point code may select circuits in increasing order of CIC values, with the other exchange selecting in the reverse order.

Method 2 involves dividing the both-way circuits between the two exchanges into two equal groups. If, for example, circuits with even-numbered CIC values are organized in one group and the odd numbered circuits in the other, then each exchange has priority in the control of one of the groups. The exchange makes a selection from among the circuit in its priority group on the basis of first in, last out; that is, the circuit that has been idle for the longest time is selected. When all the circuits in the priority group of the exchange are busy, the selection can be made from the nonpriority group (which is the priority group for the other exchange). Contrary to the criteria of selection in the priority group, in this case, the circuit that has been released most recently (last in, first out) is selected.

Even if a dual seizure occurs, the exchange should detect this condition and perform the necessary follow-up action. The criteria for detection of dual seizure is shown in Figure 9–27. Exchange A detects dual seizure when it receives an IAM for the same circuit for which it had previously sent an IAM before receiving a valid backward signal. Figure 9–27 refers to the case where the calls are 64 kbps connections. The exchanges also check for cases of dual seizure where the CIC is different for the two IAMs. This may happen in calls involving multirate connections because in such a connection, only the circuit with the lowest-numbered CIC is indicated in the IAM.

On dual seizure, of the two connections attempted on the same circuit, one should be released and the other allowed to continue. The exchange whose call origination is permitted to continue is referred to as the control exchange and the other is the noncontrol exchange. When both calls relate to 64 kbps connections, the exchange with the higher signaling point (SP) code functions as the control exchange. Thus, in the example of Figure 9–27, exchange A is the control exchange. Call A is allowed to mature, whereas call attempt B is released. The IAM received at the control exchange is discarded.

9.6.2 Errored, Unexpected, or Unrecognized Messages

In rare cases, errored, unexpected, or unrecognizable messages may be received by the ISUP in an exchange. Several possibilities can cause this situation. The MTP is designed to transfer messages with a high degree of reliability without missequencing, repetition, or loss. Malfunctions cannot be entirely ruled out, however; therefore, ITU-T recommendation Q.706 [7] specifies the following MTP performance figures:

- Not more than 1 in 1E + 7 messages should be lost.
- Not more than 1 in 1E + 10 messages should be delivered out of sequence or duplicated.
- Not more than 1 in 1E + 10 signal unit errors should remain undetected.

The repetition, loss, or missequencing of messages by the MTP may result in an unexpected message arising in the ISUP call control message sequence.

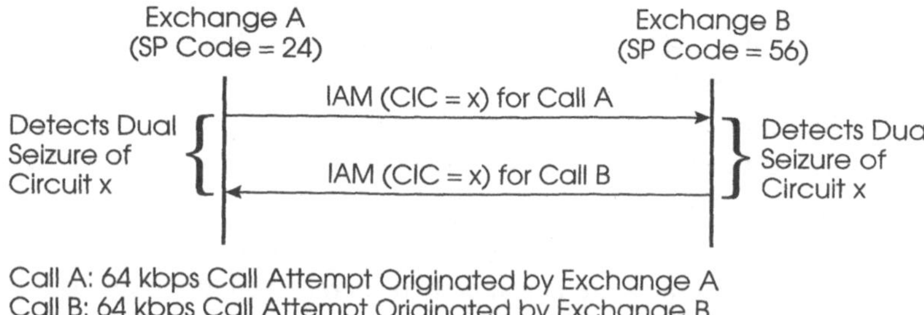

Figure 9–27 Detection of dual seizure.

Errored ISUP messages may occur due to errors that remain undetected in the MTP. An errored message is one whose message type parameter is recognized by the ISUP but whose contents are inconsistent and do not conform to the ISUP message format. Two examples are a message whose total length is less than the number of octets required for the mandatory parameters and a message with wrong pointer settings.

Unexpected or unrecognizable messages may also be received due to interworking problems between different versions of the ISUP protocol implementations or by incorrect or inconsistent optional parameter settings in the exchanges.

An unrecognized message is one that cannot be identified by the receiving ISUP; the contents of the message type parameter do not match any of the ISUP messages known to the exchange. Another possibility is that even though the message may be recognizable, it may contain a parameter that is unrecognizable; the parameter name may be unknown to the exchange. As explained in Section 9.2, the names of mandatory parameters are not included in the message, since these parameters are identified by their order of occurrence or pointer values. Thus, unrecognized parameters are always optional parameters. Furthermore, a parameter name may be recognizable, but it may be received in a message in which it is not expected to occur. Both these cases are treated as unrecognized parameters. Finally, a parameter may be recognized, but the parameter value may be unrecognized if the contents correspond to a spare or reserved value.

Thus, the following cases need to be considered:

- Errored messages
- Unexpected messages
- Unrecognized messages
- Unrecognized parameters
- Unrecognized parameter values

9.6.2.1 Actions for Errored Messages

An errored message is discarded by the ISUP.

9.6.2.2 Actions for Unexpected Messages

Handling of unexpected REL and RLC messages received at an exchange is illustrated in Figure 9–28. For all other unexpected messages, the following actions are specified:

- If the unexpected message is received for an idle circuit, a reset message for that circuit is sent.
- The same action is performed, except for the case of dual seizure, when an unexpected message is received for a circuit that is busy on a call setup and no backward message has been received so far.
- If the unexpected message is received for a circuit that is busy in a call setup and a backward message has already been received, then the message is discarded and call processing proceeds as if the message were never received. For multirate call, a circuit group reset message is sent.

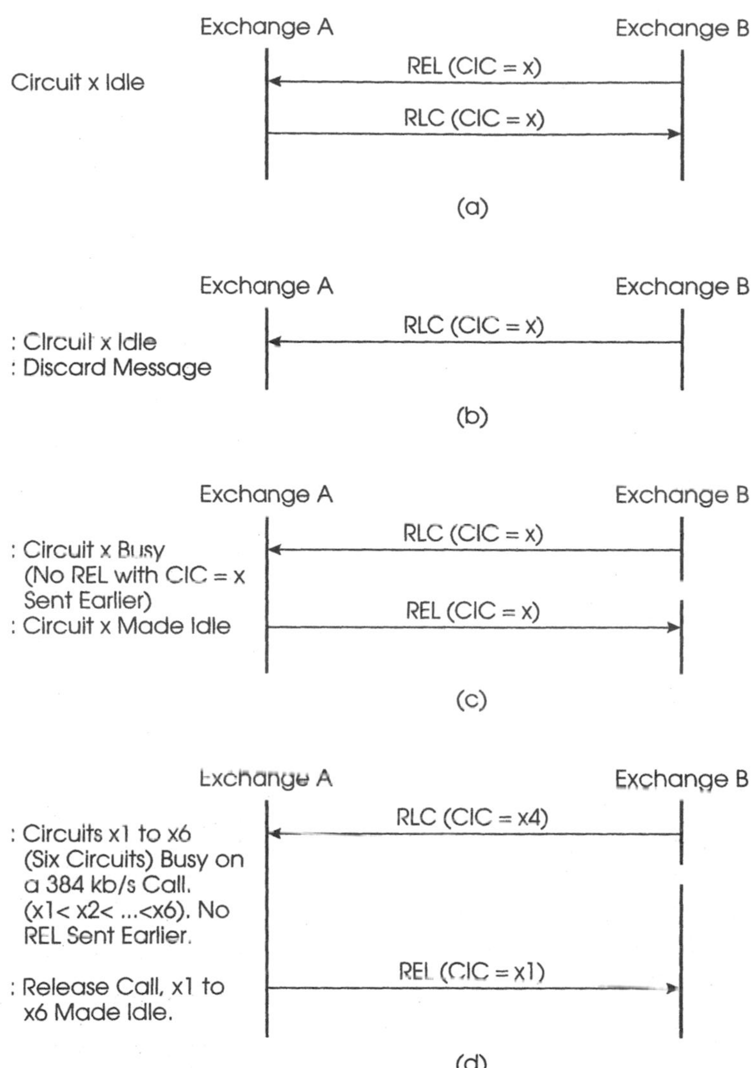

Figure 9–28 Actions for unexpected REL and RLC messages: (a) unexpected REL message received for an idle circuit; (b) unexpected RLC for an idle circuit; (c) unexpected RLC for a circuit busy on a 64 kbps connection; (d) unexpected RLC for a circuit busy on a multirate connection (for example, 384 kbps connection).

- Dual seizure is, in fact, an example of reception of an unexpected IAM. In this case, the handling follows the procedure described in Section 9.6.1.

9.6.2.3 Actions for Unrecognized Messages

If the message is found to be unrecognizable, the exchange first examines whether the unrecognized message itself contains any instructions on how to handle it. Two optional parameters may exist (either singly or jointly) in the message for this purpose:

1. Message compatibility information to provide instructions if the message is unrecognizable
2. Parameter compatibility information to handle situations where one or more parameters within the message are unrecognizable

The message compatibility information parameter has a single-octet instruction indicator. Refer to Figure 9–29. Bits are set in the instruction indicator to provide guidance regarding the course of action that the receiving exchange should follow. Refer to Table 9–12. Thus, for example, the receiving exchange may be asked to release the call (bit B = 1), send a notification to the exchange that generated the message (bit C = 1), discard the message, or pass it on transparently to the next exchange (depending on the value of the D bit). The role of bit A will be discussed shortly. The notification is sent by means of a confusion message whose format is shown in Figure 9–30.

The actions required also depend on the type of exchange receiving the unrecognized message. For this purpose, exchanges may be classified into two categories, type A and type B.

Type A exchanges are

1. Originating and destination exchanges
2. Interworking exchanges, that is, those exchanges where interworking between signaling systems is involved (interworking of ISUP with other user parts or a different signaling system)
3. Incoming and outgoing international exchange

Type B exchanges are all national and international transit nodes, except those where interworking is involved. Figure 9–31 illustrates the classification.

Bit A of the instruction indicator is not examined at exchanges of type A; only bits B, C, and D are examined to determine the actions required. The possible alternatives are summarized below.

1. The message may not be discarded but instead be transferred transparently to the next exchange (that is, passed on, if bit D is received as 0). This is applicable to outgoing international and incoming international exchanges only.

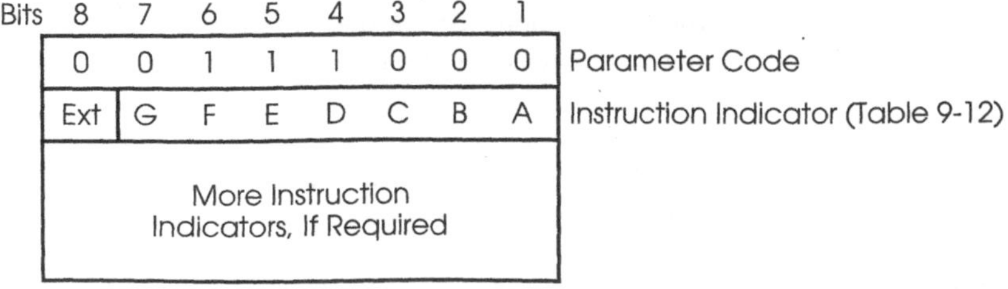

Figure 9–29 Message compatibility information parameter.

Table 9-12 Format of Instruction Indicator and List of Actions

Bit A	
0	Transit interpretation
1	End node interpretation
Bit B	
0	Do not release call
1	Release call
Bit C	
0	Do not send notification
1	Send notification
Bit D	
0	Do not discard message (pass on)
1	Discard message
Bit E	Pass on not possible indicator
0	Release call
1	Discard information
Bits F and G	Spare
Extension bit	
0	Next octet exists
1	Last octet

2. The message may be discarded and no notification may be sent.
3. The message may be discarded and a confusion message may be sent.
4. The call may be released by sending an REL message.

When a confusion or an REL message is sent, the cause value 97 (message type nonexistent, discarded) is included in the message. Also included in the diagnostic subfield is the parameter type of the received unrecognized message. (Refer to Figure 9–10 for the format of the REL message.)

Since the message compatibility information parameter is an optional parameter in various messages, it may not be sent at all. In that event, a confusion message is returned with cause value 97 along with parameter type in the diagnostic subfield. The action is identical for both type A or type B exchanges.

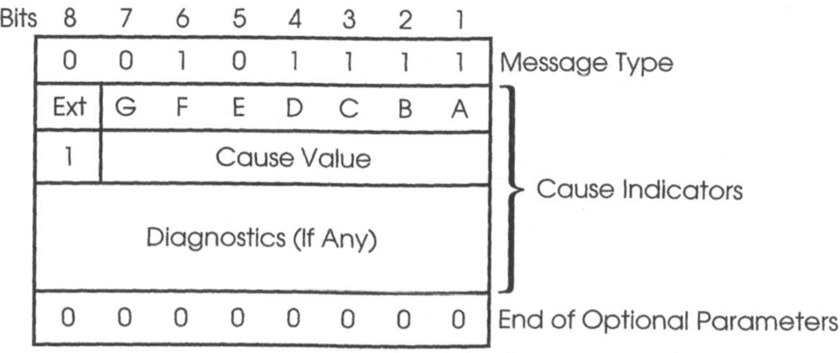

Figure 9–30 Confusion message.

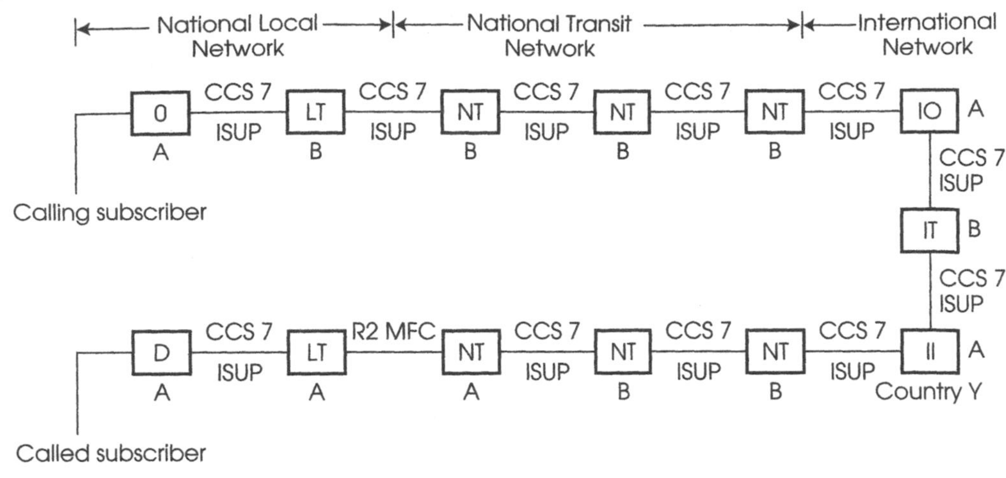

Figure 9–31 Example of type A and type B exchanges for an international call.

For type B exchanges, the unrecognized information is passed on unchanged if bit A is set to 0. If bit A is 1—that is, end node interpretation—then the other bits B, C, and D should also be examined, and actions identical to type A exchange ensue.

9.6.2.4 Actions for Unrecognized Parameters

A message may optionally contain a parameter compatibility information parameter to provide instructions on the actions to be taken in case the message contains one or more parameters not recognized by the exchange receiving the message. One parameter compatibility information parameter may contain instructions for handling several unrecognized parameters. Refer to Figure 9–32. The instruction indicator has a format similar to the one used for the message compatibility information parameter field.

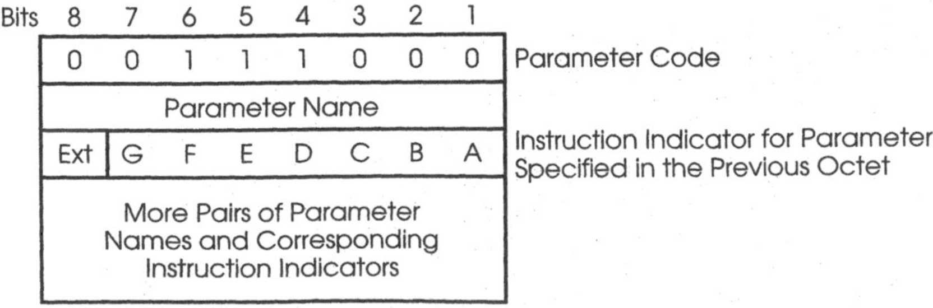

Figure 9–32 Parameter compatibility information parameter.

The procedure followed is similar to that for unrecognized messages. The confusion message uses cause value 99 (parameter nonexistent or not implemented, discarded) along with the diagnostic field indicating the message name and the name of the parameter that has not been recognized. When more than one parameter is unrecognized, only the first unrecognized parameter is included in the diagnostic field. The REL message also uses cause value 99.

9.6.2.5 Actions for Unrecognized Parameter Values

The contents of a parameter field may correspond to spare or reserved values. Spare and reserved codes exist in several cases, as noted in various tables presented in this chapter. One version of the ISUP may make use of these codes, the other may not. If both implementations coexist in a network, an exchange may receive in a message codes considered spare or reserved by it. These will be treated as unrecognized parameter values by the exchange. For these cases, actions performed at the receiving exchange can be summarized as follows:

1. For some of the unrecognized codes, a default value may be assigned by the receiving exchange. Table A.1/Q.763 of annexure A to ITU-T recommendation Q.763 specifies default interpretations. Examples of default interpretations are the following:
   - For the satellite indicator (refer to Table 9–1), if the spare code 11 is received, then the default interpretation is "two satellite circuits in the connection."
   - For the spare code of a continuity check indicator (refer to Table 9–1), the default option is "no continuity check required."
   - For the charge indicator (refer to Table 9–5), the default option is "charge."
   - For the called party's category indicator (refer to Table 9–5), the default option is "no indication."
2. Table A.1/Q.763 lists only 21 cases of default interpretation. For other cases, because an appropriate default code cannot be assigned, the parameter value has to be considered as unrecognized by the receiving exchange. For unrecognized values in the mandatory parameters, a comprehensive list of actions for various cases is presented in Tables A.2/Q.763 and A.3/Q.763 for type A and type B exchanges, respectively.
3. For unrecognized values in optional parameters, the entire parameter is considered as unrecognized, and action taken is identical to the description given in the previous section.

9.6.3 Unequipped Circuit Identification Code

A message may be received with a CIC value that does not exist in the translation tables of the exchange. In this situation, it is not possible for the exchange to identify the circuit indicated in the message. The received message may be an initial address message during a connection setup, a continuity check request (CCR) message, or one of the several messages used for the supervision of a circuit or a group of circuits. In these cases, the receiving exchange responds with a single-octet unequipped circuit identification code (UCIC) message. The UCIC code is returned in the CIC field of this message. The sending exchange then takes different actions depending on whether the original message (which contained the UCIC) was an IAM or any other message. For the IAM, the sending exchange removes the concerned circuit from service and reports to the maintenance system; the call is reattempted on another circuit. If the original message was a CCR message or a supervision message, then similar action is performed, but the call is not reattempted on another circuit.

9.6.4 ISDN User Part Unavailable

The case of the ISDN user part unavailable is illustrated in Figure 9–33.

1. Exchange A sends an ISUP message to exchange B.
2. The message discrimination function at the message transfer part (MTP) level 3 of exchange B finds that the ISUP indicated in the message is not available in the exchange. Accordingly, it generates a user part unavailable (UPU) message. Refer to Section 7.3.1. Figure 7–8 shows that two causes for unavailability may be specified in the UPU message:
   - Unequipped remote user, as in Figure 9–33(a)
   - Inaccessible remote user, as in Figure 9–33(b)
3. Upon receiving the UPU message at level 3, exchange A informs the ISUP by means of an MTP-STATUS primitive. The cause for unavailability is also indicated.
4. In the case of an unequipped remote user, the ISUP at exchange A marks the unavailability of the ISUP in exchange B and informs the management system. The procedure is complete.
5. For an inaccessible remote user, the ISUP at exchange A marks the unavailability of the ISUP in exchange B and sends a user part test (UPT) message. The UPT message has three parameters, message type and two optional parameters, *Parameter compatibility information* (Figure 9–32) and *end of optional* parameters. Timer T4 is also started to supervise the response to the UPT message.
6. Two conditions may arise when exchange B receives the UPT message. The ISUP may be found to be available now, or the ISUP may be unavailable again.

If the ISUP is found to be available, then a user part available (UPA) message is sent back to exchange A. The formats of UPA and UPT messages are identical. When the UPA message is received at exchange A, timer T4 is stopped and ISUP is marked as available.

If the ISUP is again unavailable, then the UPA message is not sent and timer T4 is allowed to expire at exchange A. Upon expiry of timer T4, the procedure is started all over again.

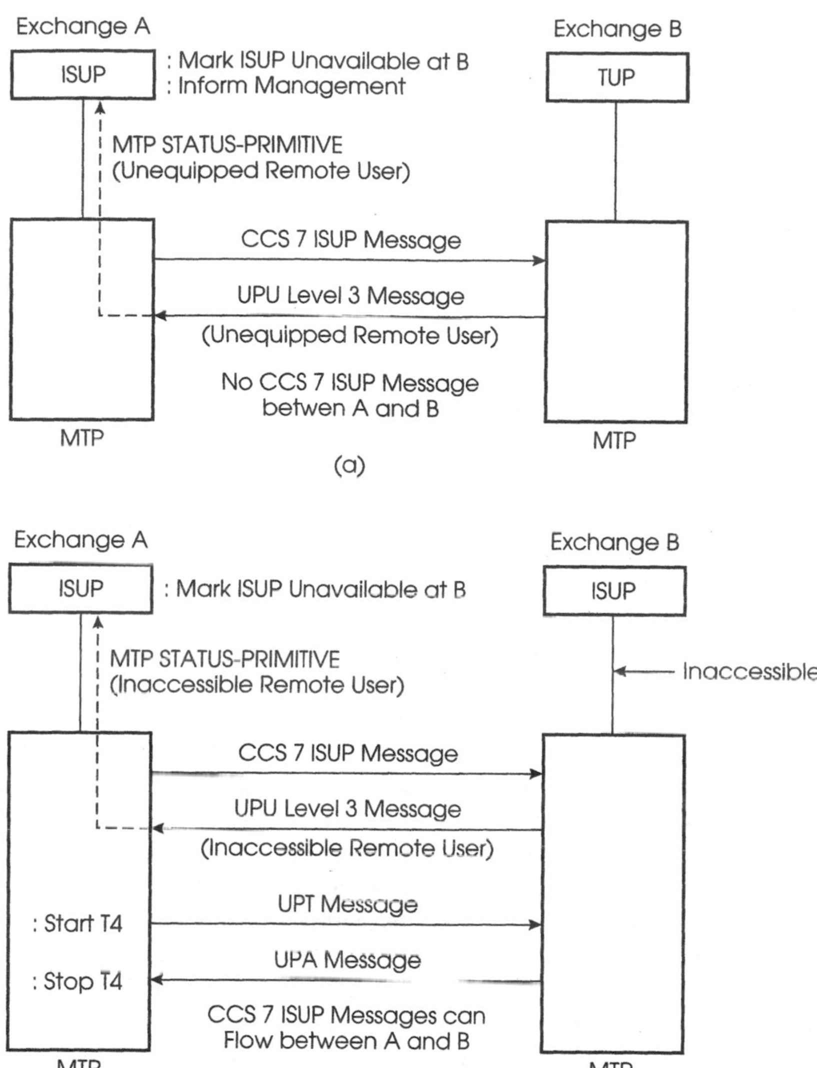

Figure 9–33 Treatment of UPU: (a) unequipped remote user; (b) inaccessible remote user.

9.7 Congestion Control

The following mechanisms of congestion control are described in this section:

- ISUP signaling congestion control
- Automatic congestion control (calling traffic overload control)
- Temporary trunk blocking

9.7.1 ISUP Signaling Congestion Control

Signaling link congestion was discussed in Section 7.6.11.1. Upon detection of congestion on the signaling link, the MTP at level 3 informs the ISUP by an MTP status primitive. The level of congestion is included where the national option with multiple congestion states is implemented. The destination toward which the signaling link congestion has occurred is also sent to the ISUP as one of the parameters associated with the MTP status primitive.

Since the volume of signaling traffic depends on the volume of speech/data traffic, to control link congestion, the ISUP begins to reduce speech/data traffic (calls) toward the destination indicated in the status primitive. The reduction of calls is carried out in steps using timers T29 and T30.

When the first congestion indication is received, ISUP timers T29 and T30 are started, and the speech/data traffic is reduced by one step. The size of this step is implementation dependent. As long as timer T29 does not expire, further MTP primitives indicating the congestion status are ignored. (The range of timer T29 is 300 to 600 ms. Timer T30 lies between 5 and 10 seconds). Thus, timer T29 ensures that the traffic is not reduced too rapidly. The first MTP status primitive after the expiry of timer T29 results in the reduction of traffic by one more step, and timers T29 and T30 are simultaneously restarted.

The reduction in speech/data traffic continues step by step, with spacing between each step provided by timer T29. After the traffic has been sufficiently reduced, the congestion indications from the MTP will cease. When timer T30 expires, the traffic is increased by one step. Thus, the restoration of traffic to its normal value is implemented by increasing traffic in steps, the spacing between steps being dictated by timer T30. The procedure is shown in Figure 9–34.

The objective of this procedure is limited to the control of signaling link congestion toward a specific destination, arising from temporary spurts in speech/data traffic. If the procedure is invoked too frequently and without a simultaneous higher-than-normal call traffic on the trunks toward the concerned exchange, then the situation may be due to under dimensioning of the signaling network. Provision of additional signaling links may remedy the situation. The procedure is not designed to control general overload conditions in an exchange; the procedure described in the next section addresses this problem.

9.7.2 Automatic Congestion Control (ACC) (Calling Traffic Overload Control)

Automatic congestion control (ACC) may be employed when the call processing software in the exchange detects traffic overload due to, for example, an exceptionally high occupancy of call processing processors. Signaling link congestion toward one or more destinations is not relevant in this context; it may or may not exist.

The ACC procedure can take into account two levels of congestion, a higher congestion condition (level 1) and a lower congestion (level 2). The degree of congestion for these levels is implementation dependent. Under congestion conditions, an additional parameter called the *automatic congestion level* parameter is added to all the REL messages generated by the ISUP. Thus, the adjacent exchanges are informed about the existence of congestion at the sending exchange. The format is shown in Figure 9–35.

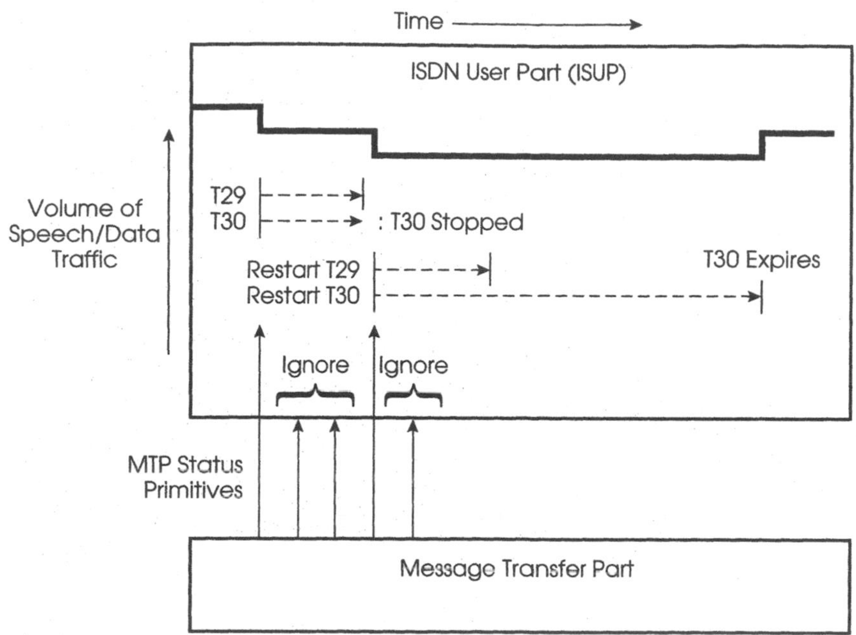

Figure 9–34 ISUP signaling congestion control.

Upon receiving congestion information, adjacent exchanges should appropriately reduce their traffic toward the overloaded exchange. When the traffic load is restored to normal, the exchange stops including the automatic congestion level parameter in the REL messages. This signals to the adjacent exchanges that overload conditions have subsided and that they may resume normal traffic after a predetermined time interval. The time interval is not part of the ISUP protocol and is implementation dependent.

9.7.3 Temporary Trunk Blocking

The temporary trunk blocking procedure is for national use. The exchange under overload employs an overload message to convey its condition to other exchanges. The overload message is a single-octet message consisting of only the parameter type.

Referring to Table 9–3, it is seen that the calling party's category parameter in the IAM contains the calling subscriber category, such as priority subscribers and ordinary

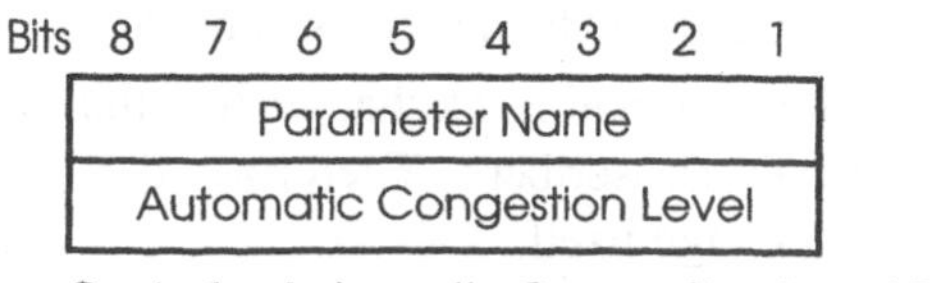

Code for Automatic Congestion Level Parameter Field:
00000000 Spare
00000001 Congestion Level 1 Exceeded
00000010 Congestion Level 2 Exceeded
All Other Combinations Are Spare

Figure 9–35 Automatic congestion level parameter.

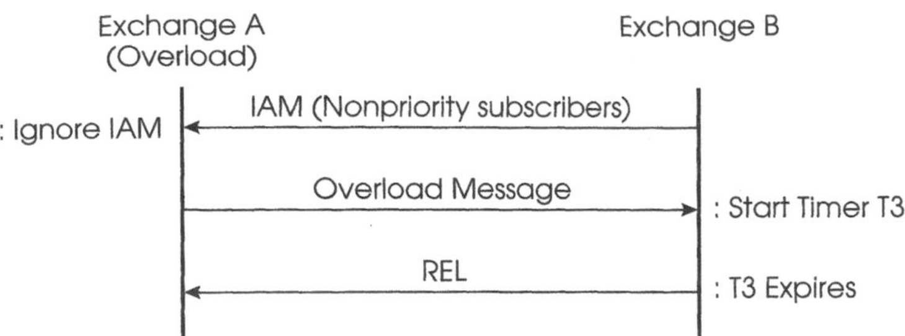

Figure 9–36 Handling of nonpriority calls at an exchange under overload.

subscribers. When an IAM is received at the overloaded exchange with the indication that the call setup is not for a priority subscriber, the IAM is not processed any further and an overload message is returned. On receipt of the overload message, timer T3 is started. On expiry of T3 (value of 2 minutes), release of the concerned circuit is initiated. The call setup is attempted if an alternative route is available. Figure 9–36 illustrates the procedure.

For priority calls, the normal procedure for call setup is followed at the exchange under overload.

9.8 ISUP Call Setup for Supplementary Services

The ISUP signaling procedures for the basic call control was described in Section 9.3. This section is devoted to ISUP procedures for calls that include supplementary services. Discussion on the call control for each and every supplementary service is too voluminous to include here. References are listed in Tables 8–3 and 8–4. Two examples are presented below.

9.8.1 ISUP Procedure for Calling Line Identification Presentation (CLIP)

The calling party's number presented to a subscriber on an incoming call may be from one of the following two sources:

1. The number may be provided by the called party's terminal and carried in the DSS 1 message to the originating exchange. This is possible only when the call is originated by an ISDN subscriber.
2. The originating exchange has the calling party number for both analog and ISDN subscribers. Therefore, the number can be provided by the originating exchange itself.

For calls originated by ISDN subscribers, one of the two options may be used. When the first option is employed, the originating exchange may either verify (that is, screen) the received calling number or may simply accept the calling party number without screening. ITU-T recommendation Q.731 [8] envisages both these possibilities. Usually, the customer-supplied calling party number is screened. The originating exchange will not screen the number, however, if an arrangement to this effect exists between the customer and the public network operator. This arrangement is called a special connection arrangement.

For analog subscriber calls, the originating exchange always provides the calling party number.

The calling party's subaddress, if supplied by the originating ISDN access, is carried transparently through the network and is presented along with the calling party's number.

The complete information necessary for the calling line identification presentation (CLIP) is included by the originating exchange in the IAM. Figure 9–3 shows the existence of up to 29 optional parameters in the IAM. The information concerning the CLIP service is carried in the following four optional parameters:

1. Access transport parameter
2. Calling party number parameter
3. Generic number parameter
4. Parameter compatibility information parameter

The calling party number parameter has the format shown in Figure 9–37. In addition to the octets provided to store the calling party number digits, other fields are devoted to providing information about the manner in which these digits should be interpreted by the succeeding exchanges in the connection. Refer to Table 9–13. For a call within the local area, it is sufficient to convey only the local directory number of the calling subscriber. In this case, the nature of address indicator is coded "subscriber number." For a national call, the area code may also be presented to the called party; therefore, the nature of address indicator will be coded "national (significant) number." The succeeding ex-

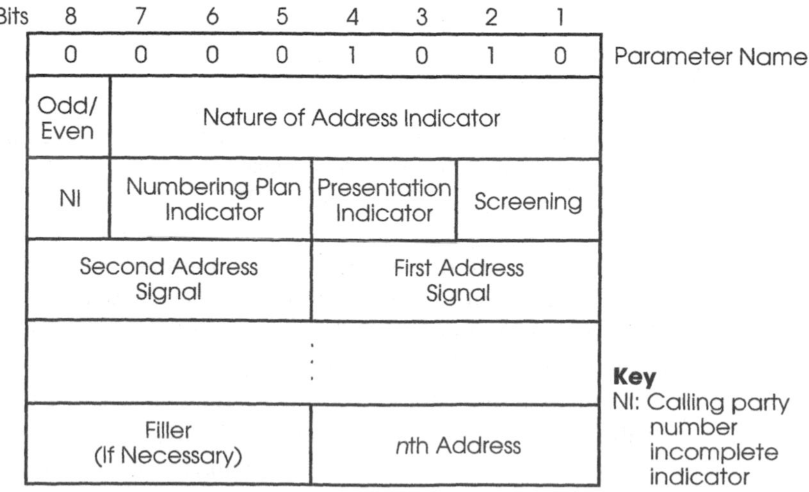

Figure 9–37 Calling party number parameter.

Table 9-13 Coding of Calling Party Number Parameter

(a) Odd/even indicator	
0	Even number of (calling party's) digits
1	Odd number of (calling party's) digits
(b) Nature of address indicator (7 bits)	
0000000	Spare
0000001	Subscriber number
0000010	Unknown
0000011	National (significant) number
0000100	International number
0000101 to 1101111	Spare
1110000 to 1111110	Reserved for national use
1111111	Spare
(c) Calling party number incomplete indicator	
0	Complete
1	Incomplete
(d) Numbering plan indicator (3 bits)	
000	Spare
001	ISDN (telephony) numbering plan (recommendation E.164)
010	Spare
011	Data numbering plan (recommendation X.121)
100	Telex numbering plan (recommendation F.29)
101 to 110	Reserved for national use
111	Spare
(e) Address presentation restricted indicator	
00	Presentation allowed
01	Presentation restricted
10	Address not available
11	Spare
When the address is not available, subfields (a), (b), (c), and (d) are coded with all 0's.	
(f) Screening indicator	
00	User provided, not verified
01	User provided, verified, and failed
10	Reserved
11	Network provided
(g) Address signal	
Consists of digits 0 to 9 from 0000 to 1001, digit 11 (1011), and digit 12 (1100). Binary combinations 1010 and 1101 to 1111 are spare.	
(h) Filler	
0000	In case of an odd number of address digits, the filler code is inserted after the last address signal.

changes in the connection are thus made aware of the nature of digits contained in the calling party number parameter. The numbering in telephony and ISDN is based on the principles and guidelines enumerated in ITU-T recommendation E.164 [9]. Therefore, the numbering plan indicator will be coded to indicate the telephony and ISDN numbering plan. The presentation indicator is coded depending on whether the calling party subscribes to the calling line identification restriction (CLIR) service. When the presentation indicator shows "presentation restricted," the destination exchange will not present the number to the called party even though it has been received in the calling party number parameter.

In Chapter 8, the subaddressing supplementary service was discussed wherein additional digits comprising the subaddress identify different terminals at an ISDN access. The subaddress is not part of the numbering plan and has only endpoint significance. Therefore, it is transported transparently through the network. In the CLIP service, the subaddress of the calling terminal may also be provided along with the directory number of the calling ISDN access. In this case, the calling party subaddress may be carried in the access transport parameter. Thus, at the originating exchange, the calling party information element in the SETUP message is directly mapped to the information elements in the access transport parameter field. Refer to Figure 9–38.

An example of a message sequence for a CLIP when ISUP is used all the way is shown in Figure 9–39. The following assumptions have been made:

1. That the calling party number consists of a three-digit area code and an eight-digit subscriber number
2. That the calling number is supplied by the network (that is, by the originating exchange)
3. That the subaddress has been supplied by the originating ISDN access

The generic number parameter is required in the IAM when a special connection arrangement exists. The parameter compatibility information parameter is also included in this case. The format of the generic number parameter is identical to the calling party number parameter format except that a number qualifier indicator of one octet is added as the first field. The number qualifier indicator in the context of the CLIP may indicate whether or not a user provided number has been screened. In the case of screening, it may also indicate whether or not the screening is successful. For a call from an ISDN subscriber with a special connection arrangement, the SETUP message received at the originating exchange has the information "user provided not verified" (that is, the calling party number is user provided and should not be verified by the originating exchange). The originating exchange loads the user received calling party number in the generic number parameter. Moreover, the number qualifier indicators are set appropriately. The screening indicator is set at "user provided, not verified."

When the IAM is received in the destination exchange, the additional calling party number, contained in the generic number parameter, is sent to the destination ISDN access. This is followed by the calling party number that is available in the calling party number parameter. The terminal at the called ISDN access thereafter presents the calling number to the user.

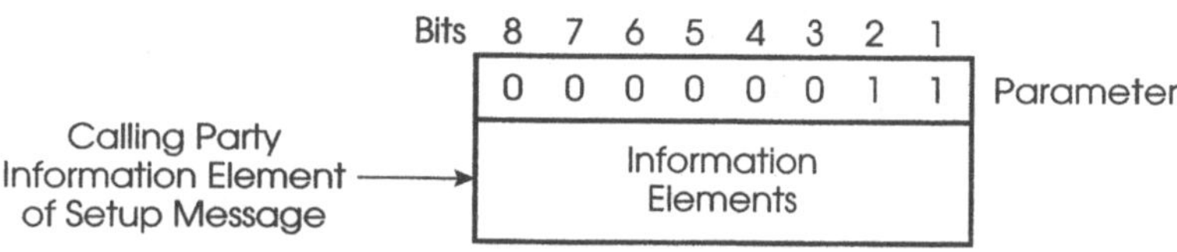

Figure 9–38 Access transport parameter.

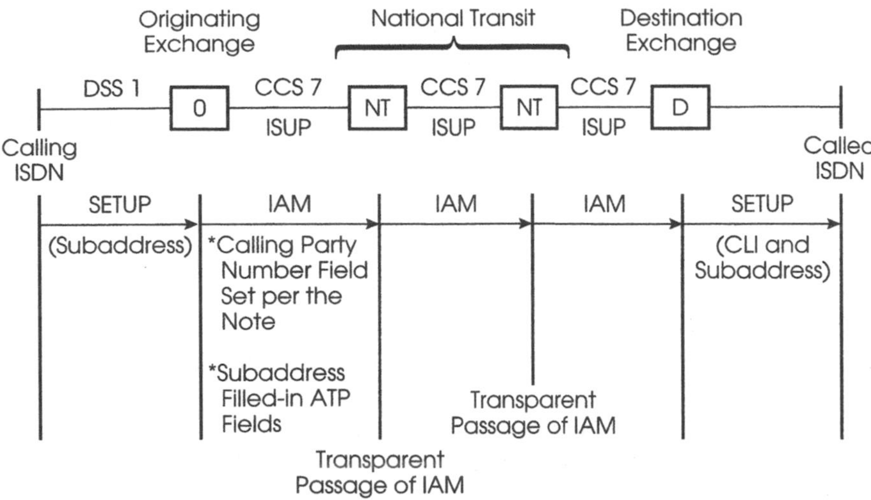

Notes:
Odd/even indicator is set to 1 since the number of digits is odd.
Nature of network indicator is set to 00000011 (national number).
Calling party number incomplete indicator (NI) is set to 0 (complete).
Numbering plan indicator is set to 001 (ISDN numbering plan).
Presentation restriction indicator (PR) is set to 00 (presentation allowed).
Screening indicator (SI) is set as 11 (network provided). Calling party number (11 digits) is filled in address signals.
Filler is inserted and set to 0000 since the number of digits are odd.

Figure 9–39 Example of CLIP-ISUP used all the way.

9.8.2 Malicious Call Identification (MCID) Supplementary Service

A description of the malicious call identification (MCID) supplementary service was provided in Chapter 8. The ISUP protocol to support this service is discussed here.

For an incoming call at the destination exchange to a user with the MCID supplementary service, the IAM is examined to determine if the complete calling party address is available. If the address is available, it is stored in the destination exchange. As an option, the subaddress may also be available in the access transport parameter of the IAM. This is also stored, if available. Thus, the information needed for the MCID service is available at the exchange and may be printed or displayed as necessary.

When the IAM does not contain the complete calling party address, however, it is necessary to obtain this information from the originating exchange. For this purpose, two additional ISUP messages are used:

1. Identification request (IDR) message
2. Identification response (IRS) message

The IDR message is sent from the destination exchange in the backward direction to request the originating exchange for the identity of the calling party. The IDR message consists of a message type and up to four optional parameters:

- MCID request indicators
- Message compatibility information
- Parameter compatibility information
- End of optional parameter

The MCID request indicators parameter contains a single-octet field in which the two least-significant bits A and B are used; the rest are spare:

Bit A: MCID request indicator
0 MCID not requested
1 MCID requested
Bit B: holding indicator
0 holding not requested
1 holding requested

A request for the calling party number is made by setting the MCID request indicator (bit A) to 1. When the national option of holding the connection is also implemented, the holding indicator (bit B) is provided in the IDR message; otherwise, this bit is spare. The destination exchange can make a request for holding the connection by setting bit B to 1.

The message compatibility and parameter compatibility parameters have the usual functions as described in Sections 9.6.2.3 and 9.6.2.4.

For time supervision, a timer Tmcid is started at the destination exchange on sending the IDR message. Tmcid has a value of 12 to 15 seconds.

The IDR message is passed without change by the transit exchanges to the preceding exchange in the connection.

At the originating exchange, upon receipt of the IDR message with A bit set to 1, an identification response (IRS) message is sent in the forward direction. The IRS message consists of the message type followed by up to seven optional parameters:

1. MCID response indicator
2. Message compatibility information
3. Parameter compatibility information
4. Calling party number
5. Access transport
6. Generic number
7. End of optional parameter

The MCID response indicator has a format similar to the MCID request indicator. The two least-significant bits are used to convey the following information (all other bits are spare):

Bit A: MCID response indicator
0 MCID not included
1 MCID included

Bit B: holding indicator
0 holding not provided
1 holding provided

The calling party address is included in the calling party number parameter, and bit A in the MCID response indicator is set to 1 to indicate this. When the MCID supplementary service is not supported, bit A is set to 0.

When holding the connection is requested, the originating exchange acknowledges the request by setting the holding indicator (bit B) to 1.

The originating exchange may also include other parameters. For example, the access transport parameter may be included to carry the subaddress of the calling ISDN access.

The IRS message is passed transparently by the transit exchanges to the succeeding exchanges in the connection. At the destination exchange, upon receipt of IRS, the Tmcid timer is stopped and the information relating to the MCID supplementary service is recorded.

The process of recording the information related to the MCID supplementary service is completed before the calling party answers the incoming call. Thus, MCID information is available to a subscriber for every incoming call of the malicious category. The printing of MCID-related information is restricted to calls for which an appropriate request has been made by the subscriber after answering the call, however.

If the IRS message is not received in response to the IDR message and timer Tmcid expires, the call is allowed to progress (without the availability of the MCID service).

9.9 Remarks

This chapter completes the description of CCS 7 protocols. The approach taken here has been to describe the various ISUP messages and their constituent parameters as they appear in a basic call between two ISDN users. Several other call scenarios are also possible, such as calls between two analog subscribers, calls requiring interworking of the ISUP with another signaling system (for example, R2 MFC), and calls between analog and ISDN subscribers. These have not been considered in this chapter. Appendix 2 provides a complete list of ISUP messages.

REFERENCES

[1] *General Function of Messages and Signals of the ISDN User Part of Signaling System No. 7.* ITU-T recommendation Q.762. International Telecommunication Union, 1994.

[2] *Formats and Codes of the ISDN User Part of Signaling System No. 7.* ITU-T recommendation Q.763. International Telecommunication Union, 1994.

[3] *Signaling System No. 7—ISDN User Part Signaling Procedures.* ITU-T recommendation Q.764. International Telecommunication Union, 1994.

[4] *Control of Echo Suppressors: Abnormal Conditions—Special Release Arrangements.* ITU-T recommendation Q.118, rev. 1. International Telecommunication Union, 1993.

[5] *Usage of Cause and Location in the Digital Subscriber Signaling System No. 1 and the Signaling System No. 7 ISDN User Part.* ITU-T recommendation Q.850. International Telecommunication Union, 1994.

[6] "Specification of signaling system no. 7." BELLCORE Technical Reference TR-NWT-000246 issue 2, June 1991; rev. 1, Dec. 1991; rev. 2, Dec. 1992.

[7] *Specifications of Signaling System No. 7. Message Transfer Part Signaling Performance.* ITU-T recommendation Q.706, rev. 1. International Telecommunication Union, 1993.

[8] *Stage 3 Descriptions for Number Identification Supplementary Services using Signaling System No. 7.* ITU-T recommendation Q.731. International Telecommunication Union, 1993.

[9] *Numbering Plan for the ISDN Era.* ITU-T recommendation E.164, rev. 1. International Telecommunication Union, 1993.

10 CCS 7 Planning and Implementation

Acronyms

ANM	answer message
ANSI	American National Standards Institute
BER	bit error rate
BHCA	busy hour call attempts
BOCs	Bell Operating companies
CCITT	The International Telegraph and Telephone Consultative Committee
CCS 7	CCITT common channel signaling system no. 7
DPC	destination point code
HSRC	hypothetical signaling reference connection
IAM	initial address message
ISC	international switching center
ISDN	integrated services digital network
ISUP	ISDN user part
ITU-T	International Telecommunication Union-Telecommunication Standardization Sector
LI	length indicator
LSSU	link status signal unit
MSU	message signal unit
MTP	message transfer part
PCR	preventive cyclic retransmission
REL	release (message)
RLC	release complete (message)
SAM	subsequent address message
SCCP	signaling connection control part
SEP	signaling endpoint
SIB	status indication busy
SIPO	status indication processor outage
SP	signaling point
SPC	stored program control
SPR	signaling point with SCCP relay function
STP	signaling transfer point
TCAP	transaction capability application part
TUP	telephone user part
UCIC	unequipped circuit identification code (message)

ABSTRACT

This chapter is devoted to the planning and implementation of the International Telegraph and Telephone Consultative Committee's (CCITT) common channel signaling system no. 7 (CCS 7) in the national network. The areas covered include:

- Definition of performance objectives for the design of CCS 7 networks
- Discussion of various CCS 7 network structures to meet performance objectives, with the specific example of the U.S. network
- Dimensioning (or provisioning) of signaling links
- Implementation strategies for CCS 7
- Monitoring the network
- Guidelines for formulation of national CCS 7 standards

10.1 Introduction

As a result of the efficiency and flexibility achieved by CCS 7, large amounts of circuit switched traffic can be controlled by the CCS 7 network. Thus, high standards of availability and performance must be ensured by the CCS 7 network. In this context, proper planning, implementation, and monitoring of CCS 7 network assumes great importance.

The introduction and subsequent expansion of CCS 7 requires careful consideration and decision making involving several technoeconomic aspects. Although the approach to planning and implementation bears a close relationship to the specific requirements and circumstances of the network, and because it is not possible to lay down precise rules that could be applied to all networks, an attempt is made here to enumerate the issues that merit examination in planning and implementation of CCS 7 networks.

10.2 Performance Objectives

The first step in planning a CCS 7 network is to specify the performance expected from the signaling network. The performance objectives are dealt with in two International Telecommunication Union-Telecommunication Standardization Sector (ITU-T) recommendations, Q.706 [1] and Q.709 [2].

The two main objectives to be met in CCS 7 planning are

1. To limit delay in signaling connections in the network
2. To achieve a high degree of availability of signaling connections

For specifying signaling performance parameters and for apportioning them between the national and international components of an international signaling connection, a hypothetical signaling reference connection (HSRC) has been defined in ITU-T recommendation Q.709. Furthermore, it is necessary to specify the performance requirements for the basic building blocks of a CCS 7 network, namely, signaling points (SPs), Signaling Transfer Points (STPs), and the signaling links. The performance of the message transfer part (MTP) is of key importance since it represents a common transport mechanism to serve the various user parts. Recommendation Q.706 deals with this subject. For the Bell operating companies (BOCs) in the U.S. network, BELLCORE TR-NWT-000246, chapter T.111.6 [3] (which is, by and large, in line with recommendation Q.706) describes the MTP performance objectives. MTP performance objectives are discussed in Section 10.2.3.

10.2.1 Hypothetical Signaling Reference Connection (HSRC)

The HSRC defines a signaling connection for international working. As pointed out in Section 4.8.1, the worldwide signaling network is generally composed of two independent types of networks, the international signaling network and the national signaling networks. In addition, Figure 7–4 illustrates the national and international CCS 7 networks. Therefore, the HSRC includes two national components and one international component. The nodes of the HSRC are the SPs and STPs, which are interconnected by signaling data links. The national component consists of the exchanges (SPs) and the STPs in the national network that are involved in the connection but excludes the international switching center (ISC) in the country. The international component includes international SPs and STPs. From the point of view of CCS 7, the ISC is considered an international SP. In addition, the ISC may also possess STP capabilities. At least one signaling point in each country should provide the STP function for international CCS 7 traffic so that the provision of international signaling links can be optimized [4].

Regarding the national signaling networks, a distinction is made between an average-sized country and a large-sized country. This categorization is based on two criteria, the geographic spread of the subscribers and the number of subscribers. An average-sized country is one where the maximum distance of a subscriber from an ISC is within 1,000 km (in exceptional cases, the maximum distance may go up to 1,500 km) or where the number of subscribers is fewer than $n \times 10{,}000{,}000$ (the value of n has not yet been specified). Countries with larger distances or number of subscribers are classified as large-sized countries.

With this definition of average- and large-sized countries, the next step is to specify the number of signaling nodes involved in an HSRC between average-sized to average-sized, average-sized to large-sized, and large-sized to large-sized countries. Furthermore, these figures must be specified for both link-by-link and end-to-end signaling. A probabilistic approach is used to specify the number of nodes involved in the HSRC to take into account the possibility of network rearrangements arising from failures. Thus, the number of nodes is not specified for all signaling connections.

For link-by-link signaling, the maximum number of SPs and STPs allowed for the international and national components of the HSRC are shown in Table 10–1. For example, for a large-sized national network, a maximum of three SPs and three STPs are allowed for 50% of all CCS 7 signaling connections. However, some CCS 7 signaling connections may involve more SPs and STPs due to network rearrangements. Therefore, it is specified that 95% of all CCS 7 signaling connections in a large national network may involve up to four SPs and four STPs. This leaves 5% of the signaling connections that may involve a higher number of SPs and STPs. The maximum figure in this case is not specified.

Table 10-1 Maximum Permissible SPs and STPs in an HSRC: Link-by-Link Signaling

For the international component:

Size	Percentage of Signaling Connections	Maximum Number of: SPs	STPs	Nodes
Large to large	50	3	3	6
	95	3	4	8
Large to average	50	2	2	4
	95	4	5	9
Average to average	50	5	5	10
	95	5	7	12

For each national component:

Size	Percentage of Signaling Connections	Maximum Number of: SPs	STPs	Nodes
Large	50	3	3	6
	95	4	4	8
Average	50	2	2	4
	95	3	3	6

Table 10–2 provides the breakup in the case of end-to-end signaling. End-to-end signaling involves a signaling relationship between the originating and the terminating signaling points, which are often called signaling endpoints (SEPs). All other signaling nodes perform signal transfer functions. A distinction is made between signaling nodes involving message transfer through the MTP (STPs in Table 10–2) and a transfer function where both the signaling connection control part (SCCP) and the MTP are involved. The latter are signaling points with SCCP relay functions (SPRs).

The number of signaling nodes in an HSRC are equal for both methods of signaling. For 50% of the connections, a maximum number of 18 nodes is permissible; for 95% of the connections, the maximum limit is 23 signaling nodes. For an HSRC between two average-sized countries, however, up to 24 signaling nodes are permitted for 95% of the signaling connections.

10.2.2 Signaling Delays

Signaling delay is an important performance parameter. The objective is to minimize signaling delays to reduce call setup time. On the basis of the HSRC and the size of the country, ITU-T recommendation Q.709 specifies the signaling delays permitted in the national and international components. The signaling delay refers to the time taken for the transfer of CCS 7 messages from the origination SP to the destination SP in the HSRC. The signaling delays for the international and national components of HSRC are given in

Table 10–2 Maximum Permissible SEPs, STPs, and SPRs in an HSRC (End-to-End Signaling)

For the international component:

Size	Percentage of Signaling Connections	Maximum Number of:		
		STPs	SPRs	Nodes
Large to Large	50	4	2	6
	95	4	3	7
Large to Average	50	6	2	8
	95	6	3	9
Average to Average	50	8	2	10
	95	8	4	12

For each national component:

Size	Percentage of Signaling Connections	Maximum Number of:			
		SEPs	STPs	SPRs	Nodes
Large	50	1	4	1	6
	95	1	5	2	8
Average	50	1	2	1	4
	95	1	4	1	6

Table 10–3 for link-by-link and end-to-end signaling. Since the message transfer time depends on the type of message, the delay figures are provided for two types of messages, simple messages and complex messages. Notice that the permissible delays for end-to-end signaling are generally less than those for link-by-link signaling. This is to be expected because in the case of link-by-link signaling, extra processing is involved in the user parts corresponding to intermediate SPs. Signaling delays for end-to-end signaling can be further minimized when the message transfer function is performed by the MTP alone, since this avoids the processing time involved in the SCCP.

A probabilistic approach is used in specifying signaling delays also. Thus, 5% of connections are permitted to suffer longer delays than specified. The upper bound for these cases is not specified. This takes care of exceptional conditions (for example, those arising from a combination of factors such as network rearrangements due to a large number of failures, excessive retransmissions, and use of satellite links).

The maximum signaling delay is a function of several parameters, such as the number of SPs and STPs that may be involved in a connection, the delay at each of the SPs and STPs, and the signaling propagation times on the signaling links. Therefore, to keep the delays within permissible limits, the signaling network should be designed with the following objectives:

- Limit the number of SPs and STPs involved in a signaling connection
- Limit the delays that may arise in each component of a signaling connection

Table 10–3 Maximum Signaling Delays (in ms) in International and National Components of an HSRC for Link-by-Link and End-to-End Signaling

Network Component	Percent of Connections	Message Type	
		Simple	Complex
For the international component:			
International (large to large)	50 95	390 (300) 410 (410)	600 (440) 620 (620)
International (large to average)	50 95	520 (340) 540 (450)	800 (480) 820 (660)
International (average to average)	50 95	650 (380) 690 (600)	1000 (520) 1040 (880)
For each national component:			
National (large)	50 95	390 (300) 520 (430)	600 (440) 800 (640)
National (average)	50 95	260 (260) 390 (300)	400 (400) 600 (440)

Note: The delays for end-to-end signaling are in parentheses.

Regarding the first aspect, the maximum number of SPs and STPs for the national component are shown in Table 10–2. The signaling network structure should be such that these values are not exceeded. Further, for the international network, usually not more than two STPs should exist between two adjacent SPs. In case of failure conditions, however, the number of STPs may reach up to four [4].

The second aspect, the signaling delays in individual components, is discussed in Section 10.2.3.3.

10.2.3 Message Transfer Part (MTP) Performance

MTP signaling performance refers to the capability of the MTP to transfer signaling messages between user parts while maintaining a high degree of availability and dependability and while keeping the message transfer time within permissible limits. These aspects are briefly discussed in the following sections.

10.2.3.1 Availability Objective

Availability is a measure of the reliability of the signaling network. For a signaling route set between an origination SP and a destination SP, the availability should be equal to or better than 99.9998%. This works out to a maximum of 10 minutes of permissible downtime for a route set in 1 year. This is illustrated in Figure 10–1 which shows a signaling route set between two nodes, SP A and SP B. The availability of a signaling route set depends on several factors, such as the following:

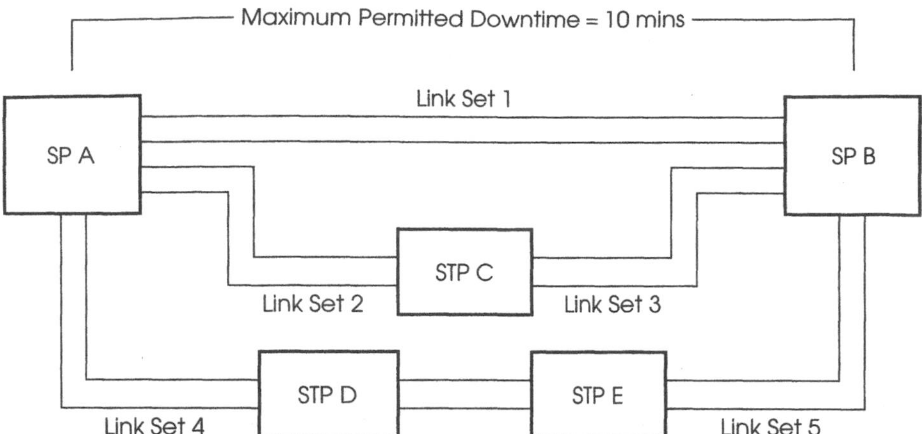

Figure 10–1 Availability requirement for a signaling route set.

- The number of signaling routes in the signaling route set (availability increases with the number of alternative signaling routes)
- The availability of individual signaling routes, composing the route set
- The availability of individual signaling routes (depends on the number of SPs, STPs, and signaling links connected serially in the signaling route and the availability figures of each SP, STP, and signaling link)

Since some of these aspects are closely related to the structure of the signaling network, to achieve the high-availability objective, the CCS 7 network should be planned to contain adequate redundancy. Redundancy may be provided in the various components comprising the signaling route set, such as by providing additional signaling links in a link set (additional signaling data links and signaling terminals) and planning more than one signaling route for a signaling relation. To improve availability, it is desirable that the redundant signaling links and routes are planned on geographically diverse paths.

For the U.S. network, which has a quad structure described in Chapter 7, the downtime allocation to different segments is shown in Figure 10–2.

10.2.3.2 Dependability Objective

The design of CCS 7 protocol provides for error detection and error correction of signal units and their transfer in proper sequence. However, malfunctioning of the MTP, although rare, cannot be entirely ruled out. ITU-T recommendation Q.706 stipulates the following objectives for the dependable transfer of messages by the MTP:

- Not more than one in 1E + 7 messages should be lost.
- Not more than one in 1E + 10 messages should be delivered out of sequence or duplicated.
- Not more than one in 1E + 10 message errors should remain undetected.

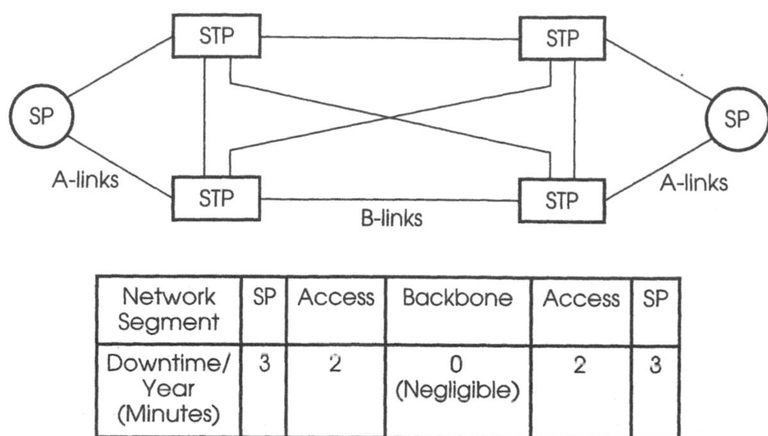

Network Segment	SP	Access	Backbone	Access	SP
Downtime/ Year (Minutes)	3	2	0 (Negligible)	2	3

Figure 10–2 Allocation of downtime.

These performance objectives are expected to be available in a CCS 7 implementation by virtue of its conformance to the specified CCS 7 protocols. Therefore, CCS 7 planning aspects are not involved in meeting the dependability objective.

10.2.3.3 Message Transfer Time

The message transfer time for a signaling relation is the interval between the time instants when the message leaves the user part at the origination SP and enters the user part at the destination SP. The message may pass through several intermediate STPs and interconnecting signaling data links.

The message transfer time is the cumulative total of the following components:

- Handling time in the MTPs of the origination and destination SPs
- Queuing delays at the SPs
- STP message transfer time
- Propagation time on the signaling data links involved in the signaling relation

Figure 10–3 shows the various components of message transfer time for messages between SP A and SP B through an STP. Although ITU-T recommendations identify the various delay components that make up the MTP transfer time, the permissible values for these components are not specified, except for the value of STP message transfer time.

When several user parts send messages to the MTP, the MTP serves the messages on a time-shared basis. A queue of messages is likely to be formed, giving rise to the delay in the MTP in accepting a message for processing. Although no objectives are specified, formulas for queuing delays have been derived in ITU-T recommendation Q.706 using the *M/G/*1 queue with priority assignment. (M/G/1 queue means that the interarrival time distribution of messages arriving in the queue is exponential (*M*), the time distribution of serving the messages is general (*G*), and there is only one server, namely the MTP.) The priority assignment refers to the transmission priority in level 2 of CCS 7 pro-

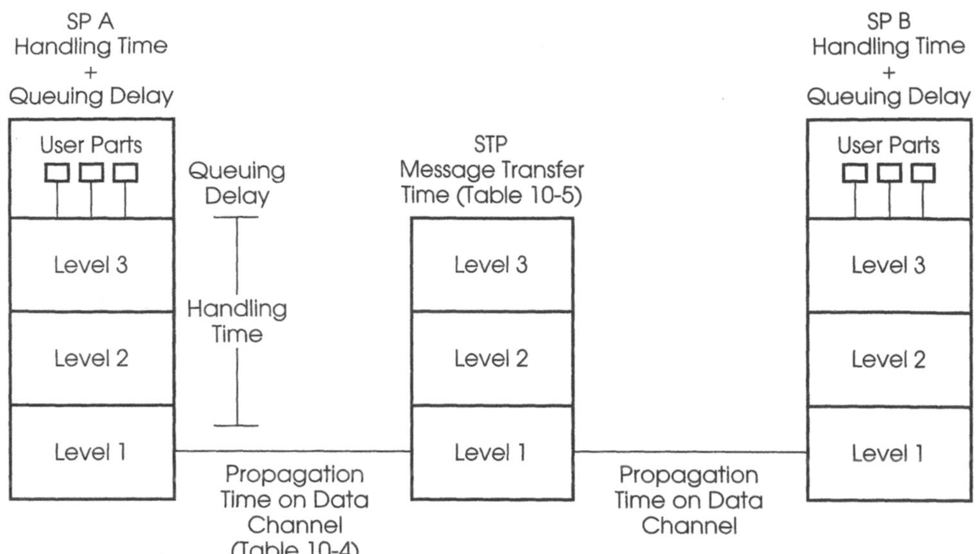

Figure 10–3 Components of message transfer time for a signaling relation.

tocol (signaling data link). Separate calculations have been made for the basic and preventive cyclic retransmission (PCR) methods of error correction in the presence and absence of disturbances (the basic and PCR methods of error correction are described in Chapter 6). Two measures of queuing delays have been considered, mean queuing delay and standard deviation. The formulas can be used by CCS 7 network designers in estimating the queuing delays.

Similarly, the formulas for computing propagation delay on data channels have been provided in annexure A to ITU-T recommendation Q.706. The calculated delays for three different types of terrestrial medium—wire, fiber, and radio—for call distances ranging from 500 km to 25,000 km are also furnished in recommendation Q.706.

The STP message transfer time is the period that begins when the last bit of a message signal unit (MSU) leaves the incoming signaling data link; it ends when the last bit of the MSU has entered the outgoing signaling data link for the first time. Thus, retransmission of the MSU is not included.

ITU-T and American National Standards Institute (ANSI) standards specify the message transfer time at an STP based on a mean signaling load of 0.2 erlang. Refer to Tables 10–4 and 10–5. These tables are based on telephone user part (TUP) messages with an average length of 15 octets. For longer messages, such as those encountered in the integrated services digital network (ISDN) user part (ISUP), the STP message transfer time will be longer.

For user parts other than the TUP, the STP message transfer time is calculated by adding the STP processing time (T_{ph}) and the outgoing signaling link delay (T_{od}). The STP processing time T_{ph} begins when the last bit of the MSU leaves the incoming signaling data link and ends when last bit of the MSU enters the level 2 transmission buffer associated with the outgoing signaling data link. The outgoing signaling link delay T_{od} begins when the last bit of the MSU enters the outgoing level 2 buffer and ends when the last bit

Table 10-4 Message Transfer Time at an STP Based on ITU-T Recommendations

Signaling Traffic Load	Message Transfer Time	
	Mean	95%
Normal	20 ms	40 ms
+15%	40 ms	80 ms
+30%	100 ms	200 ms

Reprinted from ITU-T recommendation Q.706 (1993) Message transfer part signaling performance. Rev. 1. Reproduced by permission.

Table 10-5 Message Transfer Time at an STP Based on ANSI Standards

Signaling Traffic Load	Message Transfer Time	
	Mean	95%
Normal	45 ms	80 ms
2 × Normal	55 ms	90 ms

of the MSU leaves the outgoing signaling data link. The STP processor handling time T_{ph}, as specified in ITU-T recommendation Q.706, is shown in Table 10–6. The values of T_{od} have been calculated in recommendation Q.706 for various combinations of the following parameters:

- Link loads of 0.2 and 0.4 erlang
- Basic and PCR methods of error correction
- Presence and absence of disturbances (errors)
- Loop delays TL of 30 ms (for terrestrial links) and 600 ms (for satellite links)
- Mean message lengths of 15, 23, 50, 140, and 279 bytes

Table 10-6 STP Processor Handling Time T_{ph}

Processor Load	Value	Mean Message Length			
		23 Bytes	50 Bytes	140 Bytes	279 Bytes
Normal	Mean	19 ms	22 ms	33 ms	55 ms
	95%	35 ms	40 ms	50 ms	75 ms
+30%	Mean	60 ms	70 ms	100 ms	160 ms
	95%	120 ms	140 ms	200 ms	320 ms

Reprinted from ITU-T recommendation Q.706 (1993) Message transfer part signaling performance. Rev. 1. Reproduced by permission.

Table 10-7 Outgoing Link Delay T_{od} with the Basic Error Correction Method in the Absence of Disturbances

A (ERLANG)	VALUE	OUTGOING LINK DELAY (ms) MSU LENGTH (BYTES)				
		15	23	50	140	279
0.2	Mean	2.7	4.0	8.3	21.5	39.6
	95%	9.3	14.0	30.1	66.0	61.5
0.4	Mean	3.5	5.2	10.8	27.6	46.9
	95%	12.2	18.6	40.0	88.7	87.1

Tables 10–7 and 10–8 show the T_{od} values in the absence of disturbances for basic and PCR methods of error correction, respectively.

The outgoing signaling delay in the absence of disturbances does not depend on the signaling loop propagation time when the basic error correction method is applied. Therefore, figures in Table 10–7 apply equally to both terrestrial and satellite links. The delay, of course, increases with the traffic load of the signaling link and with the length of MSUs.

When the PCR method is used, the values of T_{od} in the absence of disturbances do depend on the signaling loop propagation delay, as seen from Table 10–8.

The values of T_{od} tabulated for signaling links without disturbances do not occur in practice, since signaling links invariably suffer from a finite error rate. However, Tables 10–7 and 10–8 are useful because they provide a basis for comparison with T_{od} values in the presence of disturbances.

Two cases have been considered for presenting the values of T_{od} in the presence of disturbances: bit error rate (BER) values of $1 \times E - 5$ and $1 \times E - 7$. Table 10–9 lists the T_{od} values.

Table 10-8 Outgoing Link Delay T_{od} with the PCR Method in the Absence of Disturbances

A (ERLANG)	LOOP DELAY TL (ms)	VALUE	OUTGOING LINK DELAY (ms) MSU LENGTH (BYTES)				
			15	23	50	140	279
0.2	30	Mean	4.2	6.4	11.3	23.1	38.7
		95%	12.5	18.9	38.1	71.1	58.6
	600	Mean	4.2	6.5	14.1	35.7	56.0
		95%	12.6	19.4	42.2	93.1	86.2
0.4	30	Mean	5.0	7.6	15.3	29.9	43.8
		95%	15.0	22.9	48.3	93.8	79.8
	600	Mean	5.0	7.7	16.7	41.8	63.9
		95%	15.0	23.0	50.0	111.4	108.9

Table 10-9 Outgoing Link Delay T_{od} with the Basic and PCR Methods in the Presence of Disturbances

A (ERLANG)	LOOP DELAY TL (ms)	VALUE	DISTURBANCE	OUTGOING LINK DELAY (ms); MSU LENGTH (BYTES) 15	23	50	140	279	REMARKS
0.2	30	Mean	1 × E − 5	2.8 (4.2	4.1 6.2	8.4 11.4	21.9 24.0	40.4 41.3)	Lower delays in BEC. BEC is suitable for terrestrial links.
			1 × E − 7	2.7 (4.2	4.0 6.2	8.2 11.3	21.5 23.1	39.6 38.7)	
		95%	1 × E − 5	10.8 (12.8	15.4 19.3	31.4 39.5	68.0 80.4	64.8 84.5)	
			1 × E − 7	9.3 (12.8	14.1 18.9	30.1 38.0	66.0 71.3	61.5 59.0)	
	600	Mean	1 × E − 5	29.6 (5.0	31.2 7.4	36.9 15.5	55.0 39.3	80.3 63.0)	Lower delays in PCR. PCR is suitable for satellite links.
			1 × E − 7	3.0 (4.2	4.3 6.5	8.5 14.1	21.9 35.8	40.1 56.1)	
		95%	1 × E − 5	248.4 (27.8	254.2 34.9	275.0 60.3	329.4 127.2	363.8 140.9)	
			1 × E − 7	28.9 (13.0	32.7 19.7	46.0 42.5	79.2 93.7	76.9 87.4)	
0.4	30	Mean	1 × E − 5	3.8 (5.6	5.4 8.7	11.2 18.9	28.3 47.5	48.1 81.1)	Lower delays in BEC. BEC is also suitable for high-traffic terrestrial links.
			1 × E − 7	3.5 (5.0	5.2 7.6	10.8 15.3	27.6 30.1	46.9 44.2)	
		95%	1 × E − 5	14.3 (26.3	20.4 42.5	41.7 106.2	91.4 310.9	91.3 448.2)	
			1 × E − 7	12.3 (15.2	18.6 23.3	40.0 49.7	88.7 101.1	87.1 96.1)	
	600	Mean	1 × E − 5	86.3 (47.2	88.5 55.7	96.9 84.8	121.9 183.5	152.0 282.5)	High delay for both methods at a BER of 1 × E − 5, when satellite links are used.
			1 × E − 7	4.3 (5.3	6.0 8.0	11.6 17.1	28.5 42.8	47.9 65.3)	
		95%	1 × E − 5	490.1 (379.7	496.4 422.7	521.2 586.2	586.6 1103.0	626.9 1470.0)	
			1 × E − 7	44.0 (30.2	48.4 38.1	64.5 67.1	107.4 141.5	106.9 153.9)	

Notes: Figures in parentheses refer to delays for the PCR method.

BEC = basic error correction method.

PCR = preventive cyclic retransmission method.

Table 10–10 Transit Exchange Cross-Office Signaling Delay

Message Type	Exchange Call Attempts	Cross-Office Signaling Transfer Time (ms)	
		Mean	95%
Simple messages, for example, an answer message (ANM)	Normal	110	220
	15% overload	165	330
	30% overload	275	550
Processing intensive messages for example, an initial address message (IAM)	Normal	180	360
	15% overload	270	540
	30% overload	450	900

EXAMPLE 10–1

Assuming a signaling network with an average link loading of 0.2 erlang, a BER of 1 × E − 7, a mean MSU length of 50 octets, and the use of the basic error correction method on terrestrial links, the STP message transfer time can be calculated as follows:

STP processor handling time $T_{ph} = 22$ ms (from Table 10–6)
Outgoing link delay $T_{od} = 8.2$ ms (mean value from Table 10–9)
STP message transfer time $= T_{ph} + T_{od} = (22 + 8.2)$ ms $= 30.2$ ms

10.2.4 Performance Objectives for the ISUP

The performance objectives for the ISUP as specified in ITU-T recommendation Q.766 [5] include the following:

- Unsuccessful calls arising from signaling malfunctions should not exceed 2 calls in 1 × E + 5 calls.
- Cross-office signaling transfer time at a transit exchange should be as given in Table 10–10. (The cross-office time begins when the last bit of the message leaves the incoming signaling data link and ends when the last bit of the message enters the outgoing signaling data link.)
- Not more than one message out of 1 × E + 4 messages should be delayed by more than 300 ms due to error correction by retransmission.

10.3 CCS 7 Network Structure

To meet the stringent availability requirements, the CCS 7 network design should provide adequate redundancy. As noted earlier, redundancy may be built in several ways, for example, in the provisioning of signaling terminals, the number of signaling links in a link set, and the number of signaling routes to a specific destination. For the redundancy to be effective in the improvement of availability, physical diversity and technology diversity should be practiced.

Examples:

- If, at a signaling point, multiple signaling terminals are designed to be on the same printed board, then the redundant signaling terminals should be assigned on different boards. This will guard against failure of a board.
- Another example of physical diversity is to plan signaling links on a geographically separate transmission bearer. This gives good protection against failures due to dig-ins and pole line structural failures.
- Technology diversity is the use of bearers of different transmission technologies for signaling links. For example, signaling links to a destination may be divided on fiber-optic and radio transmission systems.
- When geographic separation and technology diversity of transmission bearers are not available, the signaling links may be planned on different systems. For example, the signaling links may be planned on time slots of different 30-channel (or 24-channel) PCM systems.

10.3.1 Mode of Signaling

The design of a signaling network is influenced by the choice of signaling mode. CCS 7 network designs vary widely, from networks based solely on the associated mode of signaling to those that are substantially based on the quasi-associated working. Associated and quasi-associated modes are explained in Chapter 4. In the associated mode, the signaling follows the same route as the circuit switched traffic. In the quasi-associated mode, on the other hand, the signaling follows a route that is different from the circuit switched traffic. STPs are employed for this purpose.

Networks operating solely on the associated mode are simple to design and operate; there are no STPs in the network, only SPs. Both signaling and speech/data traffic follow the same path. Such a signaling network is strongly tied to the telephony network. This signaling mode is uneconomic except for small-sized networks. An exchange functioning in the associated mode must have signaling links to all other interconnected exchanges. Typically, for the sake of redundancy at least two signaling links are needed toward each interconnected exchange, even when the volume of circuit switched traffic does not justify such provisioning. Thus, the number of signaling terminals required at each exchange is large, and signaling links may remain largely unused due to very low occupancy.

Networks that employ quasi-associated signaling are more efficient in the utilization of signaling links. Moreover, alternative signaling paths can be built through STPs in the network. Extensive use of quasi-associated signaling may, however, result in a complex network structure. Failures in the network may affect a large number of circuits; therefore, greater attention to security considerations is required.

In practice, a combination of associated and quasi-associated modes is used. The main consideration in design is how extensively quasi-associated signaling is to be used and under what situations. During the initial phase of CCS 7 deployment, it may be worthwhile to operate the network largely on the associated mode. For example, associated signaling may be used under normal operation—that is, in the absence of failures in the signaling network—and quasi-associated working may be used only for failure conditions. In this case, most signaling relations function in the associated mode, leading to a simple network structure. It may be stressed however, that no absolute rules of network design can be formulated because a number of factors that may differ from one national network to another are involved, such as the topology of the telephony network, the routing plan, the status of network digitalization, the availability of transmission links, the type of services, and the volume of traffic to be supported.

For quasi-associated working, STPs are required. These can be provided in two different ways:

1. Integrated STP
2. Stand-alone STP

When an exchange works as an SP for some signaling relations and provides the signaling transfer function for other signaling relations, it is said to function as an integrated STP. On the other hand, a stand-alone STP, as its name suggests, is equipment separate from the exchange that provides only the signaling transfer functions.

For an integrated STP, it is important to distinguish between the availability of the STP capability and its actual use in a signaling relation. Figure 10–4 illustrates the concept. In Figure 10–4(a), all three nodes A, B, and C are functioning as signaling points. The associated mode of signaling is solely used for signaling relations A–B, A–C, and C–B. Nodes B and C have only SP functionality, whereas node A possesses both SP and STP functionality (integrated STP). In the context of Figure 10–4(a), however, node A functions only as an SP. Figure 10–4(b) assumes the failure of signaling link BC. In this

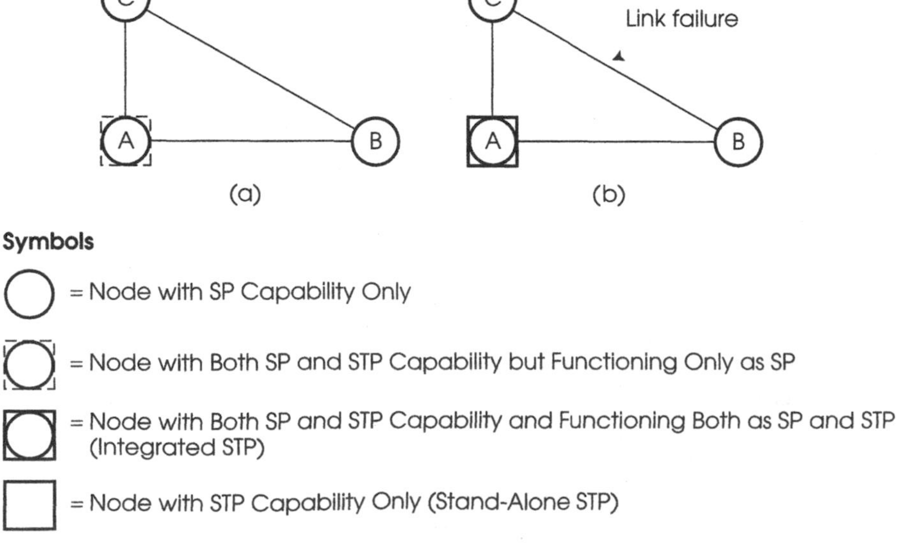

Figure 10–4 Example of quasi-associated working during link failure: (a) associated mode of working, node A functions as SP only although STP capability exists; (b) combination of associated and quasi-associated mode of working, node A functions as an integrated SP.

case, signaling in the associated mode between B and C is no longer feasible, and quasi-associated signaling takes place for the signaling relation B–C using the STP functionality available at node A. Node A continues to function as an SP for signaling relations A–B and A–C.

Quasi-associated signaling may be implemented in the network by employing either stand-alone STPs or integrated STPs. Figure 10–5 illustrates the two approaches in the event of link failures.

Because the exchanges also serve as STPs, the integrated STP approach does not require any additional equipment. On the other hand, the stand-alone approach requires an investment in STP equipment and additional signaling links to connect the stand-alone STP to the SPs in the network. Therefore, integrated STPs decidedly offer a cheaper solution. When the signaling traffic is large and the quasi-associated mode of signaling is used extensively (not just for failure conditions as in the foregoing example), however, the message transfer capacity of the STP should be large. The STP capacity is measured in terms of the number of MSUs transferred per second. Integrated STPs may not be able to provide the necessary capacity since they also have to perform SP functions concurrently. Thus, stand-alone STPs are appropriate for this situation. Another advantage with the stand-alone approach is that signaling network planning is not entirely tied down to the planning of digital exchanges. Additional signaling capacity and alternative routes can be

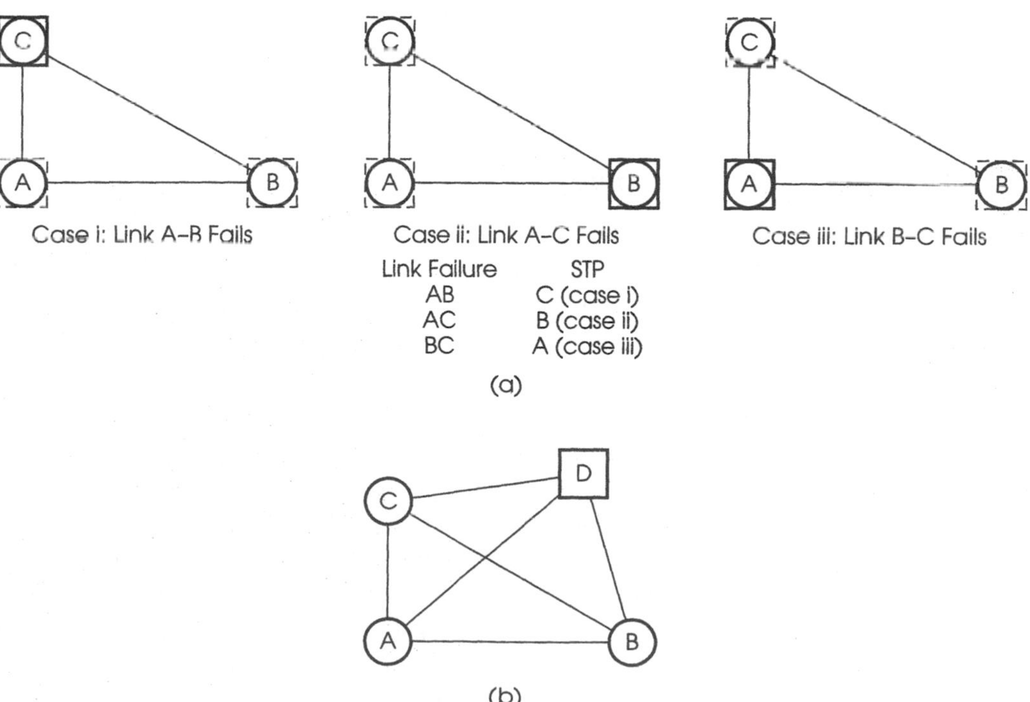

Figure 10–5 (a) Integrated STP, quasi-associated working during link failures; (b) stand-alone STP approach, quasi-associated working during link failures.

planned independently of the installation and commissioning of exchanges. Moreover, failures in an exchange do not affect the STP functions. This may not always be the case when integrated STPs are used.

Typically, during the early stages of CCS 7 implementation, the signaling traffic is low, and the main application is telephony, which is characterized by short message lengths. In this case, integrated STPs provide an adequate and economic solution. Subsequently, as the signaling needs of the network grow, particularly with the implementation of intelligent network services, stand-alone STPs can be installed. When integrated STPs are used, to avoid congestion and resultant signaling delays on particular STPs, the quasi-associated signaling traffic must be distributed over several STPs. Therefore, it is desirable that STP functionality be made available in all digital exchanges forming part of the CCS 7 network, especially in all transit exchanges, irrespective of their immediate application (as SP only or as integrated STP). This strategy provides sufficient flexibility to the network designer.

The introduction of stand-alone STPs in effect creates a hierarchical signaling network in which the STPs can be visualized as occupying a higher level than the SPs whose signaling traffic the STPs are required to transfer. To create a backbone network with multiple alternative paths for signaling, the STPs are mesh connected as far as possible. The intention is to make the unavailability of the backbone network almost negligible (refer to Figure 10–2), since failures in the backbone network have an impact on a large number of signaling relations. An SP is usually connected to at least two STPs of the mesh-connected backbone network.

The STPs may be arranged in a single level or in two levels. These arrangements are explained through the example of the U.S. network in the next section. This arrangement was described briefly in Chapter 7.

10.3.2 U.S. Signaling Network Structure

The principles on which the CCS 7 networks used by the BOCs in the United States are based are described in BELLCORE TR-NWT-000246, Chapter T1.111.5 [6]. STPs may be arranged in a single level or in a two-level hierarchy.

Figure 10–6 illustrates a single-level hierarchy. The main features are summarized as follows:

- The basic building block of the network is a pair of STPs, called a mated pair, interconnected by duplicated signaling links designated cross or C-links.
- A number of SPs are connected to both the STPs of a mated pair by signaling links called access or A-links. Thus, signaling relation between two such SPs can be established in the quasi-associated mode through either of the two STPs. This forms a signaling subnetwork. The STP pair to which an SP is connected is called the home pair for that SP. Thus, in Figure 10–6, STP pair X is the home pair for SP1. An SP may also be connected to another STP pair by means of E-links. This pair is the remote STP pair for that SP.
- Furthermore, two SPs may also be interconnected by direct signaling links (called

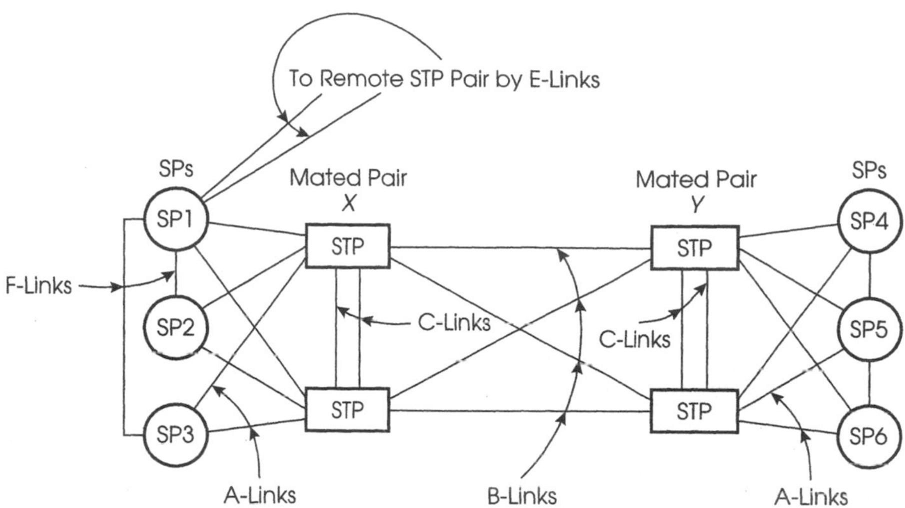

Figure 10–6 Single-level STP hierarchy.

F-links). This permits associated signaling between them. Typically, F-links are provided between SPs when the speech/data traffic between them is sufficient to justify direct signaling connection.

- One mated STP pair along with the interconnected SPs is called a primary STP pair.
- Every primary STP is connected to all other primary STP pairs in the network by means of quad signaling links, called B-links.

The number of primary STP pairs to be provided in a network depends on several parameters such as the volume of signal transfer required between connected SPs, the capacity of the STPs themselves, and the topography of the network.

As an extension to the single-level STPs, a two-level arrangement of STPs can also be implemented. An example is shown in Figure 10–7. In this case, the STP network described above is called the primary level. Pairs of STPs, designated secondary STP pairs, may be added to augment the signaling network. Secondary STPs also occur in mated pairs and are interconnected to each other by quad links called D-links. Thus, a second level of STP hierarchy called the secondary level is created. Regarding the interconnection between the two levels of STPs, a secondary STP pair is connected to a specific primary STP pair by means of D quad links. Several such secondary pairs can be connected to a primary STP pair. Several SPs can be connected to a secondary STP pair by E-links.

Based on this description, the characteristics of a one-level STP network can be summarized as follows:

- Each SP is connected to at least two STPs (an STP pair). Therefore, if access to one STP fails (due to link failure or failure of the STP itself), then the other STP is still accessible.

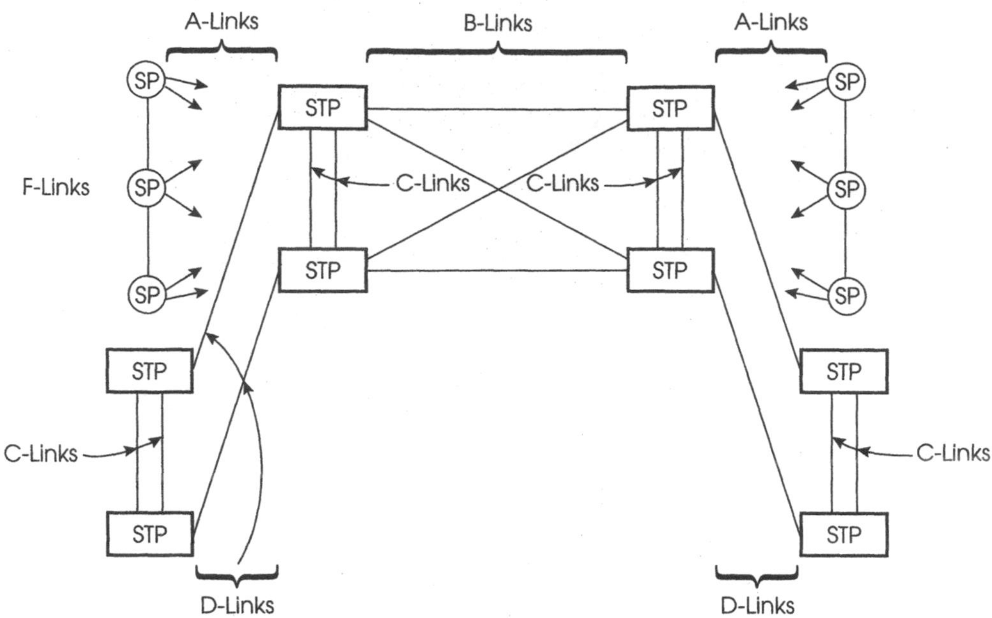

Figure 10–7 Example of two-level STP hierarchy.

- Each STP in the network is connected to every other STP to provide a highly redundant backbone network.

The main characteristics of the signaling network based on two levels of STP hierarchy are

- Each STP at the secondary level is connected to at least two STPs of the primary level.
- The STPs at the primary level are fully mesh connected.
- STPs at the secondary level may not be fully mesh connected. A secondary STP, however, is connected to one or more secondary STPs. Thus, traffic between secondary STPs need not always be routed through a primary STP.
- An SP is always connected to at least two STPs. These STPs may belong to either a primary or a secondary level.

10.3.3 Signaling Point Code

For the international network, a 14-bit-long point code has been defined as described in Chapter 4. For the national network, the administration has to decide about the length and structure of the point code. A straightforward arrangement could be the use of a 14-bit point code. This gives a possibility of addressing up to 16,344 SPs within the national CCS 7 network. However, once the 14-bit point code is implemented, a subsequent expansion in length is both expensive and undesirable from the operational point of view, since the exercise would require modifications at every SP in the network. Therefore, the administration should make a careful, long-term estimate of the likely ultimate number of the exchanges in the national network. (Stand-alone STPs also require assignment of point codes, but their number is very small compared with the number of exchanges.) For most countries, a 14-bit code should suffice. This argument is supported by the current trend of large-sized exchanges with multiple remote switching units. A single point code caters to the main exchange as well as to the remote units. Thus, as older exchanges of smaller capacities are phased out and replaced by large-capacity exchanges, the number of exchanges in the network may come down, even when there is a moderate growth in the number of subscribers. The 14-bit point code is easy to implement since it does not require any additional development or modifications in the software of switch manufacturers.

10.3.3.1 Structured versus Structureless Point Code

Another aspect to be decided is whether the point code is to be structured by subdivision of the point code bits into fields. Figure 10–8(a) shows a structureless point code. The arguments in favor of a structureless point code are as follows:

- Unlike the directory number, the point code is of no significance to the telephone subscribers. The user part (for example, the ISUP) analyzes the called party address to determine the identity of the next exchange. This identity is then translated into the destination point code (DPC). Since the point codes are handled entirely by the exchange (or stand alone STP) software, there is no requirement for a user-friendly structure.
- A structureless point code permits full use of the number of available point codes. For instance, for a 14-bit point code, it is possible to allocate all the 16,384 signaling point codes, without any gaps in numbering.

As an alternative, the point code may be divided into fields that are meaningful from an administrative point of view. An example of a structured point code is shown in Figure 10–8(b) where the point code is composed of three fields on the basis of the following assumptions:

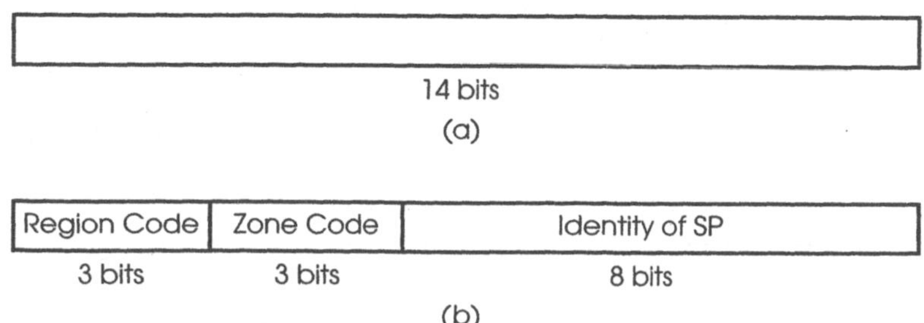

Figure 10–8 Signaling point code: (a) structureless point code; (b) example of structured point code.

1. The national telecommunication network is divided into eight regions: north, south, east, west, northeast, northwest, southeast, and southwest.
2. There can be a maximum of eight zones in each region.
3. There can be a maximum of 255 exchanges, including stand-alone STPs.

Theoretically, this arrangement also provides for 16,384 SPs ($8 \times 8 \times 256$). However, in the event of uneven growth—for example, the number of exchanges in one zone reaching 256, with a much lower number in other zones—there will be a risk of nonavailability of point codes even before the ultimate capacity of 16,384 is reached. Thus, additional parameters, such as regionwise network growth, need to be estimated while finalizing the fields and their sizes. On the contrary, the only parameter to be estimated for the unstructured point code is the ultimate number of exchanges.

Structuring provides greater convenience in allocation and administration of point codes. In the above example, once the region codes are assigned, further allotment of codes need not be managed centrally but instead may be performed at the regional level.

10.3.3.2 Numbering of Point Codes in the U.S. Network

For the U.S. network, 24-bit point codes are used. The point code is structured into three fields, each of one octet, as shown in Figure 10–9. This format permits addressing of a cluster of SPs. A cluster of SPs consists of those SPs that directly home in on a mated pair of STPs. Thus, in Figure 10–6, SP4, SP5, and SP6, which home in directly on mated STP pair Y, form a cluster.

The network identification octet is used to distinguish between different CCS 7 networks in the United States. A distinction is made between small networks, large networks, and CCS groups. A CCS 7 network consists of a set of signaling points that must include one or more STPs. A large network is one that has at least 75 SPs or that is estimated to contain at least 150 SPs in the next 5 years. One or more SPs without an STP does not qualify as a CCS 7 network. Instead, such a collection of SPs is classified as a CCS group.

Rules for assigning network identification codes may be summarized as follows:

- The network code 0 is not used. Code 255 (all 1's) is assigned for future use.
- Codes 1 to 4 are used for small networks, and code 5 is assigned to CCS groups.
- The remaining 249 codes are assignable to large CCS 7 networks. Each large network is initially assigned one network identification code. One, or in rare cases two, additional codes may be assigned subsequently.

Since only four network codes are available and since the number of small networks may be much larger, the network cluster field is also used for identifying small networks.

Network Identification	Network Cluster	Cluster Member
8 bits	8 bits	8 bits

Figure 10–9 Format of point code for the U.S. network.

In this case, code 0 is not used for the network cluster field. Thus, it is possible to assign codes to a maximum of 1020 (4 × 255) small networks. Each small network is assigned one code initially; up to three additional codes can be assigned subsequently, depending on the growth of the network.

For a CCS group, assignment is performed in blocks of four contiguous point codes, such as 5–1–0 to 5–1–3.

The assignable signaling point codes under this arrangement are 16,318,464 (249 × 256 × 256) for large networks, 2,61,120 (4 × 255 × 256) for small networks, and 65,280 (1 × 255 × 256) for CCS groups. The total theoretically assignable point codes is the summation of these three (16,644,864).

10.3.4 Dimensioning of Signaling Link Load

An important factor in signaling network design is to specify the signaling link load during normal fault-free operation. The signaling link load is the occupancy of the signaling link arising from useful signaling traffic, which consists of MSUs. For speech circuits, the occupancy of signaling links is expressed in erlangs. The network is designed on the basis of maximum signaling link load, which generally occurs during the busy hour for telephone traffic.

The network should be designed for a low signaling load per link to permit room for additional traffic that may arise from signal rerouting under failure conditions. Moreover, the signaling link load has an impact on the signaling delay. As seen in Table 10–9, to reduce the outgoing signaling link delay, the normal signaling link load must be kept low, particularly when the PCR method is used. For example, the network may be dimensioned for a signaling link load of 0.2 erlang under normal operation. The signaling load may, however, increase for short periods when some links in the network may be required to carry the diverted traffic arising from failure conditions.

Calculations for estimating the signaling traffic arising from basic calls and the number of circuits that a signaling link with 0.2 erlang occupancy can serve are presented in the following example. All messages are assumed to be ISUP messages. Both en bloc and overlap signaling are considered.

EXAMPLE 10-2

The parameters of the basic call traffic required for this calculation (along with their assumed values) are

$$\text{ratio of successful calls to total calls } (S) = 0.65$$
$$\text{ratio of unsuccessful calls to total calls } (U) = 0.35$$
$$\text{mean holding time for successful calls } (H_s) = 240 \text{ s}$$
$$\text{mean holding time for unsuccessful calls } (H_u) = 30 \text{ s}$$

Therefore, the mean duration for a call (D_m)

$$= (S \times H_s) + (U \times H_u)$$
$$= 168 \text{ seconds}$$

Assuming an occupancy of 0.8 erlang for speech circuits (not signaling circuits) during the busy hour, the number of busy hour call attempts per circuit (BHCA/circuit)

$$= \frac{3,600 \times 0.8}{168} \quad (1)$$
$$= 17 \text{ calls/circuit}$$

The percentage of successful calls, unsuccessful calls, and holding times for the two cases vary from network to network. The network designer should use the values prevailing in the network under design. Calls may be unsuccessful for a variety of reasons, including no dialing, incomplete dialing, called subscriber busy, and no answer. As a simplifying assumption, all these cases have been grouped together in this example.

The mean number of digits dialed per call (N) is the weighted value of digits dialed for successful calls (N_s) and unsuccessful calls (N_u). Again, N_s is a weighted value of digits dialed for local, national, and international calls:

$$\text{mean number of digits dialed per call } (N) = (N_s \times S) + (N_u \times U)$$

The value of N may be calculated for the network based on the numbering scheme and the proportion of local, national, and international calls. In this example, N is assumed to be nine digits.

CASE 1: En bloc signaling

Possible sequences for a successful call along with the typical length in each case are given in Table 10–11. It is assumed that the MTP overhead is seven octets for each message.

The "probability of occurrence" figures in Table 10–11 are assumed values that may vary from network to network. For example, if the ISDN terminals are of the automatic answering type, the connect message is likely to occur more often.

For the values of Table 10–11, total signaling information per successful call is

$$(1.0 \times 29) + (0.9 \times 32) + (0.05 \times 17) + (0.05 \times 48) + (1.0 \times 19) + (1.0 \times 15) = 95 \text{ octets}$$

Therefore, the mean number of octets per direction for a successful call is $\frac{95}{2}$, or 47.5.

For unsuccessful calls, the message sequence is

initial address message (IAM) $\xrightarrow{\text{29 octets}}$

release message (REL) $\xleftarrow{\text{19 octets}}$

release complete (RLC) message $\xrightarrow{\text{15 octets}}$

The total information per unsuccessful call is

$$29 + 19 + 15 = 63 \text{ octets}$$

The mean number of octets per direction for an unsuccessful call is

$$\frac{63}{2} = 31.5$$

Table 10-11 Message Sequences and Their Typical Lengths

Message Name	Length (Octets)	Probability of Occurrence
IAM ——→	29	100%
ACM ←——	17] 32	90%
ANM ←——	15]	
or		
CON ←——	17	5%
or		
ACM ——→	17]	5%
CPG ←——	16] 48	
ANM ←——	15]	
REL ——→	19	100%
RLC ←—— (calling party release is assumed)	15	100%

Note: ACM = address complete message.
ANM = answer message.
CON = connect message.
CPG = call progress message.
IAM = initial address message.
REL = release message.
RLC = release complete message.

The mean number of octets in each direction for a call (considering both successful and unsuccessful call attempts) is

$$(47.5 \times 0.65) + (31.5 \times 0.35) = 42 \tag{2}$$

From equations (1) and (2), the information transfer in each direction on a signaling link for circuit switched traffic/circuit during the busy hour is

$$17 \times 42 = 714 \text{ octets}$$

The 64 kbps signaling rate corresponds to 8,000 octets/second; therefore, a signaling link at 100% occupancy can transfer 8,000 × 3,600 or 288,000,000 octets.

The number of circuits that can be served by a signaling link with an occupancy of 0.2 erlang is

$$\frac{288{,}000{,}000 \times 0.2}{714} = 8{,}067 \text{ circuits}$$

This figure depends on the mean signaling traffic generated by each speech circuit. Higher signaling traffic reduces the number of speech circuits that can be served by a signaling link. The signaling traffic generated by a speech circuit increases with the increase in call attempts, proportion of successful calls, mean number of digits dialed per call, and amount of signaling information transferred per call. The calculations above use typical figures. The calculations for a particular network would depend on the traffic model for that network.

CASE 2: Overlap signaling

It is assumed that the IAM is followed by a single subsequent address message (SAM). The sequence for a successful call is identical to that of Table 10–11 except that the length of the IAM is reduced (assumed value of 27 octets) and the SAM (assumed value of 21 octets) follows the IAM. With these changes, the total signaling information per successful call is

$$(1.0 \times 27) + (1.0 \times 21) + (0.9 \times 32) + (0.05 \times 17) + (0.05 \times 48) + (1.0 \times 19) + (1.0 \times 15) = 114 \text{ octets}$$

The mean number of octets per direction for a successful call is 57.

For unsuccessful calls, the messages sequence is

$$\text{(IAM)} \xrightarrow{\text{27 octets}}$$
$$\text{(SAM)} \xrightarrow{\text{21 octets}}$$
$$\text{(REL)} \xleftarrow{\text{19 octets}}$$
$$\text{(RLC)} \xrightarrow{\text{15 octets}}$$

The total information per unsuccessful call is

$$27 + 21 + 19 + 15 = 82 \text{ octets}$$

The mean number of octets per direction for an unsuccessful call is 41. The mean number of octets in each direction for a call (considering both successful and unsuccessful call attempts) is

$$(57 \times 0.65) + (41 \times 0.35) = 51 \tag{3}$$

From equations (1) and (3), the information transfer in each direction on a signaling link for circuit switched traffic/circuit is

$$17 \times 51 = 867 \text{ octets}$$

The number of circuits that can be served by a signaling link with an occupancy of 0.2 erlang is

$$\frac{288{,}000{,}000 \times 0.2}{867} = 6{,}644 \text{ circuits}$$

In summary, the en bloc method is more efficient in the use of signaling links. For the same traffic model, a signaling link with 0.2 erlang occupancy will serve 8,067 circuits for en bloc signaling as opposed to 6,644 circuits for the overlap signaling.

10.4 Implementation Planning for CCS 7

The starting point in the planning of a CCS 7 network is the classification of the existing and planned switching systems on the basis of their CCS 7 capabilities. Switching systems are usually classified as follows:

- Switches that are not capable of supporting either SP or STP functions and that do not have the possibility of upgrading to include these functions. Electromechanical exchanges and SPC analog exchanges usually fall into this category.
- Switches that are not capable of supporting either SP or STP functions but that can be upgraded to include these functions by suitable addition or modification of equipment and software. Earlier versions of digital exchanges typically fall under this category since these exchanges were designed prior to the definition of CCS 7 protocols by the CCITT.
- Switches that are capable of supporting only SP functions. Some digital exchanges may be designed with only the SP functionality in view.
- Switches that are capable of supporting both SP and STP functions (integrated STP).
- Equipment capable of supporting only STP functions.

The switches that cannot be upgraded are outside the scope of CCS 7 planning. Regarding switches that can be upgraded, the decision to upgrade depends on several considerations, including the following:

1. Switch manufacturers generally tend to focus development efforts on their latest product. Thus, the most recently standardized CCS 7 protocol version may not be supported on an upgraded switch.
2. The capacity of the SP (and STP, when available) of the upgraded switch may not be sufficient. Typical parameters to be considered are
   - Maximum number of signaling links and link sets
   - Maximum number of destinations and signaling routes per destination
   - Signaling traffic capacity of the exchange in terms of messages handled per second
3. The remaining useful life of the exchange and replacement plans, if any
4. The expected cost of upgrades

Exchanges with only SP functions are appropriate when there are no immediate or long-term plans to implement integrated STPs and where stand-alone STPs have already been planned or implemented. In all other cases, it is preferable to make provision for both SP and STP functions in all digital exchanges: toll, local tandem, and local exchanges. Generally, integrated STP functions do not need any additional equipment in the exchange; the CCS 7 message handling capacity of the exchange is merely partitioned into SP and STP functions. Thus, the cost implications of this decision are not likely to be substantial. At the same time, enhanced flexibility is obtained in the designing of the CCS 7 network.

Three possible approaches to implementation of CCS 7 in the network exist:

1. Top-down approach: implementation starts from the highest level toll switches in the network.
2. Bottom-up approach: implementation of CCS 7 starts in the local exchanges.

3. Island approach: CCS 7 is implemented at different levels in the network depending on the need for CCS 7–based services. This can be seen as a pragmatic approach that strikes a balance between the top-down and bottom-up approaches.

Another factor that has bearing on CCS 7 implementation plans is the digitalization of the transmission network. The use of analog links for CCS 7, although possible, is not recommended. Thus, the growth of the CCS 7 network follows the digitalization of the transmission network. Finally, to prevent excessive retransmissions, the synchronization of the digital exchanges must precede implementation of CCS 7.

10.4.1 CCS 7 Planning Tools

As the CCS 7 network grows, it becomes increasingly difficult to plan and engineer the network manually. For making decisions during the planning process, alternative CCS 7 network structures need to be analyzed from the point of view of reliability, loading of the CCS 7 links (and link sets), and network nodes. Thus, it should be possible to analyze which network structure would best meet the performance objectives. CCS 7 planning tools are required to perform these functions. Once an appropriate network structure has been determined, planning tools are again used for generating the routing tables for each network node and for dimensioning the network. While preparing the routing tables manually, there is a risk of creating circular routings, that is, a route that results in the return of messages to the originating SP. This may happen inadvertently in a complex network due to a combination of link failure conditions and the selection of alternative links as a consequence. Planning tools, with their capability to analyze all possible failure conditions, help avoid circular routing in the network.

Planning tools are commercially available from several sources. Annexure A to ITU-T recommendation Q.780 [7] lists some of the CCS 7 planning tools. The tools are typically supported on IBM PCs and provide a user friendly man-machine interface.

10.5 Selection of User Parts: Telephone User Part (TUP) versus ISDN User Part (ISUP)

Several user parts can coexist at a signaling point. The user part should be chosen on the basis of services to be offered. While choosing, it is advisable to take into account not only the currently offered services but also those likely to be offered in the next few years. By making this provision in CCS 7 well in advance, the need for frequent CCS 7 upgrades and the attendant requirement of conducting validation tests on the new implementation can be avoided.

For ISDN services, the ISUP is the user part of choice since it includes all the functions of the TUP and provides signaling control of various ISDN services. However, because the ISUP was standardized only during the CCITT study period 1984–88, earlier implementations of CCS 7 were based on TUP. To support ISDN service on the TUP, certain enhancements on the TUP were implemented as an interim measure. Because the ISUP is well positioned to support the signaling requirements of a wide range of current and future service offerings, these implementations are likely to be upgraded to the ISUP. In North America, the ISUP is used by all carriers [8].

As discussed in Chapter 4, the SCCP has been designed to

- Enhance the addressing capability of the MTP
- Provide additional functions to support connectionless and connection-oriented services

The ISUP can be a user of both the MTP and the SCCP. ISDN services typically need limited addressing capabilities and connectionless message transfer. These requirements are adequately met by the MTP, and for the support of ISDN services it may be worthwhile to avoid the additional overhead of the SCCP. In this scenario, the user-to-user supplementary service will be realized by the pass-along method. (The pass-along method was discussed in Chapter 4.)

In a situation where some of the exchanges are already operating on the basis of the TUP or its upgrades, new exchanges may be planned in one of the following ways:

- By installing both the ISUP and the TUP in the new exchanges so that new exchanges work on the basis of the ISUP with each other and on the TUP with the existing exchanges. This is an interim solution that may be followed when the existing base of exchanges with the TUP is large and there is no urgency to provide additional ISUP-based services to subscribers served by the TUP exchanges.
- By installing only the ISUP in the new exchanges and simultaneously upgrading existing exchanges from the TUP to the ISUP. This is an ideal solution, but the feasibility of implementation depends on several factors, such as the number of exchanges with the TUP, the number of new exchanges to be installed with the ISUP, the need for ISUP-based services for existing subscribers served by TUP exchanges, and the cost of upgrade from the TUP to the ISUP.

It is a good goal to install exchanges with the ISUP for supporting both telephony and the ISDN. A single-user part avoids the problems of interworking, is easy to maintain, and affords uniformity in service provisioning throughout the network.

Regarding the version of the ISUP, it is desirable that new exchanges support the ITU-T 1992 version, which, at present, is the latest standard version. For existing exchanges that support the earlier CCITT 1988 version of the ISUP, peer-to-peer interworking is possible with the exchanges using ISUP'92, since backward compatibility has been provided in the latter. It may be worthwhile, however, to upgrade exchanges with the ISUP'88 version to ISUP'92. Recognizing the continuing need for new supplementary services in the future, ITU-T recommendation Q.761 [9] furnishes guidelines to ensure compatibility of future ISUP versions to ISUP'92. Thus, ISUP'92 will remain forward compatible and will interwork with versions of the ISUP that may be specified by the ITU-T in the future.

10.6 Monitoring CCS 7 Networks

Measurement of important CCS 7–related parameters provides a useful insight into the current availability, performance, and use of the existing CCS 7 network. In addition, these measurements provide useful inputs for estimating performance of a future network arising out of expansion plans of the current network. ITU-T recommendation Q.791 [10] stipulates that the following measurements be made on an on-line basis:

- MTP signaling link performance: measurement of signaling link failures and errors (Table 1/recommendation Q.791)
- MTP signaling link availability: measurement of duration of unavailability of signaling links (Table 2/recommendation Q.791)
- MTP signaling link utilization (Table 3/recommendation Q.791)
- MTP signaling link set and route set availability (Table 4/recommendation Q.791)
- MTP adjacent signaling point status accessibility (Table 5/recommendation Q.791)
- MTP signaling link traffic distribution (Table 6/recommendation Q.791)

The ITU-T has furnished guidelines on the possible classification and use of these "raw" or "primitive" measurements to perform operational, maintenance, and administrative functions [11].

The measurements mentioned above are performed at each node of the CCS 7 network. Thus, they provide a "local view" of the status of the network. To obtain a network-wide "global view" it is useful to plan for centralized CCS 7 monitoring facilities. Such a monitoring facility may be integrated as part of the network management system or it may be planned as a separate facility dedicated for monitoring only signaling functions.

CCS 7 monitoring facilities have a variety of functions and uses. Due to the real time nature of monitoring, early warning about impending performance deterioration or CCS 7 network failures can be obtained. Network events to look for include the following:

- SPs with an abnormally high ratio of REL to IAM messages
- Frequent invoking of ISUP overload controls at one or more SPs
- MTP restarts in the network
- SPs receiving a large number of route-set-test messages
- Frequent changeover/changeback of links
- Transfer prohibited/transfer restricted events
- Level 3 link congestion events
- Links with abnormally high signaling occupancy
- Links with high link status signal unit (LSSU) counts, with high status indication busy (SIB) LSSUs or LSSUs with status indication processor outage (SIPO)
- Unbalanced loading of links within a link set

As noted earlier, where stand-alone STPs are used to create a backbone signaling network, the availability of the backbone network should be close to 100%. Monitoring functions should therefore focus more closely on this part of the network.

10.7 National CCS 7 Standards

National CCS 7 standards are generally based on ITU-T recommendations. For countries where regional standardization bodies exist (for example, in North America and Europe), regional standards are of particular interest. Regional standards on CCS 7 draw substantially on ITU recommendations but add details and clarifications, where appropriate, to ease potential problems of interworking between different implementations. Administrations in the region, if they so chose, can adopt regional standards and use them when ordering equipment and planning services. Equipment manufacturers can also base their implementations on regional standards, secure in the knowledge that only minor modifications will be needed to meet the country or administration specific requirements. Regional standards therefore play an important role for both the administrations and the equipment suppliers in the region.

For a large number of countries, particularly in the developing world, regional standardization bodies do not exist. Moreover, many countries have multiple vendors of switching systems, and to solve the existing and potential problems of CCS 7 interworking between different systems, there is an obvious requirement of national standardization based on ITU-T recommendations. The following discussion focuses on issues to consider in the formulation of national standards on CCS 7.

CCS 7 protocol recommended by ITU-T can be applied for international and national working. At various points in the recommendations, certain aspects that can be included in a national implementation are specified as "national options" or for "national use." Clearly, these aspects are outside the scope of CCS 7 implementation for international working. Therefore, it is useful to examine each of these national options and to decide about their inclusion while formulating the national standards. Equipment suppliers, if they conform to a particular version of CCS 7 recommendations, almost invariably implement all those clauses of the recommendations that are required for international working. The implementation of specific national options usually depends on the requirements of their customers, the telecommunication administrations. Therefore, all the national options specified in a national standard may not be immediately available in an implementation. As a general principle, a national option should not be included in the national standards unless its need has been clearly established.

The choice of national options in the MTP have to do with CCS 7 network aspects and do not directly affect the range of services provided to the customers. On the other hand, the features in the user parts (for example, the ISUP) are closely linked to service provisioning. In addition to mandatory parameters, ISUP messages typically include several optional parameters. As part of the standardization exercise, the optional parameters to be used for each ISUP message must be specified. Furthermore, the code for each parameter should be finalized by specifying, where necessary, the fields meant for national use.

In the following sections, some aspects that should be specified in framing national standards are discussed. Except where stated otherwise, all references are to ITU-T recommendations of 1992.

10.7.1 The method of error correction to be used in the national network should be specified: basic, PCR, or both. Terrestrial fiber-optic links are preferable. Use of satellite links should be avoided as far as possible. If a decision has been taken to use only terrestrial links, only the basic method of error correction may be specified. Where a possibility of using satellite links cannot be entirely precluded, now or in future, both the methods should be specified (recommendation Q.703).

10.7.2 When both the methods are specified, it is advisable that within a link set the same method is applied. (The reasons are explained in Section 6.6.3.) Therefore, it is desirable that the system prevent the assignment of different methods to links within a link set. It should also be possible at an SP/STP to assign the use of the basic method for some link sets and the PCR method for others. For reasons of flexibility, this should be implemented by man-machine commands.

10.7.3 For the basic method, a national option exists to retransmit an MSU that is yet to be acknowledged (Sections 5.3.3 and 11.2.3 of recommendation Q.703). Thus, a form of forward error correction has been envisaged as a national option. The application is for links with long loop delays. This option should be considered only after study of its impact on loop delays. Note that the outgoing link delays shown in Tables 10–7 to 10–9 of this chapter do not involve this option.

10.7.4 For the PCR method, the values of $N1$ and $N2$ should be assignable by man-machine command (Section 6.4 of recommendation Q.703).

10.7.5 The status field can be either one or two octets long (length indicator LI = 1 or 2). At present, only six status indications requiring the three least-significant bits, designated A, B, and C, have been specified. A national option exists to specify one more bit, designated bit D (Section 11.1.3 of recommendation Q.703). The use of this bit may be considered when signaling nodes with only 62-octet signaling information field handling capability also exist in the network. A procedure is specified in recommendation Q.701, Section 7.2.6, to prevent sending of longer messages to these nodes using the D-bit. Although it is possible to specify a status field of two octets, the second octet will remain unused, at least in the near future since even the first octet has spare bits for future use.

10.7.6 A total of eight service indicator codes, from 1001 to 1111, are available for use in the national network. Table 7–1 lists the service indicator codes for the international signaling network. Out of 16 available codes, the use of eight codes is specified. Although the allocation of these codes can be done differently in the national network, it is desirable to follow the same allocation as for the international network for the sake of uniformity. The remaining eight service codes, from 1001 to 1111, are spare in the international network. Their use can be defined in the national network for addressing additional user parts. The network indicator may also be used for special routing, for example, to permit application of transfer prohibited, transfer allowed, and signaling route set messages for a specific user part in an SP (and not for the SP as a whole). Transfer may be prohibited not for the entire SP but only when the message is for a specified user part in the SP, whereas messages destined to other user parts may continue.

10.7.7 In the subservice field (Refer to Table 7–2), the network indicator code 11 can be used to define a second national CCS 7 network. When two versions of CCS 7 exist in a national network, two CCS 7 networks may facilitate interworking between different versions of CCS 7. Thus, all CCS 7 nodes of one version can form one CCS 7 network, and nodes of another version may be included in the second CCS 7 network. In this case, the interworking of the two versions takes place only at designated nodes interconnecting the two networks.

10.7.8 There are three possible link management procedures in level 3 MTP: basic link management, automatic allocation of signaling terminals only, and automatic allocation of both signaling terminals and signaling data link. It is necessary to specify one of these for use in the national network.

10.7.9 The transfer restricted procedure is a national option in recommendation Q.704. It should be decided whether transfer restriction applies for the national network.

10.7.10 A national option exists to define multiple congestion states for the signaling link. It has to be decided whether this option is to be included in the national standards. If so, one of the two alternatives, use of multiple congestion states with congestion priority or without congestion priority, should be specified.

10.7.11 The nominal values of all level 2 and level 3 timers should be specified. These should be within the range defined in the relevant ITU-T recommendations.

10.7.12 For level 3, heading codes of all signaling management messages, service indicator codes, and subservice field codes should be furnished in the national standards.

10.7.13 As noted earlier in this chapter, it is also necessary to specify the length of the point code (14 bits or more). Furthermore, it should be specified whether the point code is structureless or structured. In the latter case, the fields constituting the point code should be defined.

10.7.14 For the ISUP, specify whether the en bloc or the overlap method of operation is to be used. Although both en bloc and overlap signaling can coexist in a given network, it is desirable from the point of view of standardization to specify one of the two methods.

10.7.15 It is also necessary to define clearly all the ISUP messages that will form part of the national standard. For each such message, the optional parameters and their coding should also be defined.

10.7.16 It should be specified whether a continuity check is to be performed. If a continuity check is specified, whether the check is on a per call basis or on a statistical basis should be indicated.

10.7.17 To prevent dual seizure during circuit selection, two methods have been specified. In one method, an opposite order of selection is used in the two exchanges. In the other method, the both-way circuits in the two exchanges are divided into two equal groups. It should be stated which method is applicable.

10.7.18 The nominal values and range of all ISUP timers should be specified.

10.7.19 The temporary trunk blocking procedure is available as a national option to reduce traffic toward an overloaded exchange. It should be decided whether this procedure is applicable.

10.7.20 An unequipped circuit identification code (UCIC) message is available for national use. It should be stated whether this message forms part of the national ISUP.

10.7.21 A list of all the supplementary services to be supported by the ISUP and the messages, parameters, and procedures used for each service should be furnished in the national standard.

10.7.22 To meet the specific requirements of individual national networks, additional messages and procedures need to be added. A mechanism to do so exists within the framework of ITU-T recommendations. Thus, a charge information message may be required in the national network for charging of calls using the ISUP call control procedure. This is necessary when the exchange responsible for metering the call does not possess the charging information. For example, in a national network, the metering may be performed in the originating local exchange. In a network consisting of a large number of local exchanges, it may not be advisable to maintain charging information for the various destinations in each local exchange. Instead, the charging tables may be provided at the toll exchanges. In this situation, the charging information needs to be conveyed by means of this message from the toll exchange to the originating local exchange. As part of the national standard, the format and procedure for charging must be defined. A charge information message is not needed when the local exchanges maintain the charging tables.

10.8 Remarks

The guidelines for formulating national standards merely illustrate some of the key areas that should be addressed as part of this activity. A clause-by-clause examination of the relevant ITU-T recommendations would reveal several other areas that need consideration in finalizing the national standards.

REFERENCES

[1] *Specifications of Signaling System No. 7. Message Transfer Part Signaling Performance.* ITU-T recommendation Q.706, rev. 1. International Telecommunication Union, 1993.

[2] *Specifications of Signaling System No. 7: Message Transfer Part. Hypothetical Signaling Reference Connection.* ITU-T recommendation Q.709, rev. 1. International Telecommunication Union, 1993.

[3] "Message transfer part signaling performance." BELLCORE Technical Reference TR-NWT-000246, chap. T.111.6, June 1991.

[4] *Specifications of Signaling System No. 7. Signaling Network Structure.* ITU-T recommendation Q.705, rev. 1. International Telecommunication Union, 1993.

[5] *Specifications of Signaling System No. 7: ISDN User Part. Performance Objectives in the Integrated Services Digital Network Application.* ITU-T recommendation Q.766, rev. 1. International Telecommunication Union, 1993.

[6] "Message transfer part signaling performance." BELLCORE Technical Reference TR-NWT-000246, chap. T.111.5, June 1991.

[7] *Specifications of Signaling System No. 7: ISDN User Part. Signaling System No. 7 Test Specification General Description.* Annexure A to ITU-T recommendation Q.780, rev. 1. International Telecommunication Union, 1993.

[8] Kuhn, P. J., C. D. Pack, and R. A. Skoog. "Common channel signaling networks: Past, present, future." IEEE Journal on Selected Areas in Communications, vol. 12, no. 3, April 1994.

[9] *Specifications of Signaling System No. 7: ISDN User Part. Functional Description of ISDN User Part of Signaling System No. 7.* ITU-T recommendation Q.761, rev. 1. International Telecommunication Union, 1993.

[10] *Specifications of Signaling System No. 7: Monitoring and Measurements for Signaling System No. 7 Networks.* CCITT Blue Book, fascicle VI.9, recommendation Q.791. International Telecommunication Union, 1989.

[11] *Guidelines for Implementing a Signaling System No. 7 Network.* International Telecommunication Union, 1991.

11 Testing in CCS 7

Acronyms

ACM	address complete message
AERM	alignment error rate monitor
ANM	answer message
ANSI	American National Standards Institute
BHCC	busy hour completed calls
BIB	backward indicator bit
BSN	backward sequence number
CBA	changeback acknowledgment
CBD	changeback declaration
CCITT	The International Telegraph and Telephone Consultative Committee
CCR	continuity check request (message)
CCS 7	CCITT common channel signaling system no. 7
CGB	circuit group blocking (message)
CGBA	circuit group blocking acknowledgment (message)
CGU	circuit group unblocking (message)
COA	changeover acknowledgment
CON	connect, a message used in ISUP protocol
COO	changeover order
CPT	compatability testing
DPC	destination point code
DSS 1	digital subscriber signaling system 1
ECA	emergency changeover acknowledgment
ECO	emergency changeover order
FIB	forward indicator bit
FISU	fill-in signal unit
FSN	forward sequence number
IAM	initial address message
ISDN	integrated services digital network
ISUP	ISDN user part
ITU-T	International Telecommunication Union-Telecommunication Standardization Sector
LIA	link inhibit acknowledgment (signal)
LIN	link inhibit (signal)
LPO	local processor outage
LSSU	link status signal unit
MSU	message signal unit
MTP	message transfer part
OPC	origination point code
PCR	preventive cyclic retransmission
REL	release (message)
RLC	release complete (message)
RSC	reset circuit (message)
RST	route set test (message)
SCCP	signaling connection control part
SI	service indicator
SIB	status indication busy
SIE	status indication emergency alignment
SIF	signaling information field
SIN	status indication normal
SIO	status indication out of alignment. Also, service information octet
SIPO	status indication processor outage
SIOS	status indication out of service
SLC	signaling link code
SLS	signaling link selection
SLT	signaling link test
SLTA	signaling link test acknowledgment (message)
SLTM	signaling link test message
SP	signaling point

continued

SSF	subservice field	TFC	transfer controlled (message)
STP	signal transfer point	TFP	transfer prohibited (message)
SU	signal unit	TUP	telephone user part
SUERM	signal unit error rate monitor	VAT	validation testing
TFA	transfer allowed (message)		

ABSTRACT

This chapter describes the testing of the message transfer part (MTP) and the integrated services digital network (ISDN) user part (ISUP) in the International Telegraph and Telephone Consultative Committee's (CCITT) common channel signaling system no. 7 (CCS 7). Various aspects covered include:

- On-line testing in CCS 7 as described in the International Telecommunication Union-Telecommunication Standardization Sector (ITU-T) recommendation Q.707
- Functional characteristics of testers needed for validation and compatibility testing
- Validation and compatibility testing of MTP levels 2 and 3
- ISUP validation and compatibility testing

11.1 Introduction

Testing in CCS 7 is performed in several situations. When a new implementation of CCS 7 is introduced in the network, its conformance to the required protocol standard must be ensured. This objective is met by validation testing. Validation tests are performed before the signaling point is put into service. For example, while introducing a new type of switching system with CCS 7 capability, an administration would perform CCS 7 validation tests to check if the implementation in the switch conforms with the national standards. Validation testing must be as comprehensive as possible so that potential problems are identified and rectified before large-scale deployment of equipment. Once validation is successfully completed, the capability of the equipment to meet the stipulated standards is confirmed; thereafter, equipment of the same design can be installed at different sites without the need for extensive testing. Thus, validation tests are performed only once. The tests, however, need to be repeated for each change in CCS 7 version. This is necessary to validate new features and to verify that the existing features remain unaffected.

After completion of validation tests, the validated signaling point (SP) is checked for proper interworking with all other implementations of CCS 7 that may be operational in the network. This is done by performing compatibility tests. Compatibility tests check for correct interworking between two implementations of CCS 7. Therefore, if several CCS 7 implementations exist in the network, compatibility tests are performed separately with each existing implementation.

The complex nature of CCS 7 protocol dictates the need for a comprehensive test schedule. In line with the partitioning of CCS 7 functional specifications into levels, separate sets of tests are performed for validation of each level. A similar approach is followed in compatibility testing. Contrary to validation testing, however, compatibility tests are performed on in-service SPs. The ITU-T recommendations on CCS 7 testing, which cover both validation and compatibility tests, were listed in Table 4–3. In Section 11.4, CCS 7 tests for both the message transfer part (MTP) and the ISDN user part (ISUP) are described. Before discussing these tests, it is useful to examine the facilities required for CCS 7 testing. This is done in the next section.

In addition to validation and compatibility tests, where the stress is on protocol verification and protocol-related interworking issues, CCS 7 tests are also performed during the normal operation of an SP. These tests are described in Section 11.3.

11.2 Testing Equipment for CCS 7

The test equipment used for CCS 7 includes CCS 7 protocol monitors, simulators, and traffic generators. The testers vary widely in their features and sophistication, depending on the testing application. Annexure A to ITU-T recommendation Q.780 [1] lists some of the commercially available CCS 7 test equipment. Without going into the details of any particular test equipment, an attempt is made here to outline the functional characteristics of the equipment needed for CCS 7 testing. This functionality may be implemented in one or more testers.

11.2.1 Monitoring Functions

A basic requirement in testing an SP is the capability to monitor the signal units generated by the signaling point (SP) under test. When connected to a signaling link, a CCS 7 monitor records the flow of signal units (SUs) on that link without disturbing the transfer of signal units between the SPs. To record the two-way flow between a pair of SPs, it is necessary to monitor both directions. The monitored information is decoded to identify the CCS 7 SUs. A monitor typically provides several options to the user. The signaling information can be displayed on-line. Additionally, it may also be saved for later analysis. Not all the SUs flowing on the link may be of interest to the user. Therefore, monitors usually provide displays with masks to give a varying degree of detail. Depending on the testing requirement, the user can create customized displays in addition to standard display options. For example:

- Display of message signal units (MSUs) and link status signal units (LSSUs) only, excluding the fill-in signal units (FISUs)
- Display of retransmitted messages only
- Time stamping of all messages
- Display of level 3 or level 4 messages only

- Display of messages with varying format details
- Display messages for calls relating to a called or calling telephone number

For customized displays, the user specifies the necessary conditions under which messages in the recorded data should be searched and displayed. Thus, although all the SUs are logged in and saved, only those that satisfy the user-defined criteria are displayed. It may sometimes be necessary to monitor a CCS 7 link for long periods, requiring saving a large amount of raw data that may be beyond the storage capacity of the monitor. To cater to such situations, the user may instruct the monitor to capture only messages that are of interest. The conditions for capture of messages are specified prior to beginning the monitoring.

Prior to monitoring the CCS 7 link, the user specifies the standard that is implemented in the SPs. The decoding, display, and saving of CCS 7 signal units by the monitor is based on this specific protocol standard. Monitors usually provide the capability to carry out these functions corresponding to the CCITT Red Book, Blue Book, and post-1988 ITU-T recommendations on CCS 7. Regional standards such as the North American and European as well as a few national standards are included. Generally, several user parts are supported. Monitors may also identify those messages that are not in conformance with the specified standards. Therefore, monitors can be used to a certain extent to detect cases of nonconformance in an implementation.

Depending on their sophistication, monitors may have the capability of monitoring one or more signaling links. The statistical information concerning the monitored link(s) usually includes the following:

- Number of MSUs transferred per second
- Fill-in signal unit (FISU) and link status signal unit (LSSU) count per second
- Link occupancy, in erlangs
- Number of retransmissions in either direction

Monitors may also be employed in routine troubleshooting and maintenance of CCS 7 networks. Another application is in verifying the interworking of digital subscriber signaling system 1 (DSS 1) and CCS 7 protocols. For ISDN calls, the DSS 1 and CCS 7 messages may be monitored simultaneously to verify conformance to ITU-T recommendation Q.699 [2].

11.2.2 Simulation Functions

The test equipment performing simulation of CCS 7 protocols is referred to as a CCS 7 simulator. It replaces a signaling entity—for example, an SP—insofar as the protocol actions are concerned. It performs protocol functions according to a specified CCS 7 protocol standard. Simulation of level 2 and level 3 functions, such as signaling connection control part (SCCP) and user parts such as telephone user part (TUP) and ISUP, are normally included.

CCS 7 simulators are necessary testing tools for CCS 7 validation and compatibility tests. A single piece of equipment may incorporate one or more SP simulators, possibly with CCS 7 monitoring capabilities.

As for monitors, the CCS 7 simulation may be performed according to various international, regional, or national standards. Commercial simulators typically provide options of conformance to the CCITT Red Book and Blue Book and to ITU-T's 1993 version of CCS 7 protocol. Among regional standards, the American National Standards Institute (ANSI), BELLCORE, and European standards may be included. To tailor the simulator to include national variants, programming facilities are generally available.

Simulators may also be required to generate incorrect CCS 7 messages under the control of a test sequence. This ability to perform incorrect protocol actions is necessary for several validation and compatibility tests, as will be noticed in Section 11.4.

Simulators may also provide preprogrammed test sequences that may be readily applied to an SP whose conformance has to be verified. For example, for level 2 and level 3 testing, simulators may be preprogrammed to conduct tests specified in ITU-T recommendations Q.781 [3] and Q.782 [4], respectively. This eliminates the need for programming individual test scenarios. Moreover, to check for conformance to national options for which test scenarios may not be available, facilities for programming user-specified test scenarios are also provided.

A range of simulators are commercially available. However, the complete range of capabilities necessary to perform validation testing of MTP levels 2 and 3, SCCP, and the various user parts is usually available only in more sophisticated and expensive simulators.

11.3 On-Line Signaling Link Test Procedure

An on-line signaling test procedure is described in ITU-T recommendation Q.707 [5]. Corresponding BELLCORE standards are provided in TR-NWT-000246 [6]. Recall the signaling link activation procedure described in Section 7.5.2. As part of the procedure to perform link activation, following successful initial alignment, a signaling link test is carried out. Only upon the successful completion of this test is the link brought into service. The purpose of the test is to verify the mapping of signaling link code (SLC) to the physical link for the SPs at both ends of the link. Any corruption in the mapping is detected by the test. The signaling link test should also be periodically performed on signaling links already in service. The periodicity is determined by timer T2, which is kept in the range of 30 to 90 seconds.

The signaling link test (SLT) employs two messages, the signaling link test message (SLTM) and the signaling link test acknowledgment (SLTA) message. These messages are classified as signaling network testing and maintenance messages with the service indicator (SI) code of 0001. (Refer to Table 7–1.) Under this classification, only these two messages have been specified so far. For testing purposes, the CCS 7 protocol stack has an MTP testing user part at level 4. The messages are generated by this user part. The format of the messages is shown in Figure 11–1.

The SP initiating the signaling link test sends the SLT message on the signaling link under test. Simultaneously, timer T1, which has a range of 4 to 12 seconds, is started. As

			DCBA	0001		
Test Pattern	Length Indicator (n)	Spare	Heading Code H1	Heading Code H0	Label	
$n \times 8$	4	4	4	4	32	Bits

Notes:

1. The length indicator n gives the number of octets in the test pattern; n is in the range of 1 to15.
2. The heading code H1 distinguishes between the SLTM and SLTA as follows:

   D C B A

   0 0 0 1 Signaling link test message (SLTM)
   0 0 1 0 Signaling link test acknowledgment (SLTA) message
3. The label consists of three fields:
   Origination point code (OPC): 14 bits
   Destination point code (DPC): 14 bits
   Signaling link code (SLC): 4 bits

Figure 11–1 Format for SLTM and SLTA.

seen in Figure 11–1, the message contains a test pattern. The test pattern is not specified in ITU-T recommendations, and different implementations may use different test patterns. The SP at the other end of the link sends the SLTA message with the same test pattern as that received in the SLTM. BELLCORE recommends that the acknowledgment message must be sent on the same link, that is, the link under test. ITU-T recommendations, however, specify that the acknowledgment message be routed over the signaling link corresponding to the SLC contained in the SLTM. Therefore, the link used for returning the acknowledgment message may or may not be the same as the link under test.

The SLT is taken as passed by the SP that initiated the test if all the conditions mentioned below are satisfied in the received SLTA:

- The SLC in the SLTA correctly identifies the physical link on which the acknowledgment message has been received and is identical to the SLC in the SLT message sent earlier.
- The origination point code (OPC) correctly identifies the SP at the other end of the link.
- The test pattern in the SLTA matches the one sent in the SLTM.

The test is considered to have failed if the above criteria are not met or if the SLTA message is not received within time T1 of sending the SLTM (expiry of timer T1). In case of failure, the test is repeated once more. If the SLT test is being applied on a link following activation, then the link continues to stay out of service after a second failure and the management system is informed. A successful completion of the test results in bringing the link into service.

When the SLT test is performed periodically on an in-service link, the course of action to be followed in the event of failure of the test is not specified [5,6].

11.4 Validation and Compatibility Testing

Validation and compatibility testing for conformance to ITU-T recommendations is described for the following:

- Level 2 MTP testing (Section 11.4.1)
- Level 3 MTP testing (Section 11.4.2)
- ISUP testing (Section 11.4.3)

11.4.1 Level 2 MTP Testing

This description is based on ITU-T recommendation Q.781, which specifies the test sequences necessary for validation and compatibility testing of level 2 functions of an SP according to ITU-T recommendation Q.703. The tests are specified in ITU-T recommendation Q.781 under the following classification:

- Link state control for expected signal units/orders (35 tests, numbered 1.1 to 1.35)
- Link state control for unexpected signal units/orders (eight tests, 2.1 to 2.8)
- Transmission failure testing (eight tests, 3.1 to 3.8)
- Processor outage control (three tests, 4.1 to 4.3)
- SU delimitation, alignment, error detection, and correction (five tests, 5.1 to 5.5)
- Signal unit error rate monitor (SUERM) check (four tests, 6.1 to 6.4)
- Alignment error rate monitor (AERM) check (four tests, 7.1 to 7.4)
- Transmission and reception control (basic method of error correction) (13 tests, 8.1 to 8.13)
- Transmission and reception control (preventive cyclic retransmission, or PCR, method of error correction) (13 tests, 9.1 to 9.13)
- Congestion control (three tests, 10.1 to 10.3)

The test configuration for level 2 testing is shown in Figure 11–2. SP A is the SP whose level 2 is under test. SP A may have only SP functionality, only signal transfer point (STP) functionality, or a combination of the two. The level 2 tests to be performed

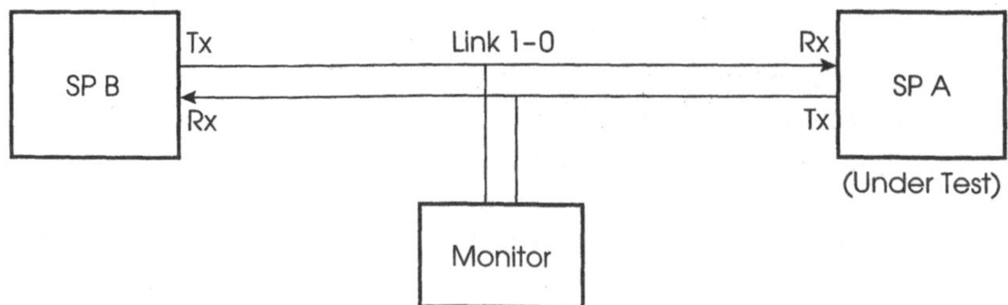

Figure 11–2 Level 2 test configuration.

are identical for all three cases. SP A is connected by a single link to SP B. SP B may be a simulator performing level 2 simulation functions according to the standard against which SP A is to be tested (in this case, ITU-T recommendation Q.703). Alternatively, SP B may be a digital exchange or a stand-alone signal transfer point (STP) whose level 2 functions have been tested earlier for conformance.

To test the level 2 functions of SP A adequately, it is necessary that SP B include capabilities of generating and receiving a certain abnormal sequence of signal units. Examples include SUs with more than seven 1's between the opening and closing flag, MSUs longer than the maximum length, MSUs shorter than the minimum length, and FISUs with an abnormal backward sequence number (BSN). Commercial simulators generally incorporate the capability to generate abnormal SUs.

In addition, it is necessary to monitor the signaling link between the SP under test and the simulator. This capability may be integrated in SP B; alternatively, a separate monitor may be used on the link.

The ITU-T recommendations use a tabular format, shown in Figure 11–3, to specify various tests. The format is common to tests for level 2, level 3, and different user parts.

From among a large number of tests prescribed for level 2, a few tests are described in the next section by way of illustration. The test numbers indicated in parentheses refer to recommendation Q.781.

11.4.1.1 Level 2 Test Examples

EXAMPLE 11-1

This test checks that the CCS 7 terminal equipment enters the correct state upon power-up (test 1.1). This test is recommended both for validation testing (VAT) and compatibility testing (CPT). Refer to Figure 11–4.

Test Number:	Page:
Reference:	
Title:	
Subtitle:	
Purpose:	
Pretest Conditions:	
Configuration:	Type of Test:
Expected Signal Unit Sequence:	
Test Description:	

Figure 11–3 Format for specifying CCS 7 tests.

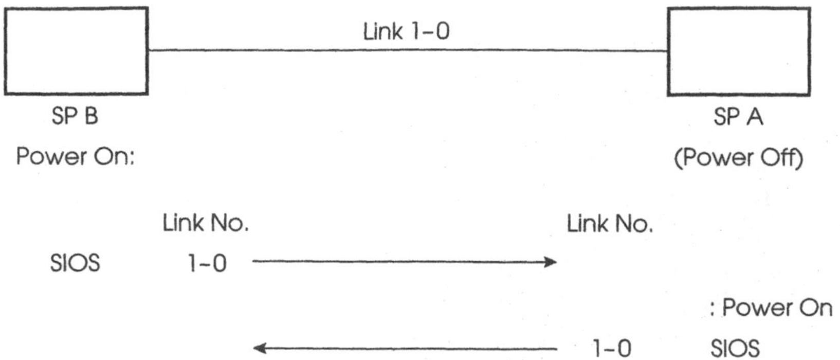

Figure 11–4 Expected SU sequence for test 1.1.

As mentioned in Section 6.7, the signaling terminal upon "power on" is expected to continuously send LSSUs with the status indication out of service (SIOS). Furthermore, upon power on, the values of forward indicator bit (FIB) and backward indicator bit (BIB) should be equal to 1, and the backward sequence number (BSN) and forward sequence number (FSN) must equal 127 (HEX 7F).

First, the power supply to the CCS 7 equipment is kept "on" at SP B while SP A is powered off. The link between the SPs is monitored. LSSUs containing status indication out of service (SIOS) flow only in one direction, SP B to SP A. No signal units are expected in the reverse direction. Then, the power at SP A is turned on. As a consequence, SIOS must be received continuously in both directions with the contents indicating FSN = BSN = 127 and FIB = BIB = 1 for each SIOS. Figure 11–4 shows the expected signal unit sequence for this test.

EXAMPLE 11-2

This test checks the "not aligned" timer T2 (test 1.2). This test is prescribed both for VAT and CPT. Refer to Figure 11–5.

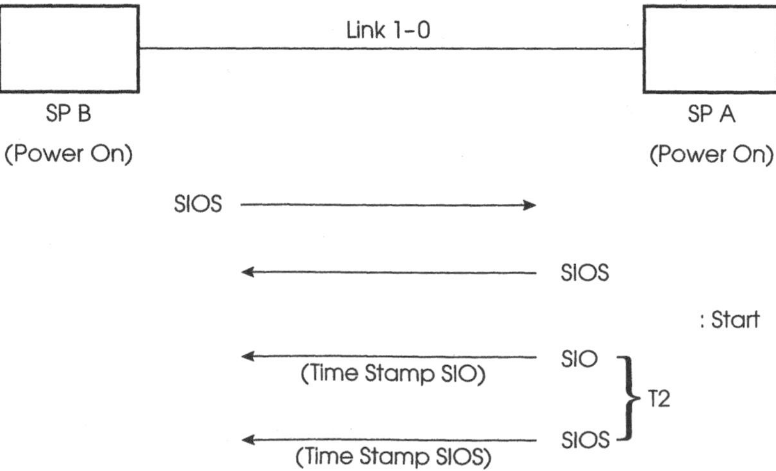

Figure 11–5 Expected SU sequence for test 1.2.

The value of timer T2 must be in the range of 5 to 150 seconds (Table 6–1). While the link is out of service, with SIOS flowing in both directions, a "start" is given at SP A. This should lead to the sending of a status indication out of alignment (SIO) by SP A and the starting of timer T2.

As stated earlier in this chapter, CCS 7 monitors can time stamp the signal units flowing on the link. The time stamp of the first SIO sent by SP A indicates when timer T2 starts.

SP B continues to send SIOS since a "start" is not given at SP B. After some time, timer T2 expires at SP A, which results in the sending of SIOS by SP A. The time stamp of the first SIOS in the A to B direction indicates the expiry of timer T2. Thus, by knowing the absolute times of the starting and expiry of timer T2, the value of timer T2 can be computed and checked against the permissible range.

EXAMPLE 11-3

This test checks for aligned timer T3 (test 1.3). This test is used only during validation testing. The expected signal sequence is shown in Figure 11–6. Notice that to make timer T3 expire at SP A, LSSUs containing SIO are sent continuously from SP B. The measured value of timer T3 must be in the range of 1 to 1.5 seconds.

EXAMPLE 11-4

This test checks the alignment ready timer T1 and the proving period timer T4 (normal proving) (test 1.4). This test is applicable to validation testing only. The expected signal unit sequence is shown in Figure 11–7. After normal proving is completed at SP A, timer T1 is started and FISUs are sent continuously to SP B. To force the expiry of timer T1 at SP A, continuous transmission of LSSUs containing status indication normal alignment (SIN) is maintained at SP B. The measured value of timer T4 must be in the range of 7.5 to 9.5 seconds (nominal value of 8.2 seconds), whereas timer T1 must be in the range of 40 to 50 seconds.

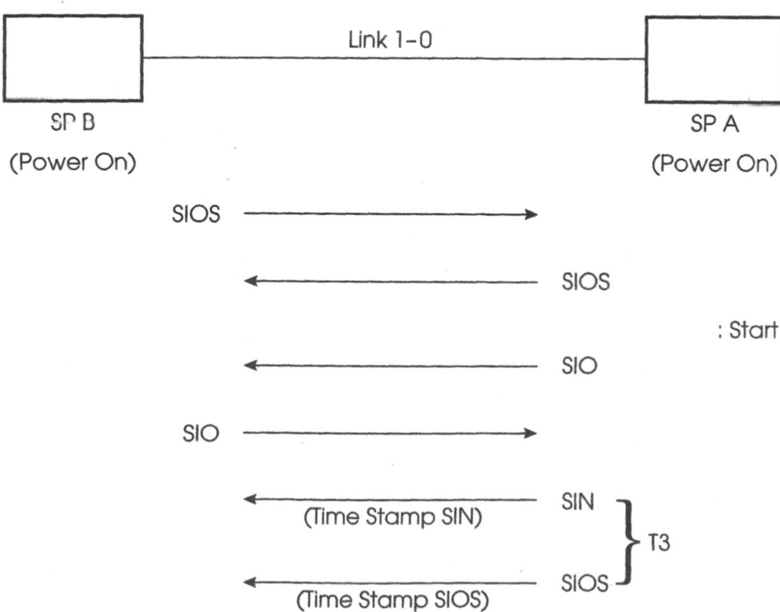

Figure 11–6 Expected SU sequence for test 1.3.

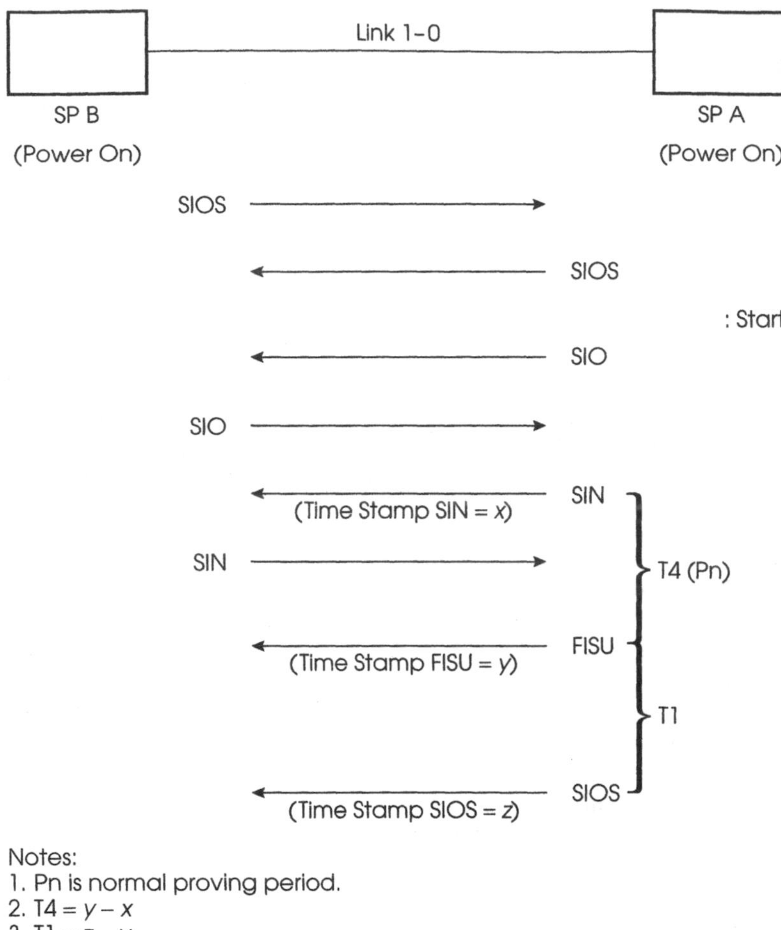

Figure 11–7 Expected SU sequence for test 1.4.

EXAMPLE 11-5

This test checks the normal alignment procedure (test 1.5). Beginning from the link out of service state, an attempt is made to bring the link into service. The signal unit sequence is identical to that shown in Figure 6–8. The test is successful if the link enters and remains in the in-service state. This test is prescribed for both validation and compatibility testing.

EXAMPLE 11-6

This test checks the emergency alignment procedure and the value of timer T4 when the emergency is set at both ends of the link (test 1.21). This test is similar to the test described in Example 5 except that an emergency condition is set at both ends of the link. Consequently, LSSUs containing status indication emergency alignment (SIE) are expected to be exchanged on the link during emergency proving. The value of timer T4 is measured to ensure that it corresponds to the emergency proving time (400 to 600 ms). The test sequence is shown in Figure 11–8.

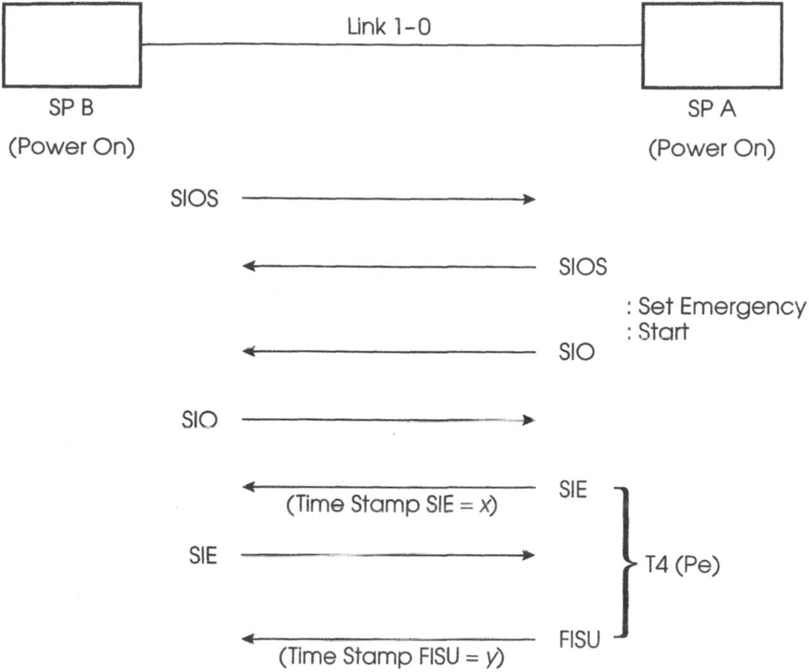

Figure 11–8 Expected SU sequence for test 1.21.

EXAMPLE 11-7

This test checks the emergency alignment procedure when an emergency is set at the other end and the SP under test perceives normal condition (test 1.22).

The alignment should be performed using emergency proving, with LSSUs containing SIN sent by SP A and LSSUs containing SIE sent by SP B. This test is performed only during validation. The expected SU sequence is shown in Figure 11–9.

EXAMPLE 11-8

In this and the following example, two tests relating to the effect of the stop command during the initial alignment procedure are described. Figure 6–7 showed that as top command during not aligned and aligned states results in the entry to the idle state in both cases. These cases correspond to tests 1.25 and 1.26, respectively.

The signal unit sequence for the first case is shown in Figure 11–10. Timer T2 is started at SP A when it sends the first LSSU containing SIO. SP B continues to send LSSUs containing SIOS. Before the expiry of timer T2, a stop command is given at SP A. This should result in SP A sending LSSUs containing SIOS on the link. The test is prescribed both for validation and compatibility testing.

In the second case, an aligned state is reached at SP A on the receipt of an LSSU containing SIO from SP B. Timer T3 is started at SP A, and it repeatedly sends SIN on the link. Before the expiry of timer T3 (1 to 1.5 seconds), a stop command is given at SP A. This should result in SP A sending LSSUs containing SIOS on the link. The test is prescribed only for validation testing. The expected signal unit sequences are shown in Figure 11–11.

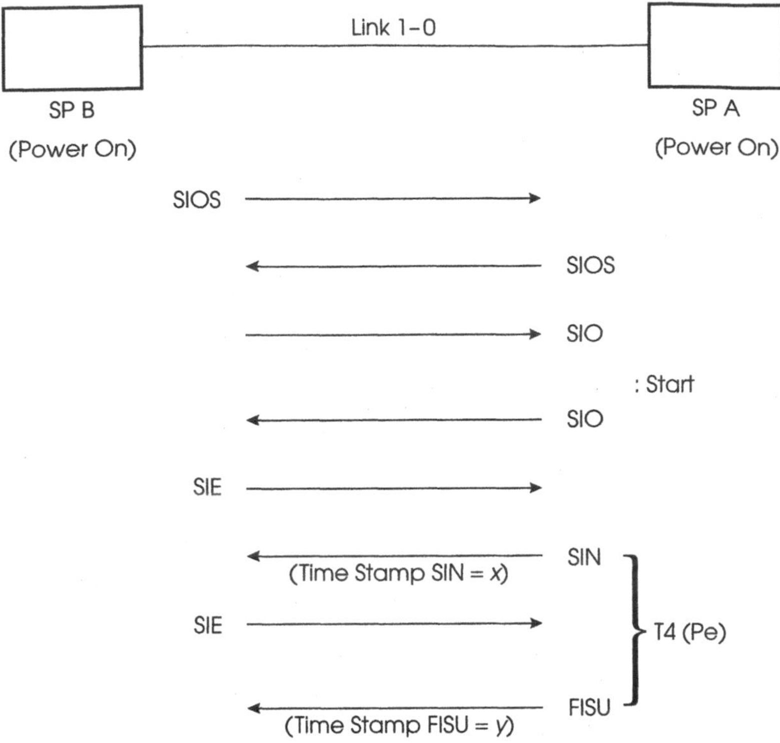

Figure 11–9 Expected SU sequence for test 1.22.

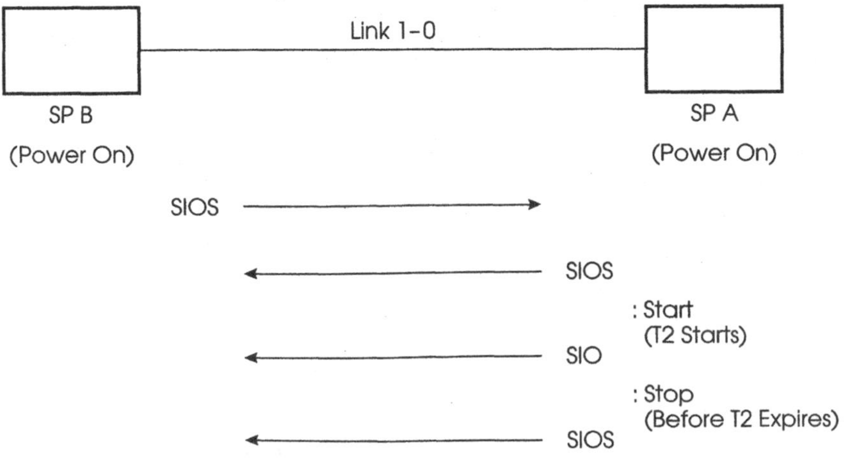

Figure 11–10 Expected SU sequence for test 1.25.

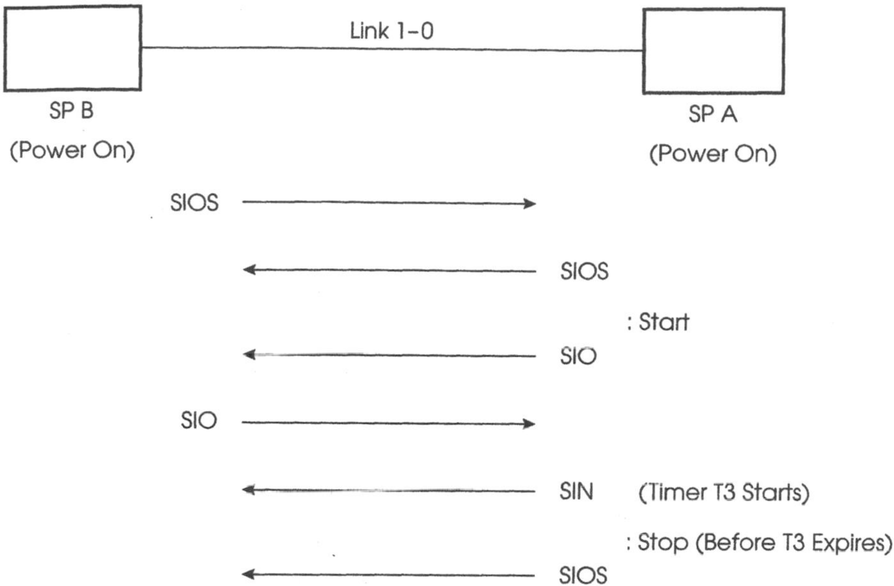

Figure 11–11 Expected SU sequence for test 1.26.

EXAMPLE 11-9

This test checks that (1) any unexpected signal units received by the SP while it is in an aligned state are ignored and (2) the level 2 ignores unexpected orders received from level 3 (test 2.5).

Commencing from the out-of-service state, the link is brought into the aligned ready state. The signal units expected at SP A are SIN, since proving of the link is continuing at SP B. As part of this test, however, unexpected LSSUs consisting of a status indication busy (SIB) and an aberrant LSSU are sent by SP B. This should have no impact, and SP A should continue to send FISUs.

To further check that the reception of unexpected orders has no impact on SP A, the following actions are taken at SP A:

- Set emergency
- Clear emergency
- Clear local processor outage (LPO)
- Start (if the link has gone out of service due to expiry of timer T6)

SP A should continue sending FISUs. Figure 11–12 shows the signal unit sequences.

EXAMPLE 11-10

This example illustrates some of the tests that may be performed to check that the link goes out of service in response to a transmission failure.

Typically, a tester can be programmed to create a transmission failure condition. Programmed means of link restoration is also provided by the tester because certain tests require a break in the transmission link only for a specified duration. In the test setup of this example, SP B is programmed to create a transmission failure condition. In this situation, SP B stops sending SUs on the link. The signal unit error rate monitor (SUERM) in SP A should detect the transmission failure condition created at SP B and take the link out of service by sending LSSUs containing SIOS toward SP B.

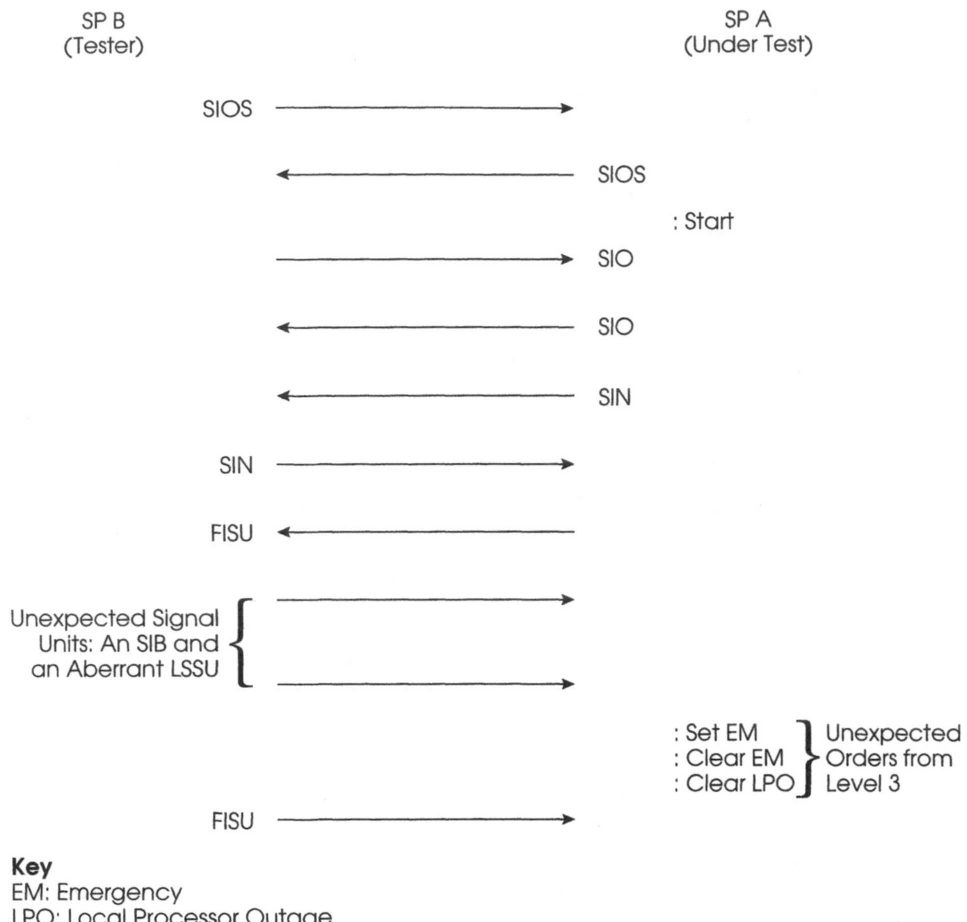

Figure 11–12 Signal unit sequence for Example 11–9 (test 2.5).

Figure 11–13 shows the signal unit sequence when the transmission failure is created in an aligned ready state. This test is prescribed only for validation testing.

The signal unit sequence for a transmission failure created during the in service state of the link is shown in Figure 11–14. This test is prescribed for both validation and compatibility testing.

Another test, performed only during validation, relates to transmission failure when a processor outage occurs at SP A (test 3.7). Refer to Figure 11–15.

EXAMPLE 11–11

This test checks the ability to perform correctly when a local processor outage occurs while the link is in service. This test is carried out only during validation (test 4.1).

As explained in Section 6.8, if a processor outage occurs while the link is in service, then an LSSU with status indication processor outage (SIPO) should be transmitted on the link and messages received from the other SP should be discarded. When the processor outage ceases, transmission of FISUs and MSUs should be resumed by the other SP (SP A). This test verifies the proper execution of these functions by SP A. The message sequence is shown in Figure 11–16.

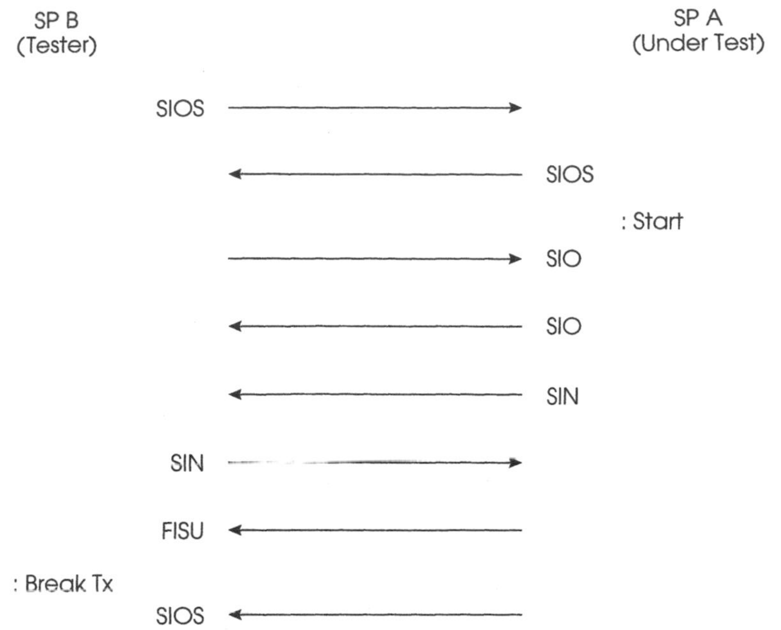

Figure 11–13 Signal unit sequence for transmission failure during an aligned ready state (test 3.1).

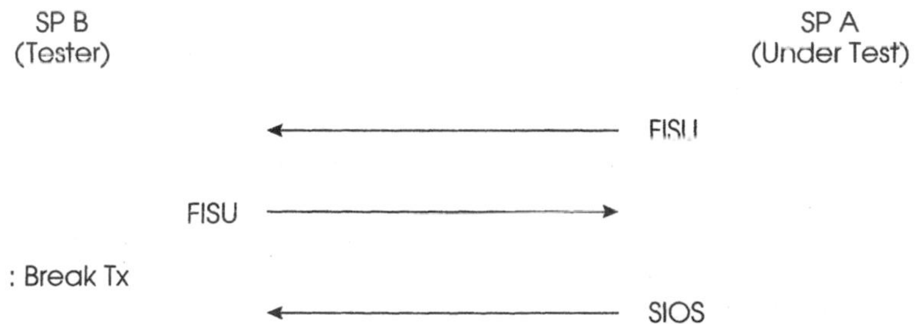

Figure 11–14 Signal unit sequence for transmission failure during an in service state (test 3.5).

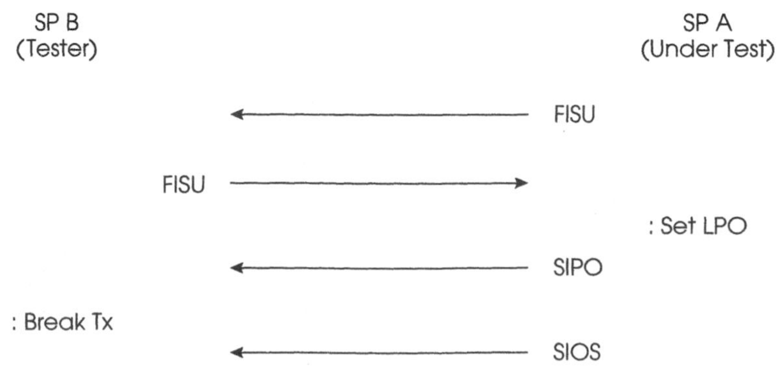

Figure 11–15 Signal unit sequence for transmission failure during processor outage at an SP under test (test 3.7).

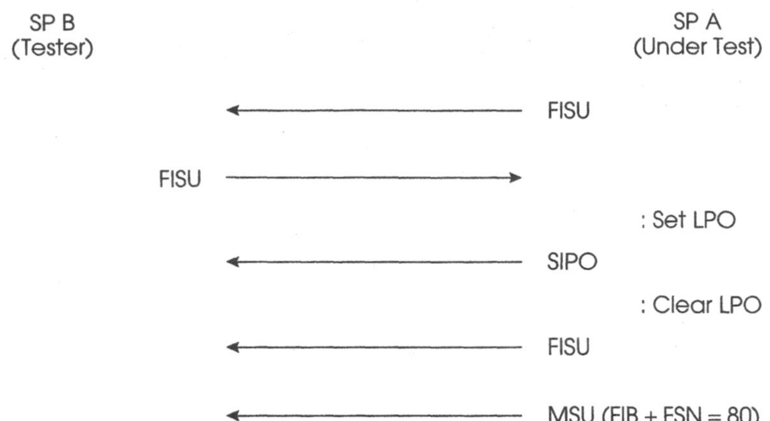

Figure 11–16 Signal unit sequence for setup and clearing of processor outage at an SP under test (test 4.1).

EXAMPLE 11-12

This example describes tests related to signal unit delimitation, alignment, and error detection.

A corrupt message signal unit (MSU) containing seven consecutive 1's is generated by the tester and sent to the SP under test (SP A) to verify that the error is detected and the MSU is discarded by SP A (test 5.1). SP A should then enter the octet counting mode. (Refer to Sections 6.4 and 6.9.1. The expected signal unit sequence for this test is shown in Figure 11–17. If the corrupt MSU is discarded by SP A, then the BSN in the FISU sent immediately following the receipt of the corrupt MSU should remain unchanged. A correct FISU is sent next by the tester. Upon receipt of the correct FISU, the SP A should leave the octet counting mode, and the link should remain in the in service state. This test is prescribed for validation testing only.

Similarly, tests are prescribed wherein the tester sends an MSU corrupted in two different ways, namely, an MSU longer than the maximum permissible length (test 5.2) and shorter than the minimum length (test 5.3).

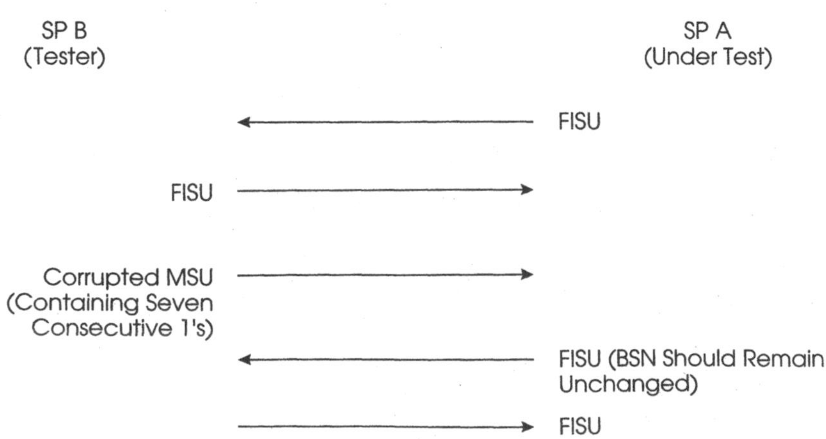

Figure 11–17 Signal unit sequence on receipt of an MSU with seven consecutive 1's at an SP under test (test 5.1).

EXAMPLE 11-13

As long as the signal unit error rate is equal to or better than 1 in 256 (refer to Figure 6–10), the link should remain in service. This is verified by sending FISUs generated by the tester with one corrupt FISU generated in every 256 FISUs (test 6.1). The value of SUERM is expected to remain unchanged at SP A, and the link should continue to remain in service. The expected message sequence is shown in Figure 11–18. This test is prescribed for validation testing only.

Another test to check the SUERM is to send FISUs that are corrupted at a marginally increased rate of 1 error in 254 to SP A. In this case, the value of SUERM should eventually equal 64. Assuming that SUERM is 0 at the beginning of the test, the link should be put out of service after about 8,192 FISUs (test 6.2). If every FISU sent by the tester is corrupted, then the link should go out of service after the transmission of 64 FISUs (test 6.3).

EXAMPLE 11-14

Recall the operation of the alignment error rate monitor (AERM) described in Section 6.9.2. AERM is used during proving of the link and is incremented each time an LSSU is received in error. During normal proving, if fewer than four corrupted LSSUs are received, then the proving is successful. To test this capability, fewer than four corrupt LSSUs are generated by the tester during the normal proving of the link (test 7.1). The expected test sequence is shown in Figure 11–19.

To check the operation of AERM, three more tests are prescribed in Q.781. One test is with an error rate equal to the normal threshold (that is, equal to four), for normal proving. In this case, when SP A receives the fourth LSSU in error, it should abort the current proving and begin a second proving. Because no corrupt LSSUs are sent by the tester during the second proving, the second proving should be successful and the link should be aligned at SP A (test 7.2). Another test involves increasing the corrupted LSSUs generated by the tester above the normal threshold during each proving period. It is checked that SP A undergoes five provings (M = 5, as indicated in Section 6.9.2) before the link is put out of service (test 7.3). The last test in this category is to test the operation of AERM during emergency proving (test 7.4).

EXAMPLE 11-15

In this example, tests on generation and receipt of MSUs in the basic error correction method are discussed.

A total of 13 tests are prescribed in recommendation Q.781 (tests 8.1 to 8.13). In this example, test 8.3 is described. This test is designed to check that MSUs are buffered when acknowledgments are not received from the other end. The steps in the test are as follows:

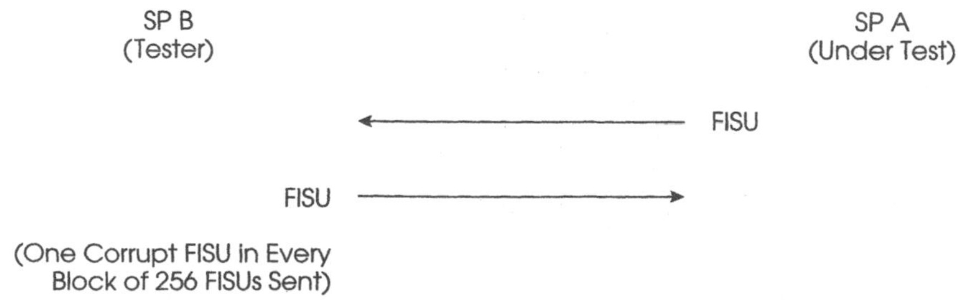

Figure 11–18 Signal unit sequence to check the SUERM of an SP under test at a signal unit error rate of 1 in 256 (test 6.1).

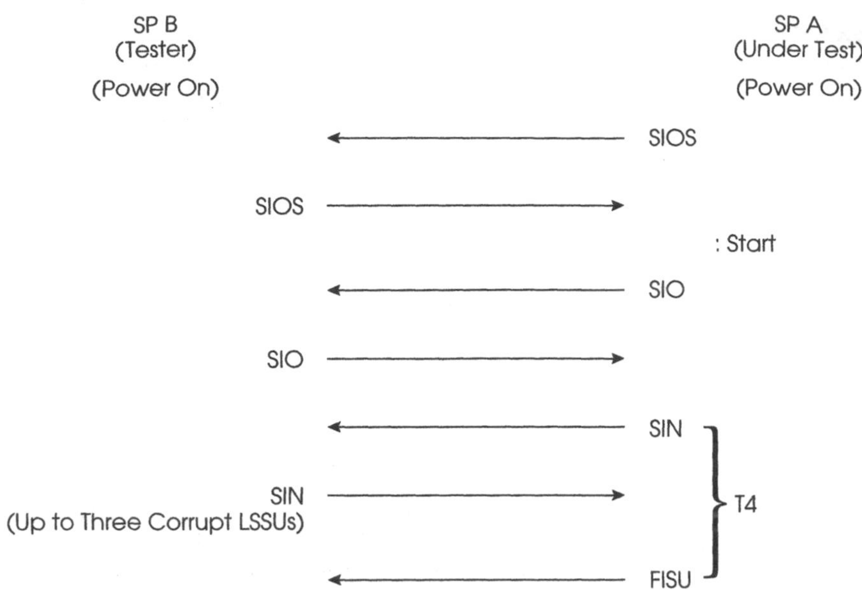

Figure 11–19 Expected SU sequence for test 7.1.

- Bring the link between SP A and SP B into service.
- Send as many MSUs from SP A as required to fill the retransmission buffer. These MSUs must be sent for a period well within the value of timer T7. To do so, a rate of 100 MSUs/second is specified. (Timer T7 has a range of 0.5 to 2 seconds. Refer to Section 6.6.1.2 and Table 6–1.)
- No acknowledgments, either positive or negative, are sent by the tester (SP B) for the received messages. To avoid the expiry of timer T7 at SP A, the tester is programmed to send a negative acknowledgment for the first message before T7 could expire at SP A.
- All unacknowledged messages should be saved in the retransmission buffer at SP A. On receipt of the negative acknowledgment for the first message, all message should be retransmitted by SP A.

The expected signal unit sequence for the test is shown in Figure 11–20.

EXAMPLE 11-16

In this example, tests to check the response to the expiry of timer T7 for the basic and PCR error correction methods are briefly discussed.

For the basic method (test 8.12), an MSU is generated at SP A while the link is in service, and no acknowledgment is sent by the tester for this MSU. As a result, timer T7 expires at SP A. It is checked that upon the expiry of timer T7, the link is taken out of service by SP A by sending an SIOS.

A similar procedure is followed for the test corresponding to the PCR method (test 9.11). No positive acknowledgment is sent by the tester, and following the expiry of timer T7, SIOS should be sent by SP A.

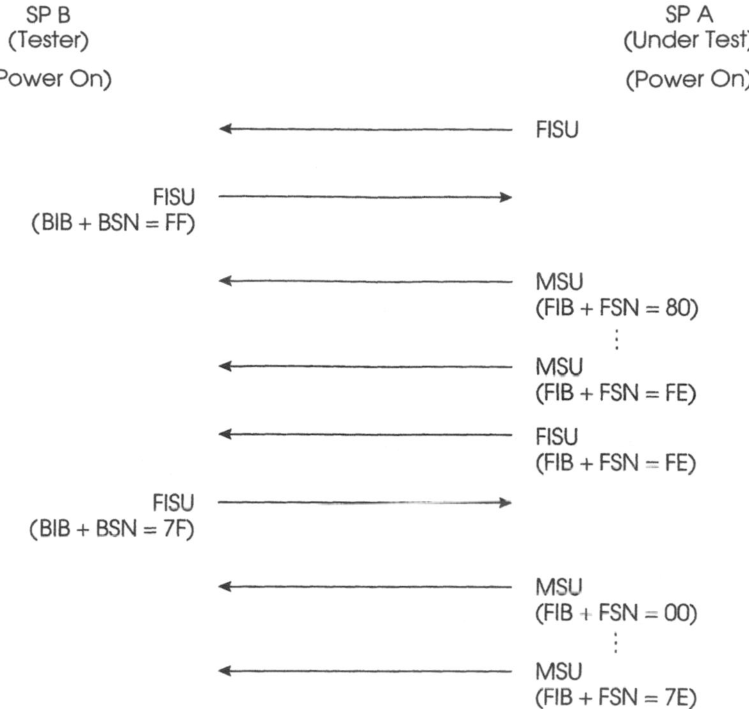

Figure 11–20 Message sequence to check buffering of MSUs (test 8.3).

EXAMPLE 11-17

Three tests are specified to check the congestion (or flow) control procedures in level 2 (tests 10.1 to 10.3). Refer to Section 6.10 for flow control procedures at level 2.

Test 10.1 is designed to check the behavior of SP A under congestion onset and congestion abatement conditions. Congestion is created, and it is checked that SP A sends an SIB with a periodicity of timer T5. Upon the clearing of the congestion, sending of SIB should be stopped. The expected signal unit sequence for the test is shown in Figure 11–21. This test is prescribed for validation testing only.

Test 10.2 checks that SP A restarts timer T7 every time an SIB is received from the other end. The test is carried out for a time interval of less than T6 so that the expiry of timer T6 does not occur at SP A.

Test 10.3 checks the value of timer T6. For this purpose, LSSUs with SIB are sent by SP B until timer T6 expires at SP A. When timer T6 expires, the link should be put out of service at SP A.

11.4.2 Level 3 Tests

Level 3 tests are prescribed in ITU-T recommendation Q.782. All tests are validation tests; a subset is prescribed for compatibility testing. Each test relates to one of the following three cases:

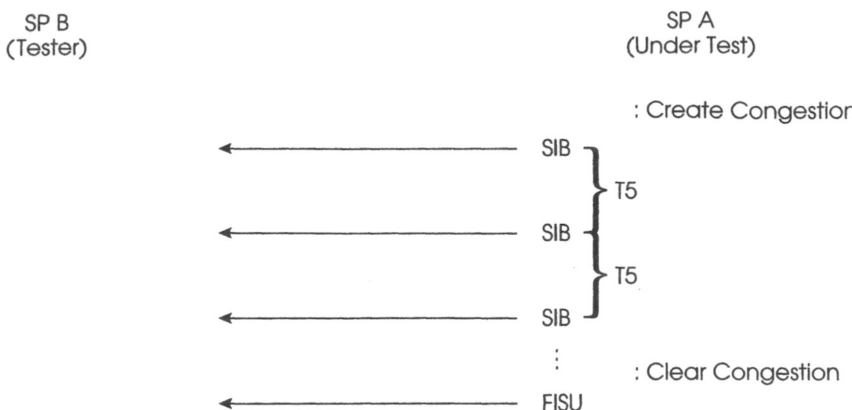

Figure 11–21 Signal unit sequence to check congestion onset and abatement (test 10.1).

1. Test node has only SP functions (SP)
2. Test node has only STP functions (STP)
3. Test node has both SP and STP functions (all)

Since level 3 relates to network functions, many level 3 tests require multiple SPs in the test configuration. The node under test is connected to the test configuration. Four configurations (designated configurations A through D) are specified. For every configuration, SP A is the signaling node under test, and the other SPs (designated SPs B, C, D, E, and F) represent the test environment. The other SPs in the configuration may be actual SPs or may be simulated using CCS 7 simulators. The rules for routing signaling traffic for each configuration have also been specified in recommendation Q.782 by means of routing tables. The configurations and the associated routing tables are described in the next section, along with a few examples of level 3 tests.

The traffic for performing level 3 tests is not generated by user parts such as the ISUP or the TUP. Instead, test traffic is generated, typically by the MTP testing user part. Refer to Figure 11–22(a). The format of the test traffic messages is shown in Figure 11–22(b).

11.4.2.1 Level 3 Test Examples

Level 3 tests are specified under the 13 categories listed in Table 11–1.

Out of the large number of tests specified for level 3 testing, a few tests are described in this section to serve as illustrative examples. The test numbers indicated in the parentheses refer to recommendation Q.782. The "TRAFFIC" in the figures associated with the following examples relates to a sequence of messages coded according to Figure 11–22(b).

EXAMPLE 11-18

The purpose of this test is to check for successful activation of the first signaling link (test 1.1). The test is prescribed for both validation and compatibility testing and may be applied to test all types of SPs. Configuration A, shown in Figure 11–23, is used. Only one link in link set 1 (L1) is employed for this test.

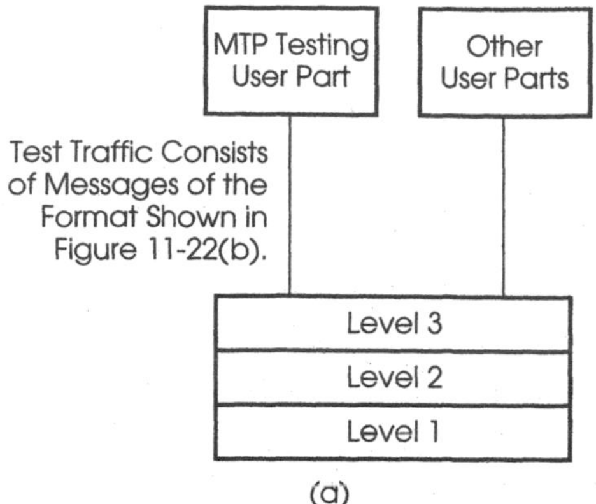

Order of Transmission ←

Up to 272 Octets	7	9	32	4	14	14	8 Bits
DATA	Spare	L	N	SLS	OPC	DPC	SIO

Notes:

1. Before transmission on the signaling link, level 2 of the traffic generating node prefixes the flag, BSN, BIB, FSN, FIB, and LI fields and suffixes the check field.
2. SI in SIO is coded 1000. SSF can have any value.
3. The label consisting of the DPC, OPC, and SLS corresponds to nodes A, B, C, D, E, or F, depending on the signaling relation in the test.
4. N indicates the serial number of the message in the test traffic. The number is useful for ready identification of message missequencing during testing.
5. L indicates the length of the data field in octets.
6. The spare field is coded with all zeros.
7. The DATA field corresponds to the SIF in ISUP messages. It has a maximum length of 272 octets. The field is filled with all zeros.

(b)

Figure 11–22 (a) MTP testing user part, generation, and reception of test traffic; (b) format of test traffic messages.

The procedure for link activation was described in Section 7.5.2. The signaling link test, which is part of the activation procedure, was discussed earlier in this chapter (Section 11.3).

After the link reaches active state, the SLTM and SLTA messages are exchanged between SP A and SP B for testing the link. Upon successful completion of the link test, the link should become available. Up to this point, the test is common for both validation and compatibility. Test traffic is now applied on the link. For the compatibility test, the signaling relation is between SP A and SP B. For the validation test, the signaling relation is established between SP A and SP C and SP B acting as an STP. In either case, the correct reception of messages is checked; that is, messages should not be lost, duplicated, or missequenced.

The test is repeated with different SLC values. Figure 11–24 shows the expected message sequence.

Table 11-1 Classsification of Level 3 Tests

TEST CATEGORY	NUMBER OF TESTS	TEST CONFIGURATION
Signaling link management	3	A
Signaling message handling	16	A, B, C
Changeover	21	A, B
Changeback	11	A, B
Forced rerouting	1	B
Controlled rerouting	1	B
Managment inhibiting	27	A
Signaling traffic flow control	4	A, C
Signaling route management	11	D
MTP restart	10	A, B, D
Traffic test	1	C
Signaling link test	6	A
Invalid messages	12	A

EXAMPLE 11-19

This test illustrates signaling message handling (test 2.5.1).

This test checks the load sharing between two link sets when all the link sets and routes are available. Configuration B, shown in Figure 11–25, is used. The test is specified for both validation and compatibility testing.

For compatibility testing, a signaling relationship exists between SP A and SP E. The routing label in the test traffic messages therefore contain the following values:

OPC = A
DPC = E (for the A to E direction)

and

OPC = E
DPC = A (for the E to A direction)

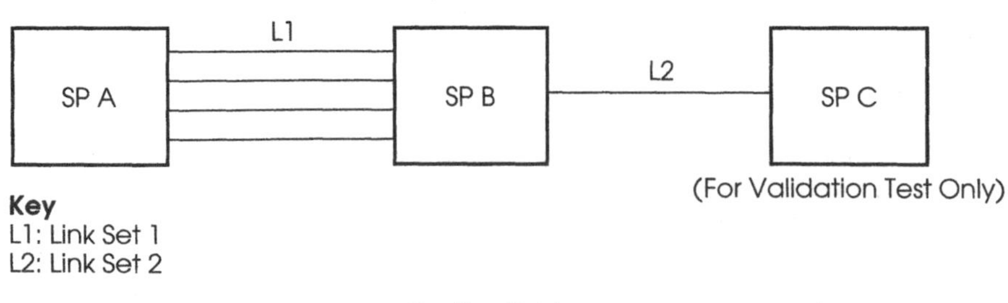

Routing Table

	A	B	C
A	—	L1	L1
B	L1	—	L2
C	L2	L2	—

Figure 11–23 Configuration A.

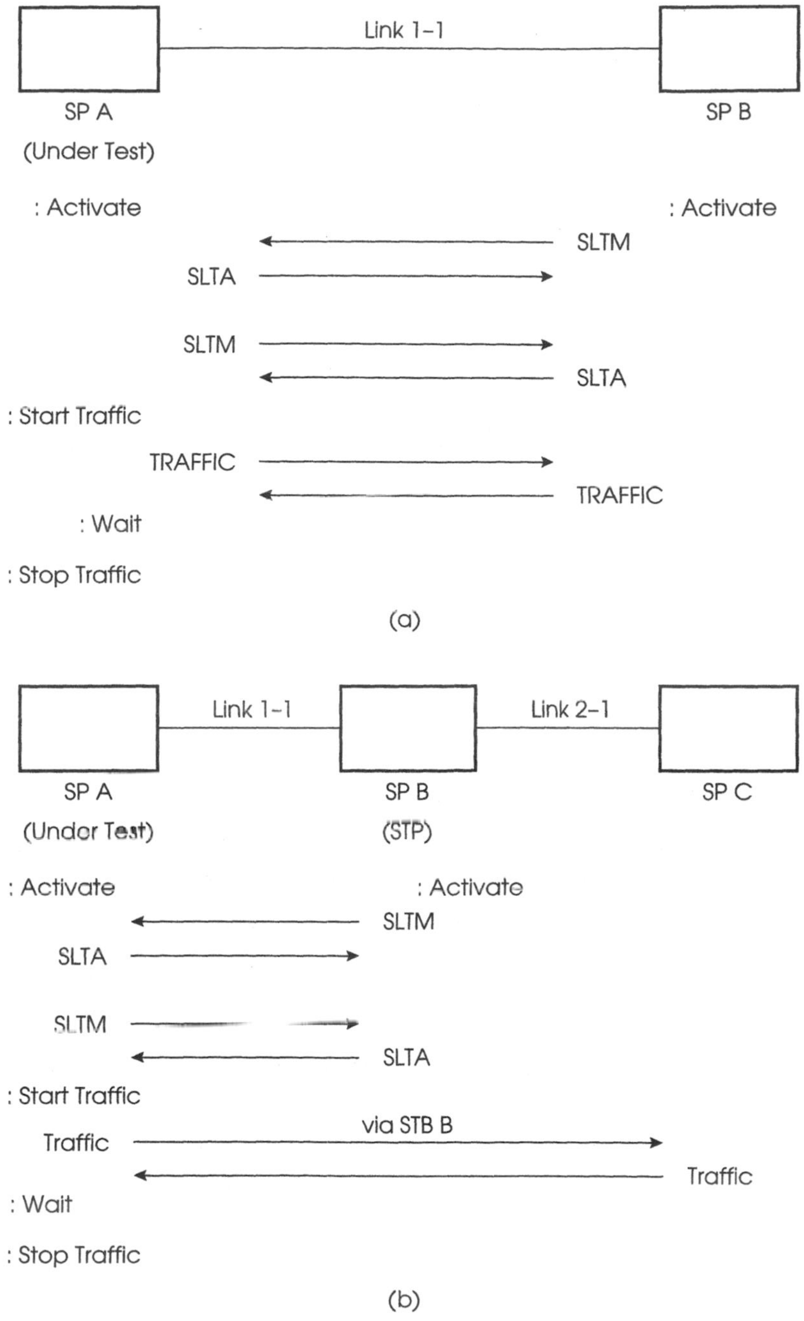

Figure 11–24 Expected message sequence for first link activation (test 1.1): (a) compatibility test; (b) validation testing.

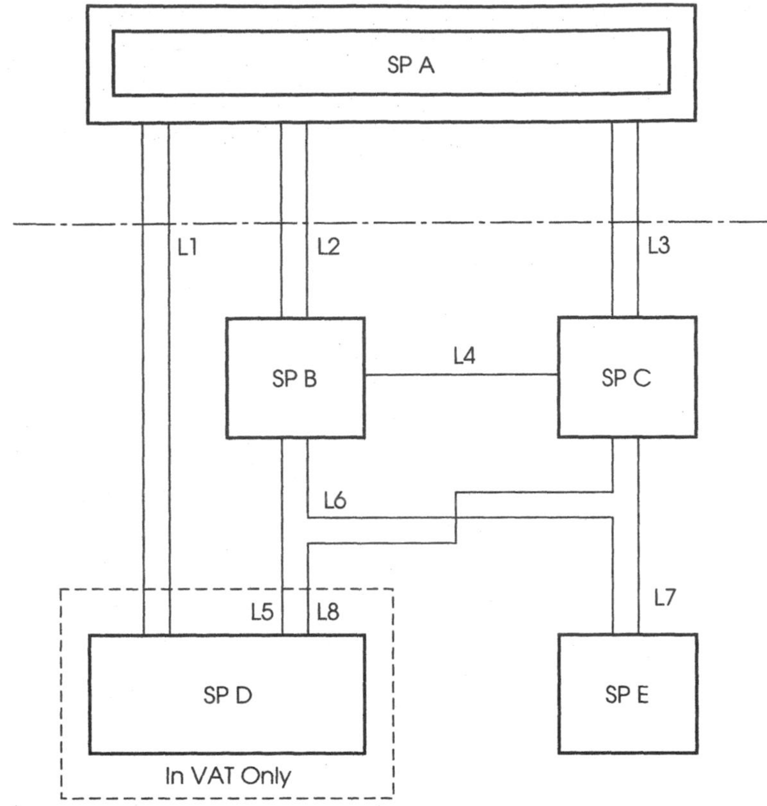

[Reprinted from ITU-T recommendation Q.782. (1993) Message transfer part level 3 test specification. Rev. 1. Reproduced by permission.]

Figure 11–25 Configuration B.

For validation testing, an additional SP D exists in the configuration. Therefore, a signaling relationship also exists between SP A and SP D. For the routing label of messages pertaining to this relationship,

OPC = A
DPC = D (for the A to D direction)

and

OPC = D
DPC = A (for the D to A direction)

The test involves sending test traffic from the SP under test, SP A, to SP E using the various signaling link selection (SLS) codes. SP E also generates test traffic to SP A. The routing of the test traffic is based on the rules defined in Table 11–2.

In the A to E direction, the traffic should be shared between link sets L2 and L3. For the traffic on link set L2, SP B acts as an STP to route the traffic on link set L6 toward destination SP E. For

Table 11-2 Routing Table for Configuration B

	A	B	C	D	E
A	—	L1 (normal) L2 (alternative)	L3 (normal) L2 (alternative)	L1–L2–L3 in load sharing	L2–L3 in load sharing
B	L2 (normal) L4 (alternative)	—	L4	L5 (normal) L4 (alternative)	L6 (normal) L4 (alternative)
C	L3 (normal) L4 (alternative)	L4	—	L8 (normal) L4 (alternative)	L7 (normal) L4 (alternative)
D	L1–L5–L8	L5 (normal) L8 (alternative)	L8 (normal) L5 (alternative)	—	Any
E	L7 (normal) L6 (alternative)	L6 (normal) L7 (alternative)	L7 (normal L6 (alternative)	Any	—

traffic on link set L3, SP C acts as an STP. In the reverse direction, the test traffic is routed on link set L7 to SP C, which acts as an STP. The test traffic is transferred by SP C on L3 to destination SP A.

During the flow of test traffic, the messages are monitored and stored for subsequent analysis. After the test traffic is stopped, the messages sent by SP A are examined to check that they have been transmitted on correct links based on the SLC and DPC values. It is also checked that there is no loss, duplication, or missequencing of messages during the exchange of test traffic.

EXAMPLE 11-20

This test covers signaling message handling (test 2.6.2).

The test is designed to check that when a destination is indicated as inaccessible upon reception of a transfer prohibited (TFP) message, traffic to this destination is stopped. Forced rerouting is not checked as part of this test. The test is prescribed only for validation testing and requires test configuration A, shown in Figure 11–23.

The main steps in the test are as follows:

- Traffic is started at SP A toward destinations SP B and SP C. Node B acts as an SP for traffic destined to it and as an STP for traffic to destination SP C.
- A TFP is sent by SP B to SP A indicating SP C as the inaccessible destination. This message may be sent on any one of the four links available in link set L1.
- It is checked that SP C has become inaccessible to SP A; that is, traffic from SP A to destination SP C should be stopped upon receipt of the TFP message.
- It is also checked that traffic to destination SP B is not disturbed.

EXAMPLE 11-21

This test checks the normal changeover procedure (test 3.1).

This test uses test configuration A, with only links 1–1 and 1–2 (out of the four links in L1) being available. The test corresponds to checking the changeover procedure as described in case 2, Section 7.6.1.

As shown in Figure 11–26, traffic is started from SP A to SP B on both links 1–1 and 1–2. Simultaneously, traffic is sent to SP C via the STP function at SP B on routes 1–1, 2–1, and 1–2, 2–1. To initiate the changeover order (COO) at SP A, one link in L1 (for example, 1–1) is deactivated.

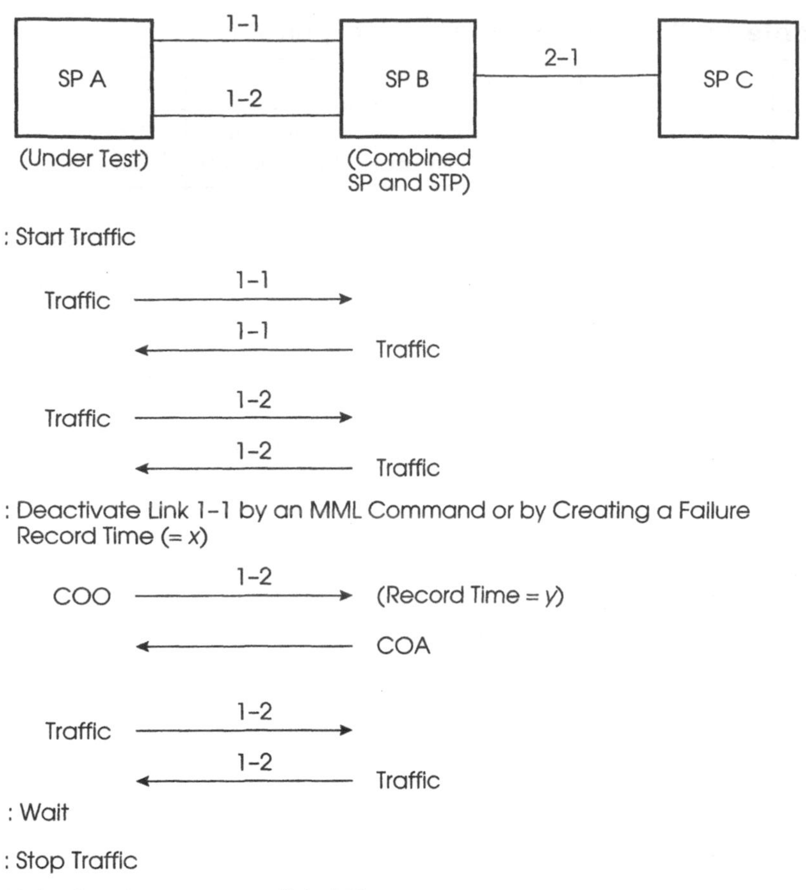

Figure 11–26 Expected test sequence for test 3.1.

The time of deactivating link 1–1 is recorded. Since another link 1–2, which is already carrying traffic, is available within the same link set L1, the changeover procedure in this test corresponds to case 2 of Section 7.6.1. The COO should be sent on link 1–2 by SP A. It is checked that the COO is sent within 500 ms of the deactivation of link 1–1. Upon receipt of the COO, SP B in the test configuration is programmed to send a changeover acknowledgment (COA) within 300 ms. Upon receipt of the COA, SP A should divert traffic normally carried by link 1–1 to link 1–2 without loss, duplication, or missequencing of messages. Moreover, the existing traffic on link 1–2 should not be disturbed.

To check that SP A responds to a COO message by a COA within 300 ms, the test is repeated by sending the COO from SP B to SP A.

EXAMPLE 11–22

This test checks the changeover procedure when no COA is received in response to the COO sent previously (test 3.3).

When no COA is received in response to a COO, the changeover procedure should be initiated after the expiry of timer T2. Refer to Section 7.6.1. The configuration and procedure for this test are identical to the test described in Example 11–21 except that SP B is programmed so that it does not respond with a COA upon receipt of a COO message. Both the time of sending the COO message by SP A and the time of the commencement of the changeover procedure at SP A are recorded. The difference between the two values is a measure of timer T2 at SP A. It is checked that this time is within permissible limits. It is also verified that the changeover procedure is completed successfully and that the traffic carried earlier by link 1–1 is now carried by link 1–2.

EXAMPLE 11-23

This test checks the emergency changeover procedure when an emergency changeover order (ECO) is acknowledged by an emergency changeover acknowledgment (ECA) (test 3.10).

This test uses configuration A with two available links in link set L1, which is the same as that used for Example 11–21. The difference in procedure from Example 11–21 is that the ECO is sent by SP A, and SP B responds with an ECA. It is checked that the traffic changes over from link 1–1 to 1–2. In this case, some messages may be lost during changeover. Refer to Section 7.6.1.1 for a description of the emergency changeover procedure. The test is repeated with SP B sending the ECO. It is checked that SP A responds with an ECA.

EXAMPLE 11-24

This test checks that the changeback procedure is correctly performed on the restoration of a link within a link set (test 4.1).

The starting point for this test is the end of test 3.1 (Example 11–21). Link 1–1, deactivated as a result of test 3.1, is activated again; it is to be checked that SP A restores traffic on this link according to the changeback procedure. The test is prescribed both for validation and compatibility testing. The main steps are as follows:

- Traffic is started from SP A on the only available link, 1–2, toward destination SP B for the compatibility test and for destinations SP B and SP C for the validation test.
- Link 1–1 is activated.
- It is checked that a changeback declaration (CBD) message with an SLC field corresponding to link 1–1 is received at SP B.
- SP B sends a changeback acknowledgment (CBA) in response.
- Upon receipt of CBA, SP A should restore the concerned traffic on link 1–1.
- The traffic flow is stopped, and it is checked that messages are not duplicated, lost, or missequenced.
- The test is repeated by activating links 1–3 and 1–4.

EXAMPLE 11-25

This test checks that the system can perform forced rerouting (test 5).

This test is prescribed for both validation and compatibility testing and makes use of test configuration B (Figure 11–25) in which link sets 1 and 4 are unavailable. The main steps in the test procedure are as follows:

- Traffic is generated by SP A toward SP E for compatibility testing alone and toward SP D if validation testing is performed. From the routing rules specified for this configuration, the routes taken by traffic from SP A to SP E via the STP function in B are as follows:

  Route 2–1, 6–1

  Route 2–2, 6–1

- The only link in link set 6—that is, link 6–1—is now deactivated. STP B is no longer capable of transferring traffic to destination E. Thus, STP B sends a traffic prohibited message to SP A for destination SP E. (Refer to Section 7.6.3 for a description of the transfer prohibited message.)
- On receipt of the TFP message, SP A should stop sending traffic meant for destination SP E to STP B. SP A should also perform forced rerouting, which provides for restoration of traffic on an alternative route. (Forced rerouting is described in Section 7.6.4.) The alternative routes on which this traffic should be diverted are the following:

  Route 3–1, 7–1

  Route 3–2, 7–1
- After verifying the forced rerouting of traffic on the alternative routes, the traffic is stopped to check that messages are not duplicated or missequenced during forced rerouting. It is, however, acceptable that some messages may be lost during the procedure.
- It is also checked that there is no impact on traffic to SP D carried on link sets 2 and 3.

EXAMPLE 11-26

This test checks that the system can perform controlled rerouting correctly (test 6).

This test is performed following the test in Example 11–25. The deactivated link set 6 is restored, causing a transfer allowed message concerning SP E by SP B to SP A. It is checked that the controlled rerouting is performed correctly, thus restoring the original traffic flow prior to the deactivation of link set 6. The value of timer T6 is also measured and checked that it lies within the permissible range. Timer T6 is the time difference between the receipt of transfer allowed (TFA) message by SP A and the commencement of restored traffic on link set 2. The traffic is stopped and it is verified that messages are not lost, duplicated, or missequenced during controlled rerouting.

EXAMPLE 11-27

This test checks for a correct response when link inhibition is requested for an available link (test 7.1.1).

Management inhibition functions were discussed in Section 7.6.9. In this test, configuration A (Figure 11–23) is used. After starting the traffic, the inhibition of available link 1–1 is initiated at SP A, and it is checked that the link inhibit (LIN) message is received at SP B. SP B responds with a link inhibit acknowledgment (LIA) message before expiry of timer T14 at SP A. The time-controlled changeover is performed at SP A upon receipt of the LIA message. It is checked that the traffic carried by link 1–1 is transferred to link 1–2. It is also checked that SP A marks link 1–1 as locally inhibited.

The test is also performed in the reverse direction. In this case, in response to the LIN message from SP B, SP A must respond with an LIA message before the expiry of timer T14 at SP B.

EXAMPLE 11-28

This test checks for a correct response when link inhibition is restarted for an available link after expiry of timer T14 (test 7.3.1)

This test differs from Example 11–28 in that, upon receipt of an LIN message for link 1–1 from SP A, SP B does not send an LIA message. Thus, timer T14 at SP A expires. It is checked that SP A again sends an LIA message requesting inhibition of link 1–1. The value of timer T14 is measured by the time difference in the two LIN messages generated by SP A. It is checked that the value of timer T14 is within the permissible range. Upon receipt of the second LIN message, SP B responds with an LIA message. As a consequence, SP A should mark the link 1–1 locally inhibited and transfer traffic on link 1–2 by performing a time-controlled changeback.

Recall from the discussion in Section 7.6.9 that a maximum of two link inhibition attempts are permitted. This aspect is also checked in this test by not sending any LIA messages from SP B for the LIN messages received from SP A. After the expiry of timer T14 a second time, SP A should abandon further attempts to inhibit the link.

EXAMPLE 11-29

This test checks the detection of level 3 congestion by sending transfer controlled (TFC) messages (test 8.2).

The use of transfer controlled messages was explained in Section 7.6.12. This test employs test configuration C, shown in Figure 11–27(a). The test consists of the following steps:

- The first step is to create congestion on link set L2 (there is only one link, link 2–1, in L2). For this purpose, start traffic from SP B to destination SP C via the STP function at A. If *n* erlangs is the maximum loading capacity of link 2–1, then the traffic generated should be more than *n* erlangs. Due to load sharing, links 1–1 and 1–2 should carry a load of more than *n*/2 erlangs each.

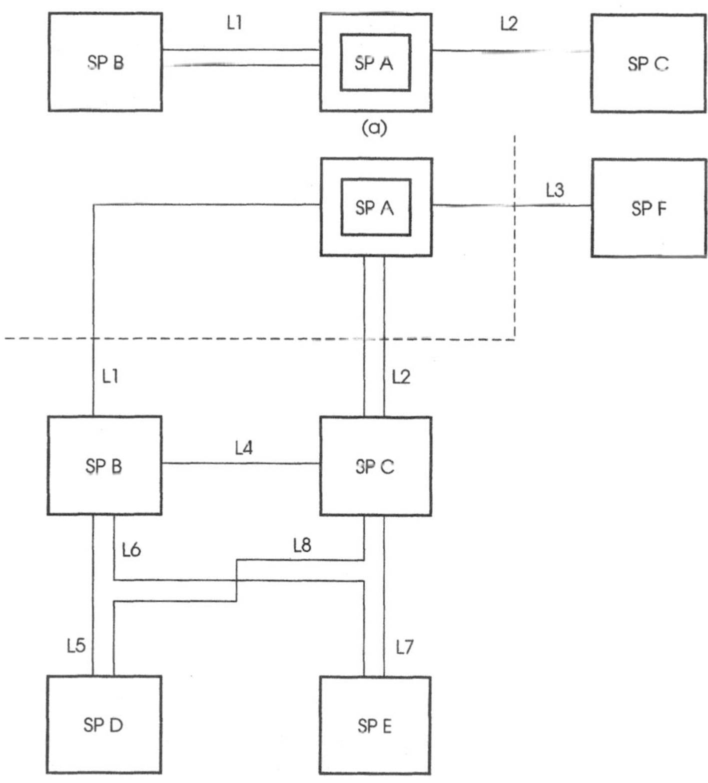

(a) Configuration C (b) Configuration D
[Part (b) reprinted from ITU-T recommendation Q.782. (1993) Message transfer part level 3 test specification. Rev. 1. Reproduced by permission.]

Figure 11–27 Configurations C and D.

- Check that the signaling traffic flow control procedure is started at SP A and that the TFC message relating to SP C is received after every eight messages from SP A to SP B.
- The traffic is now reduced so that the congestion on L2 disappears. In this situation, SP A should no longer send TFC messages.

EXAMPLE 11-30

This test checks the sending of a TFP message on an alternative route when the normal link set becomes unavailable; this concerns signaling route management (test 9.1.1).

This test, along with all the other tests related to signaling route management, require test configuration D, shown in Figure 11–27(b). SP A is under test and has both SP and STP functions. All link sets consist of only one link. The test traffic has the routing labels as follows:

- OPC = F, DPC = D, and OPC = D, DPC = F (signaling relation between F and D)
- OPC = F, DPC = E, and OPC = E, DPC = F (signaling relation between F and E)
- OPC = A, DPC = D, OPC = A, DPC = E, and OPC = A, DPC = F

The routing rules for the configuration are shown in Table 11–3.

The purpose of transfer prohibited messages was described in Section 7.6.3. The test consists of the following steps:

1. The test traffic is started. The routing, which is based on Table 11–3, is as follows:
   - For destination SP D, traffic from SP F takes link 3–1 to SP A (STP). This traffic and that originating at SP A now follow link 1–1 to SP B (STP) and, finally, link 5–1 to SP D.
   - For destination SP E, traffic from SP F takes link 3–1 to SP A (STP). This traffic along with the traffic originating at SP A is load shared on links 1–1 and 2–1. Traffic on link 1–1 is routed by SP B (STP) on link 6–1 to SP E. Traffic on 2–1 is routed by SP C (STP) on link 7–1 to SP E.

Table 11-3 Routing Table for Configuration D

	A	B	C	D	E	F
A	—	L1 (normal) L2 (alternative)	L2 (normal) L1 (alternative)	L1 (normal) L2 (alternative)	L1–L2 in load sharing (alternative)	L3
B	L1 (normal) L4 (alternative)	—	L4	L5 (normal) L4 (alternative)	L6 (normal) L4 (alternative)	L1
C	L2 (normal) L4 (alternative)	L4	—	L8 (normal) L4 (alternative)	L7 (normal) L4 (alternative)	L2
D	Any			—	Any	
E	Any				—	Any
F	L3	L3	L3	L3	L3	—

2. Link 1–1 is deactivated. SP A can no longer transfer messages to SP B and SP D. Therefore, SP A should inform SP C of its inability to transfer messages for destinations SP B and SP D. It is checked that SP A sends TFC messages to SP C concerning SP B and SP D on link 2–1. Recall from Section 7.6.3 that timer T8 is used to avoid a repetition of TFP message concerning the same destination. Accordingly, it is checked that timer T8 is started for each TFP sent.
3. It is also checked that no TFC is sent by SP A to SP C regarding SP E. This is expected, since according to the routing table, the traffic from SP A to destination SP E is load shared between links 1–1 and 1–2. Thus, SP A retains the ability to transfer messages for destination SP E despite the deactivation of link 1–1.

EXAMPLE 11–31

This test checks for the periodic sending of signaling route set test (RST) messages; this concerns signaling route management (test 9.6).

The signaling route set test procedure was described in Section 7.6.8. The procedure aims to find out when the transfer prohibited or transfer restricted conditions cease to exist. For this purpose, RST messages are to be sent to the destination at a periodicity of timer T10 until a transfer allowed message is received from the destination.

To check this procedure, the test employs configuration A (Figure 11–23). Link set 2 is made unavailable at the beginning of the test. The expected message sequence is shown in Figure 11–28.

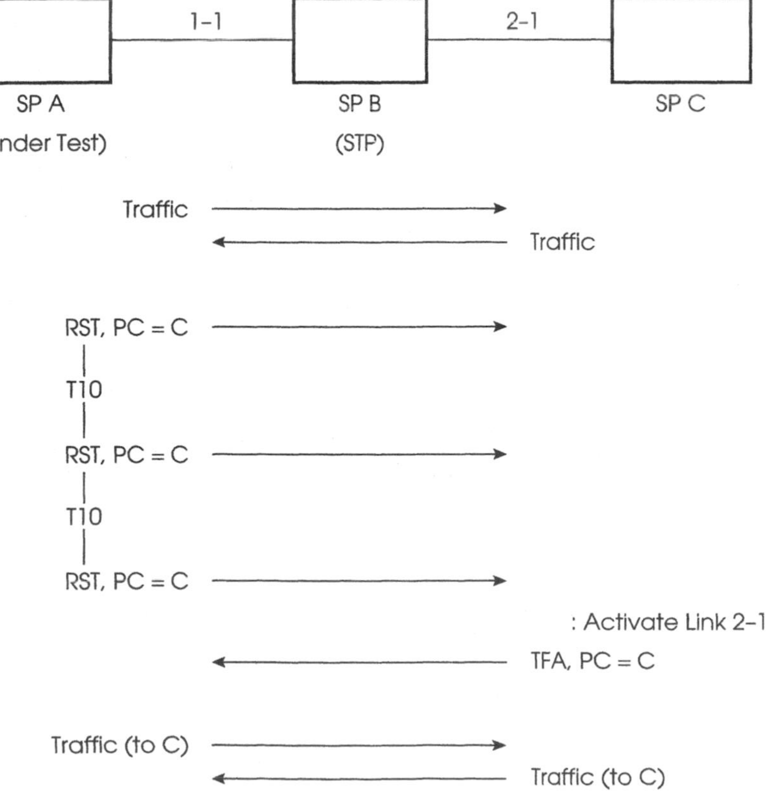

Figure 11–28 Expected message sequence for test 9.6.

The receipt of a TFP message at SP A upon deactivation of the link is not shown. By the time instants at which successive RST messages are sent, the value of timer T10 is computed. This value should be in the range of 30 to 60 seconds.

EXAMPLE 11-32

This test checks the behavior of an STP under various traffic conditions.

The criteria to be met by the STP under various traffic conditions is specified in terms of the time taken by the STP to transfer messages. According to ITU-T recommendation Q.706 [7], under normal traffic conditions, the message transfer time should be under 20 ms in 50% of the cases and twice this value in 95% of the cases.

The normal traffic is characterized by the traffic models given in Table 11–4. The mean message length in the models of Table 11–4 is typical of TUP messages. For the ISUP, longer messages are expected. Test traffic should be generated based on realistic estimates of the message lengths in the network. The format of the test traffic is the same as for other level 3 tests described so far; (see Figure 11–22(b). Configuration C, shown in Figure 11–27(a), is used for the test. Thus, the test traffic is generated in both SP B and SP C toward each other, with node A performing the STP function for both directions of traffic. The generation and reception of test traffic takes place in the MTP testing user parts of SP B and SP C, as shown in Figure 11–29.

Under the test, the message transfer time at the STP is noted, and it is checked that this delay is within stipulated limits. The test is repeated with a traffic model in which 5% of the messages have a signaling information field (SIF) equal to 272 octets.

11.4.3 ISUP Testing

The objective of ISUP testing is two fold:

1. To check that the SP under test conforms to ISUP protocol for basic call control as specified in ITU-T recommendations Q.761 through Q.764. The set of tests required for this purpose are contained in ITU-T recommendation Q.784 [8].
2. To check the ISUP implementation for the various supplementary services. These tests are described in ITU-T recommendation Q.785 [9].

The test configuration used for basic call control simply consists of the SP under test, SP A, connected to SP B. Signaling links and speech/data circuits are provided between the two nodes. SP B may be a CCS 7 digital exchange whose conformance to ISUP protocol has already been verified, or it may be a simulator. The tests for level 2 and level 3 must be completed successfully on SP A before commencing ISUP testing.

Table 11-4 Normal Traffic Models

MODEL	A	B	
Message length (bits)	120	104	304
Percent	100	92	8
Mean message length	120	120	

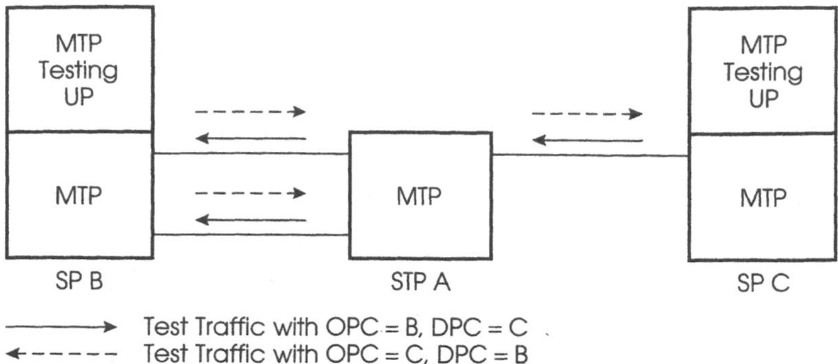

Figure 11–29 Traffic test for STP.

ISUP tests have been classified into the following eight groups:

1. Circuit supervision
2. Normal call setup, ordinary speech call
3. Normal call release
4. Unsuccessful call setup
5. Abnormal situation during a call setup
6. Special call setup
7. Bearer services
8. Congestion control and user flow control

This section describes some of these tests. The test numbers indicated in parentheses refer to recommendation Q.784.

EXAMPLE 11-33

This test checks that the circuit group blocking features can be correctly initiated (test 1.3.1.1).

Readers may recall the discussion on blocking and unblocking circuit groups in Section 9.5.3. This test is prescribed for both validation and compatibility tests. Before the commencement of the test, all circuits between SP A and SP B are idle. Under the test, SP B sends a circuit group blocking (CGB) message to SP A. The circuit group supervision type indicator is set to "maintenance oriented" (refer to Table 9–11). The range and status fields in the message are set to indicate the group of circuits between SP A and SP B that are to be blocked by the CGB message. The message sequence between SP A and SP B is monitored using a CCS 7 monitor. The expected message sequence is shown in Figure 11–30(a).

The circuits at SP B should be "remotely blocked." To verify that the circuits have actually been blocked, attempt is made to originate calls on these circuits; it should not be possible.

As the second part of this test, send a circuit group unblocking (CGU) message from SP B relating to the same circuits that were earlier blocked. The circuit group supervision type message is set to "maintenance oriented" in this message. The message sequence is again monitored, and it should correspond to Figure 11–30(b). It is expected that the circuits at SP A are in the unblocked state. This is confirmed by successfully initiating calls on the concerned circuits.

Recall that meaningful values of the range field in the CGB or CGU message lie between 1 and 31. Thus, a CGB with a range of 0 is sent by SP B, and it is then verified that SP A discards the

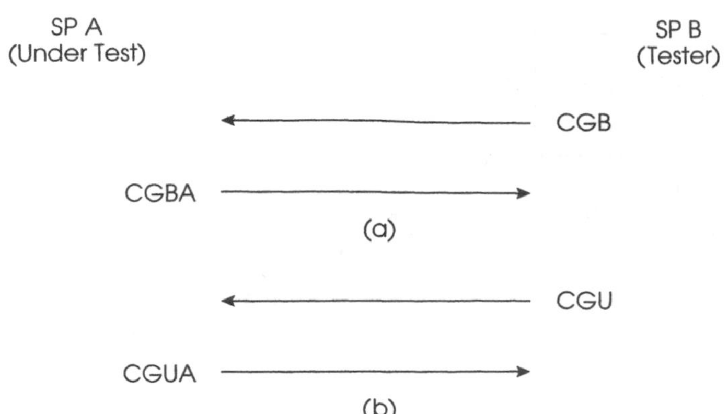

Figure 11–30 Expected message sequence for test 1.3.1.1.

message and does not respond with a circuit group blocking acknowledgment (CGBA) message. Similarly, a CGB with a range greater than 31 is sent by SP B. SP A must discard this message also.

The test is repeated with the circuit group supervision message type indicator set to "hardware oriented failure."

EXAMPLE 11-34

This test is to verify that the continuity check procedure can be correctly performed (test 1.4.1).

The continuity check procedure was discussed in Section 9.4. This test is performed during both validation testing and compatibility testing. The continuity check is initiated by SP B by sending a continuity check request (CCR) message. The expected sequence of the message is similar to Figure 9–18. The message sequence is verified by the use of a CCS 7 monitor. The associated timers are not checked as part of this test. That the circuit is in an idle state at the end of the test is also checked.

Another test (test 1.4.2) involves carrying out a similar test by initiating the continuity check at the SP under test.

EXAMPLE 11-35

This test checks for actions taken by the SP upon the receipt of unexpected messages (test 1.5.1).

Section 9.6.2.2 discussed the actions to be performed upon the receipt of unexpected messages. Four cases of the receipt of unexpected messages are verified in this test, as shown in Figure 11–31. Messages XXX and YYY represent unexpected messages. A CCS 7 monitor is used to verify the correctness of message sequence in each case. It is also checked at SPA that in each case the circuit corresponding to the unexpected message remains in the idle state.

EXAMPLE 11-36

This test is to verify that SP A can initiate an outgoing call on a both-way circuit when SP A is the controlling SP (test 2.1.1).

A call is made from SP A to SP B on a both-way circuit. After the call is established, it is cleared by SP A. The expected message sequence is shown in Figure 11–32. The sequence is verified by a CCS 7 monitor. It is also checked that the both-way circuit on which the call was established has returned to the idle state.

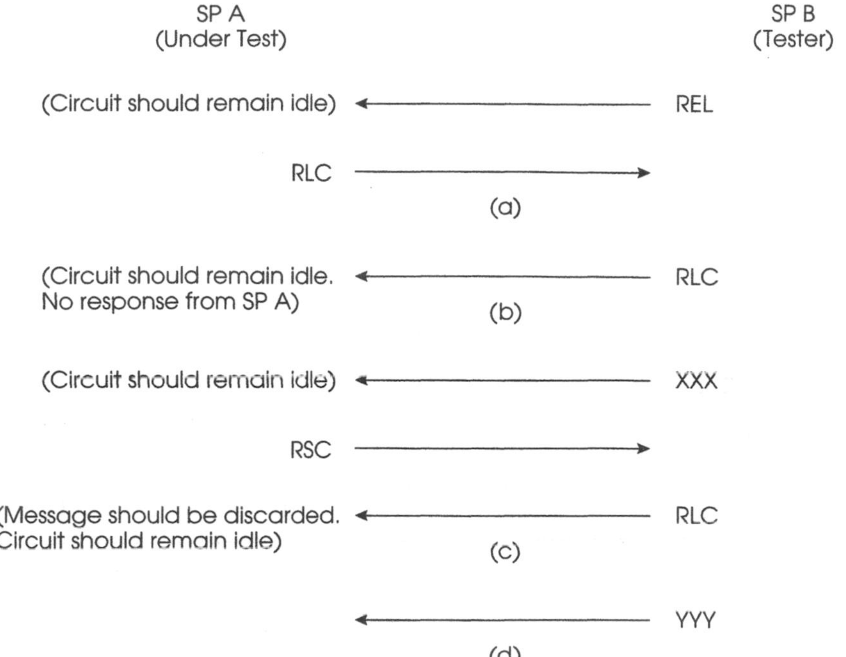

Figure 11–31 Expected message sequence for test 1.5.1.

EXAMPLE 11-37

This test checks for the en bloc operation of SP A (test 2.2.1).

The test is designed to ensure that the SP A can send all the digits of the called party address in the initial address message (IAM). Accordingly, a call is made from SP A with the IAM containing the called party address. After the call is established, call release is initiated at SP A to clear the call. The message sequence is identical to Figure 11–32. The test sequence is confirmed by monitor-

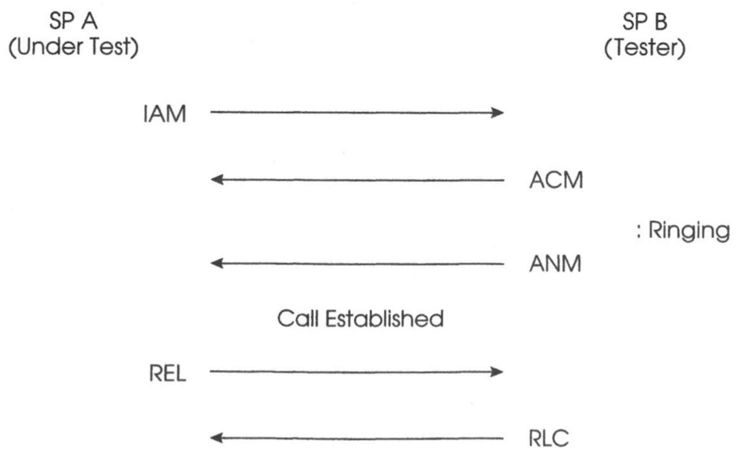

Figure 11–32 Expected message sequence for test 2.1.1.

ing the message flow. The circuit used for the call should return to the idle state. The test is performed both for validation and compatibility testing. For validation, the test is also repeated in the reverse direction.

EXAMPLE 11-38

This test checks for overlap operation at SP A (test 2.2.2).

A call is set up from SP A to SP B. The called party's address is sent in two installments; in the IAM and in the SAM. The test may also include more than one SAM. The expected message sequence shown in Figure 11–33 is verified by monitoring. This test is performed both for validation and compatibility testing.

EXAMPLE 11-39

This test verifies that a call can be successfully completed using various indications in the connect message (test 2.3.3).

A call is established from SP A to an ISDN access connected to SP B. In response to the IAM, SP B responds with a connect (CON) message. This is made possible by using a terminal with an automatic answering feature at the called access. The called party's status indicator in the CON message is set to "free subscriber." Likewise, the ISDN access indicator is set to "terminating access ISDN." After setup, the call is released by the calling party connected to SP A. The expected message sequence is shown in Figure 11–34. In addition to monitoring the messages for correctness, it is verified that the circuit used for the call has returned to the idle state. The test is repeated with the called party's status indicator set to "no indication."

As the next step, a call is made from SP A to a non-ISDN subscriber. In this case, the ISDN access indicator in the CON message is set to "non-ISDN termination." The test is again repeated. During validation testing, the test is repeated in the reverse direction.

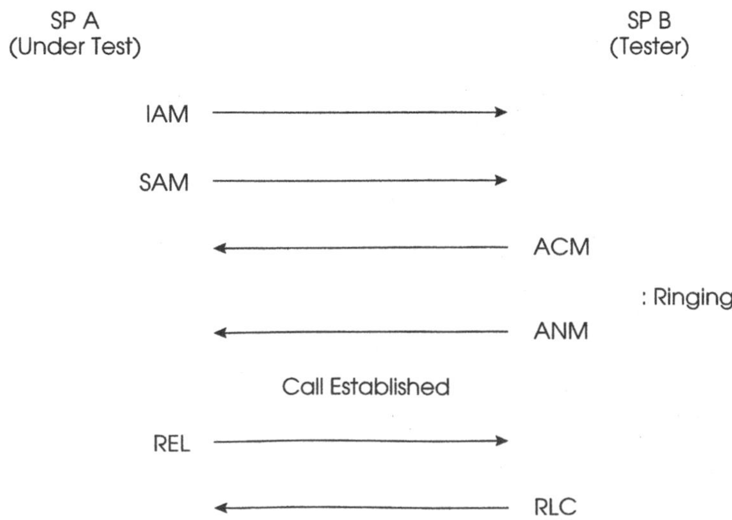

Figure 11–33 Expected message sequence for test 2.2.2.

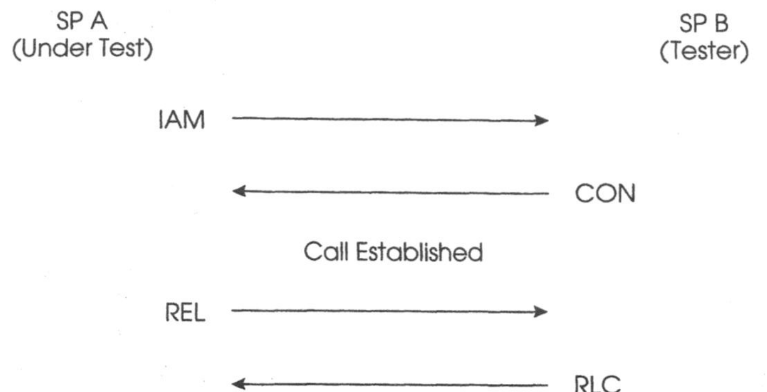

Figure 11–34 Expected message sequence for test 2.3.3.

EXAMPLE 11-40

This test verifies that the satellite indicator in the IAM is set correctly for a call switched via a satellite circuit (test 2.3.4).

A call is made from SP A to SP B. The data at SP A is so arranged that a satellite circuit is selected for the call. After the call is established, call release is initiated by the calling subscriber. The expected message sequence is the same as in Figure 11–32. The message sequence for the call is monitored. Since a satellite circuit is chosen for the call, the satellite indicator (bits BA) in the nature of the connection indicators parameter of the IAM must be set to indicate one satellite circuit in the connection. Refer to Table 9–1. The circuit used for the call should be idle.

The test is repeated in the reverse direction for validation testing.

EXAMPLE 11-41

In this example, tests for the following four cases of normal call release are considered:

1. Calling party clears before any backward message (test 3.1)
2. Calling party clears before answer (test 3.2)
3. Calling party clears after answer (test 3.4)
4. Called party clears after answer

In all these cases, calls are initiated from SP A to SP B. The expected message sequence for each case is given in Figure 11–35. For each test, the messages are monitored for correctness. It is also checked that the circuit becomes idle.

EXAMPLE 11-42

This test checks the functions of an SP when an RLC message is not received and timers T1 and T5 expire (test 5.2.3).

The role of timers T1 and T5 when an RLC message is not received during call release was explained in Figure 9–11. In this test, SP B sets up a call to SP A. After call establishment, the release is initiated by the called party connected to SP A. The data in SP B is arranged such that an RLC message is not generated in response to an REL message. The message sequence is shown in Figure 11–36. The messages are monitored, and the values of timers T1 and T5 are measured. It is checked that the maintenance system is informed upon the expiry of timer T5.

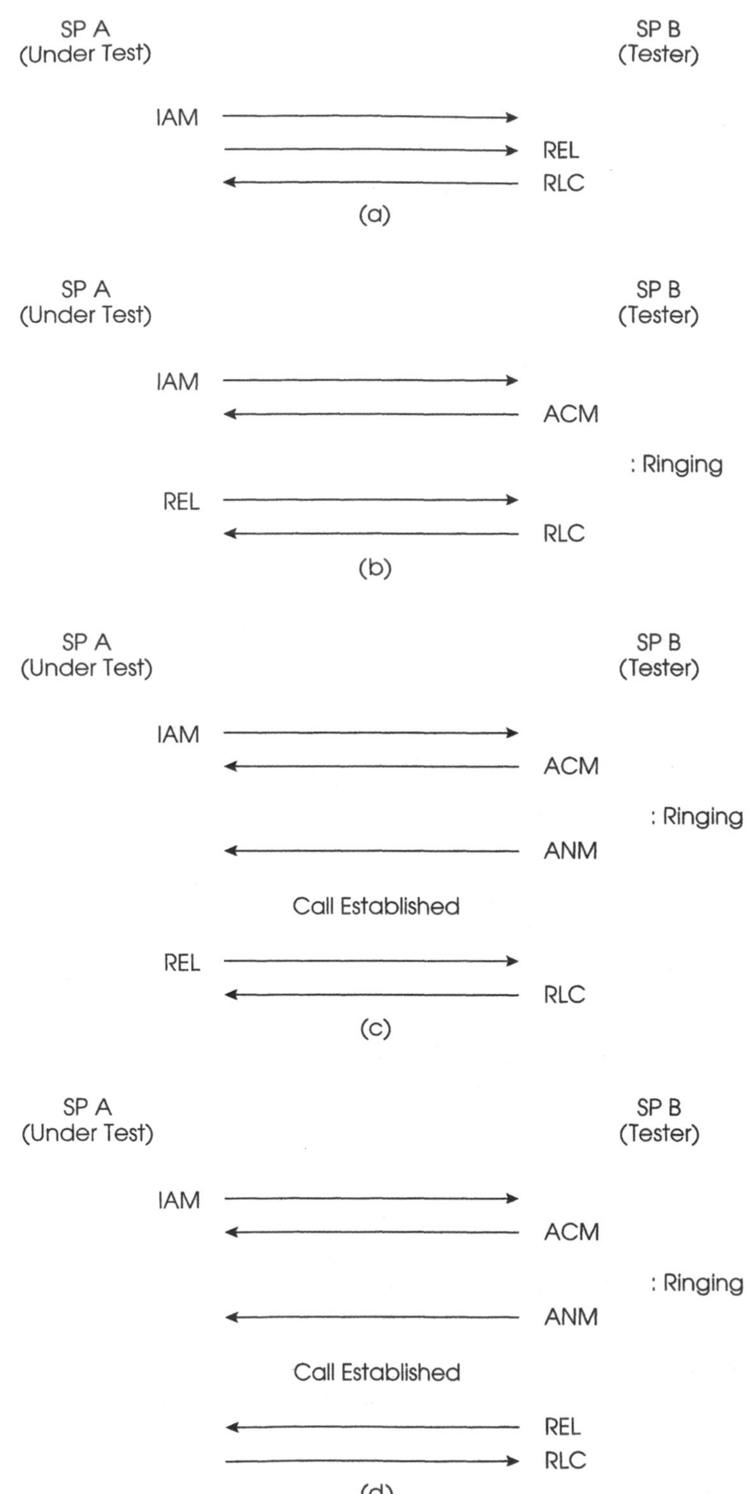

Figure 11–35 Expected message sequences for different call release scenarios: (a) calling party clears before any backward messages; (b) calling party clears before answer; (c) calling party clears after answer; (d) called party clears after answer.

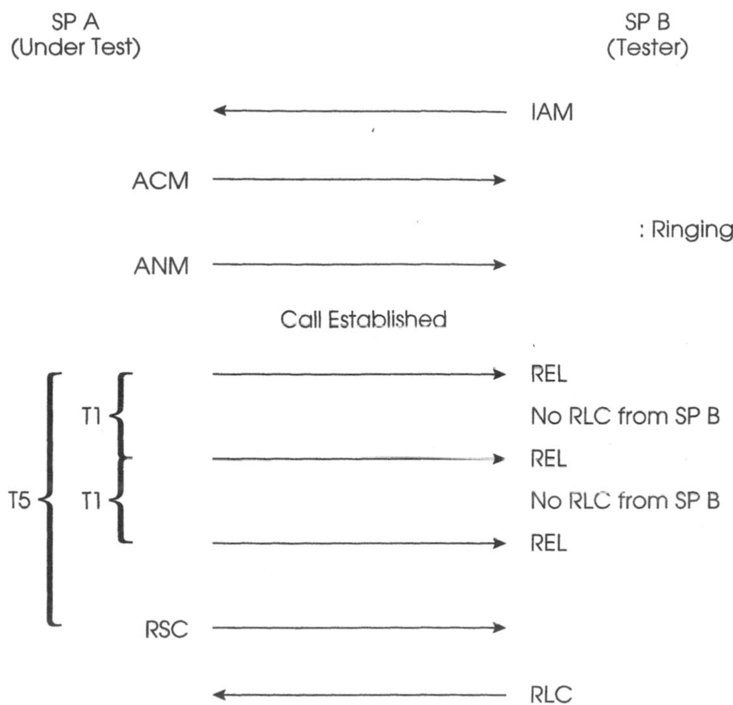

Figure 11–36 Expected message sequence for test 5.2.3.

EXAMPLE 11–43

This test checks that a call can be set up on a circuit requiring a continuity check (test 6.1.1).

Example 11–34 involved the verification of a continuity check procedure during a test call by the use of a CCR message. This test verifies the procedure when the request for continuity check is carried in the IAM. Therefore, the data at SP A is set so that the IAM contains this request when a call is made from SP A to SP B. The expected sequence of messages is verified with a CCS 7 monitor. It is also checked that the call is successfully established and released. At the end of the test, the circuit used for the call should be in the idle state. The expected message sequence is shown in Figure 11–37.

11.5 CCS 7 Testing during Testing of a Switching System

When a new type of switching system is introduced, the telecom administration usually performs validation testing for various exchange functions of the new system. Since the SP function is part of the exchange, CCS 7 validation is often performed along with the validation of other exchange functions. An important test performed on a digital switch is evaluating the call processing capability in terms of busy hour completed calls (BHCC). During this test, the exchange is loaded, by the use of call generators, to its rated call handling capability, and the occupancy of the call handling processors is measured. When the

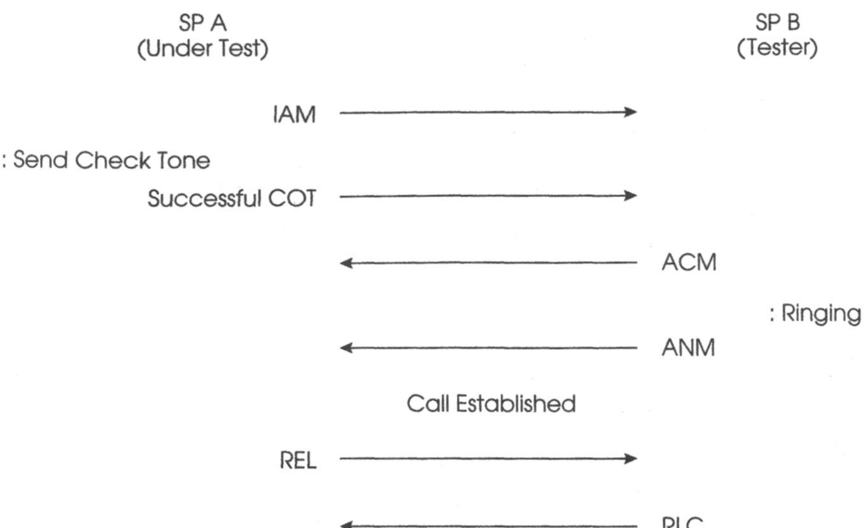

Figure 11–37 Expected message sequence for test 6.1.1.

exchange is tested on a stand-alone basis, the outgoing exchange trunks are looped back to the incoming trunks while traffic is applied to the subscriber ports. Thus, outgoing calls are looped back via the CCS 7 looped trunks and are presented to the exchange as incoming calls. Since modern digital exchanges have a very high call handling capability (of the order of one million BHCC), to load the exchange to its ultimate call handling capability with limited number of call generators, the subscriber traffic may be multiplied by using several stages of loopbacks.

A typical arrangement is shown in Figure 11–38. In addition to the looping back of speech/data circuits, the CCS 7 links should also be looped back. Because an SP has a single, unique point code during normal operation, the destination point code (DPC) contained in the routing label should be replaced by the point code of the exchange under test for each CCS 7 message in the looped signaling links. This is not necessary where provision of defining more than one point code exists in the switch for the purpose of testing.

Several useful observations can be made using the loopback arrangement. From the point of view of CCS 7 protocol, the exchange behaves as two identical SPs interconnected by signaling links. CCS 7 monitors can be connected to one or more signaling links to gather statistical information. The messages can be decoded and displayed and then logged for further analysis. The main advantage of the test setup is that CCS 7 messages that correspond to a large number of ISUP calls are available for analysis; thus, protocol errors, if any, are likely to uncover. The traffic in this case is closer to the real world, since it is generated by the ISUP and not by the MTP testing user part. The occupancy of the signaling links can be varied by changing the number of signaling links. The load sharing between links of a link set can also be observed.

It is important to note that this test is not a substitute for the CCS 7 protocol tests described in earlier sections. Rather, it supplements these tests and provides the administration with a reasonable degree of confidence in the CCS 7 implementation under test.

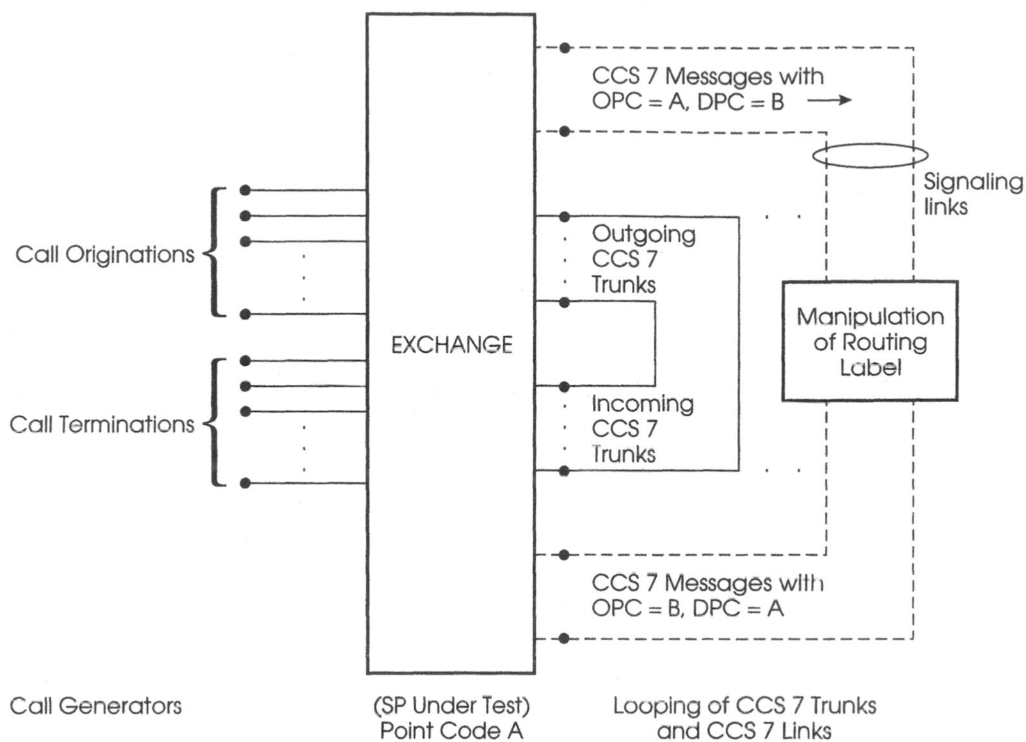

Figure 11–38 SP testing using loopback.

REFERENCES

[1] *Specifications of Signaling System No. 7. Signaling System Test Specification General Description.* ITU-T recommendation Q.780, rev. 1. International Telecommunication Union, 1993.

[2] *Interworking between the Digital Subscriber Signaling System Layer 3 Protocol and the Signaling System No. 7 ISDN User Part.* CCITT Blue Book, fascicle VI.6, recommendation Q.699. International Telecommunication Union, 1988.

[3] *Specifications of Signaling System No. 7. Message Transfer Part Level 2 Test Specification.* ITU-T recommendation Q.781, rev. 1. International Telecommunication Union, 1993.

[4] *Specifications of Signaling System No. 7. Message Transfer Part Level 3 Test Specification.* ITU-T recommendation Q.782, rev. 1. International Telecommunication Union, 1993.

[5] *Specifications of Signaling System No. 7. Testing and Maintenance.* CCITT Blue Book, fascicle VI.6, recommendation Q.707. International Telecommunication Union, 1988.

[6] "Specifications of signaling system number 7." BELLCORE Technical Report TR-NWT-000246, issue 2, June 1991; rev. 1, Dec. 1991; rev. 2, Dec. 1992.

[7] *Specifications of Signaling System No. 7. Message Transfer Part Signaling Performance.* ITU-T recommendation Q.706, rev. 1. International Telecommunication Union, 1993.

[8] *Specifications of Signaling System No. 7. ISUP Basic Call Test Specification.* ITU-T recommendation Q.784. International Telecommunication Union, 1991. Also: *TTCN Version of the Recommendation Q.784.* ITU-T recommendation Q.784A. International Telecommunication Union, 1993.

[9] *Specifications of Signaling System No. 7. ISUP Protocol Test Specification for Supplementary Services.* ITU-T recommendation Q.785. International Telecommunication Union, 1991.

12 Packet and Frame Mode Services in the ISDN

Acronyms

AU	access unit
BECN	backward explicit congestion notification (field)
BER	bit error ratio
CALL PROC	ISDN layer 3 call proceeding (message)
CCITT	The International Telegraph and Telephone Consultative Committee
CLC	X.25 clear confirm (message)
CONN	ISDN layer 3 connection (message)
CONN ACK	ISDN layer 3 connection acknowledge (message)
CR	X.25 clear request (message)
CLI	X.25 clear indication (message)
DISC	ISDN layer 3 disconnection (message)
DLCI	data link connection identifier
DL-CONTROL	data link control protocol
DL-CORE	data link core protocol
DTE	data terminal equipment
FECN	forward explicit congestion notification (field)
ISDN	integrated services digital network
ITU-T	International Telecommunication Union-International Standardization Sector
LAPB	link access protocol balanced
LAPD	link access procedure on D-channel
LAPF	link access procedures for frame mode bearer service
PH	packet handler
PSPDN	public switched packet data network
PVC	permanent virtual circuit
REL	ISDN layer 3 release (message)
RFH	remote frame handler
RLC	ISDN layer 3 release complete (message)
SABM	set asynchronous balance mode (X.25 layer 2)
SABME	set asynchronous balanced mode extended frame (ISDN layer 2)
SAPI	service access point identifier
SETUP	ISDN layer 3 setup (message)
TA	terminal adapter
TEI	terminal endpoint identifier
UA	unnumbered acknowledgment frame (both in X.25 layer 2 and ISDN layer 2)
UI	unnumbered information frame (ISDN layer 2)
VC	virtual call

ABSTRACT

This chapter presents an overview of the provisioning of packet mode and frame mode bearer services in the integrated services digital network (ISDN). The topics covered in this area include:

- Minimum integration scenario (X.31, case A)
- Maximum integration scenario (X.31, case B); packet calls on both B- and D-channels
- Frame mode bearer services with emphasis on frame relaying
- Protocols involved in the control C plane and the user U plane
- Procedures for establishing frame mode connections using recommendation Q.922 and Q.933 protocols

12.1 Introduction

The goal of designing the ISDN as a common umbrella network for various services cannot be entirely met unless packet mode services are also provided within its framework. Progress in this direction was initially slow, mainly because the digital exchanges were originally designed to perform only circuit switched functions. Thus, to truly integrate packet mode bearer services within the ISDN, it was necessary to include packet handling functions within the ISDN exchanges or as separate equipment connected to the ISDN exchanges. This is the so-called maximum integration scenario described as case B of the International Telecommunication Union-International Standardization Sector (ITU-T) recommendation X.31 [1]. While ISDN was in the process of standardization in the International Telegraph and Telephone Consultative Committee (CCITT), the public switched packet data networks (PSPDN) were implemented rather extensively in a number of countries to meet the immediate need for data services. Most of the packet traffic is on these networks, which are based on recommendation X.25 [2] of the ITU-T.

When compared with circuit switching, packet switching has several notable advantages for data calls. First, packet switching allows better use of the bearer channel capacity. Data for each call is broken into packets, and packets for several calls can share the same physical 64 kbps channel. On the other hand, a circuit switched data call engages a 64 kbps bearer for the entire call duration. Second, the use of packet switching results in an efficient use of the switching resources because the switches are used only when the packets related to the call are processed. Unlike circuit switching, there is no need for line supervision for the entire call duration. Third, packet switching flexibly serves the wide range of traffic characteristics and bit rates that are generally associated with different types of data services. Circuit switched 64 kbps connections are inefficient, especially for low bit rate interactive applications. For these applications, rate adaptation has to be performed at either end. As an illustration, assume that a data terminal equipment (DTE) is transmitting at 2.4 kbps. To carry this information on a 64 kbps B-channel, additional bits must be added to create a 64 kbps bit stream. The reverse process of removing the additional bits and restoring the original bit rate must be performed at the other end. (ITU-T recommendation V.110 specifies bit-rate adaptation [3].) For higher bit rates, the channel capacity utilization figures are somewhat better. Typically, efficiencies in the range of 40% to 50% are achieved in the direction of transmission for 64 kbps file transfer and group 4 facsimile applications. Fourth, the error control is applied on a link-by-link basis between the packet switches of a PSPDN. In circuit switching, error correction on data is not available in the network; this responsibility lies with the terminals at the two ends. With improved quality of modern transmission systems, however, this characteristic is more of a disadvantage due to processing delays in the network nodes arising from link-by-link error correction. As will be seen later in this chapter, the frame relay service dispenses with the error correction in the network nodes to achieve higher throughput. Finally, packets can be routed flexibly through the network, thereby exploiting the alternative paths that may be available. This provides better security for call completion.

Recognizing that there would be an interim period when packet handling functions will be unavailable in the ISDN exchanges, the ITU-T has specified a minimum integration scenario, generally referred to as X.31 case A. This is essentially an arrangement of interworking between the ISDN and the PSPDN since under this scenario, packet switching functions are not provided in the ISDN. The minimum integration scenario is discussed in Section 12.2. The maximum integration scenario, referred to earlier, is described in Section 12.3.

In addition to the circuit mode and packet mode bearer services, a third category of bearer services, frame mode bearer services, was also conceived on the ISDN communication platform. Thus, CCITT Blue Book recommendation I.122 [4] provided a frame work for "additional packet mode bearer." This recommendation identified the following potential services for further standardization:

- Frame relaying 1
- Frame relaying 2
- Frame switching
- X.25 based additional packet mode

During the 1988–92 study period, the process of standardization resulted in further definition of frame mode bearer services. Prominent among these is the frame relay service through the ISDN. Frame mode bearer services are discussed in Section 12.4.

12.2 Minimum Integration Scenario

The minimum integration scenario is shown in Figure 12–1. To make packet calls, an X.25 terminal along with a terminal adapter may be used. Alternatively, there could be a packet mode ISDN terminal capable of sending and receiving X.25 packets. As noted earlier, this scenario does not integrate packet mode services in the ISDN. It does, however, achieve the following:

- An integrated access for both packet and circuit switching terminals at the customer premises
- An arrangement of interworking between the PSPDN and ISDN

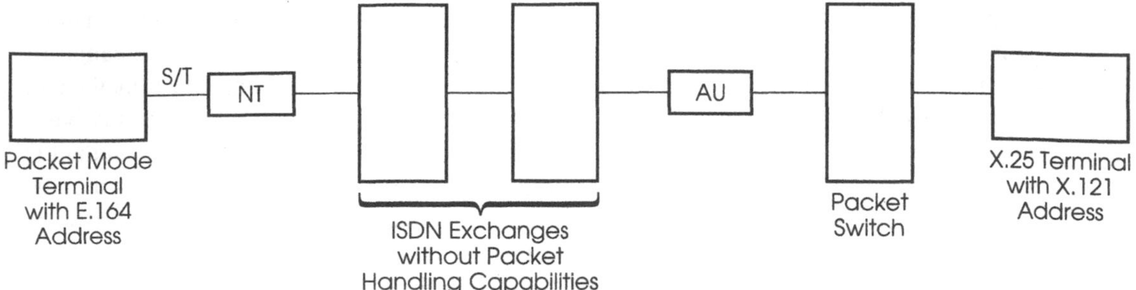

Figure 12–1 Minimum integration scenario.

The packet call is completed in two steps.

1. In the first step, a circuit switched ISDN connection is established between the originating ISDN access and an ISDN access unit (AU) in the PSPDN. An AU has an ISDN directory number; this is the number dialed by the caller to initiate a call. The AU may use either basic rate or primary rate access. The latter is normally used in conjunction with a line hunting facility. When the call arrives at an AU, it must respond by automatically answering the call. Therefore, an AU should possess the functions of an ISDN packet mode terminal (or those of an X.25 terminal and a terminal adapter combination). The protocol layers employed for the first step are

   Layer 1: I.430 [5]/I.431 [6]

   Layer 2: Q.921 [7] (link access procedure on D-channel, or LAPD)

   Layer 3: Q.931 [8]

   The bearer capability used for the call is 64 kbps unrestricted circuit mode bearer service.

2. Once the first call is set up, the calling subscriber dials the called PSPDN subscriber. The address of the called subscriber is the directory number in the PSPDN according to the numbering scheme specified in ITU-T recommendation X.121 [9]. Under this scheme, an international X.25 number consists of a total of ten digits: the first three digits for the country code and a seven-digit national number. The first three digits of the national number indicate the code of the packet exchange, and the remaining four digits identify the subscriber within the exchange. To set up the packet call, the PSPDN directory number is carried in the B-channel to the AU. The remaining signaling for call setup is also transported transparently on the B-channel. This is an example of in-band signaling. Protocols involved for the packet call are the following:

   Layer 1: I.430/I.431

   Layer 2: link access protocol balanced (LAPB)

   Layer 3: X.25

Steps 1 and 2 complete the call setup and provide access to the PSPDN through an ISDN access unit. For call release, the X.25 connection is released first. This is followed by clearing the ISDN circuit switched connection.

The X.25 terminals, although physically connected to the ISDN user network interface, are logically PSPDN users. Viewed from this angle, the minimum integration scenario provides a means of expanding the customer base of the PSPDN by inclusion of ISDN subscribers.

12.3 Maximum Integration Scenario

The maximum integration scenario allows integration of packet mode bearer services within the ISDN. The ISDN exchanges are supported by packet handlers that incorporate packet switching functions. The packet handlers may be integrated with the ISDN exchanges, or they may be placed in the network, independent of the exchange locations. Furthermore, one packet handler may serve the packet switching needs of more than one ISDN exchange. The number and location of packet handlers are based on planning considerations.

In the PSPDN, the interconnection between packet networks is based on ITU-T recommendation X.75 [10]. Inside a packet network, however, there is no standardization regarding the interconnection of packet switches, and proprietary protocols may be used by a network operator within that network. In the ISDN, a packet handler employs X.75 protocol both for interconnection to other packet handlers and for access to the PSPDN. X.75 protocol is also used between an ISDN exchange and a remotely located packet handler. When the packet handler is integrated with the ISDN exchange, internal links are used to interconnect the two.

Figure 12–2 shows one of the several possible configurations. Each ISDN exchange is shown to possess packet handling functionality. Interconnection of the ISDN to the PSPDN is also shown.

An important packet mode bearer service category supported in the ISDN is the virtual call (VC) and permanent virtual circuit (PVC) bearer service defined in CCITT recommendation I.232.1 [11]. It provides unrestricted transfer of X.25-encoded packet data between two ISDN users (packet mode ISDN terminals or X.25 terminals along with appropriate terminal adapters). At the S/T reference points on either end of the connection, either a B- or a D-channel may be used for carrying packet data. Different types of channels may be used at the two ends, such as a B-channel at the calling user end and a D-channel at the called user end.

The term *virtual* signifies that a physical dedicated connection does not exist for the call or connection. Packets of different users are interleaved on the same physical circuit. To the user, however, it appears as if the circuit is exclusively available. Thus, several logical channels, one for each virtual connection, are supported on a physical circuit. For a virtual call, the assignment and release of the logical channel on the physical circuit is performed based on appropriate call control procedures. Typically, several virtual calls may exist simultaneously on the same physical circuit, so the physical circuit is assigned during the setup of the first virtual call. Subsequent virtual calls use the same circuit.

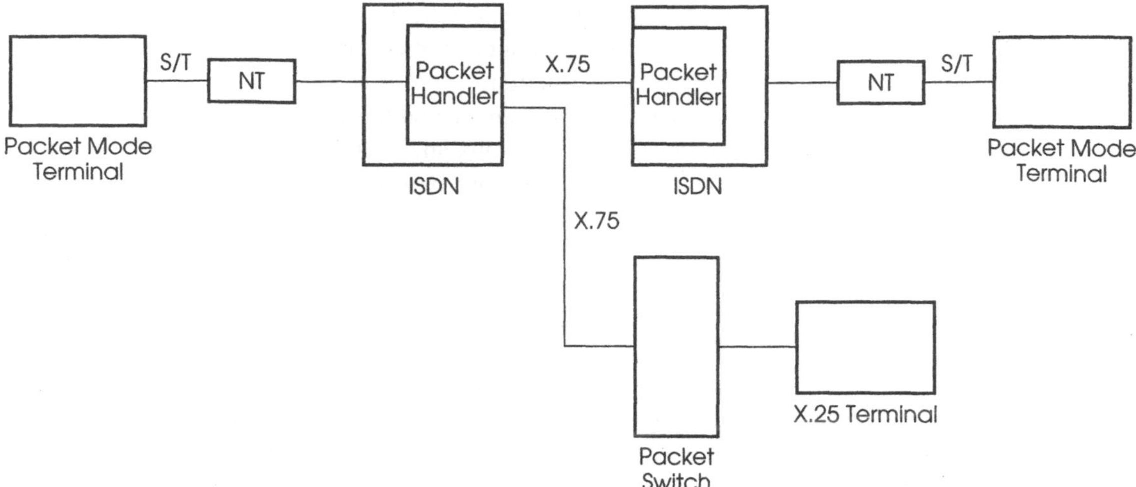

Figure 12–2 Example of a maximum integration scenario.

Likewise, the physical channel is released only when the last virtual call on the physical circuit is released.

For a permanent virtual circuit (PVC), no call setup or clearing is necessary since the logical connection between two specified terminals is assured by the network. This is analogous to the leased lines in the telephony network.

As noted earlier, either a B- or a D-channel can be used for packet calls under the maximum integration scenario. These alternatives are discussed in Sections 12.3.1 and 12.3.2.

12.3.1 Packet Calls on a B-Channel

Figure 12–3 illustrates a packet call in the B-channel. The following assumptions are made:

- Each ISDN exchange in the connection has an associated packet handler.
- The data call is the first virtual call on the B-channel at the calling user end, so B-channel setup is needed at the calling end.
- The data call is the last virtual call to be released on the B-channel at the called user end, so the B-channel release is also involved during call release.

Although the last two assumptions are likely to occur only occasionally, they have been included here to illustrate all the aspects of the call control procedure. In actual practice, as noted earlier, all calls subsequent to the first virtual call on the same B-channel do not require B-channel setup, and the B-channel cannot be released until the last virtual call is cleared. Similarly, a call on a permanent virtual circuit also does not require B-channel setup or release.

The call can be broadly divided into the following six stages, as illustrated in Figure 12–3:

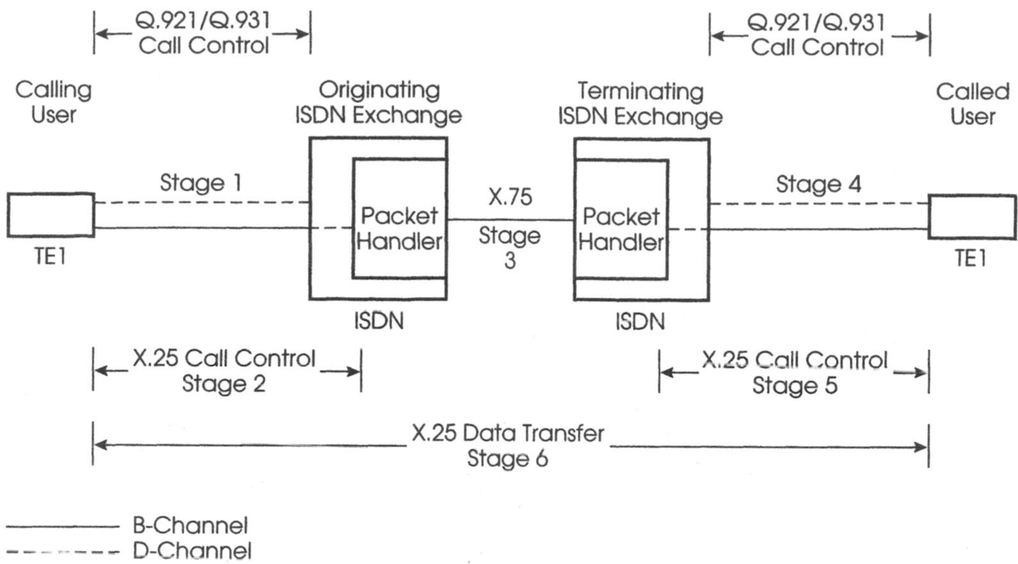

Figure 12–3 Main stages for a packet call in the B-channel: maximum integration scenario.

1. Q.921/Q.931 call control between the calling user and the originating ISDN exchange on the D-channel for assignment of a B-channel (stage 1)
2. X.25 layer 2 and layer 3 call control between the calling user and the packet handler on the B-channel (stage 2)
3. Transport of X.25 call control information through the network on X.75 links (stage 3)
4. Q.921/Q.931 call control between the terminating ISDN exchange and the called user (stage 4)
5. X.25 layer 2 and layer 3 call control between the packet handler and the called user (stage 5)
6. X.25 data flow between the calling and the called user (stage 6)

Figure 12–4 shows the detailed flow of message sequence as enumerated in the following steps:

Call setup:

1. When the packet mode ISDN terminal (hereafter referred to as the calling user) intends to make a packet call, it employs the D-channel to establish a data link connection with the originating ISDN exchange. The LAPD, described in Section 8.8, is used for this purpose. On completion of step 1, a bidirectional flow of layer 2 LAPD frames is established.

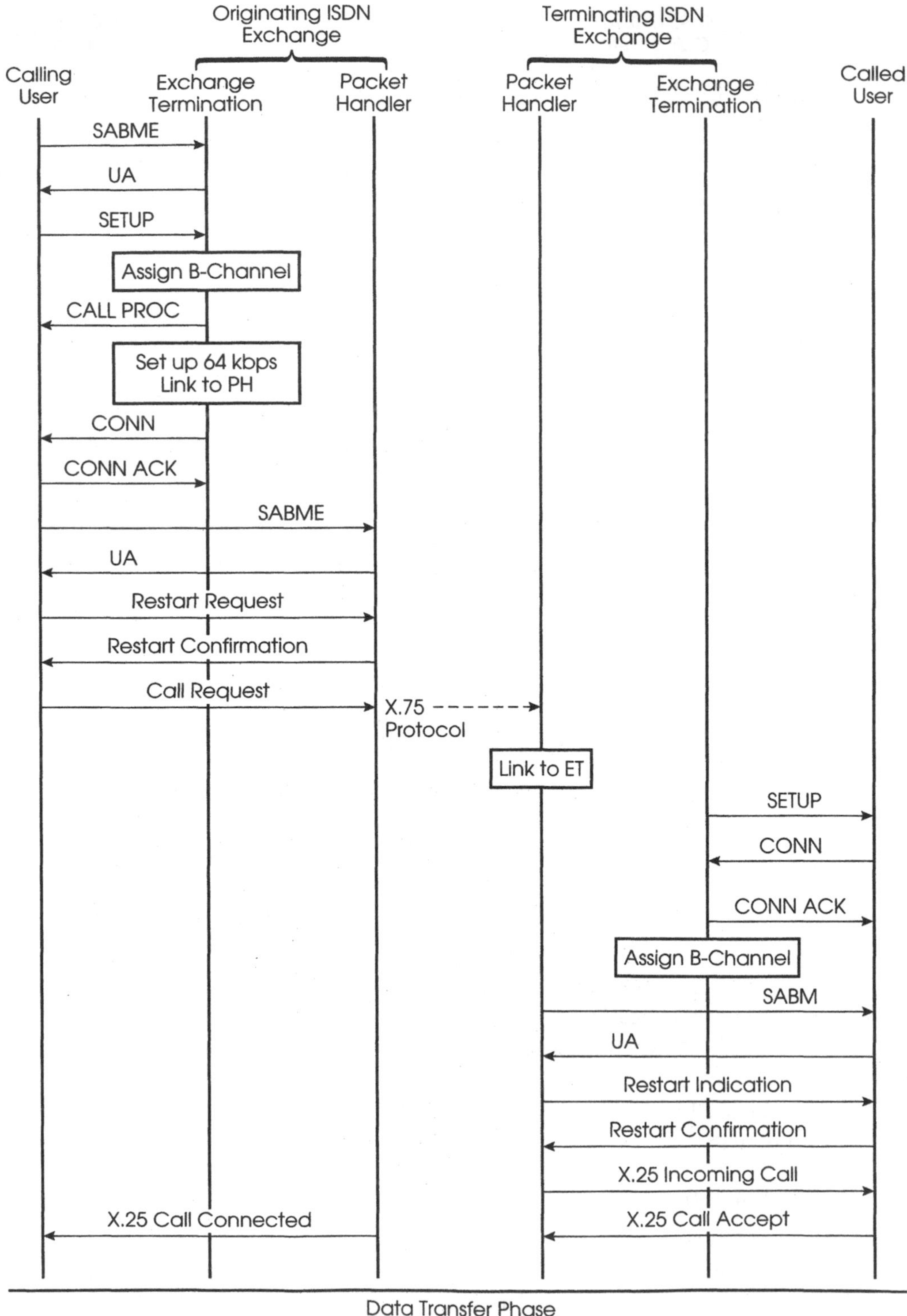

Figure 12–4 Maximum integration scenario: packet call on the B-channel.

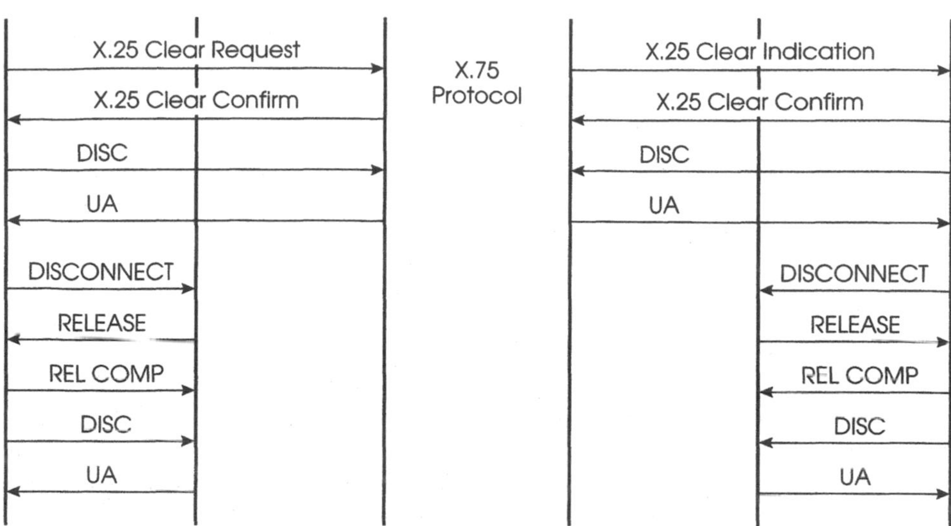

Figure 12–4 *(Continued)*

2. In the next step, the Q.931 layer 3 call control procedure is initiated to establish a B-channel connection between the calling user and the packet handler. An ISDN layer 3 setup (SETUP) message is sent on the D-channel by the calling user to the originating ISDN exchange. A notable aspect of the SETUP message is that it does not contain the called user's ISDN address. This is carried in an X.25 call control message to be sent later during call setup (refer to step 6). Thus, there is no concept of overlap operation in this case, and the SETUP message is sent only once. The bearer capability information element (Figure 8–22) in the SETUP message is coded as follows:
   - Information transfer capability field: unrestricted digital information so that packets are not modified in any manner during their transport through the network; see Figure 8–22(c)
   - Transfer mode field: packet mode; see Figure 8–22(d)
   - Information transfer rate: packet mode; see Figure 8–22(e)

   In addition, two more fields (not shown in Figure 8–22) are included in the bearer capability information element: user information layer 2 protocol, which is set to the X.25 link layer, and user information layer 3 protocol, which is set to the X.25 packet layer.
3. Upon receiving the SETUP message, the originating ISDN exchange assigns a B-channel for the packet call. This is conveyed to the calling user in the ISDN layer 3 call proceeding (CALL PROC) message.
4. By examining the bearer capability element in the SETUP message, the exchange knows that the call involves X.25 call control signaling on the B-channel between the user and the packet handler. The originating ISDN exchange establishes a link between the packet handler and the calling user. At this stage, point-to-point X.25 data link communication using LAPB can begin.

This is conveyed by the ISDN layer 3 connection (CONN) message, which is sent to the calling user by the originating exchange. The calling user may respond with an ISDN layer 3 connection acknowledge (CONN ACK) message. This message is optional.

5. X.25 layer 2 frames are exchanged between the originating ISDN access and the packet handler to establish an X.25 data link.
6. X.25 layer 3 call control messages are now exchanged on the B-channel between the calling user and the packet handler. The first X.25 layer 3 message is usually the call request message. This is sent by the calling user to the packet handler and contains the called user's ISDN address.
7. Upon examining the called user's address, the routing of the call through the network is determined. Depending on the location of the called user, the connection may require one or more packet handlers and ISDN exchanges. The X.25 call control messages are transported in the network between packet handlers on 64 kbps data links. Each such 64 kbps link is generally shared by several packet calls. As noted earlier, the protocol used between the packet handlers is X.75.
8. The terminating ISDN exchange assigns a B-channel to the called user's ISDN access. A SETUP message is included in an unnumbered information (UI) frame and sent to the terminating ISDN access in broadcast mode (terminal endpoint identifier (TEI) = 127). A compatible terminal, which in this case is a packet mode ISDN terminal, responds with a CONN message. (It is assumed that the called terminal is of automatic answering type.) The terminating ISDN exchange now sends a CONN ACK message to the called user. These messages are exchanged on the D-channel.
9. The X.25 call control procedures can now commence between the packet handler and the called user on the assigned B-channel. X.25 layer 2 messages set asynchronous balance mode (SABM) and unnumbered acknowledgment frame (UA) are exchanged to initialize the data link. After successful exchange of X.25 layer 3 messages, a packet mode connection is established between the calling and the called user, and the call enters the data transfer phase.

Call release:

10. The X.25 clear request (CR) is sent by the user to the packet handler on the B-channel. The packet handler responds with an X.25 clear confirm (CLC) message. The other user receives the X.25 clear indication (CLI) and responds with a CLC message. Thus, X.25 layer 3 procedure for packet call release is completed at either end.
11. The X.25 data link layer is now released at both ends, as shown in Figure 12–4.
12. To release the B-channel, the Q.931 procedures as described in Section 8.9.3.3 are employed at either end. For this purpose, ISDN disconnection (DISC), release (REL), and release complete (RLC) messages are used.
13. Finally, the disconnection of the data link according to Q.921 LAPD takes place to complete the release of the B-channel. (Refer to Section 8.8.5.3.)

12.3.2 Packet Calls on a D-Channel

The message sequence of an X.25 call on the D-channel is shown in Figure 12–5. In this case, Q.921/Q.931 call control procedures are not needed because the B-channel is not used. The X.25 call control procedures are used on the D-channel for call setup and release. An ISDN link layer connection is established by employing Q.921 procedures, however. The link layer connection has an SAPI value of 16. Thus, the D-channel provides a semipermanent connection for packet mode communication between the user and

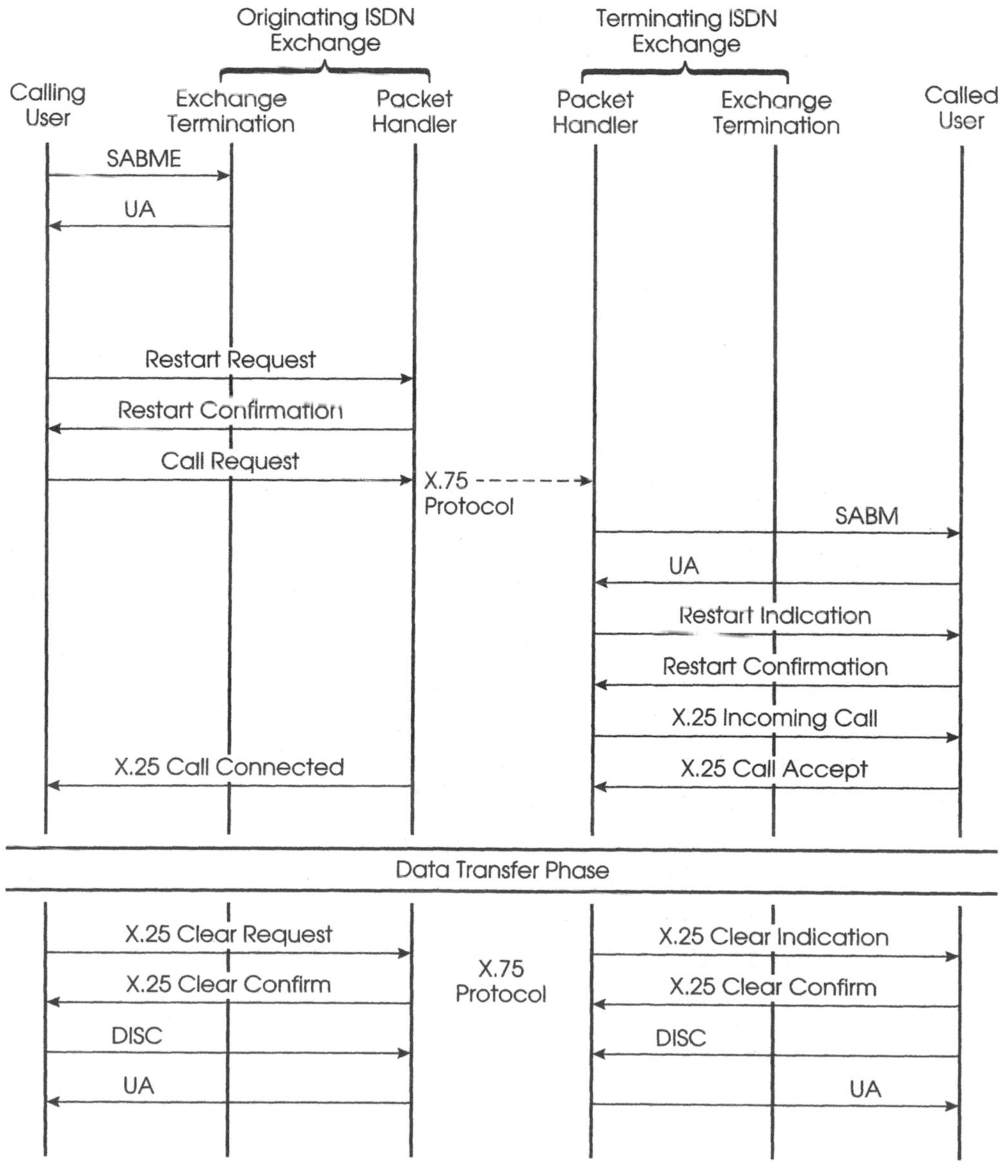

Figure 12–5 Maximum integration scenario: packet calls on the D-channel.

the packet handler (PH). Even when several packet mode terminals are communicating simultaneously over the D-channel, the SAPI value remains the same; different TEI values identify the data links.

12.4 ISDN Frame Mode Bearer Services

The two main categories of frame mode bearer services are frame relaying and frame switching. The frame relay service provides an unacknowledged transfer of frames in which error recovery and flow control functions are not implemented in the network nodes; these functions are relegated to the terminal devices. In contrast, the frame switching service provides an acknowledged transfer of frames in which error recovery and flow control functions are incorporated in the network nodes.

Table 12–1 lists the important international standards on frame mode bearer services. Prominent among the frame mode services are the frame relay services. For this reason, frame relaying is described in detail.

12.4.1 Frame Relay Services

The frame relay service is a high-speed packet switching service. Compared with X.25, a significantly higher packet throughput is achieved by exploiting the improved quality of modern transmission networks. Other than high speed, frame relaying provides much the same communication functions as the X.25 service. It should be noted that the frame relay service is not limited to the ISDN alone; it may also be supported on existing packet networks, both private and public. In fact, most of the current frame relay deployment is outside the ISDN. As the ISDN grows and expands, however, the service is likely to be supported rather extensively on the ISDN. When implemented in the ISDN, the frame relay service provides an unacknowledged transfer of frames between S/T reference points transparently through the network. The network preserves the sequence of frame transfer. It also detects transmission and frame format errors, although error correction is not performed. As noted earlier, there are two types of frame relaying, frame relaying 1 and frame relaying 2. The characteristics described so far are common to both. The difference lies in the layer 2 protocol implementation at the S/T reference points. This aspect is discussed later in this section.

Table 12–1 Important ITU-T Recommendations on ISDN Frame Mode Services

I.122	Framework for additional packet mode bearer services
I.233 [12]	Frame mode bearer services: service description
I.233.1	ISDN frame relaying bearer service: service description
I.233.2	ISDN frame switching bearer service: service description
Q.922 [13]	ISDN data link layer for frame mode bearer services
Q.933 [14]	Specification for frame mode basic call control

The ISDN environment is eminently suited to the frame relay service. Unlike X.25, which employs error and flow control on a link by link basis, the frame relay technique relies on end-to-end error and flow control. Thus, the processing involved in intermediate nodes is appreciably reduced. Figure 12–6 compares the exchange of a frame between two endpoints, A and B, for the X.25 and frame relay networks. It is seen that the transfer mechanism of frames is considerably simplified when the frame relay technique is used. Reduced delay and higher throughput are the outcome. These benefits are sensitive to the quality of transmission media, however, and are achieved only when the bit errors during transmission are low. The ISDN, with its end-to-end digital connectivity, is characterized by a low bit error ratio (BER) and is therefore a suitable platform for the frame relay service. On the other hand, the X.25 technique, which requires an acknowledgment frame at each hop, is wasteful in the context of the current widespread availability of a high-quality transmission medium.

In line with the protocol structure for circuit mode bearer services, ISDN protocols for frame relay services can be visualized to exist at two planes, the control or C plane and the user or U plane. The U plane is discussed first.

The frame relay protocols in the U plane are simple and flexible. They are simple because only two layers, the physical layer and the link layer, are required. Compare this

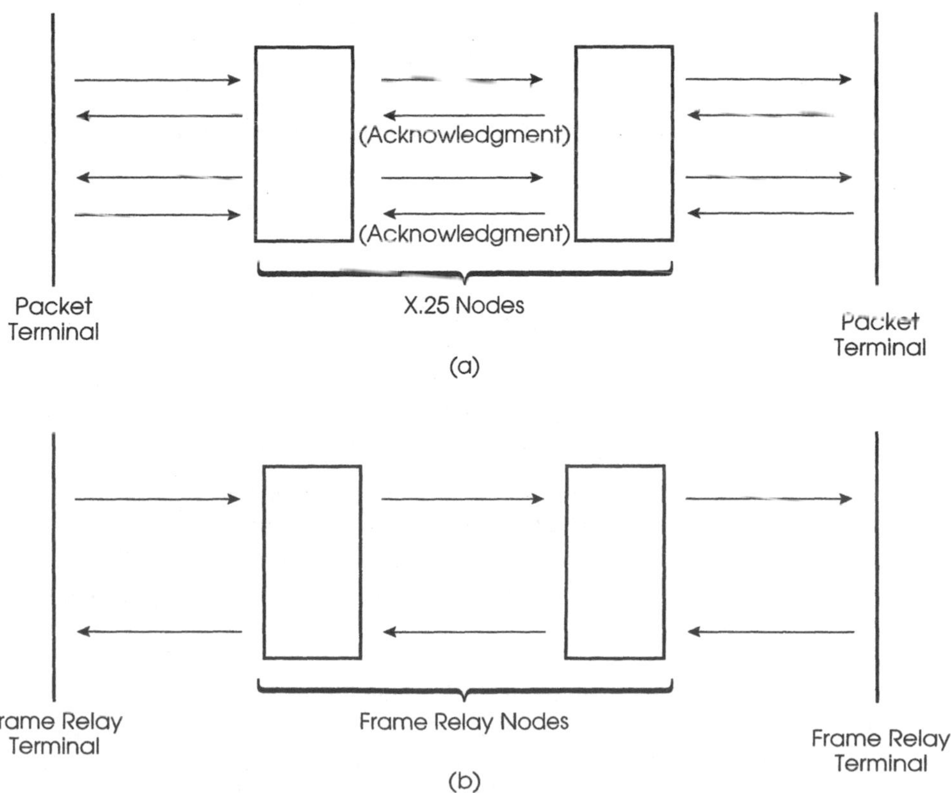

Figure 12–6 Bidirectional transfer of frames using X.25 and frame relay techniques: (a) X.25 Network; (b) Frame Relay Network.

with the three layers needed for X.25 (physical, link, and network or packet layers). Not only are the number of layers reduced, but the link layer is considerably simplified. The network nodes only implement a set of core functions; several other functions such as flow and error control are relegated to the endpoints of the connection.

The physical layer is either I.430 or I.431, depending on whether the type of ISDN access is basic or primary. The frame relay service can be provided on the B-, D-, or H-channels.

During the 1988–92 study period, the ITU-T formulated recommendation Q.922 on data link layer specifications for frame mode bearer services. These specifications, which are based on the recommendation Q.921 LAPD protocols, are designated as link access procedures for frame mode bearer service (LAPF). Since error and flow control functions are not needed at the network nodes for the frame relay service, a subset of LAPF has been described in annexure A to recommendation Q.922. The subset is called the data link core protocol (DL-CORE). The core functions include:

1. Frame delimiting, alignment, and transparency
2. Frame multiplexing/demultiplexing
3. Broad checks on the frames to confirm that they are properly bounded by flags, contain integer number of octets, and are neither too long nor too short

On the user sides—that is, at the two endpoints—additional layer 2 functions, error and flow control, must be added. Thus, layer 2 at the user sides consists of two parts:

1. A core part, DL-CORE, that communicates with the layer 2 of the network nodes
2. Additional layer 2 functions that, along with other higher layers, communicate directly with the distant user

There are two alternatives in regard to the additional layer 2 functions:

1. Additional layer 2 functions may be user specified, decided on the basis of specific congestion control and the throughput requirement. In this case, the service is referred to as frame relaying 1 service.
2. The additional layer functions may be implemented in accordance with recommendation Q.922. In this recommendation, these functions have been specified and designated as data link control (DL-CONTROL) protocol. When DL-CONTROL is used at the endpoints, the service is called frame relaying service 2.

The protocol architecture at the U plane for the frame relay service is shown in Figure 12–7. As can be seen from the figure, protocol architecture in the U plane is fairly flexible because the network nodes are transparent to the layers beyond the link layer. Layers 3 to 7 reside at the two endpoints, and the network need not be aware of protocols concerning these layers. Thus, the terminals at the two ends can flexibly implement a variety of protocols, the only requirement being the capability to operate with the "core"

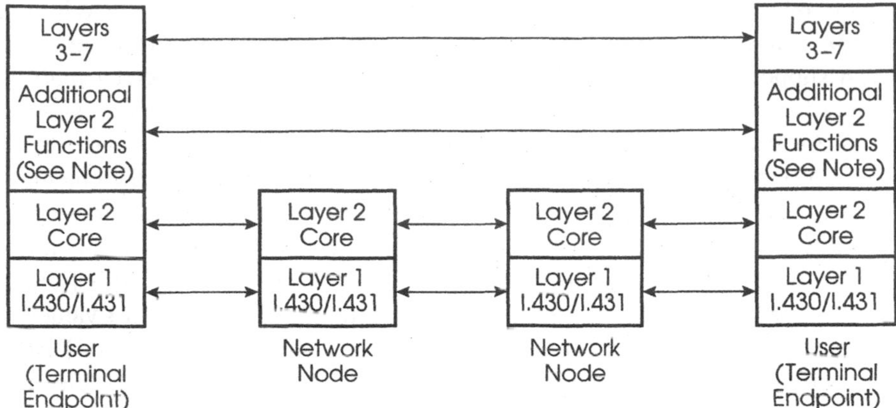

Figure 2–7 Protocol architecture for frame relay service (U plane).

layer 2 of the frame relay service, as specified in recommendation Q.922, annexure A, referred to as recommendation Q.922A. The data units generated at the higher layers must be carried in recommendation Q.922A frames. This is not a serious restriction because a large number of currently employed data protocols can operate satisfactorily with the recommendation Q.922A layer 2.

Readers may compare the U plane protocols illustrated in Figure 12–4 with the ISDN protocol architecture for circuit switched connections shown in Figure 5–4. Notice that for circuit switched services, the network nodes are completely transparent to the protocols in the U plane. The transparency of the network nodes for frame relaying is restricted to level 3 and above, however.

For the control plane, the following protocols apply:

- Recommendation I.430/I.431 for the physical layer (layer 1)
- Recommendation Q.922 for the link layer (layer 2)
- Recommendation Q.933 for the network layer (layer 3)

These protocols apply to both the frame relaying 1 and frame relaying 2 services. When frame relay services are provisioned on fixed routes that are usually specified at the time of service subscription, real-time call establishment and clearing are not involved. Consequently, layer 3 is missing in this case.

Recommendation Q.922 and Q.933 protocols are closely aligned to recommendation Q.921 and Q.931 protocols. As described in Chapter 8, the multiplexing of logical channels in the D-channel is accomplished by recommendation Q.921 using a 6-bit service access point identifier (SAPI) and a 7-bit terminal endpoint identifier (TEI) in the two-octet address field. Together, the SAPI and the TEI constitute the data link connection identifier (DLCI), which identifies a logical channel within the D-channel. On similar lines, the address field format in recommendation Q.922 contains the upper and lower DLCI fields corresponding to the SAPI and the TEI. In contrast to the two-octet address field of recommendation Q.921 (refer to Figure 8–8), the address field in recommendation Q.922 may vary from two to four octets. The default size of two octets is normally used. To support a larger DLCI address range, the three- or four-octet length address format may be employed based on prior agreement at the time of service subscription. Figure 12–8 shows the frame format for a two-octet address field. In this case, the DLCI consists of 10 bits. The DLCI identifies a virtual connection in any of the channels, D, B, or H. Since the D-channel can also be used, shared use of the D-channel concurrently with Q.921 LAPD is permissible. For example, there may be data link connections for call control of circuit switched connections in a B-channel along with frame mode virtual links on the D-channel. Readers may recall the allocation of SAPI values for the recommendation Q.921 LAPD presented in Table 8–5. Similarly, the use of DLCI values corresponding to a two-octet address field of Q.922 frames is shown in Table 12–2.

As discussed earlier, for frame relay service, the network must inform the user regarding congestion conditions as and when they arise or abate. This is necessary because congestion is managed at the two endpoints. For this purpose, the following two single-bit fields are included in the address field:

1. Forward explicit congestion notification (FECN) field
2. Backward explicit congestion notification (BECN) field

The FECN bit is set to 1 by the network to indicate to the user receiving the frame that congestion in the network exists in the direction of the received frame. This information is useful when the destination receiving the frame controls the rate of frames transmitted by the originating end.

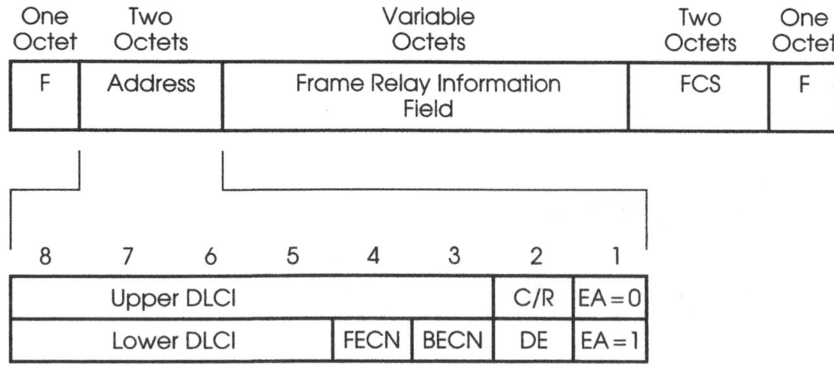

Key
C/R: Command Response bit
F: Flag
FCS: Frame Check Sequence
DLCI: Data Link Connection Identifier
EA: Address Extension Field Bit
FECN: Forward Explicit Congestion Notification
BECN: Backward Explicit Congestion Notification
DE: Discard Eligibility Indicator

Figure 12–8 Frame format for a two-octet address field.

Table 12-2 Allocation of DLCI Values

DLCI	FUNCTION
0	In channel signaling, when the channel is not a D-channel
1–15	Reserved
16–511	For support of user information, as a network option, on channels other than the D-channel
512–991	Logical link identification for support of user information
1,008–1,022	Reserved
1,023	In channel layer 2 management, when a channel other than the D-channel is used

The BECN bit is set to 1 by the network to indicate that congestion conditions prevail in the opposite direction. The function of FECN and BECN fields is illustrated in Figure 12–9.

In addition, a discard eligibility indicator bit field may be used optionally during network congestion. A frame with this indicator set to 1 can be discarded by the network, if the need arises during congestion conditions.

12.4.2 Call Control for Frame Mode Connections

The two main options for establishing frame mode connections in the ISDN are referred to as cases A and B.

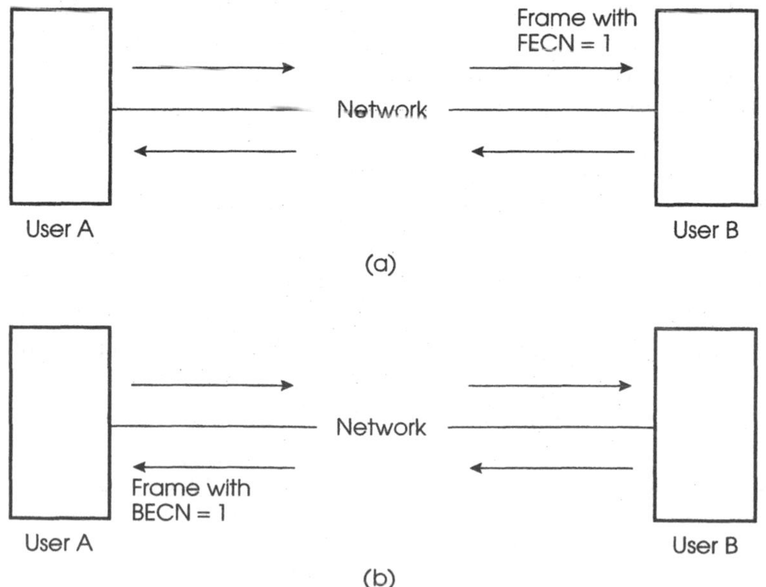

Figure 12–9 Contestion notification; with the direction of congestion from A to B: (a) using the FECN field, congestion notified to destination; (b) using the BECN field, congestion notified to origination.

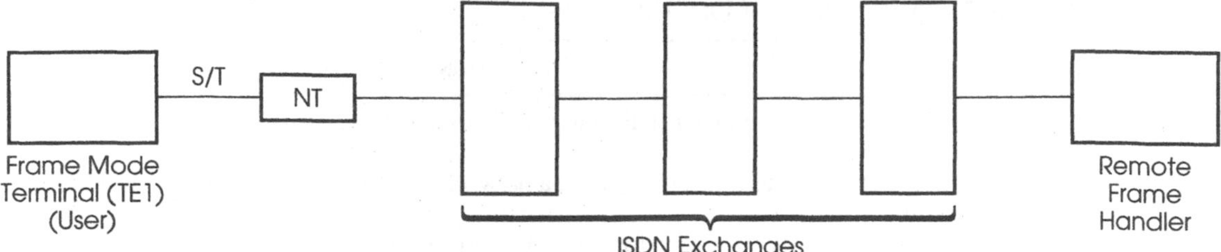

Step 1: Circuit switched connection between TE1 and the user. Signaling on the D-channel using recommendation Q.931.

Step 2: Frame mode connection on the circuit switched channel. Data link using recommendation Q. 922 with DLCI = 0 on the bearer channel. Frame mode call control employing recommendation Q.933 messages.

Figure 12–10 Frame mode call: case A.

Case A is shown in Figure 12–10. The user is connected to an ISDN exchange that has no frame handling functions. Therefore, as a first step, a circuit switched connection is established between the user and a remote frame handler (RFH), using either a B-channel or an H-channel, as illustrated in Figure 12–10. The call is originated by an ISDN frame mode terminal (TE1). An existing data terminal in association with a terminal adapter (TA) can also be used. For establishing the circuit switched connection, recommendation Q.931 call control procedures are used in the D-channel. The SETUP message sent by the user contains the address of the RFH. The bearer capability requested is "unrestricted information transfer." Once the connection is established, the second step, consisting of establishing the frame mode connection, can begin.

In the second step, a data link for the frame connection is set up in the bearer channel (B or H) employing recommendation Q.922 procedures. In-channel signaling on the bearer channel is usually used (DLCI = 0; refer to Table 12–2). The initialization of the data link is performed using, for example, set asynchronous balanced mode extended (SABME) frame/UA. The frame mode connection setup and release is based on recommendation Q.933 call control procedures. Recommendation Q.933 call control messages are a subset of those used for circuit mode connection control (recommendation Q.931), which are listed in Table 12–3. The information elements contained in these messages and the coding of each information element are defined in recommendation Q.933.

Table 12–3 Recommendation Q.933 Call Control Messages

Call Setup Messages	Call Release Messages	Miscellaneous Messages
ALERTING, CALL PROCEEDING, CONNECT, CONNECT ACKNOWLEDGE PROGRESS, SETUP	DISCONNECT, RELEASE, RELEASE COMPLETE	STATUS, STATUS ENQUIRY

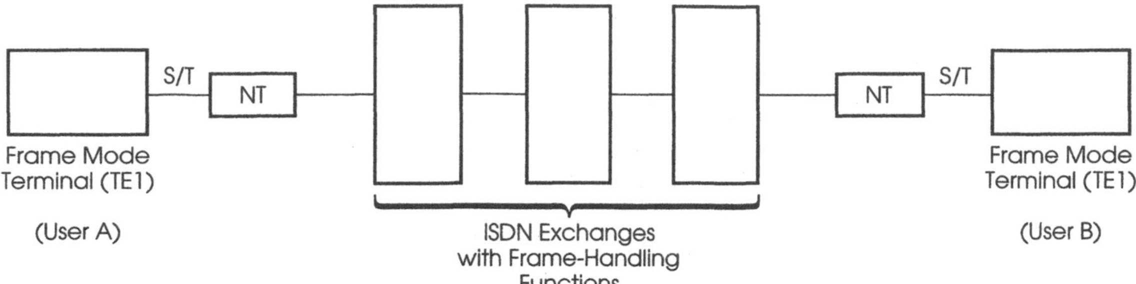

Note: This is a single-step call connection procedure for frame mode calls. Signaling in the D-channel employs recommendation Q.922 and Q.933 protocols. Physical channel for user data transport may be any channel (D, B, or H). The physical channel may be specified by the user. The DLCI identifying the logical channel for user data transport may also be indicated by the user.

Figure 12–11 Frame mode call: case B.

The user may specify the DLCI to be used for the frame mode call in the SETUP message. The channel for the user data transport is not specified, however, since the circuit switched channel is used for this purpose.

Case B provides for integrated access to frame handling functions, as illustrated in Figure 12–11. A single-step call connection procedure is used following recommendation Q.922 and Q.933 protocols. Recommendation Q.933 signaling messages are carried in the D-channel data link (SAPI = 0) for establishing a frame mode connection. Unlike case A, either the D-channel itself or any other bearer channel can be employed for user data transport. Therefore, in addition to specifying the DLCI value, the SETUP message may also indicate the bearer channel.

12.5 Remarks

Packet mode and frame mode services through the ISDN will become increasingly attractive as ISDN technology is deployed in the network on an ever-increasing basis. With this, the true potential of the ISDN as an umbrella network for various services will be finally realized.

References

[1] *Support of Packet Mode Terminal Equipment by an ISDN.* ITU-T recommendation X.31, rev. 1. International Telecommunication Union, 1993.

[2] *Interface between Data Terminal Equipment (DTE) and Data Circuit-Terminating Equipment (DCE) for Terminals Operating in the Packet Mode and Connected to Public Data Networks by Dedicated Circuit.* ITU-T recommendation X.25, rev. 1. International Telecommunication Union, 1993.

[3] *Support of Data Terminal Equipments with V-Series Type Interfaces by an Integrated Services Digital Network.* ITU-T recommendation V.110, rev. 1. International Telecommunication Union, 1992.

[4] *Framework for Providing Additional Packet Mode Bearer Services.* CCITT Blue Book, fascicle III.7, recommendation I.122. International Telecommunication Union, 1989.

[5] *ISDN User-Network Interface—Basic User Network Interface. Layer 1 Specification.* ITU-T recommendation I.430. International Telecommunication Union, 1993.

[6] *ISDN User Network Interface—Primary User-Network Interface. Layer 1 Specification.* ITU-T recommendation I.431. International Telecommunication Union, 1993.

[7] *Digital Subscriber Signaling System No. 1: ISDN User-Network Interface-Data Link Layer Specification.* ITU-T recommendation Q.921, rev. 1. International Telecommunication Union, 1993.

[8] *Digital Subscriber Signaling System No. 1: ISDN User-Network Layer 3 Specification for Basic Call Control.* ITU-T recommendation Q.931, rev. 1. International Telecommunication Union, 1993.

[9] *International Numbering Plan for Public Data Networks.* ITU-T recommendation X.121, rev. 1. International Telecommunication Union, 1992.

[10] *Packet-Switched Signaling System between Public Networks Providing Data Transmission Services.* ITU-T recommendation X.75, rev. 1. International Telecommunication Union, 1993.

[11] *Virtual Call and Permanent Virtual Circuit.* CCITT Blue Book, fascicle III.7, recommendation I.232.1. International Telecommunication Union, 1988.

[12] *Frame mode bearer services: ISDN Frame Relaying Bearer Service and ISDN Frame Switching Bearer Service.* ITU-T recommendation I.233. International Telecommunication Union, 1991.

[13] *ISDN Data Link Layer Specification for Frame Mode Bearer Services.* ITU-T recommendation Q.922. International Telecommunication Union, 1992.

[14] *Digital Subscriber Signaling System No. 1 (DSS 1)—Signaling Specification for Frame Mode Basic Call Control.* ITU-T recommendation Q.933. International Telecommunication Union, 1993.

13 Planning and Implementing the ISDN

Acronyms

AOC	advice of charge
AU	access unit
BOC	Bell operating companies
CAD/CAM	computer-aided design/computer-aided manufacture
CC	country code
CCITT	The International Telegraph and Telephone Consultative Committee
CCS 7	CCITT common channel signaling system no. 7
CFB	call forwarding busy
CFNR	call forwarding no reply
CIF	common intermediate format
CLIP	calling line identification presentation
CPE	customer premises equipment
DSS 1	digital subscriber signaling 1
EC	escape code
ETSI	European Telecommunication Standards Institute
ISDN	integrated services digital network
ISO	International Standards Organization
ISUP	ISDN user part
ITU-T	International Telecommunication Union-Telecommunication Standardization Sector
JPEC	Joint Photograph Expert Group
LAN	local area network
LCD	liquid crystal display
MCU	multipoint control units
MOU	memorandum of understanding
MPEG	Moving Pictures Expert Group
MSN	multiple subscriber number
NDC	national destination code
NIUF	North American ISDN Users Forum
NPI	numbering plan identification
PSPDN	public switched packet data network
PSTN	public switched telephone network
QCIF	quaternary common intermediate format
QOS	quality of service
RBOC	regional Bell operating companies
RLC	remote line concentrator
RSU	remote switching unit
SPC	stored program control
TMR	transmission medium requirement
TUP	telephone user part
UUS	user-to-user signaling

ABSTRACT

This chapter reviews the various aspects that need consideration when planning and implementing the integrated services digital network (ISDN). These include:

- Goals for the national ISDN
- Assessment of ISDN demand
- Selection of services and applications
- ISDN terminals
- Policy on ISDN tariffs
- Numbering and routing in the ISDN
- ISDN field trials and implementation strategies
- Quality of service and network performance issues

13.1 Introduction

An essential first step in planning the deployment of the ISDN in the national network is to precisely define the objectives that are sought to be achieved. A useful illustrative example is the national ISDN currently being implemented in the United States. The main characteristics of the national ISDN as enumerated in a BELLCORE report* [1] are the following:

- Availability of an end-to-end digital platform with standard access to circuit switched (64 kbps to 1536 kbps) and packet switched services.
- A variety of voice, data, and image service capabilities, in a standard format, available on a nationwide basis.
- Availability of innovative and cost-effective applications software and services.
- A multivendor operating environment, supported by industry and offered by multiple providers, that promotes cost-effective development, provisioning and maintenance of the network platform, as well as services on that platform.
- Standard end user equipment from many sources, that will interwork effectively and efficiently with the evolving network.

These characteristics represent a broad yet fairly comprehensive set of objectives and appear to be a good basis for planning the implementation of the ISDN.

Planning for the ISDN involves a variety of activities that can be classified into two broad categories:

1. *Market and policy-related activities,* such as assessment of demand, identification of suitable services and applications, collaborative participation between

---

multiple agencies, tariffs for the ISDN, and policy on the ownership of ISDN customer premises equipment (CPE)

2. *Technical and network-related activities,* such as technical planning, strategies for implementation of ISDN, field trials, and implementation aspects

13.2 Market and Policy-Related Issues

13.2.1 Assessment of ISDN Demand

For commercial deployment, it is necessary to assess the current and future demand for the ISDN from residential and business customers. This should include an assessment of demand for ISDN services in various sectors of national economy as well as the identification of services relevant for each sector. The exercise should also include estimates on the likely penetration of the ISDN in the network not only in quantitative terms, but also in terms of geographic spread and distribution.

The forecast for demand is usually made for the expected life span of the service. For the ISDN, the useful life will depend on two factors: the operational and technological life span of the currently deployed digital exchanges and the period for which the services offered by the ISDN remain attractive to end users. Like many other products or services, ISDN services will ultimately become obsolete. User expectations will increase progressively, fueled by the services offered by other competing technologies and the needs arising from societal changes. In the current scenario of rapid changes in technology, it is difficult to forecast too far into the future. Perhaps a period of 10 to 15 years is appropriate for demand forecasting. Demand estimates should also be made at suitable intermediate points during this period. For example, estimates may be made annually for the first 5 years and for suitably longer intervals thereafter.

The main problem in estimating demand for ISDN services arises from the lack of sufficient historical data on the service. Although the precise method for assessment of demand for ISDN services would vary from country to country, International Telecommunications Union-Telecommunication Standardization Sector (ITU-T) recommendation E.508 [2] describes the main steps that could be followed in this situation. An important step is to conduct market research for gauging the nature and extent of demand.

Market research includes market analysis and obtaining feedback from potential customers. An important parameter to be considered during market analysis is the expected rate of growth of the economy. It is useful to consider different scenarios of economic growth and compute demand estimates separately for each scenario. For more accurate estimation, sectorwise economic growth should also be taken into account. In addition to economic development, projections of the growth of telephone lines and data services should be considered. Market analysis is generally performed by a panel of economists, technical experts, and market analysts.

Feedback from potential customers is crucial to the estimation of ISDN demand. To obtain meaningful feedback, potential customers should be made aware of the services and applications that the ISDN can deliver. Dissemination of information on the ISDN is useful not only for demand estimation but also for promotion and marketing of the ISDN. The ISDN delivers a large number of services, not just a single or a few services. In the absence of familiarity with these services, end users may find some of the sophisticated features too cumbersome to use, which may result in customer resistance to the service. Advertising and distributing information on ISDN services, conducting seminars involving large potential customers, and establishing ISDN centers for demonstration of services are useful steps for creating awareness about ISDN's potential.

A common method for obtaining feedback from potential customers is to prepare questionnaires and to solicit responses. These are supplemented by other measures such as meetings and interviews. The objective should include investigation of the following aspects:

- Consumer interest in subscribing to ISDN services
- Attitudes towards existing services, such as telephone and data services
- Price sensitivity, namely, what price the customer is willing to pay for the service
- Cross-service elasticity (for example, whether a subscriber of packet network will be willing to migrate to the ISDN)

Since different categories of users may have different needs and service expectations, a separate questionnaire should be designed for each category of users. Some user categories are the following:

- Home
- Office
- Banking
- Educational institutions
- Hospitals and medical centers

Many ISDN services are of general relevance and can be offered to a broad base of customers; others may be of interest to a section or class of customers. These issues are discussed in Sections 13.2.2 and 13.2.3. Examples of popular ISDN applications are also presented in Section 13.2.3.

13.2.2 Services Relevant to a Broad Base of Customers

Many circuit mode and packet mode bearer services are available to support telephony and data transfer. Since these functions are basic to the ISDN, bearer services are needed for all categories of customers. Home users, however, usually subscribe only to basic rate access, and for them, bearer services of bit rates above 128 kbps are not meaningful. Among the teleservices, Telephony, Group 4 facsimile, Teletex, and Videotex are relevant to a broad base of ISDN customers.

There is a strong case to support as many supplementary services as technically feasible for all categories of customers. In general, supplementary services do not need any specialized terminal equipment for their provisioning. Moreover, they add value and often significantly improve the utility of the basic service to the customer. Many supplementary services can contribute to enhancing the customer's confidence in the telecommunication administration. The advice of charge (AOC) supplementary service presents one such example. In some instances, customers dispute the billing performed by the telecommunication administration, especially for long-distance calls. By displaying the charges payable by the customer for every call, the AOC service reduces the possibility of billing disputes. Although not defined in ITU-T recommendations, this supplementary service could perhaps be enhanced to include the option of displaying the customer's meter reading since last billing.

Many supplementary services have the potential to increase the revenue of the administration by improving the call success rate for the network. The call waiting supplementary service contributes significantly in this direction, particularly in networks where the busy hour calling rates are high. Often, a substantial proportion of unsuccessful calls during the busy hour result from calls made to busy subscribers. The call waiting service permits a called user to accept an incoming call even when that user is busy on another call. Therefore, this service has the potential of enhancing call success rates in the network. Call diversion services such as call forwarding no reply (CFNR) and call forwarding busy (CFB) may also improve the network call success rate and bring additional revenues to the administration. The user-to-user signaling supplementary service is another service likely to boost customer satisfaction and increase revenues in case the service is charged. The service is particularly useful when information transfer is performed during call setup. Thus, even for calls that remain unanswered, short messages can be transferred to the called user.

13.2.3 Services and Applications for Specific User Categories

Services and applications useful to home users include 64 kbps file transfer, teleshopping, and access to databases for bank transactions, railways, airlines and hotel reservations. Affluent home users will also demand PC-based videoconferencing on 64 kbps or 128 kbps. Basic access ISDN is eminently suited for home use.

For office users, 64 kbps file transfer, local area network (LAN) interconnection, videoconferencing, audioconferencing, and access to databases are useful. Both basic access and primary rate access will be required by office users, depending on the size of the establishment.

For banking, 64 kbps file transfer, electronic fund transfer, remote banking terminals and cash dispensers connected via the ISDN to host computers of the bank, and surveillance systems for security of safe-deposit vaults can be of value. Security systems require low-rate data transfer, which is typically supported on the D-channel. The data is sent periodically from remote sites to a central location to indicate the status of locking and other security devices. Both basic and primary access are required.

For educational institutions, distance learning, 64 kbps file transfer for exchange of study material, remote access to library resources, and LAN interconnection through the ISDN are popular applications.

For hospitals and health care, telemedicine is relevant. This application is briefly discussed in Section 13.2.3.1.

For research and development centers, engineering concerns, and software consultancy, LAN interconnection, 64 kbps transfer of software files, transfer of computer-aided design/computer-aided manufacture (CAD/CAM) drawings, and access to databases are useful.

For industrial establishments, LAN interconnection, 64 kbps file transfer, access to databases, telemetry, monitoring and collecting data of industrial processes from remote locations (telemetry), and control of industrial processes (telecontrol) can be useful services.

In the following section, three applications of ISDN have been chosen for discussion:

1. Telemedicine
2. Distance education
3. Videoconferencing

13.2.3.1 Telemedicine

Telemedicine is emerging as an important application of the ISDN. In remote and rural areas, expert medical advice can be obtained by general medical practitioners and other paramedical staff by use of the ISDN. The capability of the ISDN to send data, video, and voice on telephone lines is very appropriate for this application. Thus, X-ray images, electrocardiograms, case histories of patients, and other medical data can be sent over ISDN lines to medical specialists and their opinions and advice can be obtained. Remote access to medical libraries and databases is also possible. With the potential of reducing the mounting cost of medical care and improving both the quality and accessibility of medical assistance, this application is likely to be of great social relevance.

13.2.3.2 Distance Education

Another application of social relevance relates to distance education and training using ISDN lines. Audiographic ISDN terminals that combine speech with graphical images can be used for this purpose. The teacher uses the audiographic terminal to write and draw. These images are transmitted through ISDN lines and projected onto a large screen in a classroom at the other end. The teacher can also transmit previously prepared transparencies to the class. To create a classroomlike environment, it is desirable that the teacher and students have visual contact. Audiographic terminals should therefore incorporate videoconferencing equipment. The equipment in the classroom should include multiple cameras and microphones to permit interaction between students and teacher. A useful feature of distance education through the ISDN is that the study material can be readily sent by 64 kbps file transfer. The 7 kHz telephony available in the ISDN is another useful feature, since good speech quality is critical in the creation of the classroom environment. There is a growing literature on the application of ISDN for distance learning and training in different countries. Reference [3] describes several such projects.

13.2.3.3 Videoconferencing

Videoconferencing is fast emerging as an attractive application. For the corporate sector, it promises to reduce the need for long-distance travel because meetings can be set up via videoconferencing. For individual users, it significantly enriches the quality of human communication. The central problem in video communication arises from the need for very high bandwidths for transmitting encoded video images. These bandwidths are presently not supported on the ISDN, where the bit rates are limited to 2 Mbps (1.5 Mbps for North America). To reduce the communication bandwidth requirements, data-compression methods are employed to remove the redundant information before transmission on the line. Recent advances in data-compression techniques have fueled the growth of videoconferencing through the ISDN. At the heart of videoconferencing equipment lies the codec, which digitizes video and audio signals for transmission. At the receiving end, the reverse process is followed to retrieve the video and audio signals. Earlier implementations of codecs were based on the 1984 CCITT recommendation H.120 [4]. The recommendation specified the compression algorithm and the number of frames to be processed per second. Codecs implemented according to this recommendation required bandwidths in the range of 768 kbps or 2 Mbps. However, this recommendation has been superseded with new international standards on videoconferencing over the ISDN. Table 13–1 summarizes the relevant standards.

For connecting several videoconferencing terminals, multipoint control units (MCUs) are employed. The MCUs are bridging equipment that the user dials to establish a conference. In turn, the MCU interconnects different videoconferencing sites. Videoconference users with a need to interconnect several sites may procure their own MCUs. As videoconference users proliferate, however, it would be more economical for telecommunication administrations to provide the MCUs in the network. For the MCUs, the related ITU-T recommendations are H.231 [9] and H.243 [10]. Recommendation H.231 specifies the minimum requirements that must be met by the MCUs; recommendation H.243 describes the operation of video conference calls.

While the ITU-T recommendations focus on the transmission of video images, the International Standards Organization (ISO) has formulated standards for coding algorithms and compression techniques for use in video communication equipment at the two ends. Different types of coding techniques are required for still and motion pictures. Intraframe coding is used for still pictures in which the information available in a single picture frame is coded and compressed using one of several available methods. Typical compression ratios that can be achieved for still images range from 2:1 to 30:1. The Joint

Table 13–1 ITU Standards on Video Conferencing

RECOMMENDATION	SCOPE
H.261 [5]	Functions of video codec and video coding algorithms. Two video formats are defined: common intermediate format (CIF) for higher picture resolution (352 pixels by 288 lines) and quarternary common intermediate format (QCIF) with lower resolution of 176 pixels by 144 lines.
H.221 [6]	Communications framing structure for synchronization and channel multiplexing
H.242 [7]	Handshake, connection, and disconnection procedures for point-to-point connection of video telephony terminals
H.320 [8]	Technical requirements and general framework for narrowband video telephony terminals.

Photograph Expert Group (JPEG) of the ISO has recommended a method for coding still pictures that provides good picture quality coupled with a high compression ratio. For moving pictures, interframe coding is used. The information available in successive frames of a motion video is very similar in content, and this characteristic is exploited to achieve significantly higher compression ratios for moving pictures (of the order of 50:1 to 200:1). The Moving Pictures Expert Group (MPEG) of the ISO has framed the standards for moving pictures.

Videoconferencing equipment varies widely in terms of cost, sophistication, bandwidth requirement, and other features. Equipment ranges from studio videoconferencing with several high-quality cameras and microphones to PC-based desktop videoconferencing. For the ISDN, the maximum bit rate supported corresponds to the primary rate access bit rate. Video communication at 384 kbps provides reasonably good quality and is a cost-effective option for applications such as office videoconferencing and distance education. For bit rates of 384 kbps and higher, the common intermediate format (CIF) of recommendation H.261 that provides better-quality pictures is generally used. Quaternary common intermediate format (QCIF) is applied for bit rates of 64 kbps and 128 kbps. The bandwidths available should provide both video and audio communication. Thus, another issue is the bit rate to be used for audio communication; it may be 48 kbps per ITU-T recommendation G.722 [11]. However, where videoconferencing uses bandwidths of 64 kbps or 128 kbps, audio must be carried at lower bit rates, such as 16 kbps. Certain implementations of videoconferencing include simultaneous file transfer in addition to video and audio communication. In such cases, the bandwidth has to be allocated between all three.

PC-based desktop videoconferencing has great potential for future growth, since the use of the PC is ubiquitous. The equipment uses the existing PC monitor as a screen, and the only additional external pieces needed are the camera and the microphone. The camera can be placed at the top of the monitor or at any other suitable location. Thus, the equipment needs very little additional space. The PC is enhanced to function as a personal desktop video communication system by addition of one or two boards that go into the vacant slots available in the PC. The system typically works on a bit rate of 128 kbps and can be supported using two B-channels of a basic rate access with 64 kbps unrestricted digital bearer capability. For PC-based systems, a useful application along with videoconferencing is application sharing, which allows users at the two ends to display and edit a document jointly during a videoconferencing session.

For establishing a point-to-point 128 kbps video call, the videoconferencing terminal establishes two separate calls, each using 64 kbps unrestricted digital bearer capability. Thus, as far as the network is concerned, the video call is treated as two independent calls. The terminals at the two ends establish an end-to-end protocol and use the two 64 kbps channels for transmission of video and audio. The same principle is employed for establishing a 384 kbps connection. In this case, six B-channels are needed, and the video terminal establishes these connections to the other end as six independent calls. This approach is followed by many video communication equipment manufacturers because it merely requires 64 kbps unrestricted digital bearer capability from the network. A more elegant solution would be to use 2×64 kbps and 384 kbps unrestricted digital bearer service, but many existing ISDN exchanges do not support these services.

The applications of videoconferencing using the ISDN as the communications platform are many. Two applications, telemedicine and distance learning, have already been mentioned. With the availability of PC-based videoconferencing equipment, home applications are likely to pick up rapidly. Driving factors for home use are the following:

- Affordable cost of the equipment
- Widespread use of personal computers
- Possibility to employ the PC for other applications when videoconferencing is not in use
- Use of fairly inexpensive basic rate ISDN connections

13.2.4 Need for Collaborative Effort

Although telecommunication administrations have a crucial role to play, ISDN cannot succeed without the coordinated efforts of several agencies and user groups. These include:

- National standardization bodies
- Telecommunication administrations
- Switch equipment manufacturers
- ISDN customer premises equipment manufacturers
- Software houses for application development
- ISDN user groups

A striking example of cooperation between various agencies can be seen in the successful evolution of the national ISDN in the United States. The national ISDN has progressed with the active support and collaborative participation of multiple agencies, namely, the regional Bell Operating Companies (RBOCs), ISDN switch suppliers, BELLCORE, and the North American ISDN Users Forum (NIUF). The outcome of these efforts is a step-by-step evolution of network capabilities termed national ISDN-1 (1992), national ISDN-2 (1993), and national ISDN-3 (1995–96). The national ISDN stresses the standardization of user interfaces and network protocols. A key feature is the uniformity of services being offered to the users. Uniformity of services means that identical services and features are offered to the end user irrespective of the switch type through which the service is offered. Another goal met by the national ISDN is the portability of terminals so that an ISDN terminal can be used with various types of switches without any loss of functionality. This important requirement cannot be met without active cooperation between switch manufacturers, terminal equipment manufacturers, and telecommunication administrations. Portability of terminals will ensure that "islands" of the ISDN are avoided and compliant ISDN terminals are mass produced, thus pushing down terminal costs. National ISDN also stresses the development of end applications, and in this context, the role of software houses is significant.

A key objective of the national ISDN is the creation of a standard development platform for ISDN applications. The crucial importance of this requirement can be judged by considering an example from the computing world. The very large volume of application software developed for the PC is the outcome of a good and inexpensive computing platform provided by the PC. Likewise, the ISDN, by offering a standard, high-quality, ubiquitous digital communication platform, is expected to trigger the development of a large number of services and applications that will be governed only by the dynamics of the market and the creativity of application designers. A complete list of key ISDN features and attributes are described in appendix A to reference [1]. Various aspects of U.S. national ISDN are covered in references [12] to [14].

In Europe, the collaborative efforts on the ISDN have been channelized under the auspices of the European Commission. This has culminated in the implementation of Euro-ISDN based on a memorandum of understanding (MOU) reached between 26 operators in 20 European countries. The standards for Euro-ISDN have been framed by the European Telecommunication Standards Institute (ETSI). These standards permit the operation of the ISDN between member countries of the European Commission on the basis of a common set of services and features. An important implication of Euro-ISDN, like the national ISDN in the United States, is the creation of a common platform on which new software and terminals can be developed to feed the needs of the sizable European market. A European ISDN users forum was formed in 1991 with the objective of identifying ISDN applications, informing users on the current status of ISDN and development of short position papers on areas of concern in the ISDN.

13.2.5 Tariff Policy for the ISDN

Tariff policy is a matter to be decided by individual administrations. It is useful to discuss the principles that could be applied in establishing ISDN tariffs, however.

The ISDN tariff should reflect the cost of investment and ensure a reasonable return on investment. This would require detailed financial appraisal of the ISDN implementation project. Chapter VIII of the ITU GAS 9 document [15] presents a method of performing financial evaluation. But the investments in the ISDN may not always be the sole criteria in the determination of tariff. First, the ISDN is a natural evolution of the telephone network and an outcome of technological push. Thus, ISDN capabilities are being incorporated in the network to a large extent by the modernization of the telecommunication plant. Having committed themselves to this modernization exercise, administrations worldover have an obvious stake in the success of the ISDN in the marketplace. Administrations would like to ensure that the newly acquired network capabilities are exploited commercially as early as possible. These considerations of promoting the ISDN would inexorably lead to lower tariffs, at least during the introductory stage. Second, for many of the same reasons, it is not always possible to separate the ISDN from the existing network and to precisely determine the cost attributable solely to the ISDN.

While establishing the ISDN tariff, the principle of tariff harmonization should also be considered. Simply stated, harmonization means that for similar services, the charges should be the same, or nearly so, irrespective of the network through which the services are provided. Certain services that are made available through the ISDN are also offered by existing telephony and data networks. The administration should examine the existing charges for these services before fixing their tariff within the ISDN. For services that are unique to the ISDN, however, the principle of harmonization is not applicable.

The tariff structure should be simple to understand and easy to implement. Recent years have witnessed major changes in the telecommunication policy of several countries.

It is therefore advisable to recognize the possibility of future changes in regulatory policy and to implement an ISDN tariff that is flexible and easily adaptable to anticipated changes.

ISDN service should be priced so that it stimulates demand and encourages the optimum utilization of network resources. It must also take into account the paying capacity of users.

In addition, the tariff policy should also consider the socioeconomic needs of the country. For example, it should be designed to encourage those services and applications that are of social relevance.

Tariffs for teleservices using the same bearer service should be independent of the specific nature of that teleservice.

Some of the principles outlined above are also enumerated in ITU-T recommendations D.210 [16], D.211 [17], D.220 [18], D.230 [19], D.231 [20], D.250 [21] and D.251 [22]. The following three components of the ISDN tariff are identified in these recommendations:

1. Connection charge
2. Subscription charge
3. Utilization charge

The connection charge is a one-time charge to cover the installation expenses. These charges would be different for basic access and primary access connections. For basic access, the connection charges may be at least twice that of the installation charges for a normal telephone, since two simultaneous B-channel connections are available in this case. On the other hand, only one network interface is installed on the customer's premises, giving smaller labor charges for that part of the installation. There could be a justification for higher charges, where:

- An attractive set of supplementary services are included without any additional charges.
- Slow-rate data services are available on the D-channel. In this case, the customer can originate additional calls on the D-channel.

For primary access that permits 30 simultaneous calls (23 simultaneous calls in North America), a higher connection charge may be justified. The European Commission has urged the telecommunication administrations in member states to consider a ratio of ten between the connection charges for basic and primary rate access [23].

Subscription charges or rental fees are payable periodically (monthly, bimonthly, or quarterly, depending on the billing cycle) and are generally levied based on the services to which the customer subscribes. Utilization charges depend on the nature of the network resources required and the extent of their use in providing the service.

In the ISDN, the nature of network resources required are specified by the bearer capability. In a mixed analog-digital network, it may be more expensive to provide a 64 kbps unrestricted bearer service than a circuit switched bearer service for speech. Thus, a 64 kbps switched data call can be charged at a higher rate than a speech call.

The extent of utilization of network resources is estimated on the basis of the following factors:

- Duration of connection and/or volume of data transmitted. The duration of the call is usually meaningful for circuit switched connection, whereas the volume of data is an appropriate measure for a packet call.
- Distance spanned by the call
- Time of usage, for example, day, night, holidays, working days

Supplementary services often require additional processing in the network nodes and the transport of additional information in ISDN user part (ISUP) messages through the transmission network. Therefore, ITU-T recommendation D.230 stipulates that additional charges can be levied for these services by one of the following methods:

- By charging a subscription or rental for the service
- By applying a utilization charge on every call in which the service is invoked and not charging for that service when it is not invoked
- By charging both subscription and rental for the service
- By collecting a single charge for a group of services

As noted earlier, certain supplementary services may help increase revenues by increasing call success rates. The administration may consider offering such services free of charge to promote their use in the network.

13.2.6 ISDN Customer Premises Equipment

With changes in regulatory policy, the terminal equipment market has been deregulated in many parts of the world. These administrations no longer supply and maintain end user equipment, and customers are free to buy compliant terminals from the open market. This situation may be satisfactory for analog users where a fully developed competitive market for terminals already exists. In several countries, however, the market for ISDN terminals is still in a formative stage, and the customers are not fully aware of the features and sources of supply of ISDN terminal equipment. In this situation, administrations could either shoulder the responsibility of the ISDN terminal equipment supply during the introductory phase or establish a mechanism that would ensure the end user of the availability of compliant and affordable terminal equipment. Once supply sources are identified and an awareness is created among end users, the policy on ISDN terminals can be reviewed and made identical to that for analog terminals if necessary.

In keeping with the multiservice character of the ISDN, a variety of ISDN terminal equipment is required. The growth of the terminal equipment market is crucial to the success of the ISDN. Therefore, BELLCORE in the United States and the ETSI in Europe have framed guidelines and standards for the terminal equipment manufacturers. The objective of this standardization is to enable manufacturers to develop terminal equipment that would support service features uniformly, regardless of the ISDN switch to which they are connected. Table 13–2 lists some of the important BELLCORE and ETSI standards on ISDN terminals.

Some of the commonly used ISDN terminals are briefly described next.

The ISDN telephone is a basic requirement for all customers. Several models are available, which broadly fall under two categories: simple ISDN phone and ISDN feature phone. The simple ISDN phone has a liquid crystal display (LCD) for presentation of information received from the network. Examples are calling line identification presentation (CLIP), advice of charge (AOC), and short messages related to user-to-user signaling (UUS) supplementary service. The LCD is also used for the display of locally generated information. In addition are soft keys for various functions, including the invocation of supplementary services.

The feature phone is designed to take advantage of the complete range of supplementary services and other features offered by the ISDN. It usually includes a keyboard that is useful for keying short messages for the UUS supplementary service. The feature phone also incorporates an RS-232 or similar interface for connection of data terminals, a bigger LCD, and additional function keys.

As discussed in Section 8.9.4, the access to supplementary services from the telephone can be based on stimulus mode (keypad and feature key management) or functional protocol. Several administrations started out with feature key management. The current

Table 13–2 Standards on ISDN Terminals

	UNITED STATES (BOCS)
STANDARD	SCOPE
SR-NWT-002343 [24]	Customer premises equipment for ISDN primary rate access: generic guidelines
SR-NWT-002361 [25]	ISDN terminal equipment for basic rate access on National ISDN-2: generic guidelines
SR-NWT-002661 [26]	ISDN terminal equipment for basic rate access on the national ISDN: generic guidelines covering National ISDN-1 and National ISDN-2
	EUROPE (ETSI)
ETS 300 153 [27]	Attachment requirements, layer 1 and 2, for terminals connected to basic access ISDN
ETS 300 104 [28]	Attachment requirements, layer 3, for terminals connected to basic access ISDN
ETS 300 156 [29]	Attachment requirements for terminals connected to primary rate access
ETS 300 077 [30]	Terminal adaptors
ETS 300 082 [31]	End-to-end compatibility requirements 3.1 kHz telephony terminals
ETS NET 33 [32]	Attachment requirements for handset 3.1 kHz telephony terminals
prETS 300 088 [33]	Facsimile group 4 class equipment: general and service aspects
prETS 300 087 [34]	Functional specification of facsimile group 4 class 1 equipment
prETS 300 112 [35]	End-to-end protocols for facsimile group 4 class 1 equipment

trend, however, is to standardize on functional protocol, which (as pointed out in Section 8.9.4) provides a customer-friendly interface. Another notable issue about ISDN telephones is the supply of tones and announcements to the user and whether these should be provided by the network or be generated locally by the ISDN telephone. ITU-T recommendation Q.764 [36] leaves the options open. The ETSI standards ETS 300 085 [32] stipulate that the terminal should be capable of transmitting the tones and announcements received from the network. As an option, however, the terminal may locally generate tones and announcements on the basis of network information received on the D-channel. In that case, it is essential that the tones are identical to those specified for the network.

Several manufacturers supply cards that allow a PC to be connected at the S-interface. This is an attractive option, since the use of the PC is ubiquitous. Its applications and capabilities have steadily grown over the years, while the costs have declined. Moreover, a vast majority of existing and potential ISDN customers routinely use PCs. PC-based ISDN terminals have tremendous potential for growth. Several applications are already available on the PC; the 64 kbps file transfer is among the most widely used. A handset is also usually included to combine both voice and data-transfer capabilities. The use of the PC as a personal videoconferencing system was mentioned earlier. Typically, the PC-based ISDN terminal involves a cost-effective upgrade in which one or two additional boards are added in existing vacant slots. The upgrade also involves additional application software. With suitable peripheral devices, the PC can also be enhanced to provide group 4 facsimile.

Group 4 facsimile ISDN terminals are specified in the T-series recommendations of the ITU-T. Three classes of terminals have been defined: classes 1, 2, and 3. Class 1 terminals are the simplest and support end-to-end facsimile communication on 64 kbps ISDN B-channels using standardized coding and communication protocols. In addition to class 1 terminal functions, class 2 terminals can also receive teletex and mixed-mode information. Class 3 terminals have the maximum functionality: they can receive as well as transmit teletex and mixed-mode information.

Terminal adaptors that allow ISDN customers to make use of their existing terminal equipment have a useful role to play in the development of the ISDN market because they represent a bridge between the "earlier public switched telephone network (PSTN)/public switched packet data network (PSPDN)" and the "current ISDN." Examples of terminal adaptors include the following:

- Analog telephony to S-interface
- V.24 to S-interface (similar to RS-232)
- V.35 to S-interface
- RS-530 to S-interface
- X.21 to S-interface
- X.25 to S-interface

Terminal adaptors that combine several of the above in a single implementation are also available.

13.3 Technical and Network-Related Activities

13.3.1 Technical Plans

While planning the introduction of the ISDN, it is necessary to review the existing technical plans that were formulated for the PSTN such as switching, transmission, routing, numbering, and charging plans. The network synchronization and the International Telegraph and Telephone Consultative Committee (CCITT)'s CCITT common channel signaling system no. 7 (CCS 7) plans also exist for most of the national networks. When formulated for a digital network, synchronization and transmissions plans do not require any changes for the introduction of the ISDN. (The network synchronization planning aspects discussed in Chapter 3 include the requirements arising from the ISDN). CCS 7 plans may require a few changes in networks where the telephone user part (TUP) or its upgrade (for example, TUP +) was originally deployed. A program for deployment of the ISUP is necessary in such cases. CCS 7 planning aspects have already been discussed in Chapter 11.

The charging plan would need to include charging for ISDN calls based on the tariff issues discussed in Section 13.2.5. Next, the numbering and routing aspects of the ISDN are discussed.

13.3.1.1 Numbering Plan

The numbering plan for the ISDN era was described in ITU-T recommendation E.164 [37], and the numbering and addressing principles were enumerated in ITU-T recommendation I.330 [38]. The broad requirements imposed on the ISDN numbering are the following:

- Evolution from the existing PSTN numbering plan
- Provision of sufficient capacity for anticipated future expansion
- Provision of a means of discrimination in case the same area is served by multiple operators
- Arrangement for interworking with other networks, both private and public

The requirement of evolving the ISDN numbering plan from PSTN numbering is intrinsic to the evolutionary character of ISDN. Thus, the latest E.164 recommendation incorporates the Blue Book recommendation E.163 [39] meant for the PSTN. An international number in the PSTN has the following features:

- The PSTN number is composed of two parts, a country code (CC) followed by the national significant number.
- Country codes are listed in annexure A to recommendation E.164, where countries are classified under nine numbering zones. All the countries within a zone have the zone number as the first digit in their country code. For example, Japan (country code 81) appears in zone 8. The length of the country code varies from one to three digits. Country codes include the United States (country code 1), Spain (country code 34), and Hong Kong (country code 852).

- The national significant number is to be decided by the national administrations. The term *significant* has been used to exclude any prefixes that might exist for special routing of calls made between two subscribers within the same country. These prefixes are part of the national number.
- The national significant number consists of a national destination code (NDC) and the subscriber number.
- The character set 0–9 is used for forming the ISDN number.
- There are currently 12 total digits in an international PSTN number, excluding the international access code.

The above structure exists for the ISDN except that the total number of digits in this case is 15. Since there is no change in the country code, there is a possible increase in the number of digits in the national significant number by three. Thus, the addressing capability can increase a thousandfold. To incorporate this enhanced addressing capability in the switches in an orderly manner, ITU-T recommendation E.165 [40] stipulates that the 15-digit numbering scheme will come into force on the last day of 1996. This date is designated as time *T* in the recommendation. This does not imply that all administrations should increase the number of digits in the national significant number on this date. After time *T*, however, all the switches within a country must be able to store up to 15 digits to allow outgoing calls to international destinations where international numbers of 15 digits exist. Another requirement imposed on the switches is the maximum number of digits they may be required to analyze for the routing of outgoing international calls. The maximum number of digits to be analyzed should not exceed six, and these digits include the country code and part of the national significant number of the destination. Since the length of the country code varies between the one to three digits, the number of digits of the national significant number that may be analyzed varies from three to five digits.

In the ISDN era, the numbering scheme described above applies to both the PSTN and the ISDN. The stored program control (SPC) exchanges may have the flexibility of storage and number analysis; the electromechanical exchanges generally will require additional equipment (for example, more registers) to meet the above requirements.

The national destination code permits call routing to a specific area or destination. When several operators serve the same area, the numbering scheme should provide some means of identifying a specific network operator. The administration can provide this discrimination by, for example, assigning one or more digits to identify the operator.

While considering the interworking with other networks in the context of the ISDN numbering plan, it is necessary to recognize that there are multiple public networks in most countries. Each public network may have a different numbering plan. When calls span more than one network, satisfactory interworking of the numbering plans is essential for successful call completion. ITU-T recommendation E.166 [41] deals with the interworking of the ISDN numbering plan with the PSPDN and the PSTN. The following methods are available for the interworking of numbering plans:

- Dial-in method
- Escape code (EC) method
- Numbering plan identification (NPI) method

An example of the dial-in method is the dialing procedure used in X.31 case A for the interworking between the ISDN and the PSPDN. As described in Chapter 12, a two-step dialing procedure is adopted by the subscriber. An ISDN subscriber calling a subscriber in the PSPDN dials an ISDN number as the first step for connection to an access unit (AU). When the connection is established, a second dial tone (or an equivalent indication) is fed to the subscriber, who then proceeds to dial the PSPDN number following the X.121 [42] numbering plan of the PSPDN.

The EC and NPI methods provide a means of indicating to the exchange that the digits to follow belong to a different numbering plan.

In the EC method, a predefined escape code 0 is used to indicate an escape from E.164 numbering to X.121 numbering of the PSPDN. This is required, for example, when a packet mode call originates from the ISDN corresponding to X.31 case B. The EC method is an interim solution that will be superseded by the NPI method.

A more elegant solution is provided by the NPI method. The SETUP message in the recommendation Q.931 call control procedure contains a numbering plan identification (NPI) field as shown in Figure 8–29. The originating exchange is thus informed of the numbering scheme under which the calling subscriber has dialed. The originating exchange interprets the received digits appropriately and routes the call to the desired network.

Before concluding the discussion on the numbering aspects in the ISDN, it is useful to consider the directory number assignment in an ISDN customer's premises. An ISDN subscriber may need several directory numbers for a single ISDN interface. Since several terminals may be connected at an ISDN interface, there is an additional requirement of addressing a specific terminal. ISDN protocols allow distinction between terminal types by means of compatibility checking. Refer to Section 8.9.3.2 for details. Thus, a speech call is received at an ISDN telephone and a facsimile at a fax terminal. When several terminals of the same type exist at the S-interface, however, an additional addressing mechanism is required, which is provided either by the subaddressing or by the multiple subscriber number (MSN) addressing capability. In subaddressing, the additional digits needed to identify a terminal uniquely are transparently passed through the network. These digits have only endpoint significance. Therefore, subaddressing has no impact on the numbering plan. In the case of MSN, multiple directory numbers are assigned and the administration has to decide the number of multiple directory numbers that may be allocated to an ISDN interface. These numbers should, preferably, be allotted serially.

Table 13–3 lists the ITU-T recommendations on numbering in the ISDN.

Table 13–3 International Standards on the ISDN Numbering

ITU-T Recommendation	Scope
I.330	General principles on ISDN numbering
E.160 [43]	Definition of terms related to numbering
E.164	Numbering plan for the ISDN era; includes both ISDN and PSTN.
E.165	Timetable for coordinated implementation of E.164
E.166	Interworking of numbering between ISDN and public data networks

13.3.1.2 Routing Plan

Routing in the PSTN is determined on the basis of the number dialed and the network structure. Thus, in the PSTN, routing of the call does not consider the service being offered. On the other hand, the ISDN is a multiservice network where different services require different signaling and transmission capabilities. Therefore, ISDN routing must also take into account the service requested by the call, and a route should be selected with bearer capabilities that are appropriate to the service. For example, speech and data calls between the same pair of ISDN subscribers may be routed differently due to differences in the bearer capability needed in the two cases. As discussed in Chapters 8 and 9, digital subscriber signaling 1 (DSS 1) and ISUP protocols communicate the bearer capability and transmission medium requirement (TMR) through the network. Thus, taking into consideration the service associated with the call, routing decisions have to be made at various switching nodes.

The standards on ISDN routing are listed in Table 13–4.

13.3.2 ISDN Field Trials

Many administrations prefer to conduct field trials before offering commercial ISDN service. Field trials are useful in resolving technical issues and in obtaining user response to different services. They also provide real-life operational experience and help to identify glitches in the technical specifications. The lessons learned during field trials significantly contribute to the successful implementation of the ISDN.

The field trial configuration should include local and transit exchanges of all the switch types that are planned for deployment in the commercial ISDN. The exchanges in the field trial configuration should be synchronized and interconnected by CCS 7 trunks. Field trial exchanges should also support other signaling systems existing in the network so that the interworking of these signaling systems with CCS 7 is also field tried. In addition, access should be provided to other networks, such as the PSPDN.

The objectives of the field trial may include the following:

- To observe and evaluate the performance of ISDN local exchanges in the provisioning of ISDN services
- For local exchanges, to identify and resolve problems during interworking of DSS 1 protocol with ISUP protocol and with other signaling systems. For the transit exchanges, problems in ISUP protocol implementation and its interworking with other signaling systems should be examined.

Table 13–4 ISDN Routing Standards

International	U.S. Bell Operating Companies (BOC)	European
ITU-T E.172 [44]	BELLCORE TR-TSY-000448 [45]	ETSI ETS 300 100 [46]

- To evaluate the performance of various ISDN terminals, with a view to ensure uniformity of services and portability of terminals across different switch types
- To obtain feedback on customer preferences about service features
- To check whether the switch and terminal equipment specifications meet service and market requirements. The feedback is used to modify the specifications before the commercial deployment of the ISDN
- To gain experience in the operation, maintenance, and administration of the ISDN
- To examine the suitability of the local loop plant for basic rate ISDN
- To obtain data on the traffic pattern and likely demand of various ISDN services

The ITU-T has issued comprehensive guidelines on conducting ISDN field trials [47].

13.3.3 ISDN Implementation Strategies

For the commercial implementation of ISDN, several alternatives exist. One possibility is to implement an overlay ISDN network. This can be created by introducing new ISDN exchanges (or by upgrading a few existing exchanges) and connecting them by digital transmission media. The network may include both local and transit exchanges. Connectivity to the existing PSTN and other networks such as the PSPDN is provided at specified gateway exchanges. The overlay network is aimed at rapidly meeting the demand for ISDN services in a limited number of locations. This strategy, however, runs counter to the concept of the evolution of the ISDN from the existing PSTN. In addition, it is expensive to implement because a separate network has to be created. The overlay approach, however, is easy to plan and implement. Thus, it may be the only solution during the introductory phase if the current status of the network does not lend itself to a quick upgrade to the ISDN.

Another possibility is to upgrade the network toward ISDN capabilities systematically. During this process, priority is accorded to the transit network. The existing transit exchanges are either upgraded or replaced to incorporate CCS 7–ISUP signaling. Thus, signaling support for the transport of ISDN services is built into the transit network in the first step. In the second step, ISDN capable exchanges are introduced progressively (by upgrade or replacement) at locations determined by service demand. This strategy represents a natural process of evolution, but may not always be feasible. Administrations may not like to wait for the upgrade of the entire transit network, which is both expensive and time consuming, before commencing ISDN services. Therefore, to meet urgent service demands at locations where network upgrade is expected to take time, the overlay approach should also be considered. In practice, a mix of the two approaches is followed.

The strategy for implementation must also include issues concerning the penetration of the ISDN. Ideally, ISDN connections, either new or on conversion from the PSTN, should be available on demand, but this may not be feasible at all geographic locations due to technoeconomic constraints. The European Commission has set a target of 80% coverage for the European member states.

During the early stages of implementation, a few designated ISDN-capable exchanges in each city may be required to cover the entire local area. This can be achieved by a combination of the following two approaches:

1. By providing remote switching units (RSUs)
2. By ISDN multiplexers

RSUs allow savings in the local loop, since they can be located closer to the demand centers, resulting in shorter subscriber loops. Shorter loop lengths is also a technical requirement in basic rate ISDN. ITU-T recommendation G.961 [48] deals with the permissible values of different parameters associated with the two-wire local loops for basic rate ISDN. An important parameter is the total signal loss for the local loop, which should not exceed 52 db at 80 kHz. The signal loss depends on a number of factors, such as the cable gauge used, changes of cable gauge in the loop, and bridge taps. Thus, a limitation is imposed on the distance of the basic access ISDN subscriber from the exchange. The RSUs can be planned near ISDN demand centers, resulting in shorter loop lengths and greater penetration of ISDN. Currently available digital switching systems permit at least a single stage of remoting. The RSUs are connected to the main exchange by digital trunks and, like the main exchange, cater to both ISDN and analog subscribers.

Some switch types permit two levels of remoting; the RSUs can be further connected to remote line concentrators (RLCs). The RLCs can also be connected directly to the main exchange. This capability is very useful in improving ISDN penetration because, in this scenario, ISDN subscribers can be connected to the main exchange via the RSUs and the RLCs.

Most current switch implementations provide proprietary signaling protocol between the RLCs and the main exchange. A common channel signaling system, similar to CCS 7, is usually employed. Because the RLC most often has connectivity only to the main exchange, level 3 MTP functions are not needed. Due to the proprietary nature of the protocol, the RLCs of one switch type cannot connect to the main exchange of another switch type. This will change when switch manufacturers implement a standardized interface between the RLC and the main exchange. Two standards, the V5.1 and V5.2 interfaces, are being finalized in the ITU-T. The V5.1 interface, which does not support concentration and uses only one 2,048 kbps link, is described in ITU-T recommendation G.964 [49]. The V5.2 supports concentration and can support up to sixteen 2,048 kbps links.

ISDN multiplexers are useful for satisfying small pockets of demand for ISDN basic access service. An ISDN multiplexer supports the U-interface functions and is connected to the network termination of basic access subscribers on the usual two-wire metallic line. It performs multiplexing of a number of full duplex 2B + D basic accesses onto a 2 Mbps (or 1.5 Mbps) PCM system. For a 2 Mbps PCM system, up to 15 basic access subscribers can be supported by the multiplexer. The call handling capacity of the multiplexer should be designed to match the ISDN traffic needs of the connected basic access subscribers. The ISDN multiplexer may be connected to the RLC/RSU using the V5.1 interface.

13.3.4 Switch Capacity Aspects

The processing requirements for an ISDN call are considerably higher than those for an analog call. These requirements are even more pronounced when supplementary services are associated with the call. An exchange typically serves both analog and ISDN subscribers. The impact of ISDN subscribers on the call handling capacity of the exchange during the early stages of ISDN implementation is likely to be marginal, mainly because ISDN calls are a small percentage of the total calls handled by the exchange. Nevertheless, it is important to estimate the additional call handling requirements for ISDN calls, since the proportion of ISDN calls will increase with the growth of the ISDN. To estimate the call handling capacity of the exchange involving both analog and ISDN calls, a load test may be conducted. Readers may also refer to Section 11.5, where CCS 7 aspects of the load test are described.

The traffic for the load test is created by traffic generators and by call simulation. The occupancy of the various call processors is measured. Traffic is generated based on the following factors:

- Call mix, namely, the percentage of successful and unsuccessful calls. For unsuccessful calls, different call failure scenarios such as called subscriber no answer, called subscriber busy, and incomplete dialing should be included. The call mix figures are decided by the administration on the basis of traffic statistics.
- Signaling mix, namely, the percentage of calls on different signaling systems, such as CCS 7 and R2 MFC. Where the exchange is also intended to handle transit traffic, the interworking of different signaling systems such as calls on incoming R2 trunks to outgoing CCS 7 trunks and vice versa should be considered.
- Call types, namely, call originations, call terminations and transit calls (where applicable)
- Breakup between analog and ISDN calls
- Supplementary services for ISDN calls. A breakup between circuit switched and packet calls should also be included.

As part of the load test, it is useful to examine the impact of ISDN traffic on processor occupancy by taking observations for different ratios of analog and ISDN calls. As mentioned in the previous section, the geographic spread of ISDN services is provided by the RSUs. Therefore, the call handling capacity of the RSUs should also be determined during the load test.

Performing the load test requires a large number of call generators as well as an investment in time and effort. Moreover, conducting the load test on an operational exchange is not advisable because it could adversely affect the working of the exchange. Thus, load tests are usually performed only once during the validation of a switching system.

The call handling capacity of a digital switch can also be estimated by a computation method described in annexure A to ITU-T recommendation Q.543 [50].

13.3.5 Quality of Service (QOS) and Performance Requirements

Quality of service (QOS) was defined in ITU-T recommendation E.800 [51] to include the collective effect of service performance that determines a user's degree of satisfaction. This fairly broad description of QOS can be applied to ISDN services also. The

QOS aspects discussed in ITU-T recommendation I.350 [52] relate specifically to the ISDN and is restricted in scope to those parameters that can be directly measured and observed. Subjective issues like the degree of customer satisfaction are not included. A distinction is made between QOS and network performance, although network performance will clearly reflect on the quality of service. Network performance encompasses all parameters that are relevant in the design, engineering, operation, and maintenance of the system. It does not, however, include terminal features and user actions. Monitoring and maintaining network performance is the responsibility of the network provider. On the other hand, maintenance of satisfactory QOS is the responsibility of the service provider.

ITU-T recommendation I.351 [53] lists various recommendations dealing with ISDN performance issues classified under five categories: general aspects, circuit mode transfer, connection processing and packet mode transfer, connection availability, and timing. Detailed discussion on ISDN performance issues is outside the scope of this book, but readers may refer to the international standards on the subject:

- General aspects: ITU-T recommendations I.350, I.351, I.353 [54]
- Circuit mode transfer: ITU-T recommendations G.821 [55] and G.826 [56]
- Connection availability: ITU-T recommendation I.355 [57]
- Connection processing and packet mode transfer: ITU-T recommendations I.352 [58] and I.354 [59]

Recommendations on timing aspects are not listed here; they are covered elsewhere in this book.

REFERENCES

[1] "National ISDN." BELLCORE Special Report SR-NWT-002006, issue 1, Aug. 1991.

[2] *Forecasting New Telecommunication Services.* ITU-T recommendation E.508. International Telecommunication Union, Oct. 1992.

[3] Mason, R., and P. Bacsich, eds. *ISDN Applications in Education and Training.* Institution of Electrical Engineers, 1994.

[4] *Codecs for Videoconferencing Using Primary Digital Group Transmission.* ITU-T recommendation H.120. International Telecommunication Union, 1993.

[5] *Video Codec for Audiovisual Services at p × 64 kbit/s.* ITU-T recommendation H.261, rev. 2. International Telecommunication Union, 1993.

[6] *Frame Structure for a 64 to 1920 kbit/s Channel in Audiovisual Teleservice.* ITU-T recommendation H.221, rev. 2. International Telecommunication Union, 1993.

[7] *System for Establishing Communication between Audiovisual Terminals Using Digital Channels up to 2 Mbit/s.* ITU-T recommendation H.242, rev. 1. International Telecommunication Union, 1993.

[8] *Narrow-Band Visual Telephone Systems and Terminal Equipment.* ITU-T recommendation H.320, rev. 1. International Telecommunication Union, 1993.

[9] *Multipoint Control Unit for Audiovisual Services Using Digital Channels up to 2 Mbit/s.* ITU-T recommendation H.231. International Telecommunication Union, 1993.

[10] *Procedures for Establishing Communication between Three or More Audio Visual Terminals Using Digital Channels up to 2 Mbit/s.* ITU-T recommendation H.243. International Telecommunication Union, 1993.

[11] *General Aspects of Digital Transmission Systems: Transport Equipments. 7 kHz Audiocoding within 64 kbit/s.* CCITT Blue Book, fascicle III.4, recommendation G.722. International Telecommunication Union, 1988.

[12] "National ISDN-1." BELLCORE Special Report SR-NWT-001937, issue 1, Feb. 1991; plus rev. 1, Feb. 1993.

[13] "National ISDN-2." BELLCORE Special Report SR-NWT-002120, issue 1, June 1992; plus rev. 1, June 1993.

[14] "National ISDN-3." BELLCORE Special Report SR-NWT-002457, issue 1, Dec. 1993.

[15] *Case Studies on the Progressive Introduction of ISDN in a National Network, GAS 9.* International Telecommunication Union, 1992.

[16] *General Tariff Principles—Charging and Accounting in International Telecommunications Services.* CCITT Blue Book, fascicle II.1, recommendation D.210. International Telecommunication Union, 1988.

[17] *General Tariff Principles—Charging and Accounting in International Telecommunications Services.* CCITT Blue Book, fascicle II.1, recommendation D.211. International Telecommunication Union, 1988.

[18] *Charging and Accounting Principles to be Applied to International Circuit Mode Demand Bearer Services Provided over the ISDN.* ITU-T recommendation D.220. International Telecommunication Union, March, 1991.

[19] *General Tariff Principles—Charging and Accounting in International Telecommunications Services.* CCITT Blue Book, fascicle II.1, recommendation D.230. International Telecommunication Union, 1988.

[20] *General Tariff Principles—Charging and Accounting in International Telecommunications Services.* CCITT Blue Book, fascicle II.1, recommendation D.231. International Telecommunications Union, 1988.

[21] *General Charging and Accounting Principles for Non-Voice Services Provided by Interworking between the ISDN and Existing Public Data Networks.* ITU-T recommendation D.250. International Telecommunication Union, July 1991.

[22] *General Charging and Accounting Principles for Non-Voice Services Provided by Interworking between the ISDN and Existing Public Data Networks.* CCITT Blue Book, fascicle II.1, recommendation D.251. International Telecommunication Union, 1988.

[23] *Recommendations on the Coordinated Introduction of Integrated Services Digital Network (ISDN) in the European Community.* Document no. 86/659/EEC published by the European Commission, Brussels, Belgium.

[24] "ISDN primary rate interface generic guidelines for customer premises equipment." BELLCORE Special Report SR-NWT-002343, issue 1, June 1993.

[25] "Generic guidelines for ISDN terminal equipment on national ISDN-2 basic rate interfaces." Special Report SR-NWT-002361, BELLCORE issue 1, December 1992.

[26] "National ISDN generic guidelines for ISDN terminal equipment on basic rate interface." BELLCORE Special Report SR-NWT-002661, issue 1, June 1993; plus rev. 1, August 1993.

[27] *ISDN; Attachment Requirements for Terminal Equipment to Connect to an ISDN Using ISDN Basic Access.* ETSI, European Telecommunication Standard ETS 300 153:1992.

[28] *ISDN; Attachment Requirements for Terminal Equipment to Connect to an ISDN Using ISDN Basic Access. Layer 3 Aspects—(NET 3, Part 2).* ETSI, European Telecommunication Standard ETS 300 104:1991 and Amendment 1, 1994.

[29] *ISDN; Attachment Requirements for Terminal Equipment to Connect to an ISDN Using ISDN Primary Rate Access (NET 5).* ETSI, European Telecommunication Standard ETS 300 156:1992.

[30] *ISDN; Attachment Requirements for Terminal Adoptors to Connect to an ISDN at the S/T Reference Point (NET 7).* ETSI, European Telecommunication Standard ETS 300 077:1990.

[31] *ISDN; 3.1 kHz Telephony Teleservice; End-to-End Compatibility Requirements for Telephony Terminals.* ETSI, European Telecommunication Standard ETS 300 082:1992.

[32] *Integrated Services Digital Network (ISDN); 3.1 kHz Telephony Teleservice Attachment Requirements for Handset Terminals.* ETSI, Normes Europeenne de Telecommunication NET 33:1992.

[33] *ISDN; Facsimile Group 4 Class 1 Equipment on the ISDN. General and Service Aspects.* ETSI, Proposed European Telecommunication Standard prETS 300 088:1991.

[34] *ISDN; Facsimile Group 4 Class 1 Equipment on the ISDN. Functional Specification of the Equipment.* ETSI, European Telecommunication Standard ETS 300 087:1991.

[35] *ISDN; Facsimile Group 4 Class 1 Equipment on the ISDN. End-to-End Protocol.* ETSI, Proposed European Telecommunication Standard prETS 300 112:1990.

[36] *Specifications of Signaling System No. 7: ISDN User Part. Signaling Procedures.* ITU-T recommendation Q.764, rev. 1. International Telecommunication Union, 1993.

[37] *Numbering Plan for the ISDN Era.* ITU-T recommendation E.164, rev. 1. International Telecommunication Union, 1993.

[38] *ISDN Numbering and Addressing Principles.* CCITT Blue Book, fascicle III.8, recommendation I.330 International Telecommunication Union, 1988.

[39] *Numbering Plan for the International Telephone Services.* CCITT Blue Book, fascicle II.3, Vol. II, recommendation E.163. International Telecommunication Union, 1988.

[40] *Time Table for Coordinated Implementation of the Full Capacity of the Numbering Plan for the ISDN Era.* CCITT Blue Book, fascicle II.2, recommendation E.165. International Telecommunication Union, 1988.

[41] *Numbering Plan Interworking for the E.164 and X.121 Numbering Plans.* ITU-T recommendation E.166. International Telecommunication Union, Oct. 1992.

[42] *International Numbering Plan for Public Data Networks.* ITU-T recommendation X.121, rev. 1. International Telecommunication Union, 1992.

[43] *Definitions Relating to National and International Numbering Plans.* ITU-T recommendation E.160, rev. 1. International Telecommunication Union, 1993.

[44] *ISDN Routing Plan.* ITU-T recommendation E.172. International Telecommunication Union, Oct. 1992.

[45] "Digit routing and digit analysis." BELLCORE Technical Reference TR-TSY-000448, issue 1, Dec. 1988; rev. 1, July 1989; supplement 1, June 1990.

[46] *ISDN: Routing in Support of ISUP Versions/Services.* ETSI, European Telecommunication Standard ETS 300 100, June 1992.

[47] *ISDN Field Trial Guidelines Handbook.* International Telecommunication Union, 1991.

[48] *Digital Transmission System on Metallic Local Lines for ISDN Basic Rate Access.* ITU-T recommendation G.961, rev. 1. International Telecommunication Union, 1993.

[49] *V Interfaces at the Digital Local Exchange (LE)—V5.1 Interface (Based on 2048 kbit/s) for the Support of Access Network (AN).* ITU-T recommendation G.964. International Telecommunication Union, 1994.

[50] *Digital Exchange Performance Design Objectives.* ITU-T recommendation Q.543, rev. 1. International Telecommunication Union, 1993.

[51] *Quality of Service and Dependability Vocabulary.* CCITT Blue Book, fascicle II.3, recommendation E.800. International Telecommunication Union, 1989.

[52] *General Aspects of Quality of Service and Network Performance in Digital Networks, Including ISDN.* ITU-T recommendation I.350, rev. 1. International Telecommunication Union, 1993.

[53] *Recommendations in Other Series Concerning Network Performance Objectives That Apply to Reference Point T of an ISDN.* ITU-T recommendation I.351, rev. 1. International Telecommunication Union, 1993.

[54] *Reference Events for Defining ISDN Performance Parameters.* ITU-T recommendation I.353. International Telecommunication Union, 1993.

[55] *Digital Networks, General Aspects. Error Performance of an International Digital Connection Forming Part of an Integrated Services Digital Network.* CCITT Blue Book, fascicle III.5, recommendation G.821. International Telecommunication Union, 1988.

[56] *Error Performance Parameters and Objectives for International, Constant Bit Rate Digital Paths at or Above the Primary Rate.* ITU-T recommendation G.826. International Telecommunication Union, 1993.

[57] *ISDN 64 kbit/s Connection Type Availability Performance.* ITU-T recommendation I.355. International Telecommunication Union, 1993.

[58] *Network Performance Objectives for Connection Processing Delays in an ISDN.* ITU-T recommendation I.352, rev. 1. International Telecommunication Union, 1993.

[59] *Network Performance Objectives for Packet-Mode Communication in an ISDN.* ITU-T recommendation I.354. International Telecommunication Union, 1993.

14 Testing in the ISDN

Acronyms

ATS	abstract test suite
BER	bit error ratio
BOC	Bell operating companies
CCITT	The International Telegraph and Telephone Consultative Committee
CCS 7	CCITT common channel signaling system no. 7
DM	degraded minutes
DSL	digital subscriber loop
DSS 1	digital subscriber signaling system 1
EFS	error-free seconds
ETSI	European Telecommunication Standards Institute
FCS	frame check sequence
ISDN	integrated services digital network
ISUP	ISDN user part
ITU-T	International Telecommunication Union-Telecommunication Standardization Sector
IUT	item under test
LAPD	link access procedure on D-channel
LT	line termination
MFO	multiframe operation
MSP	maintenance service provider
NT	network termination
PICS	protocol implementation conformance statement
PIXIT	protocol implementation extra information for testing
PRBS	pseudorandom binary sequence
PS 1	power source 1
REJ	reject frame
RNR	receive not ready frame
RR	receive ready frame
SAPI	service access point identifier
SDL	system description language
SES	severely errored seconds
TA	terminal adapter
TE	terminal equipment
TEI	terminal endpoint identifier
TTCN	tree and tabular combined notation
UI	unnumbered information frame

ABSTRACT

This chapter focuses on the testing aspects of the ISDN, including:

- Layer 1 tests on power feeding, framing, D-channel access, activation and deactivation, timing, and electrical characteristics
- Tests on both integrated services digital network (ISDN) terminals and network termination (NT)
- Layer 2 and layer 3 tests from the point of view of routine maintenance and conformance testing
- Maintenance of ISDN subscriber access and subscriber installation

14.1 Introduction

The large-scale deployment of ISDN systems has happened only recently. Consequently, as with any other new technology, administrations have limited experience in their operation and maintenance. Testing and maintenance issues are further complicated by the complex nature of protocols and the variety of services and terminals supported in the ISDN. Thus, testing and maintenance of the ISDN is a challenging task.

Testing in the ISDN can vary considerably, from simple go/no-go tests generally associated with routine troubleshooting to highly complicated protocol conformance tests. The latter tests involve a series of predetermined tests that, if successfully completed, indicate that the implementation meets prescribed standards. These one-time tests are conducted when new equipment or functionality is introduced into the ISDN. For example, conformance testing of a new model or type of ISDN terminal is needed before it is mass marketed and supplied to customers. On the network side, if, for instance, X.31 case B packet call handling capability is introduced, then conformance testing will be required. Conformance tests are needed when a new type of ISDN capable exchange is introduced into the network. Given the layered structure of ISDN protocols, it is reasonable to specify and conduct ISDN tests separately for each layer. To verify the satisfactory execution of call control procedures, the first three layers of digital subscriber signaling system 1 (DSS 1) protocol are tested. Layer 1 tests are described in Section 14.2, and layer 2 and layer 3 tests are considered in Section 14.3.

14.2 Layer 1 Tests

The functional aspects associated with this layer were discussed in Chapter 5. The physical layer should conform to ITU-T recommendations I.430 [1] or I.431 [2]. These ITU-T recommendations also incorporate the methods of testing the physical layer. Table 14–1 lists current standards on layer 1 testing of the International Telecommunication Union-Telecommunication Standardization Sector (ITU-T), BELLCORE, and the European Telecommunication Standards Institute (ETSI).

Table 14–1 Key Standards for Physical Layer Testing

ITU-T	BELLCORE	ETSI
BASIC ACCESS ISDN		
Appendix X of I.430	TR-NWT-001329 [3]	Annexes D and E of ETS 300 012 [4]
PRIMARY ACCESS ISDN		
I.431	TR-NWT-001219 [5]	Annex C of ETS 300 011 [6]

The parameters associated with layer 1 require both analog and digital measurements. For example, the bit error ratio (BER) test involves digital signals, whereas for several other tests, analog measurements of pulse shape, transient current, and impedance are required. This is in contrast to layer 2 and layer 3 tests, which deal with testing and analysis of protocols that are logical in nature.

Some level 1 tests may require the satisfactory operation of layer 2 and 3 as a precondition for their execution. For example, before a BER test can be conducted between two ISDN interfaces, it is essential that a circuit switched connection exists between the two interfaces. This would require that layers 2 and 3 functions work satisfactorily.

The major functions that need to be tested for the physical layer in the basic rate ISDN are depicted in Figure 14–1. The item under test (IUT) represents any of the equipment that can be connected to the S-interface, such as ISDN terminal equipment (TE), terminal adapter (TA), or network termination (NT).

Testers that perform the entire range of tests enumerated in the physical layer testing standards of Table 14–1 are currently available on the market. When testing a particular type of equipment, it is essential that all other connected equipment perform according to the prescribed standards. Thus, if an NT is under test, the exchange line termination (LT) and the TEs must function satisfactorily. Thus, the tester typically incorporates sim-

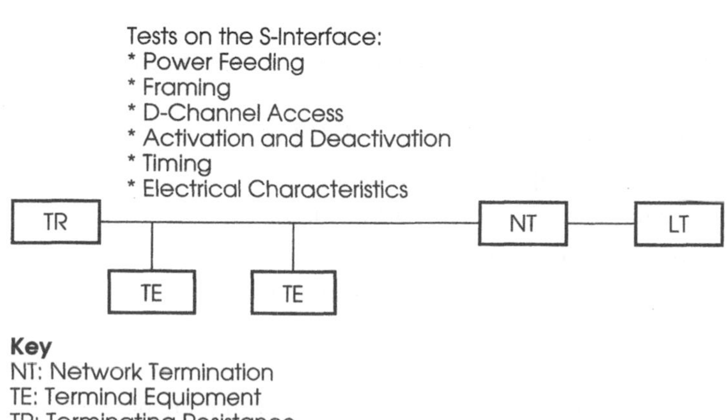

Figure 14–1 Layer 1 tests at the S-interface.

ulation functions. The need for simulation is more pronounced during the early stages of ISDN introduction. When real ISDN networks conforming to standards are firmly established, the functioning of new equipment can be verified, to a large extent, by connecting it directly to the network. Nevertheless, simulation is an important requirement during testing. The test setup should provide the following broad functions:

- Simulation functions
- Test and measurement functions

The simulation functions required depend on the item under test. For example, when a TE is to be tested, the simulator should simulate NT functions; for testing an NT, simulation of TE functions is necessary. The simulation of the digital subscriber loop (DSL) is also required in testing the physical layer. A line simulator, which replaces a real cable, is not only convenient to use but also provides a controlled test environment. Cables of different lengths and gauges can be simulated. For the tests to be useful, however, the line simulator must offer realistic simulation of the cables deployed in the local plant. Therefore, the first step is to characterize the cables used in the local plant. A nationwide survey of the local plant was undertaken in the United States in 1983 [7], which helped characterize the local loop plant of Bell operating companies (BOCs). In a random sample of 2,290 working pairs, it was found that real local loops are far from the ideal pair of two wires of uniform gauge; only about 66% of the local loops were found suitable for basic access ISDN. The physical and transmission characteristics of these loops were analyzed to characterize the local loop population generally. On this basis, 15 test loop configurations were identified that would approximate actual loops. These test loops consist of different gauges of wires of varying lengths and configurations and are presented in appendix D of BELLCORE Technical Reference TR-NWT-000393 [8]. Several manufacturers supply line simulation equipment capable of simulating these test loops.

The test and measurement function of the test setup permits a variety of measurements at the S-interface. The function may be realized using one or more pieces of test equipment. The important requirements of the test and measurement equipment connected at the S-interface can be summarized as follows:

- The capability to identify the INFO signals in either direction (NT to TE and TE to NT)
- To identify the states of the TE (F1 to F7 states) and NT (G1 to G4 states)
- To time stamp the INFO signals
- To measure the bit rate on the interface
- Jitter measurement
- To measure the input and output impedance of the NT and TEs
- To measure the pulse shape

An important piece of equipment for testing the physical layer is a digital oscilloscope, which permits the measurement and storage of the pulse shapes for individual bits of the frames. The pulse shape can then be compared with standard pulse templates. The various equipment involved in the setup may be controlled centrally by a PC using, for example, an IEEE 488 interface. This helps in automating the test process by programming the tests, recording the results, and comparing them with expected values. This method is not usable in the field, however, except possibly for one-time conformance tests.

The test categories listed in Figure 14–1 are applicable to the testing of both NT and TEs. Sections 14.2.1 and 14.2.2 describe some of the important tests pertaining to NT and TE, respectively.

14.2.1 Testing of Network Termination (NT)

Figure 14–2 shows an NT under test. The functions of an NT are limited to the physical layer. It has two interfaces: a U-interface on the network side and an S/T-interface toward the customer premises. In the figure, the objective is to test the S-interface functions of the NT. To permit the operation of the NT at the S-interface, a TE simulator conforming to recommendation I.430 is connected. A test and measurement function is also included in the test setup to monitor the activity on the S-interface. A line simulator and an LT simulator complete the test setup.

The category of tests indicated in Figure 14–1 should be performed on the NT. Some of these are described in the succeeding paragraphs. While studying these tests, readers may refer to Chapter 5, which deals with the physical layer aspects of the ISDN.

14.2.1.1 Test for Activation and Deactivation of Network Termination (NT)

In this test, the ability of the NT to perform the activation and deactivation procedures correctly is verified. An NT in a deactivated state may receive an activation request either from the network side (for example, an incoming call) or from a TE originating a call. Refer to Figure 5–14, which shows the flow of INFO signals for activation of the NT from the network side. In this case, the request for activation is conveyed to the NT by the primitive PH-AR. As a consequence, the NT is expected to send an INFO 2 signal to the TE simulator. The TE simulator responds with an INFO 3 signal. Finally, the NT should send an INFO 4 signal and reach the active state. The flow of INFO signals is recorded by the tester, and the signal sequence is verified for correctness. The NT activation time

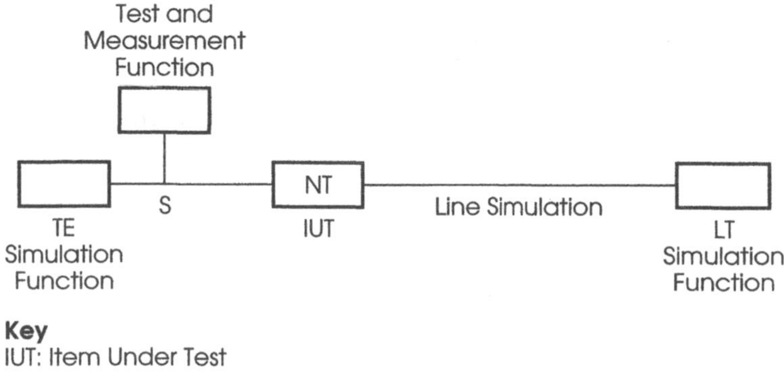

Figure 14–2 Test setup for NT.

should also be measured. This is the period between the receipt of the INFO 3 signal and the transmission of the INFO 4 signal by the NT. ITU-T recommendation I.430 stipulates that under normal conditions the NT should reach activation within 500 ms.

The test may be repeated by programming the TE simulator so that it does not respond with the INFO 3 signal upon receipt of the INFO 2 signal. This will cause timer 1 (refer to Section 5.4.3.5.2) to expire, and the NT should reach state G4.

On similar lines, the activation of the NT from the TE side can also be tested. The NT is in the deactivated state at the beginning of the test. To initiate activation, the TE simulator sends an INFO 1 signal to the NT. The NT is expected to respond with INFO 2 signals that are synchronized to the network clock. In this case, the NT activation time is the time elapsed between the receipt of the INFO 1 signal and the transmission of an INFO 2 signal by the NT. Under normal conditions, this time should be within 1 second.

Appendix X of recommendation I.430 lists the complete sequence of tests for activation and deactivation of the NT.

14.2.1.2 Test on Framing (Frame Structure in the Network Termination to Terminal Equipment Direction)

The frame structure in the NT to TE and TE to NT directions was described in Chapter 5; refer to Section 5.4.3.2 and Figure 5–12. The purpose of the test on framing is to verify the correctness of the frame structure sent by the NT in the TE direction. The TE simulator generates INFO 3 frames in the TE to NT direction. At the beginning of the test, the NT is in the active state (G3 state). The TE simulator inserts a pseudorandom pattern in both the B1- and B2-channels in the INFO 3 frames. The NT is expected to respond with INFO 4 frames. This is monitored by the test equipment, and the correctness of the binary organization is verified.

14.2.1.3 Test on D-Channel Access

The role of the NT in resolving D-channel access is to send a D-channel echo bit E; (refer to Section 5.4.3.4). This function is verified during this test. The TE simulator sends a frame with the D-channel bit of binary value 0. The NT should reflect this bit by sending a binary value 0 in the E-bit position in the next frame in the NT to TE direction. Next, the TE simulator is programmed to send the D-channel bit as 1, and it is confirmed that the NT now sends a 1 in the D echo channel.

14.2.1.4 Test on Electrical Characteristics

Two important tests for the NT relating to its electrical characteristics are the following:

1. Verification of the pulse shape for individual bits in the 48-bit frames in the NT to TE direction
2. Measurement of output impedance and input impedance of the NT

For verification of the pulse shape, the NT is kept in the active G3 state at the beginning of the test. The TE simulator sends INFO 3 signal frames in which pulses corresponding to individual bits conform to the standard pulse mask shown in Figure 5–15. The NT transmitting pair is terminated in 50 Ω. The negative and positive pulses in the frame generated by the NT are now monitored and compared with the standard template mask. The pulses should be within the mask shown in Figure 5–15. The test is repeated with a terminating impedance of 400 Ω. In this case, the pulses of the frame generated by the NT are monitored for conformance to the mask of Figure 5–16.

The measurement of output and input impedance of the NT is performed, and the measured values are compared with the prescribed impedance template of Figure 5–17. The test is conducted with the NT in deactivated state G1. In this state, it does not transmit any signals, which is equivalent to sending binary 1's. A sinusoidal voltage of an amplitude of 100 mV rms is applied. The impedance is measured for the frequency range of 2 kHz to 1,000 kHz. The measured values should exceed the impedance template shown in Figure 5–17.

14.2.1.5 Test on Timing

An important test in this category is to measure the jitter characteristics of the NT and to verify that the maximum jitter, peak to peak, is less than 5% of the bit period. Refer to Section 5.4.4. The jitter should be measured by using a high pass filter having a cut-off frequency (3 db point) of 50 Hz and an asymptotic rolloff of 20 db per decade.

Another test on timing relates to the measurement of the bit rate of INFO 4 frames transmitted by the NT. The NT is under the active state (G3) during the test, and the TE simulator sends INFO 3 frames to the NT. The bit rate of frames in the NT to TE direction is monitored.

14.2.1.6 Test on Power Feeding

The power feeding arrangement was described in Section 5.4.2. The NT has the responsibility of feeding power to the terminals across the interface, under both normal and restricted power conditions.

A test setup to verify that the NT delivers sufficient power across the interface from the local power supply and that the feeding voltage is within prescribed limits is shown in Figure 14–3. Power source 1 (PS 1) is used to supply power. The test is performed under normal power conditions when PS 1 must supply at least 10 W of power or under restricted power conditions when at least 420 mW of power should be available at the output of the NT.

In normal power conditions, to begin with, resistance R is kept infinite. In this case, no power is drawn. The voltage at the output of PS 1 is measured. Next, the value of R is slowly reduced, which results in progressive increase in power consumption across the interface. Thus, R is reduced to a point where the maximum permissible power consumption takes place. The voltage supplied by the NT is measured to verify that it is within permissible limits. (The nominal voltage is 40 V, and tolerances are 5% to −15%.)

The power supplied by the NT on the S-interface during restricted power conditions is measured by removing the local supply of power. It is verified that the polarity of supply is reversed by the NT to indicate the onset of restricted power conditions. The supply voltage is also measured to confirm that it lies within the stipulated range.

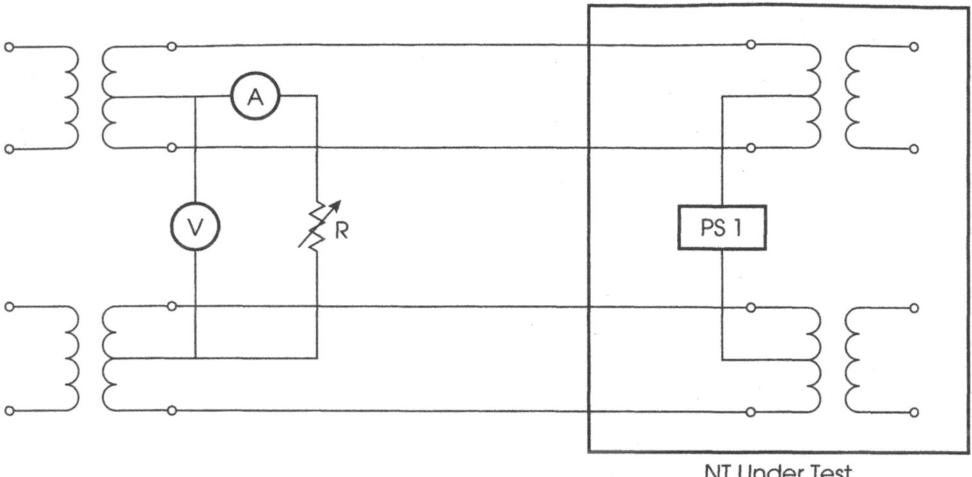

Figure 14–3 Test setup to measure the power feeding by NT 1.

14.2.1.7 Other Tests

In addition to the tests described above, a number of other tests related to power feeding by the NT have been specified in the standards listed in Table 14–1.

To test the functions of the NT toward the network, the local loop and the LT should be simulated. A line simulator that can simulate the 15 test loops mentioned earlier is usually employed. A number of measurements on the NT can be performed when connected to these test loops, including nominal impedance of the NT on the network side, return loss measurements over the frequency range of 1 kHz to 200 kHz, and resistance of NT tip and ring conductors to ground. The permissible values of these parameters are specified in BELLCORE Technical Report TR-NWT-000393 [8].

Another test is the NT metallic test. The NT is expected to provide a metallic termination to the DSL to permit the flow of sealing current provided by the LT. The metallic termination has basically two states, off (nonconducting state) and on (conducting state). A variable test voltage is applied on the tip and ring ports of the NT, and the transition between the two states is observed. The transition depends on the magnitude of the voltage and the minimum time for which it is applied. The expected characteristics of the metallic termination in terms of the applied voltage, its duration, and the resulting loop currents are defined by BELLCORE [8]. The measurements are compared with specified values.

14.2.2 Testing of Terminal Equipment

The NT and the TE are connected on the common S/T-interface. For this reason, a complementary set of tests under the same categories as those for the NT are performed for the TE as well. Refer to Figure 14–4. Some examples are the following:

- Among timing tests, the TE output jitter is measured to confirm that the maximum jitter is less than ± 7% of the bit period.

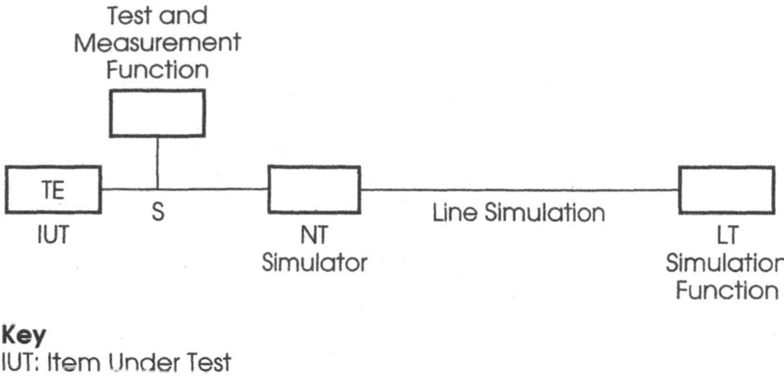

Figure 14–4 Test setup for TE.

- Output impedance of the TE is measured at frequencies between 2 kHz and 1000 kHz, and the results are compared with the standard impedance template of Figure 5–18.
- Activation and deactivation of the TE are tested. The TE is expected to function as a state machine that can take states from F1 (inactive state) to F7 (activated state), depending on the INFO signals received from the NT simulator. A simplified system description language (SDL) describing the salient features of the activation/deactivation procedure was presented in Figure 5–13. ITU-T recommendation I.430 includes a detailed SDL for the procedures, and the TE under test must perform according to this SDL.
- The shape of individual pulses, both positive and negative, are measured and compared with the standard pulse template of Figure 5–15.
- For the D echo channel, an important test is to verify that the TE under test detects collisions and stops transmission when a collision is detected. Another test is to verify that the TE correctly changes its priority level within its priority class. (Priority classes and levels were discussed in Section 5.4.3.4.)
- Tests are also performed to confirm that the TE under test, when working with normal power supplied by PS 1, does not draw excessive power. (The TE is permitted to draw no more than 1 W of power.)

14.2.3 Maintenance and Troubleshooting

The level 1 tests described so far relate to conformance testing. When the network is up and running, the focus shifts to routine maintenance and troubleshooting. The tests and measurements for these purposes should be simple to perform, because the maintenance personnel responsible for these tests are not expected to possess the same level of technical expertise as engineers in test and conformance laboratories. The testers should be simple go/no-go equipment that emphasizes quick identification of the faulty element. The testers should also be portable and robust in design. Some of the routine maintenance and troubleshooting tests are described in this section.

To test the quality of the ISDN access network, measurements of transmission parameters of the local loop are taken. The frequency range of interest in these measurements is 200 Hz to 200 kHz. Typical measurements include attenuation, crosstalk, noise, quantizing distortion, and return loss measurements.

A BER tester is also often used to test the quality of a basic access ISDN connection during installation and maintenance. The permissible value of BER is prescribed in recommendation G.821 [9]. The tester is connected to the S-interface and measures the BER (that is, the ratio of bits received in error to the total number of bits received). The BER is measured for 1-second intervals for the data carried in the B-channel. Two important modes of testing are the following:

1. *End-to-end mode,* where a circuit switched connection is established between two ISDN interfaces. Refer to Figure 14–5(a). Each tester transmits a test pattern that is received at the far end, and the BER is measured on the switched end-to-end connection in both directions. In this case, the measurements pertain to a single B-channel at the two interfaces.

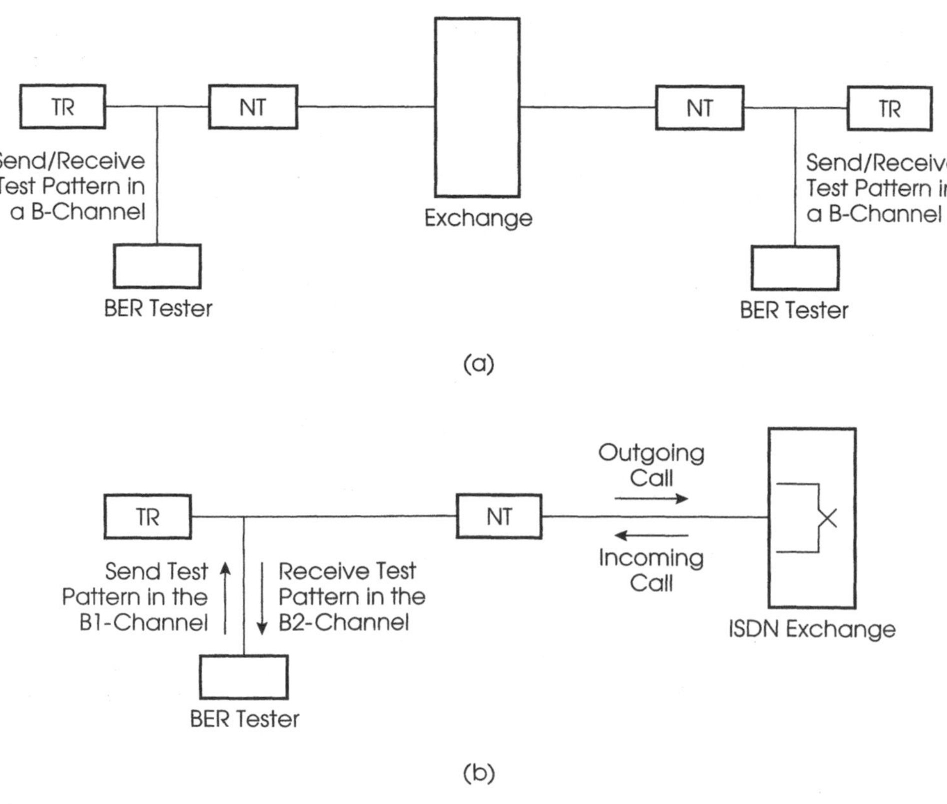

Figure 14–5 BER measurement. (a) End-to-end mode (b) Self-dial mode.

2. *Self-dial mode,* where the tester is connected at a single ISDN interface and a call is made using one B-channel and received back on the other B-channel. Refer to Figure 14–5(b). The tester sends a test pattern on one B-channel and analyzes the data received on the other B-channel. Thus, the measurements are made on two B-channels at the same ISDN interface.

As noted earlier, this test requires the establishment of an ISDN connection. Thus, the test presupposes the proper operation of layer 2 and 3 basic call control functions. The test pattern may be a pseudorandom binary sequence (PRBS) per ITU-T recommendation O.152 [10] or may be user specified. The typical recommendation G.821 error parameters measured include error-free seconds (EFS), severely errored seconds (SES), and degraded minutes (DM).

Testing the power feeding at the ISDN installation is also important for installation and maintenance. The NT and the TEs must function properly when power conditions change from normal to restricted and back to normal.

Functional tests using equipment that can automatically generate and receive ISDN calls is also useful during routine testing.

14.3 Layer 2 and Layer 3 Tests

Testing layer 2 (recommendation Q.921) [11] and layer 3 (recommendation Q.931) [12] protocols is vital to the testing and maintenance of the ISDN. Quite often, problems and anomalies noticed during operation can be traced to protocol inconsistencies. Conformance testing also involves comprehensive protocol tests. Test equipment manufacturers therefore offer a wide range of ISDN protocol testers to satisfy a variety of testing needs. The simplest protocol testers only possess monitoring functions. They are required during installation and routine maintenance. Figure 14–6 shows a tester connected on the S/T-interface of the basic access for monitoring the bidirectional flow of data. One of the two B-channels, or the D-channel, can be extracted by the tester for monitoring and analysis. Monitoring the D-channel is central to layer 2 and layer 3 testing. While doing so, a hand-

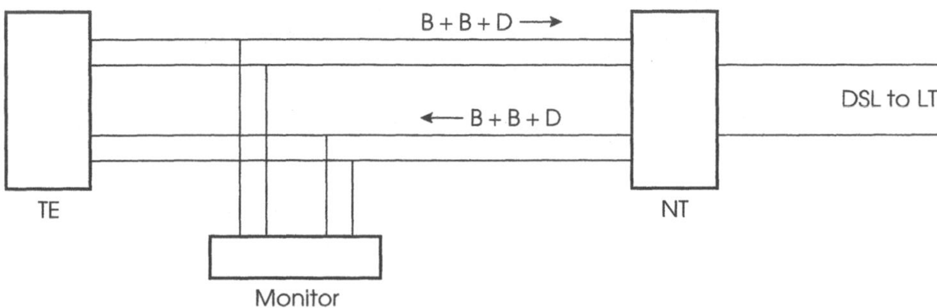

Figure 14–6 Monitoring on the S/T-interface.

set with codec may also be connected to the B-channel to check for voice communication on the switched connection. Monitoring the B-channel is particularly relevant for packet calls that are set up following recommendation X.31 case A or recommendation X.31 case B (using B-channel) procedures. Refer to Sections 12.2 and 12.3.1.

Because an interoffice ISDN call setup employs both the DSS 1 and ISDN user part (ISUP), simultaneous monitoring of DSS 1 layer 3 and ISUP messages provides a complete protocol portrait for the call and is often useful in investigating complex protocol conversion problems in the switches. This is illustrated in Figure 14–7.

The user specifies beforehand the layer to be monitored (layer 2 or 3) and the appropriate protocol standard. The monitored data is interpreted and decoded accordingly and is presented either in real time or stored for future reference.

Take the example of layer 2 monitoring. As discussed in Chapter 8, the functions of layer 2 require an exchange of frames on the 16 kbps D-channel between peer data link entities. Therefore, monitoring layer 2 functions involves identification of various types of frames, namely, information (I) frames, supervisory (S) frames, and unnumbered (U) frames. An analysis of the flow of frames helps to pinpoint any abnormality in layer 2 behavior. Two examples of abnormalities are generation of invalid frames and inopportune frames. The criteria for identifying invalid frames was enumerated in Section 8.8.3.2. Inopportune frames, although syntactically correct, do not fit into the expected sequence of responses. Monitoring layers 2 and 3 of DSS 1 is often helpful in troubleshooting protocol-related errors.

Conformance testing, being complex and comprehensive, requires sophisticated protocol testers with simulation and emulation functions in addition to the monitoring function. Protocol testers designed with conformance testing in view incorporate a set of predefined tests that can be applied on the test equipment to verify its adherence to layer 2 and layer 3 functions. Standardization efforts during the last few years have culminated in the development of abstract test suites (ATSs), whose objective is a comprehensive verification of the implementation under test (IUT). A notation to describe the tests, called the tree and tabular combined notation (TTCN), has also been standardized. The TTCN is a general notation that can be applied not only for DSS 1 layers 2 and 3 but also for describing conformance test suites for all kinds of open system interconnection protocols. ITU-T

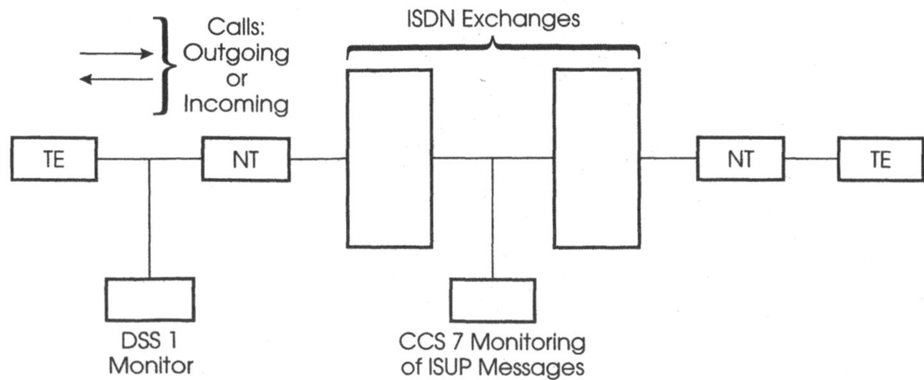

Figure 14–7 Simultaneous monitoring of DSS 1 and CCS7-ISUP.

recommendation X.292 [13] specifies the TTCN syntax. The syntax has been defined in two forms:

1. A graphical form (TTCN.GR)
2. A machine processible form (TTCN.MP)

The TTCN.GR form is designed for human use; the TTCN.MP is for programmed application. The tests are written and stored in the tester in the TTCN.MP syntax. These "test scripts" are compiled by a TTCN compiler to generate an executable test suite for the programmed execution of conformance tests. Description of TTCN syntax is outside the scope of this book, but readers may refer to ITU-T recommendation X.292 for details on this subject.

The design of the abstract test suites for layers 2 and 3 follows the general test methodology enumerated in ITU-T recommendations X.290 [14] and X.291 [15]. The test suite has a modular, four-layer hierarchical structure consisting of test groups, test cases, test steps, and test events, as shown in Figure 14–8. Test groups and test steps can be nested to any depth as required.

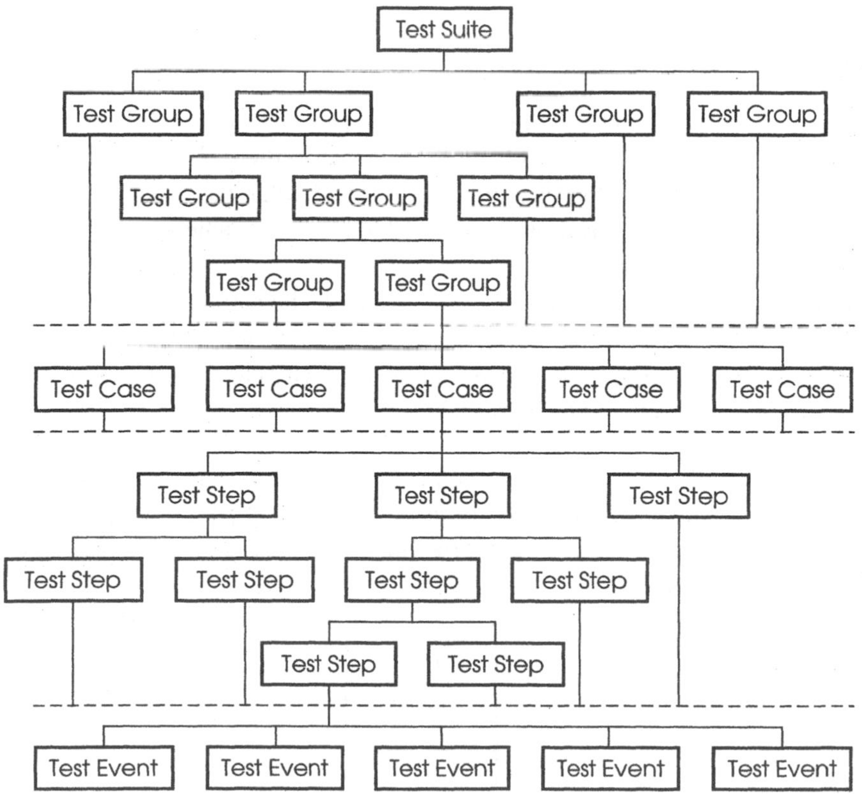

Figure 14–8 Test suite structure.
[Reprinted from CCITT recommendation X.290 (1988). Reproduced by permission.]

The ITU-T test suite for layer 2 is available in recommendation Q.921 bis [16]. The test groups comprising the test suite can be classified under three categories:

1. Management (MGMT)
2. Multiframe Operation (MFO)
3. System (SYSTEM)

The tester functions as the network side, and the IUT is layer 2 of the equipment connected on the user side, which may be an ISDN terminal, a terminal adapter, or similar equipment. It is assumed that layer 3 is available and is capable of generating I-frames. Figure 14–9 illustrates the principle.

The test cases for MGMT categories of test groups verify the terminal endpoint identifier (TEI) management functions implemented in layer 2 of the IUT. (These procedures were discussed in Section 8.8.4.) A few examples of the test cases in this category are as follows:

1. Check that when an identity remove message is sent by the tester with the Ai value that is the same as the TEI value of the IUT, the latter goes into a TEI unassigned state. (Refer to row 6 of Table 8–7 for the format of the identity remove message.)
2. Check that when an identity remove message is sent by the tester with the Ai value that is different from the TEI value of the IUT, the IUT does not respond. Thus, if the IUT has a TEI value x and a request for removal of TEI value y (Ai = y) is received from the tester, then the IUT should do nothing.
3. Check that the IUT does not respond when the tester sends an identity denied message indicating that no TEI value is available for assignment. (Refer to row 3 of Table 8–7.)
4. Check that the IUT does not respond when an ID_check request with an invalid service access point identifier (SAPI) is sent by the tester.
5. Check that the IUT does not respond when the tester sends an ID_check request with an invalid TEI address.

The bulk of the test cases fall under the multiframe operation (MFO) category. (Multiple frame operation was discussed in Section 8.8.5.2.) A few examples of tests under MFO are shown in Figure 14–10. They illustrate tests designed to verify the re-

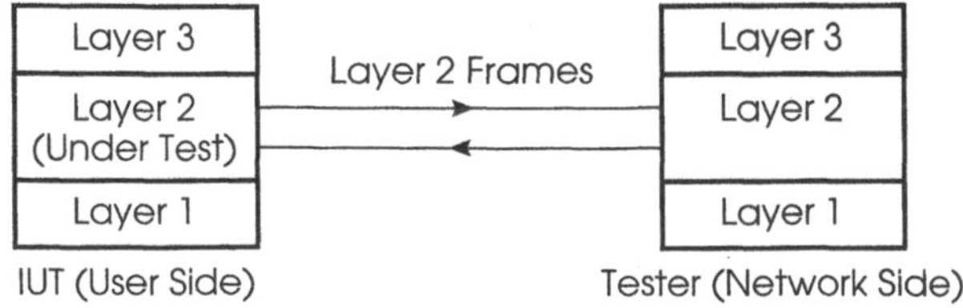

Figure 14–9 Principle of layer 2 testing.

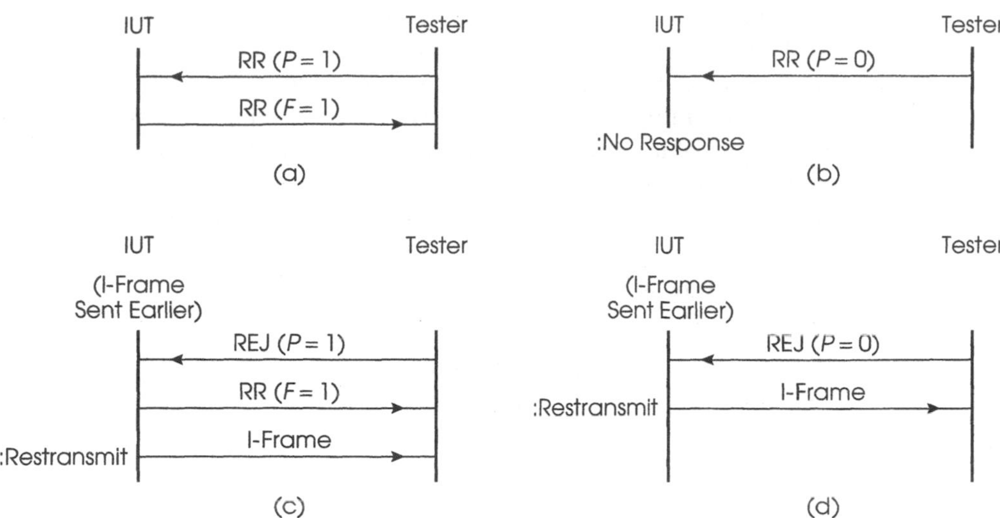

Note: IUT is in multiframe established state at the beginning and end of the test cases (a) through (d).

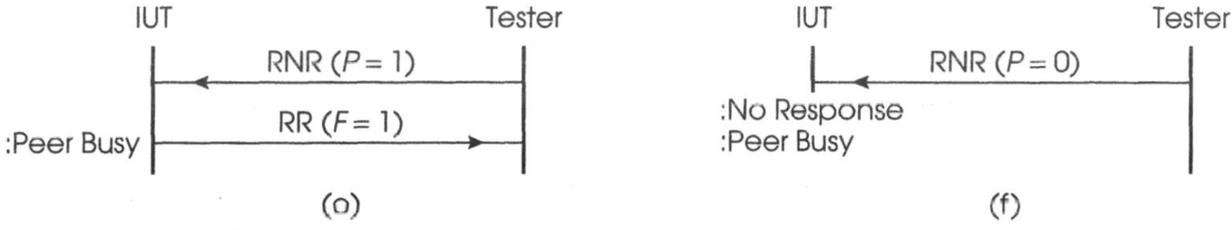

Figure 14–10 Test case examples for multiple frame operation.

sponse of the IUT to receive ready (RR), reject (REJ), and receive not ready (RNR) frames.

Examples of test cases under the system category include the following:

1. Check that the IUT does not respond when the tester sends an ID_assigned/ ID_check request/ID_denied frame containing an invalid C/R bit.
2. Check that the IUT does not respond when the tester sends an ID_assigned/ ID_check request/ID_denied frame containing an invalid octet 2 E/A-bit (= 1).
3. Check that the IUT with an unassigned TEI ignores an unnumbered information (UI) frame with a bad frame check sequence (FCS) sent by the tester.

These examples are only for illustration and represent a small fraction of the total test cases contained in the link access procedure in D-Channel (LAPD) test suite. Before concluding this discussion, certain practical considerations relating to the installation of the ATS should also be mentioned. Before testing an implementation using the ATS, it is necessary to customize the test suite according to the LAPD features available in the IUT. Certain options available in recommendation Q.921 may not be implemented in the IUT, and information in this respect must be available to permit customization of the test suite.

This information is called *protocol implementation conformance statement* (PICS). To test the IUT, more information may be needed, such as intended timer values in the IUT and a list of features that exist in the IUT but are not testable. This is called protocol implementation extra information for testing (PIXIT). Recommendation Q.921 bis includes a pro forma listing of the information that must be obtained by the testing agency from the IUT provider before commencing the tests. Listed below are a few items of information that should be sought from the IUT provider. The list is not exhaustive.

- TEI assignment: automatic or nonautomatic
- TEI value to be used during testing
- SAPI value to be used during testing
- Any unsupported SAPI number?
- IUT window size
- Maximum number of retransmissions (N200) for the IUT
- Maximum number of identity request retransmissions
- Can the IUT be forced to send the TEI identity request on demand?
- Can the IUT be forced to send one or more I-frames on demand?
- Can the IUT be forced to clear a busy condition on demand?
- Is recommendation Q.931 software available in the IUT?
- Values of timers T200 to T203

The layer 3 conformance tests for ISDN terminal equipment to be connected to the basic access consist of a series of tests designed to verify the layer 3 call states and procedures for both incoming and outgoing calls. The format and contents of the layer 3 messages, including the coding of various information elements, are also checked. The tests also include the measurement of the values of the various layer 3 timers to ensure that the values lie in the prescribed range. The behavior of the terminal on receipt of erroneous and inopportune messages is also checked. The European standards for layer 3 conformance are prescribed in ETSI standard ETS 300 104 [17]. The main body of this standard enumerates the layer 3 call control requirements that should be met by the terminals. Annexure A specifies the tests to check conformance to these requirements. These standards deal only with basic call control and do not cover the support of supplementary services by terminal equipment. Additional tests need to be performed to verify this aspect.

14.4 Maintenance of ISDN Access

The general principles for maintaining ISDN access are discussed in ITU-T recommendation I.601 [18]. The standards on the maintenance of ISDN access and ISDN subscriber installation are listed in Table 14–2. The following description is based on these standards.

The configuration to be considered for maintenance shown in Figure 14–11 consists of the following:

Table 14-2 ITU-T Standards on the Maintenance of ISDN Access and Subscriber Installation

RECOMMENDATION	SCOPE
I.601	General principles
M.3602 [19]	Application of maintenance principles to ISDN subscriber installation
M.3603 [20]	Application of maintenance principles to ISDN basic access
M.3604 [21]	Application of maintenance principles to ISDN primary access
M.3605 [22]	Application of maintenance principle to static multiplexed ISDN basic access

1. The subscriber installation (composed of the ISDN terminals, non-ISDN terminals along with the terminal adapters, and NT2) up to the T reference point or the S/T-reference if an NT2 is not used
2. The subscriber access consisting of NT1, the digital subscriber line, the LT, and the exchange termination (ET).

Maintenance functions for the ISDN subscriber installation include the following:

- Supervision of the availability of power supply
- Detection of loss-of-frame alignment
- Monitoring of transmission performance
- Capability to provide loopbacks
- Internal self-tests carried out by the terminal equipment. The nature of these tests may vary depending on the type of equipment. The internal tests should not affect

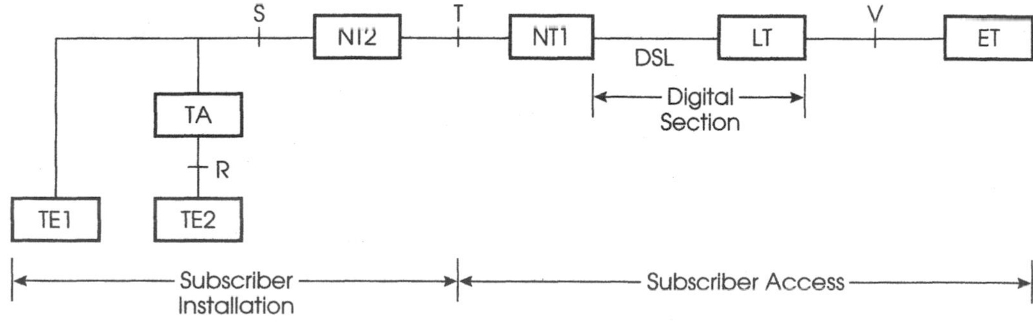

Key
TE1: ISDN Terminals
TE2: Non-ISDN Terminals
TA: Terminal Adapters
DSL: Digital Subscriber Line
LT: Line Termination
ET: Exchange Termination

Figure 14–11 Subscriber installation and subscriber access.

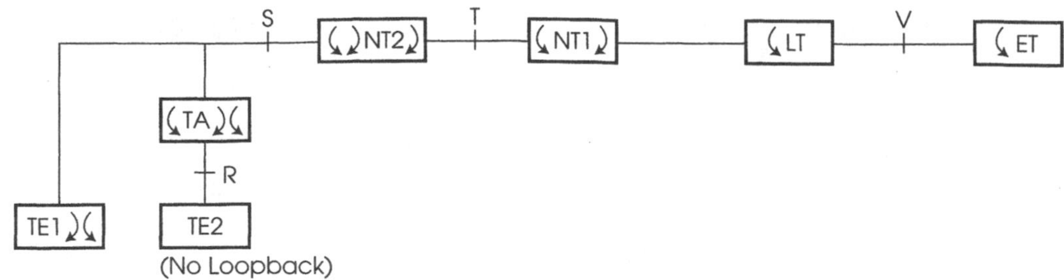

Figure 14–12 Location of loopbacks in ISDN basic access.

the normal operation of the terminals. Likewise, TAs may also perform internal tests.

- Test calls by the NT2 to various terminals in the ISDN installation (when the NT2 is present)
- Supervision of layer 2 and layer 3 functions to detect DSS 1 protocol problems

Furthermore, loopbacks may be created at different locations in the ISDN subscriber installation: at TE1, TA, NT2, and NT1. They are useful in fault localization.

The functions just described may be performed by the equipment available at the subscriber installation. Recommendation I.601 also envisages the possibility of a maintenance service provider (MSP), which may be the administration itself or another private party. The MSP may access and control the subscriber installation equipment to support the maintenance functions listed above.

The ISDN exchange performs the maintenance activities related to ISDN access, both basic and primary, as the case may be.

For basic access, when NT1 is in an active state, continuous monitoring of layer 1 functions up to NT1 are performed by the exchange. When NT1 is inactive, a periodic test for continuity up to NT1 is carried out. Supervision of layer 2 and 3 functions on the exchange side is also performed.

The location of loopbacks for basic access are shown in Figure 14–12. In addition, loops are also extended to any regenerators on the digital section.

REFERENCES

[1] *ISDN User-Network Interfaces. Basic User-Network Interface—Layer 1 Specification.* ITU-T recommendation I.430, rev. 1. International Telecommunication Union, 1993.

[2] *ISDN User-Network Interfaces. Primary Rate User-Network Interface—Layer 1 Specification.* ITU-T recommendation I.431, rev. 1. International Telecommunication Union, 1993.

[3] "Generic requirements for ISDN basic rate interface verification (BRIV)." BELLCORE Technical Report TR-NWT-001329, issue 1, Nov. 1992.

[4] *ISDN Basic User-Network Interface Layer 1 Specification and Test Principles.* ETSI, European Telecommunication Standard ETS 300 012:1992.

[5] "ISDN primary rate access testing requirements." BELLCORE Technical Report TR-NWT-001219, issue 1, Aug. 1992.

[6] *ISDN Primary Rate User-Network Interface Layer 1 Specification and Test Principles.* ETSI, European Telecommunication Standard ETS 300 011:1991.

[7] *Characterization of Subscriber Loops for Voice and ISDN Services.* BELLCORE, ST-TSY-000041, issue 1, July 1987.

[8] "Generic requirements for ISDN basic access digital subscriber lines." BELLCORE Technical Report TR-NWT-000393, issue 2, Jan. 1991.

[9] *Error Performance of an International Digital Connection Forming Part of an Integrated Services Digital Network.* CCITT Blue Book, fascicle III.5, recommendation G.821. International Telecommunication Union, 1988.

[10] *Error Performance Measuring Equipment for Bit Rates of 64 kbit/s and N × 64 kbit/s.* ITU-T recommendation O.152, rev. 1. International Telecommunication Union, 1992.

[11] *ISDN User-Network Interface—Data Link Layer Specification.* ITU-T recommendation Q.921, rev. 1. International Telecommunication Union, 1993.

[12] *Digital Subscriber Signaling System No. 1 (DDS 1)—ISDN User-Network Interface Layer 3 Specification for Basic Call Control.* ITU-T recommendation Q.931, rev. 1. International Telecommunication Union, 1993.

[13] *OSI Conformance Testing Methodology and Framework for Protocol Recommendations for CCITT Applications—The Tree and Tabular Combined Notation (TTCN).* ITU-T recommendation X.292. International Telecommunication Union, 1992.

[14] *OSI Conformance Testing Methodology and Framework for Protocol Recommendations for CCITT Applications—General Concepts.* ITU-T recommendation X.290, rev. 1. International Telecommunication Union, 1992.

[15] *OSI Conformance Testing Methodology and Framework for Protocol Recommendations for CCITT Applications—Abstract Test Suite Specification.* ITU-T recommendation X.291. International Telecommunication Union, 1992.

[16] *Abstract Test Suite for LAPD Conformance Testing.* ITU-T recommendation Q.921 bis. International Telecommunication Union, 1993. (*Note:* Copies of the *Abstract Test Suite* on diskette are available from the ITU.)

[17] *ISDN: Attachment Requirements for Terminal Equipment to Connect to an ISDN Using ISDN Basic Access. Layer 3 Aspects (NET 3, Part 2).* ETSI, European Telecommunication Standard ETS 300 104:1991 and Amendment 1, 1994.

[18] *General Maintenance Principles of ISDN Subscriber Access and Subscriber Installation.* CCITT Blue Book, fascicle III.9, recommendation I.601. International Telecommunication Union, 1988.

[19] *Application of Maintenance Principles to ISDN Subscriber Installations.* ITU-T recommendation M.3602. International Telecommunication Union, 1992.

[20] *Application of Maintenance Principles to ISDN Basic Rate Access.* ITU-T recommendation M.3603, rev. 1. International Telecommunication Union, 1992.

[21] *Application of Maintenance Principles to ISDN Primary Rate Access.* ITU-T recommendation M.3604, rev. 1. International Telecommunication Union, 1992.

[22] *Application of Maintenance Principles to Static Multiplexed ISDN Basic Rate Access.* ITU-T recommendation M.3605, rev. 1. International Telecommunication Union, 1992.

15 Timing in SONET and SDH

Acronyms

ADM	add/drop multiplexer	PDH	plesiochronous digital hierarchy
ANSI	American National Standards Institute	PRS	primary reference source
AU	administrative unit	SDH	synchronous digital hierarchy
AUG	administrative unit group	SEC	synchronous equipment clock
BITS	building-integrated timing supply	SONET	synchronous optical network
ETSI	European Telecommunication Standards Institute	SPE	synchronous payload envelope
GNE	gateway network element	SSMB	synchronous status message byte
ITU-T	International Telecommunication Union-Telecommunication Standardization Sector	SSU	synchronous supply unit
MRTIE	maximum relative time interval error	STM	synchronous transport module
NE	network element	STS	synchronous transport signal
OC-N	optical carrier N	TU	tributary unit
		TUG	tributary unit group
		UI	unit interval
		VC	virtual container
		VT	virtual tributary

ABSTRACT

This concluding chapter describes the timing aspects in synchronous optical network (SONET) and synchronous digital hierarchy (SDH). The main points considered are

- Frame format for SONET and SDH networks
- Pointer adjustment mechanism
- Clock requirements in SONET/SDH
- Timing distribution in SONET/SDH

15.1 Introduction

SONET, which stands for synchronous optical network, is a standard developed in North America to support broadband transmission based on optical-fiber technology. The detailed SONET specifications are contained in ANSI standards

Table 15-1 Signal Hierarchy in SONET and SDH

SONET	SDH	BIT RATE (MBPS)	OPTICAL CARRIER LEVEL
STS-1	—	51.84	OC-1
STS-3	STM-1	155.52	OC-3
STS-9	STM-3	466.56	OC-9
STS-12	STM-4	622.08	OC-12
STS-18	STM-6	933.12	OC-18
STS-24	STM-8	1244.16	OC-24
STS-36	STM-12	1866.24	OC-36
STS-48	STM-16	2488.32	OC-48

[1]–[6]. The complementary international standard finalized by the International Telecommunication Union-Telecommunication Standardization Sector (ITU-T) is synchronous digital hierarchy, or SDH. SONET and SDH, which are compatible to each other, are a result of an intensive standardization process.

Chapters 2 and 3 dealt with the synchronization of networks working on the basis of a plesiochronous digital hierarchy (PDH). In this concluding chapter, network synchronization is revisited in the context of SONET and SDH networks. As seen in the earlier chapters on network synchronization, timing issues can be satisfactorily resolved in the conventional PDH by proper planning and engineering of the synchronization network. The introduction of SONET and SDH, however, has created renewed interest in network synchronization and has raised several new timing issues. In this chapter, the timing requirements arising from the introduction of SONET and SDH are examined. But before considering them, it is useful to briefly discuss the frame formats and the principle of multiplexing in SONET and SDH.

The basic building block of SONET is a 51.84 Mbps signal referred to as synchronous transport signal level-1 (STS-1). The corresponding building block for SDH is synchronous transport module level 1 (STM-1), which has a bit rate of 155.52 Mbps. Both STS-1 and STM-1 can be synchronously multiplexed to create higher rate signals. Table 15–1 lists the signal hierarchy in SONET and SDH.

During multiplexing, several low-rate signals are combined to form a higher-rate bit stream. Each low-rate signal is called a *tributary* of the higher-rate multiplexed signal. The key feature of SONET and SDH is the synchronous multiplexing of signals, wherein the position of a tributary is fixed in the higher-order multiplexed signal. This is in contrast to the PDH, where multiplexing is performed asynchronously. As a consequence, to obtain a lower-order tributary, the entire PDH signal must be demultiplexed. For example, to obtain a particular DS1* signal from a DS3 signal, the latter must be demultiplexed to DS2 and then to DS1. On the other hand, synchronous multiplexing permits direct access to the required lower-order signal since its position in the higher-order signal is visible due to the absence of stuff bits.

Another notable feature of SONET/SDH is that the PDH signals of both the North American and European hierarchies can be multiplexed in a SONET or SDH frame. Thus,

*DS stands for digital signal. DS1, DS2, DS3, and DS4 represent different bit rates as indicated in Table 15–2.

Table 15-2 North American and European Signals in the PDH

North American		European	
Signal	Bit Rate (Mbps)	Signal	Bit Rate (Mbps)
DS1	1.544	E1	2.048
DS2	6.312	E2	8.448
DS3	44.736	E3	34.368
DS4	274.176	E4	139.264

SONET and SDH unify the divergent North American and European digital hierarchies by providing a common broadband platform for their transmission. Table 15–2 lists the signal names and bit rates for the two hierarchies.

A frame in SONET and SDH consists of two parts:

1. An overhead part, which permits functions such as framing, error monitoring, and pointers indicating the position of the payload within the frame
2. The payload, which contains the information being transported

Although synchronous multiplexing is achieved by byte interleaving the lower-order signals, the position of the payload is not rigidly fixed inside the frame. The payload is allowed to "float" inside the frame within a small tolerance. The beginning of the payload is indicated by the pointers in the overhead part of the frame. This flexibility in positioning the payload helps in overcoming the effects of small frequency deviations between individual network elements (NEs) of SONET/SDH. The frequency offset between NEs is kept small by synchronizing each NE of SONET/SDH to an external timing reference. Therefore, flexible positioning of the payload within a small tolerance is sufficient. This aspect is central to the timing of SONET/SDH networks.

In contrast, asynchronous multiplexing performed in the PDH involves bit stuffing (also called justification) to account for variations in the bit rates of tributaries. These stuff bits are removed during demultiplexing. Thus, timing is passed transparently through the PDH. Individual multiplexing/demultiplexing equipment operates on its internal clock, which is not timed to an external clock. Figure 15–1 illustrates the transport of timing between two digital switches through PDH and SDH.

15.2 SONET and SDH Frame Structures

15.2.1 SONET Frame Structure

The STS-1 frame structure is shown in Figure 15–2. The frame can be visualized as a table of bytes consisting of 9 rows and 90 columns. The 810 (9 × 90) byte frame is transmitted in 125 μs, yielding a bit rate of 51.84 Mbps. The transmission takes place row by row, beginning with the byte corresponding to the first row and first column.

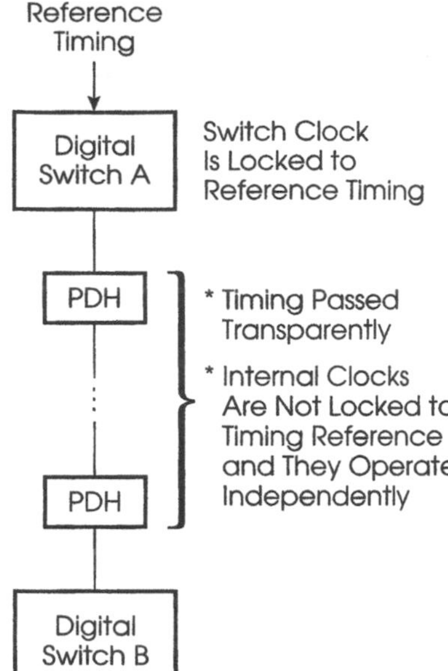

Figure 15–1 Example of timing transport between two digital switches.

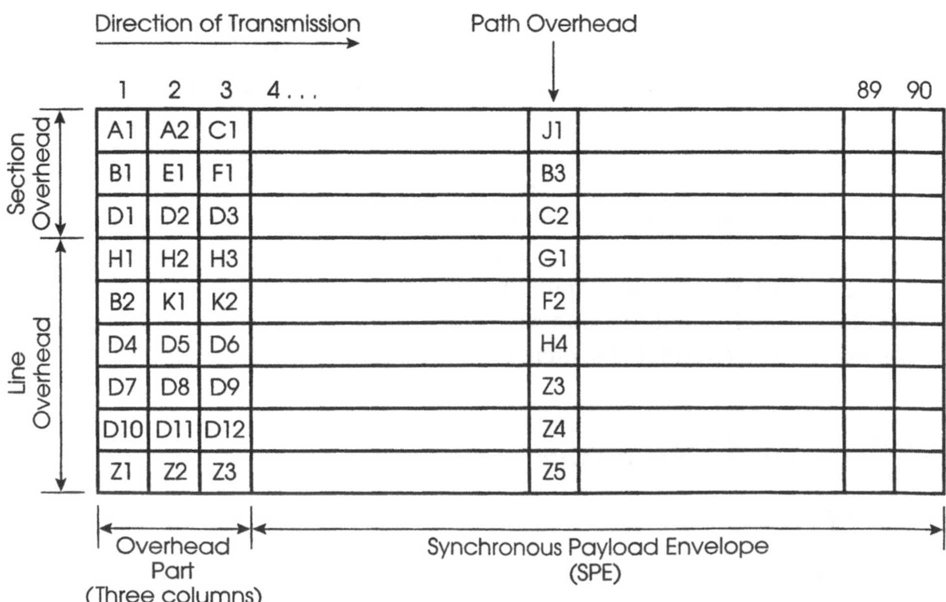

Figure 15–2 SONET frame structure.

A SONET frame consists of two parts:

1. A line and section overhead part consisting of 27 bytes of the first three columns
2. An STS-1 synchronous payload envelope (SPE) composed of the remaining 783 bytes from columns 4 to 90

In addition to the line and section overheads, the payload also contains a 9-byte path overhead, as shown in Figure 15–2. These overhead bytes are related to the section, line, and path components of a SONET network.

The basic building block of a SONET network is a "section" that consists of two NEs directly connected by optical fiber. Examples of NEs are regenerators, add/drop multiplexers (ADMs), synchronous multiplexers, and cross connects. A "line" consists of several sections. The signal structure remains unaltered during its transport through a line. A path is simply an end-to-end connection between terminals.

The 9 bytes of section overhead consists of two framing bytes (A1, A2) that indicate the beginning of an STS-1 frame, a parity check byte (B1) for section error detection, an orderwire byte (E1) for maintenance personnel, a byte (F1) for use of the operator, and three data communication bytes (D1, D2, D3) for transfer of maintenance information. The section overhead bytes are processed at every NE.

The line overhead consists of 18 bytes, which include three pointer bytes (H1, H2, H3), a parity byte (B2), two bytes (K1, K2) for automatic protection switching, nine data channels (D4 to D12), an orderwire byte (E2), and two bytes (Z1, Z2) for future growth. Except for regenerators, the line overhead bytes are processed at each NE. The pointer bytes H1, H2, and H3 are of principal interest in timing the network, and their role is discussed in Section 15.3.1.

The path overhead, which is conveyed end to end as part of the SPE, consists of a single column of 9 bytes. Included are a byte (J1) that allows a user to trace a signal through the network, a byte (B3) to perform end-to-end error monitoring by parity checking, a byte (C2) for identification of the type of payload contained in the frame, a path status byte (G1) for maintenance information, a multiframe alignment (H4) byte, and three bytes (Z3, Z4, Z5) for future growth.

Since one column is used up for path overhead, the payload has 86 columns. As noted earlier, the payload in the SPE can accommodate a variety of signals of the existing PDH hierarchies (both U.S. and European). For example, a 24-byte DS1 frame can be readily accommodated in three columns, and a 32-byte E1 frame can be carried in four columns. For carrying these signals, virtual tributaries (VTs) have been defined. Table 15–3 lists some VTs.

As seen from the table, each PDH signal is accommodated in an integer number of columns. For example, a DS1 signal of 24 bytes is carried in three columns of 27 bytes. The virtual tributary (VT1.5) carries a 24-byte DS1 payload. This payload is referred to as VT1.5 payload or VT1.5 SPE. Similarly, VT2 carries the E1 signal payload (VT2 SPE).

The VTs are mapped into the STS-1 SPE. For this purpose, similar VTs are grouped together to form a VT group. A VT group consists of 12 columns. Figure 15–3(a) shows

Table 15-3 Virtual Tributaries

TRIBUTARY NAME	LOWER-RATE SIGNAL	COLUMNS	BYTES
VT1.5	DS1 (1.544 Mbps)	3	27
VT2	E1 (2.048 Mbps)	4	36
VT3	DS1C (3.152 Mbps)	6	54
VT6	DS2 (6.312 Mbps)	12	108

examples of grouping VTs into a VT group. As shown in Figure 15–3(b), an SPE can accommodate seven VT groups.

Figure 15–4 shows the multiplexing scheme in SONET. When higher bandwidths are required, several STS-1 signals can be synchronously byte multiplexed. Thus, an STS-*N* signal is formed by multiplexing *N* STS-1 signals. The STS-*N* frame structure includes *N* structures of STS-1 signal format. It has nine rows and $N \times 90$ columns. When all the STS-1 signals in an STS-*N* follow the same path, they can be concatenated to provide a single payload of larger bandwidth. An important signal of this type is STS-3c, which is formed by the concatenation of three STS-1 signals. STS-3c includes nine column bytes of section and line overhead but only a single column byte of path overhead. Because STS-3c is equivalent to the STM-1 of SDH, it provides a common meeting ground for SONET and SDH signal hierarchies.

There are two possible ways of carrying VT payload (VT SPE) within the VT. One way is to allow the SPE to float within the VT in a manner similar to floating the payload within the STS-1 frame. This requires a VT pointer that points to the beginning of the VT

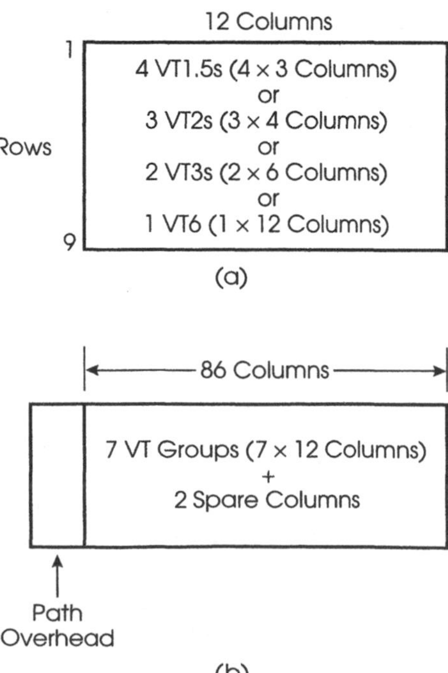

Figure 15–3 Mapping of tributaries in SPE: (a) a VT group; (b) VT groups in an SPE.

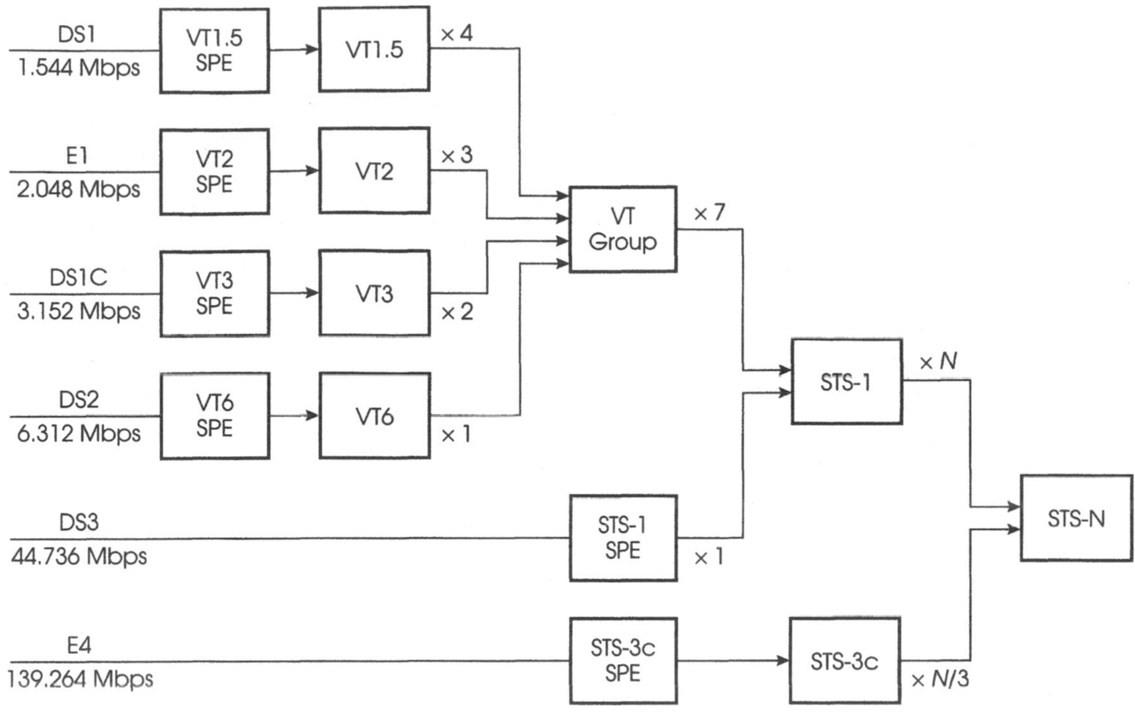

Figure 15–4 Multiplexing in SONET.

SPE in the VT. Another way is to lock the payload within the VT. In this case, a VT pointer is not needed.

DS1 and E1 PDH signals can be mapped in different ways. Mapping is a procedure by which PDH signals are adapted to the VT SPE at the boundaries of the SONET network. The gateway NE in SONET performs the mapping function. DS1 and E1 signals arriving from the PDH network are mapped into the VT1.5 SPE and VT2 SPE, respectively, at the SONET gateway NE. Three possibilities of mapping exist: asynchronous mapping, byte synchronous mapping, and bit synchronous mapping.

Asynchronous mapping involves mapping the PDH signal into an appropriate VT SPE by the use of stuff bits. Stuff bits are needed to accommodate the timing differences between the PDH signals and the SONET gateway NE. The VT SPE is then floated within the VT using a VT pointer. Locked mode of operation is not specified for asynchronous mapping. This option is mostly used for mapping DS1 and E1 signals to VT SPE.

Byte synchronous mapping does not include stuff bits. It permits direct access to 64 or $N \times 64$ kbps channels of the DS1 or E1 signals in the VT SPE. In the absence of stuff bits, the DS1 or E1 signals must be synchronous with the VT SPE. The byte synchronous mapping is specified both for floating and locked modes.

Bit synchronous mapping also does not include stuff bits. It provides bit sequence independent support for 1,544 and 2,048 kbps primary rate signal. Thus, no assumption is made regarding the structure of the primary rate signal. The mapping does not provide visibility of 64 kbps or $N \times 64$ kbps channels of the primary rate signal in the VT SPE.

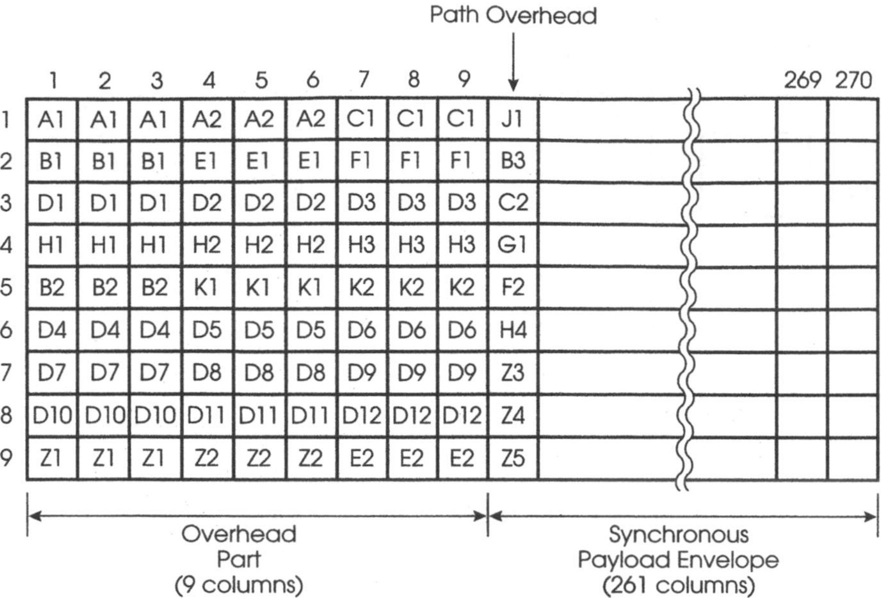

Figure 15–5 SDH frame structure.

15.2.2 SDH Frame Structure

An STM-1 frame is the modular unit for SDH. The frame format of an STM-1 frame has been specified in ITU-T recommendations G.708 [7] and G.709 [8]. It consists of 270 columns and nine rows. Refer to Figure 15–5. With the frame periodicity of 125 μs, a 155.52 Mbps bit rate is achieved. The frame can therefore readily carry a 139.264 Mbps E4 signal. An examination of the STM-1 frame reveals that it can be considered to consist of three STS-1 signal structures. Thus, as pointed out earlier, an STM-1 signal is equivalent to three concatenated STS-1 signals (STS-3c).

The VT SPEs of SONET correspond to virtual containers (VCs) in SDH, and identical to the virtual tributaries (VT) of SONET are the tributary units (TUs) in SDH. Similarly, tributary unit groups (TUGs) in SDH correspond to VT groups in SONET. Table 15–4 de-

Table 15–4 Correspondence between SONET and SDH

SONET	SDH
STS-3c	STM-1
VT SPE	Virtual containers (VCs)
VT1.5 SPE	VC-11
VT2 SPE	VC-12
Virtual tributary (VT)	Tributary unit (TU)
VT group	Tributary unit group (TUG)
VT1.5	TU-11
VT2	TU-12
VT6	TU-2

Table 15-5 Mapping of Lower-Rate Payloads

VC Name	Lower Rate Signal
VC-11	DS1
VC-12	E1
VC-2	DS2
VC-3	DS3
VC-4	E4

picts this correspondence. Basically, the signals are identical in format but have different nomenclature.

The lower-rate payloads are mapped into VCs as shown in Table 15–5.

Figure 15–6 shows the multiplexing arrangement in the SDH. At this stage, it is useful to introduce the concept of administrative units (AUs). The floating VC is called an administrative unit. Thus, an AU consists of the VC and a pointer that indicates the beginning of the VC. Two types of AUs, AU-3 and AU-4, are defined in SDH. AU-3 is built from VC-4, which is the same as the SPE (261 columns and nine rows) shown in Figure 15–5. AU-3 is used in Europe and for international working. AU-4 corresponds to VC-4, which is identical to the STS-1 SPE (87 columns and nine rows). AU-4 is used widely in

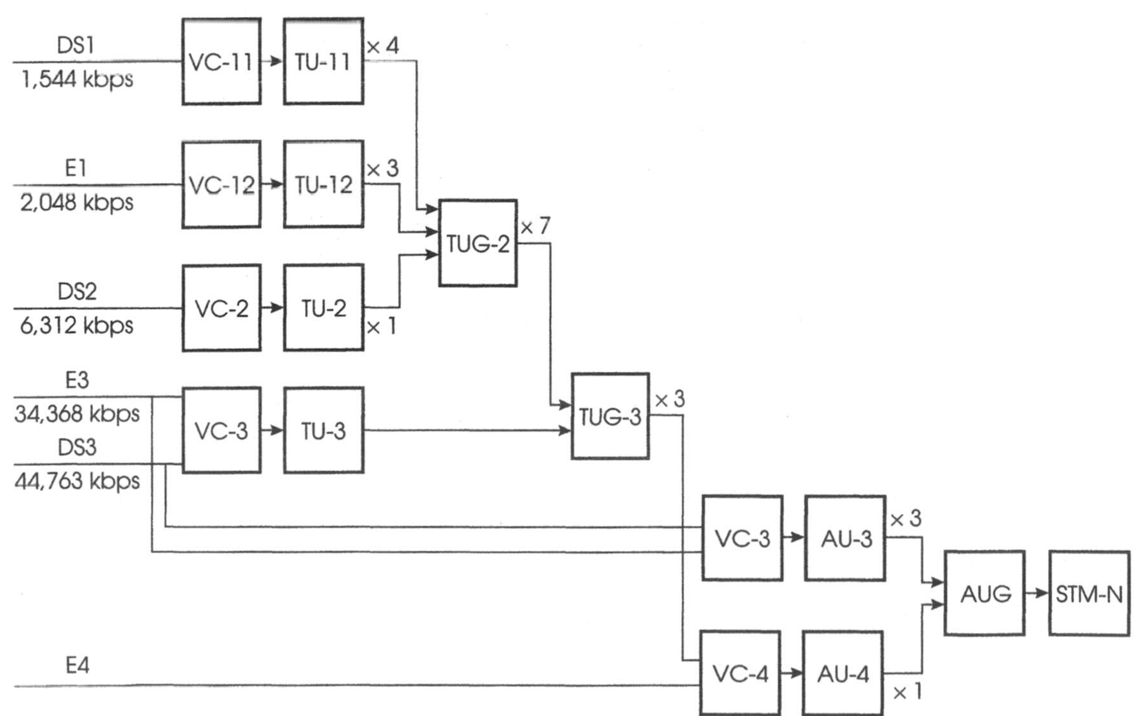

Figure 15–6 Multiplexing in SDH.

the United States. AUs may be byte interleaved to form an administrative unit group (AUG). For example, three AU-4s may be byte interleaved to form one AUG.

15.3 Network Synchronization in SONET and SDH

15.3.1 Pointer Adjustments

The nodes of SONET/SDH are supplied with timing traceable to a primary reference source (PRS). Various aspects of PRS were discussed in Chapters 2 and 3. The PRS may be common to the digital switches and all other NEs of the SONET/SDH network. When the SDH/SONET network is operated by several network operators, different operators may use different PRSs. Regardless of the single or multioperator character of the network, though, the basic requirement remains that all nodes receive a reference timing traceable to a PRS.

Although SONET/SDH NEs are synchronized to a reference timing traceable to a PRS, events causing timing impairments may result in frequency differences between NEs. The pointer mechanism in SONET/SDH has been designed to take care of these situations. As noted earlier, the position of the payload is not rigidly fixed inside the frame; rather, it floats in the frame within a small tolerance. This is achieved by means of a pointer that points to the beginning of the SPE in a frame. Thus, the position of the SPE inside the frame can be adjusted by changing the value of the pointer. The pointer adjustment is performed to accommodate frequency differences at a SONET NE. Figure 15–7 shows how pointer adjustments are performed.

Two cases may arise, as follows:

1. The sending NE clock is faster than the receiving NE clock. Thus, the received STS-1 payload rate will be higher than the frame rate of the receiving NE. In this case, the receiving NE introduces a negative pointer adjustment; that is, the pointer is decremented by 1 as shown in Figure 15–7(a). Moreover, the H3 byte is used to carry 1 byte of payload data. This is called *negative stuff byte.*
2. The sending NE clock is slower than the receiving NE clock, and therefore the received STS-1 payload rate is lower than the frame rate of the receiving NE. In this case, the receiving NE introduces a positive pointer adjustment by incrementing the pointer by 1. The byte position immediately following the H3 byte is nulled (positive byte stuffing). Refer to Figure 15–7(b).

In Figure 15–7, the pointer adjustment and byte stuffing (positive or negative) are shown to take place in frame $n + 1$. In subsequent frames, the modified pointer value continues.

A similar mechanism of pointer adjustment exists in SDH NEs. In this case, an AU3 pointer adjustment involves incrementing or decrementing the pointer by 3 bytes. The pointer adjustment is accompanied by stuffing (positive or negative) of 3 bytes.

The pointer adjustment mechanism just described eliminates the need for slip buffers. This is an advantage, because buffers introduce signal delay. When all the NEs in a SONET-SDH network receive timing from a reference traceable to a PRS, there is very

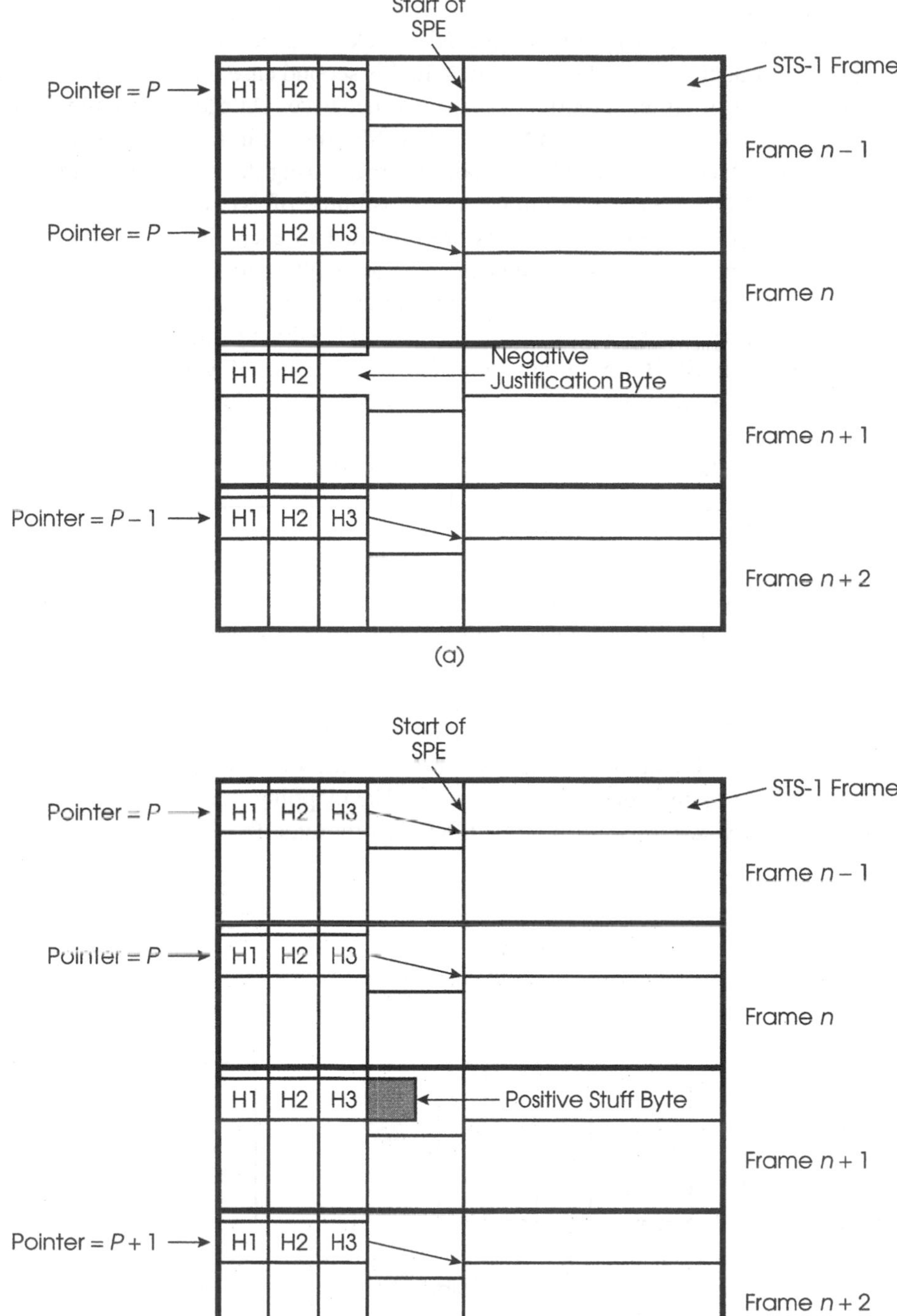

Figure 15–7 Pointer adjustments in SONET: (a) payload rate is higher than frame rate; (b) Payload rate is lower than frame rate.

little frequency offset between the NEs. Yet, pointer adjustment events may still occur due to short-term instability of the NE clocks and because phase differences brought about by transmission delay variations. In this second case, pointer adjustments take place occasionally in either direction, positive or negative. On the other hand, a sustained frequency offset in one direction between two NEs results in frequent pointer adjustments of the same polarity. This would typically happen during the holdover mode of operation of a SONET/SDH NE. To minimize the possibility of NE clocks entering the holdover mode, redundant timing references are provided to each SONET/SDH node. Failure of one timing reference results in a switchover to an alternative reference.

A major problem with pointer adjustments is that they cause large phase shifts. For SONET, every pointer adjustment involves a full 1-byte timing adjustment; AU-3 pointer adjustments in SDH are 3 bytes long. The introduction of SONET and SDH in the existing PDH network creates one or more SONET/SDH islands, and PDH signals have to pass through these islands. Upon entry to the SONET/SDH island, PDH signals are mapped into the SPE payload. Due to pointer adjustments, PDH signals accumulate jitter during their conveyance through SONET/SDH. For example, consider transporting of DS1 signals through the SONET network. Every single byte pointer adjustment introduces 8 unit intervals (UIs) of jitter. This is clearly excessive, since the DS3 equipment in the PDH is designed to tolerate no more than 5 UI of jitter at their input. Therefore, SONET equipment must perform filtration of jitter to bring it within acceptable levels before the DS3 signal leaves the SONET network.

Figure 15–8 shows a mixed PDH-SDH network. The asynchronous signals from the PDH network enter the SDH network at an input gateway network element (input GNE) and leave SONET at the output GNE. Between these two GNEs may be several other NEs that perform pointer-processing functions. The mapping function is performed at the originating GNE, whereas the output GNE incorporates the desynchronizing function. No

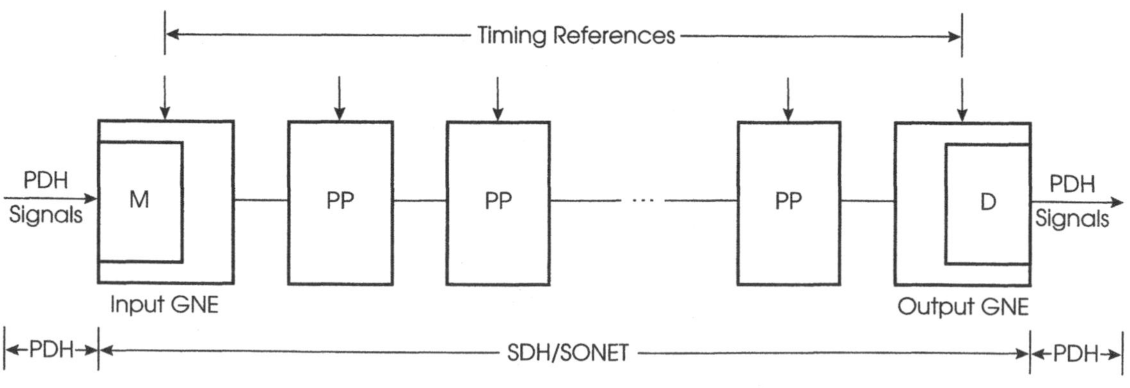

Figure 15–8 Mixed PDH-SONET/SDH network.

pointer adjustments are involved at the input GNE, but they may take place at all other NEs occasionally for various reasons. Clock noise (short-term instability of the clock), switchover to an alternative timing reference at an NE, and entry of an NE clock in the holdover mode may result in pointer adjustments. As noted earlier, clock noise at the NE induces random pointer adjustments in both positive and negative directions. When clock noise is present at several NEs in the SONET/SDH chain, a burst of pointer adjustments results. When there is a failure of all timing references at one of the NEs, a sustained frequency offset develops and continuous pointer adjustments of the same polarity occur at that NE. A switch of timing reference at an NE may result in sudden phase shift, thereby causing a pointer adjustment event. Since each pointer adjustment involves a substantial phase shift, with repeated pointer adjustments, jitter may accumulate to unacceptable levels and ultimately result in payload errors. Therefore,

- The jitter caused by pointer adjustments should be filtered out.
- Pointer adjustment events should be minimized.

Not all pointer adjustments propagate to the output GNE of SDH/SONET. The jitter arising at an NE due to pointer adjustments is removed at a subsequent NE that is locked to the timing of the input GNE. When failure of timing reference takes place at the input or the output GNE, however, the jitter accumulated due to continuous pointer adjustments is passed on to the desynchronizer at the output GNE. The function of the desynchronizer is to filter out jitter to values acceptable at the PDH interface. Therefore, the desynchronizer should be capable of handling individual pointer adjustment events as well as bursts of pointer adjustments.

Short-term stability of NE clocks is an important factor in determining the frequency of pointer adjustments in SDH/SONET. (Long-term instability does not have any significant impact on pointer activity.) Since the slave clocks specified in ITU-T recommendations G.812 [9] do not possess the needed short-term stability, a new specification for clocks with enhanced short-term stability has been formulated. For SONET, the stratum 3E clock has been defined, and a new ITU-T recommendation G.81s [10] for SDH provides the clock specifications. This aspect is discussed further in the next section.

15.3.2 Synchronization Network Reference Chain and Clock Quality in SDH

In Chapter 2, two principal methods for synchronization of digital switches were discussed: master-slave and mutual synchronization. For reasons described there, the master-slave technique has emerged as a method of choice for network synchronization in the PDH environment. For SONET/SDH also, the master-slave method is recommended by the ITU-T. BELLCORE and European Telecommunication Standards Institute (ETSI) standards also stipulate use of the master-slave method.

For SDH, a synchronization network reference chain, shown in Figure 15–9, is specified in ITU-T recommendation G.803 [11]. The PRS is at the apex of the chain, which contains two types of slave clocks:

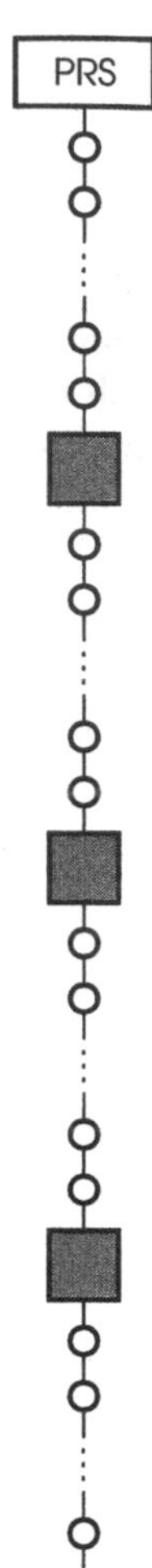

SSU (G.812): Maximum Number = 10

SEC (G.81S): Maximum Number = 60
Maximum Number in a Subchain = 20

Figure 15–9 Synchronization network reference chain.

1. Clocks conforming to G.812, generally referred to as synchronous supply units (SSUs) or simply G.812 clocks. Major network nodes in the SDH, such as digital cross connects, are equipped with G.812 clocks.
2. Clocks conforming to ITU-T G.81s recommendations, usually called synchronous equipment clocks (SECs) or simply G.81s clocks. The SDH NEs contain these clocks.

The quality of timing deteriorates as the number of clocks in tandem increases. Based on theoretical calculations, recommendation G.803 stipulates that in the worst case, the synchronization reference chain should contain no more than ten G.812 clocks, and each subchain between G.812 clocks should not contain more than 20 G.81s clocks. Furthermore, the total number of G.81s clocks in the chain should not exceed 60. These figures should never be exceeded, and in a practical synchronization network, the number of clocks in tandem should be as small as possible.

The characteristics of G.812 clocks were discussed in Chapter 2, where two categories of G.812 clocks, local and transit, were identified. In SDH, however, a G.812 clock is considered a single clock type. The difference in holdover performance of the local and transit clocks is not relevant for the SDH network since the latter is not sensitive to long-term stability characteristics.

The SSUs support the distribution of timing in the SDH network in two important ways. First, SSUs have low filter bandwidth, not more than 0.1 Hz. This low filter bandwidth enables SSUs to filter out jitter and wander accumulated by the SECs. Second, SSUs check whether the received timing reference can be traced to the PRS. This identification of the clock quality is available in the synchronous status message byte (SSMB) carried in the STM-N signal. If the timing reference is not traceable to a PRS, the SSU goes into the holdover mode. Compared with G.81s clocks, G.812 clocks have high frequency stability in the holdover mode, which helps in limiting the frequency offset during timing reference disruptions.

It is pointed out in recommendation G.81s that the pointer mechanism in SDH is not sensitive to phase variations that occur for observation periods longer than 1,000 seconds. SDH equipment is sensitive to phase variations in the range of 0.1 to 1,000 seconds, and therefore more stringent clock specifications are required for this range. The short-term stability of G.81s clocks is specified in terms of the maximum relative time interval error (MRTIE). The MRTIE is specified to rise linearly from about 20 nanoseconds at the beginning of the observation period to 40 nanoseconds in 0.03 second. Thereafter, the MRTIE is constant. These figures of short-term stability apply when there is no impairment of the reference timing or when the clock is in the holdover mode.

G.81s also provides specifications regarding phase transients at the output of the clock in the event of short disruptions of up to 10 seconds in the reference timing supply. Examples of short disruptions include short outages of timing reference and switchover to alternative timing reference. (For disruptions of more than 10 seconds, specifications for clock behavior in the holdover mode apply.)

Short-term phase variations at the output of the clock when reference timing is lost for a period of less than 10 seconds are summarized in the following:

1. The relative phase variations over a period T of up to 15 seconds should not exceed 5 × (10E-8) × T. Furthermore, additional phase shifts of up to 122 nanoseconds, with a temporary offset of 7.5 ppm, are permissible during entry or exit to the holdover mode.
2. The relative phase variation over any period T greater than 15 seconds should not exceed 1 μs.

The frequency accuracy recommended for G.81s is ± 4.6 × 10E-6. Compared with the SSU, which is based on recommendation G.812, the G.81s clock has lower holdover mode stability. Typical figures are 5 × 10E-7 per day for holdover stability and an initial frequency offset of 5 × 10E-8. Readers may compare these figures with those for the SSU (transit and local clocks) furnished in Table 2–4. Another difference between the SSU and the SEC lies in the large bandwidth of the latter, which is typically 1 to 10 Hz. Appendix D to ANSI T1.101 [12] provides a comparison of the stratum clocks (clocks at stratums 1,

2, 3, 4, and 4E) specified for the North American network to the clocks specified by the ITU-T (clocks according to G.811, G.812, and G81s).

15.3.3 Synchronization Reference Distribution in SONET

The synchronization reference timing chain of Figure 15–9 represents the synchronization distribution arrangement in the SDH, but the reference distribution arrangement in SONET is based on building-integrated timing supply (BITS) implementation. BITS was discussed in Chapter 3. In offices where SONET is deployed, both stratum 2 and stratum 3E clocks are suitable for BITS clocks. They correspond to the SSU discussed in the previous section. Both stratum 2 and stratum 3E clocks incorporate phase noise filtering. They are capable of filtering out short-term instability in the reference timing input. In fact, stratum 3E clocks were specifically introduced by BELLCORE [13] with the SONET requirement of short-term stability in view.

SONET NE clocks (which correspond to the SEC of SDH) have a narrow filtering bandwidth of 0.1 Hz due to the fast phase transients of the BITS clock. The holdover stability requirements are, however, identical to those of SEC of SDH.

The synchronization distribution arrangement between two offices deploying SONET is illustrated in Figure 15–10. The BITS clock at office A synchronizes the SONET NE. In turn, the SONET NE controls the frequency of the output optical carrier N (OC-N) signal. The SONET NE at office B receives the OC-N signal and uses it to derive a DS1 signal, which synchronizes the BITS clock. Thus, the BITS timing is distributed between offices via SONET terminals. The timing distribution consists of a chain of BITS clocks and SONET NEs. Notice that timing distribution in SONET is OC-N–based in contrast to the DS1-based timing distribution in the PDH. One important reason is that when DS1 signals are transported through the SONET network, they suffer serious short-term stability degradation due to SONET mapping and VT1.5 pointer adjustments. Therefore, references that are payload on SONET should never be used for timing. Furthermore, SONET NE clocks are designed for better short-term stability. As the SONET network expands, OC-N–based timing will progressively replace the DS1-based distribution.

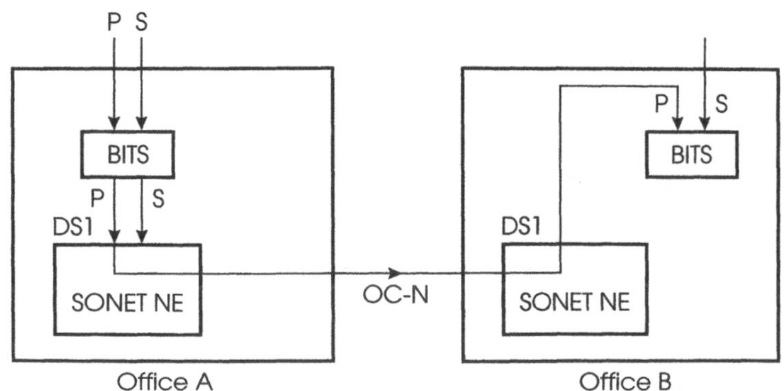

Note: BITS clocks are stratum 2 or stratum 3E clocks.

Figure 15–10 Timing distribution in SONET.

Another important factor to consider in timing distribution is the extent of cascading of timing reference through the network. As timing is passed through a series of clocks, it suffers degradation. Therefore, synchronization chains in SONET networks should be kept short, although no figure has been specified by American National Standards Institute (ANSI).

15.4 Remarks

Many of the guidelines for planning the timing of SONET/SDH are similar to those discussed in Chapter 3 in the context of PDH. Redundant timing references are planned for the NEs to improve the security of the synchronization network. Furthermore, timing loops must be avoided in the distribution of timing. Finally, the clocks for the NEs must be planned in accordance with the SEC specifications.

As SONET/SDH is progressively deployed and the network evolves from the PDH to SONET/SDH, the problem of excessive jitter caused by pointer adjustments may at times cause problems in meeting the jitter specifications in the PDH. This can be remedied by improvements in the design of the desynchronizers. Furthermore, DS1/E1 PDH signals that are payloads in SONET/SDH should not be used for timing distribution. As transmission systems turn predominantly SONET/SDH-based and timing is increasingly transported on SONET/SDH line rates, the quality of network synchronization is bound to improve. The delays associated with slip buffers in the PDH will also be avoided. Another notable feature will be the transmission of synchronization timing markers enabling better monitoring and management of timing in the network.

References

[1] American National Standard for Telecommunication. *Digital Hierarchy—Optical Interface Rates and Format Specifications (SONET).* ANSI T1.105-1991.

[2] American National Standard for Telecommunication. *Synchronous Optical Network (SONET)—Automatic Protection Switching.* ANSI T1.105.01-1994.

[3] American National Standard for Telecommunication. *Synchronous Optical Network (SONET)—Jitter at Network Interfaces.* ANSI T1.105.03-1994.

[4] American National Standard for Telecommunication. *Synchronous Optical Network (SONET)—Tandem Connection Maintenance.* ANSI T1.105.05-1994.

[5] American National Standard for Telecommunication. *Digital Hierarchy of Optical Interface Specifications (Single Mode).* ANSI T1.106-1988.

[6] American National Standard for Telecommunication. *Digital Hierarchy—Format Specifications.* ANSI T1.107-1988 (including supplements ANSI.T1.107a-1990 and ANSI.T1.107b-1991).

[7] *Network Node Interface for the Synchronous Digital Hierarchy.* ITU-T recommendation G.708, rev. 2. International Telecommunication Union, 1993.

[8] *Synchronous Multiplexing Structure.* ITU-T recommendation G.709, rev. 2. International Telecommunication Union, 1993.

[9] *Timing Requirements at the Output of Slave Clocks Suitable for Plesiochronous Operation of International Digital Links.* CCITT Blue Book, fascicle III.5, recommendation G.812, International Telecommunication Union, 1988.

[10] *Timing Characteristics of Slave Clocks Suitable for Operation of SDH Equipment.* ITU-T COM XVIII-R-128-E, recommendation G.81s. International Telecommunication Union, Feb. 1993.

[11] "Architecture of transport networks based on the synchronous digital hierarchy." ITU-T recommendation G.803. International Telecommunication Union, 1993.

[12] American National Standard for Telecommunications. Synchronization Interface Standard. ANSI T1.101-1994.

[13] "Clocks for the synchronized network: Common generic criteria." BELLCORE Technical Advisory TA-NWT-001244, issue 2, Nov. 1992.

Appendix 1: Ordering Information

ITU-T Recommendations

Orders for ITU-T recommendations should be sent to the following address:

International Telecommunication Union
General Secretariat—Sales Section
Place des Nations
CH-1211
Geneva 20
Switzerland
Telephone: 41 22 730 5285
Fax: 41 22 730 5194
Telex: 421 000 uit ch
Telegram: Burinterna Geneva

For ANSI Standards

Orders within the United States should be directed as follows:

American National Standards Institute, Inc.
1430 Broadway
New York, NY 10018
Telephone: 212-642-4900
Fax: 212-302-1286

Orders from outside the United States should be directed as follows:

Customers in countries other than the United States, including Canada and Mexico, should order American National Standards directly from the national standards organizations in their country or from ANSI's sales agents in England, India, or Japan:

American Technical Publishers Ltd
68A Wilbury Way
Hitchin, Herts SG40TP
England

Book Supply Bureau
D44 South Extension Part I
New Delhi 110049
India

Japanese Standards Association
1-24, Akasaka 4-Chome, Minato-Ku
Tokyo 107
Japan

For BELLCORE Documents

BELLCORE
Customer Relations
8 Corporate Place, Room 184A
Piscataway, NJ 08854-4156
Telephone for calls from the United States and Canada: 800-521-CORE (2673)
Telephone for calls from all other locations: 908-699-5800
Fax: 908-336-2559 or 908-336-2692

For ETSI Standards

ETSI Publications Office
Bolte Postale 152
Sophia Antipolis
06561 Valbonne Cedex
France
Fax: + 33 93 65 47 16
Telephone for more information and a personalized service:
Sharon on + 33.92.94.42.41 for (I-)ETSs and ETRs and other documents, or
Anja on + 33.92.94.42.58 for GSM Technical Specifications

Appendix 2: List of ISUP Messages

MESSAGE TYPE	CODE
Address complete	00000110
Answer	00001001
Blocking	00010011
Blocking acknowledgment	00010101
Call progress	00101100
Circuit group blocking	00011000
Circuit group blocking acknowledgment	00011010
Circuit group query	00101010
Circuit group query response	00101011
Circuit group reset	00010111
Circuit group reset acknowledgment	00101001
Circuit group unblocking	00011001
Circuit group unblocking acknowledgment	00011011
Charge information	00110001
Confusion	00101111
Connect	00000111
Continuity	00000101
Continuity check request	00010001
Facility	00110011
Facility accepted	00100000
Facility reject	00100001
Facility request	00011111
Forward transfer	00001000
Identification request	00110110
Identification response	00110111
Information	00000100
Information request	00000011
Initial address	00000001
Loopback acknowledgment	00100100
Network resource management	00110010
Overload	00110000
Pass-along	00101000
Release	00001100
Release complete	00010000
Reset circuit	00010010
Resume	00001110
Segmentation	00111000
Subsequent address	00000010
Suspend	00001101
Unblocking	00010100
Unblocking acknowledgment	00010110
Unequipped CIC	00101110
User part available	00110101
User part test	00110100
User-to-user information	00101101

Index

T

U

V

W

X

Z

About the Author

After obtaining a master's degree in electrical engineering from the University of Roorkee, India, P. K. Bhatnagar joined the Indian Department of Telecommunication (DOT) in 1972. From 1972 to 1981, he worked in the Telecommunication Research Centre at New Delhi in the design and development of Stored Program Control (SPC) electronic exchanges. Areas of his work included diagnostic, maintenance, and administrative software. During this period, he actively participated in the CCITT on the standardization of CCITT high-level language (CHILL). From 1981 to 1984, he served as principal engineer of the Switching School of the Nigerian Post and Telecommunications at Lagos.

Upon his return to India, Mr. Bhatnagar served as deputy director (digital switching) of the Telecommunication Research Centre, New Delhi. His areas of work included development of telecommunication software and collaboration with M/s Alcatel of France on the design of a new digital switching system. From 1988 on, as director of the Telecommunication Engineering Centre, New Delhi, he formulated the network synchronization plan for the Indian telecommunication network. He was also responsible for standardization, planning, and engineering of the CCITT common channel signaling system no. 7 (CCS 7) and contributed significantly to the development of national specifications for digital switching systems. From 1991 to 1993, with the liberalization of the telecommunication sector, he became responsible for the validation and technical evaluation of several major digital switching technologies for the purpose of technology selection. While serving as deputy director general, from 1993 to 1995, Mr. Bhatnagar was responsible for the planning and standardization of new services in the Indian telecommunication network. In this capacity, he completed the numbering plans for mobile and paging services and supervised the planning and implementation of the national ISDN in India. His other areas of work included network planning, technical evaluation of value-added services (VAS), network management systems, the resolution of interoperability issues for seamless service provisioning, and the introduction of intelligent network services. During a brief stint as general manager, he was responsible for the development of the telecommunication network of the Indian province of Himachal Pradesh. In 1996, he became director of the Centre for Development of Telematics (CDOT), a premier telecommunication research and development center. His current areas of work include digital switching systems for both rural and urban applications, intelligent networks, V5.1/5.2 interfaces, ATM systems, CCS 7, ISDN, and Telecommunication Management Network (TMN).

Because of different professional assignments, Mr. Bhatnagar has traveled widely. In 1988, he visited Japan, Australia, the United States, Germany, France, and the United

Kingdom to study digitalization and network synchronization aspects under a UNDP assignment. In 1989, as part of a European Commission project, he visited Denmark, Belgium, and the European Telecommunication Standard Institute (ETSI) to study the status of digitalization and ISDN in Europe. He was an ITU consultant to Telephone Organization of Thailand in 1992 and an Asia Pacific Telecommunity (APT) consultant to the same organization in 1994. In 1996, he was an APT consultant on CCS 7 to Sri Lanka and Thailand.

Mr. Bhatnagar has lectured in several seminars and has published many papers. He is also associate editor of the IEEE Telecommunications Handbook Series.

Lightning Source UK Ltd.
Milton Keynes UK
UKOW07n2015150216

268407UK00001B/21/P